Arthur A. Thompson, Jr.
The University of Alabama

4th Ed.

ECONOMICS OF THE FIRM

Theory and Practice

Prentice-Hall, Inc., Englewood Cliffs, New Jersey 07632

Library of Congress Cataloging in Publication Data

Thompson, Arthur A. (date)
   Economics of the firm.

   Includes bibliographies and index.
   1. Microeconomics.   2. Managerial economics.
I. Title.
HB171.5.T34   1985   338.5   84-18018
ISBN 0-13-231499-1

Editorial/production supervision and
   text design: Barbara Grasso
Chapter opening design: Maureen Eide
Cover design: Maureen Eide
Manufacturing buyer: Ed O'Dougherty

© 1985, 1981, 1977, 1973 by Arthur A. Thompson, Jr.

Printed in the United States of America

10 9 8 7 6 5 4 3 2

ISBN 0-13-231499-1   01

Prentice-Hall International, Inc., *London*
Prentice-Hall of Australia Pty. Limited, *Sydney*
Editora Prentice-Hall do Brasil, Ltda., *Rio de Janeiro*
Prentice-Hall Canada Inc., *Toronto*
Prentice-Hall Hispanoamericana, S.A., *Mexico*
Prentice-Hall of India Private Limited, *New Delhi*
Prentice-Hall of Japan, Inc., *Tokyo*
Prentice-Hall of Southeast Asia Pte. Ltd., *Singapore*
Whitehall Books Limited, *Wellington, New Zealand*

CONTENTS

THE ROLE OF FIRMS AND MARKETS IN THE MICROECONOMY / 22

HOW BUSINESS FIRMS FIT INTO THE MICROECONOMICS PICTURE.
THE FIRM AND THE MARKETPLACE.   The Concept of the Market.
How a Market Functions: A Simple Model.   Is "The Market" a Place?
THE FIRM AND ITS STRATEGY.
The Relevance and Importance of a Firm's Strategy.
How a Firm's Strategy Often Evolves.
GENERIC TYPES OF CORPORATE STRATEGIES.
Concentration on a Single Business.   A Strategy of Vertical Integration.
Related and Unrelated Diversification Strategies.
Corporate Turnaround and Retrenchment Strategies.
Abandonment, Divestiture, and Liquidation Strategies.   Combination Strategies.
THE CONCEPT OF THE FIRM RECONSIDERED.

APPLICATIONS CAPSULES
Kellogg's Concentration Strategy in the Ready-to-Eat Cereals Business
Vertical Integration in the Oil Industry
Beatrice Foods' Diversification Strategy
Retrenchment and Corporate Restructuring at Pillsbury

THE DEMAND SIDE OF THE MARKETPLACE
The Cardinal Utility Model / 51

THE CONCEPT OF UTILITY.   TOTAL UTILITY FUNCTIONS.
THE CONCEPT OF MARGINAL UTILITY.
Utility Functions for Related Products.
CONSUMER BEHAVIOR IN THE MARKETPLACE.
Some Simplifying Assumptions.   The Maximization of Utility.
The Conditions for Utility Maximization.   Evaluation of the Maximizing Rules.
CONSUMER SOVEREIGNTY IN THE MARKETPLACE: FICTION OR REALITY?
SUMMARY AND CONCLUSIONS.

APPLICATIONS CAPSULE
How Advertising Can Influence Consumer Demand

THE DEMAND SIDE OF THE MARKETPLACE
The Indifference Curve and Product Attribute Models / 82

DEMAND FUNCTIONS, REVENUE FUNCTIONS, AND ELASTICITY / 118

THE SUPPLY SIDE OF THE MARKETPLACE
The Technological Dimension / 165

THE SUPPLY SIDE OF THE MARKETPLACE
Production Efficiency and Returns to Scale / 189

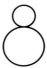

THE SUPPLY SIDE OF THE MARKETPLACE
Cost Behavior and Economies of Scale   /   242

THE GOALS OF THE FIRM
Profit and Other Considerations   /   292

HOW MARKETS FUNCTION
The Model of Perfect Competition / 319

HOW MARKETS FUNCTION
The Model of Monopolistic Competition / 348

GENERAL EQUILIBRIUM

PREFACE

This edition continues to stress solid coverage of microeconomic theory, complemented with a heavy dose of easy-to-relate-to examples and pragmatic discussions of how a competitive enterprise economy functions. What sets the fourth edition apart from its predecessors is its greatly enhanced coverage of the competitive process—the forces that drive competition and market change, generic types of competitive strategies, sources of competitive advantage, competitive behavior in various types of generic industry environments, and new ways to analyze competition and competitors. A fuller treatment of rivalry in the marketplace is in step with the realization that competition is alive and well domestically and globally; moreover, fresh techniques for industry and competitive analysis are fast developing into a hotspot for pushing beneath the general implications of the traditional market models and digging into what shapes the competitive maneuvers of rival firms. The newly emerging tools of competition analysis are so incisive and so instructive about the hows and whys of rivalrous competition that they are well on their way to becoming standard topics in microeconomics courses.

HOW THE BOOK APPROACHES MICROECONOMICS

Because of its strong microtheory content, the book is suitable for courses populated with economics majors. Because of its strong focus on the economics of firms, markets, and competitive behavior, the book is especially appropriate for courses where the audience consists mainly of MBA students and undergraduate business majors. Business school faculty frequently urge that intermediate microeconomics courses give some attention to the economics of business decisions rather than being slanted solely towards economics majors. The reasonableness of such urgings, together with my own belief that economics and business majors both benefit from a strong understanding of competitive market economics, have guided my choices of what to include and what to highlight. I have tried to follow the rules of including concepts and examples especially pertinent to analyzing the behavior of firms and competitive markets and de-emphasizing topics that either have a "purist" flavor or else relate more directly to nonmarket sectors of the economy. Moreover, the primary unit of analysis is the business firm. Readers are exposed again and again to how the conclusions of microeconomic analysis guide firms into one course of action rather than another. The economics of the firm is looked at from the inside as concerns production, cost, profitability, and competitive strategy considerations, and it is examined from the outside as concerns the influences of consumer demand, competition, market structure, and resource supply.

The result is a microtext (1) that is strong on theory and analysis, (2) that takes as its focal point the economics of the firm in a competitive market environment, and (3) that uses examples and applications to bridge the gap between theory and practice. In the overall scheme of approaches to microeconomics, the aim has been to place the text more or less mid-way between "pure theory" texts and "managerial economics" texts and, further, to achieve uniquely strong coverage of competitive forces, competitive markets, competitive strategy, and techniques of competition analysis.

TRADITIONAL TOPICS WITH A MENU OF EXTRAS

All major aspects of microeconomic theory are explored. The standard models of utility theory, indifference analysis, basic supply and demand, elasticity, production and cost functions, monopoly and perfect competition, resource pricing, and general equilibrium are given painstaking exposure. But there are differentiating extras that can be covered or not as the instructor sees fit:

- A fresh, contemporary survey of the methods of economic analysis (including "scientific testing," deductive logic, argument by example, diagrammatic models, and the use of mathematical proofs), what a theory is, the role of assumptions and abstraction, and the relevance of theory to explaining real-world economic phenomena.
- A chapter-length examination of the concept of a market, how a market functions in simple demand-supply terms, how firms and markets fit into the microeconomics picture, and the corporate strategy options of firms to vary their business make-up *from* concentrating on a single business *to* becoming partially or fully integrated *to* pursuing narrow, related diversification *to* achieving broad, unrelated diversification (Chapter 2).
- Coverage of the product attribute model of consumer demand (Chapter 4).
- Important new sections dealing with the technological aspects of production, learning and experience curve effects, how technical change can shape competitive rivalry,

and the ins and outs of technological leadership versus technological followship (Chapter 6).

- An in-depth look at profit concepts, profit theories, the debate over profit maximization, and what kinds of goals besides profit can shape the behavior of firms (Chapter 9).
- Full exposure of the models of oligopolistic competition, with special emphasis on the competitive strategies and tactics that corporate oligopolists use to establish their market positions (Chapter 12).
- A survey of multiple-goal models of business behavior (Chapter 14).
- A major new chapter on techniques for analyzing industries and competition, the highlight of which is Michael Porter's insightful model for diagnosing the nature and strength of the competitive forces that exist in a given industry (Chapter 15).
- A major new chapter surveying generic types of competitive strategies and the ways firms compete in such generic types of market environments as infant industries, mature industries, stagnant or declining industries, fragmented industries, and globally competitive industries (Chapter 16).
- Sections dealing with a firm's cost competitiveness vis-a-vis rivals, diversification, multiproduct pricing, price signaling through the media, the social costs of monopoly power, taxing excess profits, the competitive effects of advertising and product differentiation, first-mover advantages, switching costs, driving forces, strategic group mapping, competitor analysis, conducting an industry analysis, the wage-employment effects of unions, the impact of minimum wage legislation, and the economics of productivity changes.

The use of in-depth "applications capsules" to highlight actual applications of microtheory was well-received in previous editions and has been continued. As before, these aim at keeping the integration of theory and practice always before the student without disjointing the theoretical discussion. The applications capsules have been "boxed off" from the text narrative to enhance highlighting and continuity. The capsule topics were drawn from the mainstream of how a competitive enterprise economy works in actual practice; their applied nature can be easily seen by glancing through the Table of Contents. Many of the applications capsules can be used as a basis for extended class discussion. In addition to the applications capsules, summaries of empirical findings and dozens of brief examples are scattered throughout each chapter.

The attention paid to application and examples has several justifications. Students are more likely to buckle down and master theoretical material when they are convinced it has a payoff and is not just something that must be tolerated to get a degree. More fundamentally, though, the worth of microeconomic theory is best proven by its power of broad application. Indeed, unless microeconomic analysis is directed at explaining, predicting, and otherwise illuminating the economic behavior of consumers, firms, and markets, its value doesn't go much beyond an exercise in mental gymnastics and intellectual curiosity.

As has now become customary and proper, the theoretical concepts are presented in a modestly mathematical vein in belief that most students, given that they are required to take introductory calculus, are well-equipped to handle nothing more mathematically complex than first derivatives. All mathematical concepts requiring more than basic algebra are explained fully and in terms that can be grasped by the mathematically unsophisticated. The more advanced mathematical treatments of microeconomics have been placed in self-contained "capsules'' at appropriate places in the book and can be omitted without a loss of continuity.

Like any new edition, this one too has undergone important revision and updating. Chapter 1 on methodology has been extensively revised to incorporate ideas that have recently appeared in the literature. The coverage of the theory of demand has been expanded to include Kelvin Lancaster's product attribute model. Chapter 6 on the technological aspects of production now features coverage of learning curve and experience curve effects, new material on how technological change affects markets and competition, and a treatment of first-mover advantages and disadvantages. A section on ''strategic cost analysis'' has been added to Chapter 8. Chapters 2, 15, and 16 infuse this edition with its distinctive treatment of competition analysis, competitive strategy, and the nature of rivalry in various generic types of market environments. Chapter 2 acquaints students with the concept of corporate strategy and the numerous ways a firm can structure its business makeup and product portfolio. Chapter 15 covers the concept of driving forces, techniques for mapping different types of competitors and competitive strategies, the concept of competition as a strategic process, and Michael Porter's ''five forces'' model for diagnosing the extent to which competitive conditions in an industry are influenced by rivalry among industry participants, the threats posed by potential entrants, the availability of attractive substitutes, the bargaining power of customers, and the leverage that can be exercised by powerful suppliers. Chapter 16 surveys the generic approaches to building a competitive advantage and staking out a defendable position in the marketplace, explores techniques for analyzing competitors, and surveys competitive patterns in a variety of commonly encountered industry and market environments. The usual efforts have been made to improve the clarity of presentation in all chapters. In addition, the coverage of some ideas and concepts has been condensed to make room for newly added material.

All in all, the fourth edition strives for effective and comfortable balances between ''bare bones'' coverage versus in-depth analysis, theory versus application, classical versus contemporary models, mathematical versus verbal/graphical exposition, and conceptual simplicity versus the need to instill students with *some* technical proficiency and analytical skill.

The hoped-for blend is (1) a book that suits the ''need-to-know'' requirements of business school undergraduates, first-year MBA students, and economics majors and (2) a book that is a coherent and teachable synthesis of the best of all that is old and new in microeconomics. Whether I have succeeded is quite fittingly, for ''the market'' to decide. Your comments regarding coverage and emphasis will be most welcome, as will your calling my attention to specific errors.

ACKNOWLEDGMENTS

My intellectual debt to both the classical and contemporary economists whose fertile contributions have been weaved into the presentation will be obvious to any reader familiar with the literature of microeconomics; I have been particularly influenced by the recent works of F. M. Sherer and Michael E. Porter. All of the scholarly sources and materials that I have drawn upon are cited in the footnotes and bibliographical references. I genuinely hope that no violence has been done to anyone's ideas in my effort to synthesize them into the body of microeconomic analysis.

Both this edition and previous editions have benefited greatly from the comments of students, reviewers, and adopters. Special thanks are due to the reviewers of all four editions: Professor Keith Lumsden (Stanford), Robert Clower (UCLA), Howard Dye (University of South Florida), Lloyd Valentine (University of Cincinnati), Richard Hoffman (formerly of University of Buffalo), Frank Falero (California State at Bakersfield), Dwight Anderson (Arizona State University), Ralph Gray (DePaul University), Thomas C. Anderson (East Michigan University), Jay G. Chambers (University of Rochester), Larry G. Beall (Virginia Commonwealth University), Melvin C. Fredlund (California State at Hayward), Wesley Magat (Duke University), Donald J. Roberts (Northwestern University), Ernest Koenigsberg (University of California), Stephen L. Shapiro (University of North Florida), Stephen Buckles (University of Missouri), John Stevens (Babson College), William A. Hayes (DePaul University), Sharon G. Levin (University of Missouri, St. Louis), Walter Rice (California Polytechnic State University), and Charles P. Blitch (Old Dominion University).

Naturally, however, I alone am responsible for whatever blunders or inadequacies you find—I will be grateful if you will call them to my attention at P. O. Box J, University, Alabama, 35486.

Arthur A. Thompson, Jr.
Tuscaloosa, Alabama

NOTE TO THE STUDENT

Courses in intermediate microeconomics have the reputation of being among the most challenging in any college curriculum. The reputation is well deserved—this might as well be admitted at the outset. But despite the analytical rigor that characterizes the course, the road ahead is worth exploring, and I have tried to clear the way of unnecessary obstacles. Pains have been taken to make the text readable and interesting, to provide step-by-step explanations of each concept, to keep the graphs uncluttered and the mathematics simplified. Examples and applications consistently include enough detail to make them meaningful. Chapter-end problems and questions have been included as a self-test of your command of the material and to increase your mechanical proficiency with important concepts.

Because students begin the course with widely varying backgrounds and degrees of preparation, the treatment of each new topic is begun at the lowest level of analysis. No prior knowledge of economics is assumed. Thus, while this course is probably not your first exposure to economics, those of you who remember little about previous courses or who feel poorly prepared in economics will find yourselves at no serious disadvantage.

All of this has resulted in a book with more pages and lengthier explanations. But longer may still be quicker and easier. The intended effect is a more comprehensible presentation that will not only help you to hurdle the more difficult material in less time but that will also convince you of the value and power of economic analysis. A textbook is, after all, primarily for the student, not the professor and, in the final analysis, you are an excellent judge of how well the book performs its job of helping you understand the subject matter. I will be pleased to receive your praises and/or criticisms at P. O. Box J, University, AL 35486.

1

INTRODUCTION TO MICROECONOMICS
Scope and methods of analysis

George Bernard Shaw is credited with the observation that any reasonably intelligent parrot, provided that it was not tongue-tied, could be instructed in economics; it need only be taught to say "demand" and "supply." This simplification strikes at a basic economic truth: What happens in the economic marketplace depends largely on how the actions and decisions of suppliers mesh with the needs and wants of consumers. Indeed, the central task of economic analysis is exploring the ins and outs of how society's pool of scarce economic resources (land, natural resources, technology, labor, capital goods, managerial talents) can be utilized to produce a stream of goods and services that promotes the greatest consumer and societal fulfillment.

But getting a firm grip on how society can do its economic best with what it has to work with quickly runs afoul of a maze of considerations and transactions. Millions of individuals and households are constantly deciding how to budget a limited income for food, apparel, housing, medical care, transportation, and other goods and services. Millions of business firms are continuously allocating and reallocating the available amounts of time, money, and human effort across such alternative activities as more efficient manufacturing operations, new product research and development, investment in cleaner and cheaper production technologies, sales promotion, a search for new market opportunities, or improved customer services to produce an everchanging mix and array of goods and services. There are hundreds of thousands of government agencies and not-for-profit organizations involved in funding programs to supply goods and services to the public at large and to special groups (the underprivileged, the aged, the unemployed, veterans, farmers). All are drawing in one way or another upon the available resource base and causing them to be used in one way rather than another.

Moreover, the actions of each individual, household, business, or public agent are largely autonomous of one another and are based upon different values, preferences, and priorities. Each individual has his or her own notion of how best to spend a limited income and what life-style to try to live. Each business firm has its own strategies and plans for competing against rival firms and trying to improve its share of consumer patronage; a maker of telephone equipment does one set of things to compete effectively while a pest control firm's set of competitive strategies is different yet again. The state government of New York confronts different economic problems from those of Texas and is likely to adopt different kinds of economic policies to solve them. In short, each economic unit behaves on the basis of its own perceptions and employs its own specific criteria about what is best in light of its own circumstances. No reference is made to any grand economic plan for guidance, nor does any such economywide plan even exist. The economic outcome is an incredibly complicated network of demand-supply actions and production patterns—the task of economic analysis is to try to make sense out of all these transactions and to explain how the overall economic system and its many subparts actually work.

WHAT IS MICROECONOMICS?

There are two essentially different levels at which the study of economics takes place. *Microeconomics* deals with the behavior and activities of specific economic units: individuals, households, firms, industries, and resource owners. Microeconomics zeros in on such things as the prices and outputs of particular industries, the rational economic choices of individuals in buying goods and services, the economics of technological change, production efficiency and costs, competitive behavior, and the adjustment of markets to new conditions. The focus is on the trees, not the forest. In *macroeconomics*, the chief concern is with the economy as a whole and the major economic sectors that make up the whole. Macroeconomic analysis tends to view all households as a unit (the household sector), all business as an aggregate unit (the business sector) and all state, local, and federal agencies as a unit (the governmental sector) in an effort to obtain an overview of the structure and functioning of the whole economy. The key macroeconomic variables include the overall level of economic activity, total employment, national income, total consumer spending, aggregate levels of saving and investment, the size of the money supply, and the general level of prices.

In this text, we shall focus almost exclusively on microeconomics, or "the theory of the firm" as it is sometimes described. Our agenda will cover a broad front: What determines whether the demand for a firm's product will be weak or intense? How will consumers probably react to a price increase or to an increase in their disposable incomes? How can a firm tell if its use of resource inputs is efficient? What are economies of scale, and what causes them? What factors govern a firm's cost behavior? What is a market, and how does it function? How do markets differ from one another? What causes competition to be strong or weak? What are the ways in which firms compete against each other? Are large corporations monopolistic? Why is profit important in a competitive enterprise economy? Do business firms seek to maximize profits? What determine the prices firms charge for their products? What has productivity got to do with how much persons ought to be paid for their labor services? Do unions cause wages to be higher than they otherwise would be? What determines the prices of resource inputs? How does a firm decide how much of a resource input to use? These questions not only convey a sampling of what microeconomics is about but they also indicate its relevance to practical economic events.

THE METHODS OF ECONOMIC ANALYSIS

The approaches economists use to making sense out of the mass of everyday economic events involve (1) discovering good reasons for why economic events happen as they do, (2) carefully weighing a more-or-less sound set of economic facts to arrive at more-or-less plausible cause-effect economic relationships, (3) formulating a formal body of *economic theory*, and (4) building empirically based *economic models*. Many economists place great stock in taking a "scientific" approach to economic analysis, believing that a theoretically oriented, model-building approach strongly undergirded by mathematical-statistical testing is essential if there is to be any progress in understanding the intricate workings of economic variables and in evaluating alternative economic policies. As a prelude to beginning our study of microeconomics, let's take a brief look at what models are, where theories come from, and how economists tackle their job of explaining economic events and economic behavior.

The Process of Theory Formulation and Model Building

Although there is no singular method of economic analysis, many economists (in the tradition of natural scientists) have endeavored to adopt the "scientific research method" in formulating economic theories and building economic models. This method consists of five phases:

1. Defining the scope of the problem or the exact phenomena to be investigated.
2. Formulating a hypothesis about the relationships among the relevant variables.
3. Deducing testable conclusions and/or predictions from the hypothesis.
4. Testing the appropriateness of the conclusions and/or the accuracy of the predictions by reference to empirical data.
5. Accepting or revising the theory or model on the basis of the tests conducted.

Defining the Problem. Defining the problem involves isolating the exact economic phenomena of interest to the analyst and framing the specific questions to be explored. Usually, research inquiry is directed toward the whys and hows underlying the behavior of economic phenomena, the process of economic adjustment to new conditions, and the impacts which these adjustments may produce. The analyst may also be concerned with how a specific set of economic variables ties in with the broader body of economic knowledge.

Formulating the Hypothesis. The next phase consists of a search for regularity and order in the economic phenomena under investigation. This, of course, presumes that some sort of economic order in fact exists and that cause-effect economic relationships have some degree of stability over time. Such a presumption rests upon the notion of a universal order, with the job of the scientist in effect being one of differentiating among classes of uniform behavior, relating these to one another, and thereby broadening and deepening understanding of whatever universal order exists.

Consequently, once the research questions have been tightly posed, the task of the economic analyst is to discover which economic variables are important and which are not, to learn how the key variables are related, and to pinpoint cause–effect relationships—thereby allowing the analyst to understand, explain, and predict what happens and why it happens. In the course of this search, many economic happenings and factual details are, and should be, ignored because they have no important bearing upon the problem at hand. But even after the relevant has been sifted from the irrelevant, the number and complexity of economic relationships can still make it infeasible to explore so many things at once. Then the processes of abstraction and generalization are relied upon to bring the inquiry down to manageable proportions.

Abstraction involves sifting through, distilling, selecting, and restricting the variables and information considered, endeavoring to condense an otherwise cumbersome number of factors and details into a reduced set that can be handled and understood. Abstraction may consist, for example, of simplifying the study by focusing only on a manageable, but representative, subgroup or sample having the desired attributes. Or it may mean making some simplifying *assumptions* that specify the essential features of the economic environment which the analyst wishes to zero in on or that indicate basic behavioral traits about the economic units being investigated. Thus many economic models of business behavior are based upon the assumption that firms behave as if they seek to maximize profits, the rationale being that, of all the factors that motivate business decisions, profit maximization is likely to be the overriding or governing consideration. Frequently, in specifying the relationships among economic variables, it is customary to assume that all other relevant factors remain constant so that any influence that these other factors may have will not contaminate the study of the variables and relationships of primary concern.

Assumptions need not be in *exact* accord with reality; it is enough that they be *reasonable* representations of real-world conditions. One of the arts of abstraction is to employ assumptions that are (1) easy to handle, (2) sufficiently realistic, and (3) not so restrictive as to impair the scope and value of the research. If the assumptions are too detailed and too numerous, the model becomes unmanageable and/or of limited import. On the other hand, if the assumptions are gross oversimplifications of reality, even though very interesting conclusions may be drawn, the resulting analysis is likely to fail miserably in explaining real-life behavior.

What constitutes a reasonable abstraction may be illustrated in terms of the study of consumer behavior. Here it is customary for economists to assume that consumers behave as if they seek to maximize the satisfaction obtainable from their incomes. In fact, this assumption may not be literally true, at least for all consumers in each and every situation. Nevertheless, if over a reasonably interesting range of circumstances many consumers do behave as if they attempt to maximize satisfaction, then the assumption that "consumers seek to maximize the satisfaction obtainable from their incomes" is a justifiable and reasonable simplification. To restate the link between assumptions and reality in another way, even though the assumptions of a model may not be literally exact and complete descriptions of real-world behavior, as long as they are sufficiently realistic to allow for a valid analysis of the phenomena being investigated, no harm is done to reality.

After the stage has been set with abstracting, making assumptions, and simplifying comes the actual formulation of hypotheses. A *hypothesis* consists of a *tentative* identification of key variables and a *tentative* specification of how these variables may be related in terms of cause-effect or interaction. Hypotheses may be suggested to the analyst by the existing body of knowledge, by experience and familiarity with the problem, by clues uncovered in preliminary investigation, or even by intuition and hunch. The hypothesized relationships are often summarized in graphical or mathematical form to allow systematic analysis and ready determination of how changes in some variables will affect others. Verbal logic and deductive reasoning are used as well. However, research standards require that a hypothesis be logical and also subject to empirical verification or disproof. Without these qualities there is no way of judging how good it is at advancing the ability to understand real-world behavior, at predicting future events, or in formulating economic policies.

The Deduction of Predictions. Hypotheses do more than suggest explanations for behavior and cause-effect relationships. If properly formulated, they serve as the basis for deriving predictions about future economic impacts and changes. These predictions (forecasts) or conclusions stem mainly from logical deductive reasoning. To take a concrete example, we might hypothesize that the quantity purchased of an item tends to increase as the level of advertising expenditures on that item is increased, other factors remaining constant. To test whether a cause-effect relationship actually exists between advertising and sales volume, we might logically predict that in the absence of changes in other relevant factors, if IBM increases its promotional expenditures on its models of personal computers, the sales of IBM personal computers should rise. An even stronger prediction based on the same hypothesis would entail investigating the extent to which higher levels of advertising are associated with higher levels of unit sales for a broad sample of firms and products. The ability to evaluate predictive accuracy is generally believed to be an essential feature of all "soundly constructed" hypotheses and analytical procedures. The conventional wisdom is that unless hypotheses yield predictions or conclusions which are capable of being rigorously tested with empirical data, there is no appropriate way to judge their validity.

Testing the Accuracy of the Predictions. Once tentative relations among the variables are established and predictions are obtained, a multistage process of testing the theoretical model begins. First, facts and data must be collected for evaluating the accuracy of the predictions derived from the hypothesized relationships. Likely sources include published statistics from either governmental or private institutions, the results of previous research studies, or entirely new information generated from questionnaire surveys, interviews, original source documents, or field studies. For example, if the specific economic problem being studied is the nature of consumer demand for frozen orange juice concentrate, one would need to obtain statistics on the recorded quantities of frozen orange juice concentrate purchased, the prices at which these quantities were sold, the prices of other substitute breakfast drinks, the income of consumers, advertising expenditures, and population. Institutional information about the functioning of the market for frozen orange juice concentrate might also be useful. The items to be included in the actual compilation of information would necessarily depend upon the nature of the problem and the researcher's judgment. When the data are of a quantitative character (as they usually are), it may be useful to bring forth the weaponry of *descriptive statistics* and organize the data in the form of charts and tables for systematic presentation and analysis.

After the necessary data have been assembled, the precise nature of the relationships among the variables must be specified. When quantitative relationships are present in the hypothesis, equations may need to be constructed and values estimated for the coefficients and parameters. Since most of the concepts with which economists deal are empirically based (prices, costs, wage rates, revenues, profits, incomes, production rates, and so on, are all quantifiable), the use of quantitative techniques of one form or another is the rule rather than the exception. For this reason, econometric techniques often enter the picture. *Econometrics* involves (1) expressing the relationships among economic variables in mathematical form, (2) using historical data and statistical procedures to measure the hypothesized relationships, and (3) testing the accuracy of predictions derived from the hypothesized relationships. Even when quantitative expressions are not absolutely necessary, economists use them to facilitate the analysis or to render it more precise. Following the estimation of whatever quantitative and nonquantitative relationships are implied comes formal testing and evaluation of predictive accuracy.

Evaluating the Results of the Test. If the prediction is confirmed by real-world events—that is, it corresponds to what is observed—the hypothesis is *accepted.* However, it would not be correct to state that the hypothesis has been *proved;* one can only say that events have failed to *disprove* it. According to one eminent authority, hypotheses can never be proved; they can only be tested by seeing whether predictions made from them are in accord with experimental and observational facts.[1] A favorable finding on the accuracy of predictions derived from a hypothesis does not confirm the truth of the hypothesis because there is room for circumstantial evidence to produce correct predictions from a false or flawed hypothesis.

For instance, the truth of the hypothesis that a corporation's profits arise from the hiring of wise managers is not established by correctly predicting that a change in the management of Corporation XYZ will be followed by a rise in XYZ's profits; other factors not related to astute management are perfectly capable of generating higher profits. Strictly speaking, then, a hypothesis is never proved and remains on probation indefinitely. But the more it survives attempts at disproof, the more it is accepted in practice, especially when it is compatible with related theoretical systems.[2] Thus, after a hypothesis successfully survives a number of tests it becomes part of the knowledge of the discipline until evidence appears which shows that it no longer yields an acceptable degree of accuracy in its predictions.

If the observed facts contradict the predictions, the hypothesis is *disproved* or *rejected* and attempts can then be made to revise the hypothesis in accordance with the empirical evidence.[3] The modified hypothesis is retested and again modified if the test results are unsatisfactory. The process is continued until the investigator is satisfied that the analysis accounts for the observed facts with sufficient accuracy for the purpose at hand.

Figure 1-1 summarizes the facets of the scientific approach to economic research, indicating the close interaction between the real world and the theoretical world. Note that the process of economic investigation begins by observing the real world and finishes by observing the real world. This is as it should be since the major purpose of economic research is to improve the ability to understand, explain, and predict real-world economic phenomena.

Thoughtful reflection reveals that the "scientific" approach to economic analysis is grounded in several key beliefs:[4]

1. All sure knowledge is achieved via a scientific approach where the dominant theme is that we know only what we cannot doubt.
2. Prediction is the core objective of rigorous research—the ability to predict is all that really counts.
3. The really decisive test of a hypothesis about the hows and whys of economic behavior is its ability to predict.
4. Predictive power is measured by constructing objective, reproducible experiments; if the experimental implications of a hypothesis prove false, the hypothesis is proved false.

[1] W. I. B. Beveridge, *The Art of Scientific Investigation* (New York: Random House, Inc., The Modern Library, 1957), p. 118.

[2] *Ibid.*

[3] Academic lore has it that Max Weber was interrupted during a lecture once by a student protesting "The facts are not in accord with your theory." Weber replied, "So much the worse for the facts," and continued his presentation.

[4] Donald N. McCloskey, "The Rhetoric of Economics," *Journal of Economic Literature*, Vol. 21, No. 2 (June 1983), pp. 484–485. The remainder of this section and much of the next section is based on and inspired by this article.

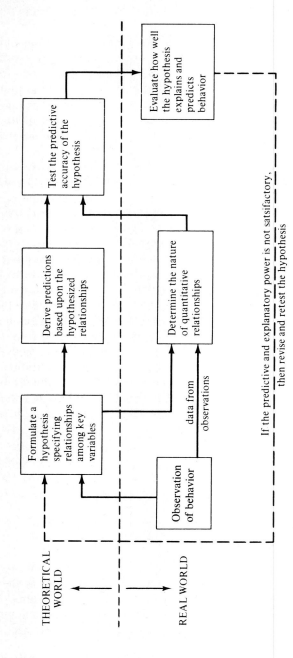

FIGURE 1-1
Relationship between theory and the real world

8

5. Reasoned argument, deductive logic, and subjective observation may well figure in the discovery of a hypothesis but they cannot figure in its confirmation—only objective, controlled, and repetitive testing can produce scientific and trustworthy knowledge.

While such beliefs have inherent appeal, they are not unshakable. In fact, a substantial, respectable, and growing number of philosophers (albeit still a minority) have doubts about the entire enterprise of the so-called scientific method as the basis for *all* knowledge. Certainly there is a basis for arguing that the study of economics is not tied as rigorously to the strict scientific approach as many economists like to believe. The official rhetoric of economists is that their methodology is scientific and that much economic knowledge possesses strong predictive powers.

Yet the predictive power of economics is open to doubt; as one noted economist put it, predicting the economic future is "beyond the power of any mortal."[5] The formal arguments for this condition are lengthy and complex but three intuitively appealing observations illustrate why the predictive powers of economic knowledge are suspect in a rigorously scientific sense: If an economist (or anyone else) has sufficient command of economics to be able to predict the economic future with confidence, why does this not result in the person acquiring the unlimited wealth that such predictive abilities can surely bring? The second telling point is that content of books about economics includes much information and analysis that has not been arrived at by strict adherence to the scientific method. Third, because virtually all economic behavior undergoes more-or-less constant change and economic conditions are seldom the same from one year to the next (one day to the next?), it is usually not feasible to subject many economic hypotheses to repeated experimental testing under conditions that closely approximate "controlled laboratory observation." Rather, the circumstances surrounding each observation of economic behavior and each application of economic policy options tend to be "one of a kind" and the assumption that all other relevant things remain constant is seldom met in actual practice. Thus although it is accurate to say that much economic research draws upon the approach of the scientific method and while the field of economics has some of the aspects of a science, the study of economics is not a *science* in the way we came to understand that word in high school.[6]

How Economists Explain: Some Alternatives to the Scientific Method

Just because the scientific objectivity of economic research may be a bit overstated, it does not follow that the barbarians are at the gates and that little confidence can be placed in what we think we know about economic behavior. There are some attractive methodological options to achieving pregant economic knowledge besides total dependence on the scientific method. People are per-

[5] Ludwig von Mises, *Human Action* (New Haven, Conn.: Yale University Press, 1949), p. 867.
[6] McCloskey, "The Rhetoric of Economics," p. 491.

suaded of things in more than one way and certainly most people do not choose to believe something or not depending on whether it comes from supposedly scientific research. This trait is just as characteristic of our beliefs about economics as about our beliefs of anything else.

So what are the methodological options to the scientific method? One is the use of verbal argument, deductive logic, and persuasive reasoning. The practice of economic debate often takes the form of commonsense reasoning, buttressed by examples and points of "fact." Economists, like other dealers in ideas, are active practitioners of the art of mutual persuasion; they spend much of their time probing for good reasons, discovering evidence to support their conclusions, citing bits of empirical data and examples drawn from observable experience, and weighing what evidence can be marshaled in support of their interpretation of what happened and why. They do these things at least as regularly as they engage in repeated testing of already established propositions to see if they can be shown to be false by newly available sets of empirical data. Indeed, many (most?) of the really significant propositions of economics sprung from this methodology and gained credibility *before* they had been tested repeatedly; comparatively few widely accepted economic propositions owe their standing to having come through rigorous application of the scientific method unscathed.[7]

The second methodological alternative to the scientific method is to construct simplified economic *models* to illustrate and isolate the links among selected economic variables. Economists have a strong affinity for using diagrams and mathematical expressions, laced with verbal discussion, to gain an understanding of how particular economic variables behave and why certain economic phenomena happen as they do. Using diagrammatic models and mathematical formulations of economic relationships constitutes an efficient, effective means of representing how specific segments of the economic puzzle fit together. The advantage of such models is that they reduce the analysis to manageable proportions (it is impossible to consider everything at once!). Simplified models of economic reality serve a pedagogical purpose and an explanatory purpose, as well as offering the potential of predictive power. Models are useful for pedagogical purposes because they permit complex, multifaceted events to be simplified to the point where the analyst can zero in on the links between two or three or four variables to expose how changes in one affect the others. To the extent that a model allows basic relationships to be understood and interactions among variables to be traced down, it serves to *explain* economic cause and effect and to reveal the reasons for why changes in one area spill over to impact another. The

---

[7] Why this is so is not hard to explain. If economists, or other scientists, waited for repeated testing of every proposition before they formed their beliefs, the outcome would be a paralysis of research and understanding. In order for propositions about economics to be tested a few times, much less repeatedly, some economists must care enough about the proposition to bother with testing it. They care only when it is believed by enough economic analysts to create a demand for testing. Often, therefore, quantitative studies rely heavily on hypotheses (or theories) which are widely enough accepted to warrant testing. But even this testing may turn out to be fairly limited in scope and frequency (as opposed to being extensive) because the pretesting arguments are so powerfully persuasive as to produce widespread belief with not much room left for doubt. See McCloskey, "The Rhetoric of Economics," pp. 489–490.

"realism" of simple models can often be extended (1) by introducing other relevant variables into the picture and exploring their effects, and/or (2) by posing a number of "what if" questions and analyzing how sensitive the results or conclusions of the model are to different magnitudes of change in one or more of the key variables. Both diagrammatic models and mathematically formulated economic models are popular among economists, chiefly because of their versatility and analytical agility.

A Perspective View about Methodology. The study of economic behavior, as currently practiced by economists, is a mixture of methodological approaches: the scientific method, rational argument, diagrammatic models, and mathematically formulated models containing anywhere from few to many economic variables. Most economists endorse the scientific approach as the official methodology for achieving knowledge about economics. Yet economic debate and economic analysis often take the form of deductive logic, argument by example, diagrammatic models, and mathematical expressions of economic relationships. The methodological standard of economists often ends up being governed by pragmatic considerations: use any of several analytical approaches as long as it has demonstrable capacity to illuminate economic behavior.

In this book, we shall rely on diagrammatic models and on logical, deductive argument as our primary analytical tools. Numerous examples will be cited as evidence of the capacity of these approaches to illuminate microeconomic relationships.

WHAT IS A THEORY?

We are now in a better position to indicate more precisely what is meant by the terms hypothesis, theory, principle, and model. It should be noted, however, that authorities are not in strict agreement on the "definitions" of these terms, with the result that how these terms are used varies somewhat from discipline to discipline and writer to writer. Nonetheless, what follows represents what is believed to be a general consensus among economists and, in any event, serves to delineate how the terms will be used in this text.

A *hypothesis* is a plausible, but largely untested explanation of how phenomena are related. It attempts to pinpoint the key variables in a behavior pattern and describe in tentative fashion how they interact. A hypothesis may be formulated on the basis of informed speculation, ordinary common sense, logical reasoning, or observable example. Supporting evidence for a hypothesis is lacking or is scanty or inconclusive. It may or may not be widely believed, but it is definitely "unproven" and thus does not stand as part of the formally accepted body of knowledge.

A *theory* is a widely accepted and presumably valid explanation of the behavior of real-world phenomena. For the most part, a theory gains its status from the process of formulating a hypothesis, logically deducing predictions from the hypothesis, and testing and retesting the accuracy of the predictions a sufficient number of times to produce a general confidence in its *predictive power*. However, a hypothesis can cross over the line to become a theory any time the weight of evidence as to its accuracy is deemed preponderant enough to accord it a place in the formally accepted body of knowledge—there is no rigid standard as to the number of tests a hypothesis must survive to become a theory. Moreover, the widespread acceptance of a theory can occur as much because of a theory's perceived *explanatory power* as because of its oft-tested predictive power. The explanatory power of a theory arises from its ability to account logically for cause-effect relationships, its capacity to illuminate why the variables are related in the manner which evidence suggests, and its compatibility with other generally accepted knowledge. The really significant difference between a hypothesis and a theory thus concerns the confidence that may be placed in it; a hypothesis is tentative and untested, whereas the evidence in support of a theory is deemed sufficient to warrant much confidence in both its predictive and explanatory powers.

The twin features of explanatory power and predictive power are *equally* important theoretical considerations. Predictive power is essential because it signifies whether a theory has empirical validity and is in accord with the available evidence. But while predictive power is necessary, it is not sufficient. Establishing a level of confidence in the predictions cannot be divorced from whether the theory is logical and consistent with other knowledge about behavior. More confidence resides in a theory whose composition can be defended on logical grounds and on the high degree to which it corresponds with related theory and evidence. One simply cannot have faith and reliance in a theory that offers no plausible explanation and has little common sense connection with the event being predicted. Prediction without explanation is sterile. Only when a theory has adequate explanatory powers does it generally gain widespread standing in the body of economic knowledge.

When a theory has been subjected to scrupulous testing and when its explanatory power is deemed sufficiently profound and universal, it may be termed a *principle* or *law*. A principle implies a very strong degree of empirical regularity; accompanying it is an explanation for its existence and reasons the principle should continue to hold in the future. Thus in terms of the predictive and explanatory confidence that can be placed in it, a theory is somewhere between a hypothesis and a principle.

Often one hears the complaint that theory is "unrealistic" and "impractical."[8] Such complaints can be valid only in the case of "bad" theory. "Good" theory cannot be unrealistic in an important sense because it does explain and predict real-world behavior. Nor can good theory be "impractical"; on the con-

---

[8] According to one wag, an "ivory tower" economic theorist is said to have remarked upon completing the construction of a new model, "And the beauty of this model, which will particularly endear it to the hearts of purists, is that under no conceivable circumstances can it be of any possible practical value." Economic theory is not without its actual examples in this regard. According to John Kenneth Galbraith, "Much economic instruction, and notably so in such fields as advanced theory, foreign trade, and monetary policy, depends not on the relevance of the subject matter but on the existence of an intellectually preoccupying theory." J. K. Galbraith, *The New Industrial State* (Boston: Houghton Mifflin Company, 1967), p. 46.

trary, it can serve as a pragmatic guide to what is happening and why since it has a demonstrated ability to explain relationships and to predict phenomena. When a theory truly has appropriate amounts of both explanatory power and predictive power, criticisms of impracticality and lack of realism contain little merit. If a theory is subject to legitimate claims of impracticality and lack of realism, the time has come to reevaluate the theory in light of current empirical evidence and to review its predictive and explanatory powers relative to alternative hypotheses and theories.

Some users of theory find the constant review of existing theory to be a nuisance. Of course, it would be nice if the need for reverification ceased. But in economics it is especially necessary to review the existing body of theory on a regular basis. A moment's reflection is enough to convince one that a nineteenth-century theory of business behavior could easily be lacking in its powers to explain and predict business behavior in the 1980s. The emergence of the giant corporation, the international dimensions of competition, and the imperatives of technological change have made the business environment today significantly different from what it was decades earlier. Thus, emerging economic developments force economic theorists to keep a close check on the explanatory and predictive powers of the existing body of economic theory.

The term *model* is much harder to describe in unambiguous fashion. In scientific/theoretical investigations there are physical models, conceptual models, mathematical models, simulation models, diagrammatic models, input-output models, benefit-cost models, and experimental models, to mention only a few. Although each of these has its own distinguishing features, there is also a common ground. The unifying feature of models, as they have been used in many branches of science, is their attempt to describe the essential features of a system in a way that is simple enough to understand and manipulate, yet close enough to reality to yield meaningful results. Usually, it is neither practical nor possible to represent the system in its original complexity; abstraction must be used, and selecting the appropriate degree of abstraction can greatly enhance the model's value. If the level of abstraction is too low, so that the model has an overabundance of specific detail, the advantages of realism are offset by the unwieldiness of the model and a lack of generalized application. On the other hand, if the model is highly abstract, the advantages gained from its analytic properties may be more than counterbalanced by its dubious connection with the real world. For example, in analyzing how a market works, if one were to assume complete buyer-seller rationality, full knowledge of economic information, perfect mobility of labor and capital resources, and instantaneous market adjustment to equilibrium, the result could be an economic model which is easily manipulated and which yields intellectually appealing conclusions but which might well lack significant ties to realities of the marketplace.

In the case of a theory-oriented model, the goal is to develop a tool that presents simply and accurately the major variables and relationships of an inadequately understood system—in which case the terms "theory" and "theoretical model" are, for many intents and purposes, synonymous. Both attempt to specify key variables and establish relationships among them. Both provide a logical framework or skeleton in which the complexities of the real world can be understood with greater insight. Both involve predictions or forecasts about phenomena, and both are judged by their accuracy in predicting and explaining the behavior of an actual system. As long as the system that the model is attempting to describe is of sufficient scope and importance, a theory and a model can stand at the same rank.

THE REALISM OF ASSUMPTIONS

One analytical problem remains to be discussed. This concerns the question of the validity of a theory which contains what some investigators consider to be "unrealistic assumptions." Consider, for example, a theory that is based upon the assumption that business firms behave as if they seek to maximize profits. Suppose further that this theory is judged to predict rather well but that there is a serious question as to whether the firms involved actually are trying to maximize profits. Is the theory then "invalid" because it is based upon an assumption that appears to be false? How does one determine whether the assumption of profit-maximizing behavior is, in fact, an accurate description of reality? Does it even make any difference whether the assumption of profit maximization is descriptively accurate or not as long as the predictive power of the theory is judged to be satisfactory for the purpose at hand? Does a theory that predicts behavior also explain behavior? These are very thorny questions, and attempts to answer them have generated a heated debate among some prominent economists.[9]

One of the principals in this debate is Milton Friedman, who, in an essay on "The Methodology of Positive Economics," maintained that whether the assumptions made in the course of formulating a hypothesis were either "realistic" or "unrealistic" may not really be significant. Friedman argued that the only relevant way to test a hypothesis is to compare its predictions with experience. He stated that there is no meaningful way to test the validity of a hypothesis by comparing its assumptions directly with reality. In support of his position, Friedman said:

> In so far as a theory can be said to have "assumptions" at all, and in so far as their "realism" can be judged independently of the validity of predictions, the relation between the significance of a theory and the "realism" of its "assumptions" is almost the opposite of that suggested by the view under criticism. Truly important and

---

[9] Milton Friedman, "The Methodology of Positive Economics," *Essays in Positive Economics* (Chicago: University of Chicago Press, 1953), pp. 3–43. Friedman's article has provoked a wealth of comment and rebuttal. See, for example, Eugene Rotwein, "On 'The Methodology of Positive Economics,'" *Quarterly Journal of Economics*, Vol. 73, No. 4 (November 1959), pp. 554–575; R. M. Cyert and E. Grunberg, "Assumption, Prediction, and Explanation in Economics," Appendix A in R. M. Cyert and J. G. March, *A Behavioral Theory of the Firm* (Englewood Cliffs, N.J.: Prentice-Hall, Inc., 1963), pp. 298–311; J. W. McGuire, *Theories of Business Behavior* (Englewood Cliffs, N.J.: Prentice-Hall, Inc., 1964), pp. 7–11; and the papers published in the *American Economic Review, Papers and Proceedings*, Vol. 52, No. 2 (May 1963), pp. 204–236.

significant hypotheses will be found to have "assumptions" that are wildly inaccurate descriptive representations of reality, and, in general, the more significant the theory, the more unrealistic the assumptions (in this sense). The reason is simple. A hypothesis is important if it "explains" much by little, that is, if it abstracts the common and crucial elements from the mass of complex and detailed circumstances surrounding the phenomena to be explained and permits valid predictions on the basis of them alone. To be important, therefore, a hypothesis must be descriptively false in its assumptions; it takes account of, and accounts for, none of the many other attendant circumstances, since its very success shows them to be irrelevant for the phenomena to be explained. To put this point less paradoxically, the relevant question to ask about the "assumptions" of a theory is not whether they are descriptively "realistic" for they never are, but whether they are sufficiently good approximations for the purpose in hand. And this question can be answered only by seeing whether it yields sufficiently accurate predictions.[10]

Here Friedman is saying that the degree of "realism" in the assumptions is often not apparent in the assumptions themselves but becomes apparent only after the theory is constructed and its predictive power evaluated. In other words, if a theory predicts accurately, then the assumptions are realistic enough despite appearances to the contrary.

Other economists have not found it hard to take issue with Friedman. Naturally, an assumption is "unrealistic" if one is applying the standard that it does not *exhaustively* describe a situation and instead mentions only some of the traits that are present. Yet it is unlikely that any statement of finite length would suffice to identify the totality of the set of characteristics embodied in a real situation. And it tests the imagination to conceive of uses for such a statement were it constructed. It is in this somewhat trivial sense that Friedman seems to be defending the legitimacy of "unrealistic" assumptions.

There are, however, two more worthy instances in which assumptions may be said to be unrealistic. First, an assumption may be unrealistic because it holds only for hypothetical or idealized circumstances. On occasion, models of theories with intentionally unrealistic assumptions are developed: for example, the frictionless world often posed in physics and the perfectly competitive market model in economics, the latter containing such "ideal" conditions as perfect knowledge on the part of the buyers and sellers, perfect flexibility and mobility in the use of economic resources, and complete freedom of entry and exit of producers into the market. The environmental systems portrayed in these models are admittedly hypothetical and serve as intellectual experiments. Their primary purpose is often to highlight the nature of the interaction among key variables, particularly when they are unaffected by numerous other factors whose influence may never be eliminated in the real world but whose effects vary in magnitude with differences in attendant circumstances. They may also be used as a standard of comparison against which the functioning of actual environmental systems can be measured. Models of this type are unique in the sense that when observations do not conform

[10] Friedman, "The Methodology of Positive Economics," pp. 14–15.

to the predictions given by the model, it is indicative that the conditions upon which the model is predicated are not being met—*not* that the model is invalid.

Second, an assumption can be termed "unrealistic" because it appears false or improbable on the basis of available evidence. Here we find the real bone of contention. Ernest Nagel, an eminent authority on methodological matters, has observed that a theory which contains an unrealistic assumption in the sense that it is false is "patently unsatisfactory, for such a theory entails consequences that are incompatible with observed fact, so that on pain of rejecting elementary logical canons the theory must also be rejected."[11] This view supports the consensus that scientific standards require theories and models to possess logical consistency and to provide explanation as well as prediction. One can scarcely be confident in the explanatory power of a theory which contains false or empirically discredited assumptions—regardless of its ability to predict. Unless the assumptions of a theory or model have been subjected to empirical testing, have not been rejected, and are generally agreed upon as having empirical validity, one has at best *proposed* explanation, not *actual* explanation; moreover, the accuracy of predictions might well be properly ascribed to mere fortuitous circumstances or uncanny chance happenings. Thus, it is imperative that we understand *why* a theory predicts before we give it credence.

Nor, as Friedman's position implies, does it follow that if a theory containing "unrealistic" assumptions has an impressive degree of predictive power, that the theory also possesses satisfactory explanatory power and that the assumptions acquire an acceptable degree of "realism." Cohen and Cyert have adequately demonstrated that Friedman's position can lead to prediction without explanation.[12] A theory or model which seems to predict well enough but which explains poorly should arouse suspicion about whether the true variables are correct represented. In such a case, any predictive power that the model may have could arise from unknown relationship(s) among variables in the model and/or the influence of unknown variables not included in the model.

It is especially important that a theoretical model possess both predictive power and explanatory power when it is to be used as a guide for control. To properly employ a theory as a basis for formulating control devices, e.g., economic policy, the user must be acutely aware of just how the values of one or more variables must be altered to bring about the desired environmental changes. This clearly requires predictive power, for the user must be able to forecast accurately the consequences of changing the selected control variables. But were the analyst to rely upon a theoretical model which generated accurate predictions without explanation, it is conceivable that the prescribed changes in the control variables could also trigger changes in some of the unspecified variables and/or relationships that had previously led (for reasons unknown) to accurate predictions, thus causing future predictions to be modified in an unpredictable fashion—for the better *or for the worse*.

---

[11] Ernest Nagel, "Assumptions in Economic Theory," *American Economic Review, Papers and Proceedings*, Vol. 52, No. 2 (May 1963), pp. 214–215.

[12] K. J. Cohen and R. M. Cyert, *Theory of the Firm: Resource Allocation in a Market Economy*, 2nd ed. (Englewood Cliffs, N.J.: Prentice-Hall, Inc., 1975), pp. 22–24.

APPLICATIONS CAPSULE

THE WIZARD WHO OVERSIMPLIFIED: A FABLE

In a certain kingdom, there was a school for the education of princes approaching manhood. Since the king and his court spent much of their time playing chess—indeed, chess was called the sport of kings—it was decided that the subject called "games" should be added to the curriculum of this school. A wizard was engaged to develop the course.

Never having played chess himself, the wizard was a little uncertain about what to teach in this course. (Only a *little* uncertain because his ignorance of chess was outweighed by his strong confidence in his general ability.) He sought the advice of a colleague in another kingdom and from him received the following communication:

"Above all else, a course in games should be rigorous and intellectually challenging. We wizards long ago concluded that chess, as actually played, is so complicated that it is impossible to formulate a body of principles and decision rules; these are essential to the rigorous analysis of any subject. We have therefore introduced a few simplifying assumptions. For example, in chess, the pieces move in a bewildering fashion—some forward, some on the diagonal, and some even at a right angle; we have tidied up this confusion by assuming that all pieces move according to the same rule. With such assumptions, we have been able, albeit with great difficulty, to develop a model, a set of principles, and decision rules which are teachable, and intellectually challenging. A 700-page treatise describing these is enclosed."

The wizard was much impressed by the 700-page treatise, and used it in his course. He found that it was teachable, and that the task of learning this model and solving problems with the decision rules was indeed rigorous and intellectually challenging, as proved by the fact that good students did well on their examinations, while poor students failed them.

The wizard maintained an active correspondence with wizards in other kingdoms about the model and its decision rules. In this correspondence, the game was referred to as "chess" although this was solely for convenience of expression; it was taken for granted that everyone knew that their game was not quite like chess as played in the real world. Eventually, some of this correspondence came to the king's attention. Although he didn't understand the formulas and the jargon, he did notice that the word "chess" was mentioned, so he commanded the wizard to appear before him.

At this audience, the wizard asked, "How can I serve you, O King?"

And the king replied: "I understand that you are teaching the princes how to play chess. I wish to improve my own game. Can you help me?"

"What we call chess may not be exactly like your game, your majesty. So before answering your question, I must analyze the problem. Please describe chess as you play it."

So the king explained the game of chess. As he did so, the wizard noted that it had the same physical layout, the same number of pieces, and apparently the same objective as the game he taught in school. It seemed clear therefore that the solution was simply to apply the decision rules for this game, although he of course

cont.

cont.

did not immediately reveal this fact to the king for he wanted to preserve his reputation for wizardry. Instead, he said thoughtfully: "I will study the problem and return in ninety days."

At the appointed time, the wizard appeared again, carrying a crimson pillow on which lay a spiral-bound report with a Plexiglas cover. It was a paraphrase of the 700-page manuscript. "Follow the rules in this report, your majesty, and you will become the best chess player in the world," he said.

The king avidly studied the report, but soon ran into difficulty. He summoned the wizard again. "I see reference to kings, and men, and squares, which are familiar terms to me; but what is all this about 'jumping,' and 'double jumping,' 'countervailing force,' and 'suboptimization'; and where do you mention queens, rooks, bishops, and knights?"

"But your majesty, as I have clearly explained in the introduction, it was necessary to simplify the environment a trifle. I doubt that these simplifications lessen the practical usefulness of what I have written, however."

"Have you by chance watched some chess players to find out?" asked the king.

"Oh, no, your gracious majesty, but I do carry on an extensive correspondence with other wizards. This is better than observing actual practice because it is generally agreed that wizards are smarter than chess players."

"And your princes. Are they equipped to play chess in the real world because of what they have learned in your course?"

"No offense intended, sir, but we wizards do not believe this to be a proper question. The purpose of our course is to teach princes to think, not to prepare them for a mere vocation."

At this point, the king lost his patience, but since he was a kindly king, he sent the wizard back to his school room rather than to a dungeon.

Moral for economics professors: An education in checkers does not prepare one for a life of chess.

Moral for operations researchers: Half a loaf is not necessarily better than no bread; it may be only chaff.

Moral for businessmen: A consultant who wants to play his own game rather than yours is worthless.

Source: Harold Peterson, "The Wizard Who Oversimplified," *Quarterly Journal of Economics*, Vol. 79, No. 2 (May 1965), pp. 210–212. Copyright © 1965 by the President and Fellows of Harvard College. Reprinted by permission of John Wiley & Sons, Inc.

SUMMARY AND CONCLUSIONS

The methodological approaches of economists in analyzing economic behavior and constructing economic theories are varied enough to preclude making an unequivocal statement about just how we have come to know and not know about what makes an economy function as it does. Some economic knowledge is grounded strongly in the methods of science and is undergirded with sufficient empirical and behavioral evidence to warrant great confidence. But repeated testing of economic relationships, under conditions akin to controlled laboratory testing, is nigh unto impossible because the forces of economic change are at work continuously—a characteristic that makes it difficult to replicate economic experiments under exactly the same conditions each time. As a consequence, to the extent that economics is a science it is a science in a different sense from the "hard" natural sciences. Thus while the research preference of many economists is to employ the scientific method whenever feasible, many times it is incumbent upon economists to use deductive logic, rational argument, the evidence of examples, and model building to probe economic cause-effect relationships. In this sense, some economic propositions are "soft," a bit imprecise, and somewhat shy on ironclad empirical evidence. Nonetheless, it would be a mistake to view the study of economics as anything other than a rigorous exercise. Economics is a discipline strongly grounded in theory, in analysis, and in conceptual rigor.

Economic theory is a term that merits careful understanding. It refers to a generally accepted analytical framework whereby the behavior of economic phenomena can be explained and predicted. Economic theory attempts to account for the hows and whys of economic change; it endeavors to explain what happens and why it happens. Good economic theory is very realistic because it has demonstrably high degrees of power to explain economic cause-effect relationships and to predict how changes in one economic variable will affect other economic variables.

Most economic theories contain one or more assumptions describing key aspects of the economic situation being analyzed and specifying certain behavioral conditions. The consensus is that any such assumptions need to be accurate representations of real-world economic behavior. Unless the assumptions upon which a theory is based are reasonable abstractions of reality and are consistent with observed behavior, the explanatory power of a theory is suspect and so is its usefulness as a guide for formulating economic policy. Whatever predictive power a theory containing "unrealistic" assumptions may have could well be due to circumstance or to undetected cause-effect relationships.

SUGGESTED READINGS

BLAUG, M., *The Methodology of Economics: Or How Economists Explain* (Cambridge: Cambridge University Press, 1980).

BOLAND, L. A., "A Critique of Friedman's Critics," *Journal of Economic Literature*, Vol. 17, No. 2 (June 1979), pp. 503–22.

COHEN, K. J., AND R. M. CYERT, *Theory of the Firm: Resource Allocation in a Market Economy*, 2nd ed. (Englewood Cliffs, N.J.: Prentice-Hall, Inc., 1975), Chapter 2.

CYERT, R. M., AND E. GRUNBERG, "Assumption, Prediction, and Explanation in Economics," Appendix A in R. M. Cyert and J. G. March, *A Behavioral Theory of the Firm* (Englewood Cliffs, N.J.: Prentice-Hall, Inc., 1963), pp. 298–311.

FRIEDMAN, M., "The Methodology of Positive Economics," *Essays in Positive Economics* (Chicago: University of Chicago Press, 1953), pp. 3–43.

LEONTIEF, W., "Theoretical Assumptions and Nonobserved Facts," *American Economic Review*, Vol. 61, No. 1 (March 1971), pp. 1–7.

McCLOSKEY, D. N., "The Rhetoric of Economics," *Journal of Economic Literature*, Vol. 21, No. 2 (June 1983), pp. 481–517.

McGUIRE, J. W., *Theories of Business Behavior* (Englewood Cliffs, N.J.: Prentice-Hall, Inc., 1964), Chapter 2.

MACHLUP, F., *Methodology of Economics and Other Social Sciences* (New York: Academic Press, Inc., 1978).

NAGEL, E., "Assumptions in Economic Theory," *American Economic Review, Papers and Proceedings*, Vol. 52, No. 2 (May 1963), pp. 211–219.

ROTWEIN, E., "On 'The Methodology of Positive Economics'" *Quarterly Journal of Economics*, Vol. 73, No. 4 (November 1959), pp. 554–575.

QUESTIONS FOR DISCUSSION

1. Characterize each of the steps of economic analysis. How do they compare with "the scientific method?" Which of these steps encompass what might be termed "theorizing?" Explain.

2. What is the difference among the terms "hypothesis," "theory," and "model"?

3. Distinguish carefully between "theory" and a "theoretical model."

4. On what grounds should a theory be evaluated? Which of these are more important, and why?

5. What is the role of assumptions in theory construction?

6. Defend Milton Friedman's position regarding the realism of assumptions. How would one go about measuring or assessing the amount of explanatory power inherent in a theory? Does this have anything to do with Friedman's emphasis on predictive power as the main criterion for judging the worth and merit of a theory?

7. On what grounds, if any, is the presence of explanatory power a desirable feature in a theory?

8. When might it be appropriate to build an analysis around assumptions that are extremely simplistic? Could such an analysis still be useful?

9. Can a model intended for explanatory purposes differ from one intended for predictive purposes?

10. (a) In a recent article, a *Wall Street Journal* columnist raised the economic question of why a pack of cigarettes obtained from a cigarette machine costs more than a pack of cigarettes bought over the counter. Feeling that it should be just the opposite, he observed:[13]

    > Everyone knows that a machine is a labor-saving device. It does things faster and easier and, one would expect, cheaper than people can. The cigaret machine at my corner luncheonette can stand there all day, every day without getting fallen arches. It never catches flu or has hangovers or sneaks off for an afternoon at the local ballpark. It doesn't require heating or lighting or air-conditioning or five-minute breaks to go the restroom. No one has to worry about the cigaret machine getting shortchanged (quite the opposite), or even slipping a couple of packs into its pocket when no one is looking. No, the cigaret machine would seem to be a classic example of an ideal form of people-replacing automation—wageless, undemanding, highly reliable.

[13] Quoted from John Tracy McGrath, "Ways to Stump an Economist," *The Wall Street Journal,* November 15, 1974, p. 14.

So, how come a pack of cigarets from the candy store costs 52 cents and a pack of cigarets from the cigaret machine a couple of doors away costs 65 cents?

Can you identify the variables that might be pertinent in accounting for the puzzlement of the columnist? What hypothesis would you offer as an explanation? How might your hypothesis be tested?

(b) In the same article, the columnist raised the question of why orange soda costs more than gasoline. His analysis ran as follows:[14]

> Gasoline starts with exploration in some God-forsaken part of the world. If oil is found, it has to be drilled for and then pumped out of the ground by pretty expensive equipment. Then it must be sent through a pipeline (a hefty capital investment), loaded into a tanker (ditto), transported over a vast expanse of water, offloaded to another pipeline, and pumped to a refinery (horrendous capital investment). After a complex refining process, what is now gasoline is loaded into railroad tank cars ($$$) and taken to a distributor's tank farm ($$). Now into tank trucks for delivery to gas stations ($). Finally the stuff is pumped into your automobile for about 60 cents a gallon, of which 12 cents is state and federal taxes. Everyone, including the laissez-faire heirs of Adam Smith and John Stuart Mill, agree that this net price of 48 cents a gallon, 12 cents a quart, is a cruel ripoff by greedy oil-producing countries and-or greedy oil companies.
>
> Now, orange soda. Like gasoline, soft drinks are produced largely by automated processes. But the equipment is relatively simple and inexpensive. The bottler puts ordinary tap water (sometimes from his own artesian well) into a can or bottle, adds some sugar syrup which also contains flavoring, coloring and a preservative, carbonates the mixture with a shot of carbon dioxide, seals the containers and delivers them by truck to our friend at the candy store. Friend sells soda for 50 cents a quart, $2 a gallon, no tax.
>
> Yes, I know. The price of sugar has risen sharply. But when sugar (and soda) were cheaper, so was gasoline. In just about the same ratio. And bottlers are now using corn syrup along with sugar to sweeten their soft drinks. But most tantalizing is the fact that quinine water and club soda and artificially sweetened diet drinks, none of which contains any sugar at all, also sell for $2 a gallon.

Identify the economic variables that could help explain why orange soda is more expensive than gasoline. What hypothesis would you offer as a possible explanation to the columnist? How would you test the validity of your hypothesis?

[14] *Ibid.*

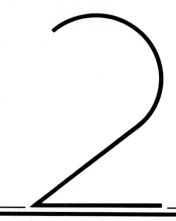

THE ROLE OF FIRMS
AND MARKETS
IN THE MICROECONOMY

One way to cut directly into the study of microeconomics is to look at what an economic system is and the basic economic activities that have to take place. Any economic system, no matter how it works, has to be concerned with such fundamental economic questions as:

- What and how much should be produced?
- How should the desired levels of production of each good and service be achieved?
- Who is to receive how much of the available supply of goods and services?
- What mechanism will exist to accommodate the need to change both the production of goods and services and the ways they are distributed to various members of society?

In a *traditional economic system* these four basic economic questions are answered by doing things in the same way as they have been done before. Custom, habit, "tried and true" methods, and social mores reign supreme and govern how things are done year after year. Economic change and technological change are slow moving. Tradition and the status quo are perpetuated. New ways of doing things are accepted very gradually and become "standard" only over a comparatively long time frame. Traditional economic systems were dominant until the eighteenth century and they still characterize the economies of many Third World nations.

   A *command economic system* relies upon public ownership and centralized control of the basic means of production; severe limitations are placed on the freedom of consumers and producers to make economic choices which conflict with government-determined economic priorities. The questions of what and how much to produce and how to distribute the fruits of production are decided by an economic commander-in-chief (a king, czar, prime minister, chairperson, or central planning authority). Heavy use is made of governmental economic directives so as to achieve planned economic outcomes. The thesis underlying a centrally planned economy is that the government is in the best position to decide what economic choices and policies are most beneficial for the economy and its component parts. Both socialistic and communistic nations are examples of command economies.

A *capitalistic* or *market economic system* emphasizes private ownership of economic resources and the means production, individual freedom of choice, competition, the profit motive, and prices determined by demand and supply conditions. Consumer wants and needs dominate what and how much to produce. The question of how best to achieve the desired levels of production is a function of the technological options, the costs of the various resource inputs which are required for each technological recipe, and the general need of producers to be efficient and cost competitive. The distribution of the available goods and services is based on incomes and the ability of consumers to buy what they choose. Most economic transactions take place in markets, where price is the ruling force and demand-supply conditions interact to determine price. The mechanism for eco-

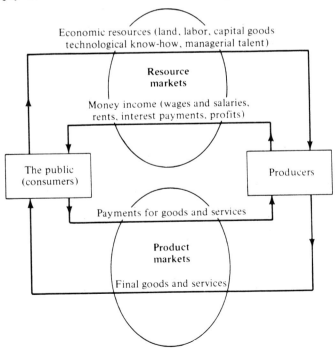

FIGURE 2-1
Economic activities in a modern market economy

nomic change is also the marketplace; changes in what consumers want to buy and are willing to pay are reflected on the demand side of the marketplace, while changes in technology, in the costs and availability of resources, in competitive pressures, and in productive efficiency are reflected on the supply side. A simplified picture of the market process is presented in Fig. 2-1. A key feature of the market system is the freedom of consumers and producers to make their own economic decisions and to pursue their own individual economic preferences, the thesis being that in encouraging the drive for individual economic self-interest, the outcome more often than not works out to be in the overall best interests of society as well.

The U.S. economy and the economies of most industrial nations in the Free World have a strong market orientation. No economy is purely and completely organized on market or capitalistic principles since all nations have governments which, to one degree or another, intervene in the economic process on behalf of society and thereby inject an element of command into their economic systems. In this sense the economies of the major industrialized nations are properly described as "mixed economic systems" with the relative doses of market and command elements varying from case to case. It is fair to say, however, that in the United States and in most of the rest of the industrialized nations *the firm is the principal economic agent for producing goods and services.*

HOW BUSINESS FIRMS FIT INTO THE MICROECONOMICS PICTURE

Although it is not always well recognized, business firms exist by public consent. In a market economy, where society grants business firms broad operating privileges (not the least of which is the opportunity to seek a profit), firms are implicitly obligated to serve the economic wants and needs of society—to the satisfaction of society. As society's principal vehicle for supplying goods and services, business firms, more than any other economic unit, become the hub of economic activity. They build new production facilities, invest in more efficient equipment, implement new technologies, market new and better products, oversee choices as to what kinds of economic resources will be engaged in what kinds of productive activities, and serve as the main source of jobs and income. So crucial is the economic role of business firms that the effectiveness with which they carry out their activities becomes a key determinant of society's economic well-being. Consequently, by focusing attention upon *the economics of the firm*—its decisions, its behavior, and its impact on society—it is possible to arrive at a basic understanding and perspective view of the inner workings of a modern market-oriented economy.

THE FIRM AND THE MARKETPLACE

The conventional wisdom in economics instructs that in a market economy the firm and its business are nearly always governed by competition and pressures in the marketplace. The firm is depicted as reacting and responding to competition and to market demand and supply conditions—forces that are beyond its purview to control. The market, not the firm, is generally viewed as the hub of economic activity and the focus of analytical concern.

Conventional business theory, in sharp contrast, looks upon markets and economic forces as limits to what a firm can do. Present and future market conditions are construed as creating opportunities (and threats) for business action. But market and economic forces are not thought of as absolute in determining what a firm does or what its business consists of. A firm's business mission, its objectives, and its strategy for competing in the marketplace are held to be well within the firm's sphere of influence; moreover, it is held to be within a firm's power to shape what happens in the marketplace with a well-conceived strategy. In fact, a particularly powerful business strategy is viewed as having the potential for generating a major impact on markets, buyers, rival firms, and the directions in which an industry is headed.

In actuality, there is validity in both views and no need to make an exclusive choice between the two different views. Markets affect firms and firms affect markets. Let's see why, starting with the role of markets and then looking at the role of firms in the microeconomy.

The Concept of the Market

In a competitive enterprise system "the market" is a factor to be taken into account by all other economic units. Its economic role is akin to that of the sun in solar system—all really important economic activities revolve around market considerations. The market is where buyers and sellers transact their business. The market is, at once, the basic mechanism for organizing an orderly exchange of goods and services and, through competitive interplay, the master over all voluntary economic transactions. The market is two-sided: it reflects both demand and supply conditions—and does so simultaneously. Through the market consumers make known their decisions to buy or not to buy and on what terms; through the market firms make known their willingness and ability to produce or not to produce and on what terms. According to an old Russian proverb, "once you have gone to market you have told the whole world." The market functions as an elaborate network through which the preferences and freely made decisions of buyers and sellers are communicated, recorded, totaled, and balanced against one another. The market, better than any firm, individual, or governmental agency, is able to signal what the current states of supply and demand are. The market is the first to receive and reflect the winds of economic change. So it is that the market's judgment about the balance between supply and demand and its verdict regarding the terms of exchange between buyers and sellers comprise an impartial and potent economic force to be reckoned with.

How a Market Functions: A Simple Model

The demand side of a market reflects the intensity with which buyers want and are willing to pay for the good or service in question. This intensity, which can be weak or strong or anywhere in between, can be represented graphically as a line showing the various quantities that buyers are willing to purchase at each of various possible prices, all other things being equal—see line *DD* in Fig. 2-2. Since buyers typically are willing to purchase less at higher prices than at lower prices, the relationship between price and quantity demanded is an inverse one (which makes the demand curve a down-sloping line). Events such as rising incomes, changes in the prices of substitute products, and shifts in preferences and life-styles can and do shift the shape and position of the demand curve, thereby creating a revised level of demand intensity (either higher or lower).

The supply side of a market depicts the extent to which sellers are willing and able to make supplies of a good or service available. Although many factors can enter into how much suppliers are willing to offer for sale at any given moment of time, supply conditions are usually such that sellers are inclined to produce more of a good or service at higher prices than at lower prices. In other words, the economic relationship between price and quantity supplied tends to be a direct one, resulting in an upward-sloping supply curve—line *SS* in Fig. 2-2. The reason for this is that, other things being equal, sellers will find it more profitable to intensify their production efforts when price is higher than when price is lower.

The interaction of demand and supply determines both the going market price and the quantity that changes hands. As depicted in Fig. 2-2, the demand and supply curves intersect at price P_1 and quantity Q_1. Competition guarantees that any other price-quantity combination will be unstable. If sellers, either deliberately or inadvertently, elect to charge a price above P_1, the surplus conditions that arise will induce competing sellers to shade their prices to work off the excess inventory buildups. As market price drops, buyers are stimulated to

$
D \qquad\qquad S

At prices above P_1, surplus
conditions will emerge,
resulting in downward
pressure on market price

At prices below P_1, shortage
conditions will emerge, and market
prices will be driven upward

$S \qquad\qquad D$

Quantity
(in units per
period of time)

FIGURE 2-2
The market mechanism: determination
of market price and the quantity sold

increase their purchases, whereas the quantity supplied (because of reduced profitability) will tend to contract, thereby acting to eliminate surplus conditions.

If the prevailing market price should for some reason turn out to be below P_1, the quantity demanded will exceed the quantity supplied such that shortages will appear. Those buyers who are most anxious to avoid doing without the product will, when confronted with shortage conditions, be inclined to accept a move on the part of sellers to alleviate a shortage via higher prices. Thus, in periods of shortage a competitive scramble among buyers for the available supplies tends to drive price upward—an outcome which automatically acts to eliminate the shortage, owing to the fact that higher prices serve to reduce the overall quantity demanded and to increase the quantity supplied.

In Fig. 2-2, only at price P_1 and quantity Q_1 will the market be cleared. At this price-quantity combination, neither surplus nor shortage conditions exist. A price-quantity *equilibrium* will prevail in the sense that no economic forces are currently operating to bring about a change in the market result. The tendency of a competitive market to establish a price at which the quantity demanded will equal the quantity supplied is called the *rationing function* of the price system and "the market mechanism" is the vehicle through which it all works.

Is "The Market" a Place?

Figuratively, the market is where buyers and sellers come together to effect their voluntary, freely made transactions. In this regard, one often hears mention made of "the marketplace," but strictly speaking, a market is seldom a single, precisely defined geographical place. In some markets buyers and sellers do indeed come face to face at a particular time and place to strike their bargain. A vegetable market and a shopping mall have such attributes. But many, maybe even most, markets range beyond a particular locale and assume area-wide, regional, national, or worldwide dimensions. A newsprint firm's market typically extends over a multistate region, thereby putting it in direct competition with other newsprint mills where market coverage overlaps. A major international oil company such as Exxon does business in many, many parts of the world and thus competes head-on with nearly every other oil company in one place or another. The markets for wheat, coffee, cotton, wool, gold, copper, rubber, aluminum, nickel, iron ore, and cocoa all assume global proportions. In the case of these and other highly standardized commodities, the market can function quite effectively without buyers and sellers standing over the goods and haggling over price and other conditions of exchange.

According to Alfred Marshall, a distinguished nineteenth-century British economist, the geographical limits of a market are defined by "an area within which buyers and sellers are in such close communication with each other that price tends to be the same throughout the area." However, Marshall's classic definition of a market proves troublesome today. Suppose that two supermarkets located across the street from each other are selling a particular brand of toothpaste at different prices—one for 79 cents and the other for 89 cents. Are we then to infer that the two grocery stores are not in the same market? Or suppose that

Avis typically rents cars at prices slightly below Hertz (perhaps because its fleet of cars consists of the less expensive, more economically equipped models). Can we conclude that Avis and Hertz are not head-on rivals competing in the same market? Would it not be more accurate to view Avis and Hertz as operating within the same market but endeavoring to appeal to different market segments through price competition? Consequently, it is fair to say that the size and extent of a market cannot be delimited solely on the criterion of price uniformity. The boundaries of a market have to be determined on a case-by-case basis, looking at both demand side and supply side characteristics.

What is indisputable, however, is that a market of some sort exists for all goods and services and all resources. There is a market for natural gas, a market for personal computers, a market for spark plugs, a market for life insurance, a market for quick copying services, a market for real estate, a market for business school graduates, a market for municipal bonds, a market for pro football players, and a market for the labor services of people skilled in operating bulldozers. It is also possible to describe a market by certain conditions that prevail as well by the product or service being exchanged. Thus, there are "buyers' markets" where conditions of oversupply and excess capacity allow buyers to drive especially good bargains with sellers. There are "sellers' markets" where demand is so strong relative to supply that sellers can command an attractive asking price. There are "perfectly efficient markets" where a large number of buyers deal with a large number of sellers, no one of which buys or sells more than an insignificant fraction of the total exchanged, where the commodities being offered by sellers are regarded by buyers as essentially identical, where the only criterion for a transaction is that no better bargain is available (that is, no buyers have a loyalty or preference for dealing with a particular seller), and where all traders are aware of all offers and deals available. Finally, there are "inefficient markets" where some or all of the foregoing conditions are absent.

Moreover, markets are linked and interconnected with each other. Markets are linked vertically since some products pass through a series of markets on their way to the final user—farmers sell cotton to ginners, who sell baled cotton fiber to cloth manufacturers, who sell yard goods to garment firms, which sell articles of clothing to department stores, which supply consumers in the retail market. Markets are linked horizontally in the sense that substitute or complementary products create relationships between and among markets for different products. What happens in the market for beef affects the market for pork. Prices in the gasoline market affect the travel and recreation business. Money market conditions affect residential construction activity. Yet each market retains a semblance of uniqueness since its operation is governed by the specific preferences and decisions of the specific buyers and sellers who participate in it as well as by the specific customs and patterns of doing business in that market.

The nature of the markets in which a firm does business is a matter for its management to study carefully. The firm's sales, profits, and growth potential are a function of both current market conditions and which way the winds of market change are blowing. A firm's success hinges upon its ability to analyze the marketplace accurately and position itself as strategically as possible so as to be in the right place, at the right time, with the right products (or services), offered at the right price. The role and function of a firm's *strategy* is to specify how this is to be accomplished.

THE FIRM AND ITS STRATEGY

Any firm has to pose and seek answers to a number of basic strategic questions: What products or services will the firm offer for sale? What buyer needs and buyer groups should the firm try to serve? How should the firm try to compete against rival firms? Should the firm concentrate on a single line of business or should it be diversified? A firm's answer to these questions defines its *strategy* and "the game plan" for approaching customers, competing against rivals, and settling upon the scope and makeup of its business interests—that is, strategy is a managerial action plan for positioning the firm in its environment and otherwise trying to operate the enterprise in a successful manner.

There are numerous ways for a firm to approach the marketplace and develop feasible answers to the questions of "what is our business, what will it be, and what should it be?" It may simply think of its business as being defined by the character of its main product or service; thus, a cement company may view itself as being in the cement business, a loan company as in the loan business, and a pizza villa as in the pizza business. Some firms describe their business by the principal ingredient in their products, as with steel companies, aluminum companies, and paper companies—even though their respective products come in a wide variety of sizes and forms and perform quite different functions. The unifying theme of other enterprises is technology, an example being General Electric, whose thousands of products are related in one way or another to electricity.

Still other firms prefer a concept based upon an expansive view of the customers or markets they serve. For example, electric utilities often construe their business as one of serving the full range of electric energy needs of any and all customers within their geographic territory. A sporting goods manufacturer may see its economic mission as supplying all types of sporting equipment to recreation enthusiasts. A home appliance manufacturer may view its business mission as one of supplying effort-saving and timesaving devices to households.

In many cases, however, a firm may employ a more explicit and narrowly focused strategy, endeavoring to zero in on a specific group of customers or a selected set of customer needs. For instance, a book publisher who does nothing but supply engineering and mathematics textbooks to college students is in a business quite distinct from that of publishing potential bestsellers sold to the general public through retail channels. Similarly, the target clientele of a small private liberal arts college is narrower and more restricted then that of a major comprehensive state university. And the business of a neighborhood convenience food mart is intended to serve fewer people and fewer needs as compared to a large supermarket.

Often, the business a firm is in defies strict classification. A firm may sell the same product to different types of customers in distinctly different ways, or it may utilize a number of different distribution channels in gaining access to markets and customers, or it may engage in a diversified set of businesses. This makes it hard to pin down exactly what a firm does and what its strategy is. For example, a hospital may say that it "provides comprehensive health care to the residents of the surrounding community," but this broad concept raises issues as to whether it is to include filling cavities and pulling teeth, making examinations for eyeglasses, nursing the aged, furnishing annual checkups, and engaging in rehabilitation services for the handicapped—all of which are often performed by medical professionals outside hospitals. A state university is unquestionably in the business of "higher education," but does this mean that it should be offering the full range of programs in higher education, including career-specific training, associate degrees similar to those of junior colleges, adult and continuing education, as well as undergraduate and graduate programs in all disciplines and professions? A railroad company may see itself as being in the "transportation business," but is this to mean getting into long-haul trucking or air-freight services or fleet car leasing or intercity busing or rapid transit?

In general, the business a firm is in is defined in terms of three dimensions: (1) customer groups, or *who* the firm is attempting to satisfy; (2) customer needs, or *what* is being satisfied; and (3) technologies, or *how* customer groups and customer needs are being served. Thinking of a business being defined in terms of only products offered and markets served is incomplete. A product, in reality, is only a physical manifestation of the application of a particular technology to the satisfaction of a particular function or need for a particular group of buyers. The definition of a firm's business, therefore, is a joint combination of technologies, functions, and customers to serve, not simply of products to offer for sale in the marketplace.

The Relevance and Importance of a Firm's Strategy

The approach that a firm takes in shaping the nature and direction of its business—as revealed by its strategy—is important from several standpoints. To begin with, the strategic course a firm charts for itself is the product of external market opportunities (or threats) and internal resources, skills, and management preferences. A whole host of factors, some related and some not, go into the firm's strategy formulation process. These include consumer buying trends and purchasing habits, technological change, competitive pressures, capital investment requirements, relative profit expectations, the firm's financial condition, an assessment of whether the firm's skills and management know-how qualify it to run a particular business successfully, preferences regarding diversification, the personal values and aspirations of management, the firm's obligations to segments of society other than stockholders, government regulations, and the social, political, and cultural constraints imposed on the firm's scope of action.

Second, the firm's strategy has a definite bearing on its competitive posture, market behavior, and range of business interests. For instance, some firms are (or try to be) technological leaders, while others are content with being technological followers. Some firms are self-acknowledged aggressive risk-takers, while others deliberately are more conservative and embrace a strategy of risk avoidance. Some firms emphasize quality and service, while others aim at the low-price, budget-conscious end of the market. Some firms position themselves as forward satellites of other companies, specializing in channeling the mass-produced items of these other companies forward to the final user; examples include automobile dealers, wholesale distributorships, and the retail chain stores. Other firms station themselves as backward satellites and make their business out of supplying one or more enterprises with raw materials, intermediate goods, or component parts (the apparel firm supplying Sears and the local logging operator whose business is furnishing wood to large paper mills serve as good examples). Some firms base their strategy on carving a niche for themselves on the "competitive fringe" of markets dominated by well-known, brand-name firms; the producers of so-called "off-brands" exemplify this type of firm. Some firms stick to a single line of business while others strive for broad diversification.

Third, strategy is the foundation for such fundamental areas of economic decision making within a business as (1) choosing which of several customer groups and customer needs to cater to, (2) selecting the most resource-efficient and cost-efficient technology and production process, (3) determining the optimum production scale and plant location, (4) trying to gain a competitive edge and win a profitable market share, and (5) responding to new market opportunities and changing demand-supply conditions.

All of this is a way of saying that insights into a firm's strategy help explain its behavior in the marketplace and provide a basis for assessing its chances for competitive survival. Whether a firm is an economic success or an economic failure is in part a function of the caliber of its strategy and not entirely just the economics of the marketplace. A well-managed firm will always seek to influence the markets for its products with a timely, perceptive, opportunistic strategy. Indeed, a major part of formulating a good strategy is concerned with how to *initiate* and *influence* rather than just *respond* and *react* to the product-customer-technological-economic changes taking place. The acid test of a good strategy, in fact, is the extent to which the firm's strategy (1) improves the firm's ability to compete successfully in the marketplace, (2) propels it to a position of market leadership, and (3) influences market trends and competitive forces. In addition, an understanding of the interplay between a firm's strategy and economic forces in the marketplace enters the picture in judging the effectiveness with which a competitive private enterprise system serves the overall economic welfare of consumers.

How a Firm's Strategy Often Evolves

In many instances a firm develops and its strategy evolves in a fairly standard pattern. Starting from a single-product, limited-market base, a firm first seeks to increase its sales volume, improve its market share, and build customer loyalty in the line of business where it first starts out. Initially, the firm's strategic emphasis is on growth and on building a stronger competition position vis-à-vis rival firms. Price, quality, service, and promotion are fine-tuned to respond more precisely to a detailed market need. The product line is broadened to meet minor variations in customer tastes and preferences. Opportunities for geographical market expansion are pursued; usually, the sequence of geographic expansion proceeds from local to regional to national to international markets, although the degree of penetration may be uneven from area to area because of varying profit potentials and may, of course, stop well short of global or even national proportions.

When the opportunities for profitable expansion of the original line of business start to peter out, the second strategic phase may be toward opportunities for vertical integration—either *backward* into the business of supplying one's own materials or component parts (rather than purchasing them from outside suppliers) or *forward* into the next manufacturing stage or channel of distribution. For some companies vertical integration is a natural strategic move, owing to the benefits vertical integration has upon the firm's ability to compete in its core business and to the potential for improving internal operating efficiency.

Once a firm has reached the practical limits of geographic market expansion in its original line of business and has also come to terms with the possibilities of forward and backward integration, the strategic options are either to attempt a more intensive implementation of the current line of business strategy or to begin to focus on diversification opportunities and building a portfolio of businesses.

A strategy of diversifying into a range of different businesses brings to the fore the issue of what new businesses and industries to enter. Obviously, there are many, many ways that a firm can address the issue of "what kind and how much diversification?" An almost infinite number of combinations of different business can be entered and become part of a firm's sphere of interest. Once a firm has invested in several different businesses and has assembled a diversified business portfolio, there arises the question of "what businesses should we get out of?"—planned abandonment, divestiture, and liquidation of *some* businesses become potential strategic options. Somewhere along the way and for any number of reasons, a firm's collection of businesses may fall into disarray and start to perform poorly; then, management's strategic challenge becomes one of concocting a game plan to restructure and rebuild the firm's portfolio of business interests to fit new conditions and new corporate priorities.

GENERIC TYPES OF CORPORATE STRATEGIES

This brief sketch of the evolutionary phases of a firm's strategy opens the door to examine the basic approaches to tailoring a corporate-wide strategic plan. Seven generic types of corporate strategy options stand out:

1. Concentration on a single business.
2. A strategy of vertical integration.
3. A strategy of related diversification.
4. A strategy of unrelated diversification.
5. Corporate retrenchment, turnaround, and repositioning strategies.

6. Abandonment, divestiture, and liquidation strategies.
7. Combination strategies.

Let's look at each of these generic corporate strategies to get a flavor of how firms can affect markets and also to begin to see some of the whys and hows of business behavior.

Concentration on a Single Business

The number of firms that have become household words concentrating in one line of business is impressively long. The power of a single-business concentration strategy is testified to by the blue-chip performance of such familiar companies as McDonald's, Holiday Inn, Coca-Cola, BIC Pen Corp., Apple Computer, Timex, Campbell Soup Co., Anheuser-Busch, Xerox, Dr Pepper, Gerber, and Polaroid, all of which gained their reputations in a single business.

A concentration strategy offers some impressive strengths and advantages. To begin with, a single business enterprise is more manageable. With the efforts of the *total* organization zeroed in on a particular technology-customer-product combination, efficiency objectives can be paramount and competitive strategy can be fine-tuned to the winds of market change and to specific customer needs and preferences. There is less chance that limited organizational resources will be spread thinly over too many activities. The firm's managers can develop first-hand, in-depth knowledge of the business and stay tuned in to all the subtle nuances of the marketplace and new developments affecting customers, technological options, and the actions of rival firms.

The power of concentrating on a single business cannot be taken lightly. A concentration strategy offers excellent potential for a firm to:

1. Become proficient at doing *one* thing *very well*, thereby building a distinctive competence and promoting a high degree of internal efficiency.
2. Acquire a solid reputation through its identification with a particular technology-customer group-product application combination.
3. Pioneer fresh approaches in meeting customer needs, responding to stiffer competition, and influencing industry trends and developments.
4. Use its accumulated experience and expertise to gain a sustainable competitive edge.

A concentration strategy in no way means that an enterprise is constrained to do the same thing in the same ways. Some actual examples of how a concentration strategy can be kept fresh and effective are given below:

1. *Create and promote more uses for the product.* Arm & Hammer baking soda sales increased markedly after the product was promoted for freshening refrigerators, cat litter boxes, and swimming pools.
2. *Take a standard commodity item and make a broader differentiated product out of it.* Frank Perdue succeeded in convincing people that his brand of chickens tasted better; Sunkist has done the same with oranges and lemons.
3. *Use advertising and promotional efforts to stimulate demand.* International Playtex and Johnson & Johnson discovered that tampons were "underadvertised" and scored major sales gains with increased television advertising.
4. *Attract nonusers to buy the product.* Procter & Gamble reversed declining Ivory soap sales in 1971 after promoting it for adults instead of just for babies.

5. *Turn an apparent disadvantage into an advantage.* J. M. Smucker put its funny-sounding name to good use with an advertising slogan: "With a name like Smucker's, it has to be good."

6. *Use price cuts to build volume, market share, and profitability.* Johnson & Johnson made its Tylenol analgesic a market success after it reduced Tylenol's price to match what Bristol-Myers was charging for Datril. Telephone companies increased the use and profitability of their long-distance call business by giving substantial rate discounts on night and weekend calls.

7. *Seek market outlets for complementary by-products.* Several lumber and wood products firms have made use of scrap materials and started marketing pine bark for landscaping purposes and cat litter and wood shavings for household pets.

8. *Develop a more compelling sales appeal.* Procter & Gamble's Pampers disposable diapers were only a modest success when touted as a convenience item for mothers, but sales took off after ads were changed to say that Pampers kept babies dry and happy.

9. *Capitalize on social concerns.* Sales of Dannon Yogurt rose sharply after ads helped health-conscious consumers "discover" the product.

10. *Make the product available through additional types of distribution channels.* Hanes captured additional sales and market share when it began to sell L'eggs panty hose in supermarkets.

Still other concentration strategy options include (1) convincing current customers to use more of a product via quantity discounts and faster rates of product innovation, (2) expanding into additional geographic markets, (3) improving quality, (4) offering more support services to customers, and (5) introducing a wider variety of models, sizes, and features to cater to specific buyer needs and preferences.

The point is that there is more than one type of concentration strategy and that there are many ways to position a firm within a single industry. For instance, the spectrum of positioning possibilities includes:

- A standard product offering⟵————————→A strongly differentiated product offering
- A single-item product line⟵————————→A full product line
- Catering to one or two customer groups⟵————————→Marketing to all types of customers
- Having one channel of distribution⟵————————→Using many channels of distribution
- Depending wholly on internal growth⟵————————→Emphasizing growth via acquisition of other firms in the same business

The strategy of concentrating on a single line of business does pose a major risk, however. Following a concentration strategy means putting all a firm's eggs in one basket. If the market for the enterprise's product or service declines, so does the enterprise's business. Changing customer needs, technological innovation, or new substitute products can undermine or virtually wipe out a single-business firm. One has only to recall what plastic bottles and paper cartons did to the market for glass milk bottles, what hand-held calculators did to the makers of slide rules, what electric typewriters did to the manual typewriter business, and what disposable diapers did to the business of cloth diaper manufacturers and to the need for diaper service companies.

APPLICATIONS CAPSULE

KELLOGG'S CONCENTRATION STRATEGY IN THE READY-TO-EAT CEREALS BUSINESS

Since 1906, when Will Keith Kellogg formed the company after accidentally discovering a way to make ready-to-eat cereal, Kellogg has aimed its strategy at being the dominant leader in the ready-to-eat cereal business. Kellogg's strategy for competing is based on product differentiation and market segmentation. The company's product line features a diverse number of brands, differentiated according to grain, shape, form, flavor, color, and taste—a something for everyone approach. Competing on the basis of low price has been deemphasized in favor of nonprice strategies keyed to extensive product variety, regular product innovation, substantial TV advertising, periodic promotional offers and prizes, and maintaining more space on the grocery shelf than rivals have.

Much of Kellogg's sales efforts are targeted at the under-25 age group (the biggest cereal eaters with an average annual consumption of 11 pounds per capita), and 33% of its cereal sales are in presweetened brands promoted almost totally through TV advertising to children. Kellogg endeavors to sidestep industry maturity and product saturation with introductions of fresh, "new" types of cereals (presweetened cereals in the 1940s, "nutritional" cereals in the 1950s, "natural" and health conscious cereals in the 1960s and early 1970s, and adult cereals in the late 1970s) and also by advertising a variety of times and places for eating cereals other than at the morning breakfast table. Product-line freshness is additionally enhanced by introduction of brands which differ only slightly from existing brands (flakes vs. shredded, plain vs. sugar-frosted, puffed vs. cocoa flavored).

In 1979, Kellogg introduced five new cereal brands—more than it had ever launched in a single year—as part of a stepped-up and redirected effort to attract consumers in the 25–50 age group (where consumption levels were only half those of the younger age groups). Kellogg also introduced its cereals in four additional countries in South America and the Middle East using campaigns that featured free samples, demonstration booths in food stores, and heavy local advertising so as to promote the use of ready-to-eat cereals as a substitute for traditional breakfast foods (corn meal and bulgur). Both of these moves were aimed at changing the eating habits of adults who had shied away from cereals or who had spurned breakfast altogether. In further support of its attempt to appeal to more customer groups, Kellogg continued to up its research budget (already the industry's most extensive) by 15% annually in an effort to develop more nutritional, health conscious cereals and breakfast foods for the older consumer segment. The whole of Kellogg's strategy in cereals had three strategic objectives: (1) increasing Kellogg's 42% market share, (2) increasing sales by 5% annually (compared to an industry growth of 2%), and (3) boosting annual cereal consumption from 8.6 pounds per capita to 12 pounds by 1985.

A Strategy of Vertical Integration

Vertical integration strategies are an offshoot of concentrating on a single business. They involve extending the scope of a single line of business backward into sources of supply and/or forward toward end users of the final product. Thus, if a manufacturer elects to make more of its own parts rather than purchase them from outside suppliers, it remains in the same industry as before—all that has changed is that its business interests extend further backward into the stages of production. Similarly, if a personal computer manufacturer elects to integrate forward by opening up a chain of retail stores to market its brands directly to users, it remains in the personal computer business even though its scope of activity within the industry has expanded.

Plainly, a firm can elect to integrate backward or integrate forward or do both. It can aspire to be fully integrated, participating in all stages of the process of getting products in the hands of final users, or it can elect to be only partially integrated. A firm can accomplish vertical integration via its own internal startup entry or it can choose to acquire an enterprise already positioned in the stage into which it wishes to integrate.

APPLICATIONS CAPSULE

VERTICAL INTEGRATION IN THE OIL INDUSTRY

Vertical integration became a way of life among the large, successful oil companies as far back as the early 1900s. The breakup of the Standard Oil trust in 1911 added impetus to vertical integration because many of the 33 newly created firms had major gaps in their business operations. During the following 10 to 15 years, with the demand for petroleum products increasing, with sales of automobiles beginning to mushroom, and with alternating periods of crude-oil shortage and oversupply, nearly all of the major companies found it less risky (and sometimes essential for competitive survival) to integrate both vertically and geographically. In the case of a refiner-marketer, there was always the threat that the feast of new crude oil discoveries would be followed by famine if and when the fields ran dry or demand increased faster than supply. So, both to preserve their profitability in the case of mushrooming supplies and to guard against possible shortages, it was desirable to integrate backward, part or all the way. This meant cultivating the goodwill of producers and drillers and making continued exploratory efforts attractive by constructing gathering lines and storage facilities as rapidly as possible and in sufficient volume to handle whatever was offered. It also meant going into production whenever and wherever necessary.

Crude-oil producers, in turn, could escape their feast-or-famine dilemma only by developing their own marketing outlets, integrating forward into both refining and retail distribution. Without assured markets, producers were necessarily subject to the randomness of crude-oil discovery and the ease of competitive entry in drilling and exploration. In both situations vertical integration contributed to the stability of the integrating company, first by providing some security against market fluctuation and instability and, second, through greater certainty of profit margins associated with a continuous utilization of producing capacity, pipelines, refinery facilities, and marketing outlets. In general, the oil companies that chose to integrate appeared to be seeking a degree of balance in their operations so as to protect them against what they perceived as an uncertain profit and competitive

cont.

cont.

position associated with heavy fixed costs and with being heavily dependent on uncontrolled intermediate markets. By maintaining a balance in each of the stages in which they did business, the operations at each stage tended to become mutually reinforcing and thus a contributor to greater operating efficiency and stability.

According to the classic study of integration and competition in the petroleum industry by Melvin de Chazeau and Alfred Kahn in 1959, the following composite paraphrase represents a rough consensus of how the executives of almost all the leading oil companies viewed the importance of vertical integration:

> We certainly try, in general, to keep a balanced operation. We will not ordinarily make major investments in one level without seeing that we are pretty well covered at other levels. So we do not expect to make the same return from our investments in production, refining and marketing. As a general rule we will not demand as high a return from prospective investments that put us in balance as from those that put us out of balance. We have a going organization, with substantial commitments at all levels: we cannot shift from one to the other with each short-term fluctuation of returns: we have to protect the positions we already have.[a]

Currently, about 50 petroleum companies in the United States can be classified as vertically integrated in that they operate in at least three stages—production, refining, and marketing.

[a] Melvin G. de Chazeau and Alfred E. Kahn, *Integration and Competition in the Petroleum Industry* (New Haven, Conn.: Yale University Press, 1959), p. 114.

Vertical integration can be a desirable strategy wherever it boosts a firm's competitive strength. Integrating backward into the business of one's suppliers offers the potential for converting a cost center into a profit producer—an attractive option when suppliers have sizable profit margins. Moreover, integrating backward spares a firm the uncertainty of being dependent on suppliers of crucial raw materials or support services, as well as lessening the firm's vulnerability to suppliers' raising the prices of important component materials.

The strategic impetus for forward integration has much the same roots. Undependable sales and distribution channels can give rise to costly inventory pileups and frequent production shutdowns, thereby undermining the economies of stable production operation. For a raw materials producer, integrating forward into manufacturing may help achieve greater product differentiation and allow escape from competing solely on the basis of price to provide a standard raw material. For a manufacturer, integrating forward may not only improve access to end-user markets but it can also produce better control over the nature and quality of services rendered to end users.

Related and Unrelated Diversification Strategies

There are two generic approaches to corporate diversification: *related* and *unrelated*. In related diversification a firm's several lines of business, although distinct, still possess some kind of "fit" based on common technology, a basic skill, common distribution channels, similar methods of operation, similar kinds of managerial know-how, product complementarity, or customer overlap—virtually any aspect of meaningful relatedness. In contrast, with unrelated diversification there is no common thread or element of fit among a firm's several lines of business; in this sense unrelated diversification is *pure* diversification.

Related Diversification Strategies. Related diversification is a very attractive way to expand a firm's field of business interests. It allows an enterprise to preserve a common core of unity in its business activities while spreading the risks out over a broader base. But more important, perhaps, when a firm has been able to build a distinctive competence in its original business, related diversification offers a way to exploit what it does best. Diversifying with the express intent of extending the firm's expertise to related businesses may carry with it a competitive advantage and above-average profit opportunities. Specific approaches to related diversification include:

- Moving into closely related products (a bread bakery buying a firm making crackers and snack foods).
- Building upon company technology (a maker of agricultural seeds and fertilizers diversifying into chemicals for insect and plant disease control).
- Seeking to increase plant utilization (an aluminum window manufacturer with idle equipment and unused plant space deciding to add aluminum siding and aluminum gutters to its product portfolio).
- Utilizing available sources of raw materials (a pulp and paper products firm electing to devote some of its timberland to plywood production).
- Acquiring a firm where the buyer has a distinctive ability to improve the operations of the seller (a successful mass-marketer of women's cosmetics buying a distributor of women's jewelry and accessories).
- Building upon the organization's brand name and goodwill (a successful coffee firm diversifying into tea).
- Acquiring new businesses which will uniquely help the firm's position in its existing businesses (a canned fruit juice firm diversifying into canned vegetables and frozen pies to give it more clout with food brokers and an expanded distribution system).

Actual examples of related diversification abound. The BIC Co., which pioneered inexpensive throwaway ballpoint pens, used its distinctive mass production and mass merchandising competences as a basis for diversifying into disposable cigarette lighters, disposable shaving razors, and panty hose. Tandy Corp. practiced related diversification when its chains of Radio Shack outlets, which originally handled mostly radio and stereo equipment, added telephones, intercoms, calculators, clocks, electronic and scientific toys, microcomputers, and peripheral computer equipment in an effort to become one of the world's leading distributors of electronic technology to individual consumers.

Unrelated Diversification Strategies. Although one might expect an overwhelming majority of firms to favor related diversification because of the benefits of having good strategic fit, unrelated diversification has nonetheless attracted some firms. A simple criterion of diversifying into "any industry in which we think we can make a profit" captures the essence of the corporate strategy of multibusiness, multi-industry firms. Textron, for example, is the corporate parent of such diverse businesses as Bell helicopters, Gorham silver, Homelite chain saws, Sheaffer pens, Fafnir bearings, Speidel watchbands, Polaris snowmobiles, Sprague gas meters and fittings, Bostitch staplers, air cushion vehicles, iron castings, milling machines, rolling mills, industrial fasteners, insurance, and missile and spacecraft propulsion systems. International Telephone and Telegraph (ITT), another pioneer of unrelated diversification, is the corporate owner of such businesses as telephone equipment, Sheraton Hotels, Wonder Bread, Smithfield Hams, Bobbs-Merrill Publishing Co., Hartford Insurance Co., Aetna Finance Co., Jabsco Pump Co., Gotham Lighting Co., Speedwriting Inc., Transportation Displays, Inc., Rayonier chemical cellulose, Bramwell Business School, South Bend Window Cleaning Co., and Scott lawn care products.

Possible ways to pursue unrelated diversification strategies include:

1. A cash-rich, opportunity-poor company seeking to acquire a number of opportunity-rich, cash-poor enterprises.
2. A firm subject to strong seasonal and cyclical sales patterns diversifying into areas with a counterseasonal or countercyclical sales pattern.
3. A debt-heavy firm seeking to acquire a debt-free firm so as to balance the capital structure of the former and increase its borrowing capacity.
4. Building a diversified portfolio of three or four unrelated groups of businesses, but striving for some degree of relatedness within each group.
5. Acquiring any firm in any line of business as long as the projected profit opportunities equal or exceed minimum criteria.

APPLICATIONS CAPSULE

BEATRICE FOODS' DIVERSIFICATION STRATEGY

Originally a local butter and egg company in Beatrice, Nebraska, the company began an effort to diversify its product line and reduce its dependence on local conditions. It started by acquiring a string of small dairies. From the outset, Beatrice followed two key principles—diversification and decentralization. Only firms headed by independent-minded entrepreneurs were brought into the fold. Although Beatrice found that the dairy business had the disadvantage of low profit margins, it had the advantage of generating a lot of excess cash (mainly because inventories of milk are provided by nature and do not require endless financing). Thus, having acquired dairies coast to coast and grown into a $200 million dairy company, Beatrice began to invest some of its cash in higher-margin food companies. LaChoy Food Products was the first acquisition and, when it worked out well, Beatrice began to push into other food lines at an accelerating rate. In the 1960s Beatrice acquired

cont.

cont.

some non-food firms and by the 1970s owned several different kinds of manufacturing operations, a warehousing division, and an insurance company. Among its acquisitions were Samsonite (luggage), Meadow Gold (dairy products), Martha White (flour), Dannon (yogurt), Clark (candy bars), Eckrich (meats), Gebhardt's (chili and tamales), and LaChoy (Chinese foods).

Beatrice's acquisition strategy followed some strict guidelines. Commodity-oriented firms were excluded because of the unpredictable price swings. Companies in head-on competition with such powerhouses as Kellogg's and Campbell Soups were avoided. In the non-food areas, Beatrice shied away from labor-intensive companies because of the risks of inflation of labor costs. Industries like steel and chemicals were avoided because of their heavy capital demands.

The basic acquisition strategy was to go after companies with at least five years of sales and profit increases, and to eliminate from consideration any firm so large that failure could seriously damage Beatrice's overall profitability. Between 1952 and 1962 most of the acquired firms had sales of about $2 million. While Beatrice sought companies with a growth rate higher than its own, it insisted on a purchase price keyed to a price-earnings multiple about one-third below Beatrice's own current price-earnings ratio. Beatrice was generally successful in buying firms it wanted at a "discount" because the Beatrice stock it was offering in return had performed so very well over the years.

Once acquired, the new businesses were managed under a decentralized structure; the general managers of each unit were given broad-ranging authority and turned loose to formulate and implement their own strategies, thereby allowing each one to be tailored to the specifics of its own market environment.

In 1977 Beatrice Foods overtook Kraft and Esmark to become the largest food-processing firm in the United States.

Source: Linda Grant Martin, "How Beatrice Foods Sneaked Up on $5 Billion," *Fortune,* April 1976, pp. 118–129.

There are several points to keep in mind about unrelated diversification strategies. First, while unrelated diversification can lead to improved sales, profits, and growth when a firm diversifies into industries where the economic potential is stronger than in its existing businesses, there are some big risks. The Achilles heel of unrelated diversification is the strain it places on corporate-level management to cope with the variety of problems encountered in a widely diversified business portfolio. Not many corporate managements are truly capable of overseeing many unrelated businesses at once. Such capability is seldom demonstrated by successfully managing one or two different businesses since the experiences and know-how gained in one often do not transfer to another. Just as the skills of an all-pro basketball player do not transfer to playing professional ice hockey, so a television manufacturer may lack the skills needed to manage a newly acquired fast-food chain. One simply cannot count upon being clever enough to hire "good management" to run many kinds of entirely different businesses and, in addition, to be clever at staying on top of how well all the different business-level managers are doing their jobs—such cleverness is easier to conceive in theory than it is to carry out in practice. In related diversification a firm can seek to extend and build on something it knows about, whereas in unrelated diversification a firm is entering "a whole new ballgame" where its prior skills and experience count for little.

Second, without some kind of strategic fit, consolidated performance of an unrelated multibusiness portfolio will tend to be no better than the sum of what the individual business units could achieve if they were independent firms, and it may be worse to the extent that centralized management policies hamstring the line of business units. This implies that pursuing a strategy of unrelated diversification adds little, if anything, to the competitive strength of the individual business units.[1] The primary value that corporate management adds in a widely diversified firm derives from an ability to do a good job of portfolio management— deciding what new businesses to add to the portfolio, which ones to get rid of, and how to allocate financial resources to the ones that are to be kept. Third, although unrelated diversification might seem to offer the potential of greater sales-profit stability over the course of the business cycle, there is not much evidence that widely diversified firms consistently suffer milder reversals in periods of recession and economic stress.

The Vehicles for Accomplishing Diversification.   Entry into new businesses can take any of three forms: acquisition, internal startup, and joint ventures. *Acquisition of an existing business* is a popular approach to corporate diversification. The buying (and selling) of companies to accomplish diversification has produced a very active market. The market for companies is well organized, rather sophisticated, and fairly efficient, involving finders, brokers, and investment bankers, all seeking to match potential buyers with willing sellers and often securing large commissions for their services and advice. Multiple bids for companies up for sale are commonplace, and both friendly mergers and unfriendly *takeovers* are much in vogue.[2] There are several reasons why an organization may prefer acquisition of an existing enterprise to launching its own grass-roots development of a new business. Acquiring an established organization has the advantage of much quicker entry into the target market while offering a way to hurdle such barriers to entry as patents, technological inexperience, the need to seek out reliable sources of supplies, the need to match rival firms in terms of efficiency and unit costs, costly promotional expenses requisite for gaining market visibility and brand recognition, and getting adequate distribution access. Internally de-

---

[1] Evidence to this effect is given in Stanley E. Boyle, *Economic Report on Conglomerate Merger Performance: An Empirical Analysis of Nine Corporations*, Staff Report to the Federal Trade Commission, reprinted in *Mergers and Acquisitions*, Vol. 8, No. 1 (Spring 1973), pp. 5–41; Ronald W. Melicher and David F. Rush, "The Performance of Conglomerate Firms: Recent Risk and Return Experience," *Journal of Finance*, Vol. 28, No. 2 (May 1973), pp. 381–388; and Robert L. Coun, "The Performance of Conglomerate Firms: Comment," *Journal of Finance*, Vol. 28, No. 3 (June 1973), pp. 754–758.

[2] In recent years, takeovers have become an increasingly used approach to acquisition. The term *takeover* refers to the attempt (often sprung as a surprise) of one firm to acquire ownership or control over another firm against the wishes of the latter's management (and perhaps some of its stockholders).

veloping the knowledge, resources, scale of operation, and market reputation necessary to become an effective competitor can take years and entails all the problems of startup. In addition, using acquisition as the vehicle for diversification has particular merit when:

- The buyer has a distinctive ability to improve the operations of the firm being acquired.
- The acquiring firm is buying into an industry with unusually attractive outlook and potential.
- The new acquisition will uniquely help the acquiring firm's position in its existing businesses.[3]

Yet there are some important drawbacks to acquisition. Finding the right kind of company to acquire can sometimes present a problem. Conceivably, an acquisition-minded firm may face the dilemma of buying a successful company at a high price or a struggling company at a low price. In the first case, the seller is in position to demand a generous compensation for the risks that have been faced, for the effort expended in putting together a successful organization, and for gaining whatever competitive position/distinctive competence is being acquired. If the buying firm has very little knowledge about the industry it is seeking to enter but has ample capital, it may be better off acquiring a capable firm— irrespective of the higher price. On the other hand, it can be advantageous to acquire a struggling firm at a bargain price when the new parent sees promising ways for transforming the weak firm into a strong one and has the money and know-how to transform it into a much stronger competitor.

Achieving diversification through *internal development* involves creating a new business entity in the desired industry and, starting from scratch, establishing new production capacity, finding sources of supply, developing channels of distribution, building a customer base, and so on. Determining the balance between the benefits and costs of internal entry entails some wide-ranging considerations:

- The firm's ability to handle the capital requirements of establishing a new business of minimum efficient size.
- How hard it will be to overcome the prevailing entry barriers (for example, will it be hard to gain access to needed technology, overcome the established name and reputation of existing firms, raise the money to fund up-front investments and cover startup losses, and secure broad enough buyer acceptance to capture a sufficient market share?).
- The effect the entrant's new production capacity will have on the supply-demand balance in the industry.
- The reactions that can be expected from incumbent firms. (Will the entrant's presence trigger price cutting and aggressive retaliation by existing firms to defend their entrenched position, or will the presence of a new firm not make much of a dent in the market and thereby not provoke much notice?)
- The profits and cash flows that can be expected from successfully participating in the industry.

[3] Michael E. Porter, *Competitive Strategy: Techniques for Analyzing Industries and Competitors* (New York: The Free Press, 1980), pp. 354–355.

Joint ventures are a useful way to gain access to a new business in at least three types of situations. First, a joint venture is a good device for doing something which is uneconomical for an organization to do alone. The Alaskan pipeline, for instance, is a joint venture in raw material supply which not only was beyond the prudent financial strength of any one oil giant but which also was, in its most economic size, designed to carry more crude oil than one company could produce from its oil land holdings. For each oil company owning oil reserves on the Alaskan North Slope to build its own pipeline to the size of its own production capability would have made little business or environmental sense. But participating in a jointly financed and jointly operated pipeline made economic fits out of misfits and enhanced the value of the partners' Alaskan oil reserves. Second, the strategy of joint venturing carries the advantage that risk is shared and therefore reduced for each participating firm. This is no small matter in a relatively large undertaking. Third, joint ventures make sense when the skills of two or more firms are needed in order to succeed; in such cases each company brings to the deal special talents which, when pooled, give rise to a new enterprise with stronger capabilities than the parents. For example, when in the 1920s General Motors developed tetraethyl lead to cure engine-knocking problems, it decided not to start its own gasoline production and distribution business to exploit the advantages of tetraethyl lead but, instead, chose to enter into a joint venture with Standard Oil of New Jersey (now Exxon), which already knew the gasoline business and had the missing expertise. Thus was born Ethyl Corporation, which grew into a worldwide supplier of tetraethyl lead for all the large gasoline marketers. With its joint venture strategy GM, in effect, made money on every gallon of tetraethyl lead gasoline sold—an effective outcome as compared to that of entering the gasoline business on its own and trying to compete directly against the oil companies.

Corporate Turnaround and Retrenchment Strategies

The thrust of corporate turnaround and retrenchment strategies is to restore an ailing firm to good health. The first task of a *turnaround* is diagnosis of the underlying reasons for poor corporate performance. The causes can be as diverse as having large losses in one or more business units which pull overall performance down, having a disproportionate number of businesses in increasingly unattractive industries, a bad economy which has adversely impacted many of the firm's business units, or having weak management. The nature of a turnaround strategy necessarily depends on the causes of poor performance and the degree to which the firm is "sick." Generally speaking, there are seven ways to try to turn around a diversified enterprise: (1) work to restore profitability in the money-losing business units, (2) deemphasize poorly performing lines of business and allocate money and resources to expanding the better performing business units, (3) institute across-the-board budget cuts in all business units, (4) revamp the composition of the firm's business interests by selling off weak businesses and replacing them with new acquisitions in more attractive industries, (5) replace key management personnel, (6) launch profit improvement programs in all business units, and (7) a combination of these. The specifics of how to overhaul and rebuild a poorly performing diversified firm, plainly enough, are a function of a firm's own problems and business portfolio composition.

Corporate *retrenchment* is a common short-run strategy for firms during periods of recession, corporate financial strain, and other adverse situations. Retrenchment at the corporate level can assume either of two variations: (1) stringent across-the-board internal economies aimed at wringing out waste and improving efficiency, and (2) a selective pruning and revamping of the weakest performing businesses in the corporate portfolio.

In the first instance, a firm that finds itself in a defensive or overextended position elects to remain in most or all of its current businesses and tries to weather the storm with various internal economy measures. Ordinarily, this type of corporate retrenchment strategy is highlighted by corporate-wide directives to reduce operating expenses, improve efficiency, and boost profit margins. It can involve curtailing the hiring of new personnel, trimming the size of corporate staff, postponing capital expenditure projects, stretching out the use of equipment and delaying replacement purchases so as to economize on cash requirements, retiring obsolete equipment, dropping marginally profitable products, closing older and less efficient plants, reorganizing internal work flows, reducing inventories, and the like.

The second variation of corporate retrenchment singles out the weak-performing parts of the corporate business portfolio for major strategy revisions, internal overhaul, and whatever else may be necessary to restore them to good health. Performing radical surgery on those units that are least profitable is nearly always a by-product of poor overall corporate performance and/or persistently poor performance in the targeted business units. Many diversified firms have found it necessary to launch drastic cutbacks in one or more of their business units because of severe trouble managing so many different businesses which do not "fit," or because of operating problems in one or more businesses which proved intractable or beyond their expertise, or because of a lack of funds to support the investment needs of all the businesses in their corporate portfolios.

Corporate retrenchment is a typical reaction to adversity from within or without the organization. Ordinarily, it is a temporary or short-run strategy for riding through bad times; once it becomes feasible to renew growth and pursue expansion opportunities, retrenchment strategies are usually discarded in favor of some other strategy.

APPLICATIONS CAPSULE

RETRENCHMENT AND CORPORATE RESTRUCTURING AT PILLSBURY

During the 1960s many companies initiated strategies for broadly diversifying their activities. During the 1970s, when it became painfully apparent that many of the newly-acquired businesses were not performing up to expectations or else did not "fit in" very well, a sizable number of these very same companies changed their

cont.

cont.

strategies from pure diversification to one of related diversification. Pillsbury was one of the companies which retreated from a conglomerate approach to a conceptual approach to diversification.

When William H. Spoor became chairman of the board of Pillsbury in January 1973, he moved quickly to narrow Pillsbury's product base to the area he felt the company knew best—food. In short order Pillsbury moved to divest its low-growth, cyclical business in poultry, its minority housing unit (Pentom Builders), its interest in magazine publishing (*Bon Appetit*), its computer service business, and its money-losing wine business (Souverain Winery). Mr. Spoor was quoted as saying, "I am only interested in businesses that fall into three categories. We should only be in consumer foods, food away from home, and agri-products."

Pillsbury's original base of business from which it first launched its diversification efforts revolved around flour milling (it is the largest miller in the U.S.), producing bakery mixes (some 300 varieties), commodity merchandising, grain exports, and grocery items for consumers (including flour, cake mixes and frostings, pancake mix, quick bread mixes, and a wide assortment of refrigerated dough products). Most of these businesses generated healthy profits and cash flows but were in markets where growth was slower. Volume gains, particularly in the consumer products categories, were largely dependent on taking business away from rival brands—a costly process with little prospect of major gains in profitability. This was what motivated the original diversification strategy.

Under Spoor's leadership, however, Pillsbury's acquisitions reverted to a more focused direction and reflected the decision to become an international food company participating in the three major areas of agribusiness, household food items, and restaurants. Firms acquired by Pillsbury under its new corporate concept included:

1. Wilton Enterprises, Inc. (acquired in 1973)—the nation's leading marketer of cake decorating products.
2. Totino's Pizza (acquired in 1976)—the second largest maker of prepared pizzas, with just over a 20% market share.
3. Fox Deluxe Foods (acquired in 1976)—operator of a pizza manufacturing plant in Joplin, Missouri.
4. American Beauty Macaroni Company (acquired in 1977)—manufacturer of a broad line of high-quality pasta products.
5. Speas Company (acquired in 1978)—a manufacturer of apple juice, cider vinegar, and pectin.
6. Green Giant Co. (acquired in 1978)—maker of frozen and canned foods.

The Green Giant acquisition was a major strategic effort by Pillsbury to gain a product mix that would put the company on a par with Kellogg Co. and H. J. Heinz, and to prepare it for a later capability to compete more broadly with General Mills and General Foods. By acquiring Green Giant, Pillsbury gained some strategic leverage in capturing shelf space in supermarkets for Pillsbury's less widely distributed lines (cake decorating sets, Funny Face and Squoze powdered drink mixes, Erasco food products, American Beauty pasta, and Sprinkle Sweet artificial sweetener). Green Giant's canned and frozen food lines were popular and thus attractive lines for supermarkets to carry. A key to success in gaining distribution through supermarkets is for a manufacturer to have products with dominant first or second

cont.

cont.

positions in fast-growing sales areas—something Pillsbury had not been able to accomplish as well as some other manufacturers. Green Giant products were tagged to fill this gap.

Besides its new acquisitions, Pillsbury continued to be active in expanding its interests in the restaurant business. Burger King Corp., acquired in 1967, was turned into the company's main revenue producer. Shortly after the acquisition, when Burger King failed to keep pace with its fast-growing market, Spoor hired the No. 3 man at McDonald's, Donald Smith, to revitalize the chain—specifically to double the number of outlets and triple earnings by 1983. During the 1973–1978 period, 70% of Pillsbury's capital improvements budget, or $385 million, was allocated to the Burger King division. A grow-and-build strategy was also used in Pillsbury's Steak and Ale restaurants (some of which operate under the names of Jolly Ox and Bennigan's) where the number of outlets rose from 52 in 1973 to 165 in 1978. At the same time, Pillsbury pushed forward in expanding its Poppin Fresh Pie Shops business; the number of units open increased from 6 in 1974 to 45 in 1978. The pie shops are mid-priced family restaurants, seating about 135 persons, featuring 27 varieties of pies and offering a limited menu of sandwiches, soups, and salads.

In its *1977 Annual Report*, Pillsbury announced that its current corporate strategy and diversification programs were aimed at producing a "repetitive, predictable, and growing" stream of earnings. The company's quantitative targets were (1) an average annual sales growth rate of 10%, (2) a minimum annual earnings per share growth rate of 10%, (3) a pretax return on average invested capital of 20%, (4) an after-tax return on stockholders' equity of 16%, and (5) an "A" credit rating.

Abandonment, Divestiture, and Liquidation Strategies

Even a shrewd corporate diversification strategy can result in the acquisition of businesses that just do not work out. Misfits or partial fits cannot be completely avoided, if only because it is impossible to predict precisely how getting into a new line of business will actually work out. Moreover, market potentials change with the times and what once was a good diversification move may later turn sour. Subpar performance by some business divisions is bound to occur, thereby raising questions of whether to get rid of them. Other business divisions may simply not mesh as well with the rest of the firm as was originally thought. Partial misfits and poorly performing divisions can also emerge, despite the presence of some strategic fit, owing to a firm's inability to manage the business or to the overload placed on internal cash resources. In still other cases, relentless changes in the customer-technology-product makeup of a business break up what once was a good strategic fit with the firm's other businesses.

When a particular line of business loses its appeal (for any of the preceding reasons), the most attractive strategy may be to get rid of it. Often such businesses are sold off to another firm. A useful guide for determining if and when to divest a particular line of business is to ask the question "If we were not in this business today, would we want to get into it now?"[4] When the answer is "no" or "probably not," getting rid of it needs to become a priority consideration.

Divestiture can take either of two forms. In some cases, it works fine to divest a business by spinning it off as a financially and managerially independent company, with the parent company retaining partial ownership or not. In other cases, divestiture is best accomplished by selling the unit outright (perhaps because this will yield more benefit to the firm's stockholders or because the business may not be able to survive as an independent operation), in which case a buyer needs to be found.

Of all the strategic alternatives, liquidation is the most unpleasant and painful, especially for a single-business enterprise, where it means terminating the organization's existence. For a multi-industry, multibusiness firm to liquidate one of its lines of business is less traumatic; the hardships of suffering through layoffs, plant closings, and so on, although not to be minimized, still leaves an ongoing organization, and perhaps one that eventually will turn out to be healthier after its pruning than before. In hopeless situations, an early liquidation effort often serves owner-stockholder interests better than an inevitable bankruptcy. Prolonging the pursuit of a lost cause merely exhausts a firm's resources and leaves less to liquidate. Unfortunately, of course, it is seldom simple for management to differentiate between when a cause is lost and when a turnaround is achievable.

Combination Strategies

The six strategy alternatives discussed above are not mutually exclusive. They can be used in combination, either in whole or in part, and they can be chained together in different sequences. For instance, one well-known company over a two-year period added 25 new lines of business to its corporate portfolio (16 through acquisition and 9 through internal startup), divested 4, and closed down the operations of 4 others. Moreover, there are endless variations of each of the six alternatives, allowing ample room for enterprises to create their own individualized strategic path. Although each firm's strategy tends to be idiosyncratic and otherwise tailor-made to its own particular situation, there are nine distinctive types of firms which are found in the population of business enterprises:

1. A single business enterprise operating in only one stage of an industry's production chain.
2. A partially integrated, single business enterprise operating in *some* of the stages of an industry's production chain.
3. A fully integrated, single business enterprise operating in *all* stages of an industry's production chain.
4. A "dominant business" enterprise with sales concentrated in one major core business but with a modestly diversified portfolio of either related or unrelated businesses (amounting to one-third or less of total corporate-wide sales).

[4] Peter F. Drucker, *Management: Tasks, Responsibilities, Practices* (New York: Harper & Row, Publishers, 1974), p. 718.

5. A narrowly diversified enterprise whose business portfolio includes a "balanced" mixture of a *few* (3 to 10) *related* business units.

6. A broadly diversified enterprise whose business portfolio includes a "balanced" mixture of many (10 to several hundred) mostly *related* business units.

7. A narrowly diversified enterprise whose business portfolio includes a "balanced" mixture of a few (3 to 10) unrelated business units.

8. A broadly diversified enterprise whose business portfolio includes a "balanced" mixture of *many* (10 to several hundred) mostly *unrelated* business units.

9. A multibusiness enterprise which has deliberately diversified into several different and unrelated areas but which has a portfolio of related businesses within each area, thus giving it several unrelated groups of related businesses.

THE CONCEPT OF THE FIRM RECONSIDERED

Traditionally, microeconomists have spoken of "the firm" as if its every action is directed by an owner-entrepreneur—a risk-taking individual who supplies financial capital, who organizes and supervises the economic resources needed for production, and who is supposedly gifted in the task of running a business. Moreover, the firm is seen as engaging in just a single line of business. The firm's behavior in this single-market, single-industry environment is said to be orchestrated by the owner-entrepreneur, with conformity to the chosen goals being purchased by payments (wages, salaries, prestige, power, security) to employees and by a system of internal controls (authority, budgets) which keeps things on track.

This concept of the firm is, of course, very appropriate for small, owner-managed enterprises, but it is at considerable variance with reality as concerns the larger corporate enterprise. The modern corporation is run by a team of professional managers who usually have a comparatively small ownership interest. The majority of the owners of corporations are absentee stockholders whose only critical role is to supply the enterprise with equity capital; the extent of stockholders' involvement seldom goes beyond an emotional concern with how much they are realizing on their financial investment (whether the company's stock price is rising or falling and the size of the dividend). Moreover, the majority of large corporate enterprises are multibusiness, multimarket, transnational firms; the scope of their operations may include related or unrelated diversification or both. Their corporate strategies can be very complex and involve a host of different competitive approaches—one for each line of business they are in.

"The firm" as a comparatively small, owner-managed, single-business small proprietorship with a localized market for its products and its stress entrepreneurship is one thing. "The firm" as a large, diversified portfolio of businesses, managed by a team of professional managers and having thousands of employees and stockholders, is another. The former is the most significant form of enterprise in terms of numbers, but the latter also has a major role in modern economies, accounting for 25 to 50% of the sales revenues of all businesses in many nations. In a real sense, corporate enterprises form the core of business activity in modern economies, dominating a number of important industries in manufacturing, transportation, utilities, retailing, services, and finance. It is their central importance which gives rise to such popular labels as "the corporate economy," "the corporate state," and "corporate capitalism."

However, all business firms, no matter how diverse their size and scope, share an important characteristic: they ultimately have to be concerned with how to compete in *each* line of business they are in. Every business has its own set of market demand-supply conditions, its own set of economic characteristics and forces of change, its own technology and cost patterns, its own competitive pressures, and so on. A firm thus needs a specific, custom-tailored strategy for competing in each line of business in which it is engaged and it has to decide how to try to position itself in the marketplace—on a market-by-market and business-by-business basis.

We shall take advantage of this business characteristic and use "the single-business firm" as the centerpiece for analyzing the economics of the firm. By looking at "the firm" as if it is only in a single line of business, we can zero in on the whys and wherefores of the behavior of a firm in a given market. It is then a not-too-large step to exploring what is different about the multibusiness, multi-industry corporate enterprise insofar as the microeconomics of firms and markets are concerned. We shall see, in fact, that we can link the economics of the single-business enterprise to the economics of the multibusiness enterprise using the concepts and ideas about corporate strategy that we surveyed earlier.

In the chapters that follow we shall analyze the microeconomic environment in greater depth, looking at how market forces shape what firms can and cannot do and looking at how firms can influence market trends and directions with a well-conceived business strategy. By focusing on the firm operating in various types of market situations and competitive conditions, we can learn about the economic relationships underlying the demand for a firm's product, efficient production technologies and resource input combinations, the behavior of production costs, the mechanisms of competition, pricing and production rates, and resource pricing and employment. Our ultimate goal is to understand thoroughly how a market economy works and to be in a position to judge the contribution of the business firm to the general economic well-being.

SUGGESTED READINGS

ANDREWS, K., *The Concept of Corporate Strategy*, rev. ed. (Homewood, Ill.: Dow Jones-Irwin, Inc., 1980), Chapters 2, 3, and 5.

BAIN, J. S., *Industrial Organization* (New York: John Wiley & Sons, Inc., 1959), Chapter 3.

CASSON, M., *The Entrepreneur: An Economic Theory* (Totowa, N.J.: Barnes & Nobel Books, 1982).

CHANDLER, A., *The Visible Hand: The Managerial Revolution in American Business* (Cambridge, Mass.: Harvard University Press, 1977).

PETERS, T. H., AND R. J. WATERMAN, JR., *In Search of Excellence* (New York: Harper & Row, Publishers, 1982).

PRESTON, L. E., "Corporation and Society: The Search for a Paradigm," *Journal of Economic Literature*, Vol. 13, No. 2 (June 1975), pp. 434–453.

SCOTT, B. R., "The Industrial State: Old Myths and New Realities," *Harvard Business Review*, Vol. 51, No. 2 (March–April 1973), pp. 133–148.

SOBEL, R., *The Entrepreneurs: Explorations within the American Business Tradition* (New York: Longman, Inc., 1979).

QUESTIONS FOR DISCUSSION

1. What is a market? What is the difference between a market and a market segment?

2. What criteria determine whether a market should be viewed as essentially being local, regional, national, or international?

3. Try to define and identify the market for each of the following products in terms of (1) market scope (local, regional, national, international), (2) the characteristics of the buyers that make up the demand side of the market, (3) whether the demand side is comprised of several distinctive market segments, and (4) any other relevant and identifiable market characteristics:
    (a) Coca-Cola.
    (b) Textbooks in economics.
    (c) Pro football.
    (d) No-return, throwaway glass containers.
    (e) Microcomputers.
    (f) Dry-cleaning services.

4. How would you characterize the strategy of
    (a) McDonald's in the hamburger and fast-food service market?
    (b) Playboy in the market for sexy magazines?
    (c) Holiday Inn in the market for hotel and motel accommodations?

5. Many of the major oil companies are beginning to redefine their businesses from one of "oil" to one of "energy." Why would this make sense from the standpoint of the oil companies? What sort of business activities would an "energy company" be in (or be getting into) that an oil company might shy away from? From a public policy standpoint, do you think it is a good thing for oil companies to become energy companies? Why or why not?

6. What qualities distinguish an entrepreneur from a professional manager? How is an entrepreneur different from the president of a diversified corporation?

7. Why does the concept of a single-product, owner-managed enterprise have questionable validity for large corporations?

8. What is the difference between a strategy of vertical integration and a strategy of diversification?

9. What is the difference between related and unrelated diversification? Why might a firm be attracted to a strategy of related diversification?

10. What are the different types of firms in terms of business makeup?

11. Explain what is meant by the following terms:
    (a) Strategy.
    (b) Joint venture.
    (c) A retrenchment strategy.
    (d) A market economic system.

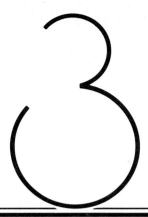

THE DEMAND SIDE
OF THE MARKETPLACE
The cardinal utility model

In modern societies the material wants of the populace tend to be characterized by two important features: (1) diversity and (2) insatiability. Consumer wants are diverse in the sense that satisfying the biological, psychological, and cultural desires of millions of people requires an immense volume and variety of goods and services. Individual tastes vary, as do individual circumstances regarding age, marital and family status, social status, income, life-style, and so on—all of which give rise to the need for a diverse, ever-changing mix of goods and services to meet consumer preferences. Consumer wants are insatiable in the sense that scarcely anyone is without a "want list." As fast as some of an individual's wants are fulfilled, new ones are activated or created to take their place. No sooner are people's basic needs for food, shelter, and clothing within their grasp than they start thinking about acquiring more elaborate creature comforts and upgrading their way of life. In addition, new wants are regularly activated by technological research and entrepreneurial efforts aimed at generating goods and services which consumers will find handy or desirable. Most people perceive themselves as having too little income rather than too much—and they find it easy to step up their expenditures for goods and services.

The constant gap between consumers' appetites for goods and services and the resource base available to satisfy them makes it necessary to install an allocation system to guide production activity. Plainly enough, when the combined want lists of consumers for goods and services exceed the capacity to supply them, there is a need to channel production efforts toward satisfying as many wants as possible and in some order of priority. In a capitalistically oriented economy the business firm is squarely in the midst of the process of deciding *what* and *how much* to produce. As a rule, competition and the profit incentive combine to induce each firm to produce only items which it perceives will be well received in the marketplace by prospective buyers.

The market process whereby a firm's product line offering becomes synchronized with consumer demand works something like this. Each individual consumer tends to spend his or her limited income on those goods and services deemed to be most necessary and most satisfying, given his or her tastes, preferences, and circumstances. Consumer expenditures are, in effect, "dollar votes" whereby buyers' priority preferences are registered in the marketplace. As long as the votes for an item are sufficiently attractive to business firms (in terms of price and potential sales volume), the profit motive takes over and induces one or more producers to supply the item to any and all who are willing and able to buy it. When the dollar votes are viewed as insufficient (or become so as consumer tastes and circumstances change), the resulting slack demand and unattractive profits act as a clear and powerful signal for firms to shift to the production of other items or face the prospect of low or negative rewards for their efforts. Through this market process of matching supply with demand item by item, resources are steered out of the production of goods and services where buyer demand is *relatively* weak and unprofitable and into the production of items where sales opportunities are expected to be more rewarding.

In effect, then, how urgently consumers desire various products and services and how able they are to back up their desires with purchasing power governs the process of what and how much to produce. Unless business firms elect to synchronize their production efforts to match the purchasing behavior of consumers (the power of advertising notwithstanding), they face the penalty of unacceptable profits and perhaps even losses and eventual bankruptcy. No firm, no matter how big or how "powerful," can survive producing something consumers do not want or will not buy.[1]

It is of the essence, therefore, that a firm understand the nature, sources, and principles of consumer demand. Indeed, consumer behavior and consumer demand are integral facets of microeconomic analysis. In this chapter we shall explore the hows and whys of consumer purchases, focusing upon the behavior of consumers in trying to maximize the satisfaction received from their incomes and upon how the demand side of the marketplace works.

---

[1] The special genius of a capitalistically oriented economic system is its power to furnish consumers with whatever goods and services they want and in whatever amounts they are willing to buy—subject *only* to the constraint that consumers be willing to pay a price high enough to make furnishing the item profitable. Proof for this assertion is readily obtained from an attempt to compile a list of products which are technologically feasible to produce and which consumers truly want and are willing to pay a profitable price for, but which are not available to those who have the money to buy them. It is a safe wager that you (or anyone else) will come up with a *very* short list of such items and even the severest critics of the profit-oriented capitalistic system would have to acknowledge the consumer benefit of this accomplishment.

THE CONCEPT OF UTILITY

Economists first began to analyze consumer behavior over a century ago when it was fashionable in psychological circles to assert that much of human behavior could be explained by people's desire to realize as much "pleasure" and to avoid as much "pain" as possible. The pleasure-pain doctrine was quickly borrowed by economists and applied to the sphere of consumer expenditures in what became the first systematic theory of motivated consumer behavior; the basic economic thesis was that rational consumers would, quite intentionally, manage their purchases of goods and services so as to realize the greatest possible amount of overall total "satisfaction." Economists labeled the want-satisfying power of goods and services as "utility."

The concept of utility refers to the pleasure or satisfaction associated with having, using, consuming, or benefiting from goods or services. The utility inherent in a good or service derives from whatever qualities it has that gives it want-satisfying capabilities. The sources and causes of utility are legion: better health, esthetic beauty or design, ease of use, flavor and taste, durability, convenience, luxury, comfort, a sense of individuality, pleasure, prestige, status, pride, security, ego gratification, and power—to mention the most obvious. Hence, utility has both objective and subjective features and, most particularly, utility is a matter of individual taste, preference, perception, personality makeup, and state of mind.

As a consequence, the utility that a good possesses or is perceived to possess is variable, not absolute. In the first place, no two people necessarily will view a good as having the same degree of want-satisfying powers—one person may derive great utility from smoking cigarettes while someone else finds them distasteful; Cadillacs may be important status symbols to some people (and hence have great utility), yet have little or no appeal to other people. Different people buy the same product for quite different uses and motivations. Peanuts, for instance, are bought by some people to serve at cocktail parties, by others to make peanut brittle, and by some to feed to squirrels, with potentially different utilities to each buyer in each case. Moreover, the utility of a good can vary from time to time, or place to place. Rising gasoline prices quickly modified the utility many people placed on small cars. Wool clothing does not have the same utility or want-satisfying powers for people living in short-winter climates as for those living in long-winter climates. But irrespective of the wide variations that different persons may place on the utility of a good or service, the utility concept offers a purposeful basis for establishing consumer preferences for what and how much they will purchase because it leads to comparisons of the amounts of satisfaction received from different consumption rates of different goods and services.

It is, of course, doubtful that the intensity of satisfaction one gains from an item can be represented precisely in *cardinal rankings* whereby numerical values (such as 14, 84.9 or −115) are assigned to represent utility. One may say that "broiled lobster is my favorite food" or "I enjoy broiled lobster more than any other seafood or meat"; but if asked "how much do you enjoy broiled lobster?", one can scarcely reply "about 17" and expect to convey understanding. The subjective nature of the utility concept is, however, susceptible to *ordinal ranking* measures. In ordinal preference patterns, one only has to be able to rank alternatives—from highest to lowest, best to worst, or most satisfying to least satisfying; no attempt is made to quantify the *amount* by which one alternative is better (or worse) than others.

Despite the fact that utility is not subject to precise quantification, it is still analytically useful to *assume* that utility can be represented by cardinal numbers. Doing so makes it easier to illuminate several important aspects of consumer behavior. We shall examine the cardinal utility approach to consumer demand in this chapter and then turn to the ordinal utility approach in Chapter 4.

TOTAL UTILITY FUNCTIONS

For illustrative purposes, assume that we can designate the amount of utility by a unit of measure called a "util." This mythical unit can be viewed as representing some arbitrary amount of satisfaction, and as such it is simply a fictional device for expressing utility in quantitative or cardinal terms.

The *total utility* which a consumer gains from a good or service may be defined as the *entire* amount of satisfaction obtained from a given amount of the item per period of time. A *total utility function* thus reflects the quantitative relationship between the satisfaction yielded by a product and its rate of consumption.[2] Total utility functions may be described in tabular form, with graphs, or with equations. Consider Table 3-1, which uses hypothetical data to illustrate the various amounts of total utility that an individual might obtain from alternative quantities of good X per period of time. As can be seen from columns 1 and 2, the more of good X consumed by the individual per period of time, the greater is his or her total utility (or total satisfaction) measured in utils, up to a consumption rate of 8 units of X. At 8 units, total utility is at its maximum value of 64 utils of satisfaction. This point is called the *saturation rate* because the consumer cannot derive any greater satisfaction from consuming more of good X per period of time. Thereoretically, at this juncture, if the consumption rate was increased to 9 or 10 units, total utility would decline, perhaps because such a consumption rate would be a nuisance (having TV sets in each room of a nine-room house) or physically debilitating (drinking nine cups of coffee a day). The point here is that while a consumer's wants in general may be unlimited or insatiable, his or her wants for specific goods or services can be totally fulfilled.

A total utility curve corresponding to the information in Table 3-1 is displayed in Fig. 3-1(a). Observe that it rises at a slower and slower rate as the consumption rate approaches 8 units of X, reaching a peak at 8 units (the saturation

---

[2] The word "function" here is nothing more than a shorthand way of referring to the way in which some factors (the independent variables) affect another factor (the dependent variable). In terms of utility functions, this literally means that the total utility obtained from a good or service varies with the amount of it consumed during some specified period of time, in which case total utility is the dependent variable and the quantity consumed is the independent variable.

TABLE 3-1 Relationships among Total Utility, Marginal Utility, and the Rates of Consumption of Good X (hypothetical data for a hypothetical person)

Units of Good X Consumed per Period of Time	Total Utility (utils)	Marginal Utility (utils)
0	0	
1	15	15
2	28	13
3	39	11
4	48	9
5	55	7
6	60	5
7	63	3
8	64	1
9	63	−1
10	60	−3

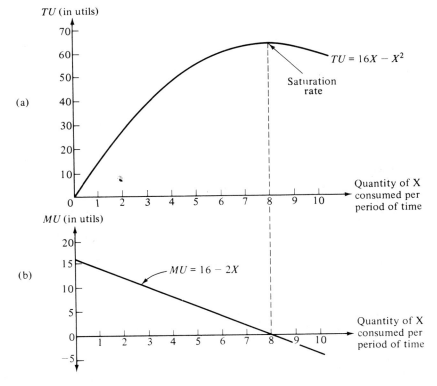

FIGURE 3-1
Total and marginal utility functions for a good whose total utility increases at a decreasing rate

rate) and then declining. The shape of the *TU* curve implies that the more of a specific product a consumer obtains, the less anxious he will be to acquire even more because the additional units yield progressively smaller amounts of *extra* satisfaction. Eventually, the amounts of extra satisfaction diminish to zero, becoming negative thereafter.

Each such total utility function can also be expressed mathematically by an equation relating total utility to the rate of consumption. It so happens that the total utility function shown in Table 3-1 and in Fig. 3-1(a) has the equation

$$TU = 16X - X^2,$$

where *TU* represents total utility in utils and *X* represents the amount of the item consumed per unit of time. Hence, if the consumption rate is 5 units of X, then

$$TU = 16(5) - (5)^2 = 80 - 25 = 55 \text{ utils.}$$

Observe that the value of 55 utils corresponds exactly to the value for total utility in Table 3-1 when the rate of consumption is 5 units and, likewise, to the value of total utility in Fig. 3-1(a) at $X = 5$ units. The use of equations to represent total utility functions allows easy calculation of total utility for any consumption rate (X).

THE CONCEPT OF MARGINAL UTILITY

Marginal utility may be defined as the change in total utility resulting from a 1-unit change in the consumption of a good or service per period of time. In the case of an increase in consumption, marginal utility refers to the *extra satisfaction* obtained from the *extra* unit of consumption per period of time. In the case of a decline in consumption, marginal utility refers to the amount of the *decline* in total utility associated with the *decline* in the consumption rate. From Table 3-1 it can be seen that when the consumption rate for good X increases from 1 to 2 units, total utility rises from 15 utils to 28 utils. Thus, the marginal utility of the second unit of X is 13 utils. In like manner the remaining values for marginal utility may be computed.

During any relatively short period of time (wherein all other relevant factors can be assumed not to change), if a consumer increases his or her consumption rate of a good or service beyond some point, the marginal utility (or extra satisfaction) which is obtained from successive units becomes smaller and smaller. This phenomenon is known as the *principle of diminishing marginal utility*, and it is held to apply to virtually all individuals for virtually all goods and services. (Can you think of any exceptions?) The values for marginal utility in Table 3-1 begin to diminish at the outset so that, in the example given, the principle of diminishing marginal utility becomes operative immediately. Each *additional* unit of X consumed per period of time gives less *extra* utility than the previous unit, thereby causing total utility to increase more slowly as the consumption rate rises. The total utility corresponding to any consumption rate can be found from the marginal utility values by calculating the cumulative marginal utility values to that point. Thus, from Table 3-1 the total utility for a consumption rate of 3 units of X equals the marginal utility of the first unit (15 utils) plus the marginal utility of the second unit (13 utils) plus the marginal utility of the third (11 utils) for a total utility of 39 utils.

The marginal utility function corresponding to the previously described total utility function can be illustrated graphically by plotting the marginal utility values given in Table 3-1. The graph of the marginal utility curve is presented in Fig. 3-1(b). In plotting the values for marginal utility from Table 3-1, it is important to note that they are plotted halfway between the two values for total utility from which they were derived. This is as it should be because the marginal utility values determined in this fashion should be representative of the *range* of consumption from which they were derived, and this is at the midpoint of that range. For the example given, the marginal utility function decreases throughout and reaches zero at the same consumption rate at which the total utility function is at its maximum height.

Actually, there is a very precise relationship between total utility functions and marginal utility functions. We shall have so frequent occasion to use these relationships, not only with reference to utility but also with reference to revenue, production, cost, and other magnitudes, that it is advantageous to master them at this point.

Consider again the total utility function described earlier:

$$TU = 16X - X^2.$$

Using this expression, we can easily obtain the value of *TU* at any consumption rate of good X by substituting the units consumed of X into the expression and evaluating the right-hand side of the equation.

However, suppose the consumption rate of good X rises from some value X to some value $X + \Delta X$, where ΔX designates an arbitrary increase of any size. We know that total utility must necessarily *change*. Let us symbolize the change that occurs in total utility by ΔTU. Rewriting the total utility function to incorporate the effect of the increase in X to $X + \Delta X$, we have

$$TU + \Delta TU = 16(X + \Delta X) - (X + \Delta X)^2,$$
$$TU + \Delta TU = 16X + 16\,\Delta X - (X^2 + 2X\Delta X + \Delta X^2),$$
$$TU + \Delta TU = 16X + 16\Delta X - X^2 - 2X\Delta X - \Delta X^2.$$

The last expression above defines the new level of total utility corresponding to a consumption rate of $X + \Delta X$ units. But our major concern is really with the *change* in total utility (ΔTU) associated with the *change* (ΔX) in the consumption rate of good X. We can obtain an expression for determining just the *change* in *TU* by subtracting *TU* from the left-hand side of the equation and its equivalent of $(16X - X^2)$ from the right hand side. This operation yields

$$
\begin{aligned}
TU + \Delta TU &= 16X + 16\Delta X - X^2 - 2X\Delta X - \Delta X^2 \\
-TU &= -16X + X^2 \\
\hline
\Delta TU &= 16\Delta X - 2X\Delta X - \Delta X^2
\end{aligned}
$$

We are now in a position to determine the additional utility per additional unit of good X by dividing both sides of the expression for ΔTU by ΔX:

$$
\frac{\Delta TU}{\Delta X} = \frac{16\Delta X - 2X\Delta X - \Delta X^2}{\Delta X} = 16 - 2X - \Delta X.
$$

The latter equation expresses the change in total utility per unit change in the consumption rate.[3]

Our interest lies yet beyond, however. Up to now all we have done is perform algebraic operations on our original expression of $TU = 16X - X^2$. Something a little different is called for at this point. In particular, we need to know what happens to $\Delta TU/\Delta X$ as the changes in ΔX become smaller and smaller and eventually became very close to zero. The mathematical way of pursuing this question is to determine the "limit" toward which the value of $\Delta TU/\Delta X$ moves as ΔX approaches zero; this limit is symbolized by dTU/dX.[4] Hence, if

$$
\frac{\Delta TU}{\Delta X} = 16 - 2X - \Delta X,
$$

it follows that as ΔX becomes infinitesimally small (approaches zero):

$$
\frac{dTU}{dX} = 16 - 2X.
$$

In terms of economics, the expression $dTU/dX = 16 - 2X$ is the equation for the marginal utility function corresponding to the total utility function $TU = 16X - X^2$. The symbol dTU/dX should be read as the *rate of change in total utility as the consumption rate changes*, which, in turn, is a more rigorous and accurate definition of marginal utility. In terms of differential calculus, marginal utility is "the first derivative of the total utility function." Consequently, if total

---

[3] More specifically, this equation defines *average marginal utility* or the average change in total utility per unit change in the consumption rate. For example, if total utility increases by 50 utils when the consumption level rises by 10 units, then $\Delta TU/\Delta X = 50$ utils/10 units = 5 utils per unit of consumption. In other words, the average change in total utility (or average marginal utility) is 5 utils for each of the 10 additional units consumed. The concept of average marginal utility is useful whenever the available data do not permit a unit-by-unit calculation of marginal utility.

[4] This is much like asking what happens to the value of y in the expression $y = (x + 1)/x$ as the value of x approaches infinity.

utility is given by the expression

$$TU = 16X - X^2,$$

marginal utility (MU) will be given by the function

$$MU = \frac{dTU}{dX} = 16 - 2X,$$

where $16 - 2X$ is the first derivative of the expression $16X - X^2$. Thus, for each and every total utility function, there is a corresponding marginal utility function. Fortunately, though, as the examples below show, there is a method for determining the marginal utility function that shortcuts the preceding laborious derivation. (The purpose of the lengthy derivation was to illustrate the logic of determining rates of change in variables for those readers not familiar with elementary differential calculus.)

The *general* procedure for finding the marginal function for any variable from the total function for that variable may be illustrated as follows. If the total function is given by

$$T = aX^n,$$

where a and n are arbitrary constants and X is any variable, then the marginal function is

$$M = \frac{dT}{dX} = naX^{n-1}.$$

EXAMPLE 1:   If $T = 16X^3$, then

$$M = \frac{dT}{dX} = 3 \cdot 16 \cdot X^{3-1} = 48X^2.$$

EXAMPLE 2:   If $T = 160 + 7X + 4X^2 - 2X^3$, then our general rule is applied to *each term* of the expression. Algebraically, the total function may be understood to be $T = 160X^0 + 7X^1 + 4X^2 - 2X^3$. Hence,

$$M = \frac{dT}{dX} = 0 \cdot 160X^{0-1} + 1 \cdot 7X^{1-1} + 2 \cdot 4X^{2-1} - 3 \cdot 2X^{3-1}$$

$$= \frac{dT}{dX} = 0 \cdot 160X^{-1} + 1 \cdot 7X^0 + 2 \cdot 4X^1 - 3 \cdot 2X^2$$

$$= \frac{dT}{dX} = 0 + 7 + 8X - 6X^2.$$

Note that the derivative (or rate of change) of the constant term in the total function turns out to be zero; this is as it should be since the rate of change in a value that is constant is necessarily zero.

EXAMPLE 3. Suppose that the total function is expressed in the form of a general algebraic equation such as $T = a + bX + cX^2$, where a, b, and c are constants. Since the total function T may be rewritten as $T = aX^0 + bX^1 + cX^2$, the corresponding marginal function M is

$$M = \frac{dT}{dX} = 0 \cdot aX^{-1} + 1 \cdot bX^0 + 2 \cdot cX^1,$$

which simplifies to

$$M = b + 2cX.$$

For readers who feel uncomfortable with the mechanics of derivatives, a number of problems and answers are provided at the end of this chapter to strengthen your ability to use this essential aspect of mathematical economics.

To summarize our brief excursion into the mathematical aspects of economic relationships, the derivative of a function is the rate of change of the dependent variable as the value of the independent variable changes; the derivative of a total function *defines* the marginal function. As applied to utility functions, *marginal utility* is the rate of change in total utility as the rate of consumption of an item changes and is calculated mathematically by finding the first derivative of the total utility function.

To return to our original example, we have found that if $TU = 16X - X^2$, then $MU = 16 - 2X$. Knowing the expression for MU allows the value of MU to be calculated easily at any value of X. Moreover, these results may be related to both Table 3-1 and Fig. 3-1. For instance, the equation of the MU function is the exact equation which describes the graph of the marginal utility function in Fig. 3-1(b). Furthermore, we can see from Table 3-1 that the value for MU between 1 and 2 units of X is 13 units (technically, at $X = 1\frac{1}{2}$, $MU = 13$ utils); if we let X assume a value of 1.5 in the equation $MU = 16 - 2X$, we get a value of 13 utils for MU, which corresponds exactly to the value in Table 3-1.

The most significant relationship between the TU and MU functions concerns the shape of the total utility function. Defining MU as the rate of change in total utility as the rate of consumption changes is equivalent to saying that the value for marginal utility at a particular consumption rate equals the *slope of the total utility function* at that consumption rate. In other words, viewed geometrically, the derivative of the total utility function is the slope of the total utility function at any X value. When we say that marginal utility is 13 utils at a consumption of 1.5 units of X, we also are saying that at $X = 1.5$ total utility is increasing at a rate of 13 utils per unit of extra consumption, which is, by definition, the slope of the total utility function at the point where $X = 1.5$ units. When total utility is at its highest point, the slope of the TU curve is zero (because the tangent line drawn to the TU function at its highest point is horizontal). Since marginal utility, by definition, has a value equal to the slope of the total utility function, the value of MU corresponding to the peak of the TU function is also zero.

Using these ideas, the total utility function in Fig. 3-1(a) may be said to *increase at a decreasing rate*. Why? Because as the consumption rate increases, the *TU* function rises more slowly [i.e., its slope gets flatter (smaller)]. Consequently, the related values for *MU* must be decreasing since these values, by definition, are equal to the slope of the *TU* function. Fig. 3-1(b) illustrates just such a pattern of change in the values for marginal utility.

Alternative shapes for the *TU* and *MU* functions are shown in Fig. 3-2. In this case, *TU increases at an increasing rate* up to a consumption rate of X_1 units. From X_1 to X_2 units, *TU increases at a decreasing rate*. Point *A* on the *TU* curve is the point of diminishing marginal utility and corresponds to the same consumption rate as point *A'* on the *MU* curve. Point *B* on the *TU* curve defines the saturation rate as does point *B'* on the *MU* graph. Although there are many forms of equations which could represent a total utility function of this shape, the simplest is the general equation for a cubic function:

$$TU = a + bX + cX^2 - dX^3,$$

where X represents the units consumed; a, b, and c are positive constants; and d is a negative constant. Using the mathematical concepts previously developed, the corresponding general equation for marginal utility is

$$MU = \frac{dTU}{dX} = b + 2cX - 3dX^2.$$

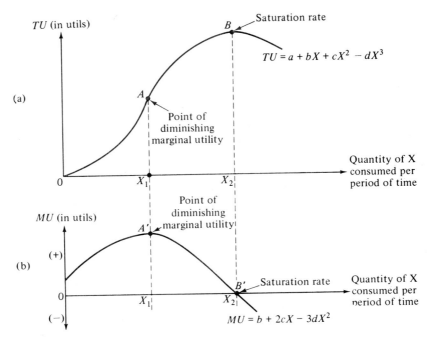

FIGURE 3-2
Generalized total and marginal utility functions for phases of increasing and decreasing returns as the rate of consumption rises

(Can you think of products or situations in which an individual's *TU* and *MU* functions might assume the shapes shown in Fig. 3-2?)

While the *TU* functions in Figs. 3-1 and 3-2 have shown total utility as being zero when the consumption rate is zero, this need not be the case; in fact, it may not even be typical. Negative amounts of utility (disutility) may arise from having none of an item as it is witnessed by the dismay of individuals who find themselves without aspirin when a headache appears or who run out of gas on a lonely road. In such cases the total utility function may start below the origin and not reach zero utility until the consumption of the item is well above the zero rate. Then, too, total utility functions for a nuisance or unwanted item may originate at a positive value, and *decrease* rapidly as more of the item comes into the possession of the consumer.

MATHEMATICAL CAPSULE 1

DETERMINING THE POINT OF DIMINISHING MARGINAL UTILITY AND THE SATURATION RATE: AN APPLICATION OF THE MATHEMATICAL CONCEPTS OF MAXIMA AND MINIMA

A maximum point on a curve is a point that is higher than its neighboring point to either side such that the curve is concave downward; a minimum point on a curve is a point that is lower than its neighboring points such that the curve is concave upward.

All maximum and minimum values of a function $y = f(x)$ occur where $dy/dx = 0$, since the first derivative of a function is indicative of its rate of change or slope. This characteristic is frequently termed the *first-order* condition.

If, at the value of *x* at which $dy/dx = 0$, the second derivative is negative, $d^2y/dx^2 < 0$, that value of *x* defines a maximum value for *y*, where $y = f(x)$. If at the value of x at which $dy/dx = 0$ the second derivative is positive, $d^2y/dx^2 > 0$, that value of x defines a minimum value for function $y = f(x)$. This requirement for distinguishing between maximum and minimum values is called the *second-order condition*.

Consider the total utility function $TU = 130X - 2.5X^2$, plotted in the accompanying graph. Suppose that we wish to determine the value of X at which TU is maximum—the saturation rate. The saturation rate corresponds exactly to that quantity consumed at which the slope of the total utility function is zero and where $MU = 0$. If $TU = 130X - 2.5X^2$, then $MU = dTU/dx = 130 - 5X$. Setting the marginal utility function equal to zero, we get

$$130 - 5X = 0.$$

Solving for the value of X which satisfies the equation, we find $X = 26$ units. This, then, is the consumption rate where TU is maximum.

Suppose that we wish to find the consumption rate of X at which diminishing MU is encountered for the total utility function presented below:

$$TU = 18X + 7X^2 - \tfrac{1}{3}X^3.$$

Diminishing MU begins at the point where the MU function is at its maximum value.

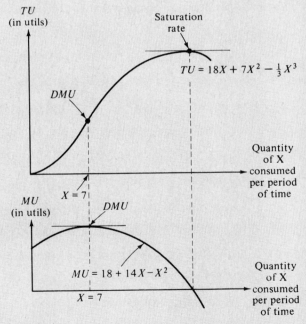

The value of X at which the slope of the MU function is zero ($dMU/dX = d^2TU/dX^2 = 0$) can be calculated as follows:

$$MU = \frac{dTU}{dX} = 18 + 14X - X^2$$

$$\frac{dMU}{dX} = \frac{d^2TU}{dX^2} = 14 - 2X.$$

Setting dMU/dX equal to zero and solving for X, we obtain $X = 7$, the consumption rate at which diminishing MU sets in.

EXERCISE

1. Determine the saturation rate and the point of diminishing marginal utility for each of the following TU functions.
    (a) $TU = 36X - X^2$.
    (b) $TU = 10X + 9X^2 - X^3$.

Utility Functions for Related Products

In many instances it is clear that the utility people obtain from one product is related to their consumption of another product. The utility derived from eating cornflakes is partially dependent on the availability of milk or cream; the satisfaction from one's automobile is related to the quantity of gasoline it uses; the enjoyment from one's binoculars is related to the frequency with which one goes to spectator events. Thus, while total utility is a function of the quantities of each product consumed per period of time, it need not be simply the sum of the utilities gained separately from each good or service.

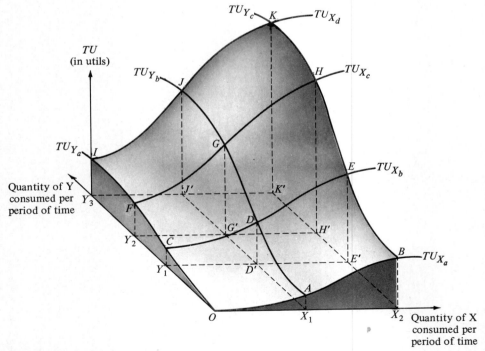

FIGURE 3-3
Total utility surface for a pair of products characterized by both increasing and decreasing marginal utility

When the satisfaction derived from one item hinges in part upon the amounts consumed of other items, the more appropriate concept of utility is that of a *total utility surface* relating total utility to the *joint rates* of consumption of all goods simultaneously. This notion is illustrated graphically for two products, X and Y, in Fig. 3-3. The consumption rates for X and Y define a horizontal plane with total utility measured as a vertical distance above it. The total utility surface is *OIKB*. If Y_1 units of product Y are consumed per unit of time along with X_1 units of product X, total utility is DD'; if the respective consumption rates are Y_2 and X_1 per period of time, total utility is GG'. The total utility surface pictured in Fig. 3-3 thus indicates how total utility changes as the rate of consumption of one product changes, given the rate of consumption of the other. The shape of the total utility surface depends upon the nature of the interrelationship among the products. In Fig. 3-3, total utility is shown as increasing at an increasing rate for a few units before diminishing marginal utility sets in, thereby making the total utility surface concave upward for this range of consumption; the surface becomes concave downward as diminishing marginal utility is realized. If diminishing marginal utility occurred from the outset for both X and Y, the total utility surface would be concave downward throughout.

MATHEMATICAL CAPSULE 2

DETERMINING MARGINAL UTILITY FOR MULTIPRODUCT TOTAL UTILITY FUNCTIONS

When the satisfaction derived from one product is related to the amounts consumed of other products, the consumer's total utility function is of the form

$$TU = f(X_a, X_b, \ldots, X_n),$$

where $X_a, X_b, \ldots, X_n$ represent the array of products available. Given such multiproduct *TU* functions, one is often called to examine the effect of a change in the consumption rate of one product upon *TU*, when the consumption rates of other products do not change. The form of the derivative which corresponds to this interest is called the *partial derivative*.

Suppose that the total utility function for two products X and Y is

$$TU = 7X + 4Y - 0.2X^2 - 0.3Y^2 - XY.$$

We find the impact of a change in the rate of consumption of X upon *TU* when the consumption of Y is kept fixed *by treating Y as a constant* and differentiating the total utility function with respect to X—this gives the partial derivative of *TU* with respect to X and is denoted by $\partial TU / \partial X$. Accordingly, we get

$$\frac{\partial TU}{\partial X} = 7 - 0.4X - Y,$$

which may be interpreted to represent *the rate of change in TU as the rate of consumption of X changes, the rate of consumption of Y being held constant.* This then is the expression for the marginal utility of product X. Similarly, the partial derivative of *TU* with respect to Y is

$$\frac{\partial TU}{\partial Y} = 4 - 0.6Y - X.$$

and it represents the expression for the marginal utility of *Y*.

EXERCISES

1. Determine the relevant marginal utility functions for each of the following total utility functions.
   - (a) $TU = 15X^2 Y^2 - X^3 Y^2$.
   - (b) $TU = 20X + 40Y - 3X^2 - Y^2$.
   - (c) $TU = 30XY + 10XZ - 3XYZ - 10Z$.
   - (d) $TU = 5.4x^{1/2} Y^{1/3}$.

2. Determine the values for MU_x and MU_y at $X = 5$ and $Y = 3$ in each of the following total utility functions.
   - (a) $TU = 16X - X^2 + 10Y - XY$.
   - (b) $TU = 33X + 2X^2 - X^3 + 4Y - XY^2$.
   - (c) $TU = 16X^2 + 15XY + 17Y^2 - 4X^2 Y^2$.

CONSUMER BEHAVIOR IN THE MARKETPLACE

Once a consumer's utility functions are known or ascertainable, it is possible to make judgments about how he or she will act in the marketplace. In approaching the whys and hows of consumer demand, economists assume that rational consumers *attempt* to arrange their purchases so as to *maximize* the total satisfaction that they can get from their money incomes. After all, consumers have no reason to deliberately try to get less than the full obtainable satisfaction from the purchasing power they have available. In reality, of course, the assumption of maximizing utility may not be literally true, at least for all consumers in each and every situation. Imperfect information about alternative purchases and about prices tends to hinder consumer attempts at utility maximization, and an exhaustive search for better information may cost more than it is worth. In addition, impulse buying and force of habit work against consumers actually identifying and purchasing the utility-maximizing combination of goods and services. Nonetheless, the assumption that consumers behave as if they seek to maximize total utility is a justifiable and reasonable abstraction for most consumers most of the time.

Confronted with a limited number of dollars to spend, the price tags on every item, thousands of items to choose among, and imperfect knowledge as to all alternatives, a consumer's task of trying to get the most for his or her money is indeed complex. Obviously, consumers cannot buy everything they want because each purchase exhausts a portion of their available money incomes. They are forced to compromise and decide what and how much of each of the many commodities within their income constraints best suit their needs and tastes. A word about the income constraint facing consumers is in order. As used here, a consumer's money income refers to the total amount of purchasing power available for spending in a given time period; this specifically includes (1) current income from whatever source, (2) any savings the consumer has accumulated from past income periods, (3) any sums the consumer wishes and is able to borrow, and (4) any other wealth the consumer may wish to allocate to current consumption.

Some Simplifying Assumptions

To keep the ensuing analysis of consumer behavior manageable, the following assumptions will be made:

1. Each consumer has full knowledge of all information pertinent to his or her expenditure decision—a definitive set of tastes and preferences, knowledge of the goods and services available, their capacity to satisfy his wants, his money income, and the prices at which specific products can be bought.
2. The consumer's preference pattern for products is one of diminishing marginal utility for each.[5]
3. The utility function for each product is independent of the rate of consumption of other products.

None of these assumptions do violence to the principles of consumer behavior we wish to derive and they make the exposition simpler.

The Maximization of Utility

For the time being, suppose that we restrict ourselves to the case of a consumer who is trying to decide what combination of two goods, X and Y, should be purchased with a weekly income of $40. We shall assume that the price of X remains at $3 per unit and the price of Y remains at $5 per unit no matter how much the consumer buys of X and Y. Table 3-2 summarizes the consumer's preference for the two items, along with the consumer's evaluation of the utility obtained from not spending the money, that is, the *marginal utility of saving*.[6]

How should the consumer allocate a $40 weekly income among buying good X, buying good Y, and saving in order to yield maximum satisfaction? To answer this question, let us proceed to ascertain what the consumer should do first. A $40 weekly income allows the consumer to buy some of either X or Y should the

---

[5] Actually, this is a more rigorous assumption than need be made. All we need assume is that the marginal utility of one good decreases *relative* to the marginal utilities of other goods as its consumption rate is increased *relative* to the consumption rate of others. Our analysis will be valid in cases where the marginal utility of a good is increasing, as long as it increases by less than proportionally to the marginal utilities of other goods.

[6] The term "saving" is used here to encompass a variety of acts associated with not spending. Consumers may rationally decide not to spend all of their money income during some period of time because (1) they place a high value on saving a portion of their income in order to provide for emergencies, accumulate an estate, or any one of a hundred other reasons; (2) they are unable to find products precisely suited to their tastes and wish to look further before making a purchase; and (3) they wish to postpone spending until some future period so that they may pay cash for the desired items. In any event, the act of not spending (i.e., saving) may bring the consumer satisfaction or utility just as does the act of consuming goods and services.

TABLE 3-2 Utility-Maximizing Combination of Goods X and Y Obtainable from an Income of $40

GOOD X (Price = $3)				GOOD Y (Price = $5)				SAVING		
Quan-tity	TU (utils)	MU (utils)	MU/Price (utils/$)	Quan-tity	TU (utils)	MU (utils)	MU/Price (utils/$)	Number of Dollars Saved	TU (utils)	MU (utils/$1)
0	0			0	0			0	10	
		54	18			75	15			9
1	54			1	75			1	19	
		45	15			60	12			7
2	99			2	135			2	26	
		30	10			40	8			3
3	129			3	175			3	29	
		9	3			25	5			2
4	138			4	200			4	31	
		3	1			15	3			1
5	141			5	215			5	32	
		−3	−1			5	1			0
6	138			6	220			6	32	

consumer decide to do so. If $3 is spent to buy the first unit of X, the consumer receives 54 utils of satisfaction; if $5 is spent to buy the first unit of Y, the consumer receives 75 utils; and if the consumer saves all $40, he or she is well past the saturation rate for money, since the marginal utility for saving a dollar becomes negative when saving exceeds $5. Of these alternatives, the purchase of X is definitely the better bargain, because it gives the consumer 18 utils of satisfaction *per dollar spent*, whereas good Y yields only 15 utils of satisfaction per dollar spent, and saving yields no greater than 9 utils per dollar saved. The proper decision variable in this instance is neither total nor marginal utility, but *marginal utility per dollar of expenditure*. It is the best indicator of value received as it combines the factor of satisfaction with the factor of cost, and both factors are requisite for valid comparisons between goods. Since the consumer receives more satisfaction for the money by buying the first unit of X instead of the first unit of Y or instead of saving, the first act should be to exchange $3 for one unit of good X. By the same reasoning, the consumer's second act can be determined. The second unit of good X will produce 14 units of satisfaction per dollar spent, as will the first of Y; both are superior to saving at this point. Since the consumer has ample funds available for spending ($37 of the original $40), the second and third acts should be to buy the second unit of X and the first unit of Y, leaving the consumer with $29. At each step the consumer must decide whether the marginal utility of a dollar's worth of spending is greater than the marginal utility of a dollar's worth of saving. If it is, the consumer should buy the good yielding the highest marginal utility per dollar of expenditure. If not, the consumer should save the money. In the example given, the consumer will maximize total utility by allocating the $40 income so as to purchase 4 units of X and 5 units of Y and to save $3.

No other allocation of the consumer's $40 weekly income will produce as much satisfaction as this one. How do we know? Suppose that our consumer were to buy one less unit of good Y, thereby freeing $5 with which to buy another unit of X and to save an additional $2. This act would reduce total utility. Giving up the fifth unit of Y entails a loss of 15 utils, whereas increasing the purchase rate of X from 4 to 5 units brings 3 utils, and saving two more dollars yields a combined 3 utils, for a total gain of 6 utils from the alternative expenditure of the $5. The consumer would therefore suffer a net loss of 9 utils of satisfaction by transferring dollars out of the purchase of Y and into X and saving. Alternatively, were our consumer to take the $3 saving and apply it to the purchase of the fifth unit of X, he or she would give up 19 utils of satisfaction and acquire only 3 utils of satisfaction, for a net loss in satisfaction of 16 utils. Any act other than buying 4 units of X and 5 units of Y and saving $3 will cause total utility to decline.

Observe carefully the characteristics of the utility-maximizing act. First, the consumer completely utilizes all available purchasing power—all income is allocated either to the purchase of commodities or to saving. There are no idle dollars; the dollars that are saved are constructively deployed every bit as much as are the dollars used for purchasing X and Y—since saving money produces utility. Thus, maximization of utility *does not require* that a consumer spend *all* his or her money—saving has utility and serves to further the motives of the consumer. Second, at the utility-maximizing combination the marginal utilities per dollar spent on the last unit of each item purchased are equal. In other words, the consumer has arranged his or her purchases to get an equivalent amount of satisfaction from the last dollar allocated to each item (including saving) bought.

The Conditions for Utility Maximization

We are now in a position to state the formal conditions for consumer maximization of utility in a multicommodity environment. Two equations will suffice:

$$P_a X_a + P_b X_b + P_c X_c + \cdots + P_n X_n + \text{saving} = \text{income}, \qquad (1)$$

$$\frac{MU_{X_a}}{P_a} = \frac{MU_{X_b}}{P_b} = \frac{MU_{X_c}}{P_c} = \cdots = \frac{MU_{X_n}}{P_n} = MU_{\text{saving}}. \qquad (2)$$

Equation (1) says that the sum of the expenditures on each commodity (X_a, X_b, X_c, . . . , X_n) plus saving must be equal to the money income (I) that the consumer has available per period of time. Total expenditures cannot *exceed* the available purchasing power; any income that is not used to buy goods and services necessarily is saved. Thus, all the consumer's money income is accounted for by either spending or saving. Equation (2) says that to maximize total utility the consumer must arrange purchases such that the marginal utilities per dollar of expenditure on the last unit of each item purchased are equal to each other and to the marginal utility of saving an additional dollar.

When the various degrees of satisfaction per dollar of marginal outlays are unequal, total satisfaction may be increased by diminishing expenditures for goods where satisfaction is less and enlarging expenditures for goods where satisfaction is greater. To illustrate, suppose that

$$MU_{X_a} = 42 \text{ utils for the last unit purchased,}$$
$$P_a = \$14 \text{ per unit,}$$
$$MU_{X_b} = 60 \text{ utils for the last unit purchased,}$$
$$P_b = \$12 \text{ per unit, and}$$
$$MU_{\text{saving}} = 4 \text{ utils for each additional dollar saved.}$$

Then,

$$MU_{X_a}/\$ \text{ spent on } X_a = MU_{X_a}/P_a = 42 \text{ utils}/\$14 = 3 \text{ utils}/\$, \text{ and}$$
$$MU_{X_b}/\$ \text{ spent on } X_b = MU_{X_b}/P_b = 60 \text{ utils}/\$12 = 5 \text{ utils}/\$.$$

The consumer is realizing more satisfaction per dollar spent on X_b than on X_a. Total utility can be increased by transferring dollars out of the purchase of X_a and into the purchase of X_b until $MU_{X_a}/P_a = MU_{X_b}/P_b = MU_{\text{saving}}$. By reducing the expenditure for X_a, the *MU* of the last unit purchased of X_a would rise (say to 56 utils), thus raising the ratio MU_{X_a}/P_a (to 4 utils per dollar). By increasing the expenditure for X_b, the *MU* of the last unit purchased would fall (say to 48 utils), thereby lowering the ratio MU_{X_b}/P_b (to 4 utils per dollar). Since X_a costs $14 and X_b costs $12, buying 1 unit less of X_a and 1 unit more of X_b would leave $2 left over either for the purchase of some other item whose *MU*/$ of expenditure exceeded 4 utils per dollar or for saving.

Sometimes the indivisibility of units of products can preclude the consumer from *exactly* equating the marginal utilities per dollar spent on the last unit for each and every item. For example, in the case above the consumer might find that there are no other goods which could be bought for $2 and receive as much as 4 utils per dollar; saving the entire $2 might reduce the *MU* of the last dollar saved to 3.8 utils. Then Equation (2) could not be precisely satisfied unless fractional units of X_a and X_b could be bought. Practically speaking, Equation (2) should be interpreted to mean that a consumer seeking maximum utility from a given money income should spend his or her dollars so as to approach *as nearly as possible* the equality of the marginal utilities per dollar spent on the last unit of each good purchased and further to approach as nearly as possible the point at which the marginal utility of spending a dollar equals the marginal utility of saving a dollar.

It follows from the utility-maximizing condition of

$$\frac{MU_{X_a}}{P_{X_a}} = \frac{MU_{X_b}}{P_{X_b}} = \cdots = \frac{MU_{X_n}}{P_{X_n}}$$

that if the price of a product falls, *other things remaining equal,* a consumer will be induced to buy more of the product. For example, if P_{X_a} declines, the ratio

MU_{X_a}/P_{X_a} becomes a larger value than the other ratios ($MU_{X_b}/P_{X_b}, \ldots,$ MU_{X_n}/P_{X_n}). To restore the utility-maximizing condition, the consumer will find it desirable to increase the quantity purchased of item X_a. Conversely, if the price of an item rises (whether it be P_{X_a} or P_{X_b} or $\cdots$ or P_{X_n}), the quantity purchased of that item will tend to fall—all other relevant demand-determining factors remaining equal. This is the basis for the *Law of Demand*, which, simply stated, holds that the price of a product and the quantity purchased of that product vary *inversely* with one another, other things being equal.

MATHEMATICAL CAPSULE 3

DETERMINATION OF THE UTILITY-MAXIMIZING COMBINATION OF PRODUCTS SUBJECT TO AN INCOME CONSTRAINT

Let $P_a, P_b, P_c, \ldots, P_n$ be the prices of products $X_a, X_b, X_c, \ldots, X_n$, I be a consumer's money income, and $TU = f(X_a, X_b, X_c, \ldots, X_n)$ be the consumer's utility function for n products which the consumer wishes to maximize subject to his or her income constraint

$$I = P_a X_a + P_b X_b + P_c X_c + \cdots + P_n X_n, \tag{1}$$

where saving here is treated as simply one kind of product. To find the utility-maximizing combination of products, a new function is generated which combines the TU function to be maximized and the constraint equation. To keep the solution determinate (as many equations as there are unknowns), an artificial unknown, called a *LaGrange multiplier*, is introduced, giving

$$\begin{aligned} Z = {} & f(X_a, X_b, X_c, \ldots, X_n) \\ & + \lambda(I - P_a X_a - P_b X_b - P_c X_c - \cdots - P_n X_n), \end{aligned} \tag{2}$$

where λ is the LaGrange multiplier. The partial derivatives of Z are found for each variable and equated to zero to establish the first-order conditions:

$$\frac{\partial Z}{\partial X_a} = \frac{\partial TU}{\partial X_a} - \lambda P_a = 0, \tag{3}$$

$$\frac{\partial Z}{\partial X_b} = \frac{\partial TU}{\partial X_b} - \lambda P_b = 0, \tag{4}$$

$$\frac{\partial Z}{\partial X_c} = \frac{\partial TU}{\partial X_c} - \lambda P_c = 0, \tag{5}$$

$$\vdots$$

$$\frac{\partial Z}{\partial X_n} = \frac{\partial TU}{\partial X_n} - \lambda P_n = 0, \tag{6}$$

$$\frac{\partial Z}{\partial \lambda} = I - P_a X_a - P_b X_b - P_c X_c - \cdots - P_n X_n = 0. \tag{7}$$

These equations may be solved simultaneously to determine the utility-maximizing purchase levels for $X_a, X_b, X_c, \ldots, X_n$. From Eqs. (3) through (6), it is seen that

$$\frac{\partial TU/\partial X_a}{P_a} = \frac{\partial TU/\partial X_b}{P_b} = \frac{\partial TU/\partial X_c}{P_c} = \cdots = \frac{\partial TU/\partial X_n}{P_n}. \tag{8}$$

The terms $\partial TU/\partial X_a$, $\partial TU/\partial X_b$, $\partial TU/\partial X_c$, . . . , $\partial TU/\partial X_n$ really are MU_{X_a}, MU_{X_b}, MU_{X_c}, . . . , MU_{X_n}, and the value of λ necessarily is equal to the marginal utility of saving. Thus, Eq. (8) translates into

$$MU_{\text{saving}} = \frac{MU_{X_a}}{P_a} = \frac{MU_{X_b}}{P_b} = \frac{MU_{X_c}}{P_c} = \cdots = \frac{MU_{X_n}}{P_n}, \tag{9}$$

which we know to be a necessary condition for consumer maximization of total utility. As an example of the foregoing, suppose that we find the utility-maximizing consumption rate for two products X and Y if the total utility function is

$$TU = 10X + 24Y - 0.5X^2 - 0.5Y^2$$

and if $P_x = \$2$, $P_y = \$6$, and $I = \$44$. Then we have

$$Z = 10X + 24Y - 0.5X^2 - 0.5Y^2 + \lambda(44 - 2X - 6Y),$$

$$\frac{\partial Z}{\partial X} = 10 - X - 2\lambda = 0,$$

$$\frac{\partial Z}{\partial Y} = 24 - Y - 6\lambda = 0,$$

$$\frac{\partial Z}{\partial \lambda} = 44 - 2X - 6Y = 0.$$

Solving $\partial Z/\partial X$, $\partial Z/\partial Y$, and $\partial Z/\partial \lambda$ simultaneously yields $X = 4$, $Y = 6$, and $\lambda = 3$.

EXERCISE

1. Determine the utility-maximizing combination of X and Y when
   (a) $TU = 12XY$,
       $P_x = \$3$,
       $P_y = \$6$,
       $I = \$60$.
   (b) $TU = 17X + 20Y - 2X^2 - Y^2$,
       $P_x = \$3$,
       $P_y = \$4$,
       $I = \$22$.

Evaluation of the Maximizing Rules

Since the foregoing discussion may seem rather formal and abstract, it is fair to ask: How realistic is this description of a consumer's disposition of income, especially considering the fact that most consumers have never heard of the conditions for utility maximization? Does the utility model meet the scientific standards of *explaining* and *predicting* real-world consumer behavior?

Basically, the answers to these two questions are "yes." The conditions for utility maximization are not as far removed from the purchase decisions of consumers as one might think at first glance. Whenever a consumer goes shopping and considers the purchase of a specific item, normally he or she will wonder (consciously or unconsciously) whether the price to be paid is "worth it." If the answer is favorable, he or she can be expected to buy the item, assuming the money is available. If the consumer decides the item is not worth the price, then he or she can be expected not to purchase it and to shop around elsewhere. Translated into the language of utility theory, this mental process is equivalent to deciding whether the *MU*/$ from consuming the item is greater than the *MU*/$ of buying some other product. If so, the consumer purchases the item; if *MU*/$ is less, the consumer elects not to buy the item; and if equality between the two prevails, the consumer is indifferent and may rationally decide to buy or not to buy.

Furthermore, it is quite reasonable to expect consumers to continue to spend their income as long as they believe the extra satisfaction that they will get from a good or service exceeds the satisfaction of keeping their money. Only when consumers believe that they will obtain more satisfaction from a dollar's worth of saving than they will from a dollar's worth of spending will saving be induced.

Viewed from this perspective, our model of consumer behavior should be more persuasive, serving at least as a plausible initial approximation. Of course, several factors operate to prevent consumers from realizing the utmost satisfaction from their money incomes. The most important obstacle is a lack of accurate information about the prices charged by various sellers and about product quality.[7] Consumers often pay more for an item at one store than is charged by another store nearby because they are unaware of the price differential. Sometimes they buy products that turn out to be less satisfactory than originally anticipated, perhaps because they mistakenly used price as a surrogate indicator of product quality or because quality was difficult to judge. In these ways they exhaust a larger share of their income than otherwise would have been the case had perfect knowledge existed. On other occasions they buy impulsively, through force of habit, out of brand loyalty, a desire for variety, or just plain curiosity. On still other occasions, they may be unduly influenced by the appeals and nuances of advertising, brand reputation, and emotion.

One of the most serious objections to the utility model concerns the postulate that the consumer's behavior consists of a steady flow of rational calculations whereby individuals systematically consider all the various conceivable purchase combinations, evaluate the utility attached to each, and then choose the package with the greatest utility. Many observers contend that this view is both oversimplified and inaccurate. Specifically, habit, loyalty, whim, impulse, inertia, and reluctance to change are held to be normal attributes of consumer behavior which invalidate the view of the consumer as a "rational economic person." Consider, for example, the consumer's purchase of groceries, gasoline, cigarettes, and personal-care items. They do not cost much per item; they are purchased frequently;

---

[7] However, it must be recognized that there are costs to consumers from searching out more accurate information. The time and expense involved in comparing the many types and features of products and in shopping around for the best buy may outweigh the associated benefits. Thus, to be completely rational, consumers should balance the costs of acquiring better information against the extra satisfaction they gain from having it.

they are available in many stores and locations; they are bought without great forethought and consultation. There is, therefore, recurring opportunity to repeat the same behavior often and develop buying habits and brand preferences. Moreover, the small expense involved in each purchase may create the feeling that what is bought and when it is bought is of no great consequence, thus dampening the concern that a significant decision problem exists and that alternatives ought to be carefully evaluated.

When different brands of the same item are viewed as essentially identical, there is an even greater tendency to make purchase a function of habit and convenience. Information seeking may go no further than scanning newspaper ads for sales and discounts and adjusting one's shopping plans accordingly. Nonetheless, weighing alternatives to buy again what has proved satisfactory in the past may, indeed, represent the simplest way to overcome the anxiety of "did I buy the right thing?" and "did I pay more than I should have?" Consumers would find it neither practical nor rewarding to repeatedly weigh alternatives; discuss and consult with family, friends, and dealers; shop around; seek out information on competing brands and substitutes; and exhibit concern with price every time they repurchase common household items. Hence, reliance upon previous experience with a brand, store loyalty, and advertising may be more "rational" than "irrational," and, as studies have shown, such loyalties and preferences seldom last long when conditions change or dissatisfaction arises.

In addition to the consumers' past experience with particular goods, brands, and stores, such personal factors as the consumers' ego needs, their emotion-colored images of goods, brands, and stores, their desire for conformity and assurance that they are doing the right thing, and their reactions (conscious or subconscious) to on-the-scene factors such as eye appeal, packaging, displays, and store layout all play a role in what they buy and what they do not. Another set of influential factors includes urgent need for an article, the notion that one has a unique opportunity to get an unusually good deal, and satisfaction with other products of the same company.

Granted that these influences exist and that they have a real impact on consumer decision making, does it follow that consumers are often "irrational" and have little interest in or capability for careful, deliberate utility maximization? Or that the consumer's perceptions of utility do not embrace these influences—at least partially? If at the instant of making a purchase decision, the consumer's actions appear to be the best or most satisfying expenditure of his or her income under the circumstances, then the consumer may be said to be rationally endeavoring to maximize utility. Certainly, there is ample reason to presume that if—at the instant of decision—the consumer knew how to spend his or her money to acquire more utility per dollar spent, he or she would do so. This is enough to give the utility model validity, even though the model, admittedly, does not reveal many of the specific factors underlying the consumer's perceptions and motivations. But significantly, there is, to date, no other tested and validated model of consumer decision which is capable of predicting and explaining detailed facets of consumer behavior—despite diligent research efforts to develop more explicit models.

CONSUMER SOVEREIGNTY IN THE MARKETPLACE: FICTION OR REALITY?[8]

The discussion above implies that the worst "enemy" of consumers in attempting to maximize the satisfaction from a limited money income is their own ignorance or irrationality. Even so, consumers are still viewed as possessing the full initiative in buying goods and services. They are assumed to respond only to wants that they originate or needs which are given to them by their environment. They are, above all, independent, and their purchasing behavior in the marketplace instructs producers as to what they want to buy; ultimately, therefore, all power over what and how much is produced is held to lie with consumers—this is what is meant by *consumer sovereignty*.

Obviously, this overstates the situation *somewhat*. Much product differentiation, advertising, and marketing strategy is designed expressly to modify individual preferences and to bend consumer demand toward the product offering of individual firms. To deny that these have any effect is untenable, and any model of consumer behavior that fails to acknowledge the role of the marketer, and, in particular, advertising is sorely lacking in its accounting for real-world purchasing patterns. The attempt to control or manage consumer demand is, in fact, a vast and sophisticated industry in its own right.

Two polar types of advertising and sales promotion strategy may be distinguished: that which is purely informational and that which is purely persuasive. Most advertising strategy incorporates both features and is therefore not pure in either sense. The persuasive type of advertising is of primary concern here.

The significance of persuasive advertising for the study of consumer behavior is that it permits sellers to try to bend consumer tastes and preferences to their own advantage. To the extent that persuasive advertising is successful toward this end, consumer behavior is not purely a response of consumers to their utility schedules. To illustrate: If an individual's satisfaction is less from additional expenditures on soft drinks than on ice cream, this can be just as well "corrected" by a change in the sales strategy of Coca-Cola as by the consumer's increasing his or her expenditures on ice cream. In terms of our utility model, when

$$\frac{MU_{\text{soft drinks}}}{P_{\text{soft drinks}}} < \frac{MU_{\text{ice cream}}}{P_{\text{ice cream}}},$$

either of two acts can restore the equality requisite for consumer equilibrium. The consumer can transfer dollars out of the purchase of soft drinks and into the purchase of ice cream, or the soft-drink manufacturers can attempt to revise upward the consumer's marginal utility for soft drinks by means of a more persuasive advertising and sales strategy. Indeed, a major purpose of advertising is to shift the consumer's utility function for the item upward such that he or she will have a more intense desire for it, thereby becoming willing to buy more of

---

[8] The material in this section draws heavily from the ideas expressed by John Kenneth Galbraith in *The New Industrial State* (Boston: Houghton Mifflin Company, 1967), Chapters 18–20.

it at a given price or else becoming willing to pay a higher price for the same amount currently being purchased.

Consumers, of course, have it well within their powers to reject persuasion. Enough consumers, by their refusal to continue to purchase items they consider unsatisfactory, can force accommodation by producers. Not even cleverly advertised products can survive when consumers find them seriously deficient. The notion of the gullible consumer, naked in the jungle of the marketplace and at the mercy of unscrupulous and misleading advertisements, is greatly exaggerated. Still, it is clear that advertising does influence consumer purchases; it can intensify consumer desire for a commodity to a point where the perceived marginal utility per dollar of expenditure becomes high enough to induce some consumers to buy the item. The public interest and the concept of consumer sovereignty are, therefore, better served by the elimination of deceitful or misleading advertising practices.

APPLICATIONS CAPSULE

HOW ADVERTISING CAN INFLUENCE CONSUMER DEMAND

Mrs. Wilson enjoys drinking freshly perked coffee made from ground coffee beans. She takes more than a normal amount of pride in making a good cup of coffee both for herself and her husband. However, Mrs. Wilson is familiar with both regular grind and instant coffee, although she is much more knowledgeable about regular coffee than instant because of her preferences for freshly ground perked coffee. Nonetheless, Mrs. Wilson does buy instant coffee occasionally because her widowed mother-in-law prefers the convenience of instant to regular coffee.

Over the years Mrs. Wilson has bought three brands of regular coffee: Maxwell House, Folger's, and the house brand at the supermarket where she shops. She has a very strong preference for Maxwell House, but she does buy Folger's and the supermarket's house brand occasionally when they are on sale or if the store where she shops happens to be out of Maxwell House. Mrs. Wilson's strong preference for Maxwell House is based upon Maxwell House's ability to satisfy her criteria of strength, flavor, aroma, and economy. Mrs. Wilson is very confident about her preference for Maxwell House because she is quite certain of her evaluations of the other brands she has tried.

One day, while watching television, Mrs. Wilson saw a television commercial from Nestlé introducing Taster's Choice freeze-dried coffee. The commercial described what freeze-dried coffee meant and how it combined the flavor of regular coffee with the convenience of instant coffee. Although she usually ignores most commercials, Mrs. Wilson paid attention to this particular one. In fact, she stopped what she was doing and watched the commercial intensely. Mrs. Wilson was exposed to the following bits of information: (1) Taster's Choice is a totally new kind of coffee, (2) made from a freeze-dry process, (3) that has the flavor and taste of regular coffee, (4) but appears and is used like instant coffee. This information led Mrs. Wilson to conclude that Taster's Choice was a new brand of instant coffee, perhaps better in taste than most other instant coffees, because it was manufactured by a new process. Nonetheless, Mrs. Wilson viewed what she heard about the freeze-dry concept with some skepticism and ambiguity. She was still convinced that she preferred regular coffee to instant coffee and decided the information about Taster's Choice was not relevant to her.

A few days later Mrs. Wilson was exposed to the same commercial. This time, she did not pay full attention, but she did listen and watch it. At the end, she concluded with greater firmness that Taster's Choice was a new brand of instant coffee, perhaps with improved taste over other instant coffees because of the new process.

The following week, Mrs. Wilson received a sample jar of Taster's Choice in the mail. While she probably would not have bought it, the free sample generated enough motivation and curiosity for her to try a cup. Mrs. Wilson was surprised to find that Taster's Choice was similar to regular coffee in taste, flavor, and aroma. Her mother-in-law, who happened to be visiting, also praised it as being better than her regular brand of instant coffee. With satisfaction, Mrs. Wilson reevaluated her attitude toward Taster's Choice and concluded that it was the most preferred brand of *instant* coffee.

When she went to her Wednesday afternoon bridge club she mentioned Taster's Choice to her friends, trying to find out how they perceived it and whether they had tried it at all. Then, a few days later, she served Taster's Choice to her husband. He, too, liked the taste and praised it. Several of Mrs. Wilson's friends also indicated that they considered it a good product. Mrs. Wilson then began to have such a high opinion of Taster's Choice that she seriously considered it as a replacement for Maxwell House regular coffee. When her sample jar of Taster's Choice was exhausted, she bought another jar to replace it.

QUESTIONS FOR DISCUSSION

1. Do you think Mrs. Wilson was inappropriately influenced by the television commercial to purchase Taster's Choice?

2. How important was advertising in reshaping Mrs. Wilson's preference for Taster's Choice as opposed to Maxwell House coffee?

3. What is there about Taster's Choice that, from Mrs. Wilson's point of view, gave it "utility?" How do you think the utility which Mrs. Wilson associated with Maxwell House compares with the utility she now associates with Taster's Choice?

4. What do you think really caused Mrs. Wilson to think more highly of Taster's Choice?

SUMMARY AND CONCLUSIONS

The utility approach to consumer behavior and the formation of individual consumer demand is grounded upon psychological principles. Rational individuals, it is said, will seek to maximize the degree of "pleasure" and minimize the degree of "pain" in choosing among alternative courses of action. In furtherance of this proposition, the concept of utility has evolved into the economist's major tool for explaining and predicting the consumer's marketplace behavior.

Utility refers to the want-satisfying power of products—that is, the amount of satisfaction a consumer receives from consuming various quantities of a good or service per period of time. A consumer's total and marginal utility functions for a product can be represented equally well by tables, graphs, and equations. Marginal utility is defined to be the rate of change in total utility as the rate of consumption of a product changes. For each total utility function, there is a corresponding marginal utility function. Every consumer has his or her own unique set of total and marginal utility functions; these vary according to his or her tastes and preferences for different products. Moreover, the satisfaction a consumer obtains from one product hinges in part upon the amounts consumed of other products.

Consumers maximize the satisfaction they can obtain from their limited money income by meeting two conditions. First, they must fully utilize all their income either by purchasing products or by saving. Second, consumers must arrange their purchases so that the marginal utilities per dollar spent on the last unit of each item purchased are equal. In other words, to maximize satisfaction, consumers must get an equivalent amount of satisfaction from the last dollar allocated to each of the items (including saving) that they choose to buy.

Few consumers probably succeed in obtaining the maximum satisfaction from their income. Impulsive buying, habit, imperfect knowledge of product prices and quality, a desire for variety, emotion and personality traits, the pressures of time and circumstances, family roles, and the persuasive powers of advertising, among others, prompt consumers to make purchases with which they may not be fully satisfied.

However, the fact that consumers do not succeed in maximizing utility is not crucial to the validity of utility theory. What is important is whether consumers act consistently on the basis of perceived utility (including both monetary and time considerations) and, accordingly, whether utility theory explains and predicts well.

SUGGESTED READINGS

ALCHIAN, A. A., "The Meaning of Utility Measurement," *American Economic Review,* Vol. 43, No. 1 (March 1953), pp. 26–50.

ELLSBURG, D., "Classic and Current Notions of Measurable Utility," *Economic Journal,* Vol. 64, No. 255 (September 1954), pp. 528–556.

FERBER, R., "Consumer Economics: A Survey," *Journal of Economic Literature,* Vol. 11, No. 4 (December 1973), pp. 1303–1342.

FRIEDMAN, M., AND L. J. SAVAGE, "The Utility Analysis of Choices Involving Risk," *Journal of Political Economy,* Vol. 56, No. 4 (August 1948), pp. 279–304.

KATONA, G., *Psychological Economics* (New York: American Elsevier Publishing Co., Inc., 1975).

STIGLER, G. J., "The Development of Utility Theory," *Journal of Political Economy,* Vol. 58, Nos. 4 and 5 (August and October 1950), pp. 307–327, 373–396.

STROTZ, R. H., "Cardinal Utility," *American Economic Review,* Vol. 43, No. 2 (May 1953), pp. 384–397.

PROBLEMS AND QUESTIONS FOR DISCUSSION

1. Find the first derivatives of each of the following functions.
   (a) $Y = 124 + 6X$.

(b) $Y = 15X^2 + 2X^3$.
(c) $TU_x = 17X - 0.5X^2$.
(d) $TU_a = 16A + 5A^2 - 0.3A^3$.
(e) $TU_b = -185 + 7B + 1.9B^2 - 0.05B^3$.
(f) $TU_c = 0.6C^{1/2}$.
(g) $TU_y = 1.5Y^{0.75}$.
  Answers: **(a)** $dY/dX = 6$.
  (b) $dY/dX = 30X + 6X^2$.
  (c) $dTU/dX = 17 - X$.
  (d) $dTU_a/dA = 16 + 10A - 0.9A^2$.
  (e) $dTU_b/dB = 7 + 3.8B - 0.15B^2$.
  (f) $dTU_c/dC = 0.3C^{-1/2}$.
  (g) $dTU_y/dY = 1.125Y^{-0.25}$.

2. Find the second derivative of each of the following functions (the second derivative is the derivative of the first derivative).
  (a) $Y = 124 + 7X^2$.
  (b) $TU_x = 9 + 14X - 0.2X^2$.
  (c) $TU_a = 130 + 14A + 15A^2 - 0.4A^3$.
  (d) $TU_b = 0.6B^{1.5}$.
    Answers: **(a)** $d^2Y/dX^2 = 14$.
    (b) $d^2TU/dX^2 = -0.4$.
    (c) $d^2TU_a/dA^2 = 30 - 2.4A$.
    (d) $d^2TU_b/dB^2 = 0.45B^{-0.5}$.

3. Explain the nature of the distinguishing features between cardinal and ordinal measures of utility.

4. Adam Smith in *The Wealth of Nations* observed: "Nothing is more useful than water: but it will purchase scarce anything; scarce anything can be had in exchange for it. A diamond, on the contrary, has scarce any value in use; but a very great quantity of other goods may frequently be had in exchange for it."
  (a) How do you account for this?
  (b) Is the term *useful* or *usefulness* synonymous with the concept of utility as we have defined it?

5. An individual's total utility function for product B is as follows: $TU = 18B - 0.5B^2$.
  (a) Graph the *TU* function, and explain the nature of the individual's utility for the product.
  (b) Calculate the equation for marginal utility, and illustrate it graphically.
  (c) How much will total utility be at a consumption rate of 10 units? At 15 units?
  (d) How much will marginal utility be at a consumption rate of 10 units? At 15 units?
  (e) How many units of product B can the individual consume and still gain additional satisfaction?

6. An individual's total utility function for product Q is as follows: $TU = 100Q + 150Q^2 - 2Q^3$.
  (a) Determine the expression for marginal utility.
  (b) Graph the total and marginal utility functions, and explain the nature of the individual's utility for the product.
  (c) How much will total utility be at a consumption rate of 5 units? How much will marginal utility be at 5 units?
  (d) At what approximate consumption rate does diminishing *MU* begin?
  (e) At what approximate consumption rate does the individual reach his saturation rate?

7. The following table shows the marginal utility, measured in utils of satisfaction, which Mr. Johnson would get by purchasing various amounts of products A, B, C, and D and by saving. The prices of A, B, C, and D are $5, $6, $8, and $20, respectively. Mr. Johnson has a money income of $95 to spend in the current period.

| Product A | | Product B | | Product C | | Product D | | Saving | |
Units	MU	Units	MU	Units	MU	Units	MU	Dollars Saved	MU
1	31	1	20	1	39	1	50	1	6
2	27	2	19	2	36	2	55	2	5
3	23	3	18	3	33	3	50	3	4
4	19	4	17	4	30	4	45	4	3
5	15	5	16	5	27	5	40	5	2
6	11	6	15	6	24	6	35	6	1
7	7	7	14	7	21	7	30	7	$\frac{1}{2}$

(a) How many units of A, B, C, and D must Mr. Johnson purchase in order to maximize total utility?

(b) How many dollars will Mr. Johnson elect to save?

(c) State algebraically the two conditions for utility maximization, and show that your answers to parts (a) and (b) satisfy these conditions.

8. Given the two conditions requisite for utility maximization, is it likely that a consumer would ever reach his saturation rate for any good or service? Why or why not? Under what circumstances *might* it occur?

9. Dr. Holt has $30 per week available to spend as he wishes on commodities A and B. The prices of A and B, the quantities of A and B he is now buying, and his evaluations of the utility provided by these quantities are as follows:

Product	Price per Unit	Quantity Purchased (units)	Total Utility (utils)	MU of Last Unit Purchased (utils)
A	$0.70	30	500	30
B	0.50	18	1,000	20

Is Dr. Holt maximizing total utility? If so, *explain why*. If not, what might he do to maximize utility? *Explain why.*

10. Suppose that Mr. Pikard has an income of $60 weekly which he is free to spend or save in any way he sees fit. Mr. Pikard believes that *each* dollar he saves gives him 5 utils of satisfaction. This past week, of the thousands of products available, Mr. Pikard purchased the following list of items and believes he obtained the indicated degrees of utility from them:

Product	Price per Unit	Quantity Purchased	Total Utility (utils)	MU of Last Unit Purchased (utils)
A	$ 2.50	1	15	15.0
B	0.75	2	16	4.5
C	0.50	10	113	3.0
D	4.00	3	248	24.0
E	3.00	6	618	18.0
F	15.00	1	90	90.0

Is it possible, given this information, that Mr. Pikard maximized the total utility he received last week from his $60?

11. The Belmont Company conducted an experiment to see how well its new typewriter would stack up against a typewriter produced by Delta Company, a firm already well established in the market. Belmont utilized three testing conditions: (1) *accurate brand labeling*, whereby both machines were placed in an office use situation with the correct company and brand names indicated; (2) *reverse brand labeling*, whereby both machines were placed in an office use situation with the company and brand names reversed; (3) *blind labeling*, whereby both typewriters were unidentified as to company and brand name. Under test condition (1), Delta's typewriter was rated moderately superior to the Belmont brand, but under test condition (2) Belmont's typewriter was rated far superior to Delta's. In the blind labeling test, the Belmont typewriter was given a slight edge over the Delta machine.

    (a) How do you account for these results?
    (b) What criteria do you think were being used to rate the two typewriters? Do you think the user's evaluations were "rational?"
    (c) Are the results consistent with the utility model of buyer behavior?

12. It has been said that "What the customer thinks he is buying, what he considers value is decisive . . . And what the customer buys and considers value is never a product. It is always utility, that is, what a product or service does for him." Comment.

4

THE DEMAND SIDE
OF THE MARKETPLACE
The indifference curve
and attribute models

While the cardinal utility approach to consumer preference offers useful insights into consumer behavior, the inability to quantify utility in a satisfactory manner caused economists to seek out an alternative mode of individual demand analysis not predicated on numerical measures of satisfaction. The search led to the development of ordinal utility analysis whereby consumer tastes and preferences are indicated by ordering or ranking the utilities of various products.[1] Interestingly enough, this seemingly slight change in approach has produced some versatile analytical tools that stand as an important extension of the cardinal utility concepts of Chapter 3.

---

[1] Although the concepts of cardinal and ordinal utility are distinct notions, it should be pointed out that there is not a wide gulf between the two. Consumers often experience considerable difficulty in deciding which products they actually prefer. For example, a consumer may have no trouble deciding that he prefers item X to item Z and that he prefers item Y to item Z, but he may have quite a hard time deciding whether he prefers item X to item Y, or vice versa. It can then be reliably hypothesized that the cardinal utility difference between the paired comparisons (X, Z) and (Y, Z) is greater than between (X, Y). To put it another way, a consumer may be able to establish an ordinal ranking among three items, X, Y, and Z, ranking X as first, Y as second, and Z as third. Yet it may be quite clear to him that Z is a poor third, while X barely edged out Y for first; this creates a strong inference that the cardinal utility difference between X and Y is much smaller than between either X and Z or Y and Z. Hence, ordinal utility rankings may permit judgments about the numerical amounts of total utility associated with various items.

THE CONCEPT OF INDIFFERENCE CURVES

The ordinal utility approach to consumer demand is usually called indifference curve analysis because "indifference curves" are its primary analytical tool. To understand the origin and meaning of indifference curves, suppose that we refocus our attention upon the utility interrelationships among goods and services.

Figure 4-1(a) depicts a total utility surface for two desirable goods X and Y. Increasing the rates of consumption of X and Y from zero levels produces the total utility surface *OEFG*. Observe that if the consumption of Y is fixed at Y_1 units, then the consumer's total utility from X and Y increases at a decreasing rate along the path *ECAF* as the consumption of X per unit of time rises from zero to X_1 units. In like manner, whenever the consumption of X is fixed, total utility increases at a decreasing rate as the consumption of Y is increased per period of time.

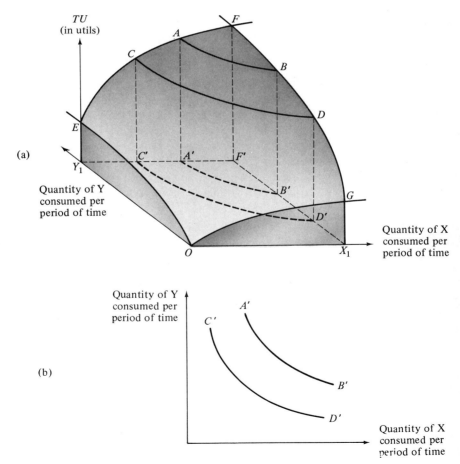

FIGURE 4-1
Derivation of indifference curves

Suppose that we connect all points on the utility surface *OEFG* which represent a total utility level of *CC'* (where *CC'* = *DD'*), thereby obtaining the contour line *CD*. Thus, all the points along *CD* are associated with a specific amount of total utility *CC'* (or *DD'*). Projecting the curve *CD* vertically downward onto the *XY* plane traces out the dashed contour line *C'D'* and defines all the combinations of products X and Y consumed per unit of time which yield an amount of total utility equal to *CC'* (or *DD'*). Logically, a consumer would be *indifferent* as to which one of the combinations of X and Y along *C'D'* he had since they all are associated with the same amount of total utility.

Following the same procedure, suppose that we move up the utility surface to a higher level of total utility *AA'* (= *BB'*). Connecting all points on the utility surface *OEFG* with a total utility of *AA'* (= *BB'*) gives the contour line *AB*. Projecting the image of *AB* perpendicularly onto the *XY* plane gives the dashed contour line *A'B'*. Any point along *AB* represents constant total utility of amount *AA'* = *BB'*, and all combinations of products X and Y lying on *A'B'* yield this amount of total utility. Again, it is reasonable to conclude that a consumer would be indifferent among the combinations of X and Y along *A'B'* because they all are equally satisfying.

Predictably enough, the contour lines *C'D'* and *A'B'* are called *indifference curves*.[2] An indifference curve is the locus of the various combinations of products that yield an equal amount of satisfaction (total utility) to the consumer, or among which the consumer is indifferent. Figure 4-1(b) illustrates indifference curves *C'D'* and *A'B'* in a two-dimensional diagram.

Although a consumer is indifferent as to the various combinations along a particular indifference curve, he is *not* indifferent as to the various combinations between indifference curves. For example, a consumer would prefer *all* combinations of X and Y on *A'B'* to those combinations on *C'D'* because the former are associated with a higher total utility (*AA'* > *CC'*). Greater degrees of total utility are shown by contour lines higher up on the utility surface, while lower degrees of total utility are shown by lower contour lines. Consequently, in a two-dimensional diagram such as Fig. 4-1(b), indifference curves lying farther from the origin represent higher levels of satisfaction than do those lying closer in. Therefore, an indifference curve may additionally be thought of as a boundary between combinations of products which a consumer views as less satisfying and those combinations which he views as more satisfying. To put it another way, a consumer is indifferent among any one of the various combinations on a given indifference curve, but he prefers all combinations on higher indifference curves to those on lower indifference curves.

There is an indifference curve associated with each distinct degree of total

---

[2] The total utility surface in Fig. 4-1(a) is mathematically defined by the general expression $TU = f(X, Y)$. The equation for one indifference curve is $TU_1 = f(X, Y)$, where TU_1 is a constant and X and Y represent all the various combinations of two products which yield a utility of TU_1. Other indifference curves on the surface are generated by assigning different values to TU. The family of indifference curves produced by letting TU assume every possible value defines the consumer's indifference map. Significantly, the values for TU need only reflect an ordered preference pattern rather than being expressed as cardinal utility (numerical) values.

utility on the total utility surface. In this sense, indifference curves are "everywhere dense," that is, an indifference curve passes through each point in the XY plane. The family of indifference curves which may be derived from the total utility surface comprises an *indifference map.* The indifference map provides a complete description of a consumer's preferences for various combinations of goods and services.

The important point to recognize at this juncture is that the specific degree of utility associated with an indifference curve is in no way crucial. In fact, the information provided by an indifference curve does not specify the *amount* of satisfaction produced by the combinations comprising it. In Fig. 4-1(b), the total utility attached to $C'D'$ and $A'B'$ could be 10 utils and 14 utils, respectively, or 112 utils and 547 utils. The *amount* by which the combinations on a higher indifference curve are preferred to those on a lower indifference curve is unspecified—it could be a little or a lot. All that is necessary for deriving an indifference curve is for the consumer to know his or her preferences well enough to be able to distinguish whether he or she prefers one combination of goods to another or whether the consumer views them as equally satisfying.[3] It is in this sense that ordinal utility or indifference curve analysis is free of the need to express utility in numerical terms.

THE SHAPES OF INDIFFERENCE CURVES

Although the height of the total utility surface is immaterial, its *shape* is not. In fact, it is the *shape* of the utility surface which determines the shape of the indifference curves, thereby describing a consumer's taste and preference pattern. Any set of consumer tastes can be portrayed by indifference curves and utility surfaces. Several examples may be given in support of this statement.

First, consider the taste and preference pattern of an individual who enjoys good X immensely (prime ribs) but considers good Y devoid of want-satisfying qualities (parsnips). Figure 4-2(a) depicts a utility surface and indifference map for such a situation. Having more of Y neither raises nor lowers total satisfaction (its marginal utility is zero); only good X has the power to change the level of total utility. The effect is to make each indifference curve in the bottom half of Fig. 4-2(a) a vertical line. As the consumption rate of X is increased per unit of time, utility increases; hence, on the indifference map higher levels of satisfaction are shown by moving rightward along the X-axis.

Figure 4-2(b) illustrates a total utility surface and corresponding indifference map for a pair of products that are *perfect substitutes.* Products are said to be perfect substitutes when their qualities are so similar that a consumer would just as soon have more of one as more of the other. Examples could be nickels and dimes (at a constant ratio of 2:1), competing brands of pencils, or competing

---

[3] The consumer must be able to avoid being thrust into a position similar to that of Buridan's ass. The ass, it may be recalled, stood midway between two equally sized bundles of hay and finally died of hunger because it could not decide which bundle to eat.

brands of essentially identical food products—milk, eggs, sugar, and black pepper. The indifference curve for perfect substitutes is a straight line because the consumer considers them as being absolutely equivalent and is willing, therefore, to substitute one for the other at some *constant* ratio, no matter how much he or she has of either.

In Fig. 4-3 is the indifference map for a pair of products that have a rigid one-to-one complementary relationship in the mind of the consumer (right and left shoes, nuts and bolts). Each indifference curve is a right angle because the

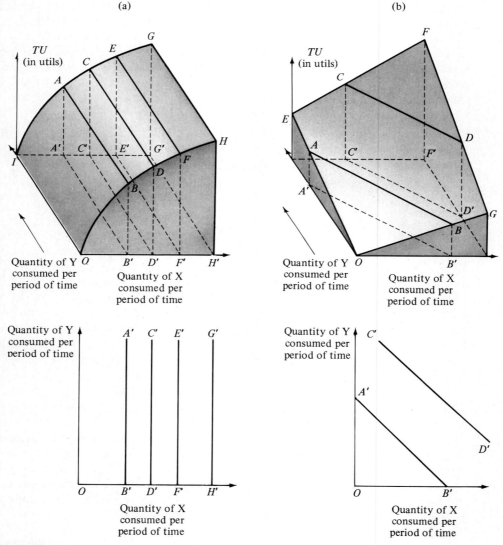

FIGURE 4-2
Total utility surfaces and indifference maps for special types of products

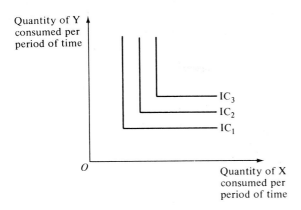

Quantity of Y
consumed per
period of time

IC$_3$

IC$_2$

IC$_1$

O

Quantity of X
consumed per
period of time

FIGURE 4-3
Indifference map for perfect complements

consumer is no better off having more of one without the other; this means more units of one complementary item have a marginal utility of zero unless combined with more units of the other complementary item. Therefore, total satisfaction can be increased only by having more of both items. (The shape of the utility surface from which these curves are derived is left as an exercise at the end of this chapter.)

THE CHARACTERISTICS OF TYPICAL INDIFFERENCE CURVES

To simplify the exposition of indifference curve analysis it is customary to make three assumptions:

1. All products are continuously divisible into subunits so that a consumer is not constrained by the size of the units in which the item is sold.
2. The consumer's tastes and order of preference among combinations of products is well defined and consistent.
3. The consumer views products as being desirable—having more is always preferred to having less; this means that the marginal utility of additional consumption is positive and, further, that useless and nuisance items are disregarded.[4]

Given these assumptions, indifference curves exhibit four characteristics. From the first assumption it follows that (a) indifference curves are continuous functions rather than collections of discrete points and (b) indifference curves are "everywhere dense"—some indifference curve will pass through every point in the *XY*-plane (or *commodity space,* as it is sometimes called).

The second assumption, in conjunction with the third, ensures that indifference curves will be nonintersecting. Consider Fig. 4-4, in which two indifference curves, IC$_1$ and IC$_2$, are shown intersecting. A moment's reflection should

---

[4] It is easy enough to redefine a nuisance item to make it a desirable item. Instead of garbage, the item can be called garbage removal; instead of polluted water, the item can be defined as clean water.

Quantity of Y
consumed per
period of time

Quantity of X
consumed per
period of time

FIGURE 4-4
Logical inconsistency of intersecting
indifference curves

indicate that it is quite illogical for combination *A* to produce simultaneously two levels of satisfaction—as would be the case were it to lie on two different indifference curves. Thus, intersecting indifference curves deny the condition of consistency (or transitivity).[5] But to say that indifference curves are nonintersecting is *not* to say that indifference curves must be equidistant from one another. Two indifference curves may or may not be the same distance apart throughout. The curves for many, even most, pairs of items may become progressively closer (or farther apart) because of differing *MU* functions.

The third assumption causes indifference curves to slope downward to the right (i.e., have a negative slope). Negatively sloped indifference curves reflect the general principle that a consumer is willing to give up units of one product if the loss in satisfaction is compensated for by having more of another product. Stated differently, by having more of one good (say X) and by giving up an appropriate amount of another good (say Y), the consumer can be made to feel just as well off as originally (when he had less of X and more of Y). By *substituting* one item for another in such a way that the gain in satisfaction from consuming more of one is exactly offset by the loss of satisfaction from consuming less of another, the consumer's overall satisfaction level can be held constant.

THE MARGINAL RATE OF SUBSTITUTION

Except in the case of perfect substitutes and perfect complements, indifference curves for desirable products not only slope downward to the right, but they are

[5] Transitivity is a scale of preference such that if *A* is preferred to *B* and *B* is preferred to *C*, then *A* must be preferred to *C*. Clearly, transitivity cannot be present if (1) *A* and *B* are viewed as equivalent, (2) *A* and *C* are viewed as equivalent, and (3) *B* is preferred to *C* (because combination *B* contains more of both goods *X* and *Y*)—this is precisely the illogical condition depicted in Fig. 4-4.

also *convex* to the origin of the indifference map. The reasons for this convexity derive from the concept of the marginal rate of substitution of one good for another.

The *marginal rate of substitution* (MRS) is the rate at which a consumer is agreeable to trading off some of one good for more of another good while at the same time holding the overall level of satisfaction constant. Consider the indifference curve shown in Fig. 4-5. The consumer is indifferent among combinations X_1Y_1, X_2Y_2, X_3Y_3, X_4Y_4, and X_5Y_5. The horizontal axis is measured so that distances $OX_1 = X_1X_2 = X_2X_3 = X_3X_4 = X_4X_5 = 1$ unit of X. Starting at combination X_1Y_1 and proceeding down the indifference curve, observe that initially the consumer is willing to give up Y_1Y_2 units of Y to get an additional unit of X and yet have just as much satisfaction as before. But as he or she acquires more and more of X and has less and less of Y left, the amount of Y he or she is willing to give up to get another unit of X becomes progressively smaller. We can express the ratio at which a consumer is willing to exchange one product for another algebraically as

$$MRS_{xy} = \frac{\Delta Y}{\Delta X},$$

where ΔY represents the number of units of Y the consumer is willing to give up and ΔX represents the number of units of X it will take to compensate the consumer for his or her loss of Y. The expression $\Delta Y/\Delta X$ thus defines the exchange ratio or marginal rate of substitution between Y and X that will precisely maintain

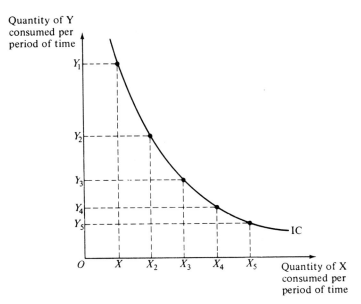

FIGURE 4-5
Marginal rate of substitution along an indifference curve

the consumer's level of satisfaction. Clearly the exchange ratio is not constant all along an indifference curve: The ratio becomes smaller going down the curve, and this is what makes the indifference curve convex. Why does the value of MRS_{xy} diminish going down the curve? One explanation for diminishing MRS_{xy} is that as we move down an indifference curve, the remaining units of Y become dearer and the additional units of X yield smaller amounts of extra satisfaction; that is, the marginal utility of the remaining units of Y rises, whereas the marginal utility from additional units of X decreases. This argument, although quite plausible since a state of diminishing marginal utility for X and Y is fairly normal, is not always sufficient. When the utility derived from good Y is partially dependent on the amount consumed of X, increasing the consumption of X may decrease the marginal utility from Y and spoil the argument. Fortunately, more powerful evidence for convexity exists. It can, for example, be demonstrated that if the consumer buys some of each of two products, his or her indifference curves must be convex to the origin; otherwise, only one of the products would be bought.

But there is more to be learned about the marginal rate of substitution. We know that in moving from one point to another on the same indifference curve there is no change in total utility. Consider, for example, the situation in going from point $X_1 Y_1$ to point $X_2 Y_2$ in Fig. 4-5. We can say that the amount of utility "lost" from consuming fewer units of Y (Y_1 to Y_2) is exactly compensated for by the "gain" in utility from consuming more units of X (X_1 to X_2). In more formal terms,

$$-\Delta Y \cdot MU_y \;=\; \Delta X \cdot MU_x.$$

"loss" in utility from consuming $Y_1 Y_2$ (or ΔY) fewer units of good Y	"gain" in utility from consuming $X_1 X_2$ (or ΔX) units more of good X

Dividing both terms of this equality by $\Delta X \cdot MU_y$ gives

$$\frac{-\Delta Y \cdot MU_y}{\Delta X \cdot MU_y} = \frac{\Delta X \cdot MU_x}{\Delta X \cdot MU_y},$$

which reduces to

$$-\frac{\Delta Y}{\Delta X} = \frac{MU_x}{MU_y} \quad \text{or} \quad \frac{\Delta Y}{\Delta X} = -\frac{MU_x}{MU_y}.$$

But since $MRS_{xy} = \Delta Y/\Delta X$, we have

$$MRS_{xy} = \frac{\Delta Y}{\Delta X} = -\frac{MU_x}{MU_y},$$

which says that the marginal rate of substitution of X for Y is equal to the ratio of MU_x to MU_y. This expression for MRS_{xy} holds true for any two points on an indifference curve. The negative sign in the expression reflects the fact that having more of one good (X) entails having less of the other good (Y). Additionally, it follows that if any two points on a given indifference curve become so close together that they are really one point, then the marginal rate of substitution of X for Y equals the slope of the indifference curve at that point. One final point: The marginal rate of substitution is meaningful only for movements along an indifference curve—never for movements among curves.

THE CONSUMER'S BUDGET CONSTRAINT

A consumer's indifference map indicates his or her subjective attitudes toward various combinations of products. It shows what combinations are preferred to others and the rates at which he or she is willing to substitute one producer for another. However, as was seen in Chapter 3, the extent to which the consumer is *able* to satisfy these tastes and preferences hinges upon (1) the available money income and (2) the respective prices of the products the individual is desirous of having. Taken together, these two factors define the individual's *budget constraint*.

For simplicity, suppose that we continue to restrict our analysis to a situation where there are just two goods X and Y with prices of P_x and P_y. As established previously, the consumer's money income (I) is fixed in the short run; he or she has only so much to spend per period of time. The consumer's expenditures for X will be equal to the selling price (P_x) times the amount purchased (X) or P_xX; similarly, the expenditure for good Y is P_yY. The sum of the consumer's expenditures for X and Y must be equal to or less than the available income I. Thus, we may write

$$P_xX + P_yY \leq I.$$

If the consumer elects to spend all of his or her income on X and Y and save nothing, then,

$$P_xX + P_yY = I.$$

Otherwise, saving accounts for the margin of difference between the consumer's total expenditures on X and Y and income.

Suppose that the available money income is \$50, $P_x = \$5$, and $P_y = \$2$. If the entire \$50 is spent on good X, a maximum of 10 units (I/P_x) could be bought; if the entire \$50 is spent on Y, as much as 25 units (I/P_y) can be purchased. These combinations are illustrated in Fig. 4-6. A straight line joining these two points on the graph shows *all* the other combinations of X and Y that the consumer's income will allow him to purchase at these prices. This line is called the *line of attainable combinations* because it represents the locus of combinations of X and Y that can be purchased when the consumer spends the entire amount of money

MATHEMATICAL CAPSULE 4

THE MARGINAL RATE OF SUBSTITUTION, THE CONVEXITY OF INDIFFERENCE CURVES, AND DIMINISHING MARGINAL UTILITY

Suppose that the total utility function for goods X and Y is

$$TU = f(X, Y);$$

than an indifference curve is defined by

$$TU = f(X, Y) = c,$$

where c is a constant. Finding the total differential of $TU = f(X, Y)$ gives

$$dTU = \frac{\partial TU}{\partial X} dX + \frac{\partial TU}{\partial Y} dY = 0,$$

since $TU = c$. Solving the total differential for dY/dX, we have

$$\frac{\partial TU}{\partial Y} dY = -\frac{\partial TU}{\partial X} dX,$$

$$\frac{dY}{dX} = -\frac{\partial TU/\partial X}{\partial TU/\partial Y} \quad \text{or} \quad -\frac{MU_x}{MU_y}.$$

Hence, dY/dX is the slope of the indifference curve or MRS_{xy}. The negative sign reflects the negative slope of the indifference curve. If the TU function is ordinal rather than cardinal, MU_x and MU_y have no meaningful absolute values—only their ratios are relevant and interpretable.

Diminishing MU for X and Y requires that

$$\frac{\partial^2 TU}{\partial X^2} < 0 \quad \text{and} \quad \frac{\partial^2 TU}{\partial Y^2} < 0;$$

however, convexity of the indifference curve requires that $d^2Y/dX^2 < 0$, which is not the same. Thus, the convexity of indifference curves does not depend on diminishing MU for X and Y.

income available.[6] The consumer can also buy any of the combinations of X and Y inside the line (the shaded area); however, if he or she does so, available

[6] In the literature of indifference curve analysis, the line of attainable combinations is known variously as the budget line, the price line, the budget restraint, the expenditure line, the price-income line, and the consumption possibility line.

In drawing the line as a continuous function, we continue our assumption of the preceding sections that products X and Y are perfectly divisible into subunits and can be purchased in any quantity.

Normally, an individual consumer's purchases of a product are so small relative to the total amount bought that the price of it can reasonably be anticipated to remain constant irrespective of the amount purchased. Thus, a linear line of attainable combinations may be considered typical. However, if by chance the prices of X and Y depend on the amounts the consumer buys, then the line of attainable combinations becomes curvilinear. When product prices fall as the consumer buys more units, the line of attainable combinations is bowed in toward the origin. When product prices rise with increasing purchase levels, the line is bowed out or concave toward the origin.

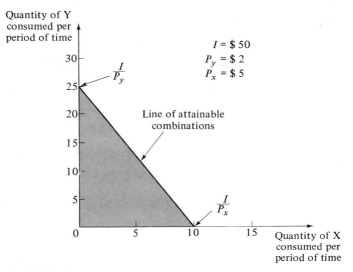

FIGURE 4-6
Line of attainable combinations

purchasing power will not be fully utilized and there will be money left over for saving (or for spending on other products). The equation of the line of attainable combinations in Fig. 4-6 is $5X + $2Y = 50, where $5 = $ the price of product X, $2 = $ the price of Y, and $50 = $ the consumer's money income. The set of values for X and Y that satisfy this equation are given by the points comprising the line of attainable combinations.

The general equation for the line of attainable combinations in a two-product economy is $P_x X + P_y Y = I$.[7] The slope of the line of attainable combinations is negative and is numerically equal to the ratio of the prices of X and Y. This is easily verified by considering the slope of the line in Fig. 4-6 between the two extreme points I/P_x and I/P_y:

$$\text{slope of the line of attainable combinations} = \frac{\text{change in the quantity of } Y}{\text{change in the quantity of } X} = \frac{-I/P_y}{I/P_x} = -\frac{P_x}{P_y}.$$

Shifts in the Consumer's Budget Constraint

Both changes in money income and changes in product prices have the effect of shifting the position of the line of attainable combinations. Consider first the effect of an increase in money income from I_1 to I_2 when the prices of X and Y

---

[7] For n number of products and where saving is indicated as a separate activity, the general equation of the line of attainable combinations may be written as

$$P_{x_a} X_a + P_{x_b} X_b + P_{x_c} X_c + \cdots + P_{x_a} X_n + \text{saving} = I,$$

where I = money income and $P_a, P_b, P_c, \ldots, P_{x_n}$ are the prices of products $X_a, X_b, X_c, \ldots, X_n$.

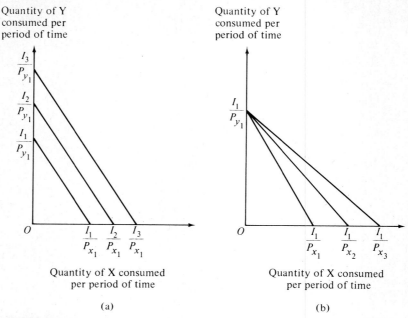

FIGURE 4-7
Shifts in the line of attainable combinations

remain constant at P_{x_1} and P_{y_1}. The larger money income permits the consumer to purchase more of X, more of Y, or more of both. The maximum amount of X which can be purchased increases from I_1/P_{x_1} to I_2/P_{x_1} as shown in Fig. 4-7(a). The maximum purchase level of Y rises from I_1/P_{y_1} to I_2/P_{y_1}. Since the prices of X and Y are fixed, the slope of the new line of attainable combinations must be identical to the slope at an income of I_1, and it must pass through points I_2/P_{x_1} and I_2/P_{y_1}. Thus, an increase in money income from I_1 to I_2, product prices remaining constant, is shown graphically by a parallel shift in the line of attainable combinations upward and to the right. Similarly, another increase in income (to I_3) will shift the line parallelwise even farther to the right. Conversely, it follows that decreases in money income can be represented by parallel shifts in the line downward and to the left.

Figure 4-7(b) displays the change in the line of attainable combinations when the price of X decreases, the price of Y (P_{y_1}) and money income (I_1) remaining unchanged. Since I_1 and P_{y_1} do not change, the maximum quantity of Y which may be purchased (I_1/P_{y_1}) is unaffected by any change in P_x. As the price of X declines from P_{x_1} to P_{x_2} the maximum quantity of X which can be purchased with I_1 is raised from its original value of I_1/P_{x_1} to I_1/P_{x_2}. Accordingly, the line of attainable combinations becomes flatter and rotates to the right about the point I_1/P_{y_1}. Should the price of X decline to P_{x_3} the line of attainable combinations rotates rightward even more. In contrast, to represent increases in the price of X the line of attainable combinations is rotated to the left around the point I_1/P_{y_1}, causing the new line to be more steeply sloped. These changes in the slope of the line follow directly from our finding that the slope of the line of attainable combinations is $-(P_x/P_y)$. Clearly, if P_y is fixed and P_x falls, the slope of the line becomes smaller (or flatter), and when P_x rises, the slope of the line becomes larger (or steeper).

THE MAXIMIZATION OF SATISFACTION

The consumer's indifference map provides a diagrammatic representation of his or her tastes and preferences; that is, it represents a subjective evaluation of the intensity of desire for different product combinations. The consumer's purchasing power (and thus ability to satisfy material wants) is reflected by the line of attainable combinations. Putting the two together provides a way for showing which of all the product combinations on the indifference map is the utility-maximizing combination.

In Fig. 4-8, the most satisfying combination among all those which can be purchased is at point C, where the consumer buys X_1 units of X and Y_1 units of Y. Combinations A and B, while attainable, are on a lower indifference curve from C and hence entail lower degrees of satisfaction. Combination D is superior to C, but it costs more than the consumer can afford and therefore is eliminated as an alternative. Indifference curve IC_2 is the highest possible indifference curve that can be reached given the consumer's income constraint, and combination C is the only obtainable combination on that curve. Consequently, C represents the most preferred combination of X and Y and may be said to represent *consumer equilibrium*. In general, the consumer's total utility is maximized *at the point of tangency between the line of attainable combinations and an indifference curve* (provided only that the products are desirable—have positive marginal utilities).

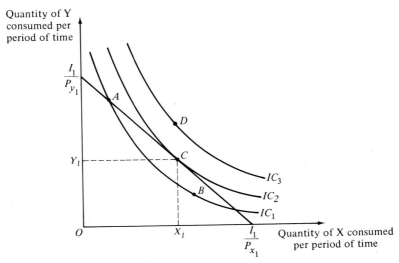

FIGURE 4-8
Determining the utility-maximizing combination of purchases

It is relevant at this point to ask: What are the conditions for maximizing satisfaction via indifference curve analysis, and how do these compare with those of cardinal utility analysis? First, we may note that the equilibrium combination of X and Y lies *on* the line of attainable combinations, rather than to the inside. This means that a consumer must *fully utilize* the available income to maximize satisfaction. Such a requirement does not preclude saving since saving may appropriately be considered as a commodity available for "purchase" by the consumer.

Second, at the equilibrium point the slope of the indifference curve is precisely equal to the slope of the line of attainable combinations. This necessarily results from their being tangent at this point. As shown earlier, the respective slopes can be expressed as

$$\text{slope of an indifference curve} = MRS_{xy} = (-)\frac{MU_x}{MU_y},$$

$$\text{slope of the line of attainable combinations} = (-)\frac{P_x}{P_y}.$$

Consequently, the second condition for maximizing satisfaction requires a consumer to so allocate purchasing power that the marginal rate of substitution of X for Y is equal to the ratio of the price of X to the price of Y. The interpretation of this condition is straightforward. The MRS_{xy} defines the *rate* at which the consumer is *willing to exchange* X for Y. The price ratio (P_x/P_y) shows the *rate* at which the consumer *can exchange* X for Y. Unless the two rates are equivalent, it is possible for the consumer to alter purchases of X and Y and achieve a greater degree of satisfaction. To illustrate: Suppose that at the current purchase combination, $MRS_{xy} = -4$, meaning that the consumer is willing to exchange 4 units of Y for 1 more unit of X. If $P_x = \$6$ and $P_y = \$2$, then the consumer need only give up 3 units of Y at \$2 each to obtain the \$6 needed to buy another unit of X. Confronted with these circumstances, the consumer will definitely be induced to make the exchange. Why? Because the preference for X and Y at this point is such that one is willing to trade off 4 units of Y for 1 unit of X, yet one has to give up only 3 units of Y to get 1 more unit of X. In general, then, consumer maximization of satisfaction requires equality between the marginal rate of substitution for any pair of products and the ratio of their prices; otherwise some exchange can be made which will increase the consumer's overall satisfaction.

However, the income allocation that will maximize consumer satisfaction can be approached from a more familiar angle. Not only is the slope of the indifference curve equal to the MRS_{xy} at any point, but it is also equal to the ratio of the marginal utilities (ordinally interpreted) of the two goods:

$$MRS_{xy} = (-)\frac{MU_x}{MU_y}.$$

Thus, we may write the second condition for maximizing satisfaction as

$$(-)\frac{MU_x}{MU_y} = (-)\frac{P_x}{P_y}.$$

This equation states that consumers' income should be allocated so as to equate the ratio of the marginal utilities with the ratio of the product prices. Rewriting the last expression, we get

$$MU_x \cdot P_y = MU_y \cdot P_x.$$

Dividing each term by $P_x \cdot P_y$ yields

$$\frac{MU_x \cdot P_y}{P_x \cdot P_y} = \frac{MU_y \cdot P_x}{P_x \cdot P_y},$$

which reduces to

$$\frac{MU_x}{P_x} = \frac{MU_y}{P_y}.$$

In an *n*-product economy, the latter expression expands to

$$\frac{MU_{X_a}}{P_a} = \frac{MU_{X_b}}{P_b} = \frac{MU_{X_c}}{P_c} = \cdots = \frac{MU_{X_a}}{P_n} = MU_{\text{saving}},$$

which, combined with the requirement for full utilization of the consumer's income, yields exactly the same conditions imposed upon the maximization of consumer satisfaction via the cardinal utility approach. Yet there is one important distinction: We reached these same conditions *without* the necessity for quantifying utility or satisfaction.

THE IMPACT OF INCOME CHANGES UPON CONSUMER PURCHASES

Changes in a consumer's money income often cause alterations in what is purchased. Suppose that we trace the impact of a change in an individual consumer's money income upon purchases of goods and services, assuming that product prices and the consumer's preference pattern remain unchanged.

Given the price of X at P_{x_1}, and the price of Y at P_{y_1}, the utility-maximizing purchase combination at an income of I_1 is shown in Fig. 4-9(a) as point A on indifference curve IC_1, where the consumer buys X_1 units of X and Y_1 units of Y. If the consumer's money income rises to I_2, the prices of X and Y remaining unchanged, the line of attainable combinations shifts in parallel fashion upward and to the right. The higher income level allows the consumer to buy more of X, or more of Y, or more of both. According to the preference pattern reflected by the shapes of the indifference curves, an increase in the consumer's money income to I_2 will result in equilibrium purchases of X_2 units of X and Y_2 units of Y at point B on indifference curve IC_2. This is a more satisfying combination of X and Y than was permitted formerly by an income of I_1 because it lies on a higher indifference curve. The consumer would realize a further gain in satisfaction should money income rise to I_3, thereby allowing him or her to reach point C on indifference curve IC_3 and to purchase X_3 units of X and Y_3 units of Y. The line joining the points of consumer equilibrium as income changes is called the *income-consumption curve.* The income-consumption curve is the locus of utility-maximizing combinations of products associated with various levels of money income and constant product prices.

When the resulting income-consumption curve is positively sloped, the products are *normal goods,* meaning that more of the goods are purchased at higher levels of income than at lower levels of income. Such is not always the case. Some items, designated as *inferior goods,* are purchased in smaller amounts when income rises, in which case the income-consumption curve is negatively sloped. Examples of goods that consumers tend to view as inferior include bologna, dried beans, recapped automobile tires, black-and-white camera film, economy or budget-priced durable goods, and reconditioned shock absorbers.

Derivation of Engel Curves.   The information provided by the income-consumption curve may be used to derive *Engel curves* for a product.[8] Engel curves show the equilibrium (utility-maximizing) quantities of a product which a consumer will purchase at various levels of income, other things remaining equal.

An Engel curve for good X is constructed in Fig. 4-9(b). From Fig. 4-9(a), we can see that at an income level of I_1 the consumer's equilibrium purchase level is X_1 units of good X. The values of I_1 and X_1 are plotted as point A' in Fig. 4-9(b). Again from Fig. 4-9(a), we see that when money income is I_2, the consumer will purchase quantity X_2; these values form point B' in Fig. 4-9(b). In like manner, point C' corresponds to a money income of I_3 and the resulting equilibrium purchase of X_3 units of X; and point D' is formed from an income of I_4 and the related purchase of X_4 units of X. Connecting points A', B', C', and D' gives the Engel curve relating purchases of X to changes in money income. An Engel curve of this shape indicates that as the consumer's money increases from very low levels, consumption of product X rises in almost equal proportion.

In other cases, as income rises a consumer's purchases of an item tend to increase less than proportionally to income; additional purchases become less and less sensitive to further gains in income, causing the Engel curve to become more steeply sloped at progressively higher incomes. Examples include newspapers, flour, light bulbs, salt, toothpaste, and most types of basic "necessities." For other normal goods, such as restaurant meals, recreation activities, travel, "lux-

---

[8] Engel curves are named for Christian Lorenz Ernest Engel, a nineteenth-century German statistician who was a pioneer in the study of consumer budgets.

FIGURE 4-9
The income-consumption curve and derivation of an Engel curve

uries," and saving, a consumer's expenditures tend to expand more rapidly than income. This increasing responsiveness of quantities purchased relative to income changes results in an Engel curve that increases at a decreasing rate. (What is the nature of the Engel curve for an inferior good?)

THE IMPACT OF PRICE CHANGES UPON CONSUMER PURCHASES

Not only do consumers typically adapt their consumption patterns to income changes, but they also react to changes in the price of goods and services. Suppose that we examine what happens to the quantity of X when we vary the price of X and hold constant the consumer's income, tastes and preferences (as reflected by the indifference map), and the price of Y.

Given the price of X at P_{x_1}, the price of Y at P_{y_1}, and money income at I_1, the consumer will maximize satisfaction by purchasing X_1 units of X and Y_1 units of Y, as shown in Fig. 4-10(a). Now suppose the price of X falls to P_{x_2}; the line of attainable combinations will pivot to the right about point I_1/P_{y_1}, allowing the consumer to purchase as much as I_1/P_{x_2} units of X were he or she to spend all income on X. The new line of attainable combinations will necessarily be tangent to a higher indifference curve than previously. Equilibrium will be reestablished by purchasing quantity X_2 of X and quantity Y_2 of Y. In like manner it can be ascertained that a further decline in the price of X to P_{x_3} will permit the consumer to reach an even higher indifference curve, maximizing satisfaction at X_3 and Y_3. The line joining the various points of consumer equilibrium is called the *price-*

FIGURE 4-10
Price consumption curve and the consumer's demand curve

consumption curve. The price-consumption curve is the locus of the utility-maximizing combinations of products that result from variations in the price of one product, when other product prices, the consumer's tastes and preferences, and money income are held constant.

Deriving the Demand Curve. The *demand curve* of an individual consumer for product X can be derived directly from the information contained in the price-consumption curve. A consumer's demand curve for a product graphically illustrates the different amounts that the consumer is willing and able to buy at various possible prices during some moment of time wherein all other factors influencing the quantity purchased are held constant. From Fig. 4-10(a) it can be seen that when the price of X is P_{x_1} the consumer's equilibrium purchase is quantity X_1 of X. This establishes one point on the demand curve for product X, shown as point *A* in Fig. 4-10(b). At the lower price P_{x_2} the consumer's purchases rise to X_2 units; this becomes a second point on the demand curve for product X—point *B* in Fig. 4-10(b). At the still lower price of P_{x_3} the consumer buys X_3 units of X, which gives a third point on the demand curve—point *C* in Fig. 4-10(b). Other points on the demand curve can be derived in analogous fashion, thereby producing line *dd* in Fig. 4-10(b).

Observe that the demand curve slopes downward to the right. This indicates that the price of X and the quantity purchased of X per period of time vary inversely. As P_x rises, the quantity demanded of X falls; or, as P_x falls, the quantity demanded rises. The fundamental principle between selling price and quantity is pure common sense—*other things remaining equal,* a person will be inclined to buy more of a product per period of time at lower prices than at higher prices. Additionally, this principle is reflected by the negative slope of the demand curve.

INCOME AND SUBSTITUTION EFFECTS

When the price of an item changes (and all other relevant factors remain constant), two forces are activated to cause the consumer to alter the quantity purchased. Take the case of a price decline. First, a decrease in price increases the consumer's real income (purchasing power), thus enhancing to some extent the ability to buy more goods and services. Second, a decrease in the price of a product induces some consumers to substitute it for other now relatively higher-priced items. Indifference curve analysis enables us to readily measure the potency of the income and substitution effects.

Consider Fig. 4-11. The consumer's money income is I_1, and the price of Y is P_{y_1}. If the price of X initially is P_{x_1}, then the original equilibrium is at point *A* on indifference curve IC$_1$ where the consumer buys X_1 units of X. When the price of X decreases to P_{x_2}, the line of attainable combinations rotates rightward; the consumer moves to a new equilibrium position at *B* on indifference curve IC$_2$, purchasing quantity X_2 of X. The overall change in the quantity demanded of X from the first equilibrium point at *A* to the second equilibrium point at *B* may be designated as the *total effect* of the price change. The total effect can, in turn, be decomposed into the substitution effect and the income effect.

Let us first isolate the substitution effect and determine its magnitude. The decline in the price of X precipitates an increase in the consumer's real income, as evidenced by the movement to a higher indifference curve even though money income remains fixed. Now imagine that we decrease the consumer's income by an amount *just sufficient* to return to the *same* level of satisfaction enjoyed before the price decline. Graphically, this is accomplished by drawing a fictitious line of attainable combinations with a slope corresponding to the *new* ratio of the product prices (P_{x_2}/P_{y_1}) so that it is just tangent to the *original* indifference curve (IC_1). This produces the line in Fig. 4-11 with extreme points I/P_{y_1} and I/P_{x_2} tangent to IC_1 at point C.

Combination C is as equally satisfying as combination A because they both lie on the same indifference curve. Yet, given the decline in the price of X from P_{x_1} to P_{x_2} the consumer will be wiser to purchase combination C instead of combination A. Why? Because it is cheaper to buy C rather than A now that the price of X has fallen to P_{x_2}. The effect of the lower price thus is to prompt the consumer to increase consumption of X and cut consumption of Y (i.e., to substitute X for Y). This increase in the consumption of X from X_1 to X_3 is the *substitution effect*; graphically, it is represented by a movement along the original indifference curve IC_1 from point A to the imaginary intermediate equilibrium at point C. More formally, the *substitution effect* refers to the *change in the quantity demanded of a product resulting exclusively from a change in its price when the consumer's real income is held constant, thereby restricting the consumer's reaction to the price change to a movement along the original indifference curve.*

The income effect is determined by observing the change in the quantity

X_1 X_2 — total effect
X_1 X_3 — substitution effect
X_3 X_2 — income effect

FIGURE 4-11
Income and substitution effects for a normal good in case of a price decline

demanded of a product that is associated solely with the change in the consumer's *real* income. In Fig. 4-11 letting the consumer's real income rise from its imaginary level (defined by the line of attainable combinations tangent to point *C*) back to its true level (defined by the line of attainable combinations tangent to point *B*) gives the income effect. Thus, the income effect is indicated by the movement from the imaginary equilibrium at point *C* to the actual new equilibrium at point *B*; the increase in the quantity of X purchased from X_3 to X_2 is the income effect. Formally, the *income effect may be defined as the change in the quantity demanded of a product exclusively associated with a change in real income.*

Comparatively speaking, the magnitude of the substitution effect is ordinarily greater than that of the income effect. Frequently, the change in the consumer's real income resulting from changes in the price of one commodity is so slight that there is little room for the consumer to alter the quantities of goods he purchased.[9] But where items can be readily substituted for one another, price changes are likely to trigger a relatively large substitution effect.

Usually, the income and substitution effects reinforce one another; that is, they operate in the same direction. A *lower* price for a product results in an *increase* in its quantity demanded due to the substitution effect and an *increase* in its quantity demanded due to the income effect. As Fig. 4-12 illustrates, when the price of a product *rises,* the substitution effect will bring about a *decrease* in quantity demanded, and the income effect likewise will bring about a *decrease* in quantity demanded. Note that in the event of either a price decrease or a price increase (Figs. 4-11 and 4-12, respectively), the quantity demanded of a product varies inversely with its price—the law of demand is operative. Second, note that in either event the change in quantity demanded stemming from the income effect moves in the *same* direction as the change in real income—if real income rises, the quantity demanded rises; if real income falls, the quantity demanded falls. These two relationships characterize the class of goods we earlier delineated as *normal goods.*

In the case of *inferior goods,* however, the income and substitution effects work in the *opposite* direction. For an inferior good, a *decrease* in the price of X causes the consumer to buy *more* of it (the substitution effect), but at the same time the higher real income of the consumer tends to cause him to *reduce* consumption of X (the income effect). The income and substitution effects for this situation are diagrammed in Fig. 4-13. Observe that the substitution effect still is the more powerful of the two; even though the income effect works counter to the substitution effect, it does not override it. Furthermore, it follows for an inferior good that in the case of a price *increase* the substitution effect causes *less* of the product to be purchased, whereas the related decline in real income

[9] For instance, if a consumer with an annual income of $10,000 finds that the price of a good he buys once a month has declined in price from 73 cents to 69 cents, then the consumer's real income has increased—but ever so slightly. The 48 cents saved on the purchase of the good over the period of a year does technically increase the consumer's real income, but it scarcely is sufficient to cause even a minor realignment in the consumer's purchases. Of course, if the item is one that is purchased frequently (cigarettes) and/or is purchased in large quantities (gasoline) and/or has a high price (automobiles), then the effect on real income may be quite significant.

FIGURE 4-12
Income and substitution effects for a normal good in case of a price increase

FIGURE 4-13
Income and substitution effects for an inferior good in case of a price decline

FIGURE 4-14
Income and substitution effects for an inferior good subject to Giffen's paradox

activates a tendency for the consumer to purchase *more* of the good. (The diagrammatics of this situation are left as an exercise for the student.)

On the very rarest of occasions, a good may be so strongly inferior that the income effect actually overrides the substitution effect. Such an occurrence means that a decline in the price of a good will lead to a *decline* in the quantity demanded and that a rise in price will induce an *increase* in the quantity demanded—in other words, price and quantity move in the *same* direction. The name given to such a unique situation is *Giffen's paradox,* and it constitutes the only exception to the law of demand. Figure 4-14 illustrates the income and substitution effects for an inferior good subject to Giffen's paradox. It should be emphasized at this point, however, that the phenomenon of Giffen's paradox is so infrequently observed in the modern world that no current examples can be offered. It does appear that one example of it did appear in the nineteenth century. According to Alfred Marshall, a Sir R. Giffen noted cases where a rise in the price of bread "makes so large a drain on the resources of the poorer labouring families and raises so much the marginal utility of money to them, that they are forced to curtail their consumption of meat and the more expensive farinaceous foods; and, bread being still the cheapest food which they can get and will take, they consume more, and not less of it."[10] But such cases are rare; when they are met with, each must be treated on its own merits. Even in the case of this outdated example one may

[10] Alfred Marshall, *Principles of Economics,* 8th ed. (London: Macmillan and Company, 1920), p. 132.

surmise that had the price of bread continued to rise, there quickly would have come a point when the purchases of bread began to decline. Thus, Giffen's paradox is likely to hold only for a fairly narrow range of prices. In our type of society Giffen's paradox is likely to be observed in at most a small minority of consuming units (individuals and households) and then only for precious few types of inferior goods.

MARKET DEMAND CURVES

The *market demand curve* for a product represents the various amounts which consumers as a group are willing and able to purchase at various alternative prices at a specific moment of time wherein other factors influencing consumer behavior are held constant. Thus, the market demand curve isolates the relationship between price and the quantity demanded by all consumers. It is found by summing the quantities of a good that each consumer is willing and able to purchase at each and every alternative price.

Figure 4-15 illustrates this process for a three-person economy with individual demands as indicated. At a price of P_1 dollars, consumer A is willing and able to buy quantity q_A per period of time; consumer B is willing and able to buy quantity q_{B_1} per period of time; and consumer C is willing and able to buy quantity q_{C_1} per period of time. Together they are willing and able to buy $q_{A_1} + q_{B_1} + q_{C_1} = Q_1$ units at a price of P_1 dollars, as indicated by the market demand curve. Similarly, at price P_2, consumer A is willing and able to purchase q_{A_2}; consumer B is willing and able to purchase q_{B_2}; and consumer C is willing and able to purchase q_{C_2}. Taken together, market demand at price P_2 is Q_2 ($= q_{A_2} + q_{B_2} + q_{C_2}$) units. Additional points on the market demand curve can be similarly determined and the market curve constructed (line DD in Fig. 4-15). Since the individual demand curves are downsloping to the right, the market demand curve must also slope downward to the right. The law of demand holds not only for individual consumer demand but also for market demand.

FIGURE 4-15
Derivation of the market demand curve for a product in a three-person economy

APPLICATIONS CAPSULE

WHICH IS LESS BURDENSOME—AN INCOME TAX OR A SALES TAX?

Suppose that a sales tax is levied on cigarettes and that each week Mr. Tanner buys a carton of cigarettes, paying a fixed sum as sales tax on the cigarettes. The payment of the sales tax effectively raises the price of cigarettes and puts him on a lower difference curve, reducing Mr. Tanner's well-being. The graphics are depicted in the accompanying figure.

Assume that Mr. Tanner has an income of OB_1 dollars and, prior to the imposing of the sales tax, that the line of attainable combinations is B_1A_1. If Mr. Tanner spent all his income on cigarettes, he could buy OA_1 units; hence, the pretax price of cigarettes is OB_1/OA_1. The initial equilibrium purchase of cigarettes is at point R on IC_1, where OQ_1 cigarettes are bought and B_1Y_1 dollars are spent to pay for them. The levying of the sales tax shifts the line of attainable combinations to B_1A_2; Mr. Tanner's new equilibrium point is at S on IC_2, with expenditures for cigarettes of B_1Y_2 dollars and consumption of OQ_2 units. Since before the sales tax was imposed, Mr. Tanner could have purchased OQ_2 units for B_1Y_3 dollars, the amount he pays in sales tax is Y_2Y_3 dollars. (An arithmetic example: Suppose Mr. Tanner formerly bought 52 cartons per year at $4 per carton but after the sales tax was imposed buys 40 cartons per year at $5. With the sales tax he is spending $200 per year for cigarettes. But if there were no sales tax, he would have had to pay only $160 for 40 cartons. Hence, the sales tax costs Mr. Tanner $40 per year.)

But how would Mr. Tanner fare if instead of imposing a sales tax on cigarettes the legislature in his state simply increased his income taxes by an equivalent amount ($40 per year) to raise the desired tax revenue? Would Mr. Tanner be better or worse off? Or would it make any difference one way or the other? Graphically, the effect of higher income taxes is shown by an inward shift of the line of attainable combinations to B_2A_3, with distance B_1B_2 being exactly equal to the dollar amount of the income tax (in our example, $40). B_2A_3 is parallel to B_1A_1 because the income tax need not disturb the price of cigarettes. Mr. Tanner's equilibrium point, given the income tax, is at point T on IC_3 with purchases of OQ_3 units. Since T is on a higher indifference curve than S, it follows that Mr. Tanner would prefer paying an income tax (of $40) rather than a sales tax of the same dollar amount ($40).

The basic reason for this perhaps surprising result is that while both taxes reduce the consumer's real income, the sales tax also triggers a substitution effect because it alters not just real income but relative prices as well. The imposition of a general income tax brings on only an income effect, and the consumer is free to spend the income he has left without any further impact or adjustment. In contrast, imposing a product-specific (or excise) tax involves both an income and a substitution effect: The sales tax reduces consumer purchasing power and also changes the price attractiveness of the taxed good relative to other goods, thereby producing a greater revision in the consumer's expenditure pattern than an income tax alone.

PROBLEMS

1. Suppose that instead of making the dollar amount of the income tax equal to the dollar amount of the sales tax, the size of the income tax is set so as to leave the consumer on the *same* indifference curve as the sales tax. Determine which of the two taxes will raise the most tax revenue.

2. If Congress decided that it was in the public interest to conserve gasoline, would it be more effective to impose a sales tax upon gasoline or to increase personal income taxes? Demonstrate graphically. What reasons can you give for this result?

However, adding together the demand curves of individuals to obtain market demand curves is not entirely valid since it implies that one consumer's purchases are completely independent of another consumer's purchase decisions. It has, for example, been noted that (1) some people buy goods not so much to satisfy inner wants as to impress other consumers with their "conspicuous consumption," (2) the buying habits of some individuals are influenced by the consumption patterns of persons with whom they associate or come into contact (the "demonstratration effect"), and (3) some consumers buy goods because of the social status they connote. Consequently, on occasions the amount of an item purchased by one consumer has a bearing upon how other consumers behave. In such cases, individual demand curves, strictly speaking, are not independent, and a more complex adding-up process must be used to obtain the market demand curve.

THE ATTRIBUTE MODEL OF CONSUMER DEMAND

Although the foregoing models of consumer behavior illuminate some of the principles underlying the demand for a good or service and the effects of changes in tastes and preferences, price levels, and income levels on the utility-maximizing purchase combinations, they are silent in pinpointing why buyers may prefer brand A over brand B for a given good or service. What is it about competing brands of the same item that causes some buyers to purchase brand A while other buyers are inclined to spend their money on brand B?

A way to explore consumer choice criteria for competing brands, called attribute analysis, emerged in the mid-1960s.[11] This extension of the theory of consumer demand applied utility and indifference curve analysis in an innovative way and was based on the argument that consumers derive utility not so much from the product itself as from its characteristics or attributes. The thesis is that the demand for an item stems chiefly from what its attributes do for the buyer. For instance, a personal computer is purchased not for its physical composition of a console, screen, and semiconductor parts but because of its speed to handle data, its user friendliness, its timesaving ability to perform complex analytical calculations, and the convenience and efficiency it has for the user—in other words, it is the personal computer's performance attributes that make it desired, not the product itself. Similarly, scuba diving equipment is purchased based on its ability to provide users a sense of exploration, exhilaration, adventure, and excitement, as well as safety features, ease of use, durability, and maintenance-free qualities. Whereas the product approach to consumer demand looks upon a consumer's preference pattern as an imponderable, individualistic given, the attribute approach seeks to explain preferences for products and brands based on the attributes and characteristics they possess. The attribute approach looks directly at what a product does for the consumer and seeks to explain consumer choice patterns in terms of a product's intrinsic features and characteristics.

Depicting the Attributes of Rival Brands

To demonstrate how a consumer might choose among brands of rival sellers, consider the case of a person intrigued with the prospects of obtaining a personal computer. In order to treat the problem of choosing among the various brands and models of personal computers on the market, let's assume that the prospective buyer has investigated the situation enough to know that the two most desirable attributes of personal computers (PCs) are user friendliness and variety of software

[11] Kelvin Lancaster, "A New Approach to Consumer Theory," *Journal of Political Economy,* Vol. 74, No. 2 (April 1966), pp. 132–57, and *Consumer Demand: A New Approach* (New York: Columbia University Press, 1971). The following treatment follows closely the treatment by Evan J. Douglas, who has cogently and systematically illuminated the trail blazed by Lancaster. See his *Managerial Economics: Theory, Practice, and Problems,* (Englewood Cliffs, N.J.: Prentice-Hall, Inc., 1979).

options. Suppose that after evaluating four major brands of PCs, the buyer comes up with the information and ratings shown in Table 4-1.

In Fig. 4-16 the four brands of PCs are shown in the "attribute space" as *rays* from the origin. The slope of each ray is the ratio of the user friendliness rating to the software options rating, as listed in Table 4-1. How far out along each ray would our personal computer enthusiast go? Given that having one PC will likely suffice, the relevant distance out along each PC ray becomes the attribute combination associated with one unit of each PC brand; the cost of acquiring each attribute combination is obviously the price of each PC brand. The consumer's "satisfaction frontier" (analogous to the line of attainable combinations) becomes points *A, B, C,* and *D* in Fig. 4-16, assuming that the consumer is willing and able to pay the price for each PC brand despite the wide price differentials (because of the differences in the attributes they possess). [*Note:* However, when a consumer needs or wishes to purchase more than one unit of an item, as in the case of shirts or beer or going to the movies, how far out each ray the consumer can go is found by (1) dividing the consumer's allotted budget for the item by the price of each brand to arrive at how many units can be purchased, and (2) calculating the total amounts of each attribute which can thus be obtained. For example, if the consumer's budget allocation is $25 and the price of brand Q is $5, it is possible to buy 5 units; further, if brand Q possesses 2 units of attribute X and 3 units of attribute Y, the consumer's budget provides access

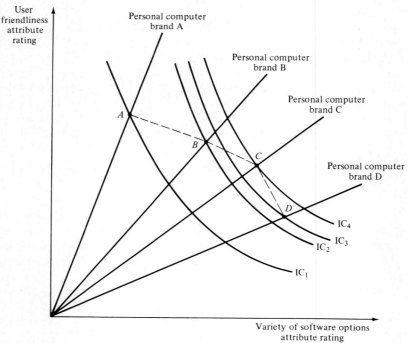

FIGURE 4-16
Maximizing the utility from product attributes

TABLE 4-1 Attributes and Prices of Four Brands of Personal Computers

| PC Brand | PC Price | Attribute Rating[a] | | Ratio of User Friendliness to Variety of Software Options |
		User Friendliness	Variety of Software Options	
A	$250	8	3	2.67
B	300	7	6	1.17
C	400	6	8	0.75
D	450	4	9	0.44

[a] On a scale of 1 to 10 where 1 = lowest and 10 = highest.

to 10 units of attribute X and 15 units of attribute Y insofar as brand Q is concerned. This combination of 10 units of X and 15 units of Y defines how far out the ray for brand Q the consumer can go given the $25 budget constraint and Q's $5 price.]

Maximizing the Utility from Product Attributes

Just as consumers can express preference or indifference between combinations of products, so can they judge the utility between combinations of attributes. Our personal computer enthusiast, in comparing the four brands of PCs, will have to evaluate the trade-off (or marginal rate of substitution) between user friendliness and software options; these evaluations produce a set of indifference curves expressing his tastes and preferences at each possible attribute combination. As before, the attribute combinations on higher indifference curves are preferred to those on lower curves and the curves slope downward to the right, are convex to the origin, and do not intersect.

Since the consumer must choose one PC brand or another and is therefore constrained to points *A, B, C,* or *D* in Fig. 4-16, utility is maximized by choosing the personal computer brand with the attribute combination on the highest indifference curve attainable. This turns out to be brand C on indifference curve IC_4.

The Effect of Price Changes

Suppose that the price of one of the brands embodying the desired attributes is changed. How will this affect the demands for this brand and the other brands? Consider Fig. 4-17 where five brands are available, the satisfaction frontier is *ABCDE* (given the initial prices of the five brands and the consumer's budget constraint), and the consumer is maximizing the utility from attributes X and Y at point *C*, where indifference curve IC_1 just touches the frontier. Now suppose that the price of brand B is reduced, shifting the satisfaction frontier out along the ray for brand B to *B'* and giving a new frontier of *AB'CDE*. The consumer can now reach the higher indifference curve IC_2 by switching to brand B. Not surprisingly, the law of demand prevails here as well: the lower price of brand B induces a greater demand for B by causing *some* consumers (those with indifference curves like those in Fig. 4-17) to switch over from now relatively higher-priced brands. Brand B offers attributes X and Y in a different combination from brand C, but those consumers who switch to B judge this to be compensated for by the lower price of B. (Can you draw a set of indifference curves on Fig. 4-17 to represent a preference pattern such that the lower price for B would *not* induce a consumer to switch from C to B?)

Pricing a Brand Out of the Market. Given a consumer's preference/indifference among the attributes of competing brands of a product, there tends to be a maximum price the consumer will pay for a brand even though it has the most desired attribute combination. In Fig. 4-18 is shown a satisfaction frontier *ABC* for three brands offering attributes X and Y. The consumer is maximizing utility on indifference curve IC_1 by purchasing only brand B. If the price of brand B rises, pulling the satisfaction frontier inward to *AB'C*, the consumer is unable to reach IC_1 and must be content with the utility level on IC_2—still purchasing only brand B but necessarily purchasing less of B because of B's higher price and an unchanged budget allocation.

However, if the price of brand B is raised still further, shifting the satisfaction frontier inward to *AB"C*, the consumer will maximize utility by shifting purchases from brand B to brand C and attaining the level of overall satisfaction associated with IC_3. Thus, brand B has been priced ''out of the market'' for this consumer even though its combination of attributes X and Y otherwise has the best fit with the consumer's taste and preference pattern. Other consumers may, however, continue to purchase brand B if (1) their income levels are nonetheless sufficient

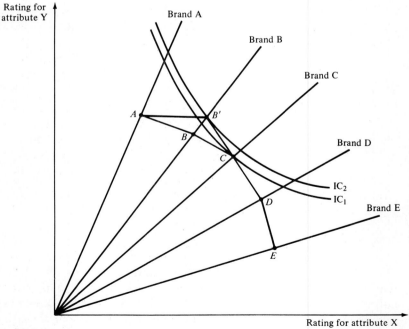

FIGURE 4-17
Effect of price changes upon brand selection

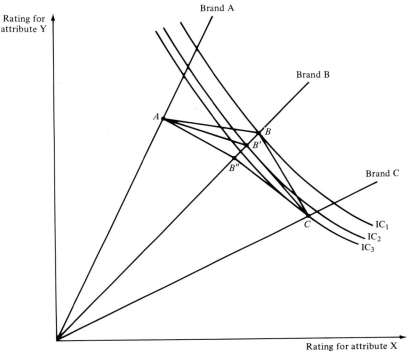

FIGURE 4-18
How a brand can get priced "out of the market"

to overcome the negative effects of the higher price; (2) they perceive the attributes of brands A, B, and C differently, such that the attributes of B are rated well above those of A and C, as compared to the ratings of our previous consumer; and (3) they purchase brand B for different attributes than those viewed as important by our previous consumer.

The law of demand thus governs the attribute model, too. As the price of one brand of a good or service falls, consumers already purchasing the brand will tend to purchase more units and other consumers will begin to buy their first units of the lower-priced brand (often at the expense of competing brands carrying higher price tags). As a brand's price rises, consumers either buy fewer units or else drop out of the market for the brand altogether and switch their purchases to lower-priced substitute brands.

SUMMARY AND CONCLUSIONS

The ordinal utility approach to consumer demand is both a supplement and an alternative to the cardinal utility approach for describing individual consumer behavior and for establishing the foundations of market demand. Indifference analysis is preferred by some economists in part because it does not require the precise quantification of utility and in part because it does not depend so heavily on the requirement of diminishing marginal utility.

A consumer's taste and preference pattern can be represented by a family of indifference curves. The shapes of the indifference curves are the critical features for displaying a consumer's set of tastes for a pair of products. Depending on the consumer's evaluation of the satisfying power of particular products, indifference curves can assume a variety of shapes and can be drawn to represent any set of tastes and preferences.

A consumer's ability to satisfy his or her tastes and preferences is represented by the line of attainable combinations. This line incorporates into the consumer's choice pattern the restraints imposed by the consumer's money income and by the prices of the goods the consumer may be desirous of purchasing. The point of tangency between the line of attainable combinations and an indifference curve defines the highest level of satisfaction which the consumer is capable of attaining, given his or her income and prevailing prices. The conditions requisite for maximizing satisfaction via the ordinal utility or indifference curve approach are exactly identical to the conditions derived from the cardinal utility approach.

By allowing income to vary, while holding product prices and the consumer's tastes fixed, the consumer's income-consumption curve can be established. The income-consumption curve illustrates the various purchase combinations that will maximize the consumer's satisfaction at different levels of income. From the data provided by the income-consumption curve, an Engel curve showing the relationship between money income and purchases of a good can be derived. Normal goods have positively sloped Engel curves; negatively sloped Engel curves are indicative of inferior goods.

The consumer's price-consumption curve can be found by observing the equilibrium path traced out by changing the price of a product and by holding money income and tastes and preferences constant. Data for plotting the consumer's demand curve are obtained from the price-consumption curve.

When the price of an item rises or falls, other relevant factors remaining unchanged, two factors are activated to prompt consumers to reassess the quantity of the item they are purchasing. The most powerful force, typically, is the substitution effect; it represents the extent to which the consumer is induced to alter what is purchased *solely* because of the change introduced in the relative prices of products. The second, and usually less powerful, force is the income effect; it represents the extent to which the consumer is motivated to buy more or less of a good because of the change in real income brought about by the price change.

In the case of normal goods the income and substitution effects operate in the same direction and reinforce one another. For inferior goods, however, the substitution and income effects work in opposite directions. For most inferior goods, the substitution effect overrides the impact of the income effect and causes the quantity demanded of a good to vary in the opposite direction from the change in the price of the good, thereby validating the law of demand. On the very rarest of occasions, a good may be so strongly inferior that the income effect overpowers the substitution effect and causes the quantity demanded to vary in the *same* direction as the change in price. Such a situation is termed Giffen's paradox and constitutes the only exception to the law of demand.

The market demand curve for a product is obtained by aggregating the quantity demanded by all individual consumers at each alternative market price.

The attribute approach to consumer behavior helps explain why buyers may rationally prefer one brand to another.

SUGGESTED READINGS

AULD, D., "Imperfect Knowledge and the New Theory of Demand," *Journal of Political Economy,* Vol. 80 (November–December 1972), pp. 1287–1294.

BAILEY, M. J., "The Marshallian Demand Curve," *Journal of Political Economy,* Vol. 62 (June 1954), pp. 255–261.

DOUGLAS, E. J., *Managerial Economics: Theory, Practice, and Problems* (Englewood Cliffs, N.J.: Prentice-Hall, Inc., 1983), Chapter 3.

FRIEDMAN, M., "The Marshallian Demand Curve," *Journal of Political Economy,* Vol. 57 (December 1949), pp. 463–495.

——, "The 'Welfare' Effects of an Income Tax and an Excise Tax," *Journal of Political Economy,* Vol. 60 (February 1952), pp. 25–33.

HENDLER, R., "Lancaster's New Approach to Consumer Demand and Its Limitations," *American Economic Review,* Vol. 65, No. 1 (March 1975), pp. 194–199.

LANCASTER, K., "A New Approach to Consumer Theory," *Journal of Political Economy,* Vol. 84 (April 1966), pp. 132–157.

——, *Consumer Demand: A New Approach* (New York: Columbia University Press, 1971).

MISHAN, E. J., "Theories of Consumer's Behavior: A Cynical View," *Economica,* New Series, Vol. 28 (February 1961), pp. 1–11.

RATCHFORD, B. T., "The New Economic Theory of Consumer Behavior: An Interpretive Essay," *Journal of Consumer Research,* Vol. 2 (September 1975), pp. 65–75.

ROTH, T. P., "On the Predictive Power of the New Approach to Consumer Theory," *Atlantic Economic Journal,* Vol. 7 (July 1979), pp. 16–25.

SAMUELSON, P. A., "Consumption Theory in Terms of Revealed Preference," *Economica,* New Series, Vol. 15 (November 1948), pp. 243–253.

PROBLEMS AND QUESTIONS FOR DISCUSSION

1. Illustrate by means of indifference curves the taste and preference pattern suggested by the following statements:
   (a) "There is not enough money to make me eat a raw oyster."
   (b) "What good is a cigarette if you don't have a light?"
   (c) "I would just as soon eat broiled lobster as filet mignon."
   (d) "What good is money if you don't spend it? After all, you can't take it with you."

2. Graphically illustrate in three dimensions the nature of the total utility surface for two goods which are perfect complements.

3. Suppose that a particular consumer has a special dislike for eating turnips but immensely enjoys eating barbecued spareribs. Draw an indifference map for these two items. Indicate the direction of higher degrees of satisfaction.

4. Explain the logical inconsistency involved were two indifference curves to intersect.

5. Suppose that the equation of an indifference curve for a consumer is as follows: $XY = 48$, where X = units of good X, Y = units of good Y, 48 = amount of utility or satisfaction expressed in utils.
   (a) Graphically determine the shape and location of this indifference curve. (Use graph paper.)

(b) Determine the consumer's MRS_{xy} at $X = 4$ and $Y = 12$.

(c) Suppose that the price of X is $10 per unit and the price of Y is $4 per unit. Determine the equation for the line of attainable combinations if the consumer's income level is $20. What is the slope of the line of attainable combinations at this income? Determine the equation and slope of the line of attainable combinations at an income of $30. Does the change in income from $20 to $30 influence the slope of the line of attainable combinations? Why or why not?

(d) Illustrate graphically the point of tangency between the indifference curve $XY = 48$ and a line of attainable combinations where $P_x = \$10$ and $P_y = \$4$. How much income will it take for the consumer to attain 48 utils of satisfaction, given these prices?

6. Is a consumer's satisfaction level increased, decreased, or unaffected when the price of a product he or she is purchasing goes down? Illustrate graphically.

7. If indifference curves for perfect substitutes are negatively sloped and linear and if indifference curves for perfect complements are right angles, is it true that the degree of convexity of an indifference curve reflects the degree of substitutability and complementarity among two products? Explain.

8. Graphically illustrate the combination of goods X and Y that will maximize satisfaction in the following set of circumstances:

(a) Goods X and Y are perfect substitutes.

(b) $MRS_{xy} = (-)1$.

(c) $P_x = \$2$, $P_y = \$2.25$, and $I = \$18$.

9. Diagrammatically illustrate the income and substitution effects for an inferior good in the case of a price increase.

10. Diagrammatically illustrate the income and substitution effects for an inferior good subject to Giffen's paradox in the case of a price increase.

11. Suppose that two goods X and Y are judged by consumers to be perfect substitutes for each other. Suppose further that the price of X is higher than the price of Y.

(a) If consumers behave rationally, what would you predict to happen to sales of the two products?

(b) Where consumers view products which compete against one another as being close or near perfect substitutes, is it surprising to find that their prices are identical or at least nearly so? Explain your answer.

12. Three frequently encountered Engel curves are shown below.

Quantity of X consumed per period of time

(a)

Quantity of X consumed per period of time

(b)

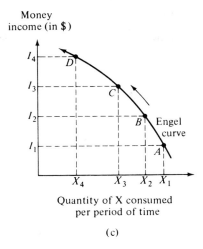

Money
income (in $)

(c)

Quantity of X consumed
per period of time

Describe the nature of the relationship between income and the quantity consumed for each of the three situations. Can you tell from the diagram whether the products in question are normal goods or inferior goods? Why or why not?

13. A beer producer is considering introducing a new super premium brand of beer to compete directly against the two leading super-premium brands, A and B. Panels of beer drinkers have rated the two leading brands in two respects—"good taste" and "lightness." Brand A was given a 7 rating (on a 1 to 10 scale) on good taste and a 2 rating on lightness. Brand B received ratings of 5 on good taste and 5 on lightness. Brand A sells for $4.25 per six-pack and brand B retails for $5 per six-pack. In taste tests for the new brand the producer is considering introducing, beer-drinking consumers have given it a 3 rating on good taste and a 7 on lightness. Plans call for the new brand to sell for $6 per six-pack.

   (a) Draw an indifference map for a representative male beer drinker which illustrates his preferences/indifference among combinations of the two attributes.

   (b) Superimpose on your hypothetical indifference map the brand attribute rays for the three brands of beer.

   (c) Which brand will the consumer select if he is willing to spend up to $25 per month on super-premium beer? (Assume that the consumer agrees with the attribute ratings cited above.)

   (d) What if the price per six-pack for the new brand is reduced from $6 to $5? Will the consumer switch brands?

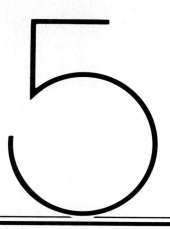

DEMAND FUNCTIONS, REVENUE FUNCTIONS, AND ELASTICITY

Utility analysis provides a good beginning to understanding the foundations of consumer demand. But one must go beyond utility theory to see how the economics of firms and markets are affected by consumer demand. The role of this chapter is to extend demand analysis to the firm, first by exploring the full complement of determinants of individual demand, second by relating the concept of demand to the firm and examining the demand curves for its products, and third by deriving the revenue functions that correspond to the firm's demand curves. In addition, attention will be focused upon the total and marginal revenue functions associated with demand curves and upon the sensitivity of demand to changes in price and consumer income.

VARIABLES THAT INFLUENCE MARKET DEMAND

Many variables influence the quantity of a good or service that all consumers in the market will purchase at some moment of time. Let's survey the main factors very briefly.

A Product's Price.   The price of a good or service is nearly always an instrumental factor in the demand picture. Other things being equal, the quantity demanded for a product varies inversely with price—buyers are willing and able to purchase more of an item at lower prices than at higher prices. In cases where a product is on sale or discounted from its regular list price or where buyers and sellers habitually haggle and negotiate over price, the appropriate measure of price is the actual amount paid rather than the initial asking price.

A Product's Attributes. Consumers are typically very interested in a product's attributes, especially in comparison to those of competing brands or substitute products. In general, the demand for a product is stronger when it possesses the attributes which the majority of consumers are seeking. In some industries, the product attributes of different firms are essentially identical, as with wool, natural gas, salt, cast iron pipe, plate glass, eggs, and paper clips; in such cases, the products of sellers are usually viewed as *standard commodities*. But where the products of rival sellers possess distinctly different attributes and are thus *differentiated* (as with soft drinks, automobiles, personal computers, restaurants, magazines, and ski equipment), the demand for one brand is very much a function of how consumers perceive its attributes in relation to the attributes of substitute brands and products. Plainly enough, rival sellers will be inclined to advertise and promote their product's attributes as a matter of information to potential buyers and in an effort to persuade buyers that their product's attributes best meet consumer needs and uses of the item.

Consumer Tastes and Preferences. The relevance of consumer tastes for determining demand is easily apparent. When consumer perceptions of a good or service become less favorable, market demand for the item weakens. By the same token, an increase in the intensity of consumer desire for an item tends to increase willingness to pay a higher price or to buy more of it or both. Needless to say, consumer taste and preference patterns undergo continuous review and are subject to change, sometimes gradual and sometimes rapid, over time. The emergence of new and better products, changing values and life-styles, new information about health and safety features of products, the business cycle, changing levels of advertising for the product, changes (up or down) in the advertising of competing brands or related items, and the number and convenience of locations in which the product is available, to mention a few, all exert a pervasive and dynamic influence upon consumer tastes and preferences.

Consumer Income. That income has an impact upon market demand in plain enough. The ability of consumers to buy goods and services, as given by their money income and purchasing power, is what permits them to satisfy their material desires. Willingness to buy is in itself insufficient; consumers must be able to pay for the products they want. Typically, the greater is consumer income the greater will be market demand for goods in general and for some items in particular. Only in the case of inferior goods is rising income accompanied by a weakening of demand.

For those items whose purchase is truly discretionary, a superior measure of consumer purchasing power may be derived by considering the consumer's *discretionary income*. This is the residual amount of income remaining after subtracting necessary living expenses and fixed payment charges from disposable personal income. Discretionary income might, for example, be found to be closely related to consumer expenditures for durables, recreation, and travel activities, therefore making it a more valid demand determinant for some goods than other income measure. The National Industrial Conference Board publishes a discretionary income series. Somewhat more refined measures of the discretionary buying power of consumers add to discretionary income such items as cash balances, near-liquid assets, and the availability of new consumer credit, thereby providing a more comprehensive indicator of consumer purchasing power for "big ticket" items and purchases where consumer credit is a factor.

Prices of Related Items. The prices of related items are an important demand variable because of the interrelationships that exist among goods. In the case of substitute goods, how the price of one compares with the price of competing brands can be a pivotal factor in the consumer's selection process. If Stroh's is cheaper than Budweiser, this fact is sure to influence the purchase decision of some buyers. In the case of items that have a complementary relationship and are demanded jointly (golf clubs and golf balls, automobiles and gasoline, toothpaste and toothbrushes), it is equally clear that the prices of both are pertinent. If the price of popcorn jumps by 50%, the demand for popcorn salt tends to be weakened; if the price of electricity rises substantially, people will tend to run their air conditioners less in the summer and may, in fact, be inclined to purchase a new energy-saving air conditioner.

Consumer Expectations. Consumers expectations with respect to future price levels, income levels, and product availability tend to influence current purchase behavior. If consumers believe that the prices of goods they expect to buy shortly are going to rise in price, they will be motivated to buy them now and escape paying the higher prices. Income expectations work much the same way. Some consumers may purchase goods currently with a view toward paying for them later out of expected increases in income; fears of a recession or impending unemployment make consumers more cautious and thrift conscious. Similarly, if consumers for some reason expect a good to be unavailable or in short supply in the near future (because of a strike, crop failures, production bottlenecks, etc.), they will be induced to increase current purchases.

The Number of Consumers and Market Size. Since the market demand for an item is the summation of individual consumer demands for the item, it is obvious that the *number of potential* consumers has a direct bearing on market demand, as well as the frequency with which they buy the product.

Some Added Demand Determinants

While the preceding factors are generally acknowledged as the "major" demand determinants, other variables can assume a significant impact on the nature and intensity of the demand for a product or service. For example, it can make a great difference in the strength of demand whether consumers view a product as a "luxury" or a "necessity." Although perceptions of an item as a luxury or a necessity is a function of individual life-styles and value judgments, the demands for luxuries and necessities tend to be different in their responses to price changes, recessionary conditions, interest rates and credit availability, and frequency of purchase. The necessity-luxury aspect explicitly recognizes the multitude of sociological influences on who buys what and with what degree of urgency; it also brings into play consideration of the ability of buyers to postpone or delay their purchases because of adverse economic circumstances.

The demand for an item may be derived from the demand for other goods, thus being known as a derived demand. For instance, the demand for steel is derived from the demand for products containing steel or requiring steel somewhere in the course of their production. The demand for newsprint is derived from the demand for newspapers. The demand for typewriters is derived from the demand for secretarial services. When the demand for a good is derived, as in the case of component parts and goods-producing tools and equipment, considerable information may be gained from examining the buying habits and characteristics of end users of the final product.

The degree of market saturation for a product can be a key factor in the sales volume and sales potential of a product, especially for durable goods. To cite a familiar case, the current market for refrigerators is largely restricted to a replacement demand with some sales going to newly formed households. Why? Because more than 95% of households today have refrigerators. In contrast, the market potential for microwave ovens is far greater. Less than 25% of American households have a microwave, thus offering producers a much larger sales potential than would be the case if the household saturation level were higher. The limited demand for items having high saturation levels has prompted some producers of durable goods to adopt a policy of "planned obsolescence," whereby their products are restyled periodically, new features are added, and consumers are in turn induced to increase the frequency with which they replace their "worn-out" and "out-of-date" models.

For those types of consumer goods which are typically purchased with the aid of credit (automobiles, appliances, furniture, houses), the level of consumer debt and prevailing interest rates may be valuable additions to the dimensions of the consumer's buying power and may, in fact, be more closely related to the demand for such items than is current money income. Logic dictates that the higher the ratio of consumer debt to consumer income and the higher the rates of interest on borrowed funds, the less able and less eager consumers will be to make additional commitments toward the purchase of such items until more favorable buying conditions present themselves.

Additional reflection would, no doubt, suggest still other factors which bear upon the demand variables for certain products. It is to be emphasized, however, that each good or service has its own peculiar set of demand determinants and that, in turn, these determinants influence demand in ways that may be unique to each specific item.

THE CONCEPT OF THE DEMAND FUNCTION

The discussion of the circumstances prompting consumers to buy or not to buy a product suggest that consumers' demand for an item is the result of the complex interaction of a wide variety of forces. In mathematical terms, the demand function

for product X can be symbolized as

$$Q_x = f(P_x, P_s, P_c, T, A_x, A_s, A_c, I, E, F, N, O)$$

where

Q_x = total quantity demanded of product X (in units),
P_x = price of product X,
P_s = measure of the prices of the brands and products that are substitutes for product X,
P_c = measure of the prices of products that are complementary to product X,
T = index of consumers' tastes and preferences,
A_x = level of advertising and promotional effort devoted to product X,
A_s = level of advertising and promotional efforts for substitute brands and products,
A_c = level of advertising and promotional efforts for complementary products,
I = measure of consumers' incomes or purchasing power,
F = features or attributes of the product in relation to other items (whether the product is a standard commodity or a differentiated product),
N = number of potential consumers (the size of the market population), and
O = other demand-related factors specific to product X.

Using the functional notation to symbolize the relationship between the quantity demanded of a particular product and specific demand-influencing variables is a more explicit and conceptually accurate way of representing the demand for a product than is the simple graphic portrayal of price-quantity relationships in the form of demand curves.

FIGURE 5-1
The nature of shifts in consumer purchases and demand intensity

Nevertheless, it is analytically convenient to segregate demand determinants into two groups: (1) the selling price of the product and (2) all other demand determinants. Using this dichotomization, variations in the purchases of a product associated solely with changes in product price are customarily termed "changes in the quantity demanded" and are represented graphically by movements *along* a given demand curve. In Fig. 5-1(a), a decrease in the price of X from P_{x_1} to P_{x_2} increases the quantity demanded from X_1 to X_2—all other factors influencing the purchase volume are assumed to remain unchanged. On the other hand, quantity variations which stem from changes in one or more of demand determinants *other than price* are referred to as "changes in demand" and are represented graphically by shifts in the demand curve [Fig. 5-1(b)].[1] For example, such factors as increases in consumer incomes, a larger advertising budget, a more intensive desire for a good, or an increase in the price of substitutes would tend to shift the position of a given demand curve to the right, say from line D_1D_1 to D_2D_2 in Fig. 5-1(b). Such events as a decline in the number of consumers, an increase in the attractiveness of substitute goods, or the expectation of a forthcoming price decrease tend to shift the demand curve to the left, as illustrated by shifting D_1D_1 to position D_3D_3 in Fig. 5-1(b).

The distinction between the two terms "change in quantity demanded" and "change in demand" correctly suggests that graphically representing the price-quantity relationship in the form of a demand curve does *not* mean that the price of an item is the sole, or even the principal, determinant of the amount purchased at some moment of time. All a demand curve purports to show is the impact that different prices will have upon the amounts purchased *when the remaining factors comprising the demand function are fixed in value.*

AVERAGE, TOTAL, AND MARGINAL REVENUE

Now suppose that we focus upon the intensity of consumer demand for a particular firm's product. Figure 5-2 depicts a hypothetical demand curve for a firm. The points along this curve represent the *maximum quantities* per unit of time that consumers are willing to buy from this firm at various alternative prices. However,

---

[1] The terms "change in the quantity demanded" and "change in demand" can be explained readily in the language of mathematics. Suppose that the equation of the demand curve is given by

$$P = a - bQ,$$

where P represents the selling price of a product and Q represents the quantity bought. As long as all the demand determinants other than P remain constant, the parameters a and b also remain constant and the equation $P = a - bQ$ defines a unique demand curve. A change in P will result in a movement along this demand curve to the corresponding value of Q—this is what has been termed a "change in the quantity demanded." However, shifts in demand determinants other than P are reflected by changes in the values of a and b. A change in the value of a shifts the level of the curve, and a change in the value of b alters the slope of the curve—either or both of which represent a "change in demand" and define the equation of a new demand curve.

it is equally accurate to view a firm's demand curve as representing the *maximum prices* that buyers are willing to pay a firm to obtain various quantities of its product. In terms of Fig. 5-2, if the firm offered quantity Q_1 for sale, P_1 is the maximum price it would be able to charge and still generate a demand of Q_1 units. (Naturally, consumers would gladly pay less for the item were the opportunity to present itself.) Moreover, it follows that price P_1 represents the *average* amount of revenue the firm will receive *per unit sold* or simply *average revenue* (*AR*). Accordingly, a firm's demand curve can with equal propriety be labeled an average revenue curve.

As with the firm's demand function, the firm's *AR* function may be expressed as a function of the quantity sold. When a firm sells all its output at the same price, its selling price and its average revenue are the same value, in which case

$$AR = P = f(Q).$$

However, if the firm sells its product at different prices to different customers, average revenue is equal to a weighted average of the selling prices, with the weights being the proportions sold at each price. Then the *AR* function becomes

$$AR = \overline{P} = f(Q),$$

where $\overline{P}$ represents the *average* selling price.

Now let us utilize the demand-*AR* concepts to examine properties of a firm's other revenue functions for each of several possible sets of demand conditions.

Average, Total, and Marginal Revenue When the Demand Curve Is Horizontal

Consider first the simple, but rather unusual, case where the firm confronts a horizontal demand curve for its product, as in Fig. 5-3(a). A horizontal demand curve means that a firm can sell all the units it wishes at the price given by the intersection of the demand curve with the price axis; in Fig. 5-3(a) this is shown as a price of \$10.[2] If the firm raises its price above \$10, no units can be sold. Obviously, if the firm can sell all it wishes at a price of \$10, it can also sell all it wishes below \$10. However, we would logically expect the firm to offer its product for sale at the maximum price of \$10, as no advantage can be gained from lowering

---

[2] Just because a firm's demand curve is horizontal, it does not follow that the law of demand is suspended. Although a firm may be able to sell all it wishes within the limits of its production capacity at a particular price, it still is true that a single consumer will prefer to buy more at lower prices than at higher prices. Similarly, it is still true that consumers as a group will prefer to buy more at lower prices than at higher prices. What may make the demand curve horizontal for a *firm* is the fact that *many* other sellers are offering consumers an *identical* product; thus, all firms may be driven by the market forces of demand and supply to sell at the same price. Because each firm is so small relative to the total market, they are able to sell all they can produce at the prevailing price, and their individual demand curves are, therefore, horizontal.

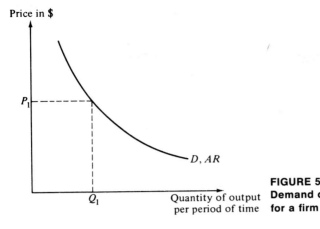

FIGURE 5-2
Demand or average revenue curve
for a firm

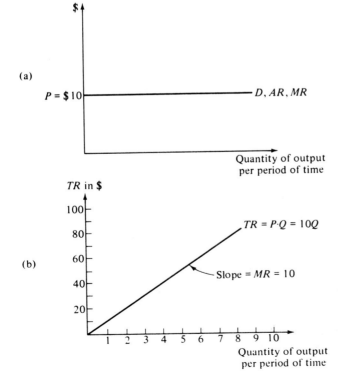

FIGURE 5-3
Average, total, and marginal
revenue function for a firm
whose demand curve is hori-
zontal

price. The equation of the firm's average revenue and demand functions in this situation is

$$AR = P = \$10.$$

The firm's *total revenue function* is found by multiplying average revenue (AR) or selling price (P) by the number of units sold (Q) and may be written as

$$TR = AR \cdot Q = P \cdot Q.$$

When the demand curve is horizontal, the corresponding total revenue curve is always a positively sloped linear function starting from the origin and having a slope equal to the product price [see Fig. 5-3(b)]. In this example, the slope of the total revenue function is equal to 10 because every time one more unit is sold, the firm's total revenue rises by $10; the related equation for TR is

$$TR = P \cdot Q = 10Q.$$

Marginal revenue is best defined as the rate of change in total revenue as the rate of output changes. This means, in mathematical terms, that the firm's *marginal revenue function* is the first derivative of the total revenue function. Thus, in our example, if

$$TR = 10Q,$$

then

$$MR = \frac{dTR}{dQ} = 10.$$

The constant value of 10 for MR means that each 1-unit increase in sales will cause total revenue to rise by $10. Geometrically, the value of marginal revenue is always equal to the slope of the total revenue function; hence, given that the firm's TR function is linear whenever the demand curve is horizontal and that linear functions have a constant slope, it follows that the value of MR for a linear TR function is necessarily a constant value no matter what the firm's volume of sales. In other words, if the firm can sell all it wishes at a price of $10, marginal revenue is fixed at $10 and is exactly equal to the firm's selling price and average revenue. The marginal revenue function corresponding to a horizontal demand-AR curve is graphically identical, therefore, to the demand-AR curve, as shown in Fig. 5-3(a).

Sometimes it is helpful to think of marginal revenue as being the change in total revenue associated with a 1-*unit* change in sales ($\Delta TR/\Delta Q$, where $\Delta Q = 1$

unit). This concept of *MR* is appropriate when one has occasion to calculate the change in total revenue associated with a *discrete* change in output; it will be referred to as *discrete marginal revenue*. But where unit volume (Q) can assume any value along continuous demand and revenue functions, it is best to define and calculate *MR* as the derivative of the firm's *TR* function. We shall refer to the latter concept of *MR* as *continuous marginal revenue*. Both concepts of *MR* will have their place in future discussions.

In the example above, the nature of the demand function is such that the values for discrete *MR* and continuous *MR* are both $10. This is typical for horizontal demand functions, but it is not true of other types of demand functions, as the next case illustrates.

Average, Total, and Marginal Revenue When the Demand Curve Is Linear and Down-Sloping

Somewhat more plausible is the product demand circumstance where the firm's demand-*AR* curve is linear and down-sloping. The general equation for linear, down-sloping demand-*AR* functions can be expressed as

$$AR = P = a - bQ.$$

The value of a in the equation is the price at which the demand curve intersects the price axis and, in economic terms, is the price just high enough so that no consumers will be willing to purchase the firm's product. The value of b in the equation is the slope of the demand curve. The minus sign ($-$) means that the demand curve is negatively sloped and that there exists an inverse relationship between P and Q, all of which is, of course, the usual case. The graph of a linear, downsloping demand-*AR* curve is shown in Fig. 5-4(a).

Since a firm's total revenue from the sale of a product equals average revenue times the quantity sold (or price times the quantity sold), the expression for *TR* can be obtained by multiplying the demand-*AR* expression by Q:

$$\begin{aligned} TR &= P \cdot Q \quad \text{(or } AR \cdot Q) \\ &= (a - bQ)Q \\ &= aQ - bQ^2. \end{aligned}$$

A total revenue function of this type is graphically portrayed by a parabola of the shape in Fig. 5-4(b).

As before, the corresponding marginal revenue function is the derivative of the total revenue function. Since $TR = aQ - bQ^2$, then

$$MR = \frac{dTR}{dQ} = a - 2bQ.$$

FIGURE 5-4
Average, total, and marginal revenue functions for a firm faced with a linear down-sloping demand curve

Plotting the *MR* function on the same diagram as the demand and *AR* functions [Fig. 5-4(a)] reveals that the *MR* curve lies below the demand curve. Both curves originate at the same value *a*, but the slope of the *MR* function is twice as great as the slope of the demand curve ($-2b$ as compared to $-b$). In geometric terms, the *MR* curve is located by drawing it so as to bisect the horizontal distance between the demand curve and the vertical axis. However, this procedure is accurate only in the case of a linear demand curve.

Marginal revenue is less than price (average revenue) because with a down-sloping demand function the firm must lower its selling price to boost the quantity sold. The lower price applies not only to the additional units sold but also to the units of output which otherwise could have been sold at a higher price. For instance, suppose that a firm can sell 50 units at a price of $1 and realize total revenue of $50. To increase sales by 1 unit to 51 units, the firm must lower its price, say to $0.99 on all units sold. The increase in total revenue is *not* the $0.99 gained from the sale of the fifty-first unit, because the firm must give up revenue of $0.01 on each of the previous 50 units formerly selling at $1. The net gain in total revenue is $0.99 − $0.50 or $0.49, as can easily be verified by multiplying 51 units times $0.99, which gives a total revenue of $50.49. Hence, the marginal revenue of the fifty-first unit is $0.49, which is less than its selling price of $0.99.

One further very important relationship remains to be pointed out. This concerns the *MR* and *TR* functions. Observe in Fig. 5-4 that the *TR* function increases at a decreasing rate up to a sales volume of Q_1 units; over this same range, *MR* is *positive* but decreasing in value. Earlier it was stated that *MR* at any sales volume *Q* equals the slope of the *TR* function at that value of *Q*. Since the *TR* function has a positive slope up to an output of Q_1, *MR* of necessity must be positive; similarly, just as the slope of the *TR* function diminishes as the sales level approaches Q_1 units, so does the value of *MR* diminish. Marginal revenue is zero at exactly the same output level (Q_1) at which total revenue is maximum. Past a sales volume of Q_1, *TR* falls and *MR* is negative. Consequently, when the slope of the *TR* function is zero, *MR* is zero, and when the slope of the *TR* function is negative, *MR* is negative.

A numerical example at this point may serve to clarify and illuminate these relationships among *AR*, *TR*, and *MR*. Suppose that a firm's demand-*AR* function can be represented by the equation

$$P = 12 - Q \quad (\text{or } AR = 12 - Q).$$

The total revenue and marginal revenue functions can be calculated as follows:

$$TR = AR \cdot Q = P \cdot Q$$
$$= (12 - Q)Q = 12Q - Q^2,$$
$$MR = \frac{dTR}{dQ} = 12 - 2Q.$$

Table 5-1 contains representative values for *P*, *Q*, *AR*, *TR*, continuous *MR*, and discrete *MR* as derived from the preceding equations. Several attributes of the values in Table 5-1 are worth noting. First, when price is $12 or higher, no consumer is willing to purchase any of the firm's product. Second, selling price and *AR* are identical; as stated earlier, this is a necessary result of a single-price policy. Third, *TR* increases rapidly at first, then more slowly, reaches a maximum at 6 units of output, and declines thereafter as sales continue to increase. Fourth, the values for continuous *MR* are positive but steadily declining for the first 5 units of output; *MR* is zero where *TR* is at its maximum value of $36, and *MR* is ever more negative as the sales volume extends beyond 6 units. Fifth, the discrete *MR* values (which are computed by subtracting successive values of *TR* in order to obtain the change in *TR* associated with a 1-unit change in *Q*) do not correspond exactly to the values for continuous *MR*. This is not because the two concepts are inconsistent but because they are really associated with different output or sales levels. For instance, when *TR* rises from $11 to $20 as a consequence of a

TABLE 5-1.   Demand and Revenue Data for a Linear Demand Function

Quantity of Output Demanded	Price $(P = 12 - Q)$	Average Revenue $(AR = 12 - Q)$	Total Revenue $(TR = 12Q - Q^2)$	Continuous Marginal Revenue $(MR = 12 - 2Q)$	Discrete Marginal Revenue $(MR = TR_Q - TR_{Q-1})$
0	$12	$12	$ 0	$12	
1	11	11	11	10	$11
2	10	10	20	8	9
3	9	9	27	6	7
4	8	8	32	4	5
5	7	7	35	2	3
6	6	6	36	0	1
7	5	5	35	-2	-1
8	4	4	32	-4	-3
9	3	3	27	-6	-5
10	2	2	20	-8	-7

rise in sales from 1 to 2 units, it is fair to say that the $9 gain in revenue is not *MR* when *TR* is $20 and sales are 2 units but is instead *MR between* 1 and 2 units of output. The values for discrete *MR* in Table 5-1 are more correctly associated with output rates of $\frac{1}{2}$, $1\frac{1}{2}$, $2\frac{1}{2}$, and so on. This can easily be confined by substituting these values of *Q* into the equation for continuous *MR*; the resulting values for *MR* correspond exactly to the values for discrete *MR* presented in the table. Thus, the discrete and continuous measures of *MR* are perfectly compatible and define the same *MR* function and curve. If the *TR* function is known, it is usually more convenient to use the continuous measure of *MR*. If *MR* must be determined from a table of *TR* values, the discrete measure of *MR* is the simplest to calculate.

Plotting the values in Table 5-1 will yield curves that possess the relationships alluded to in Fig. 5-4. The reader should verify this.

Average, Total, and Marginal Revenue When the Demand Curve Is Curvilinear

The demand curve for a product can assume a wide variety of curvilinear forms. No attempt is made here to catalog the diverse types of demand curves. We shall be content with examining two basic curvilinear demand curves with relatively simple equations.

Suppose that the demand curve for a firm's product is given by the generalized expression

$$P = a - bQ + cQ^2,$$

where a, b, and c are constants. The firm's *AR* function will likewise be

$$AR = a - bQ + cQ^2.$$

Again, the total revenue function is found by multiplying the demand equation (or AR equation) by the quantity sold as follows:

$$
\begin{aligned}
TR = P \cdot Q &= AR \cdot Q \\
&= (a - bQ + cQ^2)Q \\
&= aQ - bQ^2 + cQ^3.
\end{aligned}
$$

The marginal revenue function is the first derivative of the total revenue function,

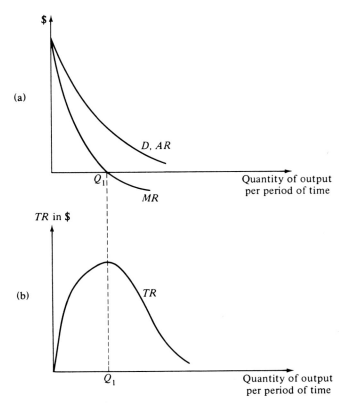

(a)

D, AR

Q_1

MR

Quantity of output
per period of time

TR in $

(b)

TR

Q_1

Quantity of output
per period of time

FIGURE 5-5
Average, total, and marginal revenue functions for a firm whose demand equation is of the general form $P = a - bQ + cQ^2$

giving

$$MR = \frac{dTR}{dQ} = a - 2bQ + 3cQ^2.$$

The shapes of these functions are pictured in Fig. 5-5. Observe that the *MR* function lies everywhere below the demand function except for their common beginning value. The values for *MR* are declining but greater than zero for the output range where *TR* is rising; *MR* is zero where *TR* is maximum. When the demand curve is convex to the origin, as in this example, the *MR* curve lies to the left of line bisecting the horizontal distance between the vertical axis and the demand curve.

Another plausible shape for the firm's demand curve to assume is that shown in Fig. 5-6 and associated with the general equation

$$P = a + bQ - cQ^2.$$

As before, the *AR* function has the same equation:

$$AR = a + bQ - cQ^2.$$

The *TR* function is again derived by multiplying the demand (or *AR*) equation by *Q*:

$$
\begin{aligned}
TR = P \cdot Q &= AR \cdot Q \\
&= (a + bQ - cQ^2)Q \\
&= aQ + bQ^2 - cQ^3.
\end{aligned}
$$

Taking the derivative of the *TR* function, we get the *MR* function:

$$MR = \frac{dTR}{dQ} = a + 2bQ - 3cQ^2.$$

Note that the graphs of these functions (shown in Fig. 5-6) portray the same basic relations among demand, *AR*, *TR*, and *MR* as stated earlier. Apart from the shapes of the curves, a significant difference between this case and the previous examples is the location of the *MR* function. Although *MR* still lies below the demand function, this time it is located to the right of a line bisecting the horizontal distance between the vertical axis and the demand curve.

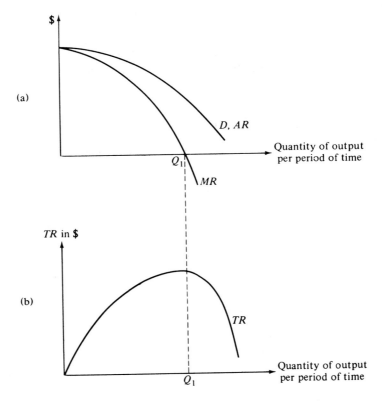

FIGURE 5-6
Average, total, and marginal revenue functions for a firm whose demand equation is of the general form $P = a + bQ - cQ^2$

ELASTICITY OF DEMAND

The concept of *elasticity* is one of the most important aspects of demand analysis. In general terms, elasticity of demand measures the magnitude of the *responsiveness* or *sensitivity* of the quantity demanded of a product to a change in some demand determinant. More specifically, elasticity concerns the extent to which a percentage change in one demand variable causes (or is associated directly with) a percentage change in the quantity demanded. Mathematically, the elasticity of demand ϵ (epilson) is calculated as

$$\epsilon = \frac{\% \text{ change in quantity demanded}}{\% \text{ change in any demand determinant}} .$$

Elasticity is *always* calculated in relative or percentage terms rather than in absolute or unit terms. This permits comparisons of demand sensitivity for different products, irrespective of the units in which products or product prices are quoted. (A 5% change has the same meaning whether it is measured in tons, dozens, crates, cans, or dollars.) And because elasticity is calculated by dividing a percentage change by a percentage change, the elasticity coefficient (ϵ) is a pure number free of any identification with the units in which the variables are expressed.

There are as many kinds of demand elasticity as there are numbers of demand determinants for a product (price elasticity, income elasticity, and so on).

Price Elasticity of Demand

The relation of product price to sales volume is of major interest to business firms as a basis for pricing policy, sales strategy, and achievement of profit and market share objectives. Consider the case of products X and Y with demand curves as shown in Fig. 5-7. The negative slopes of both curves indicate that as the prices of X and Y fall, the quantities demanded of X and Y rise. From the diagram, when the prices of X and Y are P_{x_1} and P_{y_1} (where $P_{x_1} = P_{y_1}$), the quantities purchased are X_1 units and Y_1 units, respectively. However, if the prices of X and Y decline by an identical amount to P_{x_2} and P_{y_2}, the change in the quantity demanded of X (X_1 to X_2) is greater than the change in the quantity demanded of Y (Y_1 to Y_2). In other words, the demand for X is more sensitive or responsive to a change in the price of X than the demand for Y is to a change in the price

FIGURE 5-7
Sensitivity of product demand to price changes

of Y at the indicated prices. Or, in the language of economics, we can say that the price elasticity of demand for X is greater than the price elasticity of demand for Y over the indicated price range.

Price elasticity of demand can be defined more precisely as

$$\epsilon_p = \frac{\% \text{ change in quantity demanded}}{\% \text{ change in price}}.$$

The coefficient of price elasticity is always negative. Why? Because price and quantity demanded are inversely related; when price falls the quantity demanded tends to rise and when price rises the quantity demanded tends to fall. Therefore, with one percentage change being negative and the other being positive, the price elasticity coefficient is necessarily negative.

Two distinct methods for calculating price elasticity exist: the arc elasticity method and the point elasticity method. *Arc elasticity* is a measure of the responsiveness of the quantity demanded between two separate points on a demand curve. *Point elasticity* is a measure of the sensitivity of the quantity demanded at a single point on the curve for an infinitesimal change in price.

Arc Elasticity.   To illustrate the arc technique for computing price elasticity, consider a demand curve having two points *A* and *B* with price-quantity combinations as follows:

	Price	Quantity Demanded
Point *A*	$12	30 units
Point *B*	$10	50 units

Now suppose we determine the degree of responsiveness of quantity demanded to a *decrease* in price from $12 to $10—this is equivalent to moving down along the demand curve from point *A* to point *B*. It will be recalled that the usual way of computing percentage change is to find the change in a value relative to its original value (designated below by the subscript 1) and multiply by 100 to convert the ratio to a percentage figure. Algebraically, then, our definition of price elasticity is equivalent to

$$\epsilon_p = \frac{\% \text{ change in quantity demanded}}{\% \text{ change in price}} = \frac{[(Q_2 - Q_1)/Q_1] \times 100}{[(P_2 - P_1)/P_1] \times 100},$$

where the pairs (Q_1, P_1) and (Q_2, P_2) represent, respectively, the quantity and price values *before* and *after* their change. Note, however, the multiplication by 100 of both the numerator and denominator is superfluous and can be omitted, as the terms cancel out in dividing. Substituting the appropriate values into the thus simplified formula gives

$$\epsilon_p = \frac{(Q_2 - Q_1)/Q_1}{(P_2 - P_1)/P_1} = \frac{(50 - 30)/30}{(10 - 12)/12} = \frac{20/30}{(-2)/12} = \frac{2}{3} \cdot -\frac{6}{1} = -4.0.$$

Yet, if we compute the sensitivity of the quantity demanded to an *increase* in price from \$10 to \$12 (equivalent to moving up the demand curve from point *B* to point *A*), the coefficient of price elasticity is

$$\epsilon_p = \frac{(Q_2 - Q_1)/Q_1}{(P_2 - P_1)/P_1} = \frac{(30 - 50)/50}{(12 - 10)/10} = \frac{(-20)/50}{2/10} = \frac{-2}{5} \cdot \frac{5}{1} = -2.0.$$

The discrepancy in the two elasticity coefficients arises because the percentage changes going from point *A* to point *B* are not the same as those in moving from *B* to *A*. Indeed, changing the base values for the percentage calculation from P_1, Q_1 to P_2, Q_2 gives two widely diverging measures of price sensitivity for the very same interval along the demand curve.[3]

This is a troublesome matter but not one without some remedy. The ambiguity of arbitrarily using one of the two points (*A* or *B*) as the original or base values for calculating the percentage changes can be partially overcome by using the averages of the quantity values as the base for calculating the percentage change in *Q* and the average of the two prices as the base for calculating the percentage change in *P*. Making this adjustment gives the more satisfactory

---

[3] This example demonstrates why arc elasticity calculations are only approximations. This is especially true when the shape of the demand curve is not known and data for only a few prices and quantities are given. For example, it may be observed when the price is \$8, that 250 units of the item are purchased, and when the price is \$7, that 350 units are purchased. However, as the figure below suggests, an infinite number of demand curves can pass through these two points, and these curves in general will possess slightly different elasticities at these prices.

In general, the farther apart the two points between which arc elasticity is computed, the greater is the discrepancy between the price elasticity coefficients obtained from the two-point arc formula.

formula

$$\epsilon_p = \frac{\dfrac{Q_2 - Q_1}{\left(\dfrac{Q_1 + Q_2}{2}\right)}}{\dfrac{P_2 - P_1}{\left(\dfrac{P_1 + P_2)}{2}\right)}} \cdot$$

With the modified formula it makes no difference which of the two points is point 1 and which is point 2; the same elasticity coefficient is obtained either way. For this reason, the modified formula is the accepted way of computing arc elasticity and is the one we shall use henceforth. Still, for the arc elasticity coefficient to be reliable and susceptible to meaningful interpretation, it should be computed only between points on a demand curve which are reasonably close together. In terms of our previous numerical example, the coefficient of price elasticity for a decline in price from \$12 to \$10 becomes

$$\epsilon_p = \frac{\dfrac{Q_2 - Q_1}{\left(\dfrac{Q_1 + Q_2}{2}\right)}}{\dfrac{P_1 - P_1}{\left(\dfrac{P_1 + P_2}{2}\right)}} = \frac{\dfrac{50 - 30}{\left(\dfrac{30 + 50}{2}\right)}}{\dfrac{10 - 12}{\left(\dfrac{12 + 10}{2}\right)}}$$

$$= \frac{\dfrac{20}{40}}{\dfrac{-2}{11}} = \frac{1}{2} \cdot -\frac{11}{2} = -\frac{11}{4} = -2.75.$$

Returning to our previous numerical example and using the modified formula, -2.75 should be interpreted as meaning that over the indicated range of prices and quantities a 1% change in price will cause approximately a 2.75% change in quantity demanded in the *opposite* direction.[4]

Since the sign of the price elasticity coefficient is always negative (in accordance with the law of demand), it is the *size* of the coefficient itself which is

---

[4] The student should verify at this point that exactly the same coefficient is obtained for an increase in price from \$10 to \$12 as was obtained from a decrease in price from \$12 to \$10 when the modified arc elasticity formula is used. This will confirm that the modification of averaging the prices and quantities eliminates any difference in the size of the coefficient arising from an arbitrary designation of one of the two points on the demand curve as the reference or base point. The effect of the modified formula is to produce an "average" of sorts of the two results obtained with the initial version of the arc formula. To be more exact, the modified arc elasticity formula yields an estimate of the responsiveness or sensitivity of the quantity demanded at the midpoint of the range defined by the two points on the demand curve.

most relevant. By convention, economists say that when the coefficient is a number greater than 1, demand is *elastic*, and that when the coefficient is less than 1, demand is *inelastic*. Should the coefficient turn out, by chance, to be exactly 1, demand is said to be *unitary* or of *unitary elasticity*. The rationale for this classification is straightforward. When the coefficient is greater than 1, the percentage change in quantity demanded must necessarily be *larger* than the percentage change in price. It follows, then, that the quantity demanded is relatively responsive or sensitive to price changes—or, in the language of economists, that demand is elastic. On the other hand, when the coefficient is less than 1, the percentage change in quantity demanded is *smaller* than the percentage change in price, clearly implying that the quantity demanded is relatively unresponsive or insensitive (or inelastic) with regard to price changes.

Point Elasticity. Measuring elasticity at a point eliminates the imprecision of the arc elasticity concept. Point elasticity, as the name implies, refers to the responsiveness of quantity demanded to very small price changes from a given point. Algebraically, this translates into the following:

$$\epsilon_p = \frac{\Delta Q/Q}{\Delta P/P} = \frac{\Delta Q}{Q} \cdot \frac{P}{\Delta P} = \frac{\Delta Q}{\Delta P} \cdot \frac{P}{Q}.$$

Thie expression says that price elasticity at a point equals the ratio of the change in quantity demanded to the change in price multiplied by the ratio of price to quantity demanded at that point. As the changes in price get smaller and smaller and actually approach zero, the ratio of $\Delta Q/\Delta P$ becomes equivalent to the derivative of the demand function with respect to price, or

$$\lim_{\Delta P \to 0} \frac{\Delta Q}{\Delta P} = \frac{dQ}{dP}.$$

Hence, the formula for point elasticity becomes

$$\epsilon_p = \frac{dQ}{dP} \cdot \frac{P}{Q}.$$

As illustrations of the point elasticity concept, consider the following two examples.

EXAMPLE 1: Suppose that the demand function for a commodity is defined by the equation

$$Q = 245 - 3.5P.$$

What, then, is the price elasticity of demand at a price of $10? To determine ϵ_p we need to know P, Q, and dQ/dP. At a price of $10,

$$Q = 245 - 3.5(10) = 245 - 35 = 210.$$

The rate of change in Q as P changes, dQ/dP, is found by calculating the first derivative of the demand function:

$$\frac{dQ}{dP} = -3.5.$$

Hence, we can now substitute directly into the point elasticity formula, obtaining

$$\epsilon_p = \frac{dQ}{dP} \cdot \frac{P}{Q} = -3.5 \cdot \frac{10}{210} = -\frac{1}{6} = -0.167.$$

The ϵ_p value of -0.167 says that if the price of the commodity changes by a small amount (say 1%) from its value of $10, then the quantity demanded will change by approximately 0.167% in the opposite direction. This relatively small response means demand is quite inelastic at a price of $10.

EXAMPLE 2: On occasion, the demand function may be expressed in terms of quantity rather than price. Consider the demand function

$$P = 940 - 48Q + Q^2.$$

What is the price elasticity of demand at an output of 10 units?
At $Q = 10$,

$$P = 940 - 48(10) + (10)^2$$
$$= 940 - 480 + 100 = \$560.$$

Now, it remains to find the value of dQ/dP. However, since the equation is expressed in terms of quantity rather than price, we must find dQ/dP by a slightly more circuitous route. We can determine dP/dQ quite easily as follows:

$$\frac{dP}{dQ} = -48 + 2Q.$$

It so happens (the mathematicians have formally proved it) that

$$\frac{dQ}{dP} = \frac{1}{dP/dQ},$$

thereby giving us

$$\frac{dQ}{dP} = \frac{1}{-48 + 2Q}.$$

At $Q = 10$, this becomes

$$\frac{dQ}{dP} = \frac{1}{-48 + 2(10)} = -\frac{1}{28}.$$

Substituting into the point elasticity formula, we have

$$\epsilon_p = \frac{dQ}{dP} \cdot \frac{P}{Q} = -\frac{1}{28} \cdot \frac{560}{10} = -2.$$

Again the proper interpretation of the elasticity coefficient in this case is that for a 1% price change from the current price of $560, the quantity demanded will change by about 2% in the opposite direction. And we would conclude that at a price of $560 demand is elastic.

Price Elasticity and the Slope of the Demand Curve

The concepts of slope and elasticity are frequently confused. It is sometimes fallaciously assumed that the flatter the demand curve, the greater its elasticity, and the steeper the demand curve, the smaller its elasticity. This assumption is categorically false and is so indicated in the definitions of the terms themselves. The slope of a demand curve depends entirely on the size of an absolute change in price as compared to the size of the associated absolute change in the quantity demanded. At any given point on a demand curve the slope equals dP/dQ. Yet, as we have just seen, elasticity is defined mathematically as

$$\epsilon_p = \frac{dQ}{dP} \cdot \frac{P}{Q}.$$

Elasticity is, therefore, equal to the reciprocal of the slope of the demand curve $[dQ/dP = 1/(dP/dQ)]$ multiplied by the ratio of P to Q and is a measure of the relative or *percentage* changes in P and Q. Clearly, then, since the slope (flatness or steepness) of a demand curve is based upon *absolute* changes in P and Q, whereas price elasticity has to do with *percentage* changes in P and Q, the value of the slope of the demand curve can equal the value of the coefficient of price elasticity only by the rarest of arithmetical coincidences. Moreover, in the case of a linear, downward-sloping demand curve, the slope is constant, whereas the price elasticity varies from point to point along the curve according to the value of P/Q. Thus, any notion that elasticity and slope are the same should be promptly dispelled.

Price Elasticity and Total Revenue

We are now ready to examine some of the practical applications of the price elasticity concept. Of prime interest to business firms is the effect that a price change will have upon sales volume and total revenue. Also, from the viewpoint of consumers it is pertinent to determine the effect of a price change upon the total amount of money consumers are willing and able to spend on a given product.

Consider the demand schedule in Table 5-2 and the corresponding demand curve for a firm shown as line dd' in Fig. 5-8(a). At a price of $120 ($P_1$), the firm can sell 100 units (Q_1). If price is lowered to $110 ($P_2$), sales increase to 200 units (Q_2). The *percentage* change in price obviously is small in comparison with the *percentage* change in quantity demanded—the price decline is but a fraction of its original value of P_1, whereas the increase in quantity demanded from Q_1 to

TABLE 5-2.   Elasticity and Total Revenue

Price	Quantity Demanded	Total Revenue	Coefficient of Price Elasticity	Elasticity
$120	100	$12,000		
110	200	22,000	−7.67	Elastic
100	270	27,000	−3.13	Elastic
90	330	29,700	−1.90	Elastic
85	350	29,750	−1.03	Elastic
80	370	29,600	−0.91	Inelastic
70	400	28,000	−0.58	Inelastic
60	425	25,500	−0.39	Inelastic

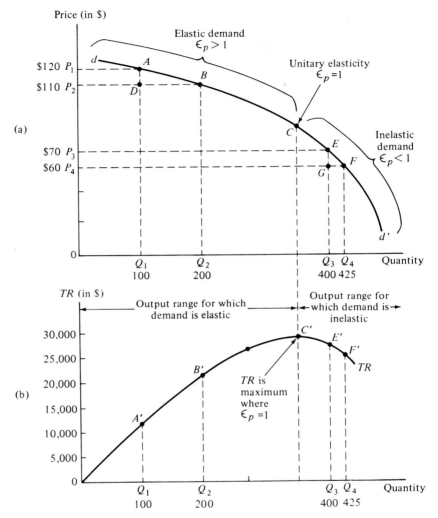

FIGURE 5-8
Relationships among demand curves, total revenue, and price elasticity

Q_2 is double the original volume of 100 units. The information in Table 5-2 verifies that the coefficient of price elasticity over this range is -7.67; thus, demand is *elastic* between points A and B. As shown in Fig. 5-8(b), total revenue increases when price is lowered from \$120 to \$110. That this is so can also be confirmed indirectly from Fig. 5-8(a). Since total revenue is price times quantity sold, the size of the area shown by rectangle OP_1AQ_1 in Fig. 5-8(a) equals *TR* at P_1. At price P_2, *TR* equals the area of rectangle OP_2BQ_2. By inspection, the area of rectangle OP_2BQ_2 exceeds that of rectangle OP_1AQ_1 and, as indicated in Table 5-2, *TR* at P_2 (\$22,000) is larger than *TR* at P_1 (\$12,000). It is larger because the *loss* of revenue due to the lower price per unit (area P_2P_1AD) is *less* than the *gain* in revenue resulting from increased sales (area Q_1DBQ_2). In other words, even though the product is sold at a lower price, the increase in sales at the lower price *more* than makes up for the smaller amount of revenue received per unit sold.

This behavior of total revenue over elastic portions of the demand curve is not merely coincidental. In fact, we may state, as a general principle, that *whenever demand is elastic, a decline in price will result in an increase in total revenue.* The reasoning is reversible: *When demand is elastic, an increase in price will result in a decline in total revenue,* because should price rise (for example, from P_3 to P_2), the gain in total revenue associated with selling the product at a higher price (area P_3P_2BE) is smaller than the loss in revenue stemming from selling fewer units (area Q_2ECQ_3).

When demand is inelastic with regard to price, a lower price will cause a decline in total revenue. This situation exists for a decrease in price from P_4 ($70) to P_5 ($60), as shown in Fig. 5-8(a). Over this price range, the coefficient of price elasticity is -0.39 (Table 5-2). At a price of $70 and sales of 400 units, *TR* is $28,000, whereas at a price of $60 and sales of 425 units, *TR* is $25,500. Graphically, at a price of P_3, *TR* is equal to the area OP_4EQ_4. Total revenue is lower because the modest increase in sales precipitated by the price decline (Q_3Q_4) is inadequate to offset the adverse impact of the fall in price; consequently, the *loss* in revenue due to the lower price (area P_4P_3EG) *exceeds* the *gain* in revenue associated with selling more units (area Q_3GFQ_4). Table 5-3 summarizes these relationships.

It follows that the positively sloped portion of the *TR* function corresponds to the elastic portion of the demand curve, and vice versa (as is illustrated in Fig. 5-8). By the same token, the negatively sloped segment of the *TR* function is associated with inelastic demand. Starting from the top of the demand curve and moving down along it, the coefficient of price elasticity is a decreasing value but remains, nevertheless, larger than 1.0; simultaneously *TR* is increasing. Where *TR* is maximum, the elasticity of demand is unitary ($\epsilon_p = 1$). As we move farther down the demand curve past the point of unitary elasticity, the coefficient of price elasticity is less than 1 and decreasing, and *TR* is declining. These relationships are typical of down-sloping demand functions.

There is a tendency, therefore, for most demand curves to be elastic at "high" prices and inelastic at "low" prices. As price falls from high levels, the response of consumers produces strong percentage gains in sales and healthy

TABLE 5-3. Price Changes, Price Elasticity, and Total Revenue

	$\epsilon_p > 1$	$\epsilon_p < 1$
$P\downarrow$	$TR\uparrow$	$TR\downarrow$
$P\uparrow$	$TR\downarrow$	$TR\uparrow$

increases in *TR*. Where $\epsilon_p = 1$ corresponds to the price at which consumers are willing to spend the greatest number of dollars on the item; at this price *TR* is maximum and $\epsilon_p = 1$. Further price cuts will not induce consumers to buy enough more units to compensate for the price decline. In other words, they are approaching their saturation level for the item, and their marginal utility for additional units is rapidly diminishing; thus, price cuts have less impact upon consumer purchases.

Furthermore, it may be noted that the more elastic demand is, the greater will *TR* rise when price falls. The more inelastic demand is, the greater will *TR* fall when price is lowered. The example in Table 5-2 verifies this.

APPLICATIONS CAPSULE

WHEN A FIRM CAN BE SURE IT'S TIME TO RAISE ITS PRICE

Whenever a firm has good reason to believe that the demand for its product is inelastic at the current selling price, profits can *always* be increased if the firm will raise its price. This outcome stems from the fact that in an inelastic demand situation, a price increase will result in a firm's experiencing (1) rising total revenue and (2) a lower total cost outlay. Whenever the coefficient of price elasticity is less than 1, a price increase will raise total revenues because the revenue gain associated with a higher selling price more than offsets the revenue decline associated with a lower unit sales volume. Also, a firm's total operating costs ought to fall as a result of a higher price, since the higher price (other things remaining equal) will tend to curtail consumer purchases of the product—thereby prompting the firm to produce fewer units, buy smaller amounts of economic resources, and, consequently, spend fewer dollars in the course of its activities. With *TR* rising and total costs falling, the overall profitability of the enterprise will, of necessity, be improved.

Pursuing the same line of reasoning, a firm contemplating a lowering of its price should beware of an inelastic demand situation. A price decrease in face of an inelastic demand will lead not only to a decline in total revenue, but also to an increase in total costs due to a rising sales volume. The firm's profits will be lowered and under such circumstances a lower selling price would seem ill-advised.

It is fair to state, therefore, that *the most profitable volume of sales lies somewhere on the elastic portion of a firm's demand curve.*

Price Elasticity and Linear Demand Curves

Although the law of demand requires only that a demand curve slope downward to the right, we shall find it convenient to represent the demand curve in its simplest form—as a straight line. Thus, it is worthwhile to be familiar with the elasticity characteristics of linear demand curves. Figure 5-9 illustrates a typical linear demand function along with its corresponding total revenue and marginal revenue function. It will be recalled that the general equations for these functions are

$$P = a - bQ,$$
$$TR = P \cdot Q = aQ - bQ^2,$$
$$MR = \frac{dTR}{dQ} = a - 2bQ.$$

Additionally, the slope of the *MR* function is twice the slope of the demand curve, and *MR* equals zero where *TR* is maximum. The geometry of the relationships among the three functions is such that the price and quantity at which *MR* = 0 and *TR* is maximum is the midpoint of the demand curve; that is, the length of the segment of the demand curve above this point is equal to the length of the segment below it.

From the discussion in the preceding section it should be evident that demand is elastic on the *upper half* of the linear demand curve and is inelastic along the *lower half* of the curve (see Fig. 5-9). The coefficient of price elasticity is one at the *midpoint* of the curve. Moreover, starting at the top of the demand curve and proceeding down along it, the coefficient of price elasticity declines from very large values to a value of one at the midpoint, becomes less than one upon passing

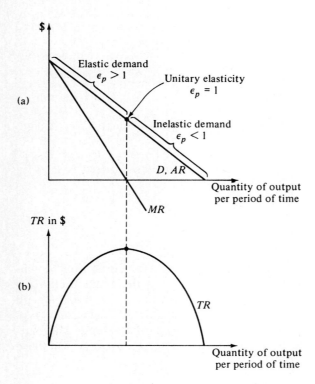

FIGURE 5-9
Linear demand curves, total revenue, and price elasticity

the midpoint, and approaches zero as price declines toward zero. As explained previously, this is because at successively lower prices and progressively larger values of Q, the percentage changes in price get larger, while the percentage changes in quantity demanded get smaller. The coefficient of price elasticity, being equal to the ratio of the percentage change in Q to the percentage change in P, thus necessarily declines as one moves down along the demand curve.

It is not accurate, therefore, to describe linear demand curves as being either elastic or inelastic; rather the upper half of the demand curve is elastic and the lower half is inelastic. It is proper to speak of the price elasticity of demand at a given point or between two given points, but it is inappropriate to speak of the price elasticity of the demand curve as a whole.

MATHEMATICAL CAPSULE 5

THE ELASTICITY OF DEMAND AT THE MIDPOINT OF A LINEAR DEMAND FUNCTION

It is relatively simple to show for a linear downsloping demand function that the price elasticity of demand at the midpoint of the demand curve is -1. All we need do is compute the coefficient of price elasticity at the midpoint utilizing the point elasticity formula.

The general equation for a linear demand curve is

$$P = a - bQ.$$

The general equations for the associated *TR* and *MR* functions are

$$TR = P \cdot Q = aQ - bQ^2,$$

$$MR = \frac{dTR}{dQ} = a - 2bQ.$$

To compute point elasticity, we must obtain values for dQ/dP, Q, and P at the midpoint of our generalized demand curve. We can find dQ/dP from the demand equation itself as follows:

$$P = a - bQ,$$

$$\frac{dP}{dQ} = -b.$$

Since

$$\frac{dQ}{dP} = \frac{1}{dP/dQ},$$

we have

$$\frac{dQ}{dP} = \frac{1}{-b} = -\frac{1}{b}.$$

The value of Q at the midpoint of the demand can be derived from the fact that at the midpoint of a linear demand curve $MR = 0$ and *TR* is maximum. Hence, the quantity at which $MR = 0$ can be found by setting the equation for *MR* equal to zero and solving for the value of Q which will satisfy this condition:

$$MR = a - 2bQ = 0,$$
$$-2bQ = -a,$$
$$Q = \frac{-a}{-2b} = \frac{a}{2b}.$$

When $Q = a/2b$, the corresponding value for P is

$$P = a - bQ$$
$$= a - b\left(\frac{a}{2b}\right)$$
$$= a - \frac{a}{2}$$
$$= \frac{a}{2}.$$

Substituting the values for dQ/dP, P, and Q into the point elasticity formula, we have

$$\epsilon_p = \frac{dQ}{dP} \cdot \frac{P}{Q}$$
$$= -\frac{1}{b} \cdot \frac{a/2}{a/2b}$$
$$= -\frac{1}{b} \cdot \frac{a}{2} \cdot \frac{2b}{a}$$
$$= -1.$$

Therefore, the coefficient of price elasticity equals -1 at the midpoint of all linear down-sloping demand functions, irrespective of the values of a and b in the general equation $P = a - bQ$.

Some Special Cases in Price Elasticity

Certain kinds of demand curves have unique price elasticity properties. Three special cases will be noted.

When the firm's demand curve is horizontal (meaning that at the going market price the firm can sell all it is able to produce but that its demand is zero at a higher price), demand is said to be *perfectly elastic* and the coefficient of price elasticity is infinity ($\epsilon_p = -\infty$). Such a demand curve is illustrated in Fig. 5-10(a). The perfectly elastic feature of the horizontal demand curve arises from the fact that should the firm raise its price above P_1, demand would fall to zero—the largest possible response to a price change. In other words, when the firm's demand curve is horizontal, there exists the highest possible degree of sensitivity to price since even if there is a small price increase above P_1, the firm's customers will reduce their purchases from the prevailing amounts to zero.

In the very improbable event that the demand curve for a product is vertical [Fig. 5-10(b)], demand is said to be *perfectly inelastic*. Quantity demanded remains

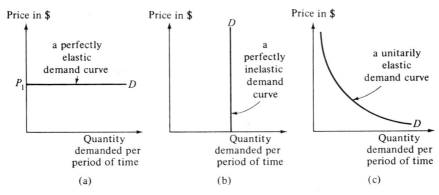

FIGURE 5-10
Special cases in price elasticity

the same despite progressively higher prices. Thus, there is *no response* whatsoever in the quantity demanded to a price change—the least possible degree of price sensitivity. The corresponding coefficient of price elasticity is zero ($\epsilon_p = 0$).

The third special case arises when consumers spend a fixed amount of dollars for a product irrespective of the price charged and the quantity bought. Every price-quantity combination results in the same amount of expenditure upon the product. The equation for such a demand curve is

$$P \cdot Q = TR = k,$$

where k is a constant and, graphically, it is illustrated by a rectangular hyperbola, shown in Fig. 5-10(c). At each and every point on the curve price elasticity is unitary ($\epsilon_p = -1$), and total revenue is constant no matter what the values of P and Q.

The Sensitivity of Market Demand to Price Changes

Just what causes the market demand for a good or service to be responsive or unresponsive to price changes? If the firms in an industry reduce prices, will there be a large expansion in market demand for the product, a moderate expansion, or very little expansion at all? The answers depend on a host of market considerations:

1. *The importance of the product to buyers.* When products are very important to consumers from the standpoint of daily living and life-styles (toothpaste, coffee, haircuts), market demand is often not very sensitive to price; as prices go up, buyers merely dig deeper in their pockets. On the other hand, there are many items which are not viewed as so crucial—going skiing in Colorado, eating T-bone steak twice a week, or buying a microwave oven. Most postponable, less

APPLICATIONS CAPSULE

"NO FRILLS" AIR FARES

As the 1974–1975 recession made inroads into passenger traffic loads of the major airlines, National Airlines persuaded the Civil Aeronautics Board (CAB) to let it try an experiment with a discount of as much as 35% from normal coach fares on certain of its regularly scheduled routes. National, in an effort to build up its load factor, tied its discount fare proposal to the offering of "no-frills" service during the flight, including doing away with complimentary meals, snacks, soft drinks, and coffee so as to reduce costs and partially offset the lower-priced fares. However, passengers using the no-frills plan could selectively purchase these items in-flight if they wished. The no-frills fares were offered only Mondays through Thursdays. The CAB gave the go-ahead to National to experiment with the no-frills fare, with the proviso that National study the plan and report back at a later date. Eastern Airlines and Delta Airlines, both competitors of National on some of the routes where National proposed to implement no-frills fares, were also permitted to use the discount fares for a trial period.

In its report to the CAB on the results of the no-frills approach, National maintained that 56% of the 133,000 passengers who used its no-frills fare from mid-April through June 30, 1975, were enticed to travel by air because of the discount fare plan. According to National, the new passenger traffic generated by discount fares increased its revenues by $4 million during that period. National said that its figures were based upon an on-board survey of 13,500 passengers and represented one of the most exhaustive studies ever conducted for a CAB investigation.

J. Dan Brock, vice president for marketing for National Airlines, was quoted at a news conference as saying that the fare had been an "unqualified success," had created a new air-travel market, and had generated more than twice the volume of new passengers required to offset revenue dilution caused by regular passengers switching to the lower fare. He said the stimulus of the fare gave National a net traffic gain of 74,000 passengers during the initial $2\frac{1}{2}$-month trial. But he also cautioned that the success claims he was making for the no-frills fare did not mean that low fares were the answer to the airline industry's excess capacity problems. Yet Brock did go so far as to state that "what no frills has proved . . . is that a properly conceived discount fare, offered at the right time in the right markets with the right controls, can help airlines hurdle traditionally soft traffic periods."

Eastern Airlines reported a much different experience. Eastern said its studies showed that only 14% of the 55,200 of its passengers who used a no-frills fare between mid-April and May 31 represented newly generated traffic, with the remaining 86% representing passengers diverted from higher fares who would have flown anyway. It said that the effect of the fare in the six major markets it studied was a net loss in revenue to Eastern of $543,000 during the initial $1\frac{1}{2}$ months. At the same time Eastern attacked the credibility of the National Airlines' survey, noting that its own data were based upon an exhaustive and scientific blind telephone survey among persons who did not know the purpose and sponsor of the survey. Eastern claimed that this type of study was more apt to produce unbiased results than National's on-board surveys.

Other airlines joined Eastern in challenging National's survey results in the

CAB's hearing to decide whether the no-frills fares should continue to be allowed. Delta Airlines, for example, claimed that the no-frills fare did not even come close to offsetting the dilution it experienced in revenues. Other airline officials observed that while National Airlines might have succeeded through its heavy promotion of the no-frills fares in diverting some business from other carriers, they felt that National's claims of generating many passengers who otherwise would not have flown were "preposterous."

Those airlines in direct competition with National on the routes where the discount fares were tried were vehemently opposed to continuing the discounts. In their view the no-frills approach constituted "economic nonsense." They announced a policy of matching National's discount fare only where forced to for competitive reasons.

QUESTIONS FOR DISCUSSION

1. Did the National Airlines' experiment suggest that the demand for airline service at discount prices is elastic or inelastic? Do Eastern's results indicate that demand is elastic or inelastic?

2. Which of the two studies, the on-board survey of National or the telephone survey of Eastern, do you think would yield the most reliable estimate as to the true elasticity of demand? Is it possible or likely that the elasticity of demand for National is different from the elasticity of demand for Eastern? Why? How would you account for the differences in the experiences of National and Eastern with discount fares?

3. Do you think it would be fair for the CAB to allow National to continue to use the no-frills fare if it wished to do so, even though Eastern Airlines and Delta Airlines and perhaps other airlines were opposed to the no-frills approach? Why?

urgent, or "luxury" types of products tend to exhibit higher degrees of price elasticity.

2. *The degree of market saturation for the product.* Market saturation has relevance to price elasticity in the sense that if nearly all households have refrigerators, it is unlikely the appliance manufacturers can stimulate the market demand for refrigerators much by cutting their average selling prices. In contrast, the use of solar water heating is far from widespread and price reductions in installed solar-water-heating equipment would probably trigger a substantial percentage gain in market sales.

3. *The income profile of current consumers of the product.* The demand for truly luxury products (such as 100-foot yachts and diamond necklaces) which are sold more or less exclusively to the very rich may be price inelastic for even fairly large percentage shifts in price. This is because the selling price tends to be a small percentage of the buyer's income—despite the size of the price tag. Yet the market demand for 16-foot fiberglass outboard runabouts, sold to the "mass market," may be fairly sensitive to price changes. When the price of an item is large in relation to income, buyers are more likely to be price-conscious and substitute-conscious; hence a given percentage change in price can be expected to have a significant demand impact, owing to the large difference it makes upon the consumer's pocketbook. From another angle, products such as videotape recorders are often initially priced well above the reach of the mass market, and the first round or so of price cuts may not generate much demand response. But as prices continue to be reduced, successively lower income levels are tapped, and market demand becomes increasingly responsive to lower prices.

4. *The number of good substitutes available at competitive prices.* The market demand for zinc castings for automotive trim may be highly price elastic because of the encroachment of cheaper plastic substitutes as zinc prices climb. On the other hand, there is as yet no good substitute for the use of glass windows and windshields in the manufacture of automobiles, and thus there is little risk of diminished demand through the substitution of other materials, as the price of automotive glass goes up.

5. *The number of uses a product has.* There is a tendency for the demand for a product to be more elastic the wider the range of uses it has. With a larger number of uses, more opportunity exists for variation in the quantity sold when price changes. Increases in price reduce the number of economical uses of a product, whereas price declines expand the range of economically feasible uses. This aspect of demand elasticity is especially pertinent for steel, aluminum, other primary metals, plastics, wool, and paper products.

APPLICATIONS CAPSULE

DO RISING GASOLINE PRICES REDUCE DEMAND?

Economists' estimates of the extent to which gasoline demand will lessen as prices rise show that in the immediate short run, the coefficient of price elasticity is −0.10—in which case the quantity of gasoline used can be expected to decline immediately about 1% for each 10% increase in retail prices at the pump. However, the elasticity picture changes substantially as the period for examining the response of motorists to higher prices is stretched out. This is because the full impact of a price change on demand does not take place immediately; the longer motorists have to make adjustments in gasoline usage, the greater is their ability to do so in terms of making basic changes in the type of car they own, in their driving habits, and in their dependence on the automobile relative to total miles driven each year. Manufacturers, moreover, have time to design and build cars with much greater fuel efficiency.

    The price elasticity estimates for periods of 2 to 3 years cluster in the neighborhood of −0.25. Professor Pindyck at MIT projects a 5-year price elasticity figure of −0.49 for the United States. Over a 10-year time frame, his estimate is −0.82 and for 15 years it is −1.03. The sharply increasing degree of price elasticity as the time of response lengthens highlights the fact that the total impact of a change in price may be much more dramatic over the long run than in the short run.

6. *The durability of the product.* Price elasticity can be partly a function of product durability because of the possibility of delaying the purchase of replacements. Postponing the purchase of new durable goods by repairing them may be an effective, albeit temporary, substitute for replacing goods whose prices are rising, thus making for a more elastic demand in the short run than would otherwise be the case.

7. *The time period under consideration.* In general, the market demand for a product tends to be more elastic in the long run than in the short run. This is primarily due to lags in consumer response to price changes and to increased chances that more good substitutes will appear as the time frame lengthens.

Plainly, more than one of these factors can affect the price elasticity of market demand simultaneously. Moreover, it is important to recognize that different classes of customers within the same market frequently have different price elasticities. For instance, industrial demand for electricity may be much more price sensitive than residential demand for electricity, owing to the greater options of manufacturers to use different fuel sources or to convert to more energy-efficient equipment. Under such circumstances, the total revenues of electric utility firms can be increased by charging higher prices to the market segment where demand is less elastic (residential users) and lower prices to price-sensitive buyers (industrial users).

A final point: When total industry demand is highly elastic at the prevailing price level, firms with access to manufacturing economies of scale are likely to try to expand the total dollar market for the product by initiating lower prices. Since the elastic nature of the market will result in unit volume increasing by greater percentages than the percentage decrease in selling prices, such a move could result in higher industry-wide profits, as well as an increased quantity demanded.

Price Elasticity and Demand for the Product of an Individual Firm

The degree to which market demand is price sensitive (elastic) or price insensitive (inelastic) does not completely carry over to the demand for the product of an individual firm. Two factors shape the price elasticity of demand for the products of an individual firm: (1) the elasticity of total *market* demand and the extent to which a firm's *pro rata* market share is affected by a change in the average *market* price, and (2) the ability a firm has to hold onto or increase its market share as it alters its prices above or below the prevailing market level. In other words, price elasticity at the level of a particular firm or brand is affected not only by the factors that govern the price elasticity of total market demand but also by how sensitive the firm's own demand is to the prices being charged by other firms in the marketplace. A couple of illustrations will highlight the reasons for this.

Consider first the case of an industry where the products of different firms are all essentially alike—as is the case with commodity-type markets (wheat, soybeans, gold, copper, oil). The key pricing feature of commodity products is uniformity of price throughout the market, although there may be minor variations depending upon location (New York or London) or time (futures or spot prices). In such markets, an individual firm has very limited pricing discretion. For example, if one coal supplier raised selling price to $30 per ton while the remaining suppliers stayed at $25, the high-priced seller would have difficulty finding buyers and demand for the firm's coal would prove quickly to be highly price elastic. Conversely, if the firm decided to undercut the prices of our coal suppliers by announcing a $20 per ton price, it would be deluged with orders—again a price-elastic condition. But this latter condition may be extremely short-lived, since other firms may be rapidly forced into matching price cuts to prevent losing customers to the low-priced firm. The strong likelihood of matching price cuts transforms what otherwise would be a highly elastic response to a firm's own price cuts into a response where the firm's price elasticity value is equal to the price elasticity of total market demand.

In general, then, when firms sell undifferentiated products using essentially the same marketing strategy, any one firm is seldom able to stray much from the prevailing industry average price. When one firm tries to change its price *independent* of other sellers, it quickly learns that the demand for its product is highly elastic above the going market price and much less elastic or even inelastic below the ruling price (depending on how the overall market demand will respond to matching price cuts by all producers).

At the other extreme, there are markets and industries in which the products of competing firms are sufficiently different (and their competitive strategies are sufficiently different in terms of product design, quality, advertising, and so on) that the demand for a particular firm's product becomes somewhat less sensitive to price. Product differentiation allows firms the room to maintain rather diverse prices; indeed, there may be no such thing as *the* industry price. In the women's dress market, for instance, there exists a broad range of prices and styles, from the bargain basement to the high-fashion salon, and each merchant is able to establish a differential market image according to the selection of dresses, decor and location of the retail shop, type of sales assistance, credit arrangements, alteration services, advertising, and so forth. High prices may be congruent with one merchant's approach, and low prices with another. In strongly differentiated product markets, the degree of price elasticity confronting the individual seller is influenced by the extent to which that firm's prices are synchronized with (1) the overall character and image of its total product offering, (2) the importance consumers attach to nonprice product features, and (3) the extent to which higher prices can be obtained through increased promotional efforts.

Therefore, in appraising the price elasticity of demand for an individual firm's product, the analyst must take into account the full dimensions along which buyers assess a product's relative attractiveness—consideration of price alone is insufficient. Particularly must one assess how the attributes of a firm's product stack up against the attributes of substitutes. Were all rival firms to have essentially comparable prices and products, one could expect price elasticity among brands to be high, since consumers would be prone to switch readily to lower-priced brands whenever one firm raised its price. But the more strongly differentiated are the products of rival sellers, the less sensitive the demand of any one firm will be to a change in its selling price. Moreover, if a firm successfully increases the degree of product differentiation between its brand and other brands, it will probably find buyers tolerant of a modest increase in prices—that is, its demand will be less price elastic than before.

Attempting to Calculate Price Elasticity for Particular Products

Attempts to develop meaningful and reliable estimates of price elasticity is a challenging empirical task. To begin with, the coefficient of price elasticity depends upon which of several prospective prices is currently being charged.

APPLICATIONS CAPSULE

WHY SOME BUYERS MAY BE LESS PRICE SENSITIVE THAN OTHERS

Buyers of products differ greatly in the degree to which they are sensitive to price changes. The demand curves of some buyers may be very elastic while other buyers may have very inelastic demands. Where buyers are insensitive to price and to price changes, one or more of the following conditions tend to prevail:

1. *The buyer is very concerned about product performance.* Buyer demand tends to be price inelastic whenever a product that "fails" or does not perform up to expectations causes the buyer to incur substantial penalties, costs, or inconvenience. The adverse risks of product failure make it worthwhile for buyers to pay a premium price for high performance characteristics and inclines them to stick with products and brands that have proven reliable in the past. A good example where this happens is in the oil-field-equipment industry. The demand for blowout preventors (a piece of oil field equipment that prevents oil from escaping a well if there is a surge in pressure) tends to be price inelastic; if the blowout preventor fails, the user faces considerable costs in terms of lost oil, lost time of skilled crews, and environmental sanctions, particularly in the case of offshore wells, where the clean up of spills is particularly expensive. As a consequence, buyers of blowout preventors are reluctant to switch from proven brand names even in the face of price increases and even when other companies seeking to penetrate the market offer lower-priced products with allegedly comparable performance features.

2. *The buyer wants a differentiated or custom-designed product and is willing to pay extra for it.* Whenever buyers want a specially designed product to fit their own particular needs, they often become locked into purchasing from a particular supplier who is willing to go to the trouble to satisfy the buyer's special design requests. In such instances, buyers may conclude that extra effort on the part of the supplier merits the compensation of a higher price. Of course, later, the supplier's willingness to accommodate the buyer's wants may provide the leverage needed to impose a price increase without much risk of losing the buyer's business.

3. *The buyer purchases the product because it is perceived to contribute to the high-quality image the buyer is trying to project on behalf of its own product.* Buyers of items that are components of the buyer's own final product often have price-

inelastic demands because they perceive that the item's quality will enhance the performance of their product, or because the brand name of the component carries prestige value which reinforces the high-quality image they are trying to project. For example, the manufacturers of expensive pieces of equipment will often use the electric motors of prestige suppliers as a component part because doing so upgrades the image of their machinery and helps enhance its market attractiveness. Manufacturers of the component part, knowing of the benefit their component gives the final product, are then in a position to ask for and get a slightly higher price when other firms cannot.

4. *The buyer obtains major savings from using a particular product or service.* Whenever a product or service can save a buyer time and money because it performs well, the buyer will tend to have an inelastic demand for the product. The same holds true when a buyer can benefit from timely delivery of a product, rapid maintenance and repair in the event of breakdowns, and technical advice. To cite an example, when a firm has high stakes in the outcome of a particular situation (such as an electric utility filing for a $200 million rate increase), the firm will be willing to pay a premium for the very best advice it can get from lawyers, accountants, consultants, and other experts having specialized knowledge and talents to offer. Another example, drawn again from the oil industry, is where a company such as Schlumberger uses sophisticated electronic techniques to detect the likely presence of oil in substrata rock formations; the information obtained from such instruments has the potential for steering oil-drilling companies away from locations where there is greater probability of a dry hole. Understandably, then, oil-drilling companies are willing to pay substantial fees for Schlumberger's services, particularly when they face difficult and costly drilling expenses because of great depth or offshore location.

5. *The cost of the item is small compared to the buyer's purchasing budget.* Many consumers do not bother to shop around for the best price and to undertake time-consuming product comparisons when the cost of the item is low. This is especially true when the buyer's major motive in purchasing the item is convenience, taste, or some other subjective preference criterion. In the case of industrial buyers, the relevant cost of an item is the firm's total expenditure for the item over some time period (a month or a year), not the cost per unit. Low unit cost is not a sufficient consideration because the number of units purchased may make the dollar costs of the item very important. In industrial purchasing, the purchase of component parts or raw materials that entail a high total dollar cost is usually handled by top executives and/or senior specialist purchasing agents who may well be very price conscious—thereby creating an elastic-demand situation.

6. *The buyer is in a position to absorb a price increase and/or can readily pass on higher costs of component parts and raw materials.* As a rule, the more a firm is in position to pass along rising costs, the less tenacious and aggressive it will be in haggling over prices and price increases. The same can hold true when an industrial buyer has a sufficiently high profit margin that it is willing to absorb a price increase rather than go to the trouble of seeking out alternative sources of supply. (However, in such instances the item is probably a sufficiently low cost item that the basic reason for price insensitivity is that the buyer falls into category 5.)

7. *The buyer is poorly informed and/or does not adhere to a policy of purchasing according to well-defined specifications.* Buyers tend to be less sensitive to prices and price increases when they are poorly informed about prevailing price conditions, demand-supply conditions, the availability and prices of substitutes, and the performance-quality-service features offered by rival brands and suppliers. More-informed buyers tend to be hard bargainers on price and other conditions of purchase. Indeed, many large purchasers make a special effort to learn the business of their suppliers so well that they know when they are getting a good price and when they are not. A poorly informed buyer is easily swayed by persuasive advertising, a good sales pitch, and efforts to downplay the performance differences among competing products.

8. *The cost to a buyer of switching from one seller to another is very high.* In some cases, an industrial user of a component part may tie the specifications of its products to that of a particular supplier, or the firm may make heavy investments in installing and using a particular supplier's equipment (as is often the case with a computer). When buyers' switching costs are high, they may well be insensitive to price changes—especially small price changes that would not make it worthwhile to switch.

Source: Michael E. Porter, *Competitive Strategy* (New York: Free Press, 1980), pp. 24–26, 114–118.

Because the price elasticity coefficient varies all along the demand curve, the elasticity estimate may not be the same for a price increase as for a price decrease. Second, it is difficult to hold all other demand determinants constant long enough to isolate the effects of a price change upon quantity demanded. Although there are a variety of econometric techniques available for dealing with situations where several variables are present and undergoing change, these are not always capable of correctly identifying and parceling out how much of the total change in quantity demanded is directly attributable to a price change and how much is attributable to changes in other demand determinants. Finally, the full impact of a price change upon demand frequently occurs after a time lag, owing to the resistance of custom, habit, life-styles, and preferences. The fact that time itself may be a real factor (in the sense that demand can be more elastic in the long run than in the short run) further confounds the calculation problem.

Nevertheless, it should be clear that firms have a definite interest in knowing how sensitive demand is to changes in selling price.

Income Elasticity of Demand

As stated in earlier chapters, the purchase levels of many items are quite sensitive to variations in consumer incomes. The responsiveness of the quantity demanded to a change in consumer income (other demand determinants being held fixed) is called *income elasticity of demand*.

Just as price elasticity was found by determining the ratio of the percentage change in the quantity demanded to some percentage change in price, so income elasticity is calculated by finding the ratio of the percentage change in quantity demanded to a percentage change in income. Hence, we may write

$$\epsilon_I = \frac{\% \text{ change in quantity demanded}}{\% \text{ change in income}}.$$

As with price elasticity, there are also two measures of income elasticity: arc elasticity and point elasticity. The arc formula for computing income elasticity is

$$\epsilon_I = \frac{\dfrac{Q_2 - Q_1}{\left(\dfrac{Q_1 + Q_2}{2}\right)}}{\dfrac{I_2 - I_1}{\left(\dfrac{I_1 + I_2}{2}\right)}},$$

where ϵ_I represents the coefficient of income elasticity and I is income. The point formula for income elasticity is

$$\epsilon_I = \frac{dQ}{dI} \cdot \frac{I}{Q},$$

where dQ/dI symbolizes the rate of change in the quantity demanded as income changes.

For all items except inferior goods, the sign of the coefficient of income elasticity is positive because for normal goods income and quantity purchased vary in the same direction. If the value of the income elasticity coefficient is greater than $+1$, the demand for the item is said to be income elastic; if it is less than $+1$, then demand is said to be income inelastic. The coefficient of income elasticity is negative for inferior goods. The greater the size of the coefficient, the greater the degree of responsiveness of the quantity demanded to a change in income.

Income elasticity varies widely from item to item. Light bulbs, dairy products, aspirin, and cigarettes are examples of products whose income elasticities are typically low. In contrast, jewelry, T-bone steak, Cadillacs, art objects, education, foreign travel, and scotch have high income elasticities. Generally, products that consumers regard as necessities have low income elasticities, while luxuries tend to have high income elasticities. Indeed, one way of designating items as either luxuries or necessities is by the size of their income elasticities.

The results of some actual studies of price and income elasticity of demand are shown in Table 5-4.

TABLE 5-4. Results of Studies of Elasticity of Demand

Product	Elasticity Finding
Air travel	
Short business-oriented routes	Price inelastic
Vacation routes	Highly income elastic
Residential electricity	
Short run (1 year)	−0.06 (price); +0.06 (income)
Long run	−0.52 (price); +0.88 (income)
Cigarettes	−0.3 to −0.4 (price); +0.5 (income)
Coffee	−0.15 (price); +0.29 (income)
China, glassware, tableware, utensils	
Short run	−1.2 (price)
Long run	−1.3 (price)
Kitchen appliances	−0.6 (price)
Tires	
Short run	−0.6 (price)
Long run	−0.4 (price)
Radio and television receivers (short run)	−1.2 (price)
Automobiles (long run)	−0.2 (price)
Legal services	−0.5 (price)
Physicians' services	−0.6 (price)
Housing	−0.40 (price)
Soybean meal	−1.65 (price)
Local residential telephone service	
Short run	−0.10 (price); +0.10 (income)
Long run	−0.14 (price); +0.14 (income)
Local telephone service, business use	
Short run	−0.08 (price); +0.10 (income)
Long run	−0.15 (price); +0.19 (income)

Sources: H. S. Houthakker and Lester D. Taylor, *Consumer Demand in the United States, 1929–1970* (Cambridge, Mass.: Harvard University Press, 1966); Philip K. Verleger, Jr., "Models of the Demand for Air Transportation," *Bell Journal of Economics and Management Science,* Vol. 3, No. 2 (Autumn 1972), pp. 437–457; James M. Griffin, "The Effects of Higher Prices on Electricity Consumption," *Bell Journal of Economics and Management Science,* Vol. 5, No. 2 (Autumn 1974), pp. 515–539; S. M. Sackrin, "Factors Affecting the Demand for Cigarettes," *Agricultural Economics Research,* Vol. 14, No. 3 (July 1962), pp. 81–88; John J. Hughes, "Note on the U.S. Demand for Coffee," *American Journal of Agricultural Economics,* Vol. 51, No. 4 (November 1969); R. W. Eberts and T. J. Gronberg, "Wage Gradients, Rent Gradients, and the Price Elasticity of Demand for Housing: An Empirical Investigation," *Journal of Urban Economics,* Vol. 12, No. 2 (September 1982), pp. 168–176; Hendrik C. Knipscheer, Lowell D. Hill, and Bruce L. Dixon, "Demand Elasticities for Soybean Meal in the European Community," *American Journal of Agricultural Economics,* Vol. 64, No. 2 (May 1982), pp. 249–253; and the New York Telephone Company.

Cross Elasticity of Demand

Insofar as their demand is concerned, goods can be related in any one of three ways:

1. They may be *competing* products or *substitutes,* in which case an increase in the purchase of one is at the expense of another. So it is with various *brands* of margarine, soap, razor blades, and gasoline; similarly, hamburgers may be a substitute for hot dogs, a trip to Florida may be a substitute for a trip to the Great Smoky Mountains, and a Toyota may be a substitute for a Cutlass.

2. They may be *complementary* products, in which case an increase in the purchase of one causes a rise in the purchase of another. Complementary implies that goods are consumed *together*. Examples include electric appliances and electric power, shoes and socks, notebook paper and ballpoint pens, and carpets and vacuum cleaners.

3. They may be *independent,* such that the purchase of one has no direct bearing upon the demand of another. Independence implies that goods are neither consumed together nor in place of each other. Pairs of items whose purchases are for all intents and purposes independent include shrimp and pillows, football tickets and a spool of thread, and fishing tackle and lingerie.

Cross elasticity of demand is a measure for interpreting the relationship between products. As between two products X and Y, cross elasticity measures the percentage change in the quantity demanded of product Y in response to a percentage change in the price of product X. In mathematical terms,

$$\epsilon_{yx} = \frac{\%\ \text{change in quantity of Y}}{\%\ \text{change in price of X}},$$

where ϵ_{yx} symbolizes the coefficient of cross elasticity between X and Y. Again, there are two ways of actually computing cross elasticity. The arc formula for calculating the coefficient of cross elasticity is

$$\epsilon_{yx} = \frac{\dfrac{Q_{y2} - Q_{y1}}{\left(\dfrac{Q_{y1} + Q_{y2}}{2}\right)}}{\dfrac{P_{x2} - P_{x1}}{\left(\dfrac{P_{x1} + P_{x2}}{2}\right)}}.$$

The point elasticity formula is

$$\epsilon_{yx} = \frac{dQ_y}{dP_x} \cdot \frac{P_x}{Q_y}.$$

The cross-elasticity coefficient may be either positive or negative. When ϵ_{yx} is positive, products X and Y are substitutes for each other. This is illustrated by a simple example. Other factors remaining constant, if the price of shipping goods by rail increases, the freight traffic via motor carrier should rise. Conversely, if the price of shipping goods by rail declines, the freight traffic via motor carrier should decrease. In either case, the percentage changes in rail rates and the volume of motor freight are in the same direction. Thus, whether the price changes are up or down, the cross-elasticity coefficient is positive.

Complementary goods have negative cross-elasticity coefficients. Automobiles and automobile insurance serve as a case in point. An increase in the price of automobiles tends to reduce purchases of automobiles and cuts back on the sales of automobile insurance. In contrast, lower automobile prices tend to stimulate car sales, thereby boosting sales of auto insurance. Hence, a change in the price of automobiles is followed by a change in sales of auto insurance in the opposite direction. As a consequence, the coefficient of cross elasticity is negative.

The strength of the relationship between substitute and complementary products is reflected by the absolute size of the cross-elasticity coefficient. The larger the coefficient, the stronger the relationship. Furthermore, it follows that the closer the coefficient is to zero (approached from either the positive or negative side), the weaker is any substitute or complementary relationship between two products and the more independent the two products are. This is so because as ϵ_{yx} approaches zero, variations in the price of one good induce no appreciable change in the quantity demanded of the other; hence, purchases of the products would seem unrelated or independent.

Measures of the cross elasticity of demand may be indicative of the boundaries of an industry. High cross elasticities indicate close relationships and suggest that the goods are part of the same industry, whereas low cross elasticities imply weak relationships and that the goods may be in different industries. If a good has a low cross elasticity with respect to all other goods, then it may be considered to constitute an industry by itself. Similarly, if several products have high cross elasticities among themselves but low cross elasticities with respect to other goods, then the product group may define an industry. For instance, various brands of TV sets have high cross elasticities among each other but low cross elasticities with other household appliances and fixtures.

However, using the cross-elasticity concept as a means of delimiting an industry is not without difficulty. In the first place, it is arbitrary as to how high cross elasticities must be to be considered in the same industry. Cross elasticities among canned vegetables may be quite high, yet the cross elasticity between canned vegetables and canned meats is liable to be rather low. Such circumstances render it difficult to define rigorously the boundaries of an industry—should it be canned vegetables or canned meats or canned foods?

A second complication arises from the existence of chains of cross relationships. The cross elasticity between a color TV console and a table model color TV may be high, as might the cross elasticity between portable color TVs and black-and-white portables. But console color TV sets and portable black-and-white sets may have low cross elasticities, thereby raising issues of just how closely related the markets for console color TV sets and portable black-and-white TV sets are to one another.

MATHEMATICAL CAPSULE 6

PARTIAL ELASTICITIES OF DEMAND: A MORE RIGOROUS CONCEPT OF DEMAND ELASTICITY

In its most general form, the demand function for a good can be expressed as

$$Q_1 = f(P_1, P_2, \ldots, P_n, I, E, R, N, T, O),$$

where

$$
\begin{aligned}
Q_1 &= \text{quantity demanded of good 1,}\\
P_1 &= \text{market price of the good,}\\
P_2, \ldots, P_n &= \text{prices of other goods,}\\
I &= \text{level of consumer incomes,}\\
E &= \text{consumer expectations regarding future prices, incomes,}\\
&\quad\text{and product availability,}\\
R &= \text{range of goods available to buyers,}\\
N &= \text{number of potential buyers, and}\\
O &= \text{all other factors relevant in influencing } Q_1.
\end{aligned}
$$

The elasticity of demand with respect to any demand determinant refers to the degree of responsiveness of the quantity demanded relative to some percentage change in that demand determinant *when the values of all other demand determinants are held fixed.*

In mathematical terms, this definition translates into the following expressions for point elasticity:

$$\epsilon_p = \frac{\partial Q_1}{\partial P_1} \cdot \frac{P_1}{Q_1}, \tag{1}$$

which is the partial elasticity of good 1 with respect to its price, P_1, or price elasticity of demand;

$$\epsilon_{12} = \frac{\partial Q_1}{\partial P_2} \cdot \frac{P_2}{Q_1}, \tag{2}$$

which is the partial elasticity of good 1 with respect to the price of good 2, or cross elasticity of demand between good 1 and good 2;

$$\epsilon_{1n} = \frac{\partial Q_1}{\partial P_n} \cdot \frac{P_n}{Q_1}, \tag{3}$$

which is the partial elasticity of good 1 with respect to the price of good n, or cross elasticity of demand between good 1 and good n;

$$\epsilon_I = \frac{\partial Q_1}{\partial I} \cdot \frac{I}{Q_1}, \tag{4}$$

which is the partial elasticity of good 1 with respect to income, or income elasticity of demand; and so on for the other demand determinants. Hence, when given the demand function for a product containing more than one variable, the procedure for determining point elasticity requires using the *partial derivative* of the demand function with respect to that demand determinant rather than the first derivative.

EXERCISES

1. Suppose that the demand function for product X is specified by the equation $Q_x = 34 - 0.8P_x^2 + 0.3P_y + 0.04I$.
   (a) Determine the price elasticity of demand for X when $P_x = \$10$, $P_y = \$20$, and $I = \$5000$.
   (b) Determine the cross elasticity of demand for X with respect to good Y when $P_x = \$10$, $P_y = \$20$, and $I = \$5000$. Are X and Y substitutes or complements?
   (c) Determine the income elasticity of demand for X when $P_x = \$10$, $P_y = \$20$, and $I = \$5000$. Is X a normal or an inferior good?

2. Suppose that the demand function for good Y is specified by the equation $Q_y = 1665 - 0.5P_y^3 - 0.1P_x^2 - 0.05I$.
   (a) Determine the price elasticity of demand when $P_y = \$10$, $P_x = \$20$, and $I = \$2500$.
   (b) Determine the cross elasticity of demand for Y with respect to good X when $P_y = \$10$, $P_x = \$20$, and $I = \$2500$. Are X and Y substitutes or complements?
   (c) Determine the income elasticity of demand for Y when $P_y = \$10$, $P_x = \$20$, and $I = \$2500$. Is Y a normal or an inferior good?

SUMMARY AND CONCLUSIONS

The analysis of the demand for a product can be approached from the standpoint of an individual consumer (individual consumer demand), from the standpoint of all consumers taken as a group (market demand), or from the standpoint of a particular business firm (product demand or firm demand). A product is determined in the main by (1) the selling price of the item; (2) consumer tastes and preferences; (3) the money income of consumers; (4) the prices of related products; (5) consumer expectations with regard to future prices, income levels, and product availability; (6) the product's attributes and what they do for the user; and (7) market size as determined by the number of consumers and the frequency with which they consume the item. Other peripheral considerations include whether the good in question is a luxury or a necessity, whether its demand is derived from the demand for other goods, the extent of market saturation, the price and availability of consumer credit, and the discretionary purchasing power of consumers. The separate impacts of the major and minor demand determinants vary in degree and intensity from product to product; each item has its own unique set of demand determinants.

   A firm's demand curve provides the basis for deriving its revenue curves. A firm's average revenue (*AR*) curve summarizes the relationship between average revenue (average price) and quantity sold; it is identical to the firm's demand curve. A firm's total revenue (*TR*) equals the total receipts it obtains from the sale of its output. A firm's marginal revenue (*MR*) is the change in total revenue that results from a very small increase or decrease in output sold. Marginal revenue may be thought of as either *continuous* or *discrete*. Continuous marginal revenue is appropriate when output changes by infinitesimally small amounts. Discrete marginal revenue is used in situations where output changes in amounts of 1 unit (or more). A firm's average revenue can be found by dividing total revenue by the number of units sold. The shapes of the various *TR*, *MR*, and *AR* functions depend on the shape of the demand curve.

Elasticity of demand measures the responsiveness or sensitivity of quantity demanded to changes in a demand determinant. Price elasticity of demand is defined specifically as a ratio of the percentage change in quantity demanded resulting from a percentage change in price. Arc elasticity is an approximate measure of demand sensitivity between two points, while point elasticity measures elasticity at a single point on the demand function. When the coefficient of price elasticity is greater than one, demand is elastic and a price decrease will cause *TR* to rise. When the coefficient of price elasticity is less than one, demand is inelastic and a price decrease will cause *TR* to fall. Total revenue is maximized at the output rate where the price elasticity coefficient is 1. The degree of price elasticity for a product varies according to (1) the region of the demand curve within which price changes, (2) the number and availability of substitures, (3) the price of the item relative to consumer income, (4) whether the item is a luxury or a necessity, (5) the number of uses for the good, (6) the length of the time period being considered, (7) the durability of the item, and (8) market saturation.

Two other elasticity concepts of particular importance are income elasticity and cross elasticity. High, positive income elasticities characterize luxury-type items; low, positive income elasticities are typical for necessities; and negative income elasticities denote inferior goods. Cross elasticity is a measure of the sensitivity of the demand for one product relative to price changes in another product. When the cross-elasticity coefficient is positive, the two goods are substitutes; when the coefficient is negative, a complementary relationship is indicated. The closer the coefficient is to zero, the more independent are the two items.

SUGGESTED READINGS

CLARKSON, G. P., *The Theory of Consumer Demand: A Critical Appraisal* (Englewood Cliffs, N.J.: Prentice-Hall, Inc., 1963).

DEAN, J., *Managerial Economics* (Englewood Cliffs, N.J.: Prentice-Hall, Inc., 1951), pp. 177–210.

HALVORSEN, R., "Residual Demand for Electric Energy," *Review of Economics and Statistics,* Vol. 47, No. 1 (February 1975), pp. 12–18.

SCHULTZ, H., *Theory and Measurement of Demand* (Chicago: University of Chicago Press, 1938).

SUITS, D. B., "The Demand for New Automobiles in the U.S., 1929–1956," *Review of Economics and Statistics,* Vol. 40 (August 1958), pp. 273–280.

WOLD, H., *Demand Analysis* (New York: John Wiley & Sons, Inc., 1953).

PROBLEMS AND QUESTIONS FOR DISCUSSION

1. The following table presents hypothetical data for the market demand for a good. Complete the table.

Price	Quantity Demanded	AR	TR	Discrete MR	Coefficient of Price Elasticity
$50	1	_____	_____	_____	_____
40	2	_____	_____	_____	_____
30	3	_____	_____	_____	_____
20	4	_____	_____	_____	_____
13	5	_____	_____	_____	_____
8	6	_____	_____		

2. Given: The demand equation is $P = 81 - 9Q$.
   - (a) What is the equation for MR?
   - (b) At what output is $MR = 0$?
   - (c) At what output is TR maximum?
   - (d) Determine the price elasticity of demand at the output where TR is maximum.
3. Suppose that the demand equation for a good is $Q = 20 - 3P$. What is the price elasticity of demand at a price of $1? At a price of $4?
4. If the demand equation for an item is $Q = 16 + 9P - 2P^2$, calculate the price elasticity of demand at a price of $4. At a price of $3.
5. If the demand equation for an item is $P = 1000 + 3Q - 4Q^2$,
   - (a) determine price elasticity of demand at $Q = 10$ units.
   - (b) determine the equations for TR and MR.
6. Given the following hypothetical data for a consumer, compute *all* meaningful elasticity coefficients (price elasticity, income elasticity, and cross elasticity). Remember that prices must be constant when income elasticity is computed and that income and the prices of other products must be constant when price elasticity is computed, and so on. In other words, the computation of elasticities of any kind is valid *only* when *all other* variables are held constant.

Period	Price of X	Quantity of X Purchased	Price of Y	Income
1	$1.00	200	$0.50	$6000
2	1.05	190	0.50	6000
3	1.05	200	0.52	6500
4	1.05	220	0.54	6500
5	1.03	210	0.53	6500
6	1.03	215	0.55	6500
7	1.03	205	0.55	6300
8	1.07	190	0.55	6300

7. Given: The market demand equation for widgets is $Q = 840 - 0.50P$, where $Q =$ quantity demanded per period of time and $P =$ price of widgets in dollars.
   - (a) If the price of widgets were lowered from $40 to $38, would you expect consumer expenditures for widgets to rise, fall, or remain unchanged?

(b) If the economy's sole producer of widgets lowered its price from \$40 to \$38, what predictions, if any, can you make about the effect the price reduction would have upon the firm's *profits*?

8. Given: The relationship between product A and product B is $Q_A = 80P_B - 0.5P_B^2$, where Q_A = units of product A demanded by consumers each day and P_B = selling price of product B.
   (a) Determine the cross-elasticity coefficient for the two products when the price of product B = \$10.
   (b) Are products A and B complements, substitutes, or independent, and how "strong" is the relationship?

9. Given the price levels now prevailing for steel products, would you expect that the price elasticity of demand for the output of U.S. Steel Corporation is higher or lower than the price elasticity of demand for the output of the steel industry as a whole? Why?

10. The Tastee Food Company estimates that the demand-income relationships for its line of frozen pies can be represented by the equation $Q = 500 + 0.10I$, where Q = cases of frozen pies and I = average family income.
    (a) Determine the point income elasticity of demand at I = \$15,000, I = \$20,000, and I = \$25,000.
    (b) The calculations in part (a) should show that ϵ_I increases as income increases. Why does this relationship exist? Would the same relationship hold if the demand-income equation were $Q = 0.10I$?
    (c) Would you characterize the demand for Tastee Foods' frozen pie line as susceptible to recessionary influences in the economy? Explain. Would sustained inflation over a period of years tend to alter the demand-income equation because of the effects that inflation has on the purchasing power of the dollar?

11. The Fairfax Apparel Company manufactures leisure shirts for men; during 1984 Fairfax sold an average of 23,000 leisure shirts for \$13 per shirt. In early January 1985, Fairfax's major competitor, Lafayette Manufacturing Co., cut the price of its leisure shirts from \$15 to \$12. The orders Fairfax received for its own leisure shirts dropped sharply, from 23,000 per month to 13,000 per month for February and March 1985.
    (a) Calculate the cross elasticity of demand between Fairfax's leisure shirts and Lafayette's leisure shirts during February and March. Are the two companies' leisure shirts good or poor substitutes?
    (b) Suppose that the coefficient of price elasticity of demand for Fairfax's leisure shirts is -2.0. Assuming that Lafayette keeps its price at \$12, by how much must Fairfax cuts its price to build its sales of shirts back up to 23,000 per month? (*Hint:* Use the arc formula for price elasticity and substitute the known values into it and solve for the unknown price.)
    (c) Would you recommend that Fairfax cut its price to the value calculated in part (b)? Why or why not?

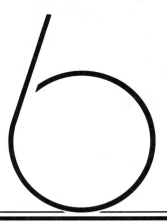

THE SUPPLY SIDE
OF THE MARKETPLACE
The technological dimension

With the insights we have gained about consumer behavior and how the demand side of the marketplace works, we are ready to switch over and look at the economics of the supply side. We begin our study of supply side microeconomics in this chapter by surveying the properties of a firm's production process and exploring why technological change ranks as one of the principal drivers of competition and market change. This chapter is organized around five topic areas: (1) the concept of production and the types of production processess, (2) the properties of the production functions of firms, (3) the role of technology and technological advance in altering a firm's costs and productive efficiency, (4) how technological change creates important new competitive forces in the marketplace, and (5) deciding whether to pursue a strategy of technological leadership or a strategy of followership.

THE CONCEPT OF PRODUCTION

It is common to think of ''production'' as being synonymous with manufacturing. With a bit of reflection, however, it is clear that quite a large number of economic functions qualify as production. Such diverse activities as collecting taxes, operating a jewelry store, drilling for oil, auditing a company's financial statements, designing a system to measure air pollution, dictating a letter, managing a United

165

Fund drive, discussing with officials of the Federal Trade Commission the factual basis for claims made in a TV commercial, driving a garbage truck, and interviewing applicants for food stamps can all be properly construed as production of one sort or another. Why? Because each involves some aspect of furnishing a good or service to some economic entity that values it.

In general, *any activity that creates value is production.* In this sense, production covers virtually every aspect of economic activity involved in furnishing a good or service to the final user—in the case of bread, the stages of production extend all the way from growing wheat to putting the loaf of bread in the buyer's sack of groceries at the supermarket. Nevertheless, because manufacturing activity illustrates the production process so well, it is convenient to focus the discussion about production and technology on manufacturing-type situations. Still, the microeconomic principles we will expose by looking at manufacturing-oriented production situations have application to virtually any enterprise or productive endeavor, irrespective of whether it is goods-oriented or service-oriented, profit-oriented or not-for-profit.

PRODUCTION ACTIVITY: TRANSFORMING INPUTS INTO OUTPUTS

If a production engineer were asked how to make some simple product, the reply might well be in terms of the kinds of raw materials needed, the proportions and order in which these ingredients should be combined, and the processing conditions and *technology* needed to produce the desired characteristics. Describing production in terms of its technology and process characteristics would serve as a beginning, although it would be incomplete. Other inputs are needed. Raw material ingredients do not get combined and processed of their own volition; these operations require human intervention or labor input. In addition, various tools, machinery, equipment, and physical facilities will probably be required to assist in the technological transformation of raw material ingredients into a finished good—these types of inputs are from a general category of economic resources called *capital.* Furthermore, production activity must occur in some location and so occupies space or land (this is particularly apparent in the case of agricultural production), and the production process takes *time*—anywhere from a few minutes to a few years. Finally, production activity requires supervision, planning, control, coordination, and leadership, or in other words, an input of *entrepreneurial* or *managerial talent* and *capability.*

In sum, *production* is a series of activities by which resource inputs (raw materials, labor, capital, land utilization, and managerial talents) are transformed through a *recipe* and *technological process* into outputs of goods or services. The time period requisite for the transformation is variable among products and from technological recipe to technological recipe for a given product. Not infrequently, a single production process yields several distinct products. In meat packing, for example, the slaughter of beef cattle produces numerous cuts of meat products, hides for leather goods, lard for cooking purposes, and ingredients for pet foods.

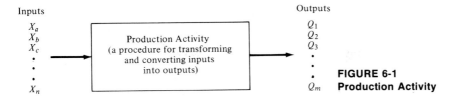

Inputs

X_a
X_b
X_c
.
.
.
X_n

Production Activity
(a procedure for transforming
and converting inputs
into outputs)

Outputs

Q_1
Q_2
Q_3
.
.
.
Q_m

FIGURE 6-1
Production Activity

Outputs produced from the same production process are designated as *joint products*.

Figure 6-1 captures the generic qualities of production activity. Of course, as concerns a specific product or technique, the size of the box and the details of what goes on inside it tend to change over time as a consequence of modifications in technology, changes in the efficiency levels of one or more inputs, and the composition of output. Since production activities are often composed of sequentially organized phase, introducing a change in one of the phases may entail changes elsewhere. Adding a new piece of laborsaving equipment, for example, can have the effect of adjusting materials specifications and of modifying the skill levels of the labor input needed to operate the new equipment. These, in turn, could necessitate changes in procurement patterns and in hiring and training programs. The increased productivity of the new equipment can cause bottlenecks at either or both ends of the phase, thereby causing even further process adjustment.

Basic Categories of Production Activity

The various types of production activities can be grouped into four categories: (1) unique-product production, (2) rigid mass production, (3) flexible mass production, and (4) process or flow production.[1] Each type has distinctive features and requirements and in understanding the production economics of a business it is important to know which type applies and to carry its principles through as efficiently as possible.

Unique-Product Production. This type of production activity is the least advanced. Each product is more or less distinct and made to specific order—a steam turbine, an office building, an aircraft carrier, the services of a law firm or an accounting firm. Production activity is labor intensive in the sense that the amount and costs of fixed assets (plant and equipment) are minor in comparison to the amount and cost of the labor involved. Unique-product production typically places high demands on skill and craftsmanship. It requires people who are good at technical functions. Unique-product production can operate at a low volume of output and it is amenable to wide fluctuation in output via adjustment in the size of the work

[1] This classification scheme and ensuing discussion is drawn from Peter F. Drucker, *Management: Tasks, Responsibilities, Practices* (New York: Harper & Row, Publishers, 1974), pp. 203–216.

force. The trigger point for production activity to commence is for an order to come in.

Moreover, work is organized more around the stage of production than around craft skill. The model is the telephone installer who, being neither a skilled carpenter nor an electrician, drills holes, installs electric wiring, makes ground connections, and tests the circuitry—everything needed within the installation stage. Another example is the construction of a single-family home, where production is grouped around the stages of setting the foundation in place; putting up the framing and roofing; installing the plumbing, wiring, and heating and cooling equipment; and doing the interior finishing. Craft skills are much in evidence but they are grouped according to the production stage of the house.

Rigid Mass Production.   As the label implies, in rigid mass production both the end product and tools, materials, and parts tend to be standardized. When Henry Ford said "The customer can have a car in any color as long as it's black," he expressed the essence of rigid mass production—the manufacture of uniform products in large quantity using a well-defined, proven, and usually inflexible technology.[2]

Rigid mass production often entails a capital-intensive technology and churns out a high and consistent volume of output; minor fluctuations in production levels adversely affect the economies of the technology-driven system. It requires high skill in the technical design of the process, as well as in its maintenance, but very little skilled labor to operate. Production planning and scheduling are of the essence in getting the in-place technology-dominated process to operate at peak efficiency. Because the nature of the final product is tightly constrained by inflexible production methods, firms making standard mass produced items have to condition customers to adapt their tastes and needs to narrow product variety—otherwise the low-cost economy of mass production cannot be realized.

Flexible Mass Production.   This production type seeks to take advantage of economical mass production by assembling the final product out of mass-produced, standardized components. The result is a diversity of end products which can readily be tailored to meet a diverse range of customer preferences. The key to making flexible mass production a viable approach is systematic analysis of customers, markets, and products to find the patterns around which diversity can be organized; this pattern then becomes the basis for taking the burden of diversity out of manufacturing and shifting it into assembly. General Motors has skillfully practiced the principle of developing many different models and sizes of cars out of fewer and fewer parts. Nearly all comparable makes of GM cars (Chevrolet, Pontiac, Buick, Oldsmobile, Cadillac) use the same frames, bodies, brakes, electrical systems, mechanical parts, and very substantially the same engines. Yet, because of different colors, body styles, fabrics, trim, and interior design, GM

---

[2] Ford realized that it would be easy enough to give buyers a color choice; all that was needed was several paint spray guns instead of one. But his argument was that the uniformity of the product would be lost once he made a concession to product diversity. To him, product uniformity was the key to mass production economies.

cars look different, have different attributes, and appeal to different customer groups and taste and preference patterns.

Flexible mass production, although generally capital-intensive and mechanized, requires a substantial amount of labor input. It also requires high skill in designing and maintaining the system—especially in terms of balancing product diversity against low-cost production of standard components. Because flexible mass production can turn out a very large variety of products and yet still capitalize upon standardized production techniques, one can predict that rigid mass production methods will become increasingly confined to a fairly small number of end products where basic uniformity is a fundamental customer need and customer specification.

Process Production.   Process production employs an integrated technology to move a continuous flow of raw material inputs through the system to produce a continuous flow of output. Typically, the system is highly automated and mechanized, thus requiring a large capital investment in facilities and equipment and only small doses of labor inputs. The continuous flow nature of the process makes for high production efficiency as long as it is operated at or near peak capacity 24 hours a day, 7 days a week; the greater the utilization of the facilities, the lower unit costs will be.

The classic example of process production is an oil refinery where crude oil is dispatched through a complex processing system to spawn a variety of refined end products for very different end uses. Process production is also the rule in the chemical industry. Other examples include milk processing, the manufacture of plate glass, and papermaking.

In many instances, process production offers the flexibility of a diverse range of products (gasoline, diesel fuel, fuel oil, motor oil, lubricants). But once built, the process itself tends to be relatively inflexible and can be changed only at major expense. Thus decisions to invest in process production facilities have to be made with an eye toward the long-range future; in particular, the prospects must be good that a firm will be able to create, maintain, and/or expand the markets for its outputs to whatever extent is needed to utilize plant capacity.[3]

THE PRODUCTION FUNCTION

Economists use the term ''production function'' to refer to the physical relationship between a firm's input of productive resources (raw materials, labor, capital, land, managerial talents) and its output of goods or services per unit of time. This relationship can be expressed symbolically as

$$Q = f(X_a, X_b, X_c, \ldots, X_n),$$

---

[3] A good example of what this means is illustrated by the famous Standard Oil story of the 1890s where the company distributed kerosene lamps free to the Chinese peasants to help create a market for kerosene.

where $X_a, X_b, X_c, \ldots, X_n$ represent quantities of various types of inputs and Q represents the quantity of output obtainable per period of time from specific combinations of the array of inputs using a given technology and production recipe. Such an expression furnishes a convenient analytical device for indicating that the quantity of a good or service produced per period of time is a function of the quantities of resource inputs used by the firm per period of time and the productive efficiency of its process for converting inputs into outputs.

The specific character of a production function thus depends partly on the quantities of resources employed and partly on the way in which they are combined (the production technology adopted by the firm). For illustration, suppose that a firm has two technologically feasible ways of combining inputs X_a, X_b, X_c, and X_d:

Production Technology	Resource Inputs	Output
Technology A	50 units each of X_a, X_b, X_c, and X_d	5,000 units
	100 units each of X_a, X_b, X_c, and X_d	10,000 units
	150 units each of X_a, X_b, X_c, and X_d	15,000 units
Technology B	50 units each of X_a, X_b, X_c, and X_d	6,000 units
	100 units each of X_a, X_b, X_c, and X_d	12,000 units
	150 units each of X_a, X_b, X_c, and X_d	18,000 units

By employing technology A the firm can produce 5000 units of output with 50 units each of inputs X_a, X_b, X_c, and X_d. Using 100 units of each input results in 10,000 units of output, and 150 units of each input yield an output of 15,000 units. However, the input-output relationship is quite different for technology B. Technology B generates more output for the same volume of input than does technology A and consequently is more efficient than A. It follows that there is a corresponding production function for *each* production technique or recipe for producing a product. A firm can alter its given production technique, by switching from one production technology to another, or by undertaking both actions. The efficiency of a production technique determines the output yield from each combination or inputs, while the state of technological know-how determines the number of available techniques.

Over the long run, competition and profit incentives induce firms to invest in the most efficient production technology available. In the short run, though, a firm is stuck with trying to utilize its current production technique in such a way as to obtain the maximum output from each alternative combination of inputs it might select. In symbolic language, for a production function of the form

$$Q = f(X_a, X_b, X_c, \ldots, X_n),$$

each numerical value of Q corresponding to specified numerical values of $X_a, X_b, X_c, \ldots, X_n$ is interpreted as being the largest possible value of Q obtainable, given the present production technology employed by the firm. For instance, in studying the production function for a firm producing red fireplugs, the most relevant output value is the *maximum* number of red fireplugs per period of time that can be produced from specific combinations of machine time, hours of skilled labor, floor space, electricity, hours of managerial input, metal casing, red paint, and so on. Anything less than the maximum output represents productive inefficiency and it is reasonable to presume that most firms in most cases are endeavoring to achieve the greatest possible level of productive efficiency rather than the largest possible amount of output for a specified set of inputs. In reality, of course, there will be occasions where mistakes, breakdowns, and inadvertent inefficiencies creep into the production process to prevent a firm from realizing its maximum productive capability.

It is equally accurate to conceive of a firm's production function as specifying the *minimum* input requirements for a designated level of output, given its production technology. To use the fireplug example again, the input-output relationship for a firm producing red fireplugs can be estimated by studying the minimum amounts of machine time, hours of skilled labor, floor space, electricity, hours of managerial input, metal casing, red paint, and so on, requisite for producing specified quantities of red fireplugs per period of time.

Whichever approach is preferred, the production function for a firm defines the limits of the firm's technical production possibilities. At any given time, when a firm producing at these limits wishes to increase output, it must use more inputs; similarly, the firm cannot use fewer inputs without decreasing its rate of output. Thus, as long as a firm is using the most efficient production technology currently available, its output rate is dependent upon (1) the quantities of resource inputs employed in the production process, and (2) how efficiently it is using these quantities of resource inputs.

Knowledge of a firm's production function permits answers to the following questions:

1. To what extent will total output change if the quantity of one input is increased and the quantity of all other inputs is held constant?
2. To what extent will total output change if the quantity of one input employed is decreased while the quantity of some other input is increased?
3. To what extent will output change if the firm increases some or all of the inputs in either equal or unequal proportions?

A firm can also ascertain from its production function whether its operating rate is technically efficient. Because the production function gives the maximum output obtainable from a given input combination, when the actual output flow is less than the potential maximum flow, the firm can produce its present output with a smaller volume of one or more inputs (and thereby reduce costs), or else it can use its present inputs to produce a larger volume of output than it is currently getting. To put it another way, unless a firm is operating at some input-output combination defined by its production function, its output rate is technically inefficient and reorganization of its operations will allow reducing inputs with no loss of output.

THE IMPACT OF TECHNOLOGICAL ADVANCE UPON PRODUCTION FUNCTIONS

It is a matter of historical fact that technological advances have over time greatly altered the ways that firms produce their products. Technological change is pertinent to production analysis because an advance in the state of technology increases the number of recipes available and alters the production functions of enterprises as they incorporate new technologies into their production methods. Just how technological advance affects a firm's production function varies from case to case:

1. A new production technology may permit the same amount of resource inputs to be combined differently so as to yield a greater output than before.
2. A new production technology may require a *smaller* quantity of one or even several inputs and *no more* of the remaining inputs to produce the same quantity of output as before, thus yielding greater efficiency and lower unit costs.
3. A new production technology may employ *less* of some inputs and *more* of others, yet with a smaller total cost and rate of input usage, to produce the same quantity of output as before.
4. A new production technology may require inputs, or yield outputs, that are of a kind not heretofore used or available at all.

Needless to say, the discovery of production technologies that are less efficient than those already known seldom has meaningful impact, since enterprises have no motive to implement them.

For several reasons, technological proficiency is often not uniform among firms producing the same product. Age differences among the plants of different firms are certain to exist, with newer plants embodying efficiency-increasing technological improvements unavailable to older plants. Also, there may be locational differences in labor efficiency and raw material quality. Managers, engineers, and technical staffs in some firms may simply have failed to keep up with current developments and may not know of better processes that other firms are using. As a consequence, rival producers may well have somewhat heterogeneous production functions and output capabilities.

How Technological Change Affects the Character of Production Processes

Let's think of the terms *production technology* as referring to the systematic application of scientific, engineering, administrative, or other organized bodies of knowledge to production activities. As the technological frontier is pushed out and innovative production methods appear, the nature of production processes tends to undergo fundamental change. For instance, the broader and deeper is society's technical capability, the more opportunities there are for further breaking down production methods into smaller pieces and bringing the full contribution of each specialized bit of knowledge to bear upon increasing efficiency and lowering costs. This in turn causes production processes to take on a new character.[4]

First, to the extent that greater production efficiency is achieved by making production methods more elaborate and sophisticated, an increasing span of time separates the beginning from the completion of production activity. An analogy may be made to the root system of a tree. Production can be thought of as being subdivided into phases which stretch back into time just as the root system of a tree penetrates and spreads through the ground. The bigger the tree, the larger and more complex its root system. Similarly, the more complex the product to be produced or the more sophisticated the production technique, the longer the time span required for its accomplishment and the larger the number of distinct phases of production. Specialized knowledge and technical expertise can then be brought to bear upon the performance of each and every phase of the whole task. As the first-level phases are completed, their results must be combined with the results of related phases so as to effect completion of the second level of the process; these second-level results must be combined again, and so on, until the phases have been put together to complete the whole process. The more complex the network, the more steps it takes to complete it and the more persons with specialized, technical, and managerial skills who are required for staffing the process.

Second, advances in production technology are typically accompanied by increases in the use of capital goods. This is because the application of more knowledge to some phase of production often involves the development of specialized tools, machinery, or equipment to perform or assist in performing the function—a trait that tends to increase a firm's dollar investment in its production activity.

Third, the added capital investment—while helping to increase output per unit of input and overall operating efficiency—sometimes has the effect of making a firm's production procedures less flexible or the composition of the final product more rigid. For instance, new equipment may be useful *only* for performing certain well-defined functions; hence, any alteration in the way they are performed may be prohibitively expensive—until a larger portion of the projected life of the specialized equipment is used up and its replacement falls within the range of economic feasibility. In the meantime, a firm finds itself "locked in" by cost constraints to using the production recipe it has already installed, whereas its rivals, if they happen to use a different and more flexible production technology, are not so constrained.

Fourth, technological advance alters the types of labor needed to staff the human element of production activity. For example, introducing computers into business operations greatly reduces the need for payroll clerks, billing clerks, bookkeepers, and similar kinds of office staff while creating entirely new demands for keypunch operators, programmers, statistical consultants, systems analysts,

---

[4] The following discussion is based largely upon the ideas expressed by John Kenneth Galbraith in Chapter 2 of *The New Industrial State* (Boston: Houghton Mifflin Company, 1967).

computer engineers, and so on. As electric utilities began to build billion-dollar nuclear plants to produce electricity, they found it necessary to hire large numbers of engineers with expertise in nuclear technology and to teach whole new teams of operating personnel the intricacies of running such a complex facility.

Fifth, when a product is complex or the production process is multistaged and sophisticated, the job of organizing and coordinating so many tasks and people becomes a major management task. In some industries, the trend to employ complex, sophisticated technology on a large scale to achieve maximum production efficiency accounts for the emergence of giant corporations. The technological imperative to subdivide production activities into manageable tasks, the organizational imperative to coordinate these tasks to effect a coherent result, and the market imperative to do so efficiently and profitably can often require that a firm be quite large in order to be successful. Big production tasks may well require big firms to do them efficiently—and at a lower cost to the ultimate customer.[5]

Where Technological Progress Comes From

Technological advance and innovation have their origins with the internal research efforts of business firms and from knowledge transfer among firms, industries, governments, and educational institutions. Some technological breakthroughs originate with basic research—investigations conducted without special concern for the usefulness of the results. But many technological discoveries emerge from purposive investigations where the intent is to obtain results for specific uses. Implicit in a firm's search for new or improved production techniques is the hope that successful research and development activities will increase the productive efficiency of the firm's operations, which in turn will give the firm a cost advantage and ultimately allow for a higher degree of profitability.

The application of *new* production techniques is not, however, the sole means of technological progress. Progress in the form of higher degrees of productive efficiency commonly derives from learning to apply existing techniques more effectively. Obviously enough, as firms obtain more experience with a given process, opportunities will be identified for improving the production technique. Particularly during the early stages of using a new technique is it possible to spot ways for improvement. This facet of technological progress is called *learning by doing* and is often neglected as a feature of progress and as a factor causing gradual, yet persistent shifts in a firm's production function.[6] A recent study of technological innovation in farm tractors, locomotives, tanker ships, aircraft, and digital computers concluded that the most important determinant of technological advance is learning by doing.[7] The gains came in small increments and often occurred in the course of implementing a technological breakthrough.

Experience in industry has shown that the "bugs" in a new technology

---

[5] This is in contrast to the view that the advance of large corporate enterprise is motivated largely by the urge for monopoly power and, ultimately, monopoly profits.

[6] Kenneth J. Arrow, "The Economic Implications of Learning by Doing," *Review of Economic Studies,* Vol. 29 (June 1963), pp. 155–173.

[7] Devendra Sahal, *Patterns of Technological Innovation* (London: Addison-Wesley Publishers Ltd., 1981), Chapter 6.

survive for sustained periods—even as much as three to ten years. Bits and pieces of complex processes do not always fit as neatly together as was originally envisioned; parts of the process may have to be torn down and rebuilt. Startup problems can prove thorny and time consuming. Moreover, once some firsthand experience has been gained, it is usually possible to identify numerous design and operating improvements. Also, it takes time for workers to learn their jobs well and reach peak labor efficiency. The gains from learning by doing and experience in working with a technology can be substantial as ideas bubble up and are gradually implemented. Even with a known technology, the period from initial startup to peak efficiency can take one to three years.

APPLICATIONS CAPSULE

THE EXPERIENCE CURVE: ITS IMPLICATIONS FOR PRODUCTION, COST BEHAVIOR, AND STRATEGY

The Boston Consulting Group (BCG) has in recent years gotten the attention of companies with a concept called "the experience curve." The experience curve is an extension of the well-known learning curve (a phenomenon discovered by an Air Force officer in the 1920s) which holds that the time needed to perform a task decreases by a constant percentage the more often it is done. The power of the learning curve is such that in some firms unit labor costs have declined 10% to 15% each time output is doubled.

In the late 1960s, Bruce D. Henderson, founder and president of Boston Consulting Group, observed that the learning curve principle seemed to apply to the *overall* unit costs of making a product as well as to just unit *labor* costs. On the basis of BCG's experiences with client firms, Henderson claimed that each time the number of units produced doubled there was a *tendency* for unit costs to also decline by a fixed percentage—usually in the 20% to 30% range. He attributed this decline in cost with each doubling of experience to the combined effect of learning, specialization, increased scale of operation, increased intensity of capital investment and incremental gains in "debugging" and improving the "state of the art" technology. The relationships were deemed predictable enough that the declines in unit cost, relative to volume, could be accurately plotted—BCG labeled the resulting graphical relationship "the experience curve."

In BCG's view, the experience curve can be a "powerful and universal tool for strategic planning," as well as a simple means of predicting and controlling a firm's costs. The rationale is as follows: the firm which has produced the greatest number of units and thus has the most accumulated experience will probably have the lowest average costs. If that firm also has the largest market share, then it should earn the greatest profits. Therefore, a firm should strive to gain a dominant share of the market for its products, even if that means temporarily lower profit margins.

The usefulness of the experience curve concept is that it permits the profitability of an increase in market share for a particular product to be calculated with more precision than otherwise. An experience curve based on actual statistics shows the decline in costs that can be anticipated with increases in volume and market share. And, as volume grows, prices can be reduced because of lower realized unit costs. Then it is merely a matter of weighing the worth of the increased market share against the investment it takes to achieve it and the probable reaction of competitors. The strategic implication of the experience curve effect is, according to BCG, that a company should strive to become a dominant force in the markets for its products, either by introducing new product variations, segmenting the market, or discouraging competitors by keeping prices low.

BCG found that some companies ignore these principles, even though they seem elementary. This particularly applies to a firm which finds itself with early leadership in market share of a product but then tries to translate lower costs into higher profit margins instead of lower prices; in BCG's view it is better to increase profits through greater volume rather than wider profit margins—as depicted in the accompanying graph. When price does not follow cost down, the door is open for rival firms to begin to gain on the market leader.

(a)	(b)
A relatively level introductory price, if held too long, encourages competitors to enter the market, triggering a steep price decline, or competitive shakeout.	If prices are lowered in step with unit costs as projected via the experience curve, entry may be discouraged and market share increased; profit margins are smaller, but long-run profits tend to be more secure.

One of BCG's first efforts at applying experience curve theory was with Norton Company of Worcester, Massachusetts. Norton was having trouble profitably penetrating the market for pressure-sensitive tape—a market dominated by 3M Company. Norton had successfully cut production costs and lowered prices, but still was unable to make a dent in increasing its market share. BCG's experience curve analysis showed that Norton, in effect, was chasing 3M Company down the cost curve, and that so long as 3M followed pricing and growth strategies to maximize market share, it was a fruitless struggle for Norton. Subsequently, Norton concluded that it could not compete successfully against 3M by trying to produce a broad range of products sold in a large number of markets; rather, the company decided it was better off concentrating in selected areas. In BCG's view the Norton situation illustrated an important experience curve commandment: if a firm cannot get enough market share to be cost-competitive, then it should get out of the business. Another instance where the same lesson applied was the effort of Allis-Chalmers

Company to compete against General Electric and Westinghouse in steam turbine engines. Between 1946 and 1963 Allis-Chalmer's market share was too small to give it a chance to be competitive on cost and therefore on price with large-volume manufacturers; thus, A-C's best decision was to withdraw from the industry.

Black & Decker, Texas Instruments, and Weyerhaeuser are among the companies which at one time or another have utilized the experience curve philosophy. In 1973, Texas Instruments described its strategy for expanding market share this way: "Follow an aggressive pricing policy, focus on continuing cost reduction and productivity improvement, build on shared experience gained in making related products, and keep capacity growing ahead of demand."

A word of caution, however. Before embarking on a strategy based on the experience curve effect, one should understand the full implications. The selection of a corporate/business strategy based on sustained cost reduction due to experience or scale entails a strategic emphasis on cost-price-efficiency over differentiation-market effectiveness considerations. For an "efficiency" strategy to succeed, one must affirm that there are significant numbers of customers that want low price as opposed to quality/service/product innovation/specialized use and other such differentiating features. Moreover, once it is decided to pursue an efficiency or price-cost leadership strategy, a firm has to guard against losing its ability to respond to product-technology-customer changes; strategies based on tight adherence to experience curve effects frequently result in creating a highly specialized work force and in relatively inflexible facilities and technologies. The outcome can be an increased difficulty and cost in (1) responding to changes in customer needs and product uses, (2) matching or bettering the product innovations of rival firms, (3) accommodating major changes in process technology and implementing technological breakthroughs, and (4) initiating these changes on one's own to drive the market in new directions.

Sources: "Selling Business a Theory of Economics," *Business Week,* September 8, 1973, pp. 85–90, and Derek F. Abell and John S. Hammond, *Strategic Market Planning* (Englewood Cliffs, N.J.: Prentice-Hall, Inc., 1979), pp. 106–121.

Another feature of technological progress is that its impact and rate of advance is uneven from firm to firm and industry to industry. Some firms are more able to finance invention and innovation efforts. A number of enterprises believe that a sounder, longer-lasting competitive edge can be achieved via technological superiority and innovation because technology-based competitive advantages are harder for rivals to overcome; hence, they value research and development activities and allocate a higher percentage of their budget for technological spending. In some cases, advancing technology seems to allow firms to purchase greater amounts of production capacity per dollar of investment. In other instances the dollar investment in production facilities per unit of output is increased. The trends of modern production technology are toward automation, robotics, computer-aided design techniques, computer-assisted operation of machinery and equipment, and "factory of the future" approaches that raise the capital intensity of many production processes.

At the same time, firms and industries have displayed a wide disparity in the rates with which they have adopted new technologies.[8] Taking into account a period of 15 years after the discovery of a new technology, it has been observed that some innovations languish in oblivion for as much as 10 years and then are rapidly adopted, that other innovations never mount a serious challenge to displace predecessor processes and facilities, and that still other innovations come quickly into general use and soon are being used to produce 80% or more of the total output of the industry. The differences in the diffusion rates of new production techniques have several root explanations. In the first place, some innovations are slow to be employed because although they are technologically possible, they are risky or are only marginally profitable. An innovation may require resource inputs which are not readily available or which have prohibitive costs, thereby undercutting the incentive to adopt it. Second, there usually is ample room for the managers of firms to possess different perceptions of the actual degree of technological superiority of an innovation, thus partially accounting for why one firm adopts an innovation and another does not. Unless an innovation has substantial technological and economic superiority over existing methods, firms are likely to switch to the technology only in the normal course of replacing worn-out equipment. Third, an innovation may require capital commitments beyond the reach of small firms; this may explain why larger firms are, on occasion, technologically superior to smaller firms. Fourth, small aggressive "high-technology" firms may build their whole business around spotting opportunities to be technological pioneers and thereby outcompeting lethargic, bureaucratic enterprises intent upon defending their position with an entrenched technology. What makes production technology unique as a strategic variable is its considerable power to shape the competitive rules of the marketplace.[9] A technological edge that translates either into a cost advantage or a product quality advantage can be a great equalizer, nullifying the reputation of entrenched incumbents and creating opportunities for the technologically proficient. Technological change is perhaps the single most important source of major market share changes among rival firms and probably the most frequent cause of the demise of long-standing dominant firms.

[8] F Lynn, "An Investigation of the Rate of Development and Diffusion of Technology in Our Modern Industrial Society," in *Studies Prepared for the National Commission on Technology, Automation, and Economic Progress*, Appendix Volume II: *Technology and the American Economy* (Washington, D.C., 1966); E. Mansfield, "The Speed of Response of Firms to New Techniques," *Quarterly Journal of Economics* (May 1963), pp. 290–311; E. Mansfield, "Size of Firm, Market Structure and Innovation," *Journal of Political Economy*, Vol. 71 (December 1963), pp. 556–576; John M. Blair, *Economic Concentration: Structure, Behavior, and Public Policy* (New York: Harcourt Brace Jovanovich, 1972); G. F. Ray, "The Diffusion of New Technology," *National Institute Economic Review*, May 1969, pp. 40–83; A. A. Romeo, "Interindustry and Interfirm Differences in the Rate of Diffusion of an Innovation," *Review of Economics and Statistics*, Vol. 57, No. 3 (August 1975), pp. 311–319; P. Dasgupta and J. E. Stiglitz, "Uncertainty, Industrial Structure and the Speed of R&D," *Bell Journal of Economics*, Vol. 11, No. 1 (Spring 1980), pp. 1–28.

[9] Michael E. Porter, "The Technological Dimension of Competitive Strategy," Working Paper, Harvard Graduate School of Business Administration, September 1981, p. 3.

How Technology Can Drive Competition in the Marketplace

Technological change is fully capable of intensifying competitive forces. The power of technology to shape competition and be a *driving force* in the marketplace stems from its ability to (1) affect the rivalry among incumbent competitors, (2) increase or decrease the ease of entry of potential newcomers to the industry, (3) change the bargaining power of customers, (4) change the bargaining power of buyers, and (5) increase or decrease the market threats of substitute products.[10]

Technological Change and Competitive Rivalry. To the extent that changes in production technology lower adopters' production costs, the pressure for price cutting grows. Lower-cost producers are in good position to use the attractiveness of a lower price to win customers away from rival sellers. While high-cost firms can try to defend their market shares by matching the lower prices of low-cost firms, they face the penalty of slim profit margins or even losses. Cost-reducing technological changes thus enhance the appeal of a competitive strategy based on *striving to be the low-cost producer* in the industry—especially when the nature of the changes can be kept proprietary (via secrecy or patents) and rival firms are blocked from implementing an imitative technological approach.

On the other hand, when changes in production technology result in enhanced product quality and product performance attributes, adopters may win customers away from rivals by following a *differentiation strategy* based on the appeal of "something better." The more that buyers are interested in a product's quality-performance attributes, the more successful that a differentiation strategy is likely to be and the more that early adopters/innovators can benefit from the changes in production technology—unless, of course, competitors find it easy to implement their own matching technological changes very quickly.

Whenever technological change involves a heavy dose of learning by doing and firsthand experience with the technology paves the way for pushing the technological frontiers out still faster, then if a firm can keep its learning proprietary, it stands to gain an important competitive edge from its technological advantage. It may well be possible to translate this technological edge in production into gains in buyer patronage, thereby increasing sales and market share at the expense of rivals.

Technological Change and the Ease of Potential Entry. There are a number of ways for changes in production technology to make it easier or harder for interested firms to enter an industry:

1. Technological change raises the barriers to entry when innovative production methods can be kept proprietary by the pioneering firm (or firms). When the requisite technical know-how and expertise is fairly easy to acquire and when the

---

[10] The discussion that follows is based on Porter, "The Technological Dimension of Competitive Strategy," pp. 4–8.

learning curve is not steeply sloped downward, it is easier for a new firm to enter the market insofar as the production part of the business is concerned.

2. Technological changes in production techniques can alter the capital requirements it takes to enter the industry by (a) requiring firms to invest heavily and continuously in research and development to remain abreast of fast-breaking technological developments (a strong commitment to R & D spending characterizes all firms in so-called high-technology businesses), and (b) affecting the capital investment it takes to build and equip a new production facility. The greater the capital requirements induced by changes in production technology, the higher the barriers to the entry of outside firms.

3. Changes in production technologies can (a) increase or decrease the need for after-sale service, (b) make it easier or harder to circumvent conventional distribution channels, (c) make it more or less expensive for buyers to switch their purchases to another seller, (d) make it easier or harder for a low-quality manufacturer to catch up with a high-quality manufacturer, or (e) make the learning curve steeper or flatter. Depending on the direction of these changes, entry barriers become higher or lower. Michelin's technological lead in producing high-quality, long-lasting radial tires proved significant enough in terms of cost-saving and product differentiation to allow it to overcome the otherwise high entry barriers associated with advertising (to acquire name recognition) and retail distribution (to gain access to the lucrative tire replacement market).

For the most part, whether advances in production technology act to make the entry of new firms easier or harder (and for that matter whether it solidifies the position of innovating firms) depends on the extent to which those firms which adopt the advances are able to prevent imitation by existing or would-be competitors. Normally, technological change that originates within a firm is easier to defend against imitation because it is proprietary and may even be patentable. But some innovations are extremely easy to copy—the know-how to build automatic drip coffee makers spread quickly and no manufacturer was without an ability to produce such products. Bausch and Lomb, however, was able to defend its low-cost spin-casting techniques for making soft contact lens for a period of several years before competitors came up with their own techniques for making a soft contact lens of comparable quality.

Plainly, when an innovating firm can protect a cost-saving or quality-enhancing technological innovation from imitation, it has potential for being translated into a competitive edge in the marketplace. However, even if a technological change triggers industry-wide imitation, lowers barriers to entry, and stimulates competitive rivalry, it can still boost the profit potential of all industry participants (including the innovating firm) enough to justify the cost of implementing the change.

Technological Change and the Power of Buyers. Changes in production technology have a way, sometimes, of tilting the bargaining and negotiating scale between producers and their customers. When technological change causes the products of producers to become more standardized, it becomes easier and less costly for customers to switch suppliers; the lower are customers' switching costs, the harder the bargain they can drive with sellers, favoring whichever supplier offers the best overall deal. Technological change can also make it easier or harder for customers to integrate backward; the easier it is for them to integrate backward, the more bargaining leverage they have over their suppliers. In some cases, technological change influences the basis of customer choice for one producer's product over another's. For example, if a producer of small electric motors discovers how to manufacture a motor that runs on less electricity, the energy-saving attribute of its product could help it win contracts to supply the motor as a component to air-conditioner manufacturers. Any time that technological change allows a seller's product to affect favorably the performance of a buyer's product, there emerges a market potential to create strong preferences on the part of the buyer and even to induce the buyer to pay a higher price. (Would you expect the demand for an energy-saving electric motor to be less price elastic in comparison with electric motors that take more electricity to run? Other things being equal, would not at least some buyers be willing to pay a higher price to enjoy the benefits of the energy-saving attribute?)

Technological Change and the Power of Suppliers. Just as technological change can shift the bargaining leverage between a firm and its customers, so can it affect a firm's competitive relationships with its suppliers. New production technologies can eliminate the need to purchase an otherwise essential component from powerful suppliers having key patents or proprietary technical know-how themselves. Conversely, technology can emerge in ways which, for reasons of either cost savings or product performance or both, force an industry to purchase component inputs from a supplier or group of suppliers. The development of plain-paper copying machines eliminated the need of users to purchase specially coated papers. The approval of aspartame as an artificial sweetener quickly swung the market over from the use of saccharin, which had been linked to causing a higher incidence of cancer. When changes in production technology give a firm more flexibility in using component parts or raw material inputs, it tends to gain bargaining leverage over suppliers and, as long as switching costs are low, is in a position to play off one supplier against another to get more favorable supply terms. On the other hand, technological change can act to raise the costs of switching suppliers, thus putting a firm into a weaker bargaining relationship with its suppliers.

Technological Change and the Use of Substitute Inputs. The degree to which technological change can induce a firm to substitute one input for another is a function of the relative price and performance of alternative inputs (something we will explore at length in Chapter 7) and the switching costs of changing between them. Production technology in containers has evolved to where soft-drink bottlers have the option of using aluminum cans, plastic bottles, or glass bottles—the options they have gives them leverage over suppliers. Changes in production technology have brought steel, aluminum, and plastic increasingly into competition as components for automobile bodies, engine parts, and interior trim. Aluminum has made inroads as a substitute for copper in the manufacture of electrical wiring products because of its lower price. Technological advances in the production of synthetic fibers have given polyester fabrics wrinkle-resistant, no-iron attributes and paved the way for them to substitute for cotton and wool in the garment trade. Technological change resulted in plastic being substituted for wood in the manufacture of chicken coops because plastic was more durable and easier to clean.

Technological Change and Industry Boundaries

The boundary of an industry is often imprecise because of the difficulty of distinguishing between incumbent firms and suppliers or buyers who may be partly vertically integrated and between an "industry's" product and its substitutes. (Given that glass bottles, paper cartons, tin cans, and aluminum cans are in competition with one another, is there such a thing as the glass bottle or tin can industry, or are both a part of the container industry?) Nevertheless, it is useful to understand that however one elects to try to draw an industry's boundaries, technological change can widen or shrink them.[11] Technological change that reduces the costs of manufacturing products tailored to meet market differences among nations can enlarge the geographic scope of an industry, turning a domestic market into a globally competitive industry. In telecommunications and data processing, technological change has caused heretofore separate industries to reform and merge—AT&T, once thought of as a telephone company, was driven by technological advances in long-distance data transmission to become involved in the information and data processing industry and thus evolved into a competitor of IBM and other data-processing companies. Technological developments in the manufacture of computerized energy management systems are bringing telephone companies, electrical equipment manufacturers, and communications firms into competition with electric power companies as concerns the conservation of electric energy. Technological changes which led to the ability to manufacture microwave ovens expanded the definition of the cooking appliance industry; similarly, the advent of solar water heating technology has expanded the boundaries of the "water-heating" industry.

Technology can narrow and fragment industry boundaries as well. The recent ability of TV manufacturers to make portable miniature TV sets with 1- to 3-inch screens created a product segment quite distinct from the table and console models which traditionally defined the industry. The technology of making "energy miser" light bulbs created a product-customer-market niche apart from "regular" light bulbs. (Would you expect the cross elasticity for these two products to be as high as for the cross elasticity between two brands of regular light bulbs?) The technology of making home computers and personal computers spawned an industry and set of firms quite apart from the industry of making large mainframe computers—only IBM has chosen to compete in both industries. Univac, Control Data, Honeywell, Amdahl, and Trilogy, together with IBM, are the big names in large computers, whereas IBM, Apple, Commodore, and Tandy are the big names

[11] Porter, "The Technological Dimension of Competitive Strategy," p. 9.

in small microcomputers. The computer industry has thus split into two fairly distinct industries because of technological advance.

The Impetus for Technological Innovations

Business firms, even if they are lucky enough to be sheltered temporarily from the cold winds of competition, are beset with a multitude of motivations and pressures for seeking out better production techniques and implementing promising innovations.[12] Naturally, the all-encompassing reason for the adoption of new technologies is to improve profitability and, ultimately, to safeguard a firm's market position and chances for competitive success. But such an explanation is a bit umbrellalike, for it hides the specific forces that drive investments in new technology and innovation.

First, product-related technological innovation (as distinct from innovations having to do with production technology) offers a major avenue for better meeting the needs and wants of buyers and, in the face of the competition for buyer patronage from rival firms, it becomes a virtual necessity for maintaining one's current market position. Firms consistently attempt to outmaneuver their rivals by introducing products with more attractive attributes—a lower price, higher quality, more after-sale service, greater durability, longer warranties, more appealing design, improved convenience, and so on. To defend successfully against such competitive tactics, a firm must be active in developing new and improved products that can win consumer favor, protect against shifts to substitute products, and build up the firm's reputation. In addition, market pressures for quality improvements, for product standardization in terms of sizes or performance, and for lower prices dictate a progressive and efficient technology.

Adverse developments in the markets for a firm's resource inputs are also a source of pressure for innovation and technological change. A portion of the trend to automate production originates from the desire of firms to escape rising labor costs and higher raw material prices associated with natural resource scarcity. Dwindling supplies of natural resources precipitate searches for technological remedies in the form of substitute resources or the ability to use lower-quality resource inputs (such as lower grades of ore). Rising fuel oil prices, rising electric rates, and natural gas scarcity have been major factors in inducing many manufacturers to install energy-saving equipment as fast as possible. The solutions to both energy and environmental pollution are clearly technological in character. In the same vein, human safety considerations and the chances of human error provide a strong motivation for technological change in some industries. Then, too, on occasion, price competition among suppliers of new capital equipment can so reduce the cost of an innovation as to make it feasible on a broader scale.

---

[12] Even firms with a stranglehold on the production of an item cannot long afford to be complacent about technological developments. Given that the threat of potential substitutes looms over every market and that technological frontiers are being pushed out along broad fronts and at accelerating rates, it is not likely that many firms, even monopolies, will choose to risk the fates of technological stagnation and obsolescence.

From an internal standpoint, the operating benefits of relieving bottlenecks in the production process can serve to motivate firms to seek technological solutions to their problems.

Rare is the firm or industry that can insulate itself successfully from the pervasive pressures to remain technologically up to date in the long run. Technical obsolescence spells almost certain competitive disaster for a firm, subject only to the propensity of government to rescue it by the granting of subsidies, protective tariffs, or regulation. On the positive side, technological prowess and virtuosity can be used to win a competitive advantage based on either lower cost or a uniquely differentiated product offering. If a firm can develop production technologies that give it a lower delivered cost of its product to the customer and can protect the source of this technological advantage from imitation, it can build a defensible competitive position and earn above-average profits. Similarly, if a firm can use technology to achieve unique product attributes, it can also have a defense against competitive forces and perhaps earn above-average profits.

TECHNOLOGICAL LEADERSHIP OR FOLLOWERSHIP?

The conceptual distinction between technological leadership and technological followership is clear enough but the two postures are empty strategic options unless they are related to their impact on the marketplace and to the sources of competitive advantage. The strategic objectives of technological leadership are usually to use technological innovation as either the vehicle for becoming the low-cost producer in the industry or the vehicle for introducing unique attributes into one's product offering that enhance its performance and differentiate it from rivals' products. The strategic appeal of being a technological follower is to try to learn from the leader's experiences, altering and adopting the new technology further to outmaneuver the leader in becoming the low-cost producer or in fine-tuning the product offering to better meet customers' needs.[13] In principle, therefore, either leadership or followership can be routes to securing a competitive advantage.

Choosing Whether to Lead or Follow

The choice of whether to pursue leadership or followership is not a simple matter. A variety of considerations have to be taken into account. In general, the attractiveness of technological leadership is governed by:[14]

1. *The extent of the technological opportunity*. High technological opportunity heightens the chance to create a significant cost or differentiation gap vis-à-vis rivals.

---

[13] Excluded from consideration here is the passive-follower type of firm, which knowingly or unknowingly ignores the competitive aspect of technological change.

[14] Porter, ''The Technological Dimension of Competitive Strategy,'' pp. 18–23.

2. *The uniqueness of a firm's technological skills.* Leadership is favored when a firm's technical expertise gives it an edge in trying to open up a technological gap; the benefits of leadership are fleeting when competitors have essentially equivalent technical skills and probably match any technological gains through parallel investments. Unique technical skills may derive from superior talent, experienced R & D capability, an ability to access technological help from customers or suppliers, accumulated technical experience, and patent protection.

3. *The fraction of the industry's technology that flows into the industry from suppliers, customers, or other industries sharing the same basic technology.* The risk of leadership increases the more that technological change flows into the industry from outside sources; this is because competitor's access to technology is decoupled from their internal technical skills and investment in R & D.

4. *The nature and size of any first-mover advantages. First-mover advantages* are factors which allow a leader to translate a technology edge into other competitive advantages that persist even if the technology gap is later closed. Potential first-mover advantages which can accrue to a technological leader include (a) being able to establish an identity and reputation as the premier producer (leading to repeat purchases by old customers and the attraction of new customers aware of this reputation) and giving the leader a differential image, (b) the existence of switching costs (if the leader makes the sale to the customer, the existence of switching costs gives the firm an advantage in gaining the customer's repeat business even if its product no longer is superior to rivals'), and (c) the existence of a steep learning or experience curve. If first-mover advantages are sizable, the leader may need to open up a one-time technological advantage to reap a substantial long-term competitive advantage. However, if first-mover advantages are slight, it becomes important to maintain technical leadership through continued innovation.

5. *Whether the movement of technology progresses along a continuous path or whether technological advance is likely to entail a shift to an entirely new path.* When technological changes involve continuity, a leader stands to retain any first-mover advantages. But when technological changes are discontinuous and produce shifts to new paths, the leader's past learning is nullified and existing facilities are obsolete—making the payoff for leadership risky and uncertain.

As the foregoing discussion hints, there are times when being a technological follower has appeal:[15]

1. *When investments in a new technology are specialized and inflexible and the pace of change in production technology is fast.* Rapid-fire technological developments, which frequently characterize young industries with immature technologies, allow followers to leapfrog leaders rather easily and quickly. Any time that investments in new plants, equipment, training, and specialized personnel are specific to a particular technique and are costly to modify, further techno-

---

[15] *Ibid.,* pp. 21–25.

logical developments require reinvestment by the leader, perhaps causing the total costs to the leader to exceed a follower's investment costs. Timely followership in such instances can be more attractive than striving to be a trailblazing pioneer.

2.   *When customer needs and purchasing behavior change quickly.* A leader's first-mover advantages are often nullified by changes in customer needs or purchasing behavior since neither repeat nor first-time buyers are likely to place as much value on past dealings. Buyer loyalty can thus be low and, in fact, an old leader can actually be disadvantaged if its identity and reputation is linked strongly with the old needs and ways.

3.   *When the nature of technological change involves sporadic shifts from one technological path to another technological path rather than moving predictably along a single path.* Here, any advantage the technological leader has is transitory and the competitive edge that the leader earns may cost more than it is worth, given that a new breakthrough on another technological branch can shift future technological and market opportunities in fairly dramatic ways.

4.   *When there is great uncertainty present about the appropriate technological direction and the ability to achieve a desired technological breakthrough.* In some industries, there can be several competing technologies with no clear indication as to which one will develop into the "best" approach or the "dominant design." There is risk in trying to be a leader and having to bet heavily on one technological approach or another (pursuing them all at once is usually not feasible); a cautious "wait and watch" strategy predicated on following quickly when the uncertainty clears and trying to improve upon the leader's efforts (while avoiding the leader's mistakes and costly experiences) becomes attractive in comparison.

5.   *When the leader's technological efforts are readily copied.* Occasions arise when new technology in an industry spreads quickly and imitation costs are low. This can occur because the technology cannot be either patented or kept proprietary and thus readily finds its way into the public domain through the activities of trade associations and trade publications, on-site inspection of new facilities and pieces of equipment, reverse engineering (where rivals tear down a leader's products part by part to learn how it was designed and engineered), and information gained from the leader's suppliers, customers, and ex-employees. In such instances, the lead-time advantage of the technological pioneer is shortened enough that followers are not really at a competitive disadvantage and are in the enviable position of being able to avoid the extra cost of pioneering (as concerns costly mistakes and false starts, redesign and reengineering, testing, and working out the bugs).

6.   *When there are major market barriers to be overcome in making the innovation a market success.* The trials and tribulations of exercising technological leadership may entail hurdling such barriers as the need to secure regulatory approval, the difficulty of educating customers to the benefits, and the need to make support investments in repair and service personnel, in sources of supply for new components and inputs, and in distribution channels. Overcoming these obstacles can be time consuming and expensive enough to make technological followership a comfortable, acceptable strategy as compared to leadership.

One other technology strategy option deserves mention and that is licensing. *Technology licensing* is a device for leaders to secure additional profits from their technological investments and for followers to gain access to a leader's technology achievements without investing in imitation. Where a leader can license technology to other firms, charging either a fixed fee or a percentage royalty, it increases the profitability and attractiveness of a leadership strategy. Although licensing a follower reduces or eliminates the technology gap between the leader and the follower, there are times when the leader can derive substantial benefits from having competitors with the same technology. This can occur in the case where (1) there are many competing technologies and the industry as a whole would benefit from a common technological approach, (2) the industry is young and the products of rival firms are so different that consumers are confused and would benefit from a more standardized product offering, and (3) the product is so new that having competitors would help develop the industry and expand the market for the leader's product. From a follower's standpoint, licensing can be attractive when licensing costs are below the cost of imitation; the follower's biggest disadvantage is that the follower is locked into the leader's technology in a way that may impede its own strategy for building a competitive edge.

SUMMARY AND CONCLUSIONS

Production, as commonly used in economics, refers to any activity that creates value. Production includes virtually all phases of economic activity except consumption. Four types of production activities are identifiable: unique-product production, rigid mass production, flexible mass production, and process production. A production function indicates, in quantitative terms, the relationship between the unit input of resources and the unit output of goods or services per period of time.

Technological change has major consequences for a firm's production function. Not only can a new technological "recipe" result in important cost savings but it also can open up opportunities to improve product performance and otherwise allow a firm successfully to differentiate its product from those of rival firms. As a consequence, changes in technology serve as an important way for firms to build a technology-based competitive advantage. Choosing whether to be a technological leader or a follower thus becomes an integral aspect of a firm's competitive strategy.

The power of technological change is readily visible in the marketplace. Innovative production technologies can alter the competitive rules of the marketplace and also serve as a great equalizer, nullifying the advantages of incumbent firms, opening up competitive opportunities for followers and newcomers, and shifting the bargaining leverage a firm has with suppliers and customers. Analyzing the competitive impact of technological changes is, therefore, an integral part of the economics of the firm.

SUGGESTED READINGS

ARROW, K. J., "The Economic Implications of Learning by Doing," *Review of Economic Studies*, Vol. 29 (June 1962), pp. 155–173.

BLAKE, S. P., *Managing for Responsive Research and Development* (San Francisco: W. H. Freeman and Company, Publishers, 1978).

DASGUPTA, P., AND J. E. STIGLITZ, "Uncertainty, Industrial Structure and the Speed of R&D," *Bell Journal of Economics*, Vol. 11, No. 1 (Spring 1980), pp. 1–28.

KAMIEN, M. I., AND N. L. SCHWARTZ, *Market Structure and Innovation* (Cambridge: Cambridge University Press, 1982).

KELLEY, P., AND M. KRANSBERG, eds., *Technological Innovation: A Critical Review of Current Knowledge*, (San Francisco: San Francisco Press, 1978).

MANSFIELD, E., *The Economics of Technological Change* (New York: W. W. Norton & Company, Inc., 1968), Chapters 2–4.

———, *et al.*, *The Production and Application of New Industrial Technology* (New York: W. W. Norton & Company, Inc., 1977), Chapters 1 and 10.

NELSON, R., M. PECK, AND E. KALOCHEK, *Technology, Economic Growth and Public Policy* (Washington, D. C.: The Brookings Institution, 1967), Chapters 1–5.

SAHAL, D., *Patterns of Technological Innovation* (London: Addison-Wesley Publishers Ltd., 1981).

SCHERER, F. M., *Industrial Market Structure and Economic Performance*, 2nd ed. (Boston: Houghton Mifflin Company, 1980), Chapters 15 and 16.

QUESTIONS FOR DISCUSSION

1. What is a production function? What are its key economic properties?
2. Describe the effects that technological change can have upon a firm's production function.
3. How have technological advances changed the basic nature of production activity during the course of the twentieth century?
4. Why is it important for business firms to keep their production techniques close to the frontier of technological know-how?
5. Explain how technology can be a driving force that shapes competition and the way a market functions. Be specific in indicating how technological change can (a) affect the rivalry among incumbent competitors, (b) change barriers to entry into the industry, (c) influence the bargaining power a firm has with its suppliers and its customers, and (d) affect the competitive pressures from substitute products.
6. How can changes in technology affect the boundaries between industries? Cite examples.
7. What incentives do firms have to be technologically progressive?
8. Under what circumstances is technological leadership an attractive strategy?
9. When may being a technological follower be attractive?
10. How can a firm use technology to create a competitive advantage?

7

THE SUPPLY SIDE
OF THE MARKETPLACE
Production efficiency and returns to scale

Having indicated the influence of technology on production processes and competition, we now turn to an in-depth examination of the economic principles underlying input-output relationships. Attention will be focused upon the conditions for achieving peak production efficiency and for optimizing the mix of resource inputs in both the short run and the long run. Analyzing the principles of production provides the foundation for understanding the economics of cost functions and cost behavior.

FIXED AND VARIABLE INPUTS

To facilitate the exposition of production analysis it is customary to classify all resource inputs into two artificial categories—fixed inputs and variable inputs. A *fixed input* is defined as one whose quantity cannot *readily* be changed in the short run in response to a desire to alter a firm's rate of output. Admittedly, inputs are seldom fixed in an absolute sense, even for very short periods of time. Practically, though, the costs of varying the use of an input may be prohibitive. Even where they are not, changing the quantity of an input may be severely impeded by the current in-place technology, by the unavailability of additional supplies of certain inputs, and/or by the length of time it takes to effect acceptable changes in their usage.[1] Examples of fixed inputs include major pieces of equipment and machinery, the space available for productive activity (buildings, factory size), and key managerial personnel.

In contrast, a *variable input* is one whose usage rate may be altered quite easily in response to a desire to raise or lower the volume of output. Resource inputs whose quantity can be easily varied within a very short time include electric power, most raw materials, transportation services, and the labor services of production and office employees. With respect to raw materials, however, there are a number of products (aspirin, cake mixes, paint, liquid bleach) where the inputs can be changed only in some fixed proportion to one another and to output; otherwise, the product's character is fundamentally changed.

THE SHORT RUN AND THE LONG RUN

Along with the concepts of fixed and variable inputs, economists distinguish between the short run and the long run. The *short run* is a time period so short that the firm is constrained from varying the quantity of its fixed inputs (major pieces of equipment, key managerial personnel, and space for production activities). Yet the short run is long enough a time period to allow for variation in the firm's variable inputs. Hence, in the short run a firm's output capability must be accomplished exclusively through changes in its usage of variable inputs.

The *long run* is defined as a period of time sufficiently long to allow *all* inputs to be varied; no inputs are fixed, including technology. Thus, in the long run a firm's output capability can be increased or decreased by altering technology or resource input usage in whatever way may be most advantageous to the firm. For instance, whereas in the short run a firm may be forced to expand production by operating its facilities at overtime rates, in the long run the firm may find it more economical to construct larger facilities or install capital-intensive machinery and avoid overtime wage rates.

The length of the short run varies from industry to industry. In industries where the quantities of fixed inputs are small or where the character of production permits fixed inputs to be changed readily, the short run may not extend beyond a period of several months. The apparel, mobile home, and food-processing industries are cases in point. For other industries the short run may be 1 to 3 years—automobiles, coal mining, aircraft, aluminum, and paper products. In the electric utility industry it takes as much as 6 to 10 years to design, construct, and start up a new generating plant.

The production significance of differentiating between fixed and variable inputs and between the short and long runs should now be more apparent. The quantities of a firm's fixed inputs determine the size of the firm's plant or its *scale of operations*. The scale of a firm's plant sets an upper limit to the amount of

---

[1] Actually, fixed inputs are not always as fixed as it might first appear. While a firm may possess a given amount of fixed input, say 10 machines, the operating pattern for the machines can be "changed" by altering (1) the speed at which the machines are operated, (2) the number of hours per day the machines are used, and (3) the number of days of operation per year. However, a firm may not have full flexibility in choosing among these options due to the constraints imposed by maintenance requirements, union work rules, and wage differentials among work shifts.

output per period of time that the firm is capable of producing in the short run. Output can, in the short run, be varied up to that limit by increasing or decreasing the usage of variable inputs in conjunction with the amount of fixed input. The limits of output can, in the long run, be raised or lowered by changing the scale of production, the technological character of the production process, and the utilization rate of any and all inputs.

SHORT-RUN PRODUCTION FUNCTIONS

The short-run production function for a firm indicates the output obtainable from combining various amounts of variable inputs with a given amount of fixed input. As stated earlier, the production function may be expressed symbolically as

$$Q = f(X_a, X_b, X_c, \ldots, X_n),$$

where Q refers to the quantity of output per unit of time and is a function of specific quantities of inputs $X_a, X_b, X_c, \ldots, X_n$.

The fundamental problem in the study of short-run production functions is to estimate the quantity of output that can be produced by combining alternative amounts of variable inputs with the available amount of fixed inputs. As an example, consider a firm operating a plant of some given size and having a fixed amount of equipment and managerial capability. Since we shall have occasion to refer to the amount of these fixed inputs, suppose that we arbitrarily designate the amounts of fixed inputs for our fictional firm's plant as constituting 2 "units." Now suppose that we conduct an experiment in which successively larger doses of variable input are combined with the 2 units of fixed input and the resulting output rates are observed and recorded.[2]

A Tabular Illustration

From Table 7-1 we see that when progressively larger doses of variable input are combined with the available fixed inputs, the quantity of output rises more rapidly at first, then more slowly, reaches a maximum, and begins to decline. The exact change in output associated with the use of one more unit of variable input per period is known in economics as the *marginal product of the variable input*.[3]

---

[2] Strictly speaking, the different amounts of variable input are best conceived as being applied to different plants of equal size and type, rather than to a progressively larger application of additional units of variable input to a single plant. Practically, however, real world implementation of this concept of measuring a firm's production function is usually not possible—many identical plants may simply not exist. The sensible alternative, therefore, is to observe the relation between input and output for a single plant operation at various points in time where the rates of variable input usage are different.

[3] It cannot be inferred from the definition of marginal product that the change in output is due just to the efforts and contribution of variable input. An increase in variable input by itself is not *the cause* of changes in output; output changes as a consequence of having more units of variable input employed in conjunction with the fixed input. An example may serve to clarify this point. Suppose a firm has five pieces of machinery, each requiring one skilled operator. As the firm increases its labor inputs from one to five skilled operators to run the five machines, it is clear that the resulting output gains are not due solely to the productive powers of labor but rather are the joint products of using more labor with the five available machines. Economists, however, customarily refer to the gains in output from using more labor as being the marginal product of labor, despite the fact that gains in output from employing more units of labor reflect the *joint* contributions of labor and the other inputs with which it is combined.

TABLE 7-1. Data for a Hypothetical Short-Run Production Function

(1) Units of Fixed Input	(2) Units of Variable Input (X)	(3) Quantity of Output $Q = 21X + 9X^2 - X^3$	(4) Discrete Marginal Product of Variable Input	(5) Continuous Marginal Product of Variable Input $MP = 21 + 18X - 3X^2$	(6) Average Product of Variable Input $AP_{vi} = 21 + 9X - X^2$	(7) Average Product of Fixed Input $AP_{fi} = \dfrac{21X + 9X^2 - X^3}{2}$
2	0	0	—	—	—	0
2	1	29	29	36	29	14.5
2	2	70	41	45	35	35
2	3	117	47	48	39	58.5
2	4	164	47	45	41	82
2	5	205	41	36	41	102.5
2	6	234	29	21	39	117
2	7	245	11	0	35	122.5
2	8	232	-13	-27	29	116
2	9	189	-43	-60	21	94.5

The change in the quantity of output per period of time resulting from a 1-*unit change* in the quantity of that input used per period of time is defined as *discrete marginal product*. In our example the values for discrete marginal product are shown in column (4) of Table 7-1; the reader should verify their derivation. Alternatively, marginal product can be calculated from the first derivative of the equation expressing the mathematical relation between the flow of output and the flow of variable input.[4] Hence, if the relationship between the quantity of output (Q) and the units of variable input (X) is

$$Q = 21X + 9X^2 - X^3,$$

then the marginal product of the variable input is

$$MP = \frac{dQ}{dX} = 21 + 18X - 3X^2.$$

This concept of marginal product is called *continuous marginal product* to distinguish it from discrete marginal product. Continuous marginal product represents the rate of change in total output as the rate of variable input changes per period of time and can be calculated in the manner shown in column (5) of Table 7-1.[5] In a mathematical sense, marginal product is meaningful only for inputs whose rate of usage can be changed; thus, there is no such thing as the marginal product of fixed inputs, since fixed inputs by definition do not change in the short run.

The average product of the variable input is shown in column (6) of Table 7-1. It is found by dividing the output rate by the required number of units of variable input:

$$AP_{vi} = \frac{\text{units of output}}{\text{units of variable input}}.$$

Thus, if $Q = 21X + 9X^2 - X^3$, where X represents the units of variable input, the expression for AP_{vi} becomes

$$AP_{vi} = \frac{Q}{X} = \frac{21X + 9X^2 - X^3}{X} = 21 + 9X - X^2.$$

---

[4] Should more than one variable input be present in the expression defining the short-run production function, the relevant concept of the marginal product of an input is the partial derivative of the production function. See Mathematical Capsule 7.

[5] The definitions and concepts of discrete and continuous marginal product are analogous to our earlier definitions of marginal utility and marginal revenue. In treating marginal product as a continuous function, we assume that both variable input and output can be varied by extremely small amounts.

Similarly, the average product of the fixed input (shown in column 7 of Table 7-1) is defined as the quantity of output divided by the available units of fixed input:

$$AP_{fi} = \frac{\text{units of output}}{\text{units of fixed input}}.$$

MATHEMATICAL CAPSULE 7

DETERMINING MARGINAL PRODUCT WHEN THE PRODUCTION FUNCTION IS COMPOSED OF SEVERAL VARIABLE INPUTS

In most production processes the quantity of output in the short run is a function of several variable inputs such that

$$Q = f(X_a, X_b, X_c, \ldots, X_n).$$

The marginal product of a specific variable input, say X_a, is found by observing the impact upon Q of a change in the usage of X_a, when the quantities of the remaining variable inputs $(X_b, X_c, \ldots, X_n)$ are held constant. Mathematically, this procedure involves determining the *partial derivative* of the production function with respect to X_a.

Suppose that the production function for a commodity is

$$Q = 7X_a^2 + 8X_b^2 - 5X_aX_b.$$

We can find the effect of a change in the rate of usage of resource input X_a when the usage of X_b is held constant by treating X_b as a constant and differentiating the production function with respect to X_a—this gives the partial derivative of Q with respect to X_a and is symbolized as $\partial Q/\partial X_a$. Thus, we obtain

$$\frac{\partial Q}{\partial X_a} = 14X_a - 5X_b,$$

which is the expression for the marginal product of input X_a. In economic terms it may be interpreted precisely to mean the rate of change in output as the usage of input X_a changes, the usage of input X_b remaining constant. In less formal terms, the expression for the marginal product of X_a tells us how changes in the use of X_a will affect the quantity of output provided X_b does not change.

Similarly, the marginal product for input X_b is the partial derivative of the production function with respect to X_b, or

$$\frac{\partial Q}{\partial X_b} = 16X_b - 5X_a.$$

It shows the impact of changes in X_b upon Q when X_a is held constant.

EXERCISES

1. Determine the marginal product functions for labor (L) and capital (C) for each of the following production functions.
   (a) $Q = 18L^2 + 14C^3 - L^2C.$
   (b) $Q = 10L^{0.5}C^{0.5}.$
   (c) $Q = 17L + 9C + 0.6L^{0.4}C^{0.5}.$

> **2.** Determine the values for MP_L and MP_C at $L = 10$ and $C = 20$ for each of the following production functions.
>   **(a)** $Q = 36L - L^2 + 20C - LC$.
>   **(b)** $Q = 5L^2 + 4LC + 6C^2 - 8(L/C)$.

Given that $Q = 21X + 9X^2 - X^3$ and that 2 units of fixed input are present, AP_{fi} can be calculated as follows:

$$AP_{fi} = \frac{Q}{FI} = \frac{21X + 9X^2 - X^3}{2}.$$

Alternatively, AP_{fi} can be computed by dividing the output values in column (3) by the number of units of fixed input given in column (1), yielding the values in column (7) of Table 7-1.

In our example, observe that marginal product increases for the first 3 units of variable input to its maximum value of 48 [column (5)]. Beyond 3 units of variable input marginal product diminishes, reaching zero at an input of 7 units per period of time and becoming increasingly negative past 8 units of variable input. The reason for this pattern of change in marginal product derives from the *principle of diminishing marginal returns*.

The principle of diminishing marginal returns has to do with the direction and the rate of change in output when increasingly larger amounts of a variable input per period of time are combined with a constant amount of fixed input. Specifically, the principle is that *as the amount of a variable input is increased by equal increments and combined with a specified amount of fixed inputs, a point will be reached (sometimes more quickly and sometimes less quickly) where the resulting increases in the quantity of output will get smaller and smaller.* In other words, as more and more variable input is added to a given fixed input, eventually the marginal product of variable input will begin to diminish. Furthermore, should the amounts of variable input applied to a given fixed input get large enough, output will reach a maximum and thereafter may *decrease* if still additional amounts of variable input are utilized.

Prior to reaching the inevitable point of diminishing marginal returns, the gains in output from larger applications of variable input may either increase at an increasing rate such that marginal product of variable input increases, or the increases in output may increase at a constant rate such that marginal product is constant. For example, in Table 7-1 the first 3 units of variable input cause the quantity of output to increase at an increasing rate. This may occur because when a small amount of variable input is combined with a relatively large dose of fixed input the fixed-variable input proportions are likely to be out of balance, causing production to be inefficient.[6] Hence, whenever variable input is being used in too

---

    [6] Examples of this condition are commonplace in manufacturing. Suppose that a plant of a given size has been designed to operate with 400 employees. If an attempt is made to operate with 50 employees, the multiplicity of functions to be performed by each employee with the attendant inefficiencies in execution, coupled with the time lost in changing from job to job, will no doubt cause output to be more than proportionately *less* than might be gotten, say, from 100 employees. Thus, up to some point, equal increments in the amount of labor used may well produce successively larger gains in the quantity of output.

sparse a proportion to the available fixed input, adding more units of variable input diminishes the associated inefficiencies and allows output to increase at an increasing rate.

A Graphic Illustration

The hypothetical data in Table 7-1 are graphed in Fig. 7-1. Since output is a function of variable input, output is the dependent variable and variable input is the independent variable. Accordingly, output per period of time is plotted on the vertical axis, and the units of variable input are plotted on the horizontal axis.

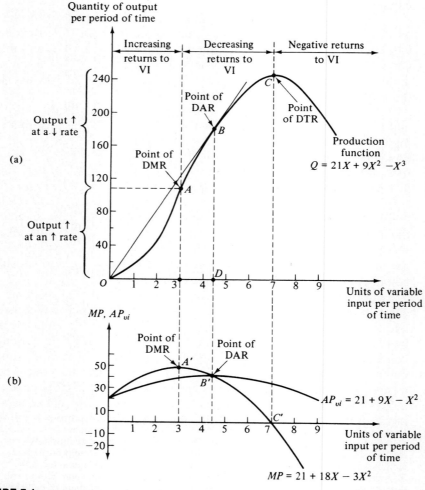

FIGURE 7-1
Short-run production function and its corresponding marginal and average product functions

Joining the points by a smooth curve yields a graphical illustration of the firm's production function for the good [Fig. 7-1(a)].

The production function of Fig. 7-1(a) conveys the same input-output relation as does the production schedule in Table 7-1.[7] Note that the production function increases at an increasing rate up to a level of usage of variable input of 3 units per period of time; accordingly, we may say that *increasing returns to the variable input* exist over this range. By this is meant that the increases in output are *more* than proportional to the increases in variable input. As the possibilities for increasing returns to variable input are exhausted, the point of diminishing marginal returns (DMR) is encountered—a point which, mathematically, corresponds to the "inflection point" on the production function. Beyond this point, heavier usage of variable inputs results in a declining marginal product (i.e., extra units of variable input yield successively smaller amounts of extra output). The curvature of the production function becomes such that it rises more slowly (i.e., output increases at a decreasing rate). Thus, between a level of usage of 3 and 7 units of variable input per period of time there exist *decreasing returns to variable input,* or, to put it another way, the increases in the quantity of output are *less* than proportional to the increases in variable input. Output is maximum when 7 units of variable input per period of time are combined with the fixed input. No further increases in output are possible without employing additional amounts of the fixed inputs in the production process. This is not feasible in the short run. For reference purposes we may label the maximum output rate in the short run as the point of *diminishing total returns* (DTR). Should more than 7 units of variable input per period of time be used in conjunction with the fixed inputs, the quantity of output would actually fall. The rationale for this derives from the existence of a limit to which fixed inputs can accommodate additional variable input and still yield additional output. Past 7 units, variable inputs are present in uneconomically large proportions relative to the available fixed input, and growing inefficiencies in resource usage cause total output to fall.

The marginal product curve corresponding to the production function described above is shown in Fig. 7-1(b). The data for deriving the shape and position of the marginal product curve comes from columns (4) and (5) in Table 7-1. Since by the marginal product of the variable input we mean the rate of change in the quantity of output as the usage rate of variable input changes, the slope of the production function at any variable input rate is the value of marginal product at that quantity of variable input. When the quantity of output is increasing at an

---

[7] In this example the production function is shown as beginning from the origin of the diagram. This is the case only when the variable input under consideration is absolutely essential to the production of the item and when output may be obtained immediately upon applying variable input. Needless to say, these characteristics do not typify all production processes or all kinds of variable inputs. For variable inputs not essential to the production of the item, the production function may begin above the origin (installing carpets in an office building to reduce noise and to enhance the esthetic quality of the working conditions, thereby boosting employee productivity is a case in point). In other situations no output may be forthcoming until substantial amounts of variable input are used with the available fixed inputs. For example, five people in a huge pulp and paper mill can produce nothing. Ten people can do little better. Where a minimum complement of variable input is requisite for any production to take place, the production function or total product curve begins to the right of the origin and at that point on the horizontal axis corresponding to the minimum input requirement.

increasing rate (as it does up to a level of 3 units of variable input), marginal product is increasing. Marginal product attains its maximum value at the point of diminishing marginal returns, which in this example is at 3 units of variable input where $MP = 48$ [point A in Fig. 7-1(a)]. Between 3 and 7 units of variable input, where the quantity of output increases at a decreasing rate, the values of marginal product are positive but diminishing. At 7 units of variable input, total output is maximum, and marginal product is zero. Beyond 7 units, additional units of variable input cause output to decline, meaning that in this range the marginal product of variable input is negative. The negative values for marginal product in the range beyond 7 units reflect the fact that the production function is declining and therefore has a negative slope.

The average product curve for the variable input originates from the same point as does the marginal product curve (in this instance, both assume a value of 21 when $X = 0$). From this point the average product curve rises until it reaches its maximum value at 4.5 units of variable input. It subsequently declines, conceivably becoming zero should variable input ever be added to such an extent that output falls back to zero. The average product curve has a definite relationship to the marginal product curve. As long as the value for MP is greater than the value for AP_{vi}, the average product curve will rise. The value for MP equals the value of AP_{vi} when AP_{vi} is at its maximum value. When the value for MP is less than the value for AP_{vi}, the average product curve falls. The explanation for this relationship is rooted in simple arithmetic; an example may suffice to illustrate it.

Consider a student who after 2 years of college has managed to earn a 2.5 overall grade average in her coursework. If *this term* she earns a 2.8 average in her courses, her new *overall* grade average will rise above the 2.5 level. However, if she earns a 2.0 average *this term,* her overall grade average will *fall* below 2.5. The overall grade average of our hypothetical student is analogous to average product, while the grade average this term is analogous to marginal product. Thus, for average product to be increasing, marginal product must exceed the average. For average product to be decreasing, marginal product must be less than average product.

The rate of variable input usage at which the AP_{vi} curve reaches its maximum value can be ascertained directly from the graph of the production function. Suppose that a ray is drawn from the origin to point B on the production function in Fig. 7-1(a). Since average product equals the quantity of output divided by the units of variable input employed, AP_{vi} at point B equals distance BD (the quantity of output) divided by distance OD (the number of units of variable input), or, more simply, BD/OD, which in turn is equivalent to the slope of the ray OB. As the number of units of variable input increases from 0 to 4.5 units (point D), the slopes of rays drawn from the origin to points on the production function become progressively greater. Since AP_{vi} is mathematically equivalent to the slope of a ray from the origin to the corresponding point on the production function, AP_{vi} is maximum at that value of variable input where the slope of such a ray is steepest. This occurs when the ray from the origin is just *tangent* to the production function (point B) or at 4.5 units of variable input. We shall designate the peak of the AP_{vi} curve as the point of diminishing *average* returns to variable input (DAR).

MATHEMATICAL CAPSULE 8

THE RELATIONSHIP BETWEEN AN INPUT'S MARGINAL AND AVERAGE PRODUCTS

That an input's marginal and average products are necessarily equal at the maximum value of average product is easily proven mathematically. Let the production function be of the general form $Q = f(X)$. Then,

$$AP_{vi} = \frac{Q}{X} = \frac{f(X)}{X},$$

$$MP = \frac{dQ}{dX} = f'(X).$$

From Mathematical Capsule 1 in Chapter 3 we know that the condition which must be satisfied for AP_{vi} to be maximum is that the slope of AP_{vi} be zero. This in turn means that the derivative of the AP_{vi} equation must be zero:

$$\frac{dAP_{vi}}{dX} = 0.$$

Using the rule of calculus for finding the derivative of a quotient, and calculating dAP_{vi}/dX, where $AP_{vi} = f(X)/X$, gives

$$\frac{dAP_{vi}}{dX} = \frac{X \cdot f'(X) - f(X)}{X^2}.$$

For dAP_{vi}/dX to equal zero requires that the numerator of the expression above be equal to zero, or that

$$X \cdot f'(X) - f(X) = 0.$$

Rewriting the condition above yields

$$f'(X) = \frac{f(X)}{X}.$$

Since $f'(X) = MP$ and $f(X)/X = AP_{vi}$, the input rate that makes AP_{vi} maximum is also the value of X at which $MP = AP_{vi}$.

Furthermore, if the expression for dAP_{vi}/dX is rewritten as

$$\frac{dAP_{vi}}{dX} = \frac{f'(X) - [f(X)/X]}{X},$$

it becomes apparent that the slope of the average product function will be positive if $f'(X)$, marginal product, is greater than $f(X)/X$, average product. This reflects the fact that as long as the value for marginal product exceeds the value for average product, the average product curve is rising. Conversely, it is clear that if marginal product is less than average product, the slope of the average product curve is negative and the value of average product is declining.

Some Alternative Types of Short-Run Production Functions

A firm's production function need not exhibit the shape illustrated in Fig. 7-1. Input-output relationships are such that other shapes are quite common. We shall look at three alternative shapes of production functions and their distinctive properties.

Constant Returns to Variable Input. As we shall verify later in this chapter, some production processes have qualities such that the firm's short-run production function is linear over the *normal* ranges of output. A linear production function, along with its corresponding marginal and average product curves, is shown in Fig. 7-2. The general equation for a linear input-output relation is

$$Q = a + bX,$$

where Q is the quantity of output, X represents the units of variable input per period of time, and a and b are constants. For the production function shown in Fig. 7-2(a) it is assumed that variable input is essential for production to occur and that some output can be obtained as soon as variable input is combined with

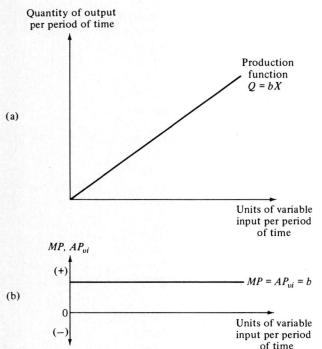

(a)

(b)

FIGURE 7-2
Production function characterized by a phase of constant returns to variable input

the available units of fixed input. The effect of this rather reasonable assumption (and we shall continue to use it in the succeeding illustrations) is that the production function begins at the origin and the value of a in the equation for the production function is zero, thereby reducing the equation of the production function to

$$Q = bX.$$

From the preceding definitions of average and marginal product, we can write

$$AP_{vi} = \frac{Q}{X} = \frac{bX}{X} = b$$

and

$$MP = \frac{dQ}{dX} = b.$$

Thus, in the case of a linear production function both marginal and average product are constants and $MP = AP_{vi}$. These relationships are illustrated in Fig. 7-2(b).

The key properties of the production function in Fig. 7-2(a) and its corresponding MP and AP_{vi} curves are as follows. A linear production function means that as additional units of variable input are combined with the given units of fixed input, the quantity of output increases at a *constant rate*—there exist *constant returns to variable input*. Each unit of variable input contributes just as much to total output as did the previous unit and as will the next unit. Since successive units of variable input are *equally* productive, their marginal products are necessarily equal. This factor makes the production function linear, because marginal product is the rate of change in the quantity of output as variable input changes. When this rate is constant, the production function is linear. Moreover, with additional units of variable input being equally productive, the average product of the units of variable input is itself a constant value equal in size to the value of the marginal product of the variable input.

It does not follow, however, that a linear production function contradicts the principle of diminishing marginal returns. Rather, linearity implies that the point of diminishing marginal returns is yet to be reached. There can be *no doubt* that if *enough* units of variable input are combined with the given amount of fixed input, diminishing returns will set in. But in production processes where a standard worker-machine ratio is employed, this point might not be encountered until the limit of the plant's capacity is approached, say around 90 to 95% of practical capacity. Thus, up to this limit, experiencing constant returns to the variable input is neither inconceivable nor unrealistic.

Decreasing Returns to Variable Input. Another type of production function displays *decreasing returns to variable input* as soon as the *first* dose of variable input is combined with the fixed input. Although several equations can be used to describe this behavior, the simplest is the quadratic equation:

$$Q = a + bX - cX^2,$$

or, more simply,

$$Q = bX - cX^2$$

if the variable input is essential for production. Here b is a positive constant and c, as indicated, is negative. The corresponding average and marginal product functions are

$$AP_{vi} = \frac{Q}{X} = \frac{bX - cX^2}{X} = b - cX,$$

$$MP = \frac{dQ}{dX} = b - 2cX.$$

These three curves are illustrated in Fig. 7-3. Observe that the MP curve lies below the AP_{vi} curve; in fact, it declines at twice the rate of AP_{vi}, as can be verified from the equations of the two functions (the slope of AP_{vi} is $-c$, and the slope of MP is $-2c$).

Here the nature of the production process is such that each additional unit of variable input adds *less* to total output than the preceding unit. Therefore, the quantity of output increases at a decreasing rate up to the maximum output. Diminishing marginal returns to variable input are encountered with the first increment of variable input. Increases in the intensity of use of the fixed input brought about by larger doses of variable input yield progressively less and less in additional output. The marginal product of variable input then is a declining, but positive, value up to X_1 units of variable input, at which point the peak of the production function is reached. Since additional usage of variable input lowers marginal product, the average product of variable input is always falling, being pulled downward by the declining values of MP.

When X_1 units of variable input have been combined with the fixed input, the units of fixed input are being utilized to their fullest extent so that no greater output can be gotten until the fixed inputs are increased. Larger applications of variable input beyond the level of X_1 will cause the quantity of output to fall and the marginal product of variable input to become negative, since the fixed input is being *overutilized* to such an extent that all inputs become less efficient and less productive.

Increasing Returns to Variable Input.   The last and least likely type of production function has the quantity of output increasing at an increasing rate as large amounts of variable input are used with the fixed input. The simplest form of this function is given by the equation

$$Q = a + bX + cX^2.$$

Again, if $a = 0$ and if b and c are positive constants as indicated, the equation

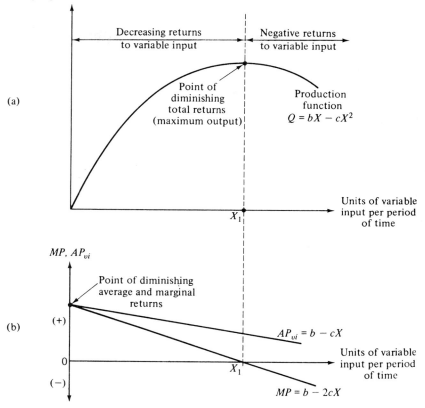

FIGURE 7-3
Production function characterized by a phase of decreasing returns to variable input

for this production function reduces to

$$Q = bX + cX^2.$$

The general equations for the corresponding average and marginal product curve can be derived as follows:

$$AP_{vi} = \frac{Q}{X} = \frac{bX + cX^2}{X} = b + cX$$

and

$$MP = \frac{dQ}{dX} = b + 2cX.$$

The graph of these three functions is shown in Fig. 7-4.

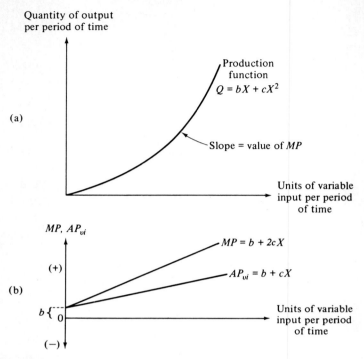

FIGURE 7-4
Production function characterized by a phase of increasing returns to variable input

For production functions of this type, output increases at an increasing rate. Adding extra units of variable input results in larger and larger gains in output as reflected by the rising marginal product of variable input. *Increasing returns to variable input* are said to prevail, because the gains in the quantity of output are *more* than proportional to the increased usage of variable input. The average product of variable input rises persistently, being pulled up by the increases in marginal product.

It is important to note that a production function of this form is likely to describe the behavior of output *only* for relatively small values of variable input, where the fixed input is being utilized far less than it could be. In other words, increasing returns to variable input are likely to prevail only for low rates of output—and then only in those instances where combining more variable input with the fixed input causes a dramatic increase in the productivity of the inputs such that output can be increased at an increasing rate. Situations of this nature can be anticipated only when the fixed inputs are being so grossly underutilized that additional variable input will permit great reductions in inefficiencies, thereby making for disproportionately greater gains in output.

A More General Type of Production Function.   When one considers the *entire* range of output of which a firm is capable, the most probable type of input-output relation is that where first is encountered a (short) range of increasing returns to variable input, then a (perhaps long) range of *approximately* constant returns to variable input, and finally a range of decreasing returns to variable input as production capacity is approached. A simple form of a production function which captures these basic elements is like that described earlier and shown in Fig. 7-1. The general equation for a production function of this shape and character is

$$Q = a + bX + cX^2 - dX^3;$$

or, given our assumption that $a = 0$, we have

$$Q = bX + cX^2 - dX^3,$$

where b and c are positive constants and d is a negative constant. The general equations for the corresponding average and marginal product curves are

$$AP_{vi} = \frac{Q}{X} = \frac{bX + cX^2 - dX^3}{X} = b + cX - dX^2$$

and

$$MP = \frac{dQ}{dX} = b + 2cX - 3dX^2.$$

The general applicability of this type of production function is wide. No doubt many production processes contain a stage of increasing returns to variable input at very low output rates, and almost every production process is certain to reflect decreasing returns to variable input as the upper limit to production capacity is approached. Moreover, for many production processes constant returns (or nearly so) to variable input can characterize the range in between. This can be seen from Fig. 7-1(a), where the production function assumes an *almost* linear shape along the range from point A to just beyond point B.

Because the cubic type of production function does incorporate the key characteristics of other production functions, we shall in future discussions use it to describe input-output relations over the entire range of a firm's output capacity. However, when there is some special reason to expect increasing, decreasing, or constant returns to the variable input to dominate the input-output relationship over the relevant range of output, we shall depart from use of the cubic form of production function and employ instead the indicated form.

THE STAGES OF PRODUCTION

Production functions of the form

$$Q = a + bX + cX^2 - dX^3$$

and the associated average and marginal product curves can be divided into three stages, as illustrated in Fig. 7-5. Stage I extends from zero usage of the variable

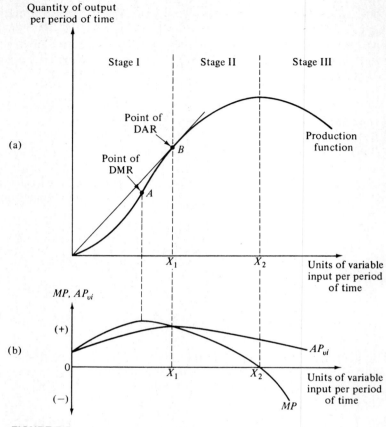

FIGURE 7-5
The stages of production

input to the point where the *average* product of variable input is maximum. Stage II extends from maximum AP_{vi} to where the quantity of output is maximum and *MP* is zero. Stage III coincides with the range of variable input where the total output is falling and marginal product is negative. These stages are of special significance for analyzing the efficiency with which resource inputs are used.

Stage I.   Included as stage I is the entire range over which AP_{vi} is increasing. Note that in stage I the point of diminishing marginal returns is reached (point *A*) and passed. Up to the point of DMR, output is increasing at an increasing rate; past this point it increases at a decreasing rate. The marginal product of variable input rises to its peak and begins to fall, yet it remains a greater value than average product throughout the stage. Stage I ends when the point of diminishing *average* returns is reached (point *B*).

   What about the efficiency with which the fixed and variable input are being used in stage I? The *efficiency* of an input is best measured by its *average* product, because it indicates the amount of output obtained *per unit* of input. An input's marginal product is a measure of the efficiency of one additional unit of variable input, but it does not reflect the efficiency of *all* the units of variable input taken as a group. Since the average product of variable input is rising throughout stage I, it is evident that variable input is being employed with *increasing* overall efficiency as the end of stage I is approached. Indeed, maximum efficiency of the variable input is attained at the border between stages I and II, where AP_{vi} is maximum. So much for variable input; now what about the efficiency of the fixed inputs in stage I? Although we have no curve representing the average product of fixed input (AP_{fi}), we still know that the quantity of output rises throughout stage I and that the level of fixed input remains unchanged. Thus, because AP_{fi} = units of output/units of fixed input, it follows that the average product of fixed input must also be rising throughout stage I.

Therefore, in stage I increasing the quantity of variable input applied to a given quantity of fixed inputs has the effect of raising the efficiency with which *both* fixed and variable inputs are being utilized. Just *why* the efficiency of both fixed and variable inputs rises in stage I stems from a relative imbalance between the fixed and variable inputs. Throughout stage I the amount of fixed input is excessive compared to the amount of variable input employed. The unduly large proportions of fixed input to variable input in stage I cause the fixed inputs to be *underutilized* and the variable inputs to be *overutilized*. Hence, as more variable input is used, the imbalance is relieved, and the efficiencies of both inputs rise.

The rising efficiencies of fixed and variable inputs have important implications for the costs of production in stage I. As will be demonstrated in the next chapter, when both the average products of fixed and variable inputs are increasing, the *unit* costs of producing more output are declining. Thus, *from the standpoint of efficiency and unit costs, a firm would always prefer to move through stage I to at least the border of stage II before ceasing to use more variable input.*

Stage II. In stage II the quantity of output rises at a decreasing rate; accordingly, the marginal product of variable input is declining, although it remains greater than zero. More significantly, the average product of variable input is falling throughout stage II. The average product of fixed input, however, continues to rise in stage II, because the quantity of output continues to rise even though the amount of fixed input is held constant. In stage II, then, additional units of variable input add to the efficiency of fixed input but diminish the efficiency of variable input.

Stage III. At the boundary between stages II and III, short-run output is maximum, and the fixed input is being utilized to its fullest extent—the efficiency of the fixed input has reached its peak level. With further doses of variable input, the amount of variable input relative to fixed input becomes so large that total output falls. There simply is too little fixed input relative to the amounts of variable input being used. Thus, the use of larger quantities of variable input per period of time reduces AP_{vi} still more, and MP becomes increasingly negative. And with total output falling, AP_{fi} is also decreasing. In sum, the efficiency of variable input and the efficiency of fixed input both diminish as stage III is entered.

The Optimum Stage.   The foregoing description of the three stages should make it apparent that operating in stage II is best from the standpoint of efficiency and unit costs. In stage I, variable input is used too sparingly with the available fixed input; increases in variable input will so increase the efficiency of all inputs that the *unit costs* of producing more output will decline. Thus, efficiency and cost considerations will induce the firm to employ at least an amount of variable input sufficient to reach stage II.

Stage III is obviously irrational. It makes no sense whatsoever for a firm to incur the added expense of purchasing and using more units of variable input per period of time when the payoff is a decline in total output and a reduction in overall operating efficiency.

Therefore, stage II is optimum from the standpoint of overall production efficiency and cost. Just where in stage II is the best rate of variable input usage depends on the prices of fixed and variable input (we shall pursue this point later on in this chapter). However, *stage II is not the stage in which profit is necessarily maximized.* Demand for a firm's product may in the short run be so low that it is actually more profitable to operate in stage I. We shall indicate this more clearly in a later chapter. Additionally, it should be apparent that stage III can never be more profitable than stage I or stage II because the decline in total output is accompanied by rising total costs (because of using more variable input) and potentially lower revenues.

Fixed Inputs and the Short-Run Production Function

In the preceding section it was shown that economical production occurs only in stage II, yet what can a firm do if its level of product demand does not warrant an output sufficiently high to reach stage II? For instance, suppose, as is shown in Fig. 7-6(a), that a firm reaches stage II at an output of Q_2 units but that the quantity demanded at the current selling price is only Q_1 units. Several alternatives are open to the firm. In the short run it can (1) tolerate the production inefficiency of operating in stage I—which may, incidentally, still allow for ample profit to be earned; (2) seek to increase product demand by lowering its selling price and/or increasing promotional and selling efforts; or (3) add new products to its product line to take up the slack in production capacity. If these prove unsatisfactory for a variety of reasons, in the long run the firm can reduce its scale of production operations by cutting back on the size of fixed inputs. Reducing the size of fixed inputs has the impact of shifting the production function down and to the left, as shown in Fig. 7-6(b).[8] Then the firm can reach stage II at a lower output (Q_3 as compared to Q_2) and with a smaller amount of variable input (X_3 as compared to X_1). Demand for the firm's product can be satisfied by using

---

[8] In the event that fixed inputs are "lumpy" and can be reduced only by a relatively large proportion, the production function conceivably could shift downward and *to the right,* meaning that the firm can reach stage II at a lower output provided its usage of variable input is increased. Whether the firm would prefer to use less fixed input and more variable input in producing its product would depend on the relative prices of fixed and variable inputs.

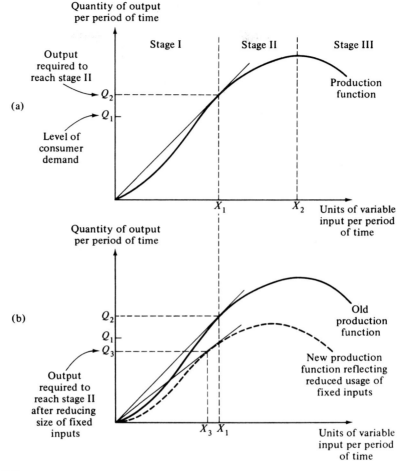

FIGURE 7-6
Impact of reductions in the use of fixed inputs upon the production function

fewer inputs, thereby cutting production costs and widening the firm's profit margin at the current price.

Similarly, when a firm encounters a level of product demand exceeding its total output capability in the short run, several options are again open. If the strong demand for the item is perceived to be temporary, a price increase to ration the available supply among potential buyers may be in order, and no increase in production capacity is warranted. But when demand seems likely to remain above production capacity on a relatively permanent and profitable basis, a price increase in the short run might well be combined with an expansion of the firm's scale of operations in the long run. To accomplish this, the size of the fixed inputs must be increased; such action has the effect of shifting the production function upward and raising the maximum obtainable rate of total output.

DETERMINING OPTIMAL INPUT PROPORTIONS

So far, the firm has been pictured as changing its rate of output in the short run by employing more or less units of variable input. In the long run, changes in the usage of fixed inputs may also be undertaken to adjust output capabilities. Although the fixed-variable input approach to output adjustment helps specify certain fundamental physical relationships of production, it does not permit determination of the precise optimal proportion of different resource inputs within stage II. To pinpoint more exactly the maximum efficiency-minimum cost combination of resource inputs, we must shift our attention away from the relationships between input-output flows to the relationships between resource inputs and resource prices.

The Production Surface

To simplify our analysis of optimal input combinations, let us begin by assuming that capital and labor are the only two types of resource inputs required in producing a good. No disservice to reality is done by this assumption since the relevant principles we shall derive for two inputs apply equally to any greater number of inputs. Capital may be thought of as symbolizing those kinds of resource inputs which are fixed in the short run and labor as symbolizing those kinds of inputs which are variable in the short run. (Letting capital be the proxy for fixed inputs in the short run and labor be the proxy for variable inputs makes it easier to indicate the optimal combination of fixed and variable inputs in the long run.)

In the three-dimensional diagram of Fig. 7-7(a), the coordinates in the horizontal plane show the alternative combinations of capital and labor. The quantity of output associated with each combination of the two types of resource inputs is measured vertically above the plane. Varying the quantities of capital and labor generates the hill-shaped production surface *OCPL*.[9] If *OC* units of capital are used, varying the quantity of labor generates the production function *CDAP*. Similarly, given *OL* units of labor, varying the quantity of capital input gives the production function *LEBP*. Notice that the shapes of the production functions generated by holding the input of one resource constant and letting the other change [lines *CDAP* and *LEBP* in Fig. 7-7(a)] correspond to the cubic type of production function, a type of production relationship which often typifies the entire output range for a plant.

Suppose that we connect all points on the production surface *OCPL* associated with an output of *AA'* units (where *AA'* = *BB'*), obtaining the contour line *AB*. All the points along *AB* are associated with the *same* amount of output (*AA'* = *BB'*). Projecting line *AB* vertically downward onto the horizontal plane gives the dashed contour line *A'B'*. The line *A'B'* defines all the combinations of capital and labor employed per unit of time that will yield an output flow of *AA'* = *BB'*;

---

[9] Observe that the concept of the production surface is analogous to the utility surface discussed in Chapters 3 and 4.

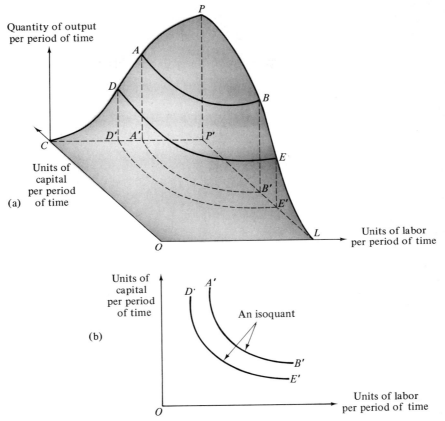

FIGURE 7-7
Derivation of isoquants from a production surface

such a line is called an *isoquant*.[10] For movements along an isoquant the rate of output remains constant, but the input ratio (in this case the ratio of capital to labor) changes continuously.

Following the same procedure, suppose we move down the production surface to a lower rate of output, say *DD'*, and connect all points on the production surface *OCPL* representing an output of *DD'* (where *DD'* = *EE'*). This gives the contour line *DE*, which, projected vertically downward onto the horizontal plane, traces out the dashed contour *D'E'*. Any point along *DE* represents constant total output, and all combinations of capital and labor lying on *D'E'* are capable of producing this amount of output. Contour line *D'E'* is also an isoquant.

---

[10] The term "isoquant" is derived from the prefix *iso-*, meaning equal, and the word *quantity*; hence, it literally means equal quantity (of output). In the literature of economics isoquants are sometimes referred to as product indifference curves, equal product curves, or isoproduct curves.

Figure 7-7(b) illustrates isoquants $A'B'$ and $D'E'$ in a two-dimensional diagram. All input combinations lying on $A'B'$ yield more output than the input combinations on $D'E'$. Higher rates of output are represented by isoquants lying farther from the origin, as indicated by the positions on the production surface of the contour lines from which isoquants are derived. A complete set of isoquants for a production surface is called an *isoquant map.*[11]

Isoquants may be viewed as analogous to the contour lines on a topographic map. Each isoquant connects all points of the same altitude or output rate. From this standpoint, the entire production surface (of which only a section is shown in Fig. 7-7) can be considered as a "production mountain" with isoquants as the contour lines encircling it.

Although a firm's production function and production surface have been displayed as being continuous, with the isoquants derived therefrom also being continuous, it is more realistic to acknowledge that the "lumpiness" of resource inputs can produce a discrete production surface with correspondingly discrete isoquants. Many resources (especially capital) do not lend themselves to being used in continuously divisible subunits. After all, anything less than a whole machine is less than satisfactory. More importantly, technology is not of such a character that an infinite number of combinations of resources can be used to produce equivalent amounts of output. A firm is necessarily constrained in its selection of resource inputs to the finite number of recipes known to exist for producing an item. Realistically, then, it is more accurate to conceive of an isoquant as a series of points, where each point represents a technically feasible combination of resource inputs that yields the specified level of output. Viewing isoquants as discontinuous or discrete functions keeps the limited potentials of substituting one resource input for another in the forefront. However, as long as the "lumpiness" of resource inputs is recognized, it does little harm to simplify our discussion by drawing isoquants as smooth curves. Certainly, our exposition of the pertinent relationships is made easier by considering a smooth curve instead of a series of points.

The Characteristics of Isoquants

The properties of isoquants are similar to those of indifference curves: (1) isoquants are nonintersecting; (2) all *rational* combinations of resource inputs lie on that portion of an isoquant which slopes downward to the right; and (3) the rational segments of isoquants tend to be convex to the origin. Each of these properties warrants brief discussion.

For two isoquants to intersect is illogical and contrary to our assumption of efficiency. Intersection would mean that two different amounts of output could be produced with the same combination of resource inputs. This could occur only if a firm uses its inputs so inefficiently that the marginal products of some of the

---

[11] Suppose that a firm's production function is $Q = f(L, C)$; then a particular isoquant is defined by assigning a value to Q and observing all the different technically feasible values of L and C which will yield that value of Q. The firm's isoquant map is derived by repeating this procedure for many values of Q.

resources are zero or negative—something that a firm is not likely to do knowingly. Hence, an isoquant shows only the maximum output obtainable from resource inputs, which precludes intersection.

As indicated above, an isoquant map consists of a series of concentric rings around the hill of production. A single such isoquant is reproduced in Fig. 7-8. All the points along the isoquant in Fig. 7-8 represent input combinations capable of producing the same level of output. Although all the combinations of capital and labor lying on this isoquant represent possible recipes for producing this output, some of the combinations are more rational than others. For example, combination B would never be chosen over combination A. Why? Combination A requires the same amount of capital input as B (C_2 units) but requires considerably less labor input (L_1 units as compared to L_3 units); hence, combination A is *cheaper* than B. Similarly, combination D is always preferable to combination C, since it requires much less capital input (C_1 as compared to C_3 units) while using the same amount of labor input (L_2 units). It follows that the economically practical resource combinations fall within the lower left quadrant of the isoquant—the boldly inscribed portion in Fig. 7-8 lying between the vertical and horizontal tangents to the isoquant at points E and F. The remaining points on the isoquant constitute economically foolish resource combinations, even though they represent technically feasible recipes. Thus, for reasons of economy in resource use and in minimizing costs, the rational segment of an isoquant is the portion sloping downward to the right and convex to the origin.

The downward slope of the economic region of an isoquant derives from the possibility of substituting one resource input for another in the production process and still maintaining the same production rate. Consider the *rate* at which one input must be substituted for another to keep output constant. From Fig. 7-9, we see that a change from input combination C_1L_1 to input combination C_2L_2

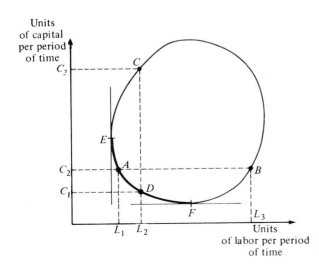

FIGURE 7-8
Economic region of an isoquant

FIGURE 7-9
Marginal rate of technical substitution

involves a substitution of labor for capital. The rate at which labor is substituted for capital over this range is

$$\frac{C_2 - C_1}{L_2 - L_1} = \frac{-\Delta C}{\Delta L}$$

and is called the *marginal rate of technical substitution* of labor for capital. The marginal rate of technical substitution (MRTS) measures the reduction in one input (ΔC) per unit increase in the other (ΔL) that is just sufficient to maintain a constant level of output.

In moving from $C_1 L_1$ to $C_2 L_2$ in Fig. 7-9, the output rate remains unchanged; consequently the "loss" in output from using fewer units of capital input is exactly compensated for by the "gain" in the output from using more units of labor input. The "loss" in output from using less capital equals the reduction in capital usage multiplied by the "average" marginal product of these units, or

$$-\Delta C \cdot MP_C.$$

By the same token the "gain" in output from using a larger dose of labor equals

$$\Delta L \cdot MP_L.$$

Since the "loss" and the "gain" are equivalent in size, we can say that

$$-\Delta C \cdot MP_C = \Delta L \cdot MP_L.$$

Dividing both sides of this equation by $\Delta L \cdot MP_C$ gives

$$-\frac{\Delta C \cdot MP_C}{\Delta L \cdot MP_C} = \frac{\Delta L \cdot MP_L}{\Delta L \cdot MP_C},$$

which reduces to

$$-\frac{\Delta C}{\Delta L} = \frac{MP_L}{MP_C} \qquad \text{or} \qquad \frac{\Delta C}{\Delta L} = -\frac{MP_L}{MP_C}.$$

Therefore, it is apparent that between combinations C_1L_1 and C_2L_2,

$$\text{MRTS}_{LC} = \frac{\Delta C}{\Delta L} = -\frac{MP_L}{MP_C}.$$

That MRTS_{LC} is negative derives from the substitution of one resource for the other and the negative slope of the isoquant; however, for our purposes it is the *size* of the ratio that is important, not its sign.

Now suppose that combination C_1L_1 in Fig. 7-9 is moved closer and closer to C_2L_2 so as to merge eventually with it to form a single point. The ratio $\Delta C/\Delta L$ will then approach the value of the slope of the tangent to the isoquant at point C_2L_2. Consequently, we may say that the *marginal rate of technical substitution of one input for another input at any point along an isoquant is equal to the slope of the isoquant at that point.*[12]

The MRTS of labor for capital *diminishes* as more and more labor is substituted for capital because the greater the extent to which labor is substituted for capital, the more labor it takes to compensate for a reduction in the use of capital. The other points along the isoquant in Fig. 7-9 make this clearer. The vertical axis in Fig. 7-9 is measured so that $C_1C_2 = C_2C_3 = C_3C_4 = C_4C_5 = OC_5 = 1$ unit of capital. Starting at resource combination C_1L_1 and proceeding down the isoquant, we find that it takes a relatively small increase in the use of labor (L_1L_2 units) to compensate for using one less unit of capital and still produce the same quantity of output. But, as we move farther *down* the isoquant and

---

[12] Mathematically, the MRTS can be found by taking the first derivative of the equation defining an isoquant. For example, if the expression

$$LC = 100$$

defines an isoquant, then the MRTS_{LC} can be found as follows:

$$C = \frac{100}{L} = 100L^{-1},$$

$$\frac{dC}{dL} = -100L^{-2} = \frac{100}{L^2}.$$

Since $\text{MRTS}_{LC} = dC/dL$, we have

$$\text{MRTS}_{LC} = -\frac{100}{L^2}$$

for any value of L in which interest may focus.

continue to substitute labor for capital, reductions in capital must be offset by progressively larger increases in labor input ($L_1L_2 < L_2L_3 < L_3L_4 < L_4L_5$). Plainly, then, the MRTS of labor for capital diminishes as the degree of substitution is increased. Where the isoquant becomes horizontal, the substitution of labor for capital has reached its maximum limit, and the $\text{MRTS}_{LC} = 0$. Further reductions in capital will cause output to *fall*; no longer is it possible to reduce the use of capital and maintain output by using more labor. The amount of capital corresponding to point S in Fig. 7-9 is the minimum amount of capital which can be used to produce an output of Q_1. By the same rationale, as we move back up the isoquant toward point R, capital is being substituted for labor, and the ratio of ΔC to ΔL is rising. At point R, capital has been substituted for labor to the maximum possible extent; the MRTS of capital for labor is infinity, and the slope of the isoquant is vertical. The amount of labor corresponding to point R is the minimum amount of labor which can be used to produce output Q_1.

It is the changing marginal rate of technical substitution that makes the isoquant convex to the origin. Should two inputs be perfect substitutes for each other, the isoquant is linear and downsloping. Such a relationship between inputs is rare, especially regarding inputs as diverse as labor and capital. That most isoquants are convex is easily demonstrated. Consider labor and capital in making fenders for automobiles. A metal-stamping machine with a single operator can transform a piece of sheet steel into the shape of an automobile fender in a matter of seconds. Within limits, less expensive stamping machines requiring more labor time can be used to make the same fender. But the more labor and the less capital used to shape sheet steel into fenders, the more difficult it becomes to carry the degree of substitution further without jeopardizing the quantity and quality of output. The hammering out of the fender, for example, would require an inordinate amount of labor time and cost, as well as entailing a major reduction in fender quality. The same reasoning applies equally well to other resource inputs; consequently, a diminishing marginal rate of technical substitution of one resource input for another is a generally encountered phenomenon in production processes.

The Isocost Curve

Isoquants concern only the possible ways that firms can combine resource inputs—no restrictions, save those of a technical nature, are brought into play. In reality, though, firms are limited in their choice of production techniques by the prices of resource inputs and by the amount of funds available for purchasing these inputs.

An *isocost curve* portrays the various alternative combinations of resource inputs which a firm can purchase, given the prices of resource inputs and the stipulated amount of expenditure on resources.[13] Continuing our assumption of only two inputs, capital and labor, let the price of labor be P_L, the price of capital

---

[13] The concept of isocost curves is analogous to the concept of lines of attainable combinations (Chapter 4). The only difference is that isocost curves deal with the resource combinations which a firm can purchase, whereas lines of attainable combinations relate to a consumer's ability to purchase goods and services.

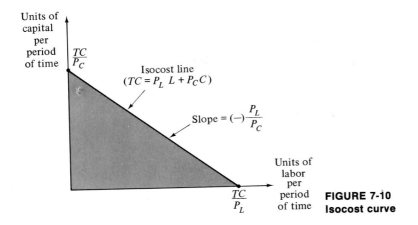

FIGURE 7-10
Isocost curve

be P_C, and the stipulated amount of expenditure on resources be TC (total cost). The firm's expenditure for labor equals the price of a unit of labor (P_L) times the amount of labor purchased (L) or $P_L \cdot L$; similarly, the firm's expenditure for capital is $P_C \cdot C$. With only two resource inputs to choose from, the sum of the firm's expenditures for labor and capital must be equal to or less than the maximum allowable expenditure (TC). Thus, the expression defining the isocost curve may be written as

$$P_L L + P_C C = TC.$$

Provided that P_L and P_C are unaffected by the quantity of labor and capital purchased, if the firm elects to spend all its cost outlay (TC) for labor, a maximum of TC/P_L units can be employed; if the firm elects to spend all its cost outlay for capital, a maximum of TC/P_C can be bought.[14] A straight line joining TC/P_C and TC/P_L shows all the combinations of capital and labor obtainable from an expenditure of TC dollars. Figure 7-10 illustrates such an isocost curve. The slope of the isocost curve can be derived from points TC/P_C and TC/P_L. Between these two points, the

$$\text{slope of isocost curve} = \frac{(-)TC/P_C}{TC/P_L} = -\frac{TC}{P_C} \cdot \frac{P_L}{TC} = (-)\frac{P_L}{P_C}.$$

[14] Resource prices need not remain constant irrespective of the amounts purchased of labor and capital. A large employer in a tight labor market may have to raise wage rates to attract and hire more labor. A large purchaser of capital goods may be able to squeeze price concessions from suppliers of capital goods as the firm's usage of capital increases. Likewise, quantity discounts may be received on raw material purchases. When the prices of resource inputs fall as the amounts purchased go up, the isocost curve is bowed in toward the origin. In the event that resource prices rise as their levels of usage are increased, the isocost curve is bowed out from the origin.

The Optimum Mix of Resource Inputs

A basic objective of firms is to realize the greatest amount of output from a stipulated total cost outlay. In terms of isoquant-isocost analysis this means getting to the highest isoquant permitted by the firm's isocost curve. In Fig. 7-11, the output rate corresponding to isoquant Q_2 is the highest output which can be attained given an outlay of TC dollars and prices P_L and P_C. Accordingly, the optimum combination of resource inputs for producing output Q_2 is C_1 units of capital and L_1 units of labor. From a slightly different viewpoint, this resource combination may also be designated as the *least-cost resource combination,* since it represents the minimum cost of producing Q_2 units of output when the prices of capital and labor are P_C and P_L, respectively. In other words, the point of tangency between the isocost and isoquant curves defines the optimum resource combination, whether interest centers upon (1) finding the maximum output for a given total cost outlay and at given resource prices, or (2) finding the minimum cost for producing a given output at given resource prices.

If capital symbolizes fixed input and labor symbolizes variable input, then the mix of capital and labor at the least-cost resource combination in Fig. 7-11 defines the optimal proportions of fixed and variable input for producing Q_2 units of output. This proportion is optimum because, given the prices of the two inputs, no other combination of fixed (capital) and variable (labor) input yields Q_2 units as cheaply—hence the term *least-cost* resource combination.

The Conditions for Optimizing the Resource Mix. There are two conditions for optimizing the combination of labor and capital inputs. First, we may note that the optimum resource combination of capital and labor lies *on* the isocost line rather than inside it. This means the firm must fully utilize its available dollars

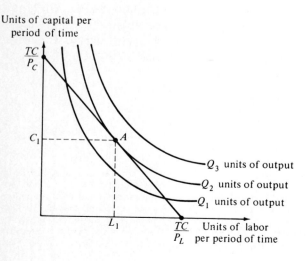

Units of capital per period of time

$\dfrac{TC}{P_C}$

C_1 A

Q_3 units of output

Q_2 units of output

Q_1 units of output

L_1 $\dfrac{TC}{P_L}$ Units of labor per period of time

FIGURE 7-11
Determining the optimum resource combination

in purchasing inputs if it is to maximize output. Translated into the language of mathematics, we can say that optimization requires

$$P_L L + P_C C = TC.$$

Second, at the point of tangency between the isocost line and the maximum attainable isoquant, the slope of the isocost line is equal to the slope of the isoquant. From prior discussions the

$$\text{slope of the isoquant} = \text{MRTS}_{LC} = (-)\frac{MP_L}{MP_C}$$

and the

$$\text{slope of the isocost line} = (-)\frac{P_L}{P_C}.$$

Since the slopes are equal, we may write

$$\text{MRTS}_{LC} = (-)\frac{P_L}{P_C}$$

which states that to optimize the resource mix a firm must allocate its expenditures so that the marginal rate of technical substitution of labor for capital equals the ratio of the price of labor to the price of capital. The interpretation of this result is straightforward. The MRTS$_{LC}$ defines the *rate* at which a firm is *technically able* to substitute labor for capital. The price ratio P_L/P_C shows the *rate* at which a firm is *economically able* to substitute labor for capital. Unless the two rates are equivalent, a firm can alter its resource mix and obtain a larger output or else reduce its costs for a given output. For example, suppose that MRTS$_{LC} = -\frac{1}{2}$, meaning that a firm is technically able to substitute 2 units of labor input for 1 unit of capital input without changing output. If $P_L = \$10$ and $P_C = \$30$, then a firm is economically able to give up 1 unit of capital in return for 3 units of labor. Giving up 1 unit of capital releases \$30, of which only \$20 is needed for purchasing labor, since 2 units of labor at \$10 each will compensate for a 1-unit reduction in capital input. The remaining \$10 can be applied to the purchase of additional resources for increasing output or else to reducing the total costs of the current output rate. In either event the firm will be better off. In general terms, therefore, optimizing the input combination requires equality between the marginal rate of technical substitution for any pair of resource inputs and the ratio of their prices; in the absence of equality some substitution of one resource for another can be initiated to increase output, or else expenditures on resource inputs can be reduced.

However, we can approach this second condition for optimizing the resource mix from another angle. Not only is the slope of the isoquant equal to MRTS at any point, but it is also equal to the ratio of the marginal products of the resource inputs:

$$\text{MRTS}_{LC} = (-)\frac{MP_L}{MP_C}.$$

Thus, we may rewrite the second condition for optimizing the resource combination as

$$(-)\frac{MP_L}{MP_C} = (-)\frac{P_L}{P_C}.$$

This equation states that the firm's total cost outlay should be allocated among labor and capital so as to equate the ratio of their marginal products with the ratio of their prices. Transforming the latter equation still further by cross-multiplying, we get

$$P_L \cdot MP_C = P_C \cdot MP_L.$$

Dividing both sides by $P_L \cdot P_C$ gives

$$\frac{P_L \cdot MP_C}{P_L \cdot P_C} = \frac{P_C \cdot MP_L}{P_L \cdot P_C},$$

which reduces to

$$\frac{MP_C}{P_C} = \frac{MP_L}{P_L}.$$

The latter expression says that a firm should arrange its input purchases so as to obtain an equivalent amount of additional output from the last dollar spent on each input. When the extra outputs per dollar spent on the last unit of each resource are unequal, the quantity of output can be increased (or total costs reduced) by diminishing expenditures where the marginal product per dollar spent is less and by enlarging expenditures where the marginal product per dollar spent is greater. For example, if

$$MP_L = 42 \text{ units output for the last unit of labor purchased,}$$
$$P_L = \$7 \text{ per unit,}$$
$$MP_C = 80 \text{ units of output for the last unit of capital purchased,}$$
$$P_L = \$10,$$

then

$$\frac{MP_L}{P_L} = \frac{42 \text{ units}}{\$7} = 6 \text{ units of output/\$ spent on labor}$$

and

$$\frac{MP_C}{P_C} = \frac{80 \text{ units}}{\$10} = 8 \text{ units of output/\$ spent on capital.}$$

The firm is realizing more extra output per dollar spent on the last unit of capital than on the last unit of labor. This situation calls for (1) reallocating dollars away from the purchase of labor, thereby raising MP_L and increasing the output per dollar spent on labor, and (2) spending more dollars on the purchase of capital thereby decreasing MP_C and decreasing the output per dollar spent on capital. Substituting capital for labor will tend to equalize the ratios MP_L/P_L and MP_C/P_C.

MATHEMATICAL CAPSULE 9

DETERMINATION OF THE OPTIMUM RESOURCE COMBINATION

Let P_L and P_C be the prices of units of labor (L) and capital (C); let TC symbolize the budget a firm has available for purchasing the two resource inputs; and let $Q = f(L, C)$ represent the firm's production function for a commodity. The issue is how to best allocate the available dollars (TC) among purchases of labor and capital input so as to maximize the quantity of output (Q) subject to the constraint that the total expenditures on inputs just exhaust TC. More formally, what values of L and C will cause $Q = f(L, C)$ to be maximum, yet just meet the constraint that

$$TC - P_L L - P_C C = 0?$$

The mathematical solution requires using the Lagrangian multiplier method of finding the maximum value of a function. A new function is generated which combines the production function to be maximized with the constraint to be met. To keep the solution determinate (as many equations as there are unknowns), an artificial unknown, called a Lagrange multiplier and symbolized by λ, is introduced into the new function, giving

$$Z = f(L, C) + \lambda(TC - P_L L - P_C C).$$

Note that the constraint has been expressed in such a way that it is satisfied when $TC - P_L L - P_C C = 0$. Next, the partial derivatives of Z are found for each variable and equated to zero to establish the first-order conditions:

$$\frac{\partial Z}{\partial L} = \frac{\partial Q}{\partial L} - \lambda P_L = 0,$$

$$\frac{\partial Z}{\partial C} = \frac{\partial Q}{\partial C} - \lambda P_C = 0,$$

$$\frac{\partial Z}{\partial \lambda} = TC - P_L L - P_C C = 0.$$

These three equations are then solved simultaneously to determine the combination of L and C which will maximize the quantity of output subject to the cost constraint. As an example of the foregoing, suppose that the production function is

$$Q = 20L + 65C - 0.5L^2 - 0.5C^2$$

and that $TC = \$2200$, $P_L = \$20$ per unit, and $P_C = \$50$ per unit. To find the maximum output obtainable from an expenditure of $2200, we generate the function

$$Z = 20L + 65C - 0.5L^2 - 0.5C^2 + \lambda(2200 - 20L - 50C).$$

Finding the partial derivatives of Z and setting them equal to zero, we have

$$\frac{\partial Z}{\partial L} = 20 - L - 20\lambda = 0,$$

$$\frac{\partial Z}{\partial C} = 65 - C - 50\lambda = 0,$$

$$\frac{\partial Z}{\partial \lambda} = 2200 - 20L - 50C = 0.$$

Solving these three equations simultaneously gives $L = 10$, $C = 40$, and a maximum Q of 1950 units.

EXERCISE

1. Determine the optimum resource combination of labor and capital when
   (a) $Q = 140L + 160C - 5L^2 - 2C^2$,
       $P_L = \$12$,
       $P_C = \$24$,
       $TC = \$732$.
   (b) $Q = 6LC$,
       $P_L = \$5$,
       $P_C = \$10$,
       $TC = \$180$.

When There Are More Than Two Resource Inputs.   The preceding conclusions are easily expanded for cases where more than two distinct kinds of resource inputs are used in a production process. In the event that a production process requires multiple types of resource inputs $(X_a, X_b, X_c, \ldots, X_n)$ obtainable at prices $(P_{X_a}, P_{X_b}, P_{X_c}, \ldots, P_{X_n})$, the optimal mix of resource inputs is attained by meeting the following two conditions:

$$P_{X_a}X_a + P_{X_b}X_b + P_{X_c}X_c + \cdots + P_{X_n}X_n = TC, \tag{1}$$

$$\frac{MP_{X_a}}{P_{X_a}} = \frac{MP_{X_b}}{P_{X_b}} = \cdots = \frac{MP_{X_n}}{P_{X_n}}. \tag{2}$$

The Expansion Path

It is not likely that a firm will maintain its output at the same rate for long. Market conditions, particularly demand, change frequently and cause firms to adjust output rates accordingly. For this reason, the firm has an interest in knowing the least-cost resource combinations for several rates of output. Especially pertinent is the issue of how much more of each input to use should market conditions warrant a long-term expansion or contraction of output.

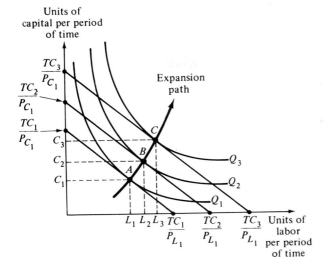

FIGURE 7-12
Determining the optimum resource combination for various output rates

Consider Fig. 7-12, where inputs of C_1 units of capital and L_1 units of labor are being used to produce an output of Q_1 units at a total cost of TC_1 dollars. Now suppose that the firm wishes to expand output to Q_2 units per period of time. Clearly, a greater total cost outlay is required. Assuming that the prices of capital and labor remain constant at P_{L_1} and P_{C_1}, an increase in the expenditure level for resource inputs will shift the isocost curve outward *parallel* to itself. Thus, an outlay of TC_2 dollars using C_2 units of capital and L_2 units of labor represents the least possible cost of producing output Q_2. Similarly, an outlay of TC_3 dollars with inputs of C_3 units of capital and L_3 units of labor is the least possible cost of producing Q_3 units of output. The line joining these and all other least-cost resource combinations is called the *expansion path* of the firm. *The expansion path shows the locus of optimum input combinations for each possible rate of output when the prices of the resource inputs remain constant.*

The shape of the expansion path for labor and capital has a certain amount of economic significance. It is probable that increasing the output of most commodities over the long run entails a technological and economic bias toward using relatively more capital than labor, meaning the expansion path is as shown in Fig. 7-13(a). Support for this stems from the readily observable tendency of large firms to use a more capital-intensive production recipe than do smaller firms producing the same item—presumably because it is almost always more efficient than labor-intensive production techniques. Occasionally, the expansion path may be linear or very nearly so [Fig. 7-13(b)]. A linear expansion path for a product implies that the costs of additional output are minimized by using more of both inputs *in the same proportion* as before, perhaps because technological requirements call for a constant ratio between inputs. In rare cases the expansion path could assume

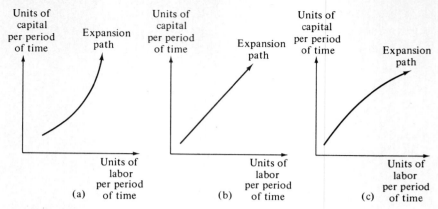

FIGURE 7-13
Alternative shapes for the expansion path

the shape of that in Fig. 7-13(c), where maximum efficiency-minimum cost requires using relatively more labor than capital to expand total output.

The expansion path shows the amounts of resource inputs which the firm should use as it expands its *long-run* rate of output. But in the short run the firm has no alternative to adjusting output rates by using more or less variable input with the given amount of fixed input. To minimize costs in the short run a firm should alter its usage of variable resources so as to keep the ratios of the marginal products per dollar spent on variable inputs equivalent. In other words, if *in the short run* a firm uses four *variable* inputs (X_a, X_b, X_c, and X_d), even though the fixed inputs cannot be changed, then optimal resource usage entails adjusting *variable* input combinations such that

$$\frac{MP_{X_a}}{P_{X_a}} = \frac{MP_{X_b}}{P_{X_b}} = \frac{MP_{X_c}}{P_{X_c}} = \frac{MP_{X_d}}{P_{X_d}}.$$

The Impact of Changes in Resource Prices

The prices of resource inputs, as with the prices of goods and services, are subject to change. When they do change, firms are prompted to alter input combinations. Suppose we examine the effect of an increase in the price of labor upon the optimum mix of capital and labor.

Given the price of labor P_{L_1}, the price of capital P_{C_1}, and the firm's total cost outlay TC_1, the firm will optimize its inputs at an output of Q_1 by combining L_1 units of labor with C_1 units of capital as shown by point A in Fig. 7-14. If the price of labor rises to P_{L_2}, then the isocost curve pivots to the left about point TC_1/P_{C_1} and restricts the maximum usage of labor to TC_1/P_{L_2} units (were the entire total cost outlay used to buy labor). The new isocost curve will necessarily be tangent to a lower isoquant than previously and it will not be possible to produce

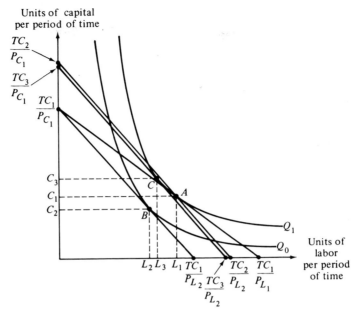

FIGURE 7-14
Adjusting to changes in resource prices

Q_1 units of output with an expenditure of TC_1 dollars. The optimum input mix becomes L_2 units of labor and C_2 units of capital (point B in Fig. 7-14) at an output of Q_0 units. The firm must choose between being content with a lower output (Q_0) or else increasing TC to permit maintenance of output at Q_1. If the latter alternative is chosen and assuming the input of capital is fixed *in the short run* at C_1 units (as can be the case in the real world), then the firm will find it most advantageous *in the short run* to continue to produce Q_1 units of output by using C_1 units of capital and L_1 units of labor (point A). Why? Because when the firm's capital input is fixed at C_1 units, the *smallest* amount of labor that can be used to produce an output of Q_1 units is L_1 units of labor. An examination of Fig. 7-14 verifies this statement. Consequently, *in the short run* point A represents the least cost of producing Q_1 units when no more than C_1 units of capital are available, despite the fact that the price of labor has risen from P_{L_1} to P_{L_2}. But, since the price of labor has gone up, it is clear that the cost of producing Q_1 units of output must be greater than TC_1. The higher cost can be illustrated graphically by drawing a new isocost line with a slope of P_{L_2}/P_{C_1} (so as to reflect the new ratio of resource prices) through point A. The extreme points of this isocost line are TC_2/P_{C_1} and TC_2/P_{L_2}, where $P_{L_2} > P_{L_1}$ and $TC_2 > TC_1$. *In the short run,* therefore, the fixed aspect of capital input may cause the firm to leave its input combination unchanged in response to an increase in the price of labor, provided it elects to continue to produce Q_1 units and provided it can afford to increase its expenditures on resource inputs from TC_1 to TC_2.

However, *in the long run* the firm has incentive to change its usage of capital and labor in response to the higher price of labor. As soon as time and money permit, the firm will be induced to produce Q_1 units of output by shifting from point A to point C in Fig. 7-14. Point C is determined by finding the point of tangency between isoquant Q_1 and an isocost line with a slope of P_{L_2}/P_{C_1}; this isocost line is parallel to the isocost line defined by extreme points TC_2/P_{C_1} and TC_2/P_{L_2}, because both lines reflect the resource inputs obtainable when the price of labor is P_{L_2} and the price of capital is P_{C_1}. The shift in the optimum resource mix from point A to point C will reduce the costs of producing Q_1 units of output from TC_2 to TC_3, an amount which is indicated graphically by the distance between the isocost line defined by extreme points TC_3/P_{C_1} and TC_3/P_{L_2} and the isocost line defined by extreme points TC_2/P_{C_1} and TC_2/P_{L_2}.

Thus, in the long run an increase in the price of labor relative to the price of capital will induce the firm to substitute capital for labor. The logic of such action is compelling. Whenever a resource becomes more expensive, it makes sense to use less of it and more of other less expensive inputs. This is precisely what many firms have proceeded to do. In manufacturing, for example, as unions and other wage-increasing forces have combined to drive up the relative price of labor, firms have put forth a concerted effort to substitute capital for labor. High labor costs are, in fact, a major motive for introducing automated production processes. Substitution of capital for labor is most evident in the steel, coal-mining, chemical, petroleum, automobile, aluminum, and pulp and paper industries, as well as in the use of computers to perform tasks formerly handled by white-collar employees.

However, the degree to which firms have substituted capital for labor has been obscured somewhat by growing output rates. Suppose that a firm simultaneously experiences a rise in the price it must pay for labor inputs and an increase in the demand for its product. As just explained, the increase in the price of labor, given the price of capital, will eventually precipitate a substitution of capital for labor. This result is shown in Fig. 7-15 as the movement from point A to point C. But should the increase in demand for the firm's product dictate a change in output from Q_1 to Q_2 units, then the firm will find it advantageous to shift from the input mix at point C to the input mix at point D. The movement from point C to point D ultimately calls for using both more capital and more labor than originally. In this case, the labor-increasing effect of raising the firm's output rate more than offsets the labor-decreasing effect of the rise in the price of labor input. But had the price of labor input not risen, the firm would have preferred to use L_4 units of labor instead of L_3 units to produce Q_2 units of output. Thus, the increase in the price of labor input served to restrict the use of labor and caused the firm to select a more capital-intensive production technology (point D) than it otherwise would have selected (point E).

Insofar as an entire economy is concerned, rising consumer demand is essential to keeping unemployment rates from rising to prohibitive levels as business enterprises shift to more capital-intensive production technologies. Nonetheless, the net effect of increases in labor input prices is still to restrict the growth of employment opportunities to less than what would be realized if rising wages did

FIGURE 7-15
Effect of simultaneous changes in resource and output rates upon the optimum resource combination

not further increase the propensity of firms to substitute capital for labor. Fortunately, in the United States the demand for goods and services has usually grown fast enough to override much of the labor-decreasing effect of automation and technological change.

RETURNS TO SCALE

Up to now, the firm and its technology have been examined primarily from a short-run point of view, where a portion of the firm's resource inputs are fixed. The concept of *returns to scale* deals with production relationships over a time span sufficiently long to allow changes in any and all inputs, especially those inputs such as plant space, major pieces of capital equipment, and managerial capability, which are typically fixed in the short run. Specifically, the phrase "returns to scale" refers to the character of changes in output when *all* resource inputs are changed in *equal* proportions.

Consider a firm using L units of labor in combination with C units of capital to obtain an output of Q units. Then

$$L + C \to Q.$$

Now suppose that the amounts of both labor and capital are increased by some arbitrary proportion a. Plainly, output will rise; the question is by what proportion. Suppose that we designate the proportion by which output increases as b. Then

$$aL + aC \rightarrow bQ.$$

1. If the change in output is more than proportional to the change in input ($b > a$), *increasing returns to scale* are said to prevail. For example, if the inputs of capital and labor are increased by 20% per period of time, and output rises by 30%, the firm enjoys increasing returns to scale.

2. If the change in output is equal to the proportional change in input ($b = a$), *constant returns to scale* are present. In this case a doubling of the inputs of both capital and labor per period of time leads to a doubling of the number of units produced.

3. If the change in output is less than proportional to the change in input ($b < a$), the firm experiences *decreasing returns to scale*. An illustration of decreasing returns to scale would be where inputs are increased by 40% but output rises by only 30%.

Given the state of technology, it is generally believed that in expanding its scale of operation a firm will pass successively through

1. A short range of increasing returns to scale,
2. A lengthy range of constant returns to scale, and
3. A range of decreasing returns to scale.

Conceivably, a firm can increase its usage of resource inputs to the point where output reaches an absolute peak; subsequent increases in input then would produce a stage of negative returns to scale where output actually falls.

However, if the concept of returns to scale is broadened to permit changes in a firm's technical capabilities as its size increases, firms may well be (and, indeed, are) able by skillful application of new technologies to expand their scale of operations without ever encountering sharply decreasing returns to scale.[15] Constant returns to scale over a wide range of output appear to characterize many manufacturing industries. The reasons for increasing, constant, and decreasing returns to scale are worth exploring further.

Factors Contributing to Increasing Returns to Scale.   Five factors combine to produce increasing returns to scale for a firm. The most pervasive of these five factors

---

[15] Several empirical studies confirm this finding. See, for example, J. Haldi and D. Whitcomb, "Economies of Scale in Industrial Plants," *Journal of Political Economy,* Vol. 75, No. 4 (August 1967), pp. 373–385; and John R. Moroney, "Cobb-Douglas Production Functions and Returns to Scale in U.S. Manufacturing Industry," *Western Economic Journal,* Vol. 6, No. 1 (December 1967), pp. 39–51.

originates with opportunities for specializing in the use of resource inputs as a firm's scale of operations is increased. The gains in efficiency from specialized use of production-type labor are well chronicled.[16]

In small-scale operations where the typical employee performs several different and perhaps diverse tasks, it is difficult for workers to attain a high degree of proficiency at each one. Mediocre performance of some tasks, with an attendant loss of efficiency, is almost unavoidable; in addition, time is lost in changing from task to task. As scale increases, however, it becomes easier to assign workers to tasks for which they are particularly adept. In concentrating upon a single, well-defined task, people tend to develop greater speed and accuracy—plus they are better at identifying shortcuts and ways for improvement. Time lost in switching from task to task is eliminated. Also, the costs of training individual workers may be reduced by increased specialization. However, specialization in the use of labor can be carried so far that the monotony of performing assembly line jobs becomes excessively fatiguing and mindless, and efficiency gains are neutralized. Hence, firms must be alert to dividing up work tasks in ways that preserve motivated effort.

Second, the larger the scale of production, the greater the feasibility of utilizing the most advanced productive equipment and technology and obtaining the benefits of using specialized capital equipment.[17] Frequently, the most efficient recipe from a technological point of view involves making a product via mass production methods. Small enterprises cannot justify the use of such large-volume

---

[16] The productive powers of specialized use of labor are amply illustrated in a famous passage from Adam Smith's *The Wealth of Nations*, written over 200 years ago: "To take an example . . . from a very trifling manufacture; but one in which the division of labor has been very often taken notice of, the trade of the pinmaker; a workman not educated to this business (which the division of labour has rendered a distinct trade), nor acquainted with the use of the machinery employed in it (to the invention of which the same division of labour has probably given occasion), could scarce, perhaps, with utmost industry, make one pin in a day, and certainly could not make twenty. But in the way in which this business is now carried on, not only the whole work is a pecular trade, but it is divided into a number of branches, of which the greatest part are likewise peculiar trades. One man draws out the wire, another straights it, a third cuts it, a fourth points it, a fifth grinds it at the top for receiving the head; to make the head requires two or three distinct operations; to put it on, is a peculiar business, to whiten the pins is another; it is even a trade by itself to put them into the paper; and the important business of making a pin is, in this manner, divided into about eighteen distinct operations, which in some manufactories, are all performed by distinct hands, though in others the same man will sometimes perform two or three of them. I have seen a small manufactory of this kind where ten men only were employed, and where some of them consequently performed two or three distinct operations. But though they were very poor, and therefore but indifferently accommodated with the necessary machinery, they could, when they exerted themselves, make among them about twelve pounds of pins in a day. There are in a pound upwards of four thousand pins of a middling size. Those ten persons, therefore, could make among them upwards of forty-eight thousand pins in a day. Each person, therefore, making a tenth part of forty-eight thousand pins, might be considered as making four thousand eight hundred pins in a day. But if they had all wrought separately and independently, and without any of them having been educated to this peculiar business, they certainly could not each of them have made twenty, perhaps not one pin in a day; that is, certainly, not the two hundred and fortieth, perhaps not the four thousand eight hundredth part of what they are at present capable of performing, in consequence of a proper division and combination of their different operations."

[17] M. A. Adelman found that employment among the 200 largest firms was about 60% more capital intensive than in the economy as a whole. See M. A. Adelman, "The Measurement of Industrial Concentration," *Review of Economics and Statistics*, Vol. 33, No. 4 (November 1951), p. 278.

production technology, let alone raise the money to install it.[18] Thus, small-scale operations often must rely upon multipurpose machinery and equipment, which seldom can attain the speed and precision of the single-purpose pieces of capital equipment used in larger-sized production units. Not only can larger-scale enterprises afford to employ mass production methods and to embrace new technologies, but they also have the organizational ability to market larger volumes of output, to diversify, to integrate vertically and horizontally (when antitrust will allow), and to decentralize. Hence, they are better positioned to capitalize upon more than proportional increases in output from their production, selling, and administrative inputs.

Purely dimensional factors are a third reason for increasing returns to scale. Doubling the diameter of a natural-gas pipeline can more than double the flow through it. A 100-watt light bulb does not require $2\frac{1}{2}$ times as much labor and materials as a 40-watt light bulb. Doubling the labor and materials in a motor can easily more than double the horsepower of the motor. To build and operate a pulp and paper plant capable of producing 5000 tons of paper products per week does not require 5 times as much labor, managerial talent, equipment, and building space as a pulp and paper plant capable of producing only 1000 tons per week. In a somewhat related fashion, tripling the rate of output of an assembly line may require only one additional inspector instead of two; a diesel locomotive may have sufficient power to pull 50 freight cars as adequately as 20; and a bookseller may be able to sell books in both economics and business administration subjects as well as just those in economics with less than a proportional increase in time, effort, and cost.

Fourth, since technologically complex production processes require several major pieces of equipment, the scale of production may have to be large to overcome potential bottlenecks in the process. Suppose two machines A and B are required for packaging a product, machine A being used to fill the package with the proper amount of the product and machine B being used to wrap the package in cellophane. If machine A can fill 15,000 packages per day and machine B can wrap 20,000 packages per day, then at an output of 60,000 units per day, where four type A machines and three type B machines are used, both types of machines can be efficiently utilized. At less than 60,000 units of output full utilization of both machine types is not possible, and some amount of idle capacity will be present.

And, finally, as its size increases a firm can afford to employ management *specialists,* thereby realizing the benefits to be gained from a specialized use of managerial talents (just as from a specialized use of labor). The added presence of management specialists can give larger firms a proficiency edge over smaller firms whose managers, being fewer in number, must spread their time over a wider range of problems. The managers of many small firms are not skilled enough or equipped for the task of large-scale strategy formulation and organization-

---

[18] For example, in the mid-1970s the rule-of-thumb estimate for the cost of a new oil refinery was about $2000 per single barrel of capacity. That meant a 100,000-barrel-a-day plant, about the smallest considered economically feasible, would require a capital investment of $200 million.

building, which increases the chances that they will be "outmanaged." In contrast, larger firms have the flexibility to staff up to just the right range and depth of skills needed. Moreover, they have the ability to apply the skills of specialists in organized, innovative ways. Decentralization, the multidivisional organizational form, matrix organizational structures, project management, and task force concepts have all been employed in their several varieties to bring about improved operating performance and results.[19] At the same time, with larger size comes an ability to utilize the efficiencies of high-speed computers; to initiate and develop new managerial techniques based upon operations research, simulation processes, and other tools of management science; and to experiment with the use of new managerial methodologies. On the whole, therefore, there is a pronounced tendency for the organizational and managerial capabilities of large firms to exceed those of small enterprises. In fact, a large firm may find that one of its strongest competitive weapons is its superior numbers of people and its potential for specializing its personnel more deeply.

Factors Contributing to Constant Returns to Scale. Increasing returns to scale cannot continue indefinitely; the factors responsible for obtaining output at rates more than proportional to the volumes of resource inputs will sooner or later be exhausted—and usually sooner. This is particularly true for the production unit of a firm—the plant. It is no secret in business that certain size plants are more efficient than others. Moreover, experts in technology and engineering can peg quite closely the most efficient plant size for producing a given product. It is then a simple matter for large-scale enterprises to build as many of these optimum-sized facilities as may be necessary to satisfy the firm's need for productive capacity for that product. For example, if the most efficient plant size is one capable of producing 100,000 units per year, a large firm selling 1 million units per year can realize constant returns to scale in producing this item by building 10 plants, each capable of producing 100,000 units. Where a firm produces several products, it can organize itself into divisions and scale them to the most efficient size. In so doing a large firm may be able to realize constant returns to scale for an almost indefinitely large volume of output. And by centralizing purchasing, selling, and administrative activities under one management, it may even be possible to realize increasing returns from these latter inputs, making the firm's overall operations more efficient than that achievable by a smaller enterprise. Since the ability to decentralize into optimum-sized plants and productions is restricted only by a firm's capacity to manage its operations, the range of output for which a firm can experience constant returns to scale in its production activities is virtually unlimited.

---

[19] Alfred D. Chandler, Jr., *Strategy and Structure* (New York: Doubleday & Company, Inc., Anchor Books edition, 1966), pp. 126–127, 156–157, 195–196, 230, 256, 321–323, 369, 382–383; Oliver E. Williamson, *Corporate Control and Business Behavior* (Englewood Cliffs, N.J.: Prentice-Hall, Inc., 1970). Chapters 7 and 8; Jay R. Galbraith, "Matrix Organizational Designs," *Business Horizons,* Vol. 14, No. 1 (February 1971), pp. 29–40; Peter F. Drucker, *Management: Tasks, Responsibilities, Practices* (New York: Harper & Row, Publishers, 1974); Henry O. Armour and David J. Teece, "Organizational Structure and Economic Performance: A Test of the Multidivisional Hypothesis," *Bell Journal of Economics,* Vol. 9, No. 1 (Spring 1978), pp. 106–122.

APPLICATIONS CAPSULE

FORD'S RIVER ROUGE PLANT:
A CASE OF DECREASING RETURNS TO SCALE

One of the most dramatic examples of pushing a plant's scale of operations beyond a point of manageable size occurred in the 1920s when Ford Motor Company built a gigantic new manufacturing and assembly plant at River Rouge outside Detroit. The River Rouge plant was intended to centralize at one site a broad spectrum of activities relating to automobile production. At this one facility Ford employed 75,000 workers producing coke, pig iron, steel, castings, forgings, and parts and components for cars and tractors, as well as assembly line activities. The plant occupied over 1000 acres and included 93 separate structures, 23 of which were main buildings. The site contained 93 miles of railroad tracks and 27 miles of conveyors. It took a maintenance force of nearly 5000 people to try to keep the plant clean; each year janitorial crews wore out 5000 mops and 3000 brooms and used 86 tons of cleaners on the floors and walls and on the 330 acres of windows.

It soon became evident that the size of the plant was well beyond the optimal point. According to some observers, the plant was so massive and complex that top-level plant managers had little contact with and understanding of what was happening from a plant-wide perspective; lower-level managers were lost in the hubub of so many large and complex activities. The constant and unremitting tempo of the huge quantities of materials coming in and automobiles going out took its toll on both workers and management. According to a former Ford official:

> Everybody was on edge. They ran around in circles and didn't know what they were doing. Physically everybody was going like a steam engine but not so much mentally. As long as their feet were on the go they were working hard. The more a man ran around the better he was . . . . Officials had no offices—only desks in the open factory at which they stood. They couldn't keep records, and lower officials could not discuss their problems together.[a]

In the final analysis, sheer bigness was the undoing of the giant plant. The coming and going of a virtual army of workers, the incoming shipment of huge volumes of raw materials, the maze of manufacturing and assembly line activities, and the shipping out of thousands of cars—all going on at one centralized site— not only created enormous problems of congestion but became a nightmare to manage and operate.

Ford soon found that it was cheaper to ship parts and components for final assembly to scattered, decentralized plants than it was to try to centralize the manufacturing and assembling of cars at one site. Within a few years Ford Motor Company began establishing branch assembly plants and by 1928 had 35 in the United States alone. For many years now, most of the mighty industrial complex at River Rouge has been shut down; in recent years only the foundry has been in use.

[a] Allan Nevins and Ernest Hill, *Ford, Expansion and Challenge: 1915–1933* (New York: Charles Scribner's Sons, 1957), p. 296.

Factors Contributing to Decreasing Returns to Scale.   The principal factor causing a firm to experience decreasing returns to scale is the limit to which the managerial function can be efficiently performed. As a firm becomes larger, the problems of integrating the many facets of its activities multiply. Decision-making is more complex, and the burdens of administration become disproportionately greater. Conventional wisdom insists that "diminishing returns" to management will be encountered as top management loses touch with the daily routine of operation and finds it increasingly necessary to delegate authority to lower-echelon managers whose level of competence may not be as great. Red tape and paper work expand with size; bureaucratic procedures creep in, causing the managerial hierarchy of larger firms to be sluggish and unwieldy in responding to the operational requirements of the organization.

This view of the limits to managerial efficiency is not without merit, yet it is not altogether valid and convincing. Many large corporate enterprises (McDonald's, General Electric, IBM, Procter and Gamble, Delta Airlines, Atlantic Richfield, Sears, 3M Corp.) are widely noted for being well-managed organizations. Big firms appear to have been quite adept at circumventing and subverting

TABLE 7-2. Some Empirical Evidence on Returns to Scale

Analyst/Author	Year	Findings and Conclusions
Moroney[a]	1967	Based upon estimates of production functions made from cross-section statistics in two-digit SIC manufacturing industries, it was concluded that a large majority of these industries were characterized by constant returns to scale.
Bain[b]	1956	In examining the optimum size of plants in the automobile industry, it was found that, in general, a volume of 300,000 cars per year is a low estimate of what is needed for productive efficiency in any one line and that there were probable added advantages to 600,000 units. In assembly alone, a range of 60,000 to 180,000 appeared to be optimal.
Hirsch[c]	1959	It was found that approximately constant returns to scale exist over a considerable range of sizes for public schools and school districts in the St. Louis area.
Riew[d]	1966	In a study of Wisconsin high schools, it was found that there are very significant scale economies up to at least a size of 2400 pupils.
Haldi and Whitcomb[e]	1967	Based upon engineering studies of production functions and scale economies in a variety of industries, it was concluded that (1) there appear to be no great scale economies concerning the use of primary raw materials; (2) efficiency gains for using gas, electricity, and other utilities in larger quantities sometimes occur because larger furnaces, motors, and other such equipment units perform more efficiently than smaller units; (3) large economies of scale in labor costs are possible for process-type plants because labor's chief function is to watch gauges, adjust valves, and perform maintenance tasks—none of which require many extra workers as capacity is added; (4) substantial economies of scale are obtainable in performing supervisory and management functions; (5) there are substantial economies of scale in maintenance performance arising from the fact that maintenance needs do not increase proportionately with capacity, nor do labor costs for this maintenance increase proportionately with output.

TABLE 7-2. *(continued)*

Analyst/Author	Year	Findings and Conclusions
Blair *et al.*[f]	1975	In fitting one linear and three nonlinear functional forms to average administrative costs, there was strong evidence of scale economies in the administrative aspects of a health insurance program.
Miller[g]	1978	Using information from the *1972 Census of Manufactures*, it was found that (1) on average, the four largest firms in an industry had an output per plant employee that was 39% greater than that for all other firms in the industry, (2) on average, the four largest firms had profits per employee that were 57% greater than those for the remainder of the industry, and (3) on average, the top four firms were able to handle 43% more raw material inputs per employee than the remainder of the industry. The study covered 448 industries (at the four-digit SIC level). The conclusion was that the leading four firms are substantially more productive than smaller firms and that there is compelling evidence of large economies of scale at the firm level for a major portion of American industry.
Caves, Christensen, and Swanson[h]	1981	Using data from the American railroad industry for the 1955–1974 period, the authors found sizable returns to scale when output changes were accompanied by changes in haul and trip lengths.
Humphrey[i]	1981	Substantial economies of scale were found to exist at a majority of Federal Reserve operated "automated clearinghouse" check-processing centers during 1978 and 1979. On average, for each 10% rise in volume, total production costs rose only by 6 to 7%.
Ball and Chambers[j]	1982	Empirical results over the period 1972–1976 indicated that the meat products industry was characterized by increasing returns to scale.

[a] John R. Moroney, "Cobb-Douglas Production Functions and Returns to Scale in U.S. Manufacturing Industry," *Western Economic Journal,* Vol. 6, No. 1 (December 1967), pp. 39–51.

[b] Joe S. Bain, *Barriers to New Competition* (Cambridge, Mass.: Harvard University Press, 1956), p. 244.

[c] Werner Hirsch, "Appendix—Economies of Scale," *Analysis of the Rising Costs of Public Education,* Study Paper No. 4, Materials Prepared in Connection with the Study of Employment, Growth, and Price Levels, for consideration by the Joint Economics Committee, Congress of the United States, November 10, 1959 (Washington, D.C.: U.S. Government Printing Office, 1959).

[d] John Riew, "Economies of Scale in High School Operation," *Review of Economics and Statistics,* Vol. 48, No. 3 (August 1966), pp. 280–287.

[e] John Haldi and David Whitcomb, "Economies of Scale in Industrial Plants," *Journal of Political Economy,* Vol. 75, No. 4 (August 1967), pp. 373–385.

[f] Roger D. Blair, Jerry R. Jackson, and Ronald J. Vogel, "Economies of Scale in the Administration of Health Insurance," *Review of Economics and Statistics,* Vol. 47, No. 2 (May 1975), pp. 185–189.

[g] Edward M. Miller, "The Extent of Economies of Scale," *Southern Economic Journal,* Vol. 44, No. 3 (January 1978), pp. 470–487.

[h] Douglas W. Caves, L. R. Christensen, and Joseph A. Swanson, "Productivity Growth, Scale Economies, and Capacity Utilization in U.S. Railroads, 1955–1974," *American Economic Review,* Vol. 71, No. 5 (December 1981), pp. 994–1002.

[i] D. B. Humphrey, "Scale Economies at Automated Clearinghouses," *Journal of Bank Research,* Vol. 12, No. 2 (Summer 1981), pp. 71–81.

[j] V. E. Ball and R. G. Chambers, "An Economic Analysis of Technology in the Meat Products Industry," *American Journal of Agricultural Economics,* Vol. 64, No. 4 (November 1982), pp. 699–709.

managerial inefficiencies via reliance on a higher order of managerial technology. Innovative organizational schemes, computerized data processing, systems analysis, strategic planning, and operations research models, coupled with superior management talent have had the effect of allowing the management function in billion-dollar corporations to be performed with good results.[20] Hence, while it is undoubtedly true that limits exist regarding efficient performance of the managerial function, it is just as true that the prevailing limits can be pushed back by the successful application of better managerial technologies. It does not appear that the limits to efficient performance of the managerial function have, in practice, been a significant factor in hindering the growth of enterprises any more than has inefficient performance of other phases of business activity.

Table 7-2 provides summary findings of several investigations of the nature and existence of returns to scale.

MATHEMATICAL CAPSULE 10

DETERMINING RETURNS TO SCALE FROM THE PRODUCTION FUNCTION

Suppose that a large, diversified enterprise carefully examines the input-output relationships for each of its three major products (X, Y, and Z) and concludes that the production functions for these products are

$$Q_X = 1.6L^{0.4}C^{0.4}M^{0.1},$$
$$Q_Y = \sqrt{0.4L^2CM},$$
$$Q_Z = 10L + 7C + M,$$

where Q represents output per period of time, L is units of labor input, C is units of capital input, and M is units of managerial input. The question immediately arises as to what returns to scale are encountered in manufacturing the three products. The answer can be determined by observing what happens to output when the inputs of labor, capital, and management are increased *in equal proportions*. The production function is "tested" by multiplying each input by a constant factor (say a) and ascertaining whether output changes (1) by an amount greater than a in which case increasing returns to scale are signified, (2) by an amount equal to a

---

[20] The rapid development of analytical and managerial techniques that stimulate and assist enterprises to find more efficient ways of accomplishing their activities is impressive. Operations research, simulation, and mathematical programming are among the more sophisticated of these new forms of managerial technology, but equally significant advances have been made concerning new and more precise accounting and budget-control procedures, better methods of market analysis, more efficient cash management procedures, refinements in business forecasting, and communications techniques. The unifying character of these new developments in managerial technology is that they bring the principles of rational problem solving to bear even more heavily upon sustaining effective organizational performance.

in which case constant returns to scale are signified, or (3) by an amount less than a in which case decreasing returns to scale are indicated.

The returns to scale indicated by the production function for product X are found in the following manner. Multiplying each of the three inputs by a, where $a > 1$ so as to indicate an increase in the inputs, we obtain

$$1.6(aL)^{0.4}(aC)^{0.4}(aM)^{0.1},$$

which becomes

$$1.6a^{0.4}L^{0.4}a^{0.4}C^{0.4}a^{0.1}M^{0.1}.$$

Factoring a out of the function gives

$$a^{0.4+0.4+0.1}(1.6L^{0.4}C^{0.4}M^{0.1})$$

or

$$a^{0.9}(1.6L^{0.4}C^{0.4}M^{0.1}).$$

The expression in parentheses defines the level of output prior to the change in input, and $a^{0.9}$ represents the proportional change in the output of product X when each input is increased by a. Because the exponent for a is less than 1, increasing the inputs by a results in a *less than proportional* increase in the output of X, and the production function for X may be said to exhibit decreasing returns to scale.

In the case of product Y, increasing each input by an arbitrary proportion a, where $a > 1$, yields

$$\sqrt{0.4(aL)^2(aC)(aM)}.$$

Simplifying this expression, we get

$$\sqrt{0.4a^2L^2aCaM} = \sqrt{0.4a^4L^2CM} = a^2\sqrt{0.4L^2CM}.$$

Hence, increasing each input by a causes output to expand by a^2—obviously, increasing returns to scale are present, since output expands at a rate more than proportional to the input increase. This result is easily confirmed by means of a numerical example. Suppose, originally, that $L = 5$, $C = 5$, and $M = 2$; then

$$\begin{aligned} Q_Y &= \sqrt{0.4L^2CM} \\ &= \sqrt{0.4(5)^2(5)(2)} \\ &= \sqrt{100} \\ &= 10. \end{aligned}$$

If all the inputs are doubled ($a = 2$), we have $L = 10$, $C = 10$, $M = 4$, and

$$\begin{aligned} Q_Y &= \sqrt{0.4(10)^2(10)(4)} \\ &= \sqrt{1600} \\ &= 40. \end{aligned}$$

Consequently, doubling the inputs of labor, capital, and management causes the output of product Y to quadruple (since $a^2 = 4$ when $a = 2$), and increasing returns to scale may be said to characterize the production function for product Y.

Increasing the inputs by a for the production function for product Z gives

$$10(aL) + 7(aC) + aM,$$

or, more simply,

$$a(10L + 7C + M).$$

Here output changes by the same proportion as input, so constant returns to scale are present.[a] Again, a simple example verifies existence of constant returns to scale for product Z. If $L = 15$, $C = 10$, and $M = 5$, then

$$Q_Z = 10L + 7C + M$$
$$= 10(15) + 7(10) + 5$$
$$= 225.$$

Doubling the inputs ($a = 2$) so that $L = 30$, $C = 20$, and $M = 10$, we get

$$Q_Z = 10(30) + 7(20) + 10$$
$$= 450.$$

Therefore, doubling each input causes the output of product Z to double—a constant-returns—to—scale situation.

The character of the production functions for the three products X, Y, and Z provides a guide to management for choosing the products upon which to concentrate its limited resources. *Other things being equal*, cost and efficiency considerations call for steering resources (financial and otherwise) to those products with the most favorable returns to scale. The most favorable, of course, is increasing returns to scale, followed in order by constant returns and decreasing returns. Hence, products Y, Z, and X in that order yield the enterprise the greatest amounts of output for a given amount of input.

However, a word of qualification must be offered. Returns to scale in no way reflect the demand side of the picture. The mere fact that the output of a commodity is characterized by decreasing returns to scale does not mean that it is unprofitable. The price which can be obtained for product X may be so favorable that it is relatively more profitable than either product Y or Z. In fact, the competitive forces prevailing in the markets for Y and Z could make those commodities unprofitable, even though they can be produced under very favorable conditions. Returns to scale indicate only the direction of change in productive efficiency and unit costs which can be anticipated if the size of the firm's production operations is increased or decreased. Also, the nature of the production function for a product can change over a period of time because of scientific and engineering developments, innovation, and advances in managerial technology. Thus, in the long run the production process for an item can be transformed from decreasing to constant or increasing returns to scale.

EXERCISE

1. Determine the returns to scale implied in each of the following production functions.
    (a) $Q = 0.4A^2 + 0.3AB + 2.0B.$
    (b) $Q = 0.7L^8C^{.3}.$
    (c) $Q = 10 + 4A + 9B.$
    (d) $Q = (10/L) + 6C.$

[a] The mathematics of production functions is not always as neat and clear-cut as the three cases above might indicate. Consider the production function

$$Q = 16L + 0.5LCM + 1.4L^{0.5}C^{0.3}M^{0.1}$$

Changing the inputs by a yields

$$16(aL) + 0.5(aL)(aC)(aM) + 1.4(aL)^{0.5}(aC)^{0.3}(aM)^{0.1},$$

which simplifies to

$$16aL + 0.5a^3LCM + 1.4a^{0.9}L^{0.5}C^{0.3}M^{0.1}.$$

Inspecting the expression above term by term, we find that the first term ($16aL$) has the characteristic of constant returns to scale, the second term ($0.5a^3LCM$) has the characteristic of increasing returns to scale, and the third term ($1.4a^{.9}L^{.5}C^{.3}M^{.1}$) displays decreasing returns to scale. Whether the entire production function exhibits increasing, constant, or decreasing returns to scale on balance depends on the relative strengths of the three terms. In this instance the strong increasing returns influence found in the second term will overpower the mildly decreasing returns shown in the third term, with the result that the entire production function shows increasing returns to scale.

SUMMARY AND CONCLUSIONS

In analyzing production processes, resources are generally divided into two categories: fixed and variable. Corresponding to the notion of fixed and variable inputs is the notion of the short run and the long run. In the short run, output can be changed only by altering the amount of variable input used in conjunction with the given fixed input. In the long run, output can be changed by altering the scale of production, the technology of the production process, and the rate of usage of any and all inputs.

The principle of diminishing marginal returns states that as the amount of a variable input is increased by equal increments and combined with a specified amount of fixed input, eventually a point will be reached where the resulting increases in the quantity of output will get smaller and smaller. Should the usage rate of variable input get sufficiently large, the quantity of output will reach a maximum and may then decrease as still larger amounts of variable input are employed.

The relationships between the production function, average product, and marginal product can be used to define three stages of production. Stage I covers the range of variable input where AP_{vi} is rising; stage II includes the range where AP_{vi} is falling *and* where MP is declining yet positive; and stage III encompasses the range where MP is negative and total output is falling.

The optimum resource combination is in stage II at the input rate where (1) the firm is fully utilizing its dollars in purchasing inputs and (2) an equivalent amount of extra output is being obtained from the last dollar spent on each input. Graphically, this condition is achieved at the point of tangency between the isocost curve and an isoquant.

If the firm increases all its inputs by a given proportion and output increases by *more* than this proportion, increasing returns to scale prevail. If the firm increases all its inputs by a given proportion and output rises by this *same* proportion, constant returns to scale characterize the production process. If the firm increases all its inputs by the same proportion and output rises *less* than proportionally, decreasing returns to scale are present. Increasing returns to scale occur because of increased specialization in use of resources, technological considerations, dimensional factors, and indivisibility of inputs. Constant returns to scale arise when the production process embodies standard man-machine ratios and when it is feasible to assimilate a number of optimum-sized production units under a single management. Decreasing returns to scale occur primarily because of limitations to efficient performance of the managerial function.

SUGGESTED READINGS

COURVILLE, L., "Regulation and Efficiency in the Electric Utility Industry," *Bell Journal of Economics and Management Science*, Vol. 5, No. 1 (Spring 1974), pp. 53–74.

HALDI, J., AND D. WHITCOMB, "Economies of Scale in Industrial Plants," *Journal of Political Economy*, Vol. 75, No. 4 (August 1967), pp. 373–385.

HUETTNER, D. A., AND J. H. LANDON, "Electric Utilities: Scale Economies and Diseconomies," *Southern Economic Journal*, Vol. 44, No. 4 (April 1978), pp. 883–912.

MAXWELL, W. D., "Short-Run Returns to Scale and the Production of Services," *Southern Economic Journal*, Vol. 32, No. 1 (July 1965), pp. 1–19.

MILLER, E. M., "The Extent of Economies of Scale," *Southern Economic Journal*, Vol. 44, No. 3 (January 1978), pp. 470–487.

———, "Size of Firm and Size of Plant," *Southern Economic Journal*, Vol. 44, No. 4 (April 1978), pp. 861–872.

MOORE, F. T., "Economies of Scale: Some Statistical Evidence," *Quarterly Journal of Economics*, Vol. 73, No. 2 (May 1959), pp. 232–245.

MORONEY, J. R., "Cobb-Douglas Production Functions and Returns to Scale in U.S. Manufacturing Industry," *Western Economic Journal*, Vol. 6, No. 1 (December 1967), pp. 39–51.

SHEN, T. Y., "Economies of Scale, Expansion Path, and Growth of Plants," *Review of Economics and Statistics*, Vol. 47, No. 4 (November 1965), pp. 420–428.

STIGLER, G., "The Economies of Scale," *Journal of Law and Economics*, Vol. 1 (October 1958), pp. 54–71.

PROBLEMS AND QUESTIONS FOR DISCUSSION

1. Fill in the values for discrete MP, AP_{vi}, and AP_{fi} based upon the information given in the table.

Units of Fixed Input	Units of Variable Input	Quantity of Output	Discrete MP	AP_{vi}	AP_{fi}
3	0	0			
3	1	120	———	———	———
3	2	270	———	———	———
3	3	390	———	———	———
3	4	480	———	———	———
3	5	540	———	———	———
3	6	560	———	———	———
3	7	540	———	———	———

2. Given: The production function $Q = 12X$, where Q = units of output per period of time and X = units of variable input.
   (a) Determine the equations for MP and AP_{vi}.
   (b) Assuming 5 units of fixed input are presently being employed in the production process represented by the production function above, determine AP_{fi} when 10 units of variable input are combined with the 5 units of fixed input.
   (c) Graphically illustrate the production function and the corresponding MP and AP_{vi} functions.
   (d) How would you describe the important properties of this production function?

3. Production managers for the Cosmic Paper Corporation estimate that their production process is currently characterized by the following short-run production function: $Q = 72X + 15X^2 - X^3$, where Q = tons of paper products per production period and X = units of variable input employed per production period.
   (a) Determine the equations for MP and AP_{vi}.
   (b) What is MP when 7 units of variable input are employed?
   (c) By how much does output rise when the usage of variable input is increased from 7 to 8 units per production period?
   (d) At what rate of usage of variable input is the point of diminishing marginal returns encountered?
   (e) What is the maximum output capability per production period? What rate of usage of variable input is required to reach the maximum output level?
   (f) Graphically illustrate this production function and the corresponding MP and AP_{vi} functions. Indicate on your graph the output ranges where output is increasing at an increasing rate and where output is increasing at a decreasing rate. Also indicate the output where the point of diminishing average returns to variable input is encountered.

4. Graphically illustrate the stages of production for each of the following general types of production functions.
   (a) $Q = bX$.
   (b) $Q = bX - cX^2$.
   (c) $Q = bX + cX^2 - dX^3$.

5. The production department of the National Cabinet Corporation employs 20 unskilled laborers, 45 semiskilled workers, and 60 skilled craftsmen. A careful assessment of the productivity of the three types of labor indicates that the marginal product of an unskilled laborer is currently 10 units of output per worker-day, the marginal product of a semiskilled worker is 20 units per worker-day, and the marginal product of a skilled craftsman is 50 units per worker-day. The wage rates for the three types of labor result in labor costs of $20 per worker-day for unskilled labor, $30 per worker-day for semiskilled workers, and $50 per worker-day for skilled craftsmen. Output is currently at the desired level. Would you suggest a change in the labor mix used by the production department? Why or why not?

6. The Fashion Dress Corporation is considering the construction of a new plant. Engineers have submitted the following possible plant designs—all of which are equally capable from a physical standpoint of producing the desired output of 1000 dresses per day:
   (a) Illustrate the technically feasible production alternatives by means of an isoquant.

Plant Design	Units of Capital	Units of Labor
1	50	500
2	75	400
3	150	200
4	250	100
5	350	50

(b) Suppose that the price of capital is $100 per unit and the price of labor is $50 per unit. Which plant design should be selected? Justify your answer with an isocost-isoquant graph.

(c) What will be the required total cost outlay for capital and labor for the selected plant design?

7. Suppose that Apex Manufacturing Corporation has its choice of three production processes for producing its product. With process A, Apex can produce 100 units of output per hour using 5 units of labor and 20 units of capital; by process B, 100 units per hour with 10 units each of labor and capital; by process C, 100 units per hour with 20 units of labor and 5 units of capital. All three processes are characterized by constant returns to scale.

(a) Graphically illustrate isoquants for outputs of 100, 200, and 300 units per hour.

(b) If the price of labor is $5 per unit and capital costs $10 per unit, which process should be selected to produce 200 units? *Illustrate* your answer by means of isoquant and isocost curves.

(c) If the price of labor is $8 per unit and the price of capital is $8 per unit, which process should be selected to produce 100 units per hour? Verify your answer with an isoquant-isocost graph.

(d) If the price of labor is $14 per unit and capital is $7 per unit, which process should be selected to produce 300 units per hour? What will be the necessary total cost outlay?

8. Jupiter Products, Inc., has derived the following production function for its operation: $Q = 0.65L^{0.42}C^{0.38}M^{0.20}Z^{0.08}$, where Q = units of output per period of time, L = hours of labor, C = hours of machine services, M = hours of managerial input, and Z = miscellaneous resource services.

(a) Assuming that Jupiter's operations are sufficiently flexible to vary the usage of L, C, M, and Z, what kind of returns are indicated by this production function? Why?

(b) What inference, if any, can you make about the firm's unit costs for producing additional units of output?

9. A diversification-minded company has employed a team of operations researchers to advise it on acquiring prospective enterprises. Four small firms, each producing the same commodity but employing radically different production technologies, are currently being carefully scrutinized for possible acquisition. The operations research team has initiated investigations of the production, marketing, and financial aspects of the four firms for the purpose of singling out one of them as the best candidate for acquisition. As part of their investigation they have sought to estimate the production functions for each of the four firms; their estimates are as follows:

$$\text{Firm A: } Q_A = 0.8L^{0.6}C^{0.2}M^{0.1}.$$
$$\text{Firm B: } Q_B = \tfrac{7}{5}L + \tfrac{3}{2}C + M.$$
$$\text{Firm C: } Q_C = \sqrt{0.09L^{0.5}C^{1.0}M^{0.5}}.$$
$$\text{Firm D: } Q_D = 6L^2 + 7C^2 - LC + 0.1M^2.$$

On the basis of these estimates alone, which of the four firms appears to offer the acquisitive company the best prospects? Why?

10. What is the difference between "returns to variable input" and "returns to scale?"

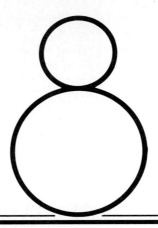

THE SUPPLY SIDE
OF THE MARKETPLACE
Cost behavior and economies
of scale

The costs of goods and services derive from the technology and the inputs used to produce them. The analysis of cost behavior is founded, therefore, upon the principles of production. In this chapter we shall translate the relationships among production technology, inputs, and outputs into cost functions. After exploring the nature of "cost," short-run and long-run cost curves will be derived for a variety of possible production functions and production technologies. Then we will conclude the chapter by looking at economies of scale and a new analytical tool called "strategic cost analysis."

DEFINING AND MEASURING COSTS

Mention of the word *cost* immediately conjures up the thought of "money outlays." In the context of business operations, costs are commonly viewed as a firm's actual or historical expenditures for resource inputs. However, for many decision purposes historical costs are of limited significance. In the first place, the costs that really matter for *business decisions* are future costs; historical costs are useful primarily as bench marks for anticipating behavior. Even so, *historical* costs should be treated warily since inflation, changing input supply conditions, and so on can make past costs an obsolete indicator of the future.

As a means of illustrating the multidimensional aspects of cost, consider the apparently innocuous statement: "General Electric's cost of producing an electric toaster in 1984 was $9.45.'' The most obvious interpretation of this statement is that the costs incurred by General Electric in operating its electric toaster divisional unit amounted to an average of $9.45 in 1984. No doubt the basis for such a figure would be the historical expenses for resources bought outright or hired by GE and which were routinely recorded in its accounts according to GE's scheme of accounting practice. These explicitly incurred expenses might consist of production labor costs, payments for component parts purchased from suppliers, managerial salaries, interest costs, payments for electric power, transportation costs, telephone services, depreciation charges, administrative expenses, property taxes, and other miscellaneous payments.

Despite the apparent accuracy and completeness of including all actual operating expenses, the figure of $9.45 per toaster will in all probability not prove to be as definitive and all-inclusive as first appears. To begin with, anyone familiar with the techniques and options of cost accounting is aware that two manufacturers of physically identical products who use different, but acceptable, methods of measuring cost could differ in their reported costs by 40% or more.[1] Historical cost statistics can thus be misleading unless one knows a great deal about the particular cost accounting system from which they are derived.

Second, it is easy to overlook allowances for equity capital supplied by the firm's stockholders as being a valid cost element.[2] If firms borrow money from banks or other financial institutions, the interest costs are shown as an expense on the profit and loss statement; yet if the same funds are raised by selling new issues of common stock, no cost for capital is entered in the firm's ledger. Nonetheless, if stockholders fail to receive a return on their invested capital equivalent to what could be earned were they to invest their funds in the best alternative investment of equal risk, then they will understandably be reluctant to supply the enterprise with financial capital in the future. Thus, if General Electric wishes to use equity capital as a source of financing for its activities (including making toasters), then in the long run GE must not only cover all actual operating expenses but also have enough revenue left over to reward stockholders with a return on their investment at least equivalent to stockholders' *opportunity costs*—the return GE's owners are sacrificing by not having invested in other ventures of comparable risk. GE must cover this opportunity cost in order to induce continued stockholder participation and confidence in the firm's activities. These oppor-

---

[1] Cost differentials can "artificially" be produced by judiciously selecting among the following options for measuring a firm's costs: (1) using an accelerated depreciation schedule instead of the straight-line method; (2) using the first-in, first-out (FIFO) method of inventory valuation instead of the last-in, first-out (LIFO) method; (3) employing a direct costing system rather than a full-cost accounting system; (4) selecting any one of several acceptable rules for determining the time period to which certain kinds of expenses will be charged; and (5) using artificial transfer prices for intermediate goods passing from one operating division to another instead of open market transfer prices.

[2] In the case of entrepreneurial or owner-managed firms the cost of other owner-supplied resources may be overlooked. For example, the proprietor may elect not to pay himself a salary but instead rely upon "profits" as payment for his services. Such a practice clearly understates the operating costs of the enterprise, since the value of the managerial skills furnished by the proprietor is not included. Similarly, if no allowance is made for the costs of land and working capital supplied by the proprietor, total costs will be underestimated.

tunity costs represent a minimum acceptable return to stockholders and are just as legitimate a cost of doing business as recorded operating expenses.

Third, for some purposes the best measure of the true economic worth (cost) of a resource input may be the resource inputs' opportunity costs rather than the dollar outlays for the input appearing in historical accounting records. As above, we use the term *opportunity costs* to represent the benefits (monetary or otherwise) foregone by not choosing the best alternative course of action. In other words, opportunity costs are the sacrifices incurred by not having done something else. Several examples may be offered to make the relevance of opportunity cost considerations more apparent. The cost to General Electric of making its own heating elements for use in GE electric toasters can correctly be viewed as the price at which GE could sell these heating elements to other firms were they not to use them in their own toasters. In periods of strong demand for GE products, the cost to GE of using available resources for toaster production is the profit GE gives up by not devoting these resources to the production of other GE appliances and products. The costs to GE of using scarce executive and managerial talents in toaster production is not so much the related salaries as it is the contribution to profits that these executives and managers could make by devoting their time to other GE activities. The cost of building a new $2 million plant to manufacture GE toasters is not just the interest that GE might have to pay on the borrowed money but rather the profits or cost savings that could be achieved by investing the $2 million in making electric skillets, vacuum cleaners, numeric-controlled process equipment, longer-lasting light bulbs, or any other of GE's many products.[3] Opportunity costs are, therefore, a measure of the sacrifice incurred from a decision not to take advantage of an alternative opportunity; putting a dollar value on opportunity costs involves a comparison between the chosen course of action and the best alternative course of action.

Although precise calculation of either implicit or opportunity costs is often subjective, considering these two aspects of cost in conjunction with historical costs can lead to a sounder analysis and determination of costs. Certainly, adjusting historical costs for implicit and opportunity cost elements improves the accuracy with which the profitability of an enterprise can be judged. For instance, unless GE's revenues from the sale of toasters exceed both the explicit and implicit costs of toaster production, GE cannot be said to be truly earning a profit on toasters. Moreover, unless GE's return on its dollar investment in toaster production is at least equivalent to what it could earn by putting this investment in another activity, GE should discontinue toaster production and shift its resources into the better alternative. Thus, while the size of a firm's opportunity costs is difficult to determine, some estimate of their size is crucial to key decisions. In

---

[3] From a broader social viewpoint, the cost of producing a toaster can be thought of as the utility consumers forego from giving up the goods that could have been produced had not some of society's existing pool of economic resources been used to manufacture electric toasters. Resources used to produce toasters cannot be used to produce other things—items from which certain segments of society may derive great satisfaction. Thus, the cost to society of a GE toaster is not $9.45 but is the sacrifice of utility associated with not having more of some other item which GE or some other firm could have produced instead.

this regard it is better to have a rough estimate of the right concept of cost than an accurate estimate of the wrong concept.

Fourth, to view the concept of cost in exclusively monetary terms is to leave out a portion of what may rightfully be considered as cost. The social costs of noise, congestion, and environmental pollution are not easily reduced to dollars and cents. Nor are psychic costs readily expressed in monetary terms; these involve the mental anguish and mental dissatisfaction associated with such activities as dismissing employees, moving one's family to accept a transfer to an undesirable location, working on holidays, pressures from one's boss for outstanding performance, and the monotony of repetitive tasks.[4] Plainly, social costs and psychic costs abound in many business situations, yet they never appear in an enterprise's financial accounts. A thread common to all the many dimensions of cost can be summed up in the word *sacrifice*. All costs entail a sacrifice of some type; the form of the sacrifice may be tangible or intangible, objective or subjective, monetary or nonmonetary. For this reason, it is not always possible in many cases to reduce costs to simple dollars and cents, nor is it possible to arrive at a single, unambiguous and universally acceptable way to calculate *the cost* of a product.

But even after adjusting historical costs in all of the ways just discussed, we end up with a cost figure of limited usefulness for making decisions. Looking again at the stated cost of $9.45 for producing a GE toaster, consider the following questions:

1. How much of the $9.45 represents costs directly related to the production of toasters (direct costs), and how much of the $9.45 represents costs not directly traceable to toasters [e.g., the chief executive's salary and other costs common to the production of several of GE's products (common costs)]?

2. How much of the $9.45 represents fixed charges associated with the plant, equipment, and management needed for toaster production (fixed costs), and how much is accounted for by direct production labor and raw materials (variable costs)?

3. To what extent would the $9.45 cost be altered by a 10% increase in GE's production of toasters (incremental costs)?

4. What portion of the $9.45 represents controllable costs (property taxes as compared to managerial salaries), and what portion represents cuttable costs (the use of skilled union labor as compared to advertising)?

5. How would a labor strike affect the costs of producing a toaster (shutdown costs and startup costs)?

6. To what extent can the $9.45 cost be expected to change in the long run (long-run versus short-run costs)?

7. How is the $9.45 cost of a toaster divided between manufacturing costs and such selling costs as salesmen's salaries and commissions, promotional expenses, maintaining distribution channels, and operating repair centers and warehouses?

---

[4] Psychic costs are not unique to business enterprise, nor can they be lightly dismissed as inconsequential. For example, few students would question that they incur significant psychic costs from preparing for and taking final exams; nor would professors deny the existence of psychic costs in preparing and grading exams and in assigning final grades. The examination process is very painful indeed, and to ignore the psychic costs which it entails would probably mean omitting the greatest of the costs of administering examinations.

8. How would the introduction of a completely automated assembly line alter the $9.45 cost?
9. What portion of the $9.45 could be postponed in the event of a decision to trim the costs of toaster production (postponable costs)?
10. How much of the $9.45 could be avoided if it became necessary to reduce toaster production by 20% (escapable versus unavoidable costs)?

These questions suffice to indicate that no one measure of the costs of production is adequate for decision-making purposes. Different decision problems call for different kinds of cost information. Depending on the purpose at hand, one may wish to determine total costs, average costs, marginal costs, fixed costs, variable costs, direct costs, common costs, historical costs, future costs, opportunity costs, controllable costs, shutdown costs, postponable costs, long-run costs, escapable costs, replacement costs, incremental costs, manufacturing costs, selling costs, administrative costs, labor costs, and so on ad infinitum.[5]

COST-OUTPUT RELATIONSHIPS

The fundamental starting point in cost analysis is that a functional relationship exists between the costs of production and the rate of output per period of time. A cost function shows the various costs which will be incurred at alternative output rates; in other words,

$$\text{cost} = f(\text{output}).$$

But, as indicated in Chapter 7, the rate of output is, in turn, a function of the rate of usage of the resource inputs:

$$\text{output} = f(\text{inputs}).$$

Since the production function establishes the relations between input and output flows, once the prices of the inputs are known the costs of a specific quantity of output can be calculated. As a consequence, the level and behavior of costs as a firm's rate of output changes is largely dependent on two factors:

1. The character of the underlying production function.
2. The prices the firm must pay for its resource inputs.

The former determines the shape of the firm's cost functions, while the latter determine the level of costs. To simplify our examination of cost-output relationships, we shall assume that the prices a firm pays for its resource inputs are not affected by changes in its output rate.

---

[5] More complete discussions of the many aspects of cost are found in J. M. Clark, *Studies in the Economics of Overhead Costs* (Chicago: University of Chicago Press, 1923), Chapters 4–6; Joel Dean, *Managerial Economics* (Englewood Cliffs, N.J.: Prentice-Hall, Inc., 1951), Chapter 5; and Milton H. Spencer, *Managerial Economics*, 3rd ed. (Homewood, Ill.: Richard D. Irwin, Inc., 1968), Chapter 7.

The Short Run and the Long Run

In discussing the relationships between cost and output it is useful to differentiate between cost behavior in the short run and cost behavior in the long run. From Chapter 7 it will be recalled that the short run refers to a period of time so short that the firm cannot readily vary such inputs as the amount of space available for production activity, major pieces of equipment, basic technology, and key managerial personnel (the so-called fixed inputs); output is alterable only by increasing or decreasing the usage of variable inputs (production labor, raw materials, and so on). In the long run, however, sufficient time exists for modifying technology *and* the usage of any and all inputs so as to maintain an optimum combination—all inputs are therefore variable in the long run, as is technology.

The classification of resource inputs as being fixed or variable in the short run and as being all variable in the long run provides a convenient approach to investigating cost behavior. We shall first examine short-run cost functions and then long-run functions.

COST-OUTPUT RELATIONSHIPS IN THE SHORT RUN

The Family of Total Cost Concepts

Three concepts of total cost are important for analyzing a firm's short-run cost structure: total fixed cost, total variable cost, and total cost.

The fixed inputs of a firm give rise to fixed costs, the amount of which depends on the quantity of each of the various fixed inputs and the respective prices paid for them. Salaries of top-management officials, property taxes, interest on borrowed money, depreciation charges, rents on office space, the implicit costs of equity capital, and insurance premiums are examples of fixed costs. A firm's fixed costs reflect the dollar value (or economic worth) of its fixed inputs. Because the amounts of fixed input do not vary with output in the short run, it follows that fixed costs also do not vary with output. In formal terms, *total fixed cost* (*TFC*) may be defined as the sum total of the costs of all the fixed inputs associated with the firm's operations.[6] Because the firm's fixed input quantities are not subject to change in the short run, *TFC* is constant unless the *prices* of the fixed inputs change (higher property taxes, increases in insurance rates or rents, and so on). Moreover, total fixed costs continue even if production facilities are idle.

---

[6] In terms of more formal mathematics, total fixed costs may be defined as

$$TFC = \sum_{i=1}^{n} p_i x_i,$$

where

p_i = price of a specified fixed input,
x_i = quantity of the specified fixed input, and
n = number of various kinds of fixed inputs.

Similarly, those inputs that are variable in the short run give rise to short-run variable costs. Since in the short run a firm modifies its output rate by buying more or less units of variable input, variable costs depend on and vary with the quantity of output. *Total variable cost (TVC)* is the sum of the amounts a firm spends for variable inputs employed in the production process.[7] Examples of variable costs include payroll expenses, raw material outlays, power and fuel charges, and transportation costs.[8] Total variable cost (*TVC*) is zero when output is zero because no variable inputs need be employed to produce nothing. However, as output increases, so does the usage of variable input; thus, *TVC* increases directly with output.

The *total cost* of a given output rate in the short run is the sum of total fixed cost and total variable cost:

$$TC = TFC + TVC.$$

At zero output, total variable cost is zero and total cost is equal to total fixed cost. As soon as output rises above zero in the short run, some variable inputs must be used, variable costs are incurred, and total cost is the sum of the fixed and variable expenses.

The Family of Unit Cost Concepts

There are four major *unit cost concepts*: average fixed cost (*AFC*), average variable cost (*AVC*), average total cost (*ATC*), and marginal cost (*MC*). All these may be derived from the total cost concepts discussed above.

Average fixed cost is defined as total fixed cost divided by the units of output, or

$$AFC = \frac{TFC}{Q}.$$

Since total fixed cost is a constant amount, average fixed cost declines continuously as the rate of production increases. For example, if *TFC* = \$1000, at an output of 10 units *AFC* = \$1000/10 = \$100; at an output of 20 units *AFC* = \$1000/20 = \$50; at an output of 50 units *AFC* = \$1000/50 = \$20; and so on. The reduction of *AFC* by producing more units of output is commonly called "spreading the overhead." The calculation of average fixed cost can also be approached from a

---

[7] Total variable costs may be defined in mathematical terms as

$$TVC = \sum_{j=1}^{m} p_j x_j,$$

where

p_j = price of a specified variable input,
x_j = quantity of the specified variable input, and
m = number of various kinds of variable inputs.

[8] A variety of expenses incurred by firms has both fixed and variable aspects. These include telephone service, advertising outlays, research and development costs, office supplies, expense account allowances, payroll taxes, and fringe benefit costs.

slightly different direction. If we conceive of a firm's inputs as consisting of a number of identical units, then total fixed cost equals the number of units of fixed input (*FI*) multiplied by the unit price of the fixed input (P_{fi}), or $TFC = (P_{fi})(FI)$. Substituting into the expression for *AFC* gives

$$AFC = \frac{TFC}{Q} = \frac{(P_{fi})(FI)}{Q} = P_{fi}\left(\frac{FI}{Q}\right).$$

Recalling that in Chapter 7 we defined average product of the fixed input as total output (*Q*) divided by the number of units of fixed input (*FI*), it follows that the term *FI/Q* equals $1/AP_{fi}$ and that

$$AFC = P_{fi}\left(\frac{1}{AP_{fi}}\right).$$

Average variable cost is total variable cost divided by the corresponding number of units of output, or

$$AVC = \frac{TVC}{Q}.$$

As with *AFC*, the concept of *AVC* may be related to the underlying production function. Total variable cost equals the units of variable input employed (*VI*) multiplied by the price per unit of variable input (P_{vi}). Assuming a single type of variable input is used, $TVC = (P_{vi})(VI)$. Hence, we have

$$AVC = \frac{TVC}{Q} = \frac{(P_{vi})(VI)}{Q} = P_{vi}\left(\frac{VI}{Q}\right).$$

Since the average product of variable input is defined as *Q/VI*, then

$$AVC = P_{vi}\left(\frac{1}{AP_{vi}}\right).$$

Average total cost is defined as total cost divided by the corresponding units of output, or

$$ATC = \frac{TC}{Q}.$$

However, since $TC = TFC + TVC$,

$$ATC = \frac{TC}{Q} = \frac{TFC + TVC}{Q} = \frac{TFC}{Q} + \frac{TVC}{Q}.$$
$$= AFC + AVC.$$

Last, *marginal cost* is the change in total cost associated with a change in the quantity of output per period of time. As with previous marginal concepts, we can make a distinction between discrete marginal cost and continuous marginal cost. *Discrete marginal cost* is the change in total cost attributable to a 1-unit change in the quantity of output. For example, the marginal cost of the 500th unit of output can be calculated by finding the difference between total cost at 499 units of output and total cost at 500 units of output. Hence, the increase in total cost of producing one additional unit of output equals the marginal cost of that unit. *Continuous marginal cost* may be thought of as the *rate* of change in total cost as the quantity of output changes, and it can be calculated from the first derivative of the total cost function. Thus,

$$MC = \frac{dTC}{dQ}.$$

However, because in the short run all output-related changes in total cost are attributable *solely* to changes in total variable cost (*TFC* is constant), it is equally accurate to measure discrete marginal cost by observing changes in total variable cost—the marginal cost of the 500th unit of output equals the difference between *TVC* at 499 units of output and *TVC* at 500 units of output. And continuous marginal cost can be calculated from the first derivative of the *TVC* function:

$$MC = \frac{dTVC}{dQ}.$$

As with the other unit cost concepts, the value of marginal cost is related to the underlying production function. Marginal costs stem from the changes in variable costs associated with altering the quantity of output. Since in the short run output is altered by increasing or decreasing the usage of variable inputs, changes in total variable cost (ΔTVC) may be calculated by multiplying the price of variable input (P_{vi}) by the associated change in variable input (ΔVI), giving

$$\Delta TVC = P_{vi}(\Delta VI).$$

As indicated above, $MC = \Delta TVC$ for a 1-unit change in output, or if output changes by several units, then

$$MC = \frac{\Delta TVC}{\Delta Q}.$$

But since $\Delta TVC = P_{vi}(\Delta VI)$, we have

$$MC = \frac{P_{vi}(\Delta VI)}{\Delta Q} = P_{vi}\left(\frac{\Delta VI}{\Delta Q}\right).$$

In Chapter 7, marginal product (*MP*) was defined as the change in output attributable to a change in variable input, or $MP = \Delta Q / \Delta VI$. It follows, therefore, that

$$MC = P_{vi}\left(\frac{1}{MP}\right).$$

Marginal cost is of central interest because it reflects those costs over which the firm has the most direct control in the short run. More particularly, MC indicates the amount of cost which can be "saved" by reducing output by 1 unit or, alternatively, the amount of additional cost which will be incurred by increasing production by 1 unit. Average cost data do not reveal this valuable bit of cost knowledge.

Now let us use these definitions to investigate the behavior of a firm's costs for a variety of production functions. Specifically, we shall examine the total, average, and marginal cost functions for each of the following types of short-run production functions:

1. $Q = a + bX + cX^2$ (increasing returns to variable input).
2. $Q = a + bX$ (constant returns to variable input).
3. $Q = a + bX - cX^2$ (decreasing returns to variable input).
4. $Q = a + bX + cX^2 - dX^3$ (increasing and decreasing returns to variable input).

Here Q is the quantity of output and X the units of variable input.

Cost Behavior under Increasing Returns to Variable Input

When a firm's production function exhibits increasing returns to variable input, each additional unit of variable input adds more to total output than does the previous unit. Graphically, then, the production function increases at an increasing rate and has, in the simplest case, the general equation $Q = a + bX + cX^2$, where $a = 0$, provided that variable input (X) is essential for any output (Q) to be produced. Figure 8-1(a) illustrates this type of production function. The corresponding marginal and average product functions are shown in Fig. 8-1(b).

As previously indicated, a firm's fixed inputs, not being easily susceptible to change in the short run, give rise to a constant amount of cost. Hence, graphically, the firm's *TFC* function is a horizontal line, reflecting the fact that *TFC* does not vary with the quantity of output—as depicted in Fig. 8-1(c). Note that, in drawing the *TFC* curve, costs (in dollars) are plotted on the vertical axis and the quantity of output is on the horizontal axis. Algebraically, the dollar amount of *TFC* can be represented by a constant, say a, making the general equation for the total fixed-cost function

$$TFC = a.$$

The total variable cost (*TVC*) function gets its shape directly from the production function. To illustrate the tie between the production function and *TVC*, consider the behavior of *TVC* as successive units of variable input per period of

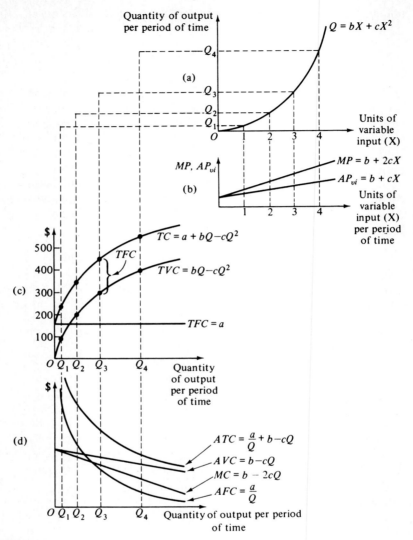

FIGURE 8-1
Production and cost behavior for an increasing-returns-to-variable-input situation

Note: The coefficients "b" and "c" in the equations for the production functions will have different values than the coefficients "b" and "c" in the cost function equations.

time are added to the given amount of fixed inputs. Suppose that the price of variable input is $100 per unit. From Fig. 8-1(a) it can be seen that employing 1 unit of variable input with the given fixed input will yield an output of Q_1 units; this translates into TVC of $100 for Q_1 units of output [Fig. 8-1(c)]. Similarly, employing 2 units of variable input yields Q_2 units of output and results in TVC of $200. Note that in panel (a) the marginal product of the second unit of variable input is larger than the marginal product of the first unit (distance $Q_1Q_2 >$ distance OQ_1) in accordance with increasing returns to the usage of variable input. Adding the third unit of variable input causes the quantity of output to increase even faster to Q_3 units (distance $Q_2Q_3 >$ distance Q_1Q_2), and *TVC* at Q_3 is $300. When the fourth unit of variable input per period of time is employed, output rises by yet a greater increment to Q_4 units (distance $Q_3Q_4 >$ distance Q_2Q_3), and *TVC* becomes $400. From Figs. 8-1(a) and (c) its is apparent that when the quantity of output increases at an increasing rate, *TVC* must necessarily increase at a decreasing rate. With each additional unit of variable input, *TVC* rises by a constant amount equal to the price per unit of variable input, yet the associated increases in output get larger and larger owing to the rising productivity of additional variable input. To put it another way, when increasing returns to variable input characterize the production function, the quantity of output rises faster than does total variable cost. The simplest equation for representing *TVC* which captures the properties of such cost behavior is

$$TVC = bQ - cQ^2.$$

[It must be emphasized that while the equations for the production function ($Q = bX + cX^2$) and the *TVC* function ($TVC = bQ - cQ^2$) are very similar in form, the values of the constants b and c in the production function *are not equal* to the values of b and c in the *TVC* equation—except in the rarest of coincidences.] Notice that *TVC* equals zero at zero output and that the *TVC* function begins at the origin. Also, the greater is the usage of variable input, the greater is both the quantity of output and the level of total variable costs.

Given that $TC = TFC + TVC$, the total cost curve is found by vertically summing the *TFC* and *TVC* functions. The equation for the total cost function in this case is

$$TC = a + bQ - cQ^2.$$

where a represents the *TFC* component of *TC* and $bQ - cQ^2$ represents the *TVC* component. From Fig. 8-1(c), it can be seen that the shapes of the *TVC* and *TC* curves are identical. At every rate of output their slopes are equal and the two curves are separated by a constant vertical distance equal to the amount of *TFC*. At zero output, $TVC = 0$ and $TC = TFC$.

The *AFC* curve decreases continually as the quantity of output increases—as indicated in Fig. 8-1(d). Its equation is

$$AFC = \frac{TFC}{Q} = \frac{a}{Q}.$$

As explained earlier, the decline in *AFC* derives from the spreading of *TFC* over a greater number of units of output. Geometrically speaking, the *AFC* curve is a rectangular hyperbola, meaning that the curve approaches the vertical and horizontal axes asymptotically. In addition, were we to pick any point on the *AFC* curve, draw lines perpendicular to the two axes, and calculate the area of the resulting rectangle, this area will be the same irrespective of the point chosen. Why? Because this area measures $AFC \times Q$ and because $AFC \times Q = TFC =$ a constant value.

The nature and behavior of average variable cost can be deduced from the total variable cost function. When the production function exhibits increasing returns to variable input and TVC is represented by the equation $TVC = bQ - cQ^2$, then

$$AVC = \frac{TVC}{Q} = \frac{bQ - cQ^2}{Q} = b - cQ.$$

The AVC curve corresponding to this type of production function is shown in Fig. 8-1(d). The significant point here is that increasing returns to variable input cause unit variable costs to *fall* as output increases. That this is so can be verified by means of the relationship between AVC and the production function:

$$AVC = P_{vi}\left(\frac{1}{AP_{vi}}\right).$$

Given increasing returns to variable input, the average productivity of variable input rises as more units of variable input are added [see Fig. 8-1(b)]. As AP_{vi} goes up (and provided that the price of variable input does not change), then AVC must necessarily fall.

The average total cost function can be derived by dividing the equation for total cost by the units of output, obtaining

$$ATC = \frac{TC}{Q} = \frac{a + bQ - cQ^2}{Q} = \frac{a}{Q} + b - cQ.$$

The equation for ATC could just as well have been found by adding together the equation for AFC (a/Q) and the equation for AVC ($b - cQ$) since $ATC = AFC + AVC$. The shape of the average total cost curve is obtained by vertically summing the AFC and AVC curves at every rate of output, as illustrated in Fig. 8-1(d). Here, ATC declines throughout because both AFC and AVC are decreasing. Observe that the ATC curve is asymptotic to the AVC curve. Why? The difference between ATC and AVC is the amount of AFC. At low rates of output AFC is relatively large, and the values of ATC are well in excess of the AVC values; however, as output increases, the values of AFC decline and the values of ATC more closely approach the values of AVC. Thus, while ATC always exceeds AVC, the greater the quantity of output, the smaller the value of AFC and the smaller the distance between the AVC and ATC curves. This asymptotic relationship between AVC and ATC is not unique to cost behavior in the instance of increasing returns to variable input but rather is a general and necessary trait for all types of production and cost situations.

The marginal cost function is obtained by finding the first derivative of the TC function (or TVC function—the result is the same in either event). If $TC =$

$a = bQ - cQ^2$ and $TVC = bQ - cQ^2$, then

$$MC = \frac{dTC}{dQ} = \frac{dTVC}{dQ} = b - 2cQ.$$

The *MC* curve is, therefore, both linear and downsloping, as shown in Fig. 8-1(d). The *MC* curve decreases here because under increasing returns to variable input the marginal product of successive units of variable input rises. In other words, since

$$MC = P_{vi}\left(\frac{1}{MP}\right),$$

it follows that if *MP* is increasing and if P_{vi} remains constant, then *MC* must necessarily be falling. Moreover, note that the slope of the *MC* curve $(-2c)$ is twice as large as the slope of the *AVC* curve $(-c)$; both curves originate at a common point (b). Further, the value of *MC* at a given output is equal to the slopes of the *TVC* curve and the *TC* curve at that output rate.

The salient feature of increasing returns to variable input is that the efficiency with which resource inputs are used rises as the quantity of output increases, with the concomitant result of declining unit costs. In other words, the larger the quantity produced, the lower the costs of each unit—clearly, a most favorable set of circumstances. But unfortunately for the firm, increasing returns to variable input are not likely to be realized except at output rates well below the normal operating range.

Table 8-1 presents hypothetical production and cost data for a production function exhibiting increasing returns to variable input. (Before proceeding, you would do well to examine the cost figures in this table to be sure that you fully understand how each one is computed.)

Cost Behavior under Constant Returns to Variable Input

When a firm's production process is characterized by constant returns to variable input, each additional unit of variable input used per period of time adds the same amount to total output as the preceding unit. The quantity of output increases at a constant rate, and the production function is linear. The related *MP* and AP_{vi} functions are horizontal lines, indicating that the values of *MP* and AP_{vi} are the same for every unit of variable input. The general equation for the production function is

$$Q = a + bX,$$

where $a = 0$. The related equations for marginal and average product are

$$MP = b, \quad AP_{vi} = b,$$

FIGURE 8-2
Production and cost behavior for a constant-returns-to-variable-input situation

Note: The coefficient "b" in the production function equations will have a different value from the coefficient "ᵬ" in the cost function equations.

where b is a constant equal to the slope of the production function. Panels (a) and (b) in Fig. 8-2 illustrate the family of product curves corresponding to a constant-returns-to-variable-input situation.

The *TFC* curve for a production process displaying constant returns to variable input is again a horizontal line [see Fig. 8-2(c)]. As before, this is because

TABLE 8-1 **Hypothetical Production and Cost Data for Increasing Returns to Variable Input**

Units of Fixed Input	Units of Variable Input	Quantity of Output	TFC^a	TVC^b	TC	AFC	AVC	ATC	"Average" MC
2	0	0	$100	$ 0	$100	—	$ 0	—	$4.00
2	1	10	100	40	140	$10.00	4.00	$14.00	2.67
2	2	25	100	80	180	4.00	3.20	7.20	2.00
2	3	45	100	120	220	2.22	2.67	4.89	1.60
2	4	70	100	160	260	1.43	2.29	3.72	1.33
2	5	100	100	200	300	1.00	1.00	3.00	

^{a} The price of fixed input is assumed to be $50 per unit.

^{b} The price of variable input is assumed to be $40 per unit.

TFC is determined by the prices and quantities of fixed input, not by the relationship between variable input and output. The equation for total fixed cost thus remains

$$TFC = a,$$

where a is a given amount of dollars and is determined by the amount and prices of fixed inputs present.

To discuss the shape of the *TVC* curve given constant returns to variable input, consider how *TVC* and output are affected when additional variable input is used. From Fig. 8-2(a) it can be seen that combining 1 unit of variable input per period of time with the given amount of fixed inputs will yield an output of Q_1 units; accordingly, the total variable cost of Q_1 units is $100, as shown in Fig. 8-2(c). Combining 2 units of variable input with the available fixed input yields an output of Q_2 units [Figure 8-2(a)]; the marginal product of the second unit of variable input equals the marginal product of the first unit $(OQ_1 = Q_1Q_2)$ in accordance with the condition of constant returns to variable input [Fig. 8-2(b)]. *TVC* at Q_2 units of output is $200 [Fig. 8-2(c)]. Adding the third unit of variable input causes the quantity of output to rise to Q_3 $(OQ_1 = Q_1Q_2 = Q_2Q_3)$, and the total variable cost of Q_3 units is $300. And so it goes. Each additional unit of variable input produces an equivalent rise in output (*MP* is constant), and *TVC* rises by a constant amount ($100 in this case) with each unit increase in variable input. Plainly then, the *TVC* curve is *linear*, begins from the origin, and has the general equation

$$TVC = bQ.$$

The *TVC* function is illustrated in Fig. 8-2(c).

Since *TC* = *TFC* + *TVC*, the shape of the total cost curve is derived by vertically adding the *TFC* and *TVC* curves [see Fig. 8-2(c)]. It follows that the equation for *TC* may be found by adding together the expressions for *TFC* and *TVC*:

$$TFC = a, \quad TVC = bQ,$$
$$TC = TFC + TVC = a + bQ.$$

Since all changes in total cost are solely attributable to changes in variable cost items, the shape of the *TC* curve is identical to the shape of the *TVC* curve. Given constant returns to variable input, the *TC* curve is therefore a linear function with a slope equivalent to the slope of *TVC*; the two curves are separated by a constant vertical distance equal to the amount of *TFC*. At zero output, *TVC* = 0 and *TC* = *TFC*.

As before, the *AFC* curve decreases continually as the quantity of output increases, and it assumes the shape of a rectangular hyperbola. Its equation is

$$AFC = \frac{TFC}{Q} = \frac{a}{Q}.$$

The reasoning is the same as previously. As a constant value (*TFC*) is divided by an increasing value (*Q*), the resulting values (*AFC*) get smaller and smaller, as depicted in Fig. 8-2(d).

The equation for *AVC* can be derived from the expression for total variable cost as follows:

$$AVC = \frac{TVC}{Q} = \frac{bQ}{Q} = b.$$

This means that with constant returns to variable input *AVC* is a constant value. That this is so can be confirmed from the relationship

$$AVC = P_{vi}\left(\frac{1}{AP_{vi}}\right).$$

With constant returns to variable input, AP_{vi} is also a constant, and assuming a given price for variable input, *AVC* must necessarily be a constant. To illustrate, suppose that variable input costs \$100 per unit and that AP_{vi} is fixed at 50 units of output. Then,

$$AVC = P_{vi}\left(\frac{1}{AP_{vi}}\right) = \$100\left(\frac{1}{50}\right) = \$2,$$

and it is \$2 at each and every output rate. Graphically, the *AVC* curve is a horizontal line with a height of *b* dollars above the horizontal axis [see Fig. 8-2(d)].

Since, by definition, average total cost equals total cost divided by the units of output, the equation for *ATC* under conditions of constant returns to variable input becomes

$$ATC = \frac{TC}{Q} = \frac{a + bQ}{Q} = \frac{a}{Q} + b.$$

Observe that since a/Q is AFC and b is AVC, the equation for ATC can be found by adding the equation for AFC to the equation for AVC. Also, because AVC is a fixed value when there are constant returns to variable input, the associated ATC curve assumes a shape precisely identical to that of the AFC curve and lies above it by the amount of AVC [see Fig. 8-2(d)]. The ATC curve is, therefore, asymptotic to the horizontal AVC curve and decreases throughout.

With marginal cost being equal to the first derivative of the TC function (or the TVC function) and the equation for TC being $TC = a + bQ$, the equation for MC becomes

$$MC = \frac{dTC}{dQ} = \frac{dTVC}{dQ} = b,$$

where b is a constant. That MC is a constant value when constant returns to variable input prevail follows from its relationship with marginal product:

$$MC = P_{vi}\left(\frac{1}{MP}\right).$$

With constant returns, MP is itself a fixed value, and if P_{vi} is also a given, then MC becomes the product of a constant times a constant. For example, if P_{vi} = \$100 and if the marginal product of every additional unit of variable input equals 50 units of output, then

$$MC = P_{vi}\left(\frac{1}{MP}\right) = \$100\left(\frac{1}{50}\right) = \$2.$$

Thus, with constant returns to variable input, $MC = AVC = b$, and the MC curve is a horizontal line. The value of MC equals the slope of the TVC and TC curves.

Figure 8-2(d) illustrates how the unit cost curves are related to one another. Table 8-2 presents hypothetical production and cost data for a production function exhibiting constant returns to variable input. Observe that the greater the output

TABLE 8-2 Hypothetical Production and Cost Data for Constant Returns to Variable Input

Units of Fixed Input	Units of Variable Input	Quantity of Output	TFC[a]	TVC[b]	TC	AFC	AVC	ATC	"Average" MC
2	0	0	\$100	\$ 0	\$100	—	\$ 0	—	\$4.00
2	1	10	100	40	140	\$10.00	4.00	\$14.00	4.00
2	2	20	100	80	180	5.00	4.00	9.00	4.00
2	3	30	100	120	220	3.33	4.00	7.33	4.00
2	4	40	100	160	260	2.50	4.00	6.50	4.00
2	5	50	100	200	300	2.00	4.00	6.00	

[a] The price of fixed input is assumed to be \$50 per unit.
[b] The price of variable input is assumed to be \$40 per unit.

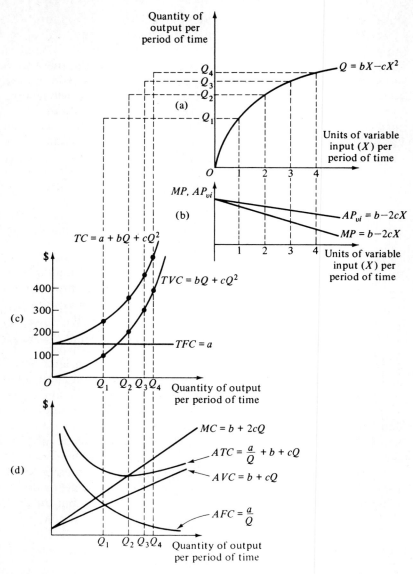

FIGURE 8-3
Production and cost behavior for a decreasing-returns-to-variable-input situation

Note: The coefficients "b" and "c" in the production function equations will have different values from the coefficients "b" and "c" in the cost function equations.

rate, the lower is average total cost. This occurs because total fixed costs are being spread over a larger volume of output and AVC and MC are constant. A number of industry studies show that constant MC and AVC and slowly declining ATC typify many production processes over the "normal" range of output (more about this presently).

Cost Behavior under Decreasing Returns to Variable Input

With a production process characterized by decreasing returns to variable input, the marginal product of variable input declines as output rises. Each additional unit of variable input used per period of time with the available fixed input adds less to total output than the previous unit, and the quantity of output increases at a decreasing rate. Both the marginal and average product functions are down-sloping. The product curves are illustrated in panels (a) and (b) of Fig. 8-3.

As is the case with all types of short-run production functions, the *TFC* curve associated with decreasing returns to variable input is again a horizontal line having the equation

$$TFC = a,$$

where a is a constant [see Fig. 8-3(c)]. *TFC* is a constant dollar value because neither the amount nor the cost of the available fixed inputs is affected by the nature of the returns to variable input embodied in the production function.

However, the shape of the *TVC* curve is very definitely affected by the nature of the underlying production function. Letting $P = \$100$ per unit, each additional unit of variable input employed will cause *TVC* to rise by $100. From Fig. 8-3(a) it is evident that combining 1 unit of variable input per period of time with the given fixed input yields an output of Q_1 units. This translates into a *TVC* of $100 at an output of Q_1 units, as shown in Fig. 8-3(c). Combining 2 units of variable input with the fixed input produces a less-than-proportional increase in output to Q_2 units ($OQ_1 > Q_1Q_2$), and *TVC* becomes $200 at an output of Q_2. Adding the third unit of variable input yields yet a smaller increment in the quantity of output ($Q_1Q_2 > Q_2Q_3$); *TVC* rises to $300. Successive additions of variable input produce similar results. The declining marginal product of variable input causes output to rise ever more slowly, while *TVC* increases by a given amount ($100 in this example) with each unit increase in variable input. Such behavior produces a *TVC* curve which increases at an increasing rate with output, as indicated in Fig. 8-3(c). The simplest equation to represent this type of function is

$$TVC = bQ + cQ^2.$$

Since $TC = TFC + TVC$, the equation for *TC* under conditions of decreasing returns to variable input becomes

$$TC = a + bQ + cQ^2.$$

The graph of this function, shown in Fig. 8-3(c), starts from the point where the *TFC* curve intersects the vertical axis and thereafter increases at an increasing rate. The shape of the *TC* curve is identical to the shape of the *TVC* and lies above it by a constant amount equal to *TFC*.

As is the case irrespective of the character of the production function, the *AFC* curve is a decreasing function that is asymptotic to the horizontal axis [see

Fig. 8-3(d)]. Its equation is

$$AFC = \frac{TFC}{Q} = \frac{a}{Q}.$$

The nature and behavior of AVC are easily established. Since the equation for TVC is

$$TVC = bQ + cQ^2,$$

the equation for AVC becomes

$$AVC = \frac{TVC}{Q} = \frac{bQ + cQ^2}{Q} = b + cQ.$$

The graph of the AVC function is linear with a positive slope equal to the value of c. Thus, when the production function exhibits decreasing returns to variable input, AVC rises as output is increased. That AVC rises throughout can be confirmed by examining the expression

$$AVC = P_{vi}\left(\frac{1}{AP_{vi}}\right).$$

With decreasing returns to variable input, AP_{vi} decreases over the entire output range [see Fig. 8-3(b)]. Assuming a constant price for variable input, as output is increased the smaller and smaller values of AP_{vi} result in larger and larger values of AVC. Aside from the mathematics of the situation, the logic for rising AVC is compelling. When the production function displays decreasing returns to variable input, both the marginal and average productivity of variable inputs decline as output is increased. Hence, the efficiency of variable input falls as more variable input is added and as output rises. Lower efficiency in the usage of variable input clearly implies higher variable costs per unit of output.

Since $ATC = TC/Q$, the equation for average total cost is

$$ATC = \frac{TC}{Q} = \frac{a + bQ + cQ^2}{Q} = \frac{a}{Q} + b + cQ.$$

However, the graph of ATC is somewhat less obvious. Whereas the AFC component of ATC (a/Q) decreases as the quantity of output rises, the AVC component of ATC $(b + cQ)$ rises continuously as output rises. Hence, whether ATC rises or falls hinges upon the decreases in AFC relative to the increases in AVC. At low output rates the declines in AFC are larger than the increases in AVC, so that the ATC curve declines up to an output of Q_2 units. At Q_2 the decline in AFC is exactly offset by the increase in AVC, and ATC is a minimum. Beyond Q_2, the increases in AVC override the decreases in AFC, with the result that the ATC curve turns upward. But despite the U-shaped behavior of ATC, the ATC curve is still asymptotic to the AVC curve for the reason previously given.

A production function displaying decreasing returns to variable input is associated with a rising marginal cost function. Given that $TC = a + bQ + cQ^2$ (and that $TVC = bQ + cQ^2$),

$$MC = \frac{dTC}{dQ} = \frac{dTVC}{dQ} = b + 2cQ.$$

The graph of such an equation is a linear function with a positive slope equal to $2c$ [see Fig. 8-3(d)]. The increasing aspect of MC stems from its relationship to marginal product:

$$MC = P_{vi}\left(\frac{1}{MP}\right).$$

By definition, decreasing returns to variable input means that the marginal product of additional units of variable input is a declining, yet positive, value. With MP falling as output rises, MC must necessarily rise. Note that in this instance the slope of the MC curve ($2c$) is twice as great as the slope of the AVC curve (c). Also, the MC curve passes through the minimum point of the ATC curve. The latter property is an inherent feature of the mathematical relationship between average and marginal values. MC is the additional cost for 1 unit of output; ATC is the average for all the units produced up to that point. As long as MC is below ATC, ATC is pulled down by the lower cost of the additional output. When the cost of an additional unit is greater than the average cost of previous units, ATC is pulled up by the higher cost of the incremental output. At the point of intersection of MC and ATC, ATC has ceased declining but has not begun to rise; this, then, is the minimum point on the ATC curve.

A production-cost structure predicated on decreasing returns to variable input (as in Fig. 8-3) is not likely to typify a firm's entire output capacity. But decreasing returns to variable input are typical of production and cost behavior at near-capacity rates of output, because the closer capacity is approached the harder it becomes to increase production without encountering the point of diminishing marginal returns; as this happens MC, AVC, and ATC will begin to rise.

Table 8-3 illustrates production and cost behavior for a situation characterized by decreasing returns to variable input throughout the indicated output range. Note that the patterns of change in the total and unit cost values parallel exactly the shapes of the cost curves in panels (c) and (d) of Fig. 8-3.

Cost Behavior with Increasing and Decreasing Returns to Variable Input

As stated in Chapter 7, the most general and pervasive type of short-run production function is the one illustrated in Fig. 8-4(a) having the general equation

$$Q = a + bX + cX^2 - dX^3,$$

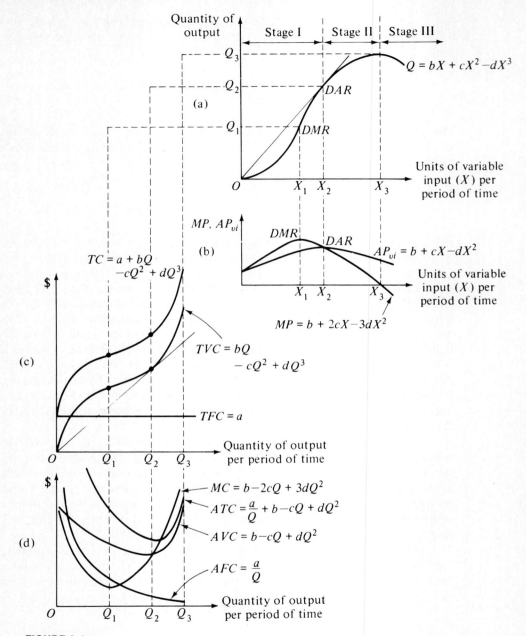

FIGURE 8-4
Production and cost behavior where both increasing and decreasing returns to variable input are present

Note: The coefficients "b", "c", and "d" in the production function equations will have different values than the coefficients "b", "c" and "d" in the cost function equations.

TABLE 8-3   Hypothetical Production and Cost Data for Decreasing Returns to Variable Input

Units of Fixed Input	Units of Variable Input	Quantity of Output	TFC[a]	TVC[b]	TC	AFC	AVC	ATC	"Average" MC
2	0	0	$100	$ 0	$100	—	$ 0	—	$ 2.00
2	1	20	100	40	140	$5.00	2.00	$7.00	2.50
2	2	36	100	80	180	2.78	2.22	5.00	3.33
2	3	48	100	120	220	2.08	2.50	4.58	5.00
2	4	56	100	160	260	1.79	2.86	4.65	10.00
2	5	60	100	200	300	1.67	3.33	5.00	

[a] The price of fixed input is assumed to be $50 per unit.
[b] The price of variable input is assumed to be $40 per unit.

and having MP and AP_{vi} functions, as shown in Fig. 8-4(b). Up to X_1 units of variable input, output increases at an increasing rate. From X_1 to X_3 units of variable input, output increases at a decreasing rate.

Again, the TFC curve is a horizontal line with the equation $TFC = a$ [see Fig. 8-4(c)]. The TVC curve for this type of production function combines the shapes of the TVC curves for both increasing and decreasing returns to variable input. From panels (a) and (c) of Fig. 8-4 it can be seen that over the range of output where increasing returns to variable input prevail (O to Q_1) the TVC curve increases at a decreasing rate, whereas over the range of output where decreasing returns to variable input are encountered (Q_1 to Q_3) the TVC curve increases at an increasing rate. At the short-run capacity rate of output (Q_3) the slope of the TVC curve becomes vertical. The explanation for this behavior of TVC rests with the principle of diminishing marginal returns. Where the quantity of output increases at an increasing rate, marginal product is also increasing, and smaller and smaller increases in variable inputs are required to produce successive units of output. This means that TVC will increase by progressively smaller amounts as output rises. But when the point of diminishing marginal returns is encountered and marginal product begins to decline, it becomes necessary to use increasingly larger amounts of variable input to obtain the same-sized output gain. Total variable costs therefore increase at an increasing rate over this output range. The general equation for a TVC curve with these traits is

$$TVC = bQ - cQ^2 + dQ^3.$$

Total cost equals the sum of TFC and TVC at each output rate and has the equation

$$TC = a + bQ - cQ^2 + dQ^3,$$

where a equals the amount of TFC and the expression $bQ - cQ^2 + dQ^3$ equals the amount of TVC at each value of Q. At zero output, $TC = TFC$, and for each successive unit produced TC varies in precisely the same fashion and at precisely the same rate as does *TVC*. As indicated in Fig. 8-4(c), the *TC* curve is the same shape as the *TVC* curve but lies above it by the amount of *TFC*.

The graph and equation of the *AFC* curve are identical to the preceding cases and are shown in Fig. 8-4(d). The behavior of *AVC* can be determined from *TVC*. Since $TVC = bQ - cQ^2 + dQ^3$, the average variable cost equation is

$$AVC = \frac{TVC}{Q} = \frac{bQ - cQ^2 + dQ^3}{Q} = b - cQ + dQ^2.$$

When plotted on a graph, an equation of this type produces a curve which declines initially, reaches a minimum, and then increases. The *AVC* curve is therefore U-shaped, as shown in Fig. 8-4(d). The rationale for this behavior of *AVC* can be seen from its relationship with AP_{vi}:

$$AVC = P_{vi}\left(\frac{1}{AP_{vi}}\right).$$

Given a fixed price for units of variable input, when AP_{vi} is rising [Fig. 8-4(b)] *AVC* must be falling; when AP_{vi} is declining *AVC* must be rising. Minimum *AVC* (an output of Q_2) corresponds to the output rate where AP_{vi} is maximum (X_2 units of variable input). At Q_2 the point of diminishing average returns is encountered, and the stage II phase of production begins. Thus, stage I rates of output correspond to the output range where *AVC* is declining, whereas stage II quantities correspond to the range of output where *AVC* is rising.

As previously indicated, *ATC* is calculated by dividing total cost by the quantity of output—or, more simply, by adding *AFC* and *AVC* at each rate of output. Here the equation for *ATC* is

$$ATC = \frac{TC}{Q} = \frac{a + bQ - cQ + dQ^3}{Q} = \frac{a}{Q} + b - cQ + dQ^2,$$

where a/Q is the *AFC* component of *ATC* and $b - cQ + dQ^2$ is the *AVC* component of *ATC*. As before, the vertical distance between *ATC* and *AVC* reflects the value of *AFC* at any output. Because *AFC* decreases as output expands, the distance between *ATC* and *AVC* gets progressively smaller. Thus, the *ATC* curve is asymptotic to the *AVC* curve and U-shaped [see Fig. 8-4(d)]. Note that the minimum point on the *ATC* curve corresponds to a quantity of output in stage II. This result is in accord with the rationale for operating in stage II presented in Chapter 7. Also, the minimum point of the *ATC* curve is at a larger volume of output than is the minimum point of the *AVC* curve. Why? *ATC* continues to fall beyond the output where *AVC* is minimum because the continuing declines in *AFC* more than offset the slight increases in *AVC*. As output expands further, however, the increases in *AVC* begin to override the decreases in *AFC*, and *ATC* turns upward. The minimum point on the *ATC* curve defines the most efficient and economical rate of operation in the short run.

Marginal cost can be determined by calculating the first derivative of the equation for either *TC* or *TVC*:

$$MC = \frac{dTC}{dQ} = \frac{dTVC}{dQ} = b - 2cQ + 3dQ^2.$$

The *MC* function in this instance is a quadratic equation which, when graphed, assumes the U-shape shown in Fig. 8-4(d). The curvature of the *MC* function reflects its relationship with marginal product. Since

$$MC = P_{vi} \left(\frac{1}{MP} \right),$$

then as long as *MP* is rising, *MC* must be declining. But when diminishing marginal returns set in and *MP* is falling, then the marginal cost of the extra unit of output is rising. Hence, assuming a constant price for variable input, increasing returns to variable input result in declining marginal costs, and decreasing returns are associated with rising marginal costs. Marginal cost is minimum at the point of diminishing marginal returns where *MP* is maximum (note that this quantity of output is in stage I). Furthermore, the *MC* curve intersects the *AVC* and *ATC* curves at their minimum points—a relationship of mathematical necessity.[9] As long as the cost of producing an additional unit is less than the average total cost of previously produced units, the newly computed values of *ATC* will fall, being pulled down by the lower *MC*. Similarly, when the cost of producing an additional unit is greater than the average total cost of the preceding units, the new value of *ATC* rises, being pulled up by the higher value of *MC*. It follows that *ATC* is

---

[9] The mathematical proof of this point is relatively simple and follows the procedure presented earlier in Mathematical Capsule 8. Let *TC* be some function of the quantity of output:

$$TC = f(Q).$$

Then, by definition,

$$MC = \frac{dTC}{dQ} = f'(Q) \quad \text{and} \quad ATC = \frac{f(Q)}{Q}.$$

For *ATC* to be a minimum value, it is necessary that the slope of the *ATC* curve be zero, which, in turn, requires that the derivative of the *ATC* equation be equal to zero:

$$\frac{dATC}{dQ} = \frac{Q \cdot f'(Q) - f(Q)}{Q^2} = 0.$$

For *dATC/dQ* to equal zero, the numerator of the above expression must be zero, or

$$Q \cdot f'(Q) - f(Q) = 0.$$

This can be rewritten as

$$f'(Q) = \frac{f(Q)}{Q}.$$

Since $f'(Q) = MC$ and $f(Q)/Q = ATC$, then the output rate that makes *ATC* minimum is also the value of *Q* at which *MC* = *ATC*.

By analogous logic, it can be shown that *MC* = *AVC* at the minimum point of the *AVC* curve when the equation for total variable cost is of the form *TVC* = *f(Q)*.

TABLE 8-4 Hypothetical Production and Cost Data for Increasing and Decreasing Returns to Variable Input

Units of Fixed Input	Units of Variable Input	Quantity of Output	TFC[a]	TVC[b]	TC	AFC	AVC	ATC	"Average" MC
2	0	0	$100	$ 0	$100	—	$ 0	—	
2	1	10	100	40	140	$10.00	4.00	$14.00	$4.00
2	2	30	100	80	180	3.33	2.67	6.00	2.00
2	3	65	100	120	220	1.54	1.85	3.39	1.14
2	4	95	100	160	260	1.05	1.68	2.73	1.33
2	5	120	100	200	300	.83	1.67	2.50	1.60
2	6	140	100	240	340	.71	1.71	2.42	2.00
2	7	155	100	280	380	.65	1.81	2.46	2.67
2	8	165	100	320	420	.61	1.94	2.55	4.00
2	9	170	100	360	460	.59	2.12	2.71	8.00

[a] The price of fixed input is assumed to be $50 per unit.

[b] The price of variable input is assumed to be $40 per unit.

minimum at the point of intersection of *MC* and *ATC*. By analogous reasoning the *MC* curve must pass through the minimum point of the *AVC* function.

Table 8-4 illustrates the patterns of change in the total and unit cost values for a production function having phases of both increasing and decreasing returns to variable input.

APPLICATIONS CAPSULE

USING MARGINAL COST CONCEPTS TO DISPATCH ELECTRIC POWER

Electric utility firms have, for more than two decades, used marginal product-marginal cost concepts to generate and dispatch electric power in a more efficient, lower-cost manner. Southern Company, the nation's third largest utility, employs a load dispatching method that is designed to provide automatic, computerized control of all the company's power production and transmission facilities. The marginal cost of delivering additional kilowatts of electricity to Southern Company customers anywhere in the company's service area is continuously calculated; then, as electricity demand rises or falls at points throughout the system, computers transmit "raise" or "lower" impulses to the company's generating units and route the correct amount of electricity along the most economical transmission path to the end user.

Periodically, Southern Company engineers test the operating efficiency of every piece of power-generating equipment the company has in service. The purpose of the test is to determine how much fuel, labor, and other variable inputs are required to produce electricity with that unit and, subsequently, to calculate a production function for that generating unit. Experience has shown that revised production function equations must be calculated from time to time because normal wear and tear, maintenance problems, and mechanical efficiency vary over time and from generator to generator, depending on who manufactured it, when it was purchased, how long it has been in service, and the reliability with which it has performed. In other words, the production function for a given generating unit shifts by sufficiently large amounts over time to make it worthwhile to update the input-output equation. The equations for the production functions of each generating unit are then fed into the computer and combined with information as to fuel prices, wage rates, and other variable input prices to obtain marginal cost functions; from these, *MC* values can be calculated for a particular generating unit at whatever rate it is being operated.

In addition, because there is a loss of electricity in the course of "shipping" it through the transmission wires, Southern engineers make studies to determine the transmission loss coefficients from generating units to distribution substations. These, too, have to be updated several times a year since the transmission loss depends not only on the distance factor but also on the varying load characteristics of the system and changes in the transmission grid.

The marginal cost equations, together with the transmission loss coefficients, are the nucleus for computerized control of power generation and transmission. When, during the course of a day, the demand for electricity picks up, the computer system is programmed to compare the marginal costs of generation at each on-line unit and then to send impulses to raise the electricity output of the unit (or units) where *MC* is lowest. Simultaneously, another computer program analyzes the transmission loss coefficients to calculate how best to allocate the increased load on the transmission grid so as to minimize transmission loss to the many substations and end-user locations. In similar fashion, when electricity demand falls off (as work shifts end and businesses close at the end of the day), the dispatch system automatically sends impulses to reduce electricity generation at those power units where *MC* is highest and reroutes the remaining load to maintain maximum transmission economy and load-generation balance. At periods of peak demand, when on-line generating units are already operating at or near their minimum cost points, and assuming that water levels in Southern's dammed reservoirs are ample, the computer sends impulses to Southern's hydroelectric facilities to open the gates and generate enough power to get across the peak.

Southern's power dispatch control center is also equipped to forecast short-term loads for the next hour, day, or week. For example, weather data from all around Southern's four-state service area are fed into the computer network several times a day to help forecast heating and air-conditioning loads. The hourly, daily, and weekly forecasts of upcoming load demands are used to preplan the mix of generating units to put on line and those to put on standby, to schedule maintenance, and to determine whether to exchange blocks of electricity with neighboring utilities. For instance, approximately 15 minutes prior to the beginning of an hour, calculations as to the next hour's generating and transmission costs are made; this information is then compared immediately with similar information obtained from adjoining utilities having interconnections with Southern's transmission network. If it is determined that it would be more economical for Southern to buy a "block" of electricity from an adjacent company than to generate the electricity needed itself (because at the forecasted generating rates the other company will have lower *MC* than Southern), then an order is placed for that unit at a price set forth in the interchange agreement between the two companies. On the other hand, if Southern's marginal costs are lower than those of its neighbors, then it may agree to sell a block. The exchange of electricity among interconnected companies based upon marginal cost calculations is common throughout the electric utility industry.

As bigger and faster computers have become available, the functions of the dispatch system have been expanded to permit

1. Reductions in unnecessary "load-chasing," with resultant savings on maintenance;
2. Monitoring the current operating status of generating units, line flows, voltages, station breakers, and switches as a basis for assessing the prevailing degree of security (reliability) within the system;
3. Altering the dispatch criteria to allow for reducing power output at a particular facility because of unexpected air or thermal pollution, yet doing so in a way which entails the least increased costs to the system;
4. Operating hydro, steam, combustion, and nuclear generating units in a mix which seeks to minimize fuel costs; and
5. Monitoring temperatures, oil pressures, stream flows, and so on at unattended hydro stations to give early notification of potential troubles.

QUESTION FOR DISCUSSION

1. Suppose you were the head of a group charged with developing estimates of the production functions and marginal cost functions for power generators. What data would you want, and how would you go about conducting a test of the equipment to obtain the production function?

SHORT-RUN COST FUNCTIONS IN THE REAL WORLD: THE EMPIRICAL EVIDENCE

Economists have conducted a great many studies of the short-run cost functions of particular firms and industries. A wide variety of accounting, engineering, and econometric methods have been used to analyze historical cost and output data. Although both the methods employed and the data used suffer from a number of deficiencies, the results of these studies point consistently to one conclusion: *In the short run a linear TC function with constant marginal cost is the pattern that best seems to describe actual cost behavior over the "normal" operating range of output.* U-shaped marginal and average cost curves have been found to exist but seem to be less general than commonly thought. Table 8-5 summarizes the findings of a number of these studies.

Despite a lack of strong empirical confirmation for a U-shaped cost structure, there is still ample reason for asserting that the closer a firm approaches its short-run maximum rate of production, the greater becomes the pressure for rising marginal and average costs. As a firm attempts to squeeze more and more output from its production facilities, the chances increase that some wage premium for overtime will be incurred. If second and third shifts are used, the productivity of labor tends to be noticeably lower than on the day shift. Intensive use of equipment induces more breakdowns, leaves less time for maintenance, and induces production bottlenecks. Marginal, and perhaps obsolete, pieces of equipment may have to be brought on stream to achieve rated capacity. Hiring standards may have to be lowered to obtain the needed labor. Hence, in striving to push output

TABLE 8-5   Results of Empirical Studies of Short-Run Cost Functions

Name	Type of Industry	Finding
Lester (1946)	Manufacturing	*AVC* decreases up to capacity levels of output.
Hall and Hitch (1939)	Manufacturing	Majority have decreasing *MC*.
Johnston (1960)	Electricity, multiple-product food processing	"Direct" cost is a linear function of output, and *MC* is constant.
Dean (1936)	Furniture	Constant *MC* which failed to rise.
Dean (1941)	Leather belts	No significant increases in *MC*.
Dean (1941)	Hosiery	Constant *MC* which failed to rise.
Dean (1942)	Department store	Declining or constant *MC*, depending on the department within the store.
Ezekiel and Wylie (1941)	Steel	Declining *MC* but large variation.
Yntema (1940)	Steel	Constant *MC*.
Johnston (1960)	Electricity	*ATC* falls, then flattens, tending toward constant *MC* up to capacity.
Mansfield and Wein (1958)	Railways	Constant *MC*.

Source: A. A. Walters, "Production and Cost Functions," *Econometrica*, Vol. 31, No. 1 (January 1963), pp. 1–66.

toward the limit there is a tendency for a firm to utilize less efficient and/or marginal capital and labor inputs. As this occurs, increases in *MC* and *ATC* can be expected.

Evidence to this effect comes from McGraw-Hill's annual survey of manufacturing firms regarding (1) what percentage of production capacity is currently being used and (2) at what percentage they would prefer to operate. The preferred rates of operation usually range in the neighborhood of 90%, which strongly implies that many firms achieve maximum efficiency-minimum *ATC* at about 90% of the capacity rate of production. Apparently, producing within the 90 to 100% range would entail, as argued, rising marginal and average costs. It could be, therefore, that the failure of empirical studies to detect rising unit costs is because the cost-output data of the firms and industries examined were, for the most part, below the output range where the pressures on capacity cause unit costs to increase.

If one combines the results of empirical cost studies with the implications of the McGraw-Hill survey, then the cost functions shown in Fig. 8-5 may represent a generalized cost structure for a number of firms and production processes. The properties of these cost functions suggest increasing returns to variable input at exceptionally low production rates, constant returns to variable input thereafter up to about 90 or 95% of capacity, and decreasing returns to variable input beyond the 90 to 95% level. Thus, while the marginal cost curve is U-shaped, the bottom of the U has a wide, flat range that encompasses the "normal" and "preferred" rates of output. *AVC* continues to fall over this entire range because *MC* is below

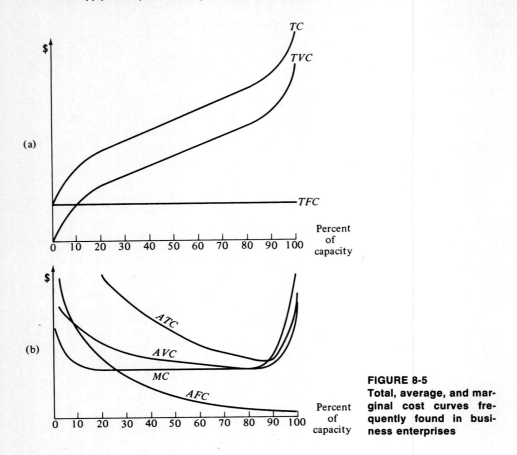

FIGURE 8-5
Total, average, and mar-ginal cost curves fre-quently found in busi-ness enterprises

AVC. This follows from the fact that the slope of *TVC* in the linear portion is a smaller value than the slope of a ray drawn from the origin of the diagram in Fig. 8-5(a) to the *TVC* curve; the former slope value equals *MC,* while the latter equals *AVC.*

COST-OUTPUT RELATIONSHIPS IN THE LONG RUN

In the long run all resource inputs are variable; a firm can alter its usage of major capital equipment, change top-management personnel, build new plant capacity, close down obsolete facilities, update its use of technology, or in any other way modify its production process and use of resources per period of time.

Such decisions are important because they determine the character of the short-run positions the firm will occupy in the future. For instance, before a firm makes a decision to change its productive potential, the firm is in a long-run position, with several options as to equipment, technology, and capital-labor mix. But once commitments are made and the new production capacity is installed, the firm's situation reverts to the short run, where the types and amounts of certain inputs are, for the time being, frozen.

Generally, a firm's long-run cost objective is to be in a position to produce the desired output at the lowest possible cost. This means adjusting its scale of production so as to be "the right size." Sometimes economies can be attained by dividing the production process into smaller production units. On other occasions lower unit costs can be achieved by enlarging the scale of production. In examining how efficiency and costs are affected by the scale of production, it is important to distinguish between *plants* and *firms* because the cost-efficiency advantages and disadvantages of each are different. Moreover, because there are no fixed inputs in the long run, the distinction between fixed and variable costs disappears—there are no *TFC* and *AFC* curves, and, in fact, we need look only at the nature and shape of the long-run average cost curve.

Cost Behavior and Plant Size

Suppose that technological constraints allow a firm the choice of constructing any one of three plant sizes: small, medium, and large. The short-run average cost curve for each of these plant sizes is represented by $SRAC_S$, $SRAC_M$, and $SRAC_L$ in Fig. 8-6. Whatever size plant the firm has currently, in the long run it can convert to or construct any one of these three plant scales. Obviously, the firm's choice of plant size is conditioned by its estimate of the production capacity needed to meet the demand for its products. For example, if the anticipated de-

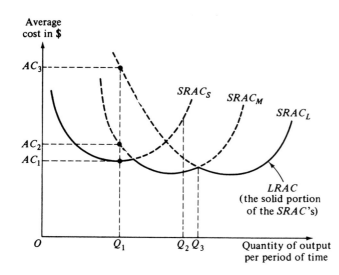

FIGURE 8-6
Long-run average cost curve when only three plant sizes are available

FIGURE 8-7
Long-run average cost curve for alternative plant sizes

mand is OQ_1, the firm should elect to build the small-sized plant since it can produce OQ_1 units of output per period of time at a cost of AC_1, which is well below either the unit cost of the medium-sized plant (AC_2) or the unit cost of the large-sized plant (AC_3). If the expected demand is OQ_2, the medium-sized plant plainly offers the lowest unit cost. On the other hand, at a demand of OQ_3 the medium- and large-sized plants are equally efficient from a unit cost standpoint. Here the final choice of plants might depend on the forecasted *trend* in consumer demand, with an expectation of strong growth tipping the scales in favor of the large plant. Otherwise, the medium-sized plant is likely to be the more attractive because of its smaller capital investment requirements.

The portions of the three short-run average costs curves which identify the optimum plant size for a given output are indicated by the solid, scalloped line in Fig. 8-6. This line is called the *long-run average cost curve (LRAC)* and shows the minimum cost per unit of producing at each output rate when all resource inputs are variable and any desired scale of plant can be built. The dashed line segments of the *SRAC* curves all entail higher average costs at each output rate than is capable of being achieved with some other plant scale.

Usually, a firm will have more than just three plant sizes to choose from. When the number of alternative plant sizes approaches infinity, the *LRAC* curve is an "envelope" of the short-run curves that is tangent to each of the short-run average cost curves (see Fig. 8-7). Here, again, the *LRAC* curve should be interpreted as representing the *least unit cost attainable for a given output rate when the firm has time to change the rate of usage of any and all inputs.* Suppose the firm estimates that an output of OQ_1 is most desirable; then the plant represented by $SRAC_1$ is the most efficient because it can produce OQ_1 units at a lower cost per unit than can a plant of any other size. If consumer demand should expand sufficiently to warrant an output of OQ_2 units, the output of the plant represented by $SRAC_1$ could be increased to meet this demand in the short run. Nevertheless, in the long run the firm would prefer to construct the plant represented by $SRAC_2$ because this slightly larger plant is capable of producing OQ_2 units at a lower cost. Should the level of demand expand even further to OQ_3, although the plant represented by $SRAC_2$ is capable of producing OQ_3 units, the plant represented by $SRAC_3$ is preferable because of its ability to produce OQ_3 units at a lower average cost.

Of all the possible plant sizes, the one which is most efficient of all is the one whose *SRAC* curve is tangent to the *LRAC* curve at the *minimum point* of the *LRAC* curve.[10] The plant capable of producing the product at the lowest unit cost of all the other plants is termed the *optimum plant size*. In Fig. 8-7 the optimum plant size is the one corresponding to $SRAC_4$—no other plant is capable of producing the item at as low an average cost as is the plant associated with $SRAC_4$. It is in this sense that $SRAC_4$ represents the optimum plant size.

Observe that the *LRAC* curve is *not* tangent to the *SRAC* curves at their minimum points except in the one case of the optimum plant size. When the *LRAC* curve is decreasing (up to an output of OQ_4 in Fig. 8-7) the *LRAC* curve is tangent to the *SRAC* curves to the left of their minimum cost points. Therefore, for outputs smaller than OQ_4, it is more economical to produce the desired output by "underusing" a slightly larger plant operating at *less* than its minimum cost output than it is to construct a plant that will produce the desired output at the minimum point of its *SRAC* curve. However, when the *LRAC* curve is rising (past an output of OQ_4 in Fig. 8-7), the *LRAC* curve is tangent to the *SRAC* curves to the right of their minimum cost points. Hence, at outputs greater than OQ_4 it is more economical to produce the desired output by overusing a slightly smaller plant than it is to build a larger plant to produce the desired output at the minimum point of its *SRAC* curve.

The U-shape of the *LRAC* curve clearly implies that up to a certain output constructing larger-sized plants results in greater efficiency and lower unit cost, but that beyond this output larger plants become progressively less efficient and entail higher unit costs. There are a host of factors which underlie *economies of scale* and *diseconomies of scale*.

Reasons for Economies of Scale at the Plant Level. At the plant level, lower unit costs basically derive from the economies of mass production. Up to a point, larger operations allow greater subdivision of the production process and greater specialization in the use of resource inputs (labor, capital equipment, and supervision). Almost invariably, specialization along functional or task-specific lines maximizes the efficiency gains and cost savings to be had from "the learning curve" (or the "experience curve") and from machine execution of simplified work elements. For example, in the automobile industry the huge presses which

---

[10] In the event that the *LRAC* curve has a horizontal segment, there will be several plant sizes which qualify as the most efficient.

stamp out automobile bodies in a matter of seconds, the automatic equipment which drills holes in the cylinder block in one operation, the large ovens which spray and bake paint on the car, the miles of computerized assembly lines, and the mechanized equipment used to transport materials and finished parts from station to station on the production floor are quite efficient. Moreover, the greater the volume of production and the more intensive the utilization of such facilities, the lower are the unit fixed costs per car because the fixed investment costs of capital-intensive techniques are being spread out over a larger number of units of output. This, together with the fact that the cost of purchasing and installing larger machines and equipment is usually *not* proportionately greater that the costs of smaller machines with less capacity, means that large plants have an inherent ability to achieve lower average fixed costs, since they produce more units of output over which to spread proportionately smaller overhead costs.[11]

Centralizing and integrating manufacturing stages into a single continuous process offers another avenue for achieving scale economies at the plant level. For instance, steel firms have found it advantageous to have pig iron, raw steel, and semifinished steel products produced in one continuous operation in order to economize on reheating materials between phases of the production process.

Also, the larger a plant, the greater the opportunities for taking advantage of and utilizing by-products. Take the case of naphtha; naphtha is a by-product of producing coke from coal and can be commercially marketed by steel plants having a large enough coking facility to make the capture of naphtha worthwhile. Other industries where by-products come into play include petroleum refining, meat packing, chemicals, and paper products. The advantage of building on a scale large enough to capture by-products is that, by gaining salable output which otherwise is waste, firms have added revenues to apply against production costs associated with the primary product.

Large-scale plants are in a position to take advantage of quantity discounts on purchases of raw materials and utility services. Similarly, larger plants can sometimes realize transportation savings by instituting their own shipping.

Eventually, of course, plants can be enlarged to the point where all economies of scale are taken full advantage of; larger plants then bring no additional savings in unit costs. It is here that the minimum level of the *LRAC* curve for plants is reached. Whether the *LRAC* curve begins to rise immediately with further increases in plant size or whether it has a flat portion before turning upward varies from industry to industry, depending on return-to-scale considerations and whether an industry's production technology requires large and indivisible units of capital input for low-cost production. Given the apparent prevalence of constant

---

[11] One of the major reasons for lower electric rates during the 1950s and 1960s was the substantial savings in investment costs which electric utility firms realized by increasing generating unit sizes from 40 megawatts to 60, 80, 120, 150, and 250 mW. In the mid-70s, a generating plant with two 300-mW coal-fired units could be installed for an investment of about $330 per kilowatt ($198 million total); doubling the size to two 600-mW units involved an investment of about $268 per kilowatt; and doubling again to two 1200-mW units entailed an investment of approximately $245 per kilowatt. However, past sizes of 800 to 900 mW, there were offsets against part of the investment savings because of higher transmission and maintenance costs and because of the need to maintain larger reserve margins as a hedge against unexpected breakdowns. Thus, the net savings associated with an increase in size from 880 mW to 1000 mW was only about $3 per kilowatt.

returns to scale, the *LRAC* curve is likely to have a flat bottom, thereby giving rise to a number of optimum-sized plants, each capable of producing at the lowest achievable unit cost. But there can be little doubt that, at some juncture, continued increases in plant size will produce diseconomies and cause *LRAC* to rise.

APPLICATIONS CAPSULE

ECONOMIES OF SCALE IN THE PIPELINE BUSINESS

The operation of oil and natural gas pipelines typically entails substantial economies of scale. According to studies made by Exxon, the relative costs of oil pipelines fall rapidly as the diameter of the pipeline increases—as shown in the diagram.

Relative Pipeline Costs versus System Throughput

The scale economies in the pipeline business are so large that they extend the efficient size beyond the level which a single company may be able to utilize. As a result, most interstate pipelines in the United States are owned by more than one company and the same pipeline system is often jointly used by many companies, owners and nonowners. This joint use allows the most efficient-size pipeline to be built and full advantage to be taken of scale economies. It has also resulted in interstate pipelines being designated as "common carriers" subject to regulation by the Interstate Commerce Commission (ICC).

The presence of large economies of scale has dictated a number of operating practices. For example, in the case of oil pipelines, owners may require throughput guarantees or some other provision for the recovery of costs incurred before they will connect a new shipper to the system. The cost of a new connection may include laying a pipeline to the new shipper or installing new metering facilities to account for shipments or building additional working tankage. Throughput guarantees commit the shipper who is requesting the connection to either ship sufficient volumes or pay sufficient tariffs to provide some reasonable assurance that the added investment by the pipeline owner will be paid off. The ICC has authority to address any abuses, including the prevention of excessive throughput guarantees. Some nonowner firms are guaranteed access to pipelines on an equal basis with large owner-users and thus crude and product transportation is available to producers, refiners, and marketers alike.

Pipeline practices such as minimum tender requirements are dictated by considerations of efficiency. Crude oils vary greatly in quality, as do the different types of refined products. To minimize mixing and contamination at the interface between sequential batches of crude or product, the pipeline sets minimum batch sizes. When a full batch is accumulated, it is pumped through the pipeline.

Whenever common carrier pipeline capacity is inadequate to meet volumes tendered, government regulations require that available capacity be allocated equitably. Pipeline proration rules allocate capacity in proportion to recent shipments or current tenders of new shippers and historic shippers alike. Deviation from the pipeline's proration rules in favor of an owner company is a violation of the law. Under ICC regulations and the common carrier status of the interstate pipelines, users have the right to appeal for relief to the ICC if they feel they have been treated unfairly.

Pipeline tariffs are regulated by the ICC and have fallen steadily since the early 1950s, mainly because new technology has allowed larger and larger diameter pipelines with their resultant economies of scale and greatly reduced costs. According to ICC statistics, the average industry revenue per barrel moved 1000 miles fell from 65 cents in 1955 to 50 cents in 1971.

Generally, the production units in aircraft, electric power production, automobiles, steel, oil refining, paper, tires, glassware, aluminum, and inorganic chemicals all involve large-scale, multimillion-dollar plant investments. On the other hand, the manufacture of garments, mobile homes, shoes, furniture, sporting goods, and precision instruments, as well as printing and publishing, coal mining, and farming, can be efficiently conducted in relatively small production units.

Reasons for Diseconomies of Scale at the Plant Level.   The more space over which a plant is spread, the greater the bottlenecks and costs of getting labor, materials, and semifinished goods from one place in the plant to another. Moreover, the larger the plant, the more likely that needed raw materials will have to be shipped from more distant suppliers, thereby driving up the transportation costs of incoming materials. Similarly, the larger the output of a plant, the farther distances outputs may have to be shipped to reach potential buyers, thereby raising the costs of transporting the product from the point of manufacture to the final consumer. To these must be added the growing difficulties of maintaining efficient supervision and coordination. As an extreme example, imagine the incredible problems that would beset General Motors were it to try to produce some 5 million Buicks, Cadillacs, Chevrolets, Oldsmobiles, and Pontiacs at a single plant site— the logistics of managing 850,000 employees, millions of component parts, and hundreds of thousands of inventoried cars would entail a colossal logjam and gross inefficiency.

Cost Behavior and Firm Size

Even after plants have been expanded to their most efficient size and all economies of plant size taken advantage of, there may arise additional cost-efficiency gains from putting a number of plants under common management. The separate units of a multiplant enterprise may perform the same kind of operation and thus be horizontally integrated—a chain of motels or a series of garment plants. Or the plants may be vertically integrated to perform successive phases of the same overall production process. Or they may involve the production of a number of unrelated products, as occurs in diversified enterprises. In all three situations, opportunities for realizing scale economies may exist.

Reasons for Economies of Scale at the Firm Level.   To begin with, putting several plants under common management economizes on top-management costs. Spreading the salaries of key executives and administrative staff over 5 million units of output a year instead of 1 million units lowers average cost. Second, multiproduct firms may derive a number of economic advantages from specializing in serving the full range of needs of a particular customer segment or market, or from using the same distribution channel to market their outputs, or from using a common technology to produce a number of different products. Third, there are mass-marketing economies associated with nationwide distribution systems and sales promotion compaigns which provide a more effective canvassing of markets and consumers per dollar spent.[12] For example, General Motors in selling 5 million cars annually can well afford to spend $90 million advertising its cars (a paltry advertising cost of only $18 per car), but for American Motors to spend $90 million on advertising to sell 300,000 cars ($300 per car) would place them at a distinct price disadvantage. Fourth, a large enterprise is better able to afford expert specialists for research, development, design, and production engineering, thereby keeping it in position to introduce new and improved products and to embrace new technologies. Fifth, with large size comes greater market visibility and recognition, which, if accompanied by growth and above-average profitability, can translate into lower borrowing and capital costs. Some large corporations are able to borrow at interest rates 1 to 3 percentage points below small and medium-sized firms. Sixth, the debt capacity and capital-raising potential that tends to accompany large size is available for (1) pioneering the development and implementation of cost-saving technological innovations; (2) withstanding the risk of cyclical downturns, sour investments in a new project, or secular decline in demand for some of its products; and (3) investing in specialized management talent proficient in solving problems and developing better managerial technologies. When fully exploited, the outcome is an *organizational economy of scale*

---

[12] This contention is documented in a study by William S. Comanor and Thomas A. Wilson, "Advertising and the Advantages of Size," *American Economic Review, Papers and Proceedings*, Vol. 59, No. 2 (May 1969), pp. 87–98.

that can produce sizable reductions in unit costs and effective strategies for competing in the marketplace.[13]

Last, but far from least, large size achieved via vertical integration and/or diversification can be a distinct asset in surviving fundamental market changes occasioned by abrupt increases in input prices, disruptions in raw material supplies (bad harvests, trade boycotts), the ups and downs of the business cycle, technological breakthroughs, shifts in consumer demand, and changing life-styles. An unintegrated, undiversified, single-plant enterprise is vulnerable to unexpected market developments. But with vertical integration, diversification, or both, an enterprise obtains a measure of security. Integrating vertically allows a firm to *internalize* the problems of securing reliable supplies of essential inputs at reliable prices and of marketing the firm's outputs. Thus, it is not without design that heavy users of coal buy and operate coal mines; that major steel firms have their own sources of iron ore; that major oil refiners maintain divisions to search out deposits of crude oil on the one hand and to market refined products at retail on the other hand; that Sears has an ownership interest in an appliance manufacturer; that General Motors has its own divisions to supply it with batteries, shock absorbers, air-conditioning units, and various other automobile parts; that A&P has a division to supply it with bakery products and canned goods; and that Goodyear, Firestone, and B. F. Goodrich all give special attention to maintaining an effective chain of retail stores, including a number of company-owned and -operated outlets. Diversifying into a variety of products and markets spreads risk and lessens the dependence a firm has on any one product, customer, market, or line of business. Both integration and product-market diversification, therefore, help to insulate a firm from adverse developments and to stabilize its base of operations.

However, one other advantage of large size is not to be minimized in explaining the success of corporate enterprise. As a firm gets larger, its *absolute* size gives it a measure of *control* or leverage over its costs, its selling prices, its production technology, its sources of financial capital, the attitudes and buying propensities of its customers, its relationships with government, and whatever other factors are crucial to successful enterprise. The mere size of a firm breeds power or, at the very least, an ability to throw its weight around on its own behalf. Motivated by an instinct for self-protection and risk avoidance, large firms often take deliberate steps to achieve some degree of control over the stability of operations. Max Weber, years ago, observed the tendency of large-scale organizations to construct buffers and control devices that guard against market and competitive adversity. To be sure, the power and influence of the giant corporation is far from absolute or unfailing in application, but where it can be brought into play it *partially* frees a firm from the grip and sometimes harsh discipline of competitive market forces.

Moreover, with bigness comes an opportunity to exercise political influence and thereby win undue favors and privileges via the governmental process. Usually, the large corporation is careful not to flaunt its power publicly, but there can be little doubt that where such power exists it will be used to protect and

[13] This point is developed in more detail in Oliver E. Williamson, *Corporate Control and Business Behavior* (Englewood Cliffs, N.J.: Prentice-Hall, Inc., 1970), especially Chapters 8 and 9.

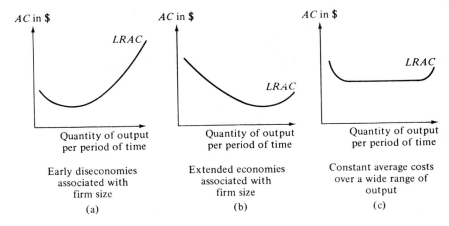

FIGURE 8-8
Alternative shapes for the long-run average cost curve

enhance the firm's interests. As a consequence, the economic benefits of large size can accrue to several groups in varying proportions—to consumers in the form of better and lower-priced goods and services and/or to stockholders in the form of higher profits, dividends, and stock prices and/or to corporate management in the form of higher salaries, luxurious office accommodations, social prestige, and political clout and/or to rank-and-file employees in the form of higher wages, more fringe benefits, and better working conditions.

Reasons for Diseconomies of Scale at the Firm Level. The chief reason why a firm's long-run average cost curve supposedly turns upward relates to the increasing difficulties and costs of managing ever-larger enterprises. Conventional wisdom instructs that beyond some size the larger a firm gets, the more likely it will become burdened down with bureaucratic red tape and unwieldy decision-making procedures; as a result, approval of key recommendations gets bogged down in costly layers of management and the time it takes for the firm to respond to new developments becomes inefficiently long. In addition, large firms may be at a price disadvantage in obtaining the services of blue-collar labor. Unions have had their greatest success in dealing with large enterprises; large firms often pay higher hourly wage rates than do small and medium-sized firms. Thus, to the extent that larger size is accompanied by an increase in the ability of unions to secure higher wage rates, the large enterprise may find itself confronted with diseconomies of scale unless it takes steps to offset them by means of automation or some other productivity-increasing strategy.

The Long-Run Average Cost Curve for Firms. In some industries economies of scale are negligible and diseconomies assume paramount importance at relatively low outputs. Figure 8-8(a) shows a long-run average cost curve for firms in such situations. The points on the curve show the lowest feasible unit cost of production for various *firm* sizes when the *firm* has sufficient time to adjust its input com-

TABLE 8-6   Results of Empirical Studies of Long-Run Cost Functions

Name	Type of Industry	Finding
Bain (1956)	Manufacturing	Small economies of scale for multiplant firms.
Holton (1956)	Retailing	LRAC is L-shaped.
Alpert (1959)	Metal	Economies of scale up to an output of 80,000 lbs per month; constant returns to scale and horizontal LRAC thereafter.
Moore (1959)	Manufacturing	Economies of scale prevail quite generally.
Lomax (1951) and Gribbin (1953)	Gas (Great Britain)	LRAC of production declines as output rises.
Lomax (1952) and Johnston (1960)	Electricity (Great Britain)	LRAC of production declines as output rises.
Johnston (1960)	Life assurance	LRAC declines.
Johnston (1960)	Road passenger transport (Great Britain)	LRAC either falling or constant.
Nerlove (1961)	Electricity (U.S.)	LRAC (excluding transmission costs) declines and then shows signs of increasing.

Source: A. A. Walters, "Production and Cost Functions," *Econometrica*, Vol. 31, No. 1 (January 1963), pp. 1–66.

binations to optimum levels.[14] Examples where small-scale firms sometimes have cost advantages over large-scale enterprises include farming, many of the retail trades, printing, and certain types of light manufacturing such as baking, electronics, instruments, concrete products, and soft-drink bottling.

In other industries economies of scale are extremely important, and the firm's *LRAC* curve declines significantly over a long range of output, as depicted in Fig. 8-8(b). Here a firm must be big in an absolute sense if it is to stay competitive. The automobile, aluminum, steel, railroad, aircraft, paper products, and farm implement industries are cases in point.

In still other industries the *LRAC* curve of firms is virtually horizontal over a wide range of output [see Fig. 8-8(c)]. Economies of scale are quickly exhausted, yet diseconomies are not forthcoming until very large outputs are produced. Or, alternatively, economies and diseconomies cancel each other out over an extended range of output. The result is that small, medium-sized, and large firms can operate with roughly an equivalent degree of efficiency. The meat packing, apparel, furniture, oil, household appliance, coal mining, textile, food products, rubber, and chemical industries are representative of this type of long-run cost behavior.

Table 8-6 summarizes the results of several major studies of long-run cost functions. None of these studies present conclusive evidence that large firms

---

[14] It is worth noting that cost curves can vary between plants and firms in the same industry because of (1) differences in the firms' products and the impact this can have on costs; (2) age differences in production facilities, with newer facilities incorporating more efficient and cheaper technology-related improvements; and (3) differences in geographic locations—where wage rates, labor productivity, transportation costs, and taxes vary from area to area.

actually encounter significant diseconomies of scale in the range of observed data. Rather, the long-run average cost curve has generally been found to decrease and then level off as output rises. However, the failure to find much evidence of diseconomies of large size does not warrant concluding that *LRAC* curves in these industries fail to turn upward at some point. Firms may simply have been wise enough to avoid becoming so large as to incur rising unit costs. Moreover, the lack of truly large firms in several industries indicates that diseconomies do exist, although it does appear that diseconomies do not begin at so small a firm size as some might have imagined.

STRATEGIC COST ANALYSIS

While the nature and behavior of a firm's internal cost curves are important, a full-blown cost analysis must also address a firm's cost competitiveness and ability to compete successfully. Competitors do not necessarily, or even usually, incur the same costs in supplying their products to end-users. The disparities in costs among rival producers can stem from:

- Differences in the prices paid for raw materials, component parts, energy, and other items purchased from suppliers.
- Differences in basic technology and the age of plants and equipment. (Because rival companies have usually invested in plants and key pieces of equipment at different points in time, they enter into competition with facilities having somewhat different technological efficiencies and different fixed costs—older facilities built when technology was less developed are typically less efficient but because they were constructed in times when it took less money to put them in place, they *may* still be reasonably cost competitive with modern facilities costing more to build. Whether older plants having lower fixed investment costs are, overall, cost competitive with newer plants having higher fixed investment costs depends on the trade-off between the lower depreciation and other fixed costs of older plants and the increased operating efficiency of newer plants.)
- Differences in internal operating costs, owing to the economies of scale associated with different-sized plants, learning and *experience curve* effects (see the Applications Capsule in Chapter 6), different wage rates, different energy costs, and the like.
- Differences in rival firms' exposure to rates of inflation and changes in foreign exchange rates (as can occur in global industries where competitors have plants located in different nations).
- Differences in shipping and forward channel distribution costs.

Plainly enough, for a company to be competitively successful, its costs must be "in line with" those of rival producers. The need to be cost competitive is not so stringent as to *require* every firm's costs to be *equal* but, as a rule, the more a firm's costs are above those of the low-cost producers the more vulnerable its

FIGURE 8-9
The Complete Production-Cost Chain

market position becomes. Given the numerous opportunities for there to be cost disparities among competing companies, it is incumbent upon firms to be alert to how their costs compare with rivals' costs and how they can remain cost competitive over the long run. This is where *strategic cost analysis* comes in.

Strategic cost analysis focuses on a firm's relative cost position vis-à-vis its rivals. The primary analytical tool of strategic cost analysis is the construction of a *complete production-cost chain* showing the makeup of costs all the way from the inception of production to the end price paid by ultimate customers.[15] The complete production-cost chain thus includes more than just a firm's own internal cost structure; it includes the buildup of cost (and thus the "value" of the product) at each stage in the whole market chain of getting the product in the hands of the final user, as shown in Fig. 8-9. Constructing a complete production-cost chain is more revealing than restricting attention to just a firm's own internal costs because a firm's overall ability to furnish end users with its product at a competitive price can easily depend on cost factors originating either *backward* in the suppliers' portion of the production-cost chain or *forward* in the distribution channel portion of the chain.

The task of constructing a production-cost chain is not an easy task. It requires breaking a firm's own historical cost accounting data out into several principal cost categories and developing cost estimates for the backward and forward channel portions of getting the product to the end user as well. It also requires estimating the same cost elements for one's rivals—an advanced art in competitive intelligence in itself. But despite the tediousness of the task and the imprecision of some of the estimates, the payoff in exposing the cost competitiveness of one's position and the attendant strategic alternatives makes it a valuable analytical tool. As an abbreviated example, consider Fig. 8-10 showing a simplified production-cost chain comparing the cost competitiveness of U.S. steel producers and Japanese steel producers over a 20-year period. The shifts in the several cost components over the period are dramatic. Most resulted from relative

[15] The ins and outs of strategic cost analysis are discussed in greater length in Michael E. Porter, *Competitive Advantage* (New York: The Free Press, 1985).

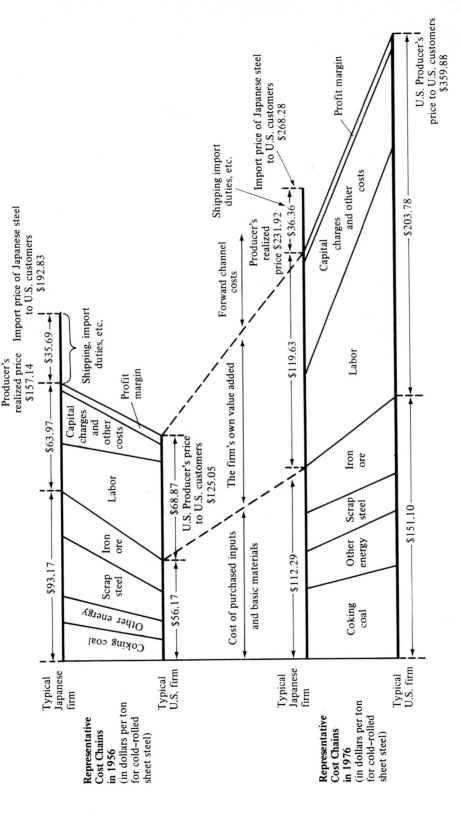

FIGURE 8-10
Illustrative Cost Chains for U.S. Steel Firms versus Japanese Firms, 1956 and 1976

Sources: Compiled by the author from data in U.S. Federal Trade Commission, *The United States Steel Industry and Its International Rivals: Trends and Factors Determining International Competitiveness* (Washington, D.C.: U.S. Government Printing Office, 1978); and Robert W. Crandall, *The U.S. Steel Industry in Recurrent Crisis* (Washington, D.C.: The Brookings Institution, 1981).

shifts in input prices which built up gradually over time, but technological changes in input requirements and labor productivity were also at work.

While Fig. 8-10 is, for illustrative purposes, constructed using national averages from published sources (specific companies obviously prefer to protect the confidentiality of their own cost data for competitive reasons), the relevant level at which to develop cost estimates is a single line of business for a given firm and not an industry or group of firms. Plainly, the makeup of each firm's total value chain is unique to its own situation and can vary from item to item in the product line, from customer group to customer group (if different distribution channels are used), and from plant to plant (if plants employ different technologies or if plants are located in widely different geographic locations—different countries, for example). Once a firm has constructed production-cost chains for itself and its major competitors, it is in position to diagnose the degree to which it is cost competitive.

Looking again at Fig. 8-9, observe that there are three main areas in the complete production-cost chain where important differences in the *relative* costs of competing firms can occur: in the suppliers' part of the cost chain, in their own respective value-added segments, or in the forward channel portion of the chain. To the extent that the reasons for a firm's lack of cost competitiveness lie either in the backward or forward sections of the overall production-cost chain, its job of reestablishing cost competitiveness may well have to extend beyond its own in-house operations. When a firm has a cost disadvantage in the area of purchased inputs, four strategic options quickly emerge for consideration:

- Negotiate more favorable prices with suppliers.
- Integrate backward to gain control over material costs.
- Try to use lower-priced substitute inputs.
- Try to make up the difference by initiating cost savings elsewhere in the production-cost chain.

When a firm's cost disadvantage occurs in the forward end of the cost chain, there are three corrective options:

- Push for more favorable terms with distributors.
- Change to a more economical distribution strategy, including the possibility of forward integration.
- Try to make up the difference by initiating cost savings earlier in the cost chain.

It is likely, of course, that a substantial portion of any relative cost disadvantage lies within rival firms' own cost structures. Here, five options for restoring cost parity emerge:

- Initiate internal budget-tightening measures aimed at using less input to generate the desired output (cost-cutting retrenchment).
- Invest in cost-saving technological improvements.
- Innovate around the troublesome cost components as new investments are made in plant and equipment.
- Redesign the product to achieve cost reductions.
- Try to make up the internal cost disadvantage by achieving cost savings in the backward and forward portions of the complete production-cost chain.

The analytical contribution of strategic cost analysis is the emphasis it places on a firm looking beyond the inner workings of its own cost structure to see how its costs stack up against the costs of competitors. Strategic cost analysis is accomplished by examining the cost makeup of one's own complete production-cost chain and comparing it against the production-cost chains of important rival firms. Such comparisons reveal whether a firm has a cost advantage or disadvantage vis-à-vis major competitors and help pinpoint which cost components in the production-cost chain are the source of the cost advantage or disadvantage. A strategic analysis of a company's cost structure and overall cost competitiveness is integral to the task of appraising how strong a grip a firm has on its market position and assessing a firm's competitive strategy options.

SUMMARY AND CONCLUSIONS

Measuring the cost of an activity means assessing the amount of sacrifice associated with conducting that activity. Completeness requires that the nature of the sacrifices considered be both tangible and intangible, objective and subjective, monetary and nonmonetary.

No one measure of cost is adequate for managerial or economic purposes. Depending on the type of problem, one may wish to calculate historical costs, opportunity costs, total costs, average costs, marginal costs, fixed costs, variable costs, direct costs, common costs, long-run costs, short-run costs, labor costs, controllable costs, shutdown costs, escapable costs, replacement costs, incremental costs, manufacturing costs, selling costs, administrative costs, and so on.

The cost-output relationships for a firm in the short run are governed by the character of the underlying production function. When the production function exhibits increasing returns to variable input, as output rises TFC remains constant, TVC and TC increase at a decreasing rate, and unit costs (AFC, AVC, ATC, and MC) decline.

When the underlying production function displays constant returns to variable input, rising output is associated with the following cost behavior: TFC is a fixed value, TVC and TC rise at a constant rate, MC and AVC are equal and constant, and AFC and ATC decline.

When the underlying production function is characterized by decreasing returns to variable input, increases in the output rate generate cost functions such that the TVC and TC functions increase at an increasing rate, TFC remains fixed, AVC and MC rise, AFC decreases, and ATC is U-shaped.

When the production function has a range first of increasing returns and then of decreasing returns to variable input, the firm's TFC function is again a horizontal line, but the TVC and TC functions both increase at a decreasing rate over the range of output where increasing returns to variable input prevail, then increase at an increasing rate over the output range where decreasing returns prevail. As usual, AFC decreases with increases in output irrespective of the nature of the returns to variable input. And the AVC, ATC, and MC are U-shaped functions, with the MC curve intersecting the AVC and ATC curves at their minimum points.

According to the best available empirical evidence, the behavior of total, average, and marginal costs in many firms embraces elements of the four preceding basic types of production-cost-output relationships. At output rates well below "normal," increasing returns to variable input are encountered, and unit costs fall as output rises. Beyond these abnormally low output rates, constant returns to variable input prevail up to approximately 85 to 90% of capacity; over this output range total costs rise linearly, *MC* is a constant, and *ATC* declines. Past 90% of capacity, decreasing returns to variable input are encountered, *TVC* and *TC* begin to rise disproportionately to the additional increases in output, and *AVC, MC,* and *ATC* rise sharply.

In the long run when there is time to alter the usage of any and all inputs, a firm will seek to become the right size to produce the desired output at the lowest possible cost. The *LRAC* curve for a *plant* shows the minimum average cost of producing a good using various *plant* sizes when all resource inputs are variable and any desired scale of *plant* can be built. The *LRAC* curve for a *firm* shows the minimum average cost of producing a product for various firm sizes when the firm has adequate time to adjust any and all of its inputs to optimal levels. By and large, the *LRAC* curves for both plants and firms are U-shaped.

The behavior of long-run costs is a key force in determining the number and size of firms in a particular industry. Generally speaking, where significant economies are associated with mass production technologies, the structure of the industry will consist of a small number of large-scale producers. When there are few cost advantages to producing in large quantities and many cost disadvantages, production units will be large in number and small in size. In those cases where unit cost is virtually unaffected by the output rate, small, medium, and large firms may be able to compete on fairly equal terms.

Strategic cost analysis is a valuable analytical tool for examining how a firm's costs compare with the costs of its competitors. The core of strategic cost analysis is the construction of complete production-cost chains exposing whether a firm is at a cost advantage or disadvantage and whether it stems from cost differences in (1) the backward portion of the cost chain, (2) the rivals' own internal cost structures, or (3) the forward portion of the cost chain. The strategic options for eliminating a net cost disadvantage depend on where the cost disparities lie in the overall chain.

SUGGESTED READINGS

ALCHIAN, A. A., "Costs and Outputs," *The Allocation of Economic Resources,* Moses Abramovitz *et al.,* eds. (Stanford, Calif.: Stanford University Press, 1959), pp. 23–40.

APEL, H., "Marginal Cost Constancy and Its Implications," *American Economic Review,* Vol. 38, No. 5 (December 1948), pp. 870–885.

BECKENSTEIN, A. R., "Scale Economies in the Multiplant Firm: Theory and Empirical Evidence," *Bell Journal of Economics,* Vol. 6, No. 2 (Autumn 1975), pp. 644–657.

CLARK, J. M., *Studies in the Economics of Overhead Costs* (Chicago: University of Chicago Press, 1923), Chapters 4–6.

DEAN, J., *Managerial Economics* (Englewood Cliffs, N.J.: Prentice-Hall, Inc., 1951), Chapter 5.

EITEMAN, W. J., "Factors Determining the Location of the Least Cost Point," *American Economic Review,* Vol. 37, No. 5 (December 1947), pp. 910–918.

JOHNSTON, J., *Statistical Cost Analysis* (New York: McGraw-Hill Book Company, 1960), Chapters 4 and 5.

KOOT, R. S., AND D. A. WALKER, "Short Run Cost Functions of a Multiproduct Firm," *Journal of Industrial Economics,* Vol. 18, No. 2 (April 1970), pp. 118–128.

SHERER, F. M., A. R. BECKENSTEIN, E. KAUFER, AND R. D. MURPHY, *The Economics of Multiplant Operation: An International Comparison Study* (Cambridge, Mass.: Harvard University Press, 1975).

TANGRI, O. P., "Omissions in the Treatment of the Law of Variable Proportions," *American Economic Review,* Vol. 56, No. 3 (June 1966), pp. 484–493.

VINER, J., "Cost Curves and Supply Curves," reprinted in *Readings in Price Theory* (Homewood, Ill.: Richard D. Irwin, Inc., 1952), pp. 198–232.

WALTERS, A. A., "Production and Cost Functions," *Econometrica,* Vol. 31, No. 1 (January 1963), pp. 1–66.

WILLIAMSON, O. E., "Hierarchical Control and Optimum Firm Size," *Journal of Political Economy,* Vol. 75, No. 2 (April 1967), pp. 123–138.

PROBLEMS AND QUESTIONS FOR DISCUSSION

1. Complete the following table:

Units of Output	TFC	TVC	TC	AFC	AVC	ATC	"Average" MC
0	___	___	$ 500	___	___	___	
100	___	___	750	___	___	___	___
200	___	___	1100	___	___	___	___
300	___	___	1500	___	___	___	___
400	___	___	2000	___	___	___	___
500	___	___	2600	___	___	___	___

2. Complete the following table. Assume that units of fixed input cost $10 each and that units of variable input cost $20 each.

Units of Fixed Input	Units of Variable Input	Units of Output	"Average" Marginal Product of Variable Input	Average Product of Variable Input	TFC	TVC	TC	AFC	ATC	"Average" MC
100	0	0		___	___	___	___	___	___	
100	20	600	___	___	___	___	___	___	___	___
100	40	1500	___	___	___	___	___	___	___	___
100	60	2000	___	___	___	___	___	___	___	___
100	80	2200	___	___	___	___	___	___	___	___
100	100	2300	___	___	___	___	___	___	___	___

3. Given the total cost function $TC = 10,000 + 9Q$, where $Q =$ units of output:
   (a) Determine the equations for *TFC* and *TVC*, and illustrate graphically the relationships among *TFC*, *TVC*, and *TC*.
   (b) Determine the equations for *AFC*, *AVC*, *ATC*, and *MC*. Graphically illustrate their relationships to one another.
   (c) What, if anything, can you infer about the nature of the underlying production function?
   (d) How much is the marginal cost of the 100th unit of output? How much is *AVC* at an output of 100 units? Explain why $MC = AVC$ at each rate of output.

4. Given the total cost function $TC = 20,000 + 4Q + 0.5Q^2$, where $Q =$ units of output:
   (a) Determine the equations for *TFC* and *TVC*. Graph the *TFC*, *TVC*, and *TC* functions, and graphically show their relationships to one another. How would you describe the behavior of *TVC* as output increases?
   (b) Determine the equations for *AFC*, *AVC*, *ATC*, and *MC*. Graph each of these functions, and graphically show their relationships to one another.
   (c) What is the nature of the underlying production function? What will its shape be?

5. Given the following information:
   (a) $Q = 6X$, where $X =$ units of variable input and $Q =$ units of output.
   (b) There are 10 units of fixed input.
   (c) Price of the fixed inputs $= \$10$/unit.
   (d) Price of the variable inputs $= \$5$/unit.
   Determine the corresponding equations for *TFC*, *TVC*, *TC*, *AFC*, *AVC*, *ATC*, and *MC*.

6. The total cost function of a shirt manufacturer is $TC = 10 + 26Q - 5Q^2 + 0.5Q^3$, where *TC* is in hundreds of dollars per month and *Q* is output in hundreds of shirts per month.
   (a) What is the equation for *TVC*?
   (b) What is the equation for *AVC*?
   (c) What is the equation for *ATC*?
   (d) What is the equation for *MC*?
   (e) Plot (or sketch) the relationships among *TFC*, *TVC*, and *TC*.
   (f) Plot (or sketch) the relationships among *AFC*, *AVC*, *ATC*, and *MC*.
   (g) What, if anything, can you infer about the nature of the underlying production function?

7. Given $TC = 2000 + 15Q - 6Q^2 + Q^3$, where $Q =$ units of output:
   (a) How much is *TFC* at an output of 2000 units? At 5000 units?
   (b) How much is *AFC* at an output of 2000 units? At 5000 units?
   (c) How much is *AVC* at an output of 20 units?
   (d) How much is *MC* at an output of 20 units?
   (e) How much is *ATC* at an output of 20 units?
   (f) At approximately what output rate is the point of diminishing marginal returns to variable input encountered?
   (g) At approximately what output rate does diminishing average returns begin?
   (h) At approximately what rate of output does stage II begin?

8. Given the production function $Q = 15X$, where $X =$ units of variable input and Q = units of output. Units of variable input cost $\$30$ each and units of fixed input cost $\$100$ each. Ten units of fixed input are available.
   (a) Determine *AFC* at an output of 400 units.
   (b) Determine *AVC* when 10 units of variable input are combined with the 10 available units of fixed input.
   (c) How much is *MC* at an output of 300 units?

9. Prove that $MC = AVC$ at the minimum point of the *AVC* curve when the equation for *TVC* is of the general form $TVC = bQ - cQ^2 + dQ^3$. (*Hint:* See footnote 10.)

10. What is the relationship, if any, between marginal costs and fixed costs?

11. Given the following cost information:
   (a) *AFC* for 5 units of output is $2000.
   (b) *AVC* for 4 units of output is $850.
   (c) *TC* rises by $1240 when the sixth unit of output is produced.
   (d) *ATC* for 5 units of output is $2880.
   (e) It costs $1000 more to produce 1 unit of output than to produce nothing.
   (f) *TC* for 8 units of output is $19,040.
   (g) *TVC* increases by $1535 when the seventh unit of output is produced.
   (h) *AFC* plus *AVC* for 3 units of output is $4185.
   (i) *ATC* falls by $5100 when output rises from 1 to 2 units.

Using this information, complete the following table:

Output	TFC	TVC	TC	AFC	AVC	ATC	MC
0	___	___	___	___	___	___	___
1	___	___	___	___	___	___	___
2	___	___	___	___	___	___	___
3	___	___	___	___	___	___	___
4	___	___	___	___	___	___	___
5	___	___	___	___	___	___	___
6	___	___	___	___	___	___	___
7	___	___	___	___	___	___	___
8	___	___	___	___	___	___	___

12. Midwest Foundry Corp. was exploring the construction of one of three types of facilities for manufacturing a new type of cast iron pipe. Estimated costs for each of the three facilities are indicated below:

Cost Component	Plant A	Plant B	Plant C
Cost of materials per unit	$3.00	$3.00	$3.00
Labor costs per unit	$0.25	$0.50	$0.75
Equipment cost (10-year life)	$750,000	$600,000	$250,000
Fixed overhead expenses	$100,000	$60,000	$20,000
Maintenance and variable overhead expense per unit	$0.15	$0.20	$0.40
Annual output capacity (in units)	500,000	375,000	125,000

   (a) Determine which plant is capable of achieving the lowest *ATC* at an output of 300,000 units. (For outputs greater than the annual capacity of plant C, assume that Midwest would simply build as many type C plants as necessary to obtain the desired output.)
   (b) What is the lowest-cost plant arrangement for an output of 1 million units?

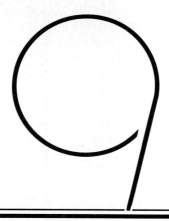

THE GOALS OF THE FIRM
Profit and other considerations

A major task of microeconomic theory is to explain and to predict how companies will behave and respond to changes in particular market forces and economic policies. This is not a simple matter in a trillion-dollar economy where the forms of enterprise range from the freewheeling independent proprietorship to the multiproduct, billion-dollar modern corporation and where competition varies from one industry to the next. However, economists have developed two complementary approaches to studying business behavior. One is to try to explain business behavior through the goals of the firm, the argument being that decision makers are prone to select the actions and strategies which they perceive best contribute to achieving the firm's goals. The other holds that market conditions and competition are the chief factors underlying (or constraining) a firm's behavior. The two are by no means exclusive and we shall find it useful to use both.

In this chapter we shall examine the considerations which can motivate and drive firms to behave as they do, concentrating mainly on the profit motive. Particular emphasis will be placed on the character, source, and use of profit, the role and functions of profit in a modern economy, and whether firms seek to maximize profit. In the last section of the chapter some major alternatives to strict profit maximization will be presented.

THE AMBIGUOUS MEANING OF PROFIT

Profit is typically defined as the difference between total revenue and total cost. In terms of symbols, $\pi = TR - TC$, where π represents profit. This definition of profit, although widely accepted and seemingly straightforward, is nonetheless ambiguous in its application. To the accountant, "profit" usually means total revenue minus actual historical costs; thus *accounting profit* is an *ex post* concept based upon past transactions and historical fact.[1] To the economist "profit" means total revenue minus *all* costs—not just the historical money expenses incurred by the firm but an allowance for a "normal" profit as well. The various approaches to what constitutes a cost and how cost should be measured give rise to the concepts of accounting profit, normal profit, and economic profit.

The most significant element of discrepancy between accounting and economic measures of profit relates to the treatment of the stockholders' capital investment in an enterprise. Economists contend that in a capitalistic economy the owners of an enterprise must, over the long run, receive a return on their investment of sufficient magnitude to induce the enterprise to remain in business. Whenever the profitability of a business consistently is below what can generally be earned in other enterprises of equivalent business risk, stockholders can be expected to seek greener pastures for their investment funds. Because additional resources and capital will tend to be withheld from an enterprise if and when realized accounting profits fall below "minimum acceptable levels" for sustained periods, it is appropriate to conceive of this minimum profitability as a "cost." It is a cost in the sense that unless revenues from a firm's operations are adequate to provide acceptable rewards to stockholders, the enterprise will be denied additional venture capital and, in time, will wither and die.[2] In other words, in the long run, *some minimum amount of profit is a condition of survival.*

How large is this minimum acceptable degree of profitability? a 10% after-tax return on stockholders' investment? or 15%? Actually, a hard and fast standard does not exist; how much profit is enough varies with the circumstances—the risk involved, the time period, the amount of required capital investment, inflation rates, the health of the economy, the type of industry, the long-run potential of the enterprise, what other firms are earning, and so on. But whatever the size of the minimum, it provides a benchmark for judging whether to remain in business or get out. Firms that cannot earn an acceptable profit doing what they are doing should "get out" and divert capital and resources into activities where *at least* a minimum acceptable profit can be earned. Accordingly, it has become customary in economics to think of the *minimum profit* that is necessary to keep a firm in business in the long run *as being a genuine cost of production.* We shall refer to this minimum return to ownership as *normal profit.* On the other hand, *economic*

---

[1] However, accounting measures of profit are by no means exact just because they are based upon past events with known monetary values. Indeed, several acceptable accounting alternatives exist for determining the "correct" revenues and costs to attribute to a given time period. There are a number of alternative techniques for calculating depreciation, valuing inventories, deciding when to write off overdue accounts receivable as bad-debt losses, and deciding how to adjust the costs of fixed assets for price level changes. In addition, while it is customary to count the costs of advertising, public relations, research and development, and training in the period in which they occur, it is clear that they affect *future* sales, production, and profits. Hence, accounting profit calculations are estimates rather than absolute truth.

[2] The actual or realized return to stockholders takes two forms: (1) dividends and (2) capital gains—increases in the value of a stock in terms of price per share.

profit can be construed as a return over and above a normal profit. The following examples illustrate how accounting profit, normal profit, and economic profit are related.

> EXAMPLE 1: Company A owns production facilities valued at $100 million. Its net earnings after taxes were $12 million—as determined by standard accounting techniques. Assuming that the "normal" rate of return for firms of comparable position is 8%, the company's normal profit should approximate $8 million (8% of $100 million). Company A's *economic profit* is thus $12 million − $8 million = $4 million. The $4 million represents that portion of the overall return to owners (stockholders) *over and above* what could be earned in comparable alternative ventures.

> EXAMPLE 2: Company X has made an equity investment of $50 million in facilities to produce high-speed copying equipment. According to conventional accounting measures, its earnings after taxes were $5 million or 10% on investment. However, an evaluation of the alternatives open to company X indicates that had the firm directed its energies to producing word processors, net earnings after taxes could have been $6 million. Hence, even though company X realized a 10% return on its investment, it lost out on an opportunity to earn 12%, thereby resulting in an *opportunity loss* of 2%.

Henceforth we shall endeavor to use the term "profit" to mean economic profit; a normal return or normal profit will be treated as part of total cost. One final point: insofar as both decision making and the analysis of firm behavior are concerned, interest centers more on *expected* profit than upon *realized* profits.[3] Realized profits are relevant as a guide to action and to behavior only to the extent that they influence future profit expectations. Realized profits can also serve as the yardstick for measuring past performance. Nonetheless, expected profit considerations serve as the basis for decisions and for predicting business behavior.

THEORIES OF PROFIT

The profit-oriented capitalistic type of economic system has provoked a wealth of controversy and discussion about profit—from whence it derives, the economic functions it performs, its ethical and moral qualities, and whether profit is socially justified. The various theories about profit and its economic role can, for convenience, be grouped into three broad categories:

1. Compensatory and functional theories of profit.
2. Friction and monopoly theories of profit.
3. Technology and innovation theories of profit.

---

[3] More precisely, managers are primarily interested in the size of the time-discounted profit flow, or to put it another way, the *present value* of the expected stream of profits. The present value of the stream of profits flowing in from an investment is the amount of money that must be invested *now*, at some rate of return, to produce a cash flow equivalent to the expected profit flow.

This grouping is indicative of historical patterns of thinking on profit issues and for our purposes offers a logical approach to examining the whys and wherefores of both normal and economic profit.

Compensatory and Functional Theories of Profit

As applied to owner-managed firms, the compensatory and functional theories of profit regard normal profit as a payment to the entrepreneur in return for services performed in coordinating and supervising the many facets of a firm's activities and in bearing the risks of enterprise. The entrepreneur is the key force in initiating, integrating, and guiding productive activities to a successful conclusion. It is entrepreneurial alertness to unnoticed product-customer-technological opportunities that catalyzes and drives market processes. The entrepreneur is held to be *the* human action element crucial to making the firm a success and to stimulating economic activity in general. Profit, therefore, arises partly as a justifiable compensation and reward to the entrepreneur for fulfilling the various economic and managerial functions successfully. Losses are the penalty for entrepreneurial failure.

From this perspective, the entrepreneur emerges as a laborer of a particular type and talent. Profit becomes the special creation of the gifted entrepreneur, who, by his or her comprehension of the marketplace, capacity for organization, administrative ability, and energy, wisdom, and economy, is most responsible for generating an excess of total revenue over total cost—an excess that may result in the realization of economic profits as well as normal profits. Profit, then, is more than something that just happens to be left over after all costs are covered; rather its existence signals astute entrepreneurship, a vitality of enterprise, and competitive strength.

While this explanation of profit provides a plausible rationale for justifying and explaining why individual proprietorships, partnerships, and small entrepreneurial corporations are entitled to at least a normal profit, it is at considerable variance with the realities of large corporate enterprise. In large corporations, salaried managers perform much of the entrepreneurial function, but the profits accrue to "absentee" stockholders, whose primary function is to supply financial capital to the firm rather than entrepreneurship. Consequently, functional and compensatory reasons other than entrepreneurship must be found for justifying why corporations should earn a normal profit.

One such basis pertains to the risk-taking function which stockholders perform even though they are absentee owners. In furnishing the corporation with venture capital, the stockholder receives no assurance of a return on his or her investment in the form of dividends and/or capital gains. The stockholder can and does lose money when the corporation's activities prove to be unprofitable. Unpredictable changes in the general economic environment combine with sudden changes in consumer tastes, resource supplies, competitive forces, government policy, and technology to produce an abundance of uncertainty that tends to enrich some firms and impoverish others. Investors willing to accept the uncertainties of enterprise are entitled to a reward for the use of their capital—a reward that rightly should be keyed to the degree of uncertainty borne by the investor. The reward for bearing uncertainty and risking one's venture capital is properly considered as normal profit and not economic profit.

At least a portion of corporate profits, then, can be looked upon as a reward to stockholders for confronting uncertainty and supplying venture capital to the enterprise. Naturally, though, a 20% *expected* return will not be valued as highly as a 20% *guaranteed* return. Depending upon the confidence investors place in the estimated profitability of a venture and depending upon their immediate inclinations toward either taking risks or avoiding them, they may evaluate a 20% expected return as equivalent to 10% on a sure thing, or just 8%, or even just 5%. Hence while stockholders are indeed absentee owners, they still perform the essential entrepreneurial functions of bearing the uncertainties of enterprise and of supplying risk capital—both of which contribute to a firm's survival and competitive success. And the element of uncertainty explains why business firms must sometimes earn ''high'' profits if they are to keep investors willing to supply risk capital—the greater the degree of uncertainty, the greater must be the prospect of reward to justify going ahead with a venture.

Another compensatory explanation as to how profit arises attaches to the service that a firm renders to its customers. To some extent, a firm's profit (normal or economic) may derive from the fact that many buyers are willing to pay a price that more than covers the cost of labor, materials, capital, taxes, and other expenses involved in furnishing the good or service because of the time it saves, or its usefulness and convenience, or status and prestige, or any other utility-related reason. The excess of price over cost thus represents compensation to the supplier for having the skill and foresight to give buyers the kind of value they wanted. The proponents of this viewpoint observe that when firms are adequately rewarded with profit for fulfilling society's material wants in the face of market uncertainties, they tend to be more efficient, more willing to innovate, more venturesome, and therefore more progressive. Why? Because when the stakes are more attractive, enterprises are more daring and their entrepreneurial spirit more vibrant. Moreover, the earning of economic profit enhances the financial ability of firms to invest in new activities and to make up for the periodic losses of those ventures that turn sour.

Friction and Monopoly Theories of Profit

A second group of theories maintains that profit can result from luck, good fortune, positions of advantage, various market frictions, and/or a lack of vigorous competition. These have the effect of allowing firms to earn ''monopoly'' profits. Ideally, competition is always sufficiently strong to preclude firms from ''exploiting'' consumers; when it is, firms are generally unable to maneuver themselves into the position of being able to influence prices or otherwise ''rig the market'' to their own advantage.

In the real world, of course, competition is not always powerful and responsive enough to foreclose any and all elements of monopolistic advantage. For example, unusually favorable locations for motels, service stations, restaurants, and similar establishments give them distinct locational advantages over less fortunately situated rivals. International trade barriers may give domestic producers a more strategic position in domestic markets. Military and other government installations may bring profit bonanzas to adjacent localities. Windfall profits may be obtained for short periods of time as the result of circumstances (labor strikes, extreme weather conditions, natural disasters) which temporarily create a sellers' market. The granting of patents, trademarks, and copyrights enables the holder to legally exclude competitors. Hence, being in a position of advantage and thereby able to realize "monopoly profits" explains how and why some firms have above-normal degrees of profitability.

However, the ability of firms to extort big profits from their customers is easily exaggerated. Competition is seldom weak enough for great numbers of firms to grab positions of monopoly power. Nor is it valid to conclude that better-than-average profits are always socially undesirable relative to the alternatives. For example, society undoubtedly benefits from the practice of granting patents (a legal monopoly); to do otherwise would surely discourage inventive and innovative activities.

Technology and Innovation Theories of Profit

The unifying feature of the third group of profit theories is the potential of technology and innovation for providing the impetus for above-average profitability.[4] New methods of production and distribution enhance profits by lowering costs or else neutralizing cost-increasing factors. New and improved products raise profits by generating favorable changes in demand and/or prices. New managerial, financial, marketing, or accounting practices promote higher profits through operating economies. Taken together, the various forms of innovation constitute perhaps the most powerful and pervasive weapon business firms have for earning sustained economic profits.

That technologically superior production techniques and product innovations are capable of producing attractive economic profits is confirmed by the profit performance of IBM, Xerox, Polaroid, DuPont, General Electric, and Eastman Kodak—all of which have emphasized innovation-related strategies. However, innovation-related profits are subject to attacks over the long run. As an innovation becomes widely adopted and/or imitated, the innovating firms gradually lose their initial advantage; competitive pressures stiffen, product prices are shaved in response to rising supply capabilities, and profits drift back down to "normal" levels. Hence, for a firm to continue to profit from innovation it must be able to bring forth new innovations to replace the shrinking profits of previous innovations. In a technologically dynamic environment, the pursuit of innovation

---

[4] The "innovation theory of profit" is chiefly associated with the late Joseph A. Schumpeter. He made a distinction between invention and innovation; the former he termed as the creation of something new, whereas the latter he viewed as the actual application of an invention in the production process. As originally expounded, Schumpeter used innovation theory to explain business cycles rather than to identify the causes and character of profits. See his *Theory of Economic Development* (Cambridge, Mass.: Harvard University Press, 1934), Chapter 6.

profits creates "a perennial gale of creative destruction" whereby something new, something better, and something different is constantly being introduced to replace older innovations whose associated profitability has already been undermined.[5]

A Perspective View of Profit Theories

The diversity among the three groups of profit theories suggests that, in practice, profit (both normal and economic) results from a variety of influences, with the mix varying from firm to firm and time to time. In a sense, profit results from any of several elements either within the firm or in its environment which differentiates it from other firms in the marketplace; or, to put it another way, *profit arises from the differential advantages among firms*. Since there are any number of kinds and degrees of advantages a firm can assemble, no single theory can adequately justify or explain above-average profit. Furthermore, the various theories themselves are not mutually exclusive. For example, the profit earned by an innovating firm derives in part from the monopoly which the superiority of its innovation provides. At the same time, innovation-related profits may be viewed partly as compensation for successful risk-taking, since, after all, a firm cannot know in advance whether an innovation will produce the results the blueprints predict.

THE SOCIAL BENEFITS OF PROFIT

Traditional theory holds that the owners of enterprise are not the sole beneficiaries of profit—major benefits accrue to society as well. The argument that private self-gain benefits society proceeds as follows. Profit-seeking enterprises find the rewards greatest for doing what society most wants done simply because it is virtually impossible for a firm to earn profits doing something for which consumer demand is lacking. The size of the profit flow acts as a feedback mechanism, informing firms clearly and quickly of what is being well received in the market and what is not. Rising profits serve as society's signal for an industry to expand. At the same time, rising profits help provide firms with the earning power needed to obtain capital and resource inputs for expansion. When profits are less than satisfactory, a reevaluation of a firm's market offering is warranted and if low profitability is viewed as permanent, a reallocation of the firm's resources to other more profitable ventures is in order. Thus, profit is *the* supreme test of a firm's performance. Profit feedback automatically regulates market processes, signaling how society's resource pool is to be allocated among alternative uses.

---

[5] The chemical and pharmaceutical industries offer classic examples of the process of creative destruction. In both these industries the pace of technological progress is rapid and competition is keen. Large profits are earned for short periods of time as new products are introduced, but the forces of competition soon cut severely into earnings as other firms develop similar products or as patents expire. Hence, the maintenance of high earnings if almost entirely dependent upon a firm's ability to sustain a steady flow of new products.

With a profit-minded business sector there is an almost ironclad guarantee that production will be in harmony with demand. One might even say that business firms behave responsibly by seeking to earn the largest practicable amount of profit, for by so doing firms will be producing what society is most desirous of having performed.[6] To put it a little differently, socially responsible business behavior requires that firms vigorously pursue the earning of profit, for it is through the profit mechanism that society signals business firms just which goods and services are most preferred by consumers. Moreover, the profit-loss discipline is extremely reliable in inducing economic resources to be used in accordance with the tastes and preferences of consumers.

Society is also a prime beneficiary of the profit stemming from innovation. Innovation is a fundamental contributor to the process of economic growth and to advances in the standard of living, and it is, of course, the prospect of profit that stimulates innovative activity. Innovation acts as a spur to expanded production capacity, to higher levels of output, and to growth in employment. These socially beneficial spinoffs from innovative activities are critical to the realization of economic progress and cannot be lightly dismissed.

But perhaps the strongest argument for profit relates to its role in allowing a firm to better serve as a useful social and economic vehicle. A firm that does not earn at least a normal profit is not a healthy firm. Firms which are losing money or which are earning subpar profits are weakly positioned to grow and prosper; the job prospects they offer are dim; they are less able to pay higher wages and salaries; they find it difficult to obtain credit; they are financially unable to commit substantial resources to innovation and technological advance; and they are thrust, sooner or later, into a weak competitive position. Consequently, they have little to contribute in terms of providing new jobs and expanding career opportunities, implementing new technologies, marketing important new products, raising living standards, and meeting societal needs—all of which are crucial to enhancing society's overall economic welfare. The earning of what is generally considered to be at least adequate profits is, therefore, an essential prerequisite for business to be able to respond to society's needs in a positive and efficient fashion.

THE PROFIT RECORD OF BUSINESS ENTERPRISES

On the whole, the notion that companies earn "high" profits is unwarranted. For instance, before-tax manufacturing profits as a percentage of sales have ranged in the neighborhood of 6 to 9% since 1960 (see Table 9-1); only 4 to 6 cents out of every sales dollar ends up as profit after taxes—based on accounting definitions of profit. The rate of return before taxes on stockholders' ownership has fluctuated from 11 to 28%, depending upon overall economic conditions; the rate of return after taxes has usually ranged from 9 to 15%—amounts that do not seem unduly

---

[6] For a more thorough discussion of this issue, see Milton Friedman, *Capitalism and Freedom* (Chicago: University of Chicago Press, 1962), pp. 133–136.

TABLE 9-1 **Profits as a Percentage of Sales and as a Percentage of Stockholders' Equity, All Manufacturing Corporations, 1950–1983**

Year	Profits as a Percentage of Sales		Profits as a Percentage of Stockholders' Equity	
	Before Federal Income Taxes	After Federal Income Taxes	Before Federal Income Taxes	After Federal Income Taxes
1950	12.8	7.1	27.9	15.4
1955	10.3	5.4	23.8	12.6
1960	8.0	4.4	16.6	9.2
1965	9.4	5.6	22.0	13.0
1970	6.8	4.0	15.7	9.3
1975	7.5	4.6	18.9	11.6
1976	8.7	5.4	22.7	13.9
1977	8.7	5.3	23.2	14.2
1978	8.9	5.4	24.6	15.0
1979	8.9	5.7	25.7	16.4
1980	7.6	4.8	21.8	13.9
1981	7.4	4.7	21.3	13.6
1982	5.7	3.7	11.3	9.9
1983	6.3	4.0	16.4	10.6

Source: The Economic Report of the President, February 1984, pp. 254–255.

excessive considering the risks and uncertainties that go with enterprise and considering the interest rates that have prevailed on virtually risk-free savings accounts and U.S. Treasury bonds. The cynical view of business executives as cigar-smoking fat cats who exploit helpless consumers to raise their firm's already high rate of return is thus at variance with the evidence—they exist, but they are not the dominant type.

DO BUSINESS FIRMS SEEK TO MAXIMIZE PROFITS?

Because of the strong profit orientation of a competitive enterprise system, it is usually accepted as an article of faith that business firms seek to earn the largest possible profits. Most theories of the firm do not just postulate that profit is *a* goal or the *chief* goal, they state unequivocally that *the* goal is *maximum* profit and that firms can be counted upon to behave *as if* they are profit maximizers. Although it would be an exaggeration to view profit maximization as meaning a firm will point its *every* action and decision in a direction coldly calculated to obtain the largest excess of revenue over cost, it does imply that *a firm faced with several alternatives having different expected profit outcomes can usually be counted upon to select the alternative with the greatest expected profit.*

A wealth of literature has sprung up regarding the validity of relying upon the assumption of profit maximization in constructing theoretical models to explain and to predict business responses to market forces.[7] Both sides have argued from positions of strength, although each appears vulnerable on certain points. Table 9-2 summarizes the main arguments in support of profit maximization. Table 9-3 presents the chief criticisms of the assumption that firms behave as if they seek to maximize profits.

A Sense of Proportion

Although a close examination of Tables 9-2 and 9-3 suggests that both the critics and the defenders of the profit maximization assumption have persuasive arguments in their favor, choosing between full acceptance or all-out condemnation of the profit-maximizing assumption is not necessary. There is merit in an intermediate position which recognizes that there are circumstances where the profit maximization assumption will suffice and circumstances where other business goals should be recognized and incorporated into the analysis of the firm.

APPLICATIONS CAPSULE

HOW BUSINESS EXECUTIVES DEFINE WHAT IS A "REASONABLE" PROFIT

Several top-level business executives were recently asked what they considered to be a "reasonable" profit. Excerpts of their answers are indicated below:

Irving S. Shapiro
Chairman of the Board
DuPont Corp.

Asking how much profit is reasonable is like asking how many eggs you should buy for breakfast. It depends on the size of your family and other factors.

By the same token, what is a reasonable profit depends on an industry's needs. Most Americans will agree that a fair profit is essential to a strong economy, but the idea that there are "needs" for earnings may be difficult to accept. It helps to understand the functions of profit.

[7] The interested reader may wish to consult the discussions by Lester, Machlup, Oliver, Blum, and Gordon beginning in the *American Economic Review* in 1946. Pertinent literature of more recent vintage includes Joseph W. McGuire, *Theories of Business Behavior* (Englewood Cliffs, N.J.: Prentice-Hall, Inc., 1964); H. A. Simon, "Theories of Decision Making in Economics and Behavioral Science," *American Economic Review*, Vol. 49, No. 3 (June 1959), pp. 253–283; William Baumol, *Business Behavior, Value and Growth*, 1st ed. rev. (New York: Harcourt Brace Jovanovich, Inc., 1967); Edith Penrose, *The Theory of the Growth of the Firm* (New York: John Wiley & Sons, Inc., 1959); Robin Marris, "A Model of the 'Managerial' Enterprise," *Quarterly Journal of Economics*, Vol. 77, No. 4 (May 1963), pp. 185–209; R. M. Cyert and J. G. March, *A Behavioral Theory of the Firm* (Englewood Cliffs, N.J.: Prentice-Hall, Inc., 1963); O. E. Williamson, *The Economics of Discretionary Behavior: Managerial Objectives in a Theory of the Firm* (Englewood Cliffs, N.J.: Prentice-Hall, Inc., 1964); R. F. Lanzilotti, "Pricing Objectives in Large Companies," *American Economic Review*, Vol. 48, No. 5 (December 1958) pp. 921–940; William L. Baldwin, "The Motives of Managers, Environmental Restraints and the Theory of Managerial Enterprise," *Quarterly Journal of Economics*, Vol. 78, No. 3 (February 1964), pp. 238–256; and Gerald L. Nordquist, "The Breakup of the Maximization Principle," *Quarterly Journal of Economics and Business*. Vol. 5, No. 3 (Fall 1965), pp. 33–46.

Profits are not pools of money that sit idle. In all business firms, profits are used—put to work—as soon as they are earned. They are plowed back into the economy through investment in new manufacturing plants and new equipment. They are used to expand production and create jobs. They improve efficiency. In sum, profits are "seed money," the means to insure a healthy, growing economy.

Profits have a second function. A portion is paid out in dividends to the stockholders or owners. These dividends are, essentially, payment for the use of stockholders' money, which has been invested in the company.

To return to the original question, a reasonable profit is an amount that allows a company to meet its obligation to its stockholders and to acquire the facilities it must have to provide goods, services, the jobs in the future.

These needs will vary among industries. In the chemical industry, stiff competition and new technology mean plants become obsolete quickly. Bigger manufacturing units are required to supply growing markets. These conditions add up to a huge demand for capital investment.

All business—not just the chemical industry—has been suffering from a shortage of capital, due in large part to a decline in profits in recent years. This situation cannot go on indefinitely. At some point, additional borrowing becomes too risky. Our economic system must be able to generate reasonable profits so we can continue to improve our standard of living.

Fletcher L. Byrom
Chairman of the Board
Koppers Company, Inc.

A profit is reasonable when it provides for the survival of an enterprise.

Survival is possible only when profits are sufficient to perform their two life-giving functions . . . to pay investors for the use of their savings and to increase the productive base of an enterprise so that it can remain a useful entity. These two functions are essential regardless of whether the enterprise is privately held or state-owned.

Marshall McDonald
President
Florida Light and Power Company

What's a reasonable profit? Let's start the answer with another question.

What does it take to keep a company in business? It takes capital—money to buy the facilities that bring in income. You must pay for the use of this money, and what you pay with is income left over after meeting expenses.

This "left-over" income is what most call "profit"; but since you must pay it to attract capital, business analysts consider it a cost—the "cost of capital." Out of this profit comes capital for reinvestment in the business. Out of profit comes the dividend that attracts shareholder capital. Out of profit comes the ability to borrow additional capital at reasonable (there's that word again) interest rates.

All this is especially critical for an electric utility because it takes a lot of capital to keep us in business. About four dollars in facilities for each dollar we collect in revenue. Now the key question: How much profit does it take to attract this necessary capital? That depends on the relation between earnings and the risk of their loss, for one thing, and on competition for investors' money, for another. Recently, the United States government issued some securities offering about $9\frac{1}{2}$ percent interest. That's tough competition for a private company that must bid even higher for an investor's savings.

Indications are that what investors consider reasonable for an electric utility company is a return on common shareholders' equity in the 14 to 16 percent range. When the United States government must offer so high a return on a virtually risk-free investment, you can see why private business has to offer 14 percent or more to attract equity capital.

Hamer H. Budge
President
Investors Group of Companies

[A reasonable profit is] one which is somewhat above a rate that will attract investors to a similar enterprise, entailing a similar risk.

Thomas A. Murphy
Chairman of the Board
General Motors Corp.

In my view, many labels have been attached to the word profit, such as reasonable, fair, and equitable, which reflected a misunderstanding of the nature of profit itself. To be specific, I view profit as a resultant of the complex of activities carried on by a business.

Profit varies from one year to the next depending upon general economic conditions, the acceptability of the products in the market, and the ability of the enterprise to produce those products efficiently.

I would underscore the fact that our market economy requires that each business must compete for customer favor both in terms of price and product. If it is successful in this competitive effort it earns a profit and if it is successful it can generate the resources for growth. Obviously, no business can maintain itself unless its earnings are adequate to attract investment.

There is one further consideration and this is the risk factor. A company may generate above-average earnings, but when consideration is given to risk its above-average earnings may be no more than is necessary to sustain the investment.

Put in other words, a "high" profit relative to some average of all profits may well be inadequate for growth when risk is considered. If, as I believe, profits are a resultant of the operation of the business, then it follows that descriptive labels such as reasonable, fair, or equitable have little or no meaning.

David Rockefeller
Chairman of the Board
Chase Manhattan Corp.

In a free economy, growing business profits are the key to reaching and sustaining a satisfactory rate of private capital spending. Profits retained by business provide capital for growth. Profiles paid out as dividends make it possible for business to raise additional funds for capital investment through the private capital markets. A good profit trend makes it easier for a business to obtain financing through the commercial banking system; this can be especially important for smaller and medium-sized companies.

These views can be summed up in the following way:

1. What size profit is "reasonable" varies from industry to industry, depending on risk, business cycles, and capital needs.

2. A reasonable profit is an amount that allows a company to meet its obligation to its stockholders and to acquire the facilities it must have to provide goods, services, and jobs in the future.

3. The essential function of profit is to allow a firm to attract enough capital to enable it to meet the needs of customers for its products and services.

Source: Downs Matthews, "Just What Is a Reasonable Profit?" *Exxon USA*, Vol. 16, No. 3 (Third Quarter 1977), pp. 27–31.

TABLE 9-2 Summary of Arguments as to Why Firms Behave As If They Seek to Maximize Profits

Arguments for Profit Maximization	Supporting Rationale
1. The profit motive is the strongest, the most universal, and the most persistent of the forces governing business behavior.	Although firms may pursue goals other than profit, the impact of such goals upon behavior is quite small. Hence, imputing "more realistic" goals to the firm yields no *significant* improvement in explanation or prediction while greatly increasing the complexity of the analysis.
2. Competition forces firms to adopt a goal of maximum profits.	Where competition is keen, firms must display a behavior pattern very closely akin to profit maximization in order to stand a chance of earning any profit at all. Knowledge that only the fittest will survive is a powerful incentive for all firms to direct their energies in profit-maximizing directions, learning whatever skills are required and emulating firms which are visibly successful in the battle for survival.
3. Assuming that business firms behave as if they seek to maximize profits is an appropriate theoretical approach as long as such an assumption allows accurate predictions to be made about behavior.	The only valid test of a theory is its predictive power. Whether an assumption is realistic enough can be settled only by examining the predictive ability of the theory. Since economists have had considerable success in using the profit-maximizing assumption as a basis for predicting the price and output behavior of business firms, the merit of using this assumption in theoretical models is well established.
4. The profit-maximizing assumption is a useful aid in obtaining a general understanding and explanation of the behavior of groups of firms.	Microeconomic theory is not designed to explain and predict the behavior of *particular* firms; instead it is designed to explain and predict changes in observed prices and outputs as consequences of particular market forces (such as changes in wage rates, resource prices, or taxes). In accomplishing this purpose, the firm serves only as a theoretical link for identifying how one gets from the causes of business behavior to the effects of business behavior. This is altogether different from conceiving of the firm as an object of study in itself and of trying to predict and explain the behavior of Texaco or Holiday Inn.

References: 1. Milton Friedman, "The Methodology of Positive Economics," *Essays in Economics* (Chicago: University of Chicago Press, 1953), pp. 22–23.

2. Fritz Machlup, "Theories of the Firm: Marginalist, Behavioral, Managerial," *American Economic Review,* Vol. 57, No. 1 (March 1967), p. 9.

3. Melvin W. Reder, "A Reconsideration of the Marginal Productivity Theory," *Journal of Political Economy,* Vol. 55, No. 5 (October 1947), pp. 453–454.

4. George J. Stigler, *The Theory of Price* (New York: The Macmillan Company, 1952), pp. 148–149.

TABLE 9-3 Summary of Arguments as to Why Firms Do Not or Cannot Maximize Profits

Arguments against Profit Maximization	Supporting Rationale
1. Uncertainty prevents firms from maximizing profits, even if they wish to do so. Because of imperfect information and uncertainty, it is usually not possible to say unequivocally which of several courses of action appears to be the profit-maximizing alternative. Hence, profit maximization becomes a meaningless goal and prescription for decision making.	Business decisions are made in a fog of uncertainty; managers are not aware of all the alternative courses of action, much less the possible outcomes associated with each known alternative. Consequently, the path along which profit can be maximized is not easily identified because of imperfect information about demand, costs, competitive responses of firms, and general economic conditions. Moreover, the "best" rule for a firm in one decision situation may not be "best" in another decision situation. Nor is the "best" rule for one firm necessarily identical to the "best" rule for another firm. If, because of uncertainty, each firm concludes that profit maximization can be attained by a different route, then the profit-maximizing assumption has little utility in predicting business behavior.
2. In the large corporation the separation of control from ownership gives managers the discretion to pursue goals other than maximum profit.	Why should managers assume the onerous task of maximizing the monetary gains of stockholders? What motive is there for them to do so? Managers rarely encounter interference from stockholders as long as earnings remain "acceptable" and show a persistent tendency to increase. Furthermore, competitive pressures are often neither powerful nor quick enough to keep firms on the tightrope of economic survival; this gives corporate managers the discretion to pursue goals other than profit.
3. Many readily observable business practices are inconsistent with profit maximization.	Separation payments to discharged employees, beautification projects around plant facilities, donations to charity, the failure of executives to spend their whole day hard at work, and the failure of cost accounting practices to generate the data required for maximizing profits are all examples of deviations from profit-maximizing behavior. Also, managers may be anxious to maintain such harmonious relations with employees that they tolerate lax work habits and agree to restrictive work practices and cost-increasing union work rules.
4. Firms find it advantageous to avoid making as large a profit as possible.	Some of the most important reasons for not maximizing profits include (1) a fear of attracting competition from firms which have the potential to enter the industry, (2) a fear of provoking antitrust action, and (3) a belief that holding profits down to "satisfactory" levels will restrain union wage demands and will promote stronger public relations.
5. Maximizing profit is too difficult, unrealistic, and immoral.	Strictly speaking, profit maximization requires businessmen to use every trick in the trade to keep wages and fringe benefits down, to charge as high a price as the consumer can and will pay, to sell as low a quality of merchandise as they can legally hoodwink the consumer into buying, to disclaim any community responsibility, to finagle the lowest prices from suppliers, and so on. Firms seldom pursue these tactics as zealously as is suggested by profit-maximizing behavior.

References: 1. R. N. Anthony, "The Trouble with Profit Maximization," *Harvard Business Review,* Vol. 38, No. 6 (November–December 1960), pp. 126–134.

2. Neil W. Chamberlain, *Enterprise and Environment* (New York: McGraw-Hill Book Company, 1968), Chapter 4.

3. John Kenneth Galbraith, *The New Industrial State* (Boston: Houghton Mifflin Company, 1967), p. 117.

4. Melvin W. Reder, "A Reconsideration of the Marginal Productivity Theory," *Journal of Political Economy,* Vol. 55, No. 5 (October 1947), p. 452.

Profit is sure to be a goal of nearly every enterprise—probably the predominant goal. Profit is a universal measure of business performance and few firms will pursue a course of action that will deliberately lead to lower long-run profits than otherwise could be earned. Nonetheless, there is room for some firms to evidence more profit-conscious and profit-oriented behavior than for others.[8]

In general, firms confronted with strong competitive pressures are prone to exhibit short-run profit-maximizing behavior; behavior resembling something other than full profit maximization is most likely to surface in firms where profits are expected to be ample enough to please stockholders, thereby opening the door for other considerations to influence managerial decisions. There are several reasons why this tends to be so. In highly competitive markets where profit margins are thin, security is shaky, and the ability of firms to absorb losses is weak, there exists (as Darwin's thesis maintains) a fierce struggle in which only the fittest will survive. Market forces allow little room for discretionary action. Under such conditions earning even a normal profit is far from a sure thing and short-run profit considerations rise to dominate the firm's economic decisions. The elected courses of action are likely to be those *perceived* to have the greatest expected profit because to do otherwise is to endanger the firm's survival. Thus, strong competitive forces can so constrict a firm's market behavior that it may have little alternative but to pursue a strategy of short-run profit maximization. A similar condition emerges when recession or inflation weaken consumer demand to such an extent that profits plunge. In methodological terms, the profit-maximizing assumption, although not always an exact representation of reality, is nevertheless a sufficiently good approximation to the actual behavior of most enterprises confronted with these situations. Certainly, it is the best *single* assumption that can be made about the goals of these firms.

On the other hand, firms enjoying adequate profits are in the best position to deviate from a short-run profit-maximizing pattern of behavior. The reason for this is that so long as profits and earnings trends are adequate to satisfy stockholders, management has some leeway to pursue objectives other than higher short-run profits. One cannot stretch this ability too far, though.[9] It would be a gross exaggeration to presume that nonprofit goals govern the market behavior of firms with above-average profits or that management loses sight of the impact that satisfaction of other goals will have on profits. All that is being implied here is that once minimum acceptable profit levels are within reach, then management has some ability and some discretion to give more emphasis to long-run profit maximization and to nonprofit goals. There is some evidence, for instance, that the pursuit of nonprofit goals is more likely to occur in large, single-product, vertically integrated firms than in large multiproduct enterprises. The former tend

---

[8] Conceivably, there are firms where the profit goal is consistently subordinate to the achievement of other goals. But the list of firms that can afford the luxury of relegating profit to positions of lesser importance in the goal hierarchy is very short and their role in the private sector of the economy is doubtless minimal.

[9] Witness, for instance, the wave of cost-cutting campaigns, reorganizations, and overall belt tightening that transcends the business community when business turns sour and profits fall. Often, it is when profits turn into losses that management discovers how much inefficiency it has overlooked or been tolerating.

to be organized along functional lines and the heads of functional units appear more prone to disagree over priorities, to resist full organizational coordination, and to bend organizational goals to their own interests.[10] On the other hand, diversified firms with decentralized, quasi-autonomous business divisions seem to have comparatively stronger profit orientations; business units are generally run as profit centers and business-unit managers are rewarded largely on the basis of short-run performance.

To summarize, then, the assumption of profit-maximizing behavior is especially suitable in those situations where (1) large groups of firms are involved and nothing has to be predicted about the behavior of individual firms; (2) competitive forces are relatively intense; (3) the *effects* of a specified change in conditions upon prices, outputs, and resource inputs are to be explained and predicted rather than the values of these magnitudes before or after the change; and (4) only the directions of change are sought rather than precise numerical results.[11] But when the behavior of specific firms is at issue, where the number of firms is small and the behavior of any one firm affects the behavior of others, where competitive pressures are not profit-threatening, and/or where precise numerical estimates are called for, an explicit identification of a firm's goals is needed before its behavior can be explained and predicted.

THE ALTERNATIVES TO PROFIT MAXIMIZATION

Dissatisfaction with profit maximization as the sole basis for motivating business behavior had led observers to propose a number of alternative goals. These alternatives are held to provide a more realistic underpinning for explaining and predicting the behavior of the firm, especially large corporations.

Satisficing Behavior

One of the most persuasive alternatives to profit maximization is the suggestion that firms aim for a "satisfactory" rate of profit rather than a "maximum" profit.[12] Said differently, firms *satisfice* rather than maximize in pursuing profitability. The thesis is that management decision makers are content to go with workable or satisfactory solutions and courses of action rather than undertaking the more burdensome chore of figuring out the very *best* alternative at each and every fork. According to Herbert Simon (winner of the Nobel prize in economics):

---

[10] See Oliver E. Williamson, *Corporate Control and Business Behavior* (Englewood Cliffs, N.J.: Prentice-Hall, Inc., 1970).

[11] Fritz Machlup, "Theories of the Firm: Marginalist, Behavioral, Managerial," *American Economic Review*, Vol. 57, No. 1 (March 1967), p. 31.

[12] For example, see Herbert A. Simon, *Models of Man* (New York: John Wiley & Sons, Inc., 1957); Simon, "Theories of Decision Making in Economics and Behavioral Science"; Cyert and March, *A Behavioral Theory of the Firm*, and other works by the same authors. Also, see Julius Margolis, "The Analysis of the Firm: Rationalism, Conventionalism, and Behaviorism," *Journal of Business*, Vol. 31, No. 3 (July 1958), pp. 187–199.

"Administrative theory is peculiarly the theory of intended and bounded rationality—of the behavior of human beings who *satisfice* because they have not the wits to *maximize*."[13]

Briefly, the advocates of satisficing view the modern corporation as aspiring to earn future profits at least as great and probably greater than current profits. When confronted with a profit-related decision, corporate managers draw upon their experiences, decision-making conventions, and whatever information is available to select an alternative from among these known to exist that is expected to produce a *satisfactory* stream of profits. But, it is contended, decision makers typically make no attempt to identify *every* possible alternative in search of *the* most profitable alternative because the search process for finding the maximizing alternative, given market uncertainty and imperfect information about demand, costs, competitive responses of rival firms, and future economic conditions, will be too complicated, time-consuming, and futile.[14]

There also exists another rationale for satisficing behavior. Contemporary corporate theory views top management as trustees of the organization, with responsibilities not only to stockholders but to employees, customers, creditors, suppliers, communities, government, and society as well. Corporate executives should, it is said, seek a statesmanlike balance among the claims of stockholders for dividends and higher stock prices, the demands of employees for higher wages and more economic security, the pressures from consumers for lower prices and higher quality products, the requests of retailers for comfortable profit margins and of suppliers for more stable purchasing arrangements, and the insistence of the public for a cleaner environment—all within a framework that is constructive and acceptable to society. According to the satisficing theorists, these considerations lead management to adopt a posture of trying to resolve organizational conflicts and competing claims and, where feasible, to advance the welfare of *all* groups who have a stake in the organization.

Moreover, within the management group itself, there are large numbers of people in middle management as well as in top management who occupy key decision-making and policy-formulating positions. Many of these people share vested interests in production, sales, personnel relations, finance, or research and development and form coalitions to promote their cause. For example, production managers (and production employees) are prone to exert organizational pressure for stable employment, ease of production scheduling, reasonable cost standards, and output expansion. The sales department and those who view marketing as critical to the firm's success can be counted upon to focus upon the importance of sales effectiveness—including sales volumes and the firm's market share. Similarly, other coalitions of interest in the corporation press for goals relating to higher wages and salaries, better inventory control, higher dividends, bigger pen-

---

[13] Herbert A. Simon, *Administrative Behavior*, 2nd ed. (New York: The Macmillan Company, 1957), p. xxiv.

[14] Satisficing has been tested in experimental goal-seeking and problem-solving situations and appears to be a verifiable trait of human behavior. See J. G. March and H. A. Simon, *Organizations* (New York: John Wiley & Sons, Inc., 1958), pp. 140–141, and R. M. Cyert and J. G. March, "Organization Factors in the Theory of Oligopoly," *Quarterly Journal of Economics*, Vol. 70, No. 1 (February 1956), pp. 44–64.

sions, nicer offices, larger expense accounts, more power and status in decision making, greater financial liquidity, technological superiority, and so on. In many respects, these various constituencies within an organization pursue their own interests and attempt to maximize their own utility subject to whatever constraints prevail.

In effect, then, the large corporation contains many centers of power of varying potency over which top management presides. According to the satisficing theorists, the outcome is to reduce corporate goals and decisions to a matter of politics, trade-offs, and compromises. In such an environment, maximizing the monetary well-being of stockholders is not feasible because the pursuit of profit is constrained by the requirement to *satisfy*, at least minimally, the demands of other competing interests. No one center of power, least of all absentee stockholders who may have no more knowledge about the organization than is contained in the annual report, normally has the organizational support needed to impose its goal on all the others and thereby *maximize* its attainment. As a consequence, satisficing behavior becomes the rule rather than the exception and is exemplified in such performance standards as seeking to earn a "satisfactory profit," charging "fair prices," obtaining a "satisfactory share of the market," and growing at an "acceptable rate."

Revenue Maximization

A second frequently mentioned alternative to profit maximization is that of constrained revenue maximization.[15] Here it is contended that once profits reach acceptable levels some firms are inclined to place higher dollar sales ahead of higher profits as the main object of concern. They are allegedly moved to do so because sales revenue is such a key yardstick of business performance. Sales revenue trends reflect consumer acceptance of a firm's products, its competitive position in the marketplace, and growth—all of which are indicative of the firm's vitality. Any position of advantage a firm has in its markets is undermined and its ability to respond effectively to competitive pressures is weakened when sales fall off. In such cases, firms become particulary vulnerable to a deterioration in general business conditions. At the same time, managerial self-interest underlies an expansive sales strategy to the extent that executive salaries evidence closer correlation with the scale of a firm's operations than with its profitability.

Nonetheless, revenue maximization is pursued with a watchful eye toward profits. Profits must be kept high enough to satisfy stockholders and to help finance an expansion of sales and output. Funds for expansion can be gotten internally from retained earnings, or they can be obtained externally from new stock issues and borrowing. However, the willingness of bankers and investors to supply the firm with money capital depends directly on the firm's earning power—the larger are profits (current and expected), the more funds a firm can attract from the capital market. Thus, while a firm is motivated to sell more output and push sales

---

[15] This goal was first proposed by William Baumol. Baumol's thesis is fully developed in Chapter 6 of his *Business Behavior, Value and Growth*, previously cited. This section draws heavily from his discussion therein.

revenues to new peaks, it is constrained from pursuing revenue maximization to such an extent that profits are seriously impaired and the firm is denied the funds it needs for sustained growth and expansion into new markets.

Market Share Goals

Many firms, because of the importance of *experience curve* effects (see the Applications Capsule in Chapter 6), have targets relating to sales volume and market share.[16] Obviously, a big market share can be a valuable asset—not only because being on top or near the top in the market share pecking order is an enviable position to defend but also because it reflects a firm's ability to compete effectively and to benefit from scale economies and being a recognized market leader. However, it is clear that achieving a big market share can easily promote greater profitability and stronger competitive position; by itself, a bigger market share is a hollow victory. For this reason, market share is not likely to be *the* principal goal of the firm. In fact, aggressive pursuit of a higher market share via price cutting and "doing whatever it takes" to win buyer patronage may endanger profitability.[17] Too successful a pursuit of an ever-larger market share may also produce a market dominance that invites antitrust action.[18]

Long-Run Survival Goals

Some economists have argued that business firms, like most other organizations and individuals, have a compelling instinct and motivation to survive.[19] The urge to survive is, allegedly, more fundamental than the profit motive because a firm could maximize profit and still not survive. An inadequate cash flow, shrinking markets, takeovers by acquisition-minded firms, and so on may spell the end, even for profitable firms. In the view of these economists, higher sales, profits, and market share are relevant because they contribute to the long-run survival and viability of the firm. Thus, it is contended, survival goals take precedence over other goals, particularly in stress situations.

The importance of long-run survival is apparent. But, as a goal, it is not very helpful in predicting and explaining business behavior. At any one time, there

[16] Robert F. Lanzilotti, "Pricing Objectives in Large Companies," *American Economic Review*, Vol. 48, No. 5 (December 1958), pp. 921–940; A. D. H. Kaplan, J. B. Dirlam, and R. F. Lanzilotti, *Pricing in Big Business: A Case Approach* (Washington, D.C.: The Brookings Institution, 1958), pp. 181–200; Burnard H. Sord and Glenn A. Welsh, *Business Budgeting* (New York: Controllership Foundation, 1958), p. 149; and Paul N. Bloom and Philip Kotler, "Strategies for High Market Share Companies," *Harvard Business Review*, Vol. 53, No. 6 (November–December 1975), pp. 63–72.

[17] See William E. Fruhan, Jr., "Pyrrhic Victories in Fights for Market Share," *Harvard Business Review*, Vol. 50, No. 5 (September–October 1972), pp. 100–107, and R. D. Buzzell, B. T. Gale, and R. Sultan, "Market Share—A Key to Profitability," *Harvard Business Review*, Vol. 53, No. 1 (January–February 1975), pp. 97–106.

[18] General Motors is said to exercise care that its share of the automobile market does not go much beyond the 55% level. General Electric officials have stated they do not wish to exceed 50% of any given market; moreover, "the company would rather be pushing to expand a 25% share than defending a 50% share." See Lanzillotti, "Pricing Objectives in Large Companies," p. 933.

[19] Kenneth E. Boulding, *A Reconstruction of Economics* (New York: John Wiley & Sons, Inc., 1950), pp. 26–27; Galbraith, *The New Industrial State*, p. 167.

exist many avenues for survival, and thus the choice of one necessarily tends to hinge on other factors. And once survival over the near term seems assured, other goals are sure to motivate managerial decisions. The primary significance of a survival goal is that it is a precondition for accomplishing other goals and objectives. As an explanation of behavior, its relevance is limited to those occasions where the firm's situation is so grave that every effort must be directed toward getting through the period ahead.

Personal Goals of Corporate Managers

The separation of ownership and control in corporations allows executives some measure of freedom to fulfill personal goals. Such motives as the glory of being the industry leader, personal vanity, the pride of being at the head of a large business empire, the desire for professional recognition in executive circles, an affinity for luxurious office accommodations, and the quest for larger salaries may divert managerial decisions down avenues other than *pure* profit maximization. The desires of managers for a quiet, easy life and for more leisure time have also been said to blunt the drive for maximization, since managers with "normal" preferences will exert something less than every ounce of their energy toward maximizing profit.[20]

Fellner has observed the tendency for there to be asymmetry in the rewards to managers.[21] In his view, when risky investments turn out badly, stockholders lose their assets and managers their jobs. But when aggressive moves turn out well, the rewards that managers receive are not always in close proportion to stockholder gains. Faced with this imbalance, Fellner asserts that managers are inclined to forgo high-risk/high-profit ventures for more secure (although still acceptable) profits associated with lower-risk endeavors. A related manifestation is the preference of managers for steadily rising profits over widely fluctuating profits, even though the latter may average higher than the former. This is because sharp earnings' declines may arouse stockholders' demands for a management change, while an outstanding rise in earnings may produce investor expectations of repeat performances and embarrassing questions when the gains are not duplicated.

In the same vein, a pride of workmanship, the urge to create, a pervasive interest in technological feats, and an ambition to demonstrate professional excellence may lead to managerial actions in conflict with the greatest possible profits. Achieving technological superiority and a leadership position in product engineering in spite of possible adverse effects on profits is said to appeal especially to executives with technical and scientific backgrounds and to firms in

[20] Tibor Scitovsky, "A Note on Profit Maximization and Its Implications," *The Review of Economic Studies*, Vol. 11, No. 4 (Winter 1943), pp. 57–60, and John R. Hicks, "Annual Survey of Economic Theory: The Theory of Monopoly," *Econometrica*, Vol. 3, No. 1 (February 1935), p. 8. Such a characterization may do considerable justice to some European business managers of past generations, but whether it describes the psychology of present-day corporate executives in either the United States or Europe is dubious indeed.

[21] William Fellner, *Competition among the Few* (New York: Alfred A. Knopf, Inc., 1949), pp. 172–173.

"high-technology" industries. Technological virtuosity meshes well with the needs of those members of the firm (engineers, technical specialists, research scientists) concerned with keeping the firm on the frontiers of technical know-how and product capability because it means opportunities for the technologists to pursue their favorite interests, as well as opportunities for personal advancement in the form of better jobs, higher salaries, and promotions.

The Goal of Social Responsibility

In recent years much has been said and written about the need for firms, particularly large corporations, to behave in a "socially responsible" manner.[22] Social responsibility has come to mean many things: having a number of diverse interest groups represented in the corporation's governance structure and decision-making process; relating the entire enterprise to the changing needs of society; balancing stockholder interests against the larger interest of society as a whole; revamping corporate policies and practices so as to promote the public welfare in a positive way; and urging firms to help solve the social ills of society while going about their regular business. In essence, the urging of social responsibility upon firms aims at creating a "corporate conscience."

The philosophy underlying social responsibility goals is that stockholder interests in the long run are best served by corporate policies that contribute to developing the kind of society in which business can grow profitability. In fact, the pursuit of profit and the pursuit of social objectives are held to be mutually reinforcing. Profits can be earned performing functions that entail primary or secondary social benefits. At the same time, social objectives can be achieved more rapidly and more efficiently by enlisting the productive power of business firms through the opportunity for profit and by imposing harsh penalties for business activities that are deemed socially harmful.

Adoption of social responsibility goals probably has the ultimate effect of containing the drive for greater short-run profits. Very likely, it makes a satisficing approach to goal formation an even more viable and more attractive managerial practice. But by no means does social responsibility mean that a firm's profitability is secondary; the earning of adequate profit is a prerequisite for giving a firm the organizational ability and the financial wherewithal to respond to social objectives.

Exhorting business firms to be socially responsible has met with resistance from some business managers and several public interest groups. It has been observed, perhaps correctly, that "the business of business is business." Corporate executives, it is said, are neither equipped to be social engineers nor charged to usurp stockholder interests and base decisions on what arguably is or is not "in the public interest." The contention is that in many situations the answer to "what is in the public interest?" or "what is socially responsible?" boils down to one's own personal value judgments and not to a clear-cut "this is best for *everybody*" approach. Still, a number of firms appear to be giving careful con-

---

[22] See *Social Responsibilities of Business Corporations*, issued by the Research and Policy Committee of the Committee for Economic Development, New York, June 1971.

sideration to how corporate strategies and policies affect society and they are definitely concerned about avoiding charges that they are "insensitive" and "bad citizens" when it comes to doing their public duty.

Growth and Diversification Goals

Business firms are usually alert to the organization dangers of stagnation and of the need to remain aggressive at seizing new opportunities. A firm's present activities can lose their sustaining power through changes in consumer tastes, technological change, the appearance of superior products, increased competition from domestic rivals and importers, and growth in the market power of suppliers and customers. A company that does not innovate and grow can eventually find itself managing a tired product line. Not many firms willingly choose "coasting along"—the only thing more damning in the business world than the status quo is decline.

There are several specific appeals for long-term growth and diversification being major corporate goals. To begin with, growth is a good defense against adversity. Growth via greater market penetration offers a firm a stronger, more secure market position vis-à-vis competitors, suppliers, and customers. To the extent that a firm can gain on or overtake its rivals, it has greater freedom for maneuver and more influence over important industry decisions. Growth by diversification into a wider range of products frees firms from too much dependence on one or a few products and serves as a hedge against the possible demise of bread-and-butter products. If one product or phase of a firm's operations slows down and becomes unprofitable, it can survive and even grow on the strength of its other activities. If research and development ventures in one area prove fruitless, as recurringly can be expected, other projects may reveal new vistas of opportunity. Thus, growth and diversification can help firms withstand short-term setbacks and overcome the uncertainties of enterprise.

Second, no other measure of business success has such almost unanimous acceptance as long-term growth (i.e., rising sales, rising production, and rising profits). Growth and successful diversification moves comprise a recurrent theme in the annual reports of large corporations and receive constant emphasis on financial pages and in journals devoted to business affairs. Investors and financial analysts tend to judge the worth of an enterprise not so much by current sales and profits as by growth potential. In almost all cases, more attention is given to the rates at which sales and profits have grown than to the absolute size of current sales and profits. Consequently, many firms have a strong compulsion to achieve a high growth rate; they almost always are eager to get into a lively market, and once they are in, many want nothing short of first place.

Finally, growth and diversification provide an effective means of pursuing other corporate goals and objectives. Growth and diversification can be very consistent with earning higher profits, expanding sales, defending and strengthening the firm's competitive position, paying higher dividends to stockholders, achieving higher stock prices, acquiring superior technological capabilities, creating a "sound corporate image," and so on. Although growth and diversification just for the sake of growth and diversification are suspect, there is still a pervasive tendency for them to complement and support the achievement of other goals. This alone suffices to put them near the top of the priority list.

Conflicts and Trade-Offs among Alternative Goals

Judging from the statements of corporate executives and the strategic plans of companies, it is typical for firms to try to pursue several goals simultaneously— a feature that can pose a host of strategic trade-offs and options:

- To emphasize short-run profits or long-run profits?
- To improve profit margins or increase market share?
- To increase penetration of existing markets or to enter new markets?
- To diversify into related products or into unrelated products?
- To compete in only low-risk environments or to move into high-risk markets?
- To emphasize profit goals or nonprofit goals?
- To seek out faster growth or ways to improve current operations?

How a firm goes about compromising and balancing competing goals and considerations obviously varies from firm to firm and time to time. And the choices can be very tough. For example, a firm whose profits are plunging may be tempted to reduce or eliminate expenditures for R&D, advertising and promotion, investment in new ventures, facilities and equipment, or product innovations—the very things on which long-term profits and growth are built. Evidence also exists to the effect that there is an inverse relationship between profits and profit margins, on the one hand, and growth and market share, on the other hand. Several years ago, DuPont and Union Carbide appear to have followed a strategy aimed at maintaining profit margins significantly above the chemical industry as a whole.[23] To do this, however, the companies had to be highly selective in their choices of markets, resulting in subpar rates of growth. Allied Chemical for a time also sacrificed growth in order to improve its below-average profit rates. The trade-offs among profits, growth, and competitive market position thus pose a very difficult choice of goals. Firms with above-average profit margins are likely to attract strong competition. Rival firms may well be willing to accept initially lower profits and therefore charge lower prices or spend more on promotion in order to gain a stronger market foothold and build a clientele. As they pull sales away, the leaders have two recourses: (1) try to maintain profit margins and tolerate eroding sales and market shares or (2) retaliate with price cutting, product innovation, or increased promotion (more and better ads)—any and all of which tend to lower profit margins.

The trade-offs between other alternative goals can be equally serious. Hence, firms with multiple goals may well adopt *satisficing* rather than *maximizing* criteria as the basis for decision making.

[23] Cited in Philip Kotler, *Marketing Management: Analysis, Planning, and Control* (Englewood Cliffs, N.J.: Prentice-Hall, Inc., 1976), p. 56.

SUMMARY AND CONCLUSIONS

Few economic concepts are used with a more bewildering variety of well-established meanings than profit. Not only is there accounting profit, normal profit, and economic profit, but each of these may be measured in several ways, depending on the specific accounting conventions employed and depending upon whether the desired profit measure is a dollar amount or a rate of return. Accounting profit is based on a firm's income statement and is conceived as the excess of revenue over historical costs after corporate taxes have been deducted. Normal profit is the minimum amount of profit (or rate of return) sufficient to keep the firm in business in the long run; normal profit is considered by the economist as part of total cost. Economic profit is a return over and above a normal profit. It is economic profit which business firms really seek and which governs much of their behavior.

Profit (both normal and economic) is a mixture resulting from a variety of influences, including business acumen, successful performance of the entrepreneurial function, services rendered to the consumer, a fortuitous coping with uncertainty, the presence of market frictions that inhibit a quick response of competitive forces, monopoly power and positions of advantage, technological superiority, and new product innovation.

Wide disagreement exists among economists over whether business firms, especially large corporations, behave as if they seek to *maximize* profits. Diffused ownership, conditions of uncertainty, and insulation from heavy competitive pressures are held to allow firms to pursue goals other than profit maximization. Among the most prominent alternatives to profit maximizing behavior are satisficing, revenue maximization, and growth via diversification. Lesser and/or corollary goals include a bigger market share, long-run survival, satisfactory and secure profits, a rising dividend rate, financial liquidity, technological leadership, attainment of a "good" image, behaving in a "socially responsible" manner, maintaining a strong competitive position, and achievement of personal goals of top management (power, prestige, sense of accomplishment, professional recognition, and big bonuses). Aggressive growth and diversification strategies offer firms an effective means of simultaneously pursuing and achieving many of these goals.

Doubtless, there can be no *single* goal that captures the *whole* truth about what underlies business behavior simply because there are too many subtle shadings of behavior and the decision constraints are far too complex. Furthermore, diversity of goals and variations in motivations are a natural outgrowth of a dynamic trillion-dollar economy populated by a variety of business firms ranging from the small proprietorship to the giant multiproduct corporation. The sizable differences among firms regarding market position, ownership and control, size, competition, uncertainty, technological capabilities, personalities of owners and managers, profitability, and diversification opportunities make it highly improbable that all firms pursue the *same* set of goals with the *same* degree of intensity and priority.

Even so, the profit motive is deeply ingrained in the folklore of modern business behavior, and rightly so. The imperatives of earning profits are pervasive and powerful influences. Certainly, profit stands foremost in the goal hierarchy of most firms and *if one were forced to choose a single goal to characterize business behavior, then the choice would have to be long-run profit maximization.* However, in the following chapters we shall find it helpful to use models that incorporate goals other than pure profit maximization in order to predict and to explain the full range of business behavior.

SUGGESTED READINGS

FARMER, R. N., "Two Kinds of Profit," *California Management Review*, Vol. 8, No. 2 (Winter 1965), pp. 21–28.

FRUHAN, W. E., JR., "Pyrrhic Victories in Fights for Market Share," *Harvard Business Review*, Vol. 50, No. 5 (September–October 1972), pp. 100–107.

FURUBOTN, E. G., AND S. PEJOVICH, "Property Rights and Economic Theory: A Survey of Recent Literature," *Journal of Economic Literature*, Vol. 10, No. 4 (December 1972), pp. 1137–1162.

GALBRAITH, J. K., *The New Industrial State* (Boston: Houghton Mifflin Company, 1967), Chapters 6, 7, 8, and 10–15.

KIRZNER, I. M., *Competition and Entrepreneurship* (Chicago: University of Chicago Press, 1973), Chapter 2.

LANZILOTTI, R. F., "Pricing Objectives in Large Companies," *American Economic Review*, Vol. 48, No. 4 (December 1958), pp. 921–940.

MACHLUP, F., "Theories of the Firm: Marginalist, Behavioral, Managerial," *American Economic Review*, Vol. 57, No. 1 (March 1967), pp. 1–33.

NORDQUIST, G. L., "The Breakup of the Maximization Principle," *Quarterly Journal of Economics and Business*, Vol. 5, No. 3 (Fall 1965), pp. 33–46.

SCHERER, F. M., *Industrial Market Structure and Economic Performance* (Boston: Houghton Mifflin Company, 1980), pp. 29–41.

SIMON, H. A., "Theories of Decision Making in Economics and Behavioral Science," *American Economic Review*, Vol. 49, No. 3 (June 1959), pp. 253–283.

WILLIAMSON, O. E., *Corporate Control and Business Behavior* (Englewood Cliffs, N.J.: Prentice-Hall, Inc., 1970).

PROBLEMS AND QUESTIONS FOR DISCUSSION

1. (a) The Vista Corporation has invested $10 million in producing greeting cards. Its after-tax profits according to conventional accounting measures amounted to $800,000. During the same period an average return of 6% would have been obtained by purchasing government securities. Do you think Vista Corporation earned an economic profit? Why or why not? Explain.

   (b) Suppose that the financial vice-president of Vista Corporation conducts a thorough study and finds that the prospects are excellent (90% chance of success) that an annual profit of $900,000 could be earned by shifting Vista's $10 million investment into the production of business forms. What implications, if any, does this estimate have for evaluating the profitability of Vista's greeting card operations? for future resource allocation within the firm?

2. How should an enterprise go about estimating normal profit?

3. In which of the following circumstances would an assumption of profit maximization be appropriate and in which would the analysis probably be improved by a consideration of goals other than profit? Justify your answer in each case:
   (a) The effect of steel import quotas on steel prices.
   (b) The effect of the UAW's winning a lucrative wage increase from General Motors upon the prices of GM cars.
   (c) The effect of increased liquor taxes upon the price of liquor.
   (d) The effect of the ban on cigarette advertising upon the sales strategy of the three largest cigarette producers.
   (e) The effect upon coal prices of the major oil firms' acquiring producers of coal and thereby gaining control over a large segment of the nation's coal deposits.
   (f) The effect of strong antipollution laws upon the prices of paper products, chemicals, steel, and other products produced by processes with a heavy pollution by-product.

4. "No single goal of business enterprise is pure in its purpose. Goals tend to be overlapping and interdependent." Discuss the validity of this viewpoint and give examples in support of your answer.

5. Is it possible to determine whether or not a particular firm is maximizing profits? Or, to put it another way, is it possible to ascertain at some moment of time what the maximum potential profit performance of a firm is, thus allowing a comparison with the firm's actual profit performance to see if the firm is maximizing profits? Justify your answer.

6. The Hall-Prentiss Corporation is weighing two alternative projects costing $50 million, one offering a best-guess profit expectation of $10 million with a 10% chance of losing $5 million, the other offering an expected profit of $20 million with a 30% chance of losing $5 million. Which is the profit-maximizing alternative? How does this decision situation illustrate the problem of trying to maximize profits under conditions of uncertainty?

7. Is there any difference between a firm's having "monopoly power" and having a "position of advantage" in the markets for its products?

8. Henry Ford II, in an address before the Michigan State Chamber of Commerce on October 2, 1962, made the following statements:

   > There is no such thing as planning for a minimal return less than the best you can imagine—not if you want to survive in a competitive market. It's like asking a professional football team to win by only one point—a sure formula for losing. There's only one way to compete successfully—all-out. If believing this makes you a greedy capitalist lusting after bloated profits, then I plead guilty. The worst sin I can commit as a businessman is to fail to seek maximum long-term profitability by all decent and lawful means. To do so is to subvert economic reason.

   (a) What do you suppose Ford meant when he claimed that to fail to try to maximize long-term profitability is a "sin" and subverts "economic reason"?
   (b) Do you agree with Ford's viewpoint? Why or why not?

9. It has been observed by Milton Friedman, one of the nation's most eminent economists, that "few trends could so thoroughly undermine the very foundations of our free society as the acceptance by corporate officials of a social responsibility other than to make as much money for their stockholders as possible."
   (a) What is the economic basis for such a statement?
   (b) Do you agree with this view? Why or why not?

10. According to Peter Drucker, noted professor of management and business consultant, "there is *no* justification and no rationale for profit as long as one talks the nonsense of profit motive and profit maximization." But he goes on to say: "Profit . . . is not the whole of business responsibility; but it is the first responsibility. The business that fails to produce an adequate profit imperils both the integrity of the resources entrusted in its care and the economy's capacity to grow. . . . Business needs a minimum of profit: the profit required to cover its own future risks, the profit required to enable it to stay in business and to maintain intact the wealth-producing capacity of its resources."

    Is Drucker's view in conflict with how economists view profit? With whom do you agree?

11. Although it is easy to pontificate about the general desirability of business enterprises behaving in "socially responsible" ways and doing what is in "the public interest," it is not so easy to translate such "principles" into concrete prescriptions. For instance:

    (a) Is it socially responsible and in the public interest for oil companies to raise their prices for gasoline or to lower them?

    (b) Is it in the public interest for electric utilities to invest in and operate nuclear-powered generating plants (given that they are more cost efficient than other types of generating plants and given that they do not create acid rain or other air pollution problems)?

    (c) Is it socially responsible or in the public interest for U.S. companies to build production facilities in foreign countries (where production costs may well be lower) and then ship the goods to the United States to be sold and used domestically? Is "exporting jobs" in the public interest even if it results in lower prices to users of the product?

10

HOW MARKETS FUNCTION
The model of perfect competition

A critical part of examining the market for a product is the structure of competition—whether there are *many* or *few* sellers in the industry. The terms "many" and "few" are delineated not so much by the numbers of firms as by the competitive interaction among firms. There are "many" sellers of a product when no one firm has a big enough volume of business or enjoys high enough standing as a market leader for the remaining firms to react to its actions. Each firm is small enough and insignificant enough in the context of the whole market that it is virtually an anonymous entity, hidden by sheer numbers from the watchful eyes of other firms. In contrast, we say there are "few" sellers of a product whenever the actions of any one firm will be noticed and reacted to by rival sellers. "Few" means few enough so that firms find it imperative to follow each other's moves closely. Fewness of sellers also means that each firm is large relative to the size of the market in which it operates; often, when firms are few in number each firm is large in absolute size as well.[1] The single-firm industry, or monopoly, is the limiting case of fewness.

A second key element in market analysis relates to whether the products of sellers are identical or differentiated. The products of sellers may be considered to be identical whenever and wherever customers evidence no particular pref-

---

[1] Fewness does not always mean bigness. A small community has only a few banks, dry cleaners, movies, florists, doctors, lawyers, and hairdressers—none of which are big in an absolute sense. General Motors, however, is big from both an absolute and a relative standpoint.

erence for one firm's product over that of another firm. This may arise because the item is produced by a process that confers certain measurable qualities which can be graded and which are unrelated to the seller producing it. For instance, choice-grade beef is choice-grade beef, and one cannot tell (nor does it really matter) whether it came from ranch A or ranch B. In such cases, the products of firms in an industry tend to be perfect substitutes; examples include cotton, sulfuric acid, natural gas, coal, cement, and coffee beans.

On the other hand, where the products of firms are distinctive and somewhat unique, they are not perfect substitutes for one another, and buyers may have good reason to prefer the product of one firm over that of another. However, the ultimate test of differentiation is in the mind of the buyer, and the perceived differences in the products of various firms may be either real or contrived. "Real" differences involving performance, materials, design, workmanship, and service are obviously important aspects of product differentiation. But "contrived" differences brought about by brand names, trademarks, packaging, and advertising can also be important to buyers; for example, even though all brands of aspirin are chemically alike, many buyers evidence preferences for one brand over others.

In addition, it should be recognized that a firm's product extends beyond the physical and functional characteristics of the item itself. Although a large number of retailers in an area may sell Crest toothpaste, they may not be viewed as equally attractive to buyers of Crest. The sales clerks in one store may be more courteous, or its location more convenient, or its checkout system faster, or its delivery service more dependable, or its credit terms more accommodating. Such factors can cause buyers to prefer one seller over another, even though the item purchased is the same. The various brands of shoes, wines, cereal, cosmetics, tires, and soft drinks are all examples of differentiated products.

As might be expected, competition proceeds along different lines, depending on whether there are "many" or "few" firms and whether their products are identical or differentiated. Viewed from this perspective, four main forms of market structure and organization stand out:

1. *Perfect competition*—many sellers of a standardized product.
2. *Monopolistic competition*—many sellers of a differentiated product.
3. *Oligopoly*—few sellers of either a standardized or a differentiated product.
4. *Monopoly*—a single seller of a product for which there is no close substitute.

In this chapter we shall examine the model of perfect competition. Chapters 11 to 13 concern pricing and production under conditions of monopolistic competition, oligopoly, and monopoly.

THE CHARACTERISTICS OF A PERFECTLY COMPETITIVE MARKET

A perfectly competitive market environment is distinguished by four main features. First, the products of firms in the industry are identical or at least so much alike that buyers do not care whether they buy the product of one firm or another.

Since the products of the firms are indistinguishable and therefore homogeneous "commodities," no buyer is willing to pay one firm a higher price than that charged by rival firms. Buyers are totally indifferent as to the firm from which they purchase as long as price is the same. In fact, differences in price constitute the *only* reason a buyer might prefer one seller to any other.

Second, in perfect competition each and every buyer and seller is without power to affect the going market price of the product. This means that a buyer's purchases must be such a sufficiently small portion of the total bought by all buyers that he cannot wrangle a lower price from sellers than can any other buyer. Similarly, the sales made by a particular firm must be such a sufficiently small portion of the total sold by all firms that the price of the product is not materially affected by any one firm's decision to increase or decrease its output rate. Only if many buyers or sellers act in concert can market prices be influenced materially.

Third, in a perfectly competitive market resource inputs of all kinds are completely mobile. In the long run, there are no important restrictions upon the freedom of firms to enter or leave the industry. Resources can be switched from one use to another very readily. Workers are willing and able to move from region to region in response to new job opportunities and changing wage rates. The supplies of raw materials are in no way monopolized but are made freely available to the highest bidders.

Fourth, perfect competition is characterized by a state of perfect knowledge. Decisions are made under conditions of *certainty*. Firms know exactly what their revenue and cost functions are. They also know the prices of all resource inputs and the various alternative technologies which can be used to produce their products. Consumers are aware of the prices charged by all firms. Resource owners are aware of the prices firms are paying for resource inputs and all relevant opportunity costs.

Obviously, these four conditions are so stringent that no market in the real world ever has or ever can meet them. A few markets (those for agricultural commodities and certain financial securities like money market funds, certificates of deposit, and government bonds) come close to satisfying the first three requirements but none meet the fourth requirement of perfect knowledge. Nonetheless, the study of perfectly competitive markets is not without value. Recall from the introductory chapter that a model may yield valid conclusions even though its assumptions are "unrealistic." As we shall see, the perfectly competitive model captures the essence of real-world markets where large numbers of relatively small firms sell identical products. In addition, it illuminates several basic principles underlying the economics of business behavior. For these reasons perfect competition is worthy of study even though the assumptions upon which it rests are not always accurate reflections of real-world conditions. We shall, however, be careful not to claim too much for the model of perfect competition, and we shall be especially judicious in applying its conclusions to the behavior of firms in actual situations. With these points fixed firmly in mind, suppose we analyze the behavior of a representative firm in a perfectly competitive market environment.

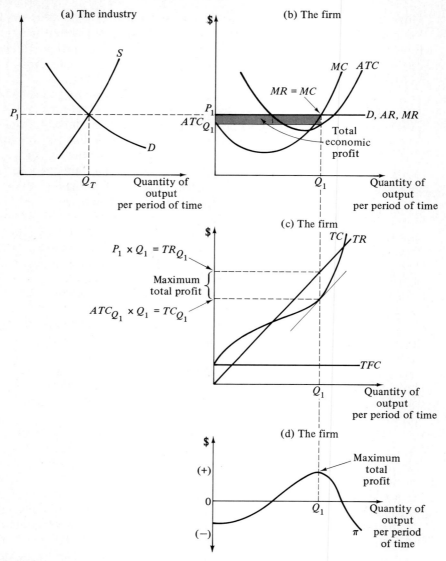

FIGURE 10-1
Profit-maximizing price and output for a firm operating in a perfectly competitive market environment

SHORT-RUN EQUILIBRIUM OF A FIRM IN A PERFECTLY COMPETITIVE MARKET

In perfect competition the prevailing market price of a product is established in classic fashion by the interaction of the market forces of demand and supply. Given the market demand and supply curves in Fig. 10-1(a), a short-run market equilibrium is attained at a price of P_1 dollars and at a total industry output of Q_T units.[2] If price were higher than P_1, then excess supply conditions would drive it downward. By the same token, if price were lower than P_1, then excess demand conditions would force it upward.

Under conditions of perfect competition, each firm has a *horizontal* demand-*AR* curve which intersects the vertical axis at the price established by market supply and market demand conditions. This is illustrated in Fig. 10-1(b). No firm can sell its output at a price even slightly higher than P_1 dollars because buyers will immediately shift their purchases to other firms selling the same item at a lower price. And since each firm is so small relative to the total market, it can sell its entire output at the market price of P_1; hence, there is no inducement whatsoever to sell at a price lower than P_1. The result is that all firms sell at the going price. At any one time a *single* price prevails throughout the market, as determined by the balance between demand and supply.

When the firm's demand-*AR* curve is horizontal, it can sell additional units of output without reducing price. Thus, marginal revenue equals price at every output rate since each additional unit sold will cause total revenue to rise by an amount equal to the price of the product. For example, if price is fixed at $10, then the sale of each additional unit causes total revenue to rise by $10; *MR* is therefore constant and equal to $10. The firm's *MR* function corresponds precisely to its demand-*AR* curve, as shown in Fig. 10-1(b). Both marginal and average revenue are equal to the market price of the product at all possible outputs of the firm.

Since the firm can sell whatever amount it wishes at the going price, its total revenue (*TR*) function will be a linear, upward-sloping curve starting from the origin, as depicted in Fig. 10-1(c). Each and every unit sold will increase *TR* by an amount equal to the selling price. Marginal revenue (*MR*) is constant, so the *TR* curve rises at a constant rate (equal to *MR* and price). The general equation for the *TR* function can be written as

$$TR = P \cdot Q.$$

Now suppose that the firm has a cost structure represented by the average total cost (*ATC*) and marginal cost (*MC*) curves in Fig. 10-1(b) and by the associated total cost (*TC*) curve in Fig. 10-1(c).[3] How much should the firm decide to offer for sale? How will the firm fare at the going price? To answer these questions first requires a consideration of the goal or goals of business enterprises in an environment of perfect competition. As was indicated in Chapter 9, profit

---

[2] The total industry output, Q_T, is the sum of the outputs of all the firms in the industry. It is important to remember that no one firm's output constitutes a significant portion of Q_T.

[3] It should be recognized that the cost curves portrayed in Figs. 10-1(b) and (c) represent just one of the several types of short-run cost functions which firms may possess. As was discussed in Chapter 8, the cubic type of *TC* function is viewed by many economists as representative of the most typical type of cost behavior. However, firms may well possess other types of cost functions depending on the character of the technology employed in the production process. The chapter-end exercises incorporate other types of cost functions to illustrate the perfectly competitive firm's output decision under a variety of cost circumstances.

is the single strongest goal of most firms, so suppose we assume that the prime objective of perfectly competitive firms is to *maximize profits* (or to minimize losses if they cannot make profits). Whether this assumption is valid will be seen shortly.

Since price is established by the market, a perfectly competitive firm has no pricing decision to make. It is a *price-taker*. The determination of price in a perfectly competitive environment is well beyond the control of any one firm; rather, each firm must live with whatever price that market demand and supply conditions establish. However, alternatives do exist regarding the firm's short-run output. The firm *is* able to exert some measure of control over its destiny by adjusting its output to any rate it is capable of producing. Assuming, then, a goal of profit maximization, consider the optimum output decision of a perfectly competitive firm.

Profit Maximization: The Total Cost-Total Revenue Approach

The easiest and most direct way to determine where profits are maximum is to compare total revenue and total costs. Logic dictates that *total profits are maximized at the output rate where TR exceeds TC by the greatest amount.* In Fig. 10-1(c) the profits of the firm are maximum at an output of Q_1 units, where the *vertical distance* between *TR* and *TC* is greatest. Geometrically, it so happens that the maximum vertical distance between *TR* and *TC* occurs at the output rate where a tangent to the *TC* curve has the same slope and is parallel to the *TR* curve, as indicated on the diagram.

The firm's profit function [Fig. 10-1(d)] is derived by subtracting *TC* from *TR* at each rate of output. It indicates how the firm's short-run profits vary with its output rate. The peak of the total profit (π) curve defines the output rate corresponding to maximum short-run profits.

Profit Maximization: The Unit Cost-Unit Revenue Approach

On a unit cost and unit revenue basis, *maximum profits are obtained at the output rate where marginal cost equals marginal revenue.* The validity of this proposition may be established as a matter of common sense. If the production and sale of one more unit of output will add more to a firm's total revenue than to its total costs, the sale of the unit must necessarily add something to the firm's total profits. If, however, the extra cost of producing and selling one more unit is greater than the extra revenues the firm gains, the firm's total profits will be reduced by selling that unit. Marginal revenue (*MR*) is defined as the *addition* to total revenue attributable to the sale of one more unit of output, while marginal cost (*MC*) is defined as the addition to total cost resulting from the production and sale of one more unit of output. Hence, to maximize profits the firm must be cognizant of the marginal revenue and the marginal cost of each successive unit of output.

Thus, in Fig. 10-1(b) the most profitable output level is at Q_1 units, where the MC curve intersects the MR curve. If the firm stops short of selling Q_1 units, then the revenue from selling an additional unit will exceed the cost of selling another unit. Plainly, the firm can increase profits by increasing its rate of output to Q_1. Should the firm produce beyond an output rate of Q_1 units, the marginal costs of all the units in excess of Q_1 will exceed the additional revenue which the firm can obtain from selling them. The firm will lose money on all the units sold past an output of Q_1 units, thereby causing total profits to be smaller than obtainable at a lesser output.

The profit-maximizing output rate in Fig. 10-1(b) corresponds exactly to the output rate in Fig. 10-1(c) where TR exceeds TC by the greatest amount. How do we know? Because at an output of Q_1 units in Fig. 10-1(c), the slope of the TR curve equals the slope of the TC curve. MR, by definition, equals the slope of TR, and MC, by definition, equals the slope of the TC function. Hence, since the values of the slopes are equal, MC must necessarily equal MR at the same output where total revenue exceeds total cost by the largest amount. Logical consistency requires further that the profit-maximizing output rate in Fig. 10-1(b) coincide with the output rate in Fig. 10-1(d) where the total profit function reaches its maximum height.

The profit-maximizing rule may be stated in yet another way: *Total profit is maximum at the output rate where marginal profit equals zero.* Marginal profit is the change in total profit resulting from a 1-unit change in output; this is equivalent to saying that

$$M\pi = MR - MC,$$

where $M\pi$ is marginal profit. More technically, marginal profit equals the rate of change in total profit as the rate of output changes, or

$$M\pi = \frac{d\pi}{dQ}.$$

Marginal profit is, therefore, geometrically equal to the slope of the total profit function. At the peak of the total profit function, its slope equals zero—hence the rationale for saying that total profit is maximized where $M\pi = 0$. As long as marginal profit is positive, the total profit function is rising, and it pays to increase output. When the profit earned on the next unit of output has shrunk to zero ($M\pi = 0$), the peak of the total profit function has been reached. If the firm produces beyond the output rate associated with zero marginal profit, marginal profit becomes negative, and the loss incurred on each of these extra units causes the total profit function to turn downward. This is evident from inspection of the total profit function in Fig. 10-1(d).

Calculation of the Profit-Maximizing Output

It is useful to examine the mathematics of determining the perfectly competitive firm's optimum output decision. Suppose the going market price for the commodity is $20 and the firm's total cost function is $TC = 75 + 17Q - 4Q^2 + Q^3$. From the preceding discussion we know that profit is maximized at the output where $MR = MC$. Both the MR and MC functions can be obtained from the information given. At a constant price of $20, MR is also $20 at every output rate. The MC function is the first derivative of the TC function, giving

$$MC = \frac{dTC}{dQ} = 17 - 8Q + 3Q^2.$$

Equating MR with MC, we have

$$20 = 17 - 8Q + 3Q^2.$$

Solving for Q yields the two roots $Q = -\frac{1}{3}$ and $Q = 3$. Since output can never be negative, the profit-maximizing rate of output is 3 units. Actually, it can be proved that the larger of the two roots is always the profit-maximizing (or loss-minimizing) output rate. It is a simple matter, however, to resolve the issue by calculating total profit at each of the values of Q for which $MR = MC$ and observing firsthand which Q yields the greatest total profit.

The profit-maximizing output can also be determined using the rule that total profit is maximum where marginal profit is zero. Again, let $P = MR = \$20$ and $TC = 75 + 17Q - 4Q^2 + Q^3$. Total profit is defined as

$$\pi = TR - TC.$$

Total revenue, being equal at every output to $P \cdot Q$, can in this case be represented by the expression $20Q$. Substituting into the expression for total profit, we have

$$\pi = 20Q - (75 + 17Q - 4Q^2 + Q^3).$$

Since marginal profit is precisely defined as the rate of change in total profit as the rate of output changes, the expression for marginal profit becomes

$$M\pi = \frac{d\pi}{dQ} = 20 - (17 - 8Q + 3Q^2).$$

Given that total profit is maximum where $M\pi = 0$, the expression above is set equal to zero, yielding

$$20 - (17 - 8Q + 3Q^2) = 0,$$
$$20 - 17 + 8Q - 3Q^2 = 0,$$
$$3 + 8Q - 3Q^2 = 0.$$

Solving for Q gives the roots $Q = -\frac{1}{3}$ and $Q = 3$, the same results given by the $MR = MC$ approach.

Total Profit or Loss

Whether the firm realizes a profit or a loss depends on the relationship between price and average total cost at the intersection of *MR* and *MC*. If price exceeds *ATC*, the firm will enjoy short-run profits, whereas if price is less than *ATC*, losses will be incurred.

In Fig. 10-1(b), selling price is P_1 dollars, and *ATC* at the profit-maximizing output of Q_1 units is ATC_{Q_1} dollars. Profit per unit is therefore $P_1 - ATC_{Q_1}$ dollars at an output of Q_1 units. Total profit is profit per unit multiplied by the number of units sold, or

$$\pi = (P_1 - ATC_{Q_1})Q_1,$$

which is numerically equivalent to the size of the shaded area in Fig. 10-1(b). This shaded area has a numerical dollar value equal to the vertical distance between *TR* and *TC* at an output of Q_1 units in Fig. 10-1(c) and equal to the height of the total profit function in Fig. 10-1(d). It should also be clear from Figs. 10-1(b) and (c) that multiplying P_1 by Q_1 gives TR_{Q_1} and that ATC_{Q_1} times Q_1 equals TC_{Q_1}.

Observe that at output Q_1, profit *per unit* is *not* maximized; in other words, total profit is not maximum at the same output at which profit per unit is maximum. Profit per unit is maximized at the output rate where price exceeds *ATC* by the greatest vertical distance, whereas total profit is maximized where $MR = MC$. These two output rates do not coincide, as an examination of Fig. 10-1(b) will confirm.

Minimizing Short-Run Losses

It does not, of course, always work out that perfectly competitive firms can earn positive economic profits in the short run. The equilibrium market price in the short run may fall below the firm's *ATC* curve at every rate of output, thereby making it impossible for the firm to cover all its costs in the short run. What, then, is the firm's optimum output decision? Should it shut down operations and wait for price to return to a more profitable level, or should it produce at a loss? If it continues to operate, at what output will the firm's losses be minimized?

The firm's decision rests on whether or not the market price is high enough to cover the firm's average variable costs (or whether enough total revenue can be obtained to cover total variable costs) at some output rate. Suppose we define *unit contribution profit* as the difference between price and average variable cost:

$$\text{unit contribution profit} = P - AVC.$$

The relevance of unit contribution profit is easily demonstrated. If a product sells for $10 per unit and average variable cost is $6, the firm is able to cover all the expenses associated with the variable inputs needed to produce the product and has $4 left over to help pay total fixed costs and to contribute to the earning of profit. Hence, even though price may not be sufficient to cover *ATC*, as long as the prevailing price is high enough to permit the firm to obtain a margin over and above *AVC*, it pays the firm to produce in the short run. Covering part of *AFC* is better than covering none of *AFC*.

A related concept is that of *total contribution profit*. Total contribution profit is the difference between total revenue and total variable costs:

$$\text{total contribution profit} = TR - TVC.$$

It should be apparent that even if *TR* is not sufficient to cover *TC*, as long as *TR* more than covers *TVC*, the firm earns some amount of total contribution profit, which can be used to pay at least a portion of the firm's total fixed costs. This is a superior outcome to the situation of shutting down. When the firm ceases selling in the short run, *TR* falls to zero, and the firm's loss will be equal to its total fixed costs. Furthermore, it stands to reason that the larger the amount of total contribution profit a firm can obtain, the better will be its short-run profit and loss position. The greater the amount by which *TR* exceeds *TVC*, the more dollars the firm will have to pay fixed costs. And when total fixed costs have all been paid, then any remaining total contribution profit represents economic profit.

We are now ready to use the concepts of contribution profit in determining a firm's optimum output decision when price temporarily falls below average total cost. Consider Fig. 10-2. Suppose supply and demand conditions establish an industry-wide price of P_1 dollars. Given the firm's *MC*, *AVC*, and *ATC* curves, what is the optimum output rate? Clearly, the firm cannot make a profit because the *ATC* curve lies above price P_1 at every output rate; the firm's decision then turns on how to minimize its losses. Observe that between output Q_1 and Q_3 in Fig. 10-2(b) price exceeds *AVC*; similarly, between the same outputs in Fig. 10-2(c), *TR* exceeds *TVC*. Thus, there are a number of output rates at which both unit and total contribution profits are positive. The significance of this finding is that the firm will minimize its losses by producing somewhere between Q_1 and Q_3, since in this output range *TR* will exceed *TVC*, and the resulting total contribution profit can be applied to the payment of total fixed costs. Common sense tells us that the firm will want to obtain as much total contribution profit as possible, so as to have the maximum number of dollars available for covering total fixed costs and thereby keeping losses to a minimum. Note in Fig. 10-2(c) that the output at which *TR* exceeds *TVC* by the greatest vertical distance occurs at output Q_2, where a tangent to the *TVC* curve is parallel to the *TR* curve; this is the output rate associated with maximum total contribution profit. It is also apparent from Fig. 10-2(c) that the vertical distance by which *TC* exceeds *TR* is less at Q_2 than at any other output rate, meaning that here the firm's short-run losses are minimized. Thus, from the standpoint of *TC-TR* analysis, *short-run losses are minimized at the output where TC exceeds TR by the smallest vertical distance*. In Fig. 10-2(d) the total profit function reaches its highest level at an output of Q_2 units; short-run losses are measured by the vertical distance from the peak of the profit function to the horizontal axis. Insofar as the firm's unit costs and revenues are concerned [Fig. 10-2(b)], an output of Q_2 units per period

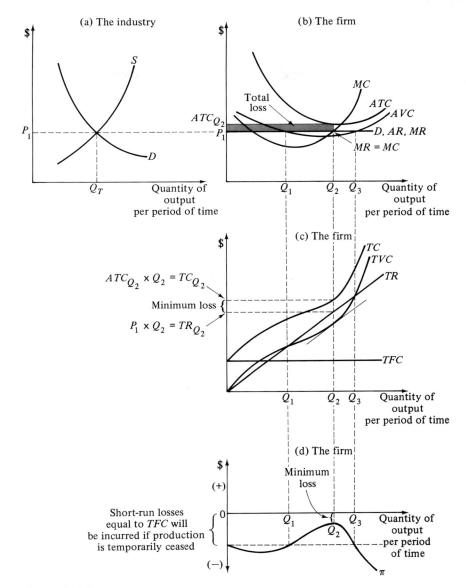

FIGURE 10-2
Short-run loss-minimizing price and output for a perfectly competitive firm

of time corresponds exactly to the output where $MR = MC$ and $M\pi = 0$. Thus, we find that the $MR = MC$ rule and its corollary, $M\pi = 0$, not only identify the short-run profit-maximizing output but also identify the short-run loss-minimizing output.

Now consider Fig. 10-3, where the forces of supply and demand combine to establish a short-run equilibrium price of P_1 dollars such that the firm's demand-

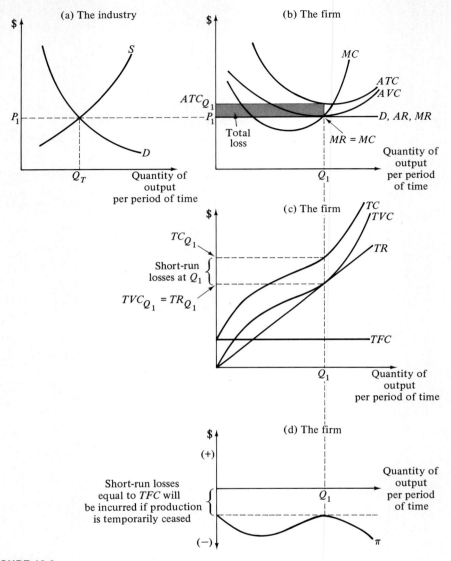

FIGURE 10-3
Short-run loss-minimizing price and output for a perfectly competitive firm when the demand curve is just tangent to the *AVC* curve

AR-MR curve is just tangent to the minimum point of its *AVC* curve. Again, there exists no opportunity for earning a normal profit, much less an economic profit, and the firm's output decision must be aimed at minimizing short-run losses. If the firm elects to produce where $MR = MC$ and where $M\pi = 0$, then it will produce Q_1 units [Fig. 10-3(b)] and will obtain total revenues of TR_1 dollars [Fig. 10-3(c)]. Price will be just equal to AVC [Fig. 10-3(b)], and total variable costs will be equal to total revenue [Fig. 10-3(c)]. Unit contribution profit will be zero, and total contribution profit will be zero. The firm's revenues will just cover variable expenses, and the firm's losses will be equal to total fixed costs. Insofar as minimizing losses is concerned, the firm will be indifferent as to producing and selling Q_1 units or closing down its operations in the short run. In either case, short-run losses will equal total fixed costs, and this is the best the firm can do. At any other output rate revenues will not even be sufficient to cover TVC, con-

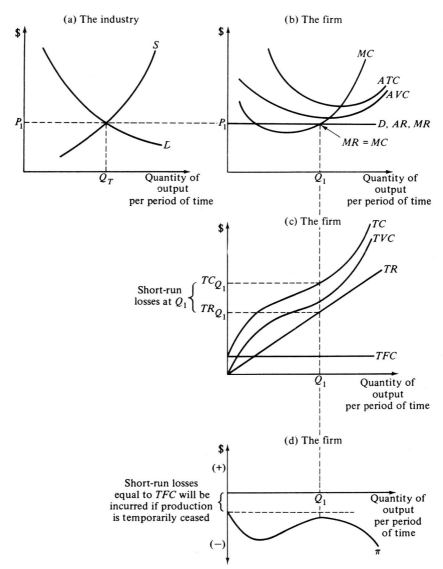

FIGURE 10-4
Short-run close-down position for a perfectly competitive firm

tribution profit will be negative, and losses will exceed *TFC* by the amount of *TVC* not covered by *TR*. However, given that short-run losses will be no more by operating at Q_1 than by closing down, the firm will in all probability elect to produce and sell Q_1 units. By so doing, the firm continues to serve its customers and to offer employment to its workers, with no difference in losses from that of the shutdown case.

However, Fig. 10-4 shows a situation where the short-run equilibrium market price falls below even minimum *AVC*. Should the firm again follow the rule of producing at the point where $MR = MC$ [Fig. 10-4(b)], then total losses will be equal to the vertical distance between *TR* and *TC* in Fig. 10-4(c). Observe that *TR* will not even cover *TVC* at this output—or any other output for that matter. The vertical spread between *TR* and *TC* is always greater at outputs above zero than at zero. Both unit and total contribution profits are negative at every output above zero. Therefore, in this instance the firm will minimize short-run losses by discontinuing production and selling nothing; losses will equal total fixed costs.

The following principles summarize the analysis: The relationship between price and *AVC* tells the firm *whether* to produce; the firm will find it advantageous to continue production if price equals or exceeds *AVC* at one or more output rates and to cease production if price falls below *AVC* at every output rate. The relationship between marginal revenue and marginal cost indicates *how much* the firm should produce when price equals or exceeds *AVC*; profits are maximized or losses are minimized at the output rate where $MR = MC$ and $M\pi = 0$. The relationship between price and *ATC* indicates the *amount of profit or loss per unit* that results from the decision to produce; total profit or loss equals the difference between price and *ATC* multiplied by the quantity produced and sold. Thus, the firm maximizes short-run profits or minimizes short-run losses by producing and selling the output at which $MR = MC$ and $M\pi = 0$. There is only one exception. When the prevailing market price is below the firm's minimum average variable costs at every output rate, losses will be minimized by stopping short-run operations altogether, holding losses to the amount of total fixed costs. As will be indicated shortly, these same principles also hold true for firms operating under conditions other than perfect competition.

THE PERFECTLY COMPETITIVE FIRM'S SHORT-RUN SUPPLY CURVE

We have just seen that a perfectly competitive firm incurring a loss in the short run will continue to produce in the short run provided it loses no more by producing than by shutting down production entirely. This proposition is useful for deriving the short-run supply curve of an individual firm in a perfectly competitive environment. The procedure is illustrated in Fig. 10-5. Suppose that market price is P_0 dollars and the firm's *AVC*, *ATC*, and *MC* curves are as shown in Fig. 10-5(a). Since P_0 is below the minimum *AVC* which the firm can achieve, the firm's short-run equilibrium rate of output is zero. Next, suppose market price is P_1. The corresponding equilibrium rate of output for the firm is Q_1 units, as

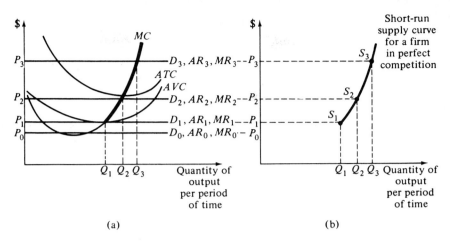

FIGURE 10-5
Derivation of the short-run supply curve for a perfectly competitive firm

this is the output at which $MR = MC$ and at which losses are minimum. Thus, the firm is ready, willing, and able to supply Q_1 units at a price of P_1 dollars; the values (P_1, Q_1) define a point (S_1) on the firm's supply curve in panel (b). Now suppose market price is P_2, generating D_2, AR_2, and MR_2. In this case, the firm's optimum output decision is to produce Q_2 units and thereby minimize its short-run losses. The values (P_2, Q_2) are associated with point S_2 in Fig. 10-5(b). Similarly, a price of P_3 leads to a profit-maximizing output of Q_3 units and point S_3. Other supply points can be derived in like fashion.

Connecting the price-output combinations in Fig. 10-5(b) gives the short-run supply curve of the perfectly competitive firm. The supply curve indicates the quantity of output per period of time which a profit-maximizing firm would supply at various alternative prices under conditions of perfect competition. It should by now be apparent that the firm's supply curve is identical in shape and position to that portion of the firm's MC curve lying above its AVC curve. This is illustrated in Fig. 10-5(a) as the boldly inscribed portion of the firm's MC curve. In other words, *the short-run supply curve for a perfectly competitive firm coincides with its marginal cost curve for all rates of output equal to or greater than the output at which AVC is minimum.* The firm's supply of output drops to zero at any price below AVC. Herein lies the link between production costs and output rates in the short run for a perfectly competitive enterprise.

THE PERFECTLY COMPETITIVE INDUSTRY'S SHORT-RUN SUPPLY CURVE

In Chapter 4 the market demand curve was derived by horizontally adding together the demand curves of individual consumers. However, factors are present which may preclude a similar determination of the short-run industry supply curve for the commodity in question. The perfectly competitive firm's marginal cost curve is derived from the underlying production function (Chapter 8) on the assumption that the price of variable input is constant, no matter how many or how few units the firm purchases. This is a reasonable assumption in the case of perfectly competitive firms, because any one firm uses such a small amount of the total supply of the variable input that changes in its rate of input usage have no perceptible effect on the market price of the variable input. In other words, a single firm can expand or reduce its output rate, and consequently its variable input usage, without affecting the price it pays for variable input.

Yet, should *all* firms in a perfectly competitive industry simultaneously decide to expand or to reduce output, there may be a marked effect upon the supply price of the variable input. For example, suppose one chicken producer decides to raise more chickens and therefore buys more chicken feed. The prevailing price of chicken feed is quite unlikely to be affected. But if all chicken producers decide to raise more chickens, upward pressure on the price of chicken feed becomes a distinct possibility, particularly in the short run when the supplies of chicken feed are limited by the available production capacity.

As a consequence, the short-run supply curve for the product of a perfectly competitive industry cannot necessarily be obtained by horizontally summing the relevant portion of the marginal cost curves of each firm. It all depends on what happens to the price of variable input when *all* firms in the industry alter their usage of variable input. In the event that the supplies of variable input to a perfectly competitive industry are perfectly elastic (the input supply curves are horizontal), then it is valid to conceive of the short-run industry supply curve for the product as being the horizontal summation of the relevant portions of the *MC* curves of the individual firms. If the use of more variable input by all firms in the industry precipitates an increase in the price of variable input, then the marginal cost curve of each individual firm will shift upward by the increase in input

(a) The industry   (b) The firm

FIGURE 10-6
Transition to long-run equilibrium for a firm operating in a perfectly competitive market environment

price, and the short-run industry supply curve will be *more steeply sloped* than had input prices remained constant. If the use of more variable input by all firms in the industry causes the price of variable input to decline (perhaps because it can be supplied more economically in larger quantities), then the marginal cost curve of each individual firm will shift downward by the decrease in input price, and the short-run industry supply curve will be *less steeply sloped* than had input prices remained constant.

But whatever happens to the price of variable input when all firms use more or less of it, we can be confident that the short-run industry supply curve is upward sloping. How steeply sloped it is depends on the factors determining the shape of the marginal cost curve of each firm and on the effect of changes in industrywide output on variable input prices. Suffice it to say at this point that to induce greater supplies of output in the short run from a perfectly competitive industry, higher prices will have to be offered. This characteristic gives rise to a short-run industry supply curve that slopes upward to the right—such then is the basis for the industry supply curves drawn in Figs. 10-1 through 10-4.

LONG-RUN EQUILIBRIUM OF A FIRM IN A PERFECTLY COMPETITIVE MARKET

Although a perfectly competitive firm finds its short-run output decision constrained by the limitations of the fixed inputs, in the long run the options are more numerous. An established firm can alter its plant size, implement new technologies, or modify the character of its products in line with changing consumer tastes. More importantly, the firm can abandon production entirely and leave the industry if below-normal profits are being earned and the prospects are dim for any improvement. On the other hand, new firms may enter the industry if the profits of established firms are sufficiently attractive. Consider now the transition of a firm from short-run to long-run equilibrium in a perfectly competitive market.

Two assumptions will greatly simplify the analysis without invalidating the important conclusions:

1. We shall suppose that all firms in the industry have comparable cost structures. By so doing we can talk in terms of a typical firm with the knowledge that all other firms in the industry will be similarly affected. (This assumption is not implausible, given that all the firms are producing identical products.)

2. We shall assume for the moment that the prices of resource inputs are unaffected (a) by changes in the long-run output rates of existing firms, (b) by the entry of firms into industry, or (c) by the exodus of firms from the industry. In other words, the firms in the industry can, singly or as a group, alter their input requirements without affecting the prices they pay for them.

Let the short-run forces of market demand (D_1) and supply (S_1) result in a market price of P_1 dollars [Fig. 10-6(a)]. Further suppose that the typical firm has a short-run cost structure represented by $SRAC_1$ and $SRMC_1$ at the indicated position on the *LRAC* curve [Fig. 10-6(b)]. With these revenue and cost functions, short-run equilibrium output for the firm is Q_1 units. At this output rate the firm realizes an economic profit because price exceeds *SRAC* at Q_1 units. Recall from Chapter 9 that an economic profit means the firm is receiving a rate of return on its investment greater than it could earn by diverting its resources into the production of other commodities. Under these circumstances the earning of an economic profit will have two significant effects. First, it will encourage the firm (if it has not already done so) to expand its production capability and take advantage of any available economies of scale indicated by the firm's *LRAC* curve. Expanding its long-run output potential (to the position defined by $SRAC_3$ and $SRMC_3$) offers the firm the prospect of even greater economic profits. Second, the existence of above-normal profits in this industry will induce new firms to initiate production of the commodity. The process of new entry may be very slow or very rapid, depending on the amount of economic profits being earned by established firms and on the length of time it takes new entrants to begin their production operations.

As time elapses and these two effects take hold, the industry supply curve will shift to the right, say from S_1 to S_3, thereby driving the market price from P_1 down to P_3 and increasing the equilibrium industry output from Q_{T_1} to Q_{T_3}. The larger volume of industry output is a result of both the entry of new firms and the expansion of firms already in the industry.

However, it is also possible that the profit attraction could be strong enough to induce the typical firm to expand its production capacity beyond $SRAC_3$ and $SRMC_3$ to the output range where it has a cost structure represented by $SRAC_2$ and $SRMC_2$. In such a case, the greater output capabilities of firms would mean a shift of the industry supply to S_2 rather than to just S_3, and the industry price would be at P_2 where D_1 intersects S_2. It is apparent from Fig 10-6(b) that at a price of P_2 dollars the typical firm will sustain losses in the short run, since market price is below $SRAC_2$ at every output rate. Obviously, then, the typical firm and the industry would have both *over-expanded;* no longer would it be possible for firms to earn normal profits. The result will be a readjustment in the industry's production rates. Given that firms can earn higher rates of return in other industries, some firms—most likely the least efficient firms, which are incurring the greatest losses—will elect to cease production of the commodity in question and shift their energies into the production of products where the profit outlook is brighter. The firms that choose to remain in the industry will find it advantageous over the long term to reduce costs by adjusting their production capabilities to the optimum size—where the *SRAC* curve is tangent to the minimum point of the *LRAC* curve. In terms of Fig. 10-6(b), the typical firm would be induced to construct production facilities having a cost structure represented by $SRAC_3$ and $SRMC_3$. The outmigration of firms, coupled with the retrenchment of the production capacity of the remaining firms, would then cause the industry supply curve to shift to the left, eventually to S_3. As the industry supply curve moves leftward, market price will rise to P_3 and total industry output will contract to Q_{T_3}. Again, the optimum output rate for the typical firm becomes Q_3 units, where MR_3 intersects $SRMC_3$.

Observe that at this output price is just equal to short-run average total cost and to long-run average cost. The typical firm earns no economic profit but is able to squeeze out a normal profit. Taken together, these conditions define long-run equilibrium for a perfectly competitive market. Given our initial assumptions of (1) perfect mobility of resources into and out of the industry and (2) a goal of profit maximization, the position of long-run equilibrium is necessarily ordained to occur at the point where price equals the minimum value of long-run average cost and where the typical firm earns no more and no less than a normal profit. This is, indeed, the only conceivable point of long-run equilibrium. The reasoning is straightforward. As long as market price is above the long-run average costs of the typical firm, economic profits can be realized. Established firms will be induced to expand provided it is profitable to do so, and new firms will be attracted into the industry. Over time the market supply curve will be shifted to the right, thereby driving market price down and lowering the horizontal demand-*AR-MR* curve confronting each firm. Economic profits will tend to vanish. On the other hand, whenever price is below the long-run average costs of the typical firm, losses will be incurred. As their plants and equipment depreciate, some firms will leave the industry, being attracted by the higher profit prospects elsewhere; the remaining firms will attempt to lower their costs by constructing more economically sized facilities. The industry supply curve shifts leftward, and market price is raised along with the horizontal demand, *AR,* and *MR* curves for the individual firms. Losses will gradually be eliminated. The number of firms in the industry and the production capacity of each firm will stabilize only when the opportunities for earning an economic profit are exhausted and when economic losses can be avoided. Therefore, since the position of long-run equilibrium must be consistent with *zero* economic profit and *zero* economic loss, it is necessary that the long-run equilibrium price be exactly equal to minimum short-run average cost and to minimum long-run average cost. Unless $P = MR = SRAC = LRAC,$ a change in firm size or in the number of firms will lead to the appearance of either economic profits or economic losses, in which case the forces of adjustment will spring into motion.[4]

It should now be apparent that we are entirely justified in our assumption made earlier that perfectly competitive firms will seek to maximize profits. Actually, perfectly competitive firms have no choice—they are placed in a position of *forced profit maximization*. Under conditions of long-run equilibrium a firm which operates at any output rate other than minimum *LRAC* will not earn a normal profit. With dismal earnings (or even losses), few firms are likely to pursue alternative goals; they simply cannot afford it. For this reason, it seems justifiable

---

[4] In practice, however, the profit thermostat regulating the number of firms and the outputs they produce works much better for expansion than contraction. Economic profits and free entry are reliable stimulants for increasing industry output, given sufficient time for firms to construct new facilities and bring new production capacity on stream. But to squeeze firms out of an over-expanded industry where profits are below normal or negative can be a slow and painful process. It takes time for entrepreneurs to accept the harsh fact that profit prospects are bleak, time for production facilities to wear out, and time to shift into other industries or else go out of business entirely. The long death of the small farmer is a case in point.

to assume that perfectly competitive firms will behave as if they seek to maximize profits.

In practice, of course, it is not really expected that a perfectly competitive industry will reach and thereafter maintain a state of long-run equilibrium. The market demand curve will certainly undergo frequent shifts as consumer tastes and preferences, incomes, and so on change. Likewise, technological progress, changing input prices, and new product availability cause periodic shifts in the firm's *SRAC* and *LRAC* curves and the industry supply curve. As a consequence, long-run equilibrium is a moving target that a perfectly competitive industry continually chases but never catches. The process of market adjustment to long-run equilibrium is dynamic and always unfolding, in response to new market circumstances of demand, supply, and prices.

Furthermore, the continual process of adjusting toward a long-run equilibrium position imposes severe constraints on perfectly competitive firms. The impersonal market forces of supply and demand are so powerful that in the long run firms are unable to make a profit any larger than that just sufficient to induce them to remain in business. The only discretionary action a firm has relates to

APPLICATIONS CAPSULE

AGRICULTURAL MARKETS: AN ILLUSTRATION OF *SOME* OF THE CHARACTERISTICS OF PERFECT COMPETITION

One sector of the American economy where perfectly competitive conditions are reasonably approximated on the supply side of the marketplace is that of agriculture. This is so for three reasons:

1. The supply side of the markets for many agricultural commodities (wheat, corn, soybeans, tobacco, cattle, hogs, cotton) is comprised of literally thousands of firms—each of which tends to be small absolutely and also relative to the market as a whole. True, some farms are much larger than others in terms of acreage, but even the largest farms are seldom as big as a moderately sized manufacturing enterprise. More important, there is virtually no instance in which a single farm produces a large enough fraction of an agricultural product to put it in a position to exert meaningful influence over either price or the total quantity supplied. Indeed, suppliers of most farm commodities are so great in number and so sufficiently equal in size that the chance to act independently and exercise market power is for all practical purposes nil.

2. Agricultural products are essentially identical from farm to farm—at least in terms of each grade and variety. Wheat, for example, is not a branded product at the farm level and carries no identification as to the farm on which it was grown. Meats, dairy products, fruits, and vegetables may carry the brand of a processor or store, but usually not the name of the farmer who raised them (exceptions where the producer's brand name does appear include eggs, bananas, and pineapples). As a result, agricultural products within the same class or grade are *highly* substitutable—so much so that each producer can rightly regard its demand curve as being horizontal at the going market price.

3. Compared to other industries, there are few barriers to the entry of new firms into the production of agricultural products. At the same time, a farmer often finds it easy to shift acreage out of the production of one item (where profit prospects are dim) into the production of another item (where profit opportunities are brighter); in such cases barriers to entry and exit are extremely low since as each new growing season rolls around farmers can readily adjust their production mix in whatever directions market conditions seem to warrant.

A combined effect of these three aspects is to make the markets for agricultural commodities very sensitive to shifts in market conditions. When bad weather produces a smaller than expected crop, market prices rise sharply. If there is an unusually bountiful harvest, the prices that farmers receive can fall drastically. A trade deal with another country can dramatically boost farm export opportunities and thus the prices of the affected products. Prices can and do fluctuate daily on the commodity exchanges, often in response to fleeting demand-supply conditions. Thus, "the market" in its role as the governing force is liable to be volatile, causing sometimes sharp swings in farm prices and farm profits. The competitive struggle becomes a contest where each seller, under conditions of considerable uncertainty, must decide whether and how it can profitably survive at the expected market prices.

The Case of Soybeans

In 1973–1974, when higher energy costs and economic recession cut into household food budgets, livestock producers began trimming back output as meat sales slacked off and, consequently, reduced their purchases of livestock feeds. Soybean meal prices tumbled from $400 a ton in 1973 to as low as $100 a ton in June 1974 and then recovered slightly to around $125 a ton throughout most of 1975. Soybean oil prices sank to around 20 cents a pound in 1975 from a peak of more than 50 cents in 1974, mainly because cautious processors started switching to competing products such as palm oil.

At planting time in spring of 1975, farmers were confronted with a hard choice of which crop to plant. Prospects for higher prices for corn, cotton, and soybeans were discouraging and the federal government offered no subsidy programs to farmers to take land out of production. Many farmers chose to plant soybeans, saying at the time that soybean prices seemed less vulnerable to a sharp decline. The soybean crop flourished because of good weather, and 1975's crop was 20% greater than 1974's. Brazil's crop, stimulated by planting newly available acreage, exceeded 350 million bushels compared to only 24 million bushels in 1968. Meanwhile the record-high soybean-product prices of previous years spurred production not only of soybeans but also of other oils and meals—from sources like cottonseed, linseed, corn, peanuts, palms, olives, and sunflowers. Particularly was soybean oil under competitive pressure from palm oil; palm oil imports were up 145% during the first 8 months of 1975.

In addition, soybean growers had another problem to contend with: because of differing production features, a farmer could grow more bushels of corn than soybeans on an acre of land. Consequently, the price of soybeans had to be higher than corn to get the same financial return per acre (many observers contended that soybeans had to be worth 2.5 to 3 times per bushel more than corn to be equally profitable). Thus, the dilemma was whether the market price of soybeans would be low enough to compete with foreign imports and substitute products and yet high enough to justify growing soybeans as opposed to alternative crops.

As the 1976 growing season approached, analysts predicted:

1. Between 2 and 3 million acres planted to soybeans in 1975 would be planted in other crops in 1976—a move that would stabilize soybean-product prices near 1975 levels, given the large inventory of soybeans in storage.

2. Soybean meal demand would improve because cattle and broiler producers were gearing up to increase outputs and consequently would need more meal for protein supplements.

3. Soybean growers would elect to be more "orderly" in marketing their soybean crops because the high prices of past years put them in a stronger financial position to hold on to their beans and finance their inventories in the hope that higher prices would return.

QUESTIONS FOR DISCUSSION

1. What economic factors are apparent in influencing short-run changes in the equilibrium price of an agricultural commodity (say soybeans)? What about the long-run equilibrium price?
2. Using the soybean market as an example, explain how "the price mechanism" acts to bring market supply and demand into balance. In what ways is competition a factor in this adjustment process?

Source: Adapted in part from *The Dow Jones Commodities Handbook 1976,* pp. 39–46.

its output decision. And in the long run even here the firm's option is taken away; it is forced to produce where $P = MR = SRAC = SRMC = LRAC$ if it wants to earn at least a normal profit. Thus, *the firm is truly a captive servant of the market.* All of this, according to conventional wisdom, works to the advantage of consumers and society as a whole. Under long-run equilibrium conditions the consumer pays a price no higher than is required to cover all costs of production, thereby obtaining products at as low a price as is economically feasible. Moreover, all firms produce at the minimum points of their cost curves, thus utilizing in the most efficient manner the pool of resources that society makes available to the industry.

A Constant-Cost Industry

In the preceding section it was assumed that the expansion or contraction of industry output had no effect on *input* prices. An industry having this characteristic is referred to as a *constant-cost* industry. The existence of such an industry has several implications which merit further exploration.

Figure 10-7 depicts long-run equilibrium under conditions of constant costs. Let D_1 and S_1 be the original short-run market demand and supply curves, with an equilibrium price at P_1 dollars. Assume that each firm in the industry is in long-run equilibrium at Q_1, where the firm's horizontal demand-AR-MR curve is

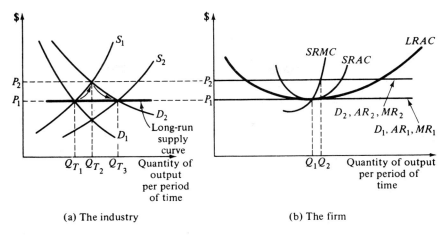

(a) The industry

(b) The firm

FIGURE 10-7
Long-run supply curve for a constant-cost industry

just tangent to the minimum points of the firm's *SRAC* and *LRAC* curves, as shown in Fig. 10-7(b). Now consider the impact of a shift in the short-run market demand curve to D_2. The market price will rise to P_2 dollars, and the profit-maximizing output for the firm becomes Q_2 units per period of time. However, at a price of P_2 dollars and an output of Q_2 units each firm will earn an economic profit, thereby triggering the entry of new firms into the industry and shifting the industry supply curve rightward, eventually to S_2. In the case of a constant-cost industry the entry of new firms and the expansion of industry output will not affect the costs of the existing firms. The reason is that the resource inputs employed by this industry are available in such sufficiently large quantities that the appearance of new firms does not bid up the prices of the inputs and raise the costs of the existing firms. As a consequence, the *LRAC* curve of established firms remains fixed, and the new firms can operate with an identical *LRAC* curve.

Long-run equilibrium adjustment to the shift in demand is accomplished when the entry of new firms has caused the market price to fall back to P_1, where $P_1 = MR_1 = SRAC = SRMC = LRAC$, and each firm is producing Q_1 units and earning only a normal profit. The important point here is that the industry has a *constant long-run supply price,* which means industry output can be expanded or contracted in accordance with market demand conditions without altering the *long-run* equilibrium price charged by the firms. To put it another way, *a constant-cost industry operating under conditions of perfect competition has a horizontal long-run supply curve.* Such a curve is illustrated in Fig. 10-7(a).

An Increasing-Cost Industry

Obviously, a situation can easily arise where changes in the output rate of an industry can cause the prices of resource inputs to change. In this section we

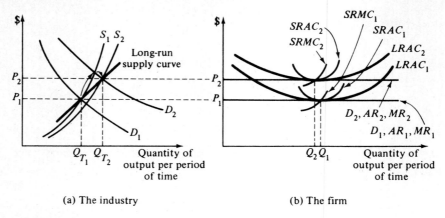

(a) The industry   (b) The firm

FIGURE 10-8
Long-run supply curve for an increasing-cost industry

examine the case where the expansion of industry output has the effect of *raising* input prices, thereby giving rise to an *increasing-cost industry*.

As illustrated in Fig. 10-8, suppose that the industry is in long-run equilibrium. D_1 and S_1 portray the initial market demand and supply conditions, market price is P_1 dollars, and each firm is operating at the output rate where price equals minimum *SRAC* and minimum *LRAC*. Now suppose that market demand increases to D_2, temporarily causing an increase in market price to the level where D_2 intersects S_1. The higher price allows established firms to earn an economic profit, which in turn attracts the entry of new firms. As output expands more resources are needed; at this point resource input prices are bid up by firms competing for the available resource supplies. The effect of rising input prices is to increase the operating costs of both established firms and new entrants. As industry output expands and input prices rise, the marginal and average cost curves for the typical firm all gradually shift upward from $SRMC_1$, $SRAC_1$, and $LRAC_1$, say to a position represented by $SRMC_2$, $SRAC_2$, and $LRAC_2$. Moreover, the short-run industry supply curve is shifted to the right by the expansion of industry output. The process of adjustment continues until all economic profits have been eliminated. In Fig. 10-8, this is depicted by the intersection of D_2 and S_2 and its associated price of P_2 dollars. Each firm selects the rate of output where $P_2 = MR_2 = SRMC_2 = SRAC_2 = LRAC_2$. The long-run industry supply curve is found by joining the points of long-run equilibrium; in Fig. 10-8 these points are represented by the intersection of D_1 and S_1 and the intersection of D_2 and S_2.

The salient feature of an increasing-cost industry is the presence of a positively sloped long-run supply curve. Whereas in a constant-cost industry the expansion of industry output has no effect on the long-run price of the industry's product, in an increasing-cost industry the effect of greater industry output is a higher product price. The long-run supply curve of an increasing-cost industry slopes upward, because greater rates of output entail rising input prices and hence rising costs. Under these circumstances, higher market prices will be required to give firms the incentive to expand output.

A Decreasing-Cost Industry

Price and output behavior in a *decreasing-cost industry* is depicted in Fig. 10-9. The initial long-run equilibrium is given by the market demand curve D_1, the short-run industry supply curve S_1, a market price of P_1 dollars, and each firm producing at the minimum points of $SRAC_1$ and $LRAC_1$. As before, suppose that market demand increases to D_2. Market price rises to the point where D_2 intersects S_1, and established firms find themselves in the position of being able to earn an economic profit. New firms are induced to enter the industry, and the short-run industry supply curve shifts rightward, say to S_2. In a decreasing-cost industry the expansion of output results in *lower* input prices and hence lower costs for the firms in the industry. Thus, as the entry of new firms causes input prices to fall, the short-run and long-run cost curves of the firm shift downward. The adjustment process will continue until a new long-run equilibrium is established. In Fig. 10-9 this occurs at the intersection of D_2 and S_2, where the resulting price of P_2 dollars is just equal to the minimum points of $SRAC_2$ and $LRAC_2$. Connecting the two points of long-run equilibrium gives the long-run industry supply curve.

Clearly, a decreasing-cost industry has a negatively sloped long-run supply curve, meaning that the equilibrium price of the industry tends to fall as industry output increases. Although it is rare for input prices to fall when industry output expands, it does occur. One example is the case of a young industry which springs up in a relatively underdeveloped area, where resource markets are poorly organized, marketing facilities are primitive, and transportation is inadequate. An increase in the number of firms and in the output of the industry may stimulate the development of marketing and transportation facilities that reduce the costs

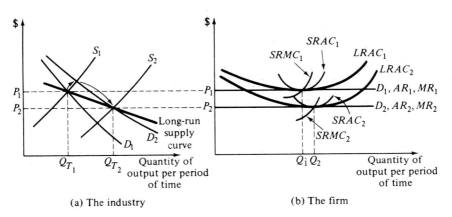

(a) The industry   (b) The firm

FIGURE 10-9
Long-run supply curve for a decreasing-cost industry

of individual firms; in addition, supplies of labor and other support services may become more dependable and more efficient. Another example arises in the case of capital goods purchases. The more firms there are in an industry and the larger its output, the more economically suppliers of capital goods may be able to provide these firms with specialized machinery, continuous-process equipment, and higher-quality tools because of their own economies of scale in producing them. By and large, the individual firm has little control over these sorts of decreasing costs; consequently, cost reductions of this type are often referred to as external economies of increasing production, or, more simply, just *external economies*. They result solely from growth of the industry and from forces outside the control of the individual firm. External economies should not be confused with internal economies of scale, which are under control of the firm and which can be secured by enlarging the scale of the firm's operations.

In the absence of technological change, most economists regard increasing-cost industries as being the most prevalent of the three types. Decreasing-cost industries are perhaps the most unusual situation. Both decreasing- and constant-cost industries are likely to evolve gradually into industries of increasing cost as they grow larger and become more mature. However, if technological change is admitted to the picture, a downsloping long-run industry supply curve becomes more probable. Technical progress in an industry can cause costs of production to fall over time, thus giving rise to a downsloping long-run industry supply curve.[5] Indeed, the industries which are most successful in lowering costs and relative prices tend to show the most dramatic increases in output over time. Technological progress can also neutralize rising input prices, thereby transforming an otherwise increasing-cost industry into a constant- or decreasing-cost industry.

IMPLICATIONS AND SIGNIFICANCE OF THE PERFECTLY COMPETITIVE MODEL

The behavior of firms and markets under conditions of perfect competition has the following features and results:

1. The chief feature of perfect competition is the existence of powerful market forces which tend to drive price to a level where each firm earns no more and no less than a normal profit and return on investment. Whenever demand and supply conditions allow firms in the industry to earn more than a normal profit, new firms are induced to enter, and where economies of scale permit, existing firms are induced to expand. Subsequently, price is driven down to the point of minimum *SRAC* and minimum *LRAC*, thereby foreclosing the opportunity to earn more than a normal return. Should demand and supply conditions result in a price that inflicts losses upon the firms in the industry, then some firms are induced to shift into the production of other commodities where the profit prospects are more

[5] The manufacture of transistors and solid-state components is an excellent example of an industry which has experienced declining costs as a result of new technologies.

favorable; the remaining firms seek to adjust their scale of operations in the direction of minimum long-run average cost. As a consequence, market forces move firms toward a "no-profit/no-loss" situation where firms earn only an accounting profit sufficient to induce them to continue in business in the industry.

2. Since every firm is subject to the discipline of the market, it must remain as efficient as the average firm in the industry, or eventually the losses that accompany inefficiency and high unit costs will force it out of business. The process of adjusting to long-run equilibrium *compels* all firms to try to produce at the lowest possible long-run average cost. A strategy of *striving to be the low-cost producer* thus becomes one of the safest routes to competitive survival.

3. Perfectly competitive firms are *price-takers and quantity-adjusters*. They have absolutely zero market power. A single firm exercises no control whatsoever over the going market price, and its only discretionary judgment is how much to produce at the prevailing market price. But even here, as long-run equilibrium adjustment occurs, the discretion over output erodes; firms which wish to earn at least normal profit find their best chance of doing so at the minimum point of the *LRAC* curve where $P = MR = SRMC = SRAC = LRAC$.

4. Both the output of specific firms and the capacity of the industry are responsive to changes in demand. If market demand increases in relation to the supply capability of the industry, market price is bid up, entry and expansion are induced, and over time additional output capacity is created. Conversely, if market demand falls or if the industry overexpands, then market price falls, expansion is discouraged, and firms may even leave the industry.

5. Perfect competition is a unique form of competition. It does not pit rival against rival; rather, it pits the firm against the market. The firm's competitive struggle is one of responding to changing market conditions and trying to stay in a cost-efficiency position to earn at least a normal profit at the going market price. Only the most cost-efficient firms survive the struggle—in the long run, and the only competitive edge a firm can hope to gain (and this is likely to be very temporary) is that of having lower costs than some or many other firms in the market.

6. With identical products, the competitive focus is on price but most particularly on the ability of firms to compete at lower market prices. In perfect competition, prices are very flexible downward. Prices fall whenever the quantity offered for sale exceeds the quantity purchased and also whenever efficiency gains, technological improvements, or lower input prices (all of which mean lower unit costs) allow firms to earn attractive profits selling at lower market prices. Those firms which rank as the industry's low-cost producers are in the strongest competitive position in the market.

7. Perfect competition provides consumers maximum protection from "exploitation" by business firms. The outcome in the marketplace results from freely made decisions of consumers to buy and freely made decisions of producers to sell. Neither is able to control the other or rig the market to his own advantage. Therefore, there can be no question of an abuse of power and, thus, no need for government intervention or regulation. In short, perfect competition is the epitome of what is meant by a *free market*.

8. The perfectly competitive model takes an overly narrow view of the competitive process because, in a sense, the entire spotlight is on low-cost production, price, and price competition. The model takes no formal cognizance of competition based on product differentiation (because the products of all firms are assumed to be identical) or of technological competition (because all firms are forced to adopt the most efficient production techniques) or of promotional competition (what is there to promote?). In fact, it is fair to say that the model of perfect competition looks upon the only "valid" and "lasting" form of competition as being competition based upon price. Such a view of competition and competitive strategy options, as we shall see in Chapters 11–16, applies only to markets where there are many sellers of a commodity product.

In conclusion, the major economic significance of the model of perfect competition concerns the benefits to consumers of perfect competition and the efficiency with which it allocates resources. Under conditions of long-run equilibrium, consumers are able to buy the product at the lowest price consistent with covering all costs of production. Since price is barely sufficient to give the firm a normal profit and keep it in business in the long run, the consumer obtains the product at as low a price as is economically feasible. In addition, every firm is forced to produce at the most efficient output rate. All scale economies are realized, and all diseconomies of size are avoided. Thus, perfectly competitive firms utilize resources in the most efficient manner possible—full production efficiency is attained. Society obtains the greatest output from the resources used in producing the commodity and at the lowest feasible price. Herein lies the social justification for a free market (or capitalistic) economy. The perfectly competitive model describes how a market economy is supposed to work in theory and provides the theoretical underpinning for laissez-faire capitalism. The model is, at least, an excellent starting point for pinpointing the benefits which society gains from a competitive marketplace.

SUGGESTED READINGS

CLARK, J. M., *Competition as a Dynamic Process* (Washington, D.C.: The Brookings Institution, 1961), Chapters 2 and 3.

KIRZNER, I. M., *Competition and Entrepreneurship* (Chicago: University of Chicago Press, 1973), Chapters 1 and 2.

MCNULTY, P. J., "A Note on the History of Perfect Competition," *Journal of Political Economy,* Vol. 75, No. 3 (August 1967), pp. 395–399.

——, "The Meaning of Competition," *Quarterly Journal of Economics,* Vol. 82, No. 4 (November 1968), pp. 639–656.

SCHERER, F. M., *Industrial Market Structure and Economic Performance, 2nd ed.* (Boston: Houghton Mifflin Company, 1980), Chapter 2.

STIGLER, G. J., "Perfect Competition, Historically Contemplated," *Journal of Political Economy,* Vol. 65, No. 1 (February 1957), pp. 1–17.

PROBLEMS AND QUESTIONS FOR DISCUSSION

1. (a) A firm's total revenue can be determined by adding the values of *MR* for each unit sold. True or false? Explain.
    (b) A firm's total cost can be determined by adding the values of *MC* for each unit produced. True or false? Explain.
    (c) A firm's total profit can be determined by adding the values of *Mπ* for each unit produced and sold. True or false? Explain.

2. Total profit is maximum at the same output at which total contribution profit is maximum. True or false? Explain.

3. Unit contribution profit $(P - AVC)$ is greatest at the same output that total contribution profit $(TR - TVC)$ is greatest. True or false? Explain.

4. Why is competition said to be "perfect" in a perfectly competitive market? Just what is so perfect about perfect competition?

5. How do perfectly competitive firms compete? In what form is "competition" present in a perfectly competitive market?

6. Graphically illustrate the short-run supply curve for a perfectly competitive firm which has a short-run production function characterized by decreasing returns to variable input over the entire range of its output capability.

7. Suppose in a perfectly competitive industry that market supply and demand forces combine to produce a short-run equilibrium price of $70. Suppose further that a firm in this industry has a weekly total cost function expressed by the equation $TC = 200 + 25Q - 6Q^2 + \frac{1}{3}Q^3$. Determine the perfectly competitive firm's profit-maximizing output rate and the amount of its short-run profits or losses.

8. Using the unit cost and unit revenue curves, graphically illustrate the short-run profit-maximizing price and output for a perfectly competitive firm which has a production function that exhibits decreasing returns to variable input over its entire range of output capability. (*Hint:* Determine the shape of the *ATC* and *MC* curves that correspond to a production function characterized by decreasing returns to variable input and then locate the price and output at which $MR = MC$.) Indicate on your graph the area that represents the firm's total profits.

11

HOW MARKETS FUNCTION
The model of monopolistic competition

In most real-world markets the products of rival firms are not standardized commodities. Rather the product offering of each firm is in some way *differentiated* from the product offerings of rivals. In fact, most enterprises devote considerable time and effort to engineering distinctive attributes into their products and to making their products unique through advertising, packaging, brand names, styling, performance features, terms of credit, service, and so on. The particular concern of this chapter is with the economics of the firm in a market environment comprised of *many* firms selling products that are very close (but not perfect) substitutes for each other. Such a market structure is labeled by economists as *monopolistic competition.*

THE DISTINCTIVE FEATURES OF MONOPOLISTICALLY COMPETITIVE MARKETS

Three factors combine to set monopolistic competition apart: (1) product differentiation, (2) the presence of large numbers of sellers, and (3) nonprice competition.

Introducing the element of product differentiation into the marketplace causes some consumers to prefer the products of particular firms over those of other firms. Each firm in devising its own unique version of the product obtains a kind of limited monopoly. There is only one producer of Budweiser beer, only one manufacturer of Hart, Schaffner, and Marx suits, and only one publisher of *Playboy*; even so, each of these firms faces competition from rival firms offering substitute brands—hence, the label "monopolistic competition." Ultimately, product differentiation has the effect of giving a monopolistically competitive firm limited influence over the price it charges for its product—the firm in a very restricted sense is a "price-maker." It derives this power from the fact that some consumers are willing, within limits, to pay a higher price to satisfy their preferences for the products of specific firms. The price differential which a firm is able to charge is a function of the firm's success in differentiating its product in the minds of consumers, thereby creating "brand loyalties" and "company loyalties." However, the price differential obtainable by any one firm is likely to be slight since close similarity among the products of rival firms makes it quite difficult to create strong brand attachment when price differences are sizable. In more formal terms, we can say that the cross elasticity of demand between products of monopolistically competitive firms is quite high; so also is the price elasticity of demand for any one firm's product.

Like perfect competition, monopolistic competition is characterized by such a sufficiently large number of firms that no one firm has the production capacity to supply a significant share of the industry's output. Monopolistically competitive firms are typically small-sized firms, both absolutely and relatively. Entry into monopolistically competitive industries is usually easy, though it is a bit more difficult than in perfect competition, because of product differentiation. A new firm must not only possess the capacity for producing the product but it must also be able to win customers away from established firms. Securing a niche in the market is likely to entail research and development costs by the new firm to discover attributes which will distinguish its product from products already on the market. Moreover, unlike perfection competition, advertising and sales promotion may be necessary to inform consumers of the availability of a new brand and to persuade enough customers to switch to the new brand. Therefore, a newcomer into a monopolistically competitive industry faces somewhat greater financial and marketing obstacles than a newcomer into a perfectly competitive market.

The final feature of monopolistic competition is the presence of vigorous *nonprice competition* among the firms. Competitive rivalry is based partially upon price and partially upon product quality, service and other conditions of sale, and sales promotion. A firm operating under conditions of monopolistic competition can simultaneously undertake three strategies for influencing its sales volume. First, the firm can change the price it charges—the strategy of *price competition*. Second, the firm can incorporate distinctive attributes into its product offering— a *differentiation strategy based on product performance, quality, service, and similar such attributes which can set a firm's product offering apart from rivals'*. Third, the firm can revise its marketing and sales promotion tactics in ways aimed at capturing greater buyer attention and buyer appeal—a *differentiation strategy based upon promotional forms of competition*. The first strategy of using price as a major competitive weapon represents an attempt to move along the demand curve confronting the firm, whereas the last two strategies involve an attempt to shift the firm's demand curve. From a theoretical standpoint all three competitive strategies can be pursued in a monopolistically competitive market without explicit regard for the behavior of rival firms and without much concern for retaliation by rival firms. The reason? *With a large number of firms in the industry, the impact of the competitive strategy of a single firm spreads itself over so many of its rivals that the effect felt by any one rival is greatly diluted and does not usually lead to the formulation of a counterstrategy or a readjustment.* Accordingly, each firm may expect its competitive approach to be unimpeded by direct counter-measures on the part of any one rival.[1]

We shall examine each of the foregoing three strategies in the sections immediately following.

PRICE AND OUTPUT DECISIONS OF FIRMS IN MONOPOLISTIC COMPETITION

Under conditions of monopolistic competition, each firm is confronted with a downsloping demand and average revenue curve. Herein lies the fundamental difference between the model of perfect competition and the model of monopolistic competition, and it stems from the presence of differentiated products. Because the particular product of each firm has certain distinguishing features which set it apart from those of other firms, a monopolistically competitive firm has a small measure of discretion in establishing the price of its product. By shaving its price to levels somewhat below the prices of rival firms, a firm can usually induce proportionately more customers to buy its product because it is a good substitute for the products of its competitors. On the other hand, a firm which raises its price can expect a significant decline in sales as many of its customers switch to lower-priced brands. Accordingly, the firm must have a downsloping demand curve, for it can sell more of its product at lower prices than at higher prices. The firm cannot raise price without losing sales, and it cannot gain sales without charging a lower price (assuming, of course, its demand curve does not shift). Moreover, *the presence of large numbers of good substitutes makes any one firm's own demand curve highly elastic over the relevant range of possible prices.*[2] Graphically, this means that a firm's demand curve tends to be *gently*

---

[1] Some economists challenge the view that a firm can rationally assume its actions will go undetected by rival firms. From a behavioral standpoint a firm can be expected to learn, sooner or later, that its strategies will in fact invoke retaliation from competitors—especially if its strategies prove successful. One must search long and hard to find a businessman who does not believe his actions will be noticed by his competitors and who, in turn, does not keep close tabs on what rival firms are doing—irrespective of how many rivals he may have. Thus, the ability to act independently is relative, not absolute. But despite this legitimate objection, it still seems fair to conclude that the larger the number of firms in an industry, the more able a firm will be to implement new strategies without provoking direct retaliation from rival firms. The fact that a firm with many rivals can act more independently than a firm with few rivals does indeed lead to differences in firm and market behavior.

[2] The results of one study showed a coefficient of price elasticity of -5.7 for different brands of frozen orange juice, -5.5 for instant coffee, -4.4 for regular coffee, and -3.0 for margarine. Indirect evidence of high elasticity also stems from the fact that rival firms in monopolistic competition

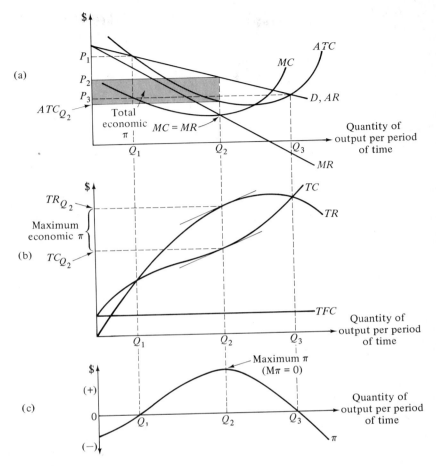

FIGURE 11-1
Short-run profit maximization for a firm in monopolistic competition

down-sloping, as depicted in Fig. 11-1(a); the demand curve is drawn as a straight line merely for simplicity and convenience. Generally speaking, the exact degree of price elasticity reflected in a monopolistically competitive firm's demand curve is a function of the number of rival firms and the degree of product differentiation which prevails among the brands of the competitors. The larger the number of competitors and the weaker the product differentiation, the greater the price elasticity of demand for any one firm's product or brand over the relevant price range.

act as though they believe that their demand curves are highly price elastic. They usually sell their products at very nearly the same price and display a distinct hesitancy to test consumer loyalty by pricing their products much above the prices charged by rival firms. For some empirical evidence as to the degree of consumer loyalty see two articles by Lester G. Telser: "The Demand for Branded Goods as Estimated from Consumer Panel Data," *Review of Economics and Statistics*, Vol. 44, No. 3 (August 1962), pp. 300–324; and "Advertising and Cigarettes," *Journal of Political Economy*, Vol. 70, No. 5 (October 1962), pp. 471–499.

When a firm's demand curve is down-sloping, its marginal revenue function does not coincide with the demand-average revenue function; rather, it lies below the demand-*AR* curve.[3] If a firm's demand-*AR* curve is linear and down-sloping, its *MR* curve is also linear and down-sloping and has a slope twice that of the demand-*AR* curve. Recall from Chapter 5 that if the demand function is given by the general linear equation

$$P = a - bQ,$$

then the equation for *TR* becomes

$$TR = P \cdot Q = (a - bQ)Q = aQ - bQ^2.$$

Since the expression for marginal revenue is found by taking the first derivative of the *TR* equation, the general equation for *MR* is

$$MR = \frac{dTR}{dQ} = a - 2bQ.$$

Both the demand-*AR* curve and the *MR* curve originate at the same value *a*, but the slope of the *MR* function is twice as great as that of the demand-*AR* curve ($-2b$ as compared to $-b$). In geometric terms, the *MR* curve is located by drawing it so as to bisect the horizontal distance between the demand-*AR* curve and the vertical axis [Fig. 11-1(a)]. The total revenue function corresponding to the demand-*AR* and the *MR* functions is depicted in Fig. 11-1(b).

Suppose that the cost structure of a typical firm in a monopolistically competitive industry is given by the *ATC* and *MC* curves in Fig. 11-1(a) and by the corresponding *TC* curve in Fig. 11-1(b). What, then, are the firm's optimal price and output levels? Since monopolistically competitive industries are composed of numerous firms that, in the main, are both small and owner-managed, it is appropriate again to assume that the firm's decisions are motivated by the desire to maximize profits. However, we cannot be completely confident about assuming firms will behave as if they seek to maximize profits, because the element of product differentiation gives each firm somewhat more discretionary decison-making power than was the case in perfectly competitive environments. As we shall see shortly, there are more variables to be considered, a greater degree of uncertainty is present, and market forces operate in ways which allow firms a modest leeway in deviating from profit-maximizing behavior. Nevertheless, a goal of profit maximization is a reasonable first approximation because of the strong competitive forces which typically inhabit a monopolistically competitive marketplace. Suppose we also assume for the moment that the firm produces a fixed product and engages in a given amount of sales promotion activity; this will allow us to pinpoint the principles underlying the price and output behavior of a mo-

---

[3] The reader is urged to refresh his or her memory on this point by reviewing the section ''Average, Total, and Marginal Revenue'' in Chapter 5.

nopolistically competitive firm. Following this, we shall relax this assumption and examine the effect of product variation and promotional expenditures upon price-output behavior.

Profit Maximization: The Total Cost-Total Revenue Approach. A firm in monopolistic competition, like the perfectly competitive firm, will maximize short-run profits at the output where total revenue exceeds total cost by the greatest amount. Given the *TR* and *TC* functions in Fig. 11-1(b), the firm will be able to earn an economic profit at any output rate between Q_1 and Q_3 units, but short-run profits will be maximum at an output of Q_2 units, where the vertical distance between *TR* and *TC* is the greatest. Geometrically, *TR* exceeds *TC* by the greatest amount at the output rate where a tangent to the *TC* curve has the same slope and is parallel to a tangent to the *TR* function. The total profit function in Fig. 11-1(c) is again derived by subtracting *TC* from *TR* at each output rate. Logic dictates that the peak of the total profit function correspond to an output rate of Q_2, where *TR* exceeds *TC* by the largest amount.

Profit Maximization: The Unit Cost-Unit Revenue Approach. On a unit cost and unit revenue basis, short-run profits are maximized at the output where $MC = MR$ and $M\pi = 0$. The reasoning is precisely the same as in the case of perfectly competitive firms. As long as an additional unit of output adds more to the firm's revenues than it does to the firm's costs, profit on that unit will be positive and total profits will be increased (or losses decreased) by producing and selling the unit. Alternatively, when *MC* exceeds *MR* and $M\pi$ is negative, total profits can be increased (or losses decreased) by decreasing the rate of output. In Fig. 11-1(a) short-run profits are maximum at an output of Q_2 units per period of time. This is the output rate at which the marginal cost curve intersects the marginal revenue curve. Moreover, it corresponds exactly to the value of Q_2 in Fig. 11-1(b). At Q_2, the tangents to *TR* and *TC* have identical slopes. Since the slope of *TC* equals *MC* and the slope of *TR* equals *MR*, *MR* must equal *MC* at exactly the output where *TR* exceeds *TC* by the greatest amount.

The highest price which the firm can charge and still sell Q_2 units is P_2 dollars. The profit-maximizing price thus corresponds to the point on the demand-*AR* curve associated with the output at which $MC = MR$. Average total cost at Q_2 units of output is ATC_{Q_2}. Total economic profit in the short run equals ($P - ATC_{Q_2})Q_2$, or the shaded area in Fig. 11-1(a). At outputs smaller than Q_2 units, *MR* exceeds *MC*, and larger outputs up to Q_2 will add more to total revenue than to total costs; accordingly, total profit will rise as the output rate is raised. At an output rate beyond Q_2, *MC* exceeds *MR*, and additional sales cause total costs to rise faster than total revenue, thereby decreasing total profit. Note that the firm can realize at least a normal profit by selling at a price as high as P_1 or as low as P_3 but that a price of P_2 dollars will yield the greatest economic profit. Prices P_1 and P_3 may be thought of as the "break-even" prices and outputs Q_1 and Q_3 may be thought of as the "break-even" output rates.

Calculating the Profit-Maximizing Output. The mathematical procedure for determining the profit-maximizing price and output for a firm with a downsloping demand function is analogous to the calculations for a firm in perfect competition.

Suppose the firm's demand function is given by the equation $P = 11,100 - 30Q$ and the firm's total cost function is given by the equation $TC = 400,000 + 300Q - 30Q^2 + Q^3$. From the preceding discussion we know that profit is maximized at the output where $MR = MC$. Both MR and MC can be obtained from the information given. If the demand function is $P = 11,100 - 30Q$, then

$$TR = P \cdot Q = (11,100 - 30Q)Q = 11,100Q - 30Q^2,$$

and

$$MR = \frac{dTR}{dQ} = 11,100 - 60Q.$$

The MC function, being the first derivative of the TC function, is

$$MC = \frac{dTC}{dQ} = 300 - 60Q + 3Q^2.$$

Equating MR with MC gives

$$11,100 - 60Q = 300 - 60Q + 3Q^2,$$

which reduces to

$$3Q^2 = 10,800.$$

Solving for Q yields the two roots $Q = -60$ and $Q = 60$. Obviously, output can never be negative; hence, the profit-maximizing rate of output is 60 units. As indicated earlier, it can be proved that the larger of the two roots is always the profit-maximizing (or loss-minimizing) output rate. It is a simple matter, however, to calculate total profit at each positive value of Q for which $MR = MC$ and see which root is associated with the greatest profit.

The profit-maximizing price is found by substituting the profit-maximizing output rate into the demand function and solving for P. In terms of our example, the profit-maximizing price is

$$
\begin{aligned}
P &= 11,100 - 30Q \\
&= 11,100 - 30(60) \\
&= 11,100 - 1800 \\
&= \$9300.
\end{aligned}
$$

Total profit at this price and output can be calculated by subtracting TC at 60 units of output from TR at 60 units of output. The reader should verify that total profit at 60 units of output will be $32,000 per period of time.

Total Profit or Loss. If demand is weak, then the monopolistically competitive firm may be unable to make an economic profit or even a normal profit. In such cases the firm must decide whether to shut down its operations in the short run and await for demand conditions to become more favorable or whether to continue operating at a loss. The firm's short-run price and output decision hinges upon whether or not demand is strong enough to allow the firm to cover variable costs at some output rate.

Consider Figure 11-2(a). Between outputs of Q_1 and Q_3 units per period, the firm's demand-AR curve lies above its AVC curve; hence, unit contribution profit $(P - AVC)$ is positive at all outputs greater than Q_1 and less than Q_3. As a consequence, between these outputs the total revenues obtained by the firm are more than sufficient to cover total variable costs, and some total contribution profit can be earned to pay at least a portion of the firm's total fixed costs [see Fig. 11-2(b)]. The firm should definitely continue to produce in the short run,

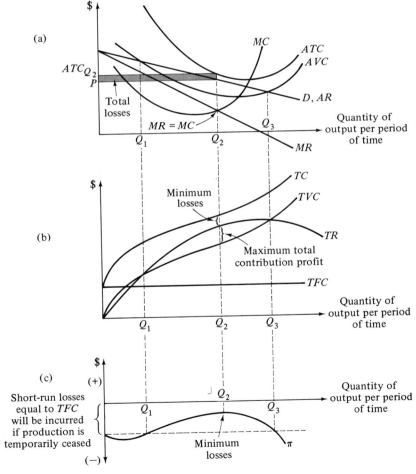

FIGURE 11-2
Short-run loss-minimizing price and output for a firm in monopolistic competition

since losses will be less than the amount of *TFC*—the amount it will lose if production and sales are temporarily discontinued. The question now is where between Q_1 and Q_3 to operate. Clearly, the firm is motivated to obtain as much total contribution profit as possible and thereby cover as large a portion of its total fixed costs as conditions will permit. Total contribution profit is maximum at the output where *TR* exceeds *TVC* by the greatest vertical distance. In Fig. 11-2(b) this occurs at an output rate of Q_2 units, where a tangent to the *TR* curve has the same slope as a tangent to the *TVC* curve. By inspection, the vertical distance by which *TC* exceeds *TR* is a minimum at Q_2, meaning that at Q_2 the firm's short-run losses are minimized. Therefore, from the standpoint of *TC-TR* analysis, short-run losses are minimized at the output rate where total contribution profit is the greatest. This output coincides exactly with the output where the vertical spread between *TC* and *TR* is smallest. The corresponding total profit function reaches its highest level at Q_2, although it still lies entirely in the negative (loss) range. Insofar as unit costs and unit revenues are concerned [Fig. 11-2(a)], an output of Q_2 units corresponds exactly to the intersection of marginal cost and marginal revenue, where marginal profit equals zero. The loss-minimizing price is *P* dollars. At an output of Q_2 units, average total cost is ATC_{Q_2}; the firm's short-run losses will equal $(P - ATC_{Q_2})Q_2$—shown as the shaded area in Fig. 11-2(a). Thus, provided that at least a portion of the demand-*AR* curve lies above the *AVC* curve (so that $P > AVC$), we see that the $MR = MC$ rule, along with its corollary, $M\pi = 0$, identifies not only the short-run profit-maximizing output but also the short-run loss-minimizing output.

Figure 11-3 illustrates a situation where the firm's demand-*AR* curve again lies below the *ATC* curve, foreclosing the opportunity for earning a normal profit in the short run. Note that the demand-*AR* curve is tangent to the *AVC* curve at a single output—Q_1 units. At Q_1, demand is just strong enough to permit the firm to sell at a price that will cover *AVC*. Unit contribution profit equals zero at Q_1; similarly, total contribution profit is zero, since $TR = TVC$ [see Fig. 11-3(b)]. From a profit-loss standpoint the firm will be indifferent as to producing and selling Q_1 units or closing down production in the short run. In either event, short-run losses will equal *TFC*, and this is the best the firm can do [see Fig. 11-3(b) and (c)]. At any other price and output combination *TR* will be insufficient to cover even *TVC*, both total and unit contribution profit will be negative, and short-run losses will exceed *TFC* by the amount of *TVC* not covered by *TR*. Given that selling Q_1 units at a price of P_1 dollars will have no adverse effects on its profit-loss position (as compared to temporarily closing down operations), the firm will undoubtedly elect to continue production. In doing so, the firm will protect its market share and, by continuing to place its product before the public, stand a better chance of realizing a favorable shift in demand conditions in the future.

Now consider Fig. 11-4, where a firm's demand-*AR* curve lies entirely below the *AVC* curve. At no output rate can sufficient revenues be accumulated to cover the variable costs of production. The vertical spread between *TR* and *TC* is always greater at output rates above zero than at zero. Both unit and total contribution profits are negative at all positive outputs. The total profit function is even more negative at positive output rates than at zero output. Therefore, in this instance

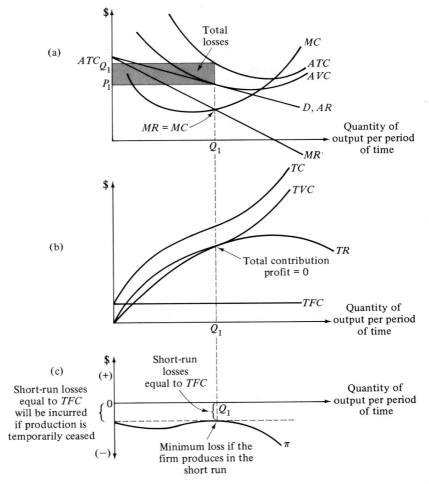

FIGURE 11-3
Short-run loss-minimizing price and output for a firm in monopolistic competition when the demand curve is just tangent to the *AVC* curve

the firm will minimize short-run losses by temporarily ceasing production and waiting for a favorable shift of the demand-*AR* curve; short-run losses will equal total fixed costs.

Of course, if the weak demand conditions are perceived as permanent and if over time the firm's costs cannot be lowered sufficiently to allow a normal profit to be earned, then the firm should begin to divert its energies and resources into the production of other more profitable commodities or else dissolve entirely. Short-run losses can be sustained only temporarily. As the time perspective lengthens, some sort of readjustment must be made.

FIGURE 11-4
Short-run close-down position for a firm in monopolistic competition

Market Demand and Supply Curves in Monopolistic Competition. Under conditions of monopolistic competition, representing industry supply and demand conditions by means of industry supply and demand *curves* is not satisfactory. Product differentiation makes the product units sold by one firm somewhat different from the product units sold by another. Bottles of hair oil differ from tubes of hair cream. Aerosol cans of hair spray are still different. Thus, there is some difficulty in constructing the quantity axis for industry curves. Furthermore, no single price prevails for the products of firms in the industry. Each firm may charge a slightly different price, according to the costs of producing its particular product and the strength of consumer demand for it. As a result of the price and product variations among firms, it is difficult to speak of a specific amount of output being supplied or demanded at a specific price. Moreover, what a firm is willing to produce at a given point in time hinges upon both *MR* and *MC*—the former varies with the demand for the product, and the latter is a function of input prices and the firm's technology. There is no unique price for each alternative output; it all depends on the shape and position of the demand-*AR* curve as to what the profit maximization price is for any given output at which *MR* = *MC*. Thus, the price-output decisions of firms cannot be meaningfully translated into an industry supply curve. The market as a whole is there, but it is better described in words than graphs.

Long-Run Adjustments of Monopolistically Competitive Firms.   We saw earlier that with free entry and exit firms in a perfectly competitive industry are unable to earn more than a normal profit. Under monopolistic competition similar forces are present, though they are not quite so powerful as to eliminate completely the earning of economic profit or to guarantee each firm as much as a normal profit. The most which can be said is that *a tendency exists* for profits to move toward normal rates of return.

The process of long-run adjustments in a monopolistically competitive industry is analogous to that of perfect competition. New firms can enter the industry without undue difficulties. When short-run economic profits exist generally throughout the industry, established firms can be expected to pursue additional economies of scale, new technologies, and other profit-enhancing, cost-reducing options. New firms, attracted by the above-normal rates of return, will be motivated to enter the industry.[4] The entry of new rivals, assuming constant market demand for the products of the industry, will cause the demand curve of each firm to shift to the left. Why? Because each firm will necessarily have a smaller market share, since more firms will be dividing the relatively constant total market among themselves. Moreover, the demand curve will become somewhat more elastic, owing to the presence of a larger number of close-substitute products. These shifts in demand will tend to narrow profit margins and cause economic profits gradually to dissipate. Provided the attraction of economic profits is sufficiently strong to induce the entry of enough new firms and provided established firms are unable to discover innovative means of earning economic profits, there will exist a tendency for all economic profits to be eliminated in the long run.

Figure 11-5 illustrates the long-run equilibrium position of the representative firm. In panel (a) the demand-*AR* curve is shown tangent to the *SRAC* curve and the *LRAC* curve at the profit-maximizing output. Output Q_1 is the long-run equilibrium output, and price P_1 is the long-run equilibrium price. Since price equals *SRAC* at Q_1 units of output, the firm is just covering *all* its costs, including implicit and opportunity costs. The accounting profit reported by the firm will be equal to a normal profit or a normal rate of return in the economic sense. In panel (b) the *TC* curve is tangent to the *TR* curve at an output of Q_1 units. The total profit function in Fig. 11-5(c) climbs just to the zero-economic-profit level at Q_1 units. Plainly, any deviation from an output of Q_1 and a price of P_1 will yield revenues

---

[4] For simplicity, we shall assume that the entry and exit of firms has no effect on input prices and, consequently, upon the *SRAC* and *LRAC* curves of the firms. In other words, the long-run adjustment process is presumed to take place in a constant-cost environment. Shifts in the *SRAC* and *LRAC* curves as firms enter or leave the industry would unduly complicate the discussion without altering the conclusions.

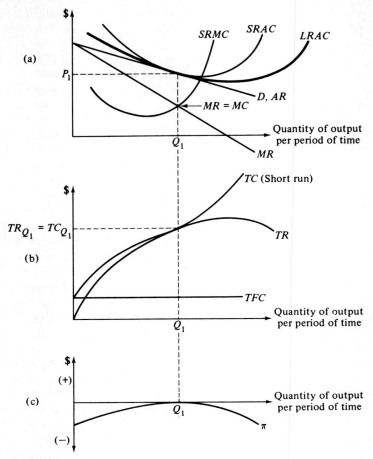

FIGURE 11-5
Long-run equilibrium for a firm in monopolistic competition

which are insufficient to cover *all* production costs including a normal profit. And since economic profits have dwindled to zero, no incentive exists for additional firms to enter the industry.

Should weak demand conditions preclude established firms from earning a normal profit (as previously illustrated in Figs. 11-2, 11-3, and 11-4), the least-efficient, highest-cost firms which are sustaining the largest losses are the most probable candidates for leaving the industry. The remaining firms can be counted upon to seek out ways to increase efficiency, reduce costs, stimulate demand, and thereby trim their losses. The exodus of firms from the industry will tend to shift the demand-*AR* curves of the remaining firms to the right, since the now fewer firms can divide the total market into larger pieces. Also, the reduction in the number of good substitutes will make the demand-*AR* curve a little less price elastic. The net result will tend to be an improvement in the profit-loss position of the representative firm to the point where at least a normal profit can be earned.

Observe that at the long-run equilibrium position, the representative firm is operating short of the minimum point on the *LRAC* curve. Each company is too small to achieve the lowest possible unit cost. In one sense there are too many firms in the industry. The same total output could be produced by a smaller number of firms, each operating at capacity. Thus, *excess production capacity* may be said to exist in the industry. Also, the long-run equilibrium price is higher than the minimum value of *LRAC*. Economists have made much of these two results; however, it is debatable how significant a criticism they constitute. The apparently excessive number of firms derives from consumer preferences for one brand over another, as reflected in the downsloping demand-*AR* curve. Consumers evidently believe they *gain* by being able to exercise their preferences for a brand or a store; otherwise, brand and store loyalty would vanish and the demand-*AR* curves of firms would tend to be horizontal (perfectly elastic).

However, the forces of long-run equilibrium adjustment in monopolistic competition are not so powerful as in perfect competition. The sequence of events leading to long-run equilibrium in monopolistic competition is readily interrupted. In the first place, some firms may be able to develop unique features in their product which are patentable and which give them a significant marketing edge over competitors, even over the long term. Second, some firms may obtain an especially favorable location for their business which allows them to earn sustained economic profits; this arises often in the case of motels, service stations, restaurants, and shopping centers. Third, through ongoing product innovation and the implementing of new technologies, firms may be able to gain advantages over their rivals which are sustainable for long periods. Finally, entry is not totally unrestricted; the added financial investment associated with product differentiation and sales promotion activities may pose some barrier to the entry of new firms, thereby allowing modest economic profits to persist in the long run. At the other end of the ladder, below-normal profits may also persist in the long run. The suburban florist may accept a return less than he could earn elsewhere because he likes living near a metropolitan area and because he likes designing floral arrangements. The proprietor of the corner grocery store may reluctantly accept subpar profits because his business is a way of life to him. Consequently, market forces will seldom be powerful enough in monopolistic competition to drive price all the way to equality with short-run and long-run average cost. Nevertheless, a *tendency* will exist for market forces to *limit* the profits and to *restrict* the losses of monopolistically competitive firms over the long run.

PRODUCT DIFFERENTIATION AND FOCUS STRATEGIES

In a monopolistically competitive marketplace, firms have the option of introducing new and different product attributes as a way to strengthen their position with buyers. Indeed, seeking to differentiate one's product from those of rival firms can be a potent competitive strategy. Setting one's own brand apart from the rest by offering improved quality and performance, new or greater convenience, more selection, extra services, greater durability, better credit terms, or distinctive design can well meet with buyer approval. In effect, successfully differentiating one's products from those of rival firms affords a firm breathing space to refrain from trying to win increased buyer patronage solely by meeting or beating the prices of competing items. And from a broader social viewpoint, *product differentiation* can be an important stimulant to technological innovation and to expanding the range of consumer choice.

Given a goal of profit maximization, our representative firm in monopolistic competition can be expected to search among the various possible combinations of product attributes for the one it perceives to be the most profitable. The problem is to select it under conditions of less than perfect knowledge about future market conditions and buyer behavior. One approach is to estimate from available market information the profitability of each of several product differentiation approaches, given the prices and product attributes of rival firms. The firm then maximizes expected profit by choosing the product differentiation theme with the highest expected profit and producing at the price and output where *MC* equals *MR*.

However, from time to time rival firms can be counted upon to incorporate new and different attributes into their own products. When they do, a firm may find further product differentiation necessary to remain competitive. A continuous sequence of product variation moves and countermoves is set in motion, often made feasible by research and development efforts aimed at generating a steady stream of potentially profitable opportunities for modifying product offerings. Rival competitors are prompted to incorporate new product features because they hope to gain a profitable, albeit temporary, competitive edge. The edge tends to be temporary because if the new attributes catch on in the market, other firms either begin to imitate the variation or to try to go it one better, in hopes of leapfrogging the competitive edge of the leaders.

In the course of this product-differentiating struggle, some firms will perceive it more profitable to adopt product attributes which appeal to price-conscious consumers, with the result that their products are slightly less expensive and of lower quality. Other firms will view it advantageous to cater to those buyers desirous of superior-quality goods, with the result that their products carry above-average prices and are claimed to have more features or above-average performance standards. Still other firms may pursue an intermediate strategy, positioning their products in between the high and low ends of the market. And some rivals may base their differentiation strategy on styling, extra service, bigger selection, easier credit terms, more convenient location, or other such features. These strategy differences reflect the fact that *markets are diverse*—being comprised in part by consumers who are strongly quality-conscious but not especially price-conscious, in part by consumers willing to sacrifice quality to get a lower price, and in part by consumers who are swayed by attributes other than price and quality. Because consumer needs and preferences are not uniform, it is feasible and profitable for firms in the same industry to pursue a *focus* or *specialization strategy* aimed at appealing to *specific* customer needs and *specific* customer groups rather than the whole market. The essence of a focus strategy is to specialize in serving a limited market segment, the premise being that by catering to the needs and preferences of a limited group of buyers a firm can gain a competitive edge in winning the patronage of this buyer group and thereby carve out its own market niche. A focus strategy has merit (1) when there are distinctly different groups of buyers who either have different needs or else utilize the product in different ways, (2) when rival firms have not attempted to specialize, opting instead to try to appeal to all types of buyers, or (3) when a firm's resources do not permit it to go after a wide segment of the total market.

From the standpoint of the consuming public, there is something to be said for a market situation where rival firms pursue different competitive strategies (cost leadership, differentiation, or focus) rather than being constrained to a single, common approach. The different strategies of competitors provide consumers with a wider range of product qualities, performance features, and prices, thereby permitting each consumer to select the brand which appears best-suited to his preferences.[5]

When a firm elects to pursue a particular differentiation or focus strategy, its *SRAC* and *LRAC* curves can shift either up or down, according to the amounts and prices of the resource inputs needed to implement the chosen competitive strategy. In the process, the demand-*AR* curves of each firm can shift both in position and slope as consumers respond to new product variations. One effect of the differences in the products and cost curves of monopolistically competitive firms is to make the long-run equilibrium positions differ from firm to firm. Higher-quality firms can exist alongside lower-quality firms. Higher-priced firms can exist alongside lower-priced firms. This condition is readily observed in the sale of drugs and cosmetics where retailers display on the same shelf the high-priced, better known brands and the lesser-known, cut-price varieties. Moreover, at a given moment, some monopolistically competitive firms may be earning sizable economic profits, others may be earning only a normal profit, and others may be sustaining losses.

---

[5] Product and strategic diversity are not, however, without their drawbacks. Critics warn that proliferation of product varieties and competitive strategies may so confuse the consumer that the exercise of rational choice becomes virtually impossible. Some consumers, confronted with a myriad of similar products, may fall into the "trap" of judging quality by price alone. Critics also point out that many product variations consist of frivolous and superficial attributes which are of dubious value in improving durability, efficiency, or usefulness. In the case of durable and semidurable consumer goods, the process of product change seems to follow a pattern of "planned obsolescence"; firms make gradual but regular changes in their products aimed at increasing the frequency with which consumers become dissatisfied with their present model and trade it in on the new model. As partial remedies for product proliferation, a number of economists propose that information about products be provided to consumers in greater amounts and that laws and penalties regarding infringement on brands and trademarks be relaxed. Increased information and a weakening of trademark protection are held to increase "competition" by promoting a greater degree of product standardization and thereby lessening the powers of producers to vend differentiated products. The end result should be a movement in the direction of perfect competition. For a more thorough argument of this point, see Edward H. Chamberlin, *The Theory of Monopolistic Competition* (Cambridge, Mass.: Harvard University Press, 1933), pp. 271–274, and George J. Stigler, "The Economics of Information," *Journal of Political Economy*, Vol. 69, No. 3 (June 1961), pp. 213–225.

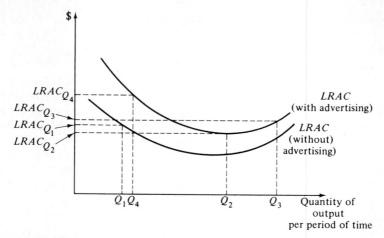

FIGURE 11-6
Effect of sales promotion expenditures upon unit costs and output rates

USING ADVERTISING AND SALES PROMOTION EFFORTS TO GAIN A COMPETITIVE EDGE

The third basic type of competitive approach which monopolistically competitive firms may employ to strengthen their market position concerns advertising and sales promotion. Advertising and promotional campaigns are a strong complement to a firm's pricing and product attribute strategies. True, sales promotion adds to a firm's costs. But if promotional efforts are well conceived, sales volume and revenues can be increased by drawing new customers away from other brands; at the same time, buyers may be persuaded that the firm's product is worth paying more for. In short, promotional expenditures can shift the firm's demand-AR curve to the right and make it slightly *less* elastic as well. As long as revenues increase by more than enough to compensate both for promotional expenses and for extra production costs associated with greater outputs, the firm will have improved its profit position.

Suppose we look closer at the possible effects of promotional expenses upon a firm's long-run average costs. Initially, for the sake of argument, suppose promotional outlays substantially increase the demand for the firm's product and, consequently, the firm's most profitable long-run output rate. What, then, is the effect on the firm's long-run average costs? As depicted in Fig. 11-6, it is obvious that sales promotion outlays will shift the $LRAC$ upward. However, if the demand-AR curve shifts such that production is more profitable at Q_2 than at Q_1, units costs will decline from $LRAC_{Q_1}$ to $LRAC_{Q_2}$ because of the economies of scale which the firm can take advantage of. Greater production efficiency more than offsets the increase in unit costs associated with promotional expenses. On the other hand, increased demand realized from sales promotion may force diseconomies of scale upon the firm, as indicated by the movement from Q_1 to Q_3; in

APPLICATIONS CAPSULE

ADVERTISING: ITS IMPACT AND ECONOMIC SIGNIFICANCE

A theoretical revolution going by the name of "the economics of information" has begun to affect economists' view of the impact and significance of advertising. The conventional economic wisdom is that advertising tends to act as the handmaiden of market power, of downside price rigidity, and of long-term price inflation. Whereas businessmen judge advertising primarily in terms of its power to increase sales and attract customers from other firms, economists judge advertising on how it affects the overall performance of markets and the economy at large. The criteria economists generally use to evaluate advertising are its effects on price competition, product prices, the achievement of large-scale economies, and the extent to which it promotes full employment and maximum production efficiency.

By and large, economists view anything but price advertising with hostility, arguing that nonprice advertising is generally aimed at convincing consumers that a firm's products are somehow different from those of rivals. This creates brand loyalty, making the buying public much less sensitive to price and thereby giving the advertiser some degree of price influence. Beyond that, economists maintain that heavy advertising erects financial barriers to the entry of new firms because, to break into a market, companies must be willing and able to spend large sums on advertising to attract buyers' attention. To the extent that advertising barriers keep out new competitors, the market power of those firms already in the industry is enhanced, with the result that prices are higher and output is smaller than would be the case if markets were more oriented toward price competition. This view is supported by statistical studies showing a correlation between the amount an industry spends on advertising and both its profitability and degree of sales concentrated in a few firms.

However, the revolution going on with respect to the economics of information holds that advertising may contain virtue as well as vice. The new view addresses the question of how advertising affects the consumer and, particularly, the kind and scope of information it provides for consumer decision making. Starting with the premise that advertising provides at least some information to consumers that they would not otherwise get, the argument is that information about a variety of products is far more likely to decrease monopoly power than to increase it.

George Stigler, of the University of Chicago, triggered the economics of information revolution in 1961, castigating economists for analyzing the prices in different markets in great depth, while relegating the analysis of consumer information about prices to "a slum dwelling in the town of economics." Whereas the customary economic view of advertising maintained that price differences for the same *type* of product were due to the ability of firms to differentiate their products and were taken as evidence that advertising gave firms too much price-making power, Stigler argued that a good part of the variability of prices, even among homogeneous products, existed because consumers did not know the prices being charged by various firms. It followed, then, that increased information about prices would enable buyers to bargain more effectively with sellers. As a consequence, reasoned Stigler, price advertising that makes search less expensive will reduce the average price consumers pay for a product.

However, in a recent study Phillip Nelson has carried Stigler's argument a step forward. Nelson claims that getting information on price is relatively easy; the difficult task for the consumer is getting a handle on quality. Nelson's study endeavors to explain how consumers get information about the quality of products from mass-media advertising, given that the information provided is likely to be self-serving and may actually be little more than image-building or boastful puffery. Nelson found that the informational content of advertising differs drastically, depending on the type of product being advertised. For what he called "search goods" (those products whose qualities can be more easily checked before purchase, such as a suit or a dress), the advertising content often consists of direct information on the quality and characteristics of the products; usually, this information is accurate since for advertisers to give misleading information invites legal action.

On the other hand, for "experience goods" (such as soft drinks, soaps, and deodorants, where ascertaining quality requires purchasing the item), advertising generally provides little or no direct quality information. For example, Nelson observes there is no direct information to "join the Pepsi generation." But even here, according to Nelson, the advertiser is saying to the consumer that he believes his product to be of high quality and well worth the consumer's dollar. And to the extent that highly advertised brands have a larger market share than less-advertised brands, there is a strong implication that the heavily advertised brand does have higher quality or yield more value to the consumer.

In support of this proposition, Nelson argues that companies will advertise their winners, not their losers, because heavy advertising of an inferior-quality product risks creating a bad image in the mind of the consumer not only of the brand but of the company as well. In the case of "experience goods" it is especially true that companies live or die from repeat purchases, so it stands to reason that over the long run the higher-quality products will win out over the lower-quality products. This leads Nelson to conclude that *on the average the best buy is the heavily advertised brand*—a proposition which traditionalists find somewhat appalling.

In addition, Nelson maintains that because advertising provides information on many similar products, consumer demand will become more responsive to price for any given product, rather than less responsive, as argued by anti-advertising critics. In other words, advertising increases information about the availability of substitutes, thereby undermining the monopoly power of any one brand—however highly advertised it may be.

Nelson's rule for buying the most advertised brand rests on two key assumptions. One, that sufficient numbers of consumers can judge quality differences between brands after they have used them. Two, that quality differences between brands would exist without advertising, given cost-efficiency differences between companies and given that companies have different opinions as to what product features consumers are looking for.

With respect to the overall market efficiency of advertising, Nelson argues that advertising permits the more efficient companies to increase their sales faster and that less efficient companies are weeded out more quickly than if there were no advertising. This yields a net economic benefit to society compared to a situation where companies do not advertise and where marginal firms may be able to hang on for longer periods of time.

The notion that advertising may be more good than bad has come under sharp attack. Perhaps the most fundamental weakness in this approach is the assumption that consumers can validate advertising claims easily and cheaply. If consumers are able to learn from experiences quickly, then it is more likely to be true that the advertised brand is the best buy—for many goods. But there are many products which require extensive testing by consumers, and other products, such as consumer durables, are purchased infrequently; in such cases, the experience information which consumers have may be too outdated to be of value. Another view is that advertising shapes and molds consumer tastes and works to the advantage of advertisers, thereby allowing firms to manage demand and to undermine consumer sovereignty. Then, too, there are studies which show that in heavily advertised consumer goods industries (such as nonprescription drugs, soaps, breakfast cereals, razors, and soft drinks) firms consistently are able to earn above-average profits. This finding has been held to confirm the existence of barriers to entry, because otherwise, it is argued, firms would be induced to enter such industries to take advantage of the above-average profit opportunities. To the extent that a new company will have to spend more than a dollar on advertising its product to counteract one dollar's worth of advertising by an entrenched firm, then the new company is at a disadvantage, and a barrier to entry exists. Moreover, it has been observed that investing in advertising is not the same as investing in tangible capital assets because if a firm fails in an industry in which it has invested heavily in capital goods, then those capital goods have a liquidation value. However, if a firm fails in an industry where it has invested heavily in advertising, its investment is water down the drain.

QUESTIONS FOR DISCUSSION

1. In your opinion, how able are consumers to validate the quality of what Nelson calls experience goods? Search goods?

2. Do you agree with Nelson that for most items, the most highly advertised brand is the best buy? Cite examples to support your answer.

3. Can you cite cases where advertising has probably tended to increase the market power of established firms? In what industries is it likely that advertising has reduced market power by facilitating the entry of new firms?

Sources: George J. Stigler, "The Economics of Information," *Journal of Political Economy*, Vol. 69, No. 3 (June 1961), pp. 213–225; Phillip J. Nelson, "Advertising As Information," *Journal of Political Economy*, Vol. 82, No. 4 (July–August 1974), pp. 729–754; William S. Comanor and Thomas A. Wilson, *Advertising and Market Power* (Cambridge, Mass.: Harvard University Press, 1974); "A New View of Advertising's Economic Impact," *Business Week* (December 22, 1975), pp. 49ff.; Phillip J. Nelson, "Information and Consumer Behavior," *Journal of Political Economy*, Vol. 78, No. 2 (March-April 1970), pp. 311–329; and Phillip J. Nelson, "The Economic Consequences of Advertising," *Journal of Business*, Vol. 48, No. 2 (April 1975), pp. 213–241.

this case, unit costs would rise from $LRAC_{Q_1}$ to $LRAC_{Q_3}$. In some cases a great portion of sales promotion efforts by firms are self-cancelling; one seller's stepped-up advertising campaign is matched by rival firms, resulting in only slight gains in sales and output—as is suggested by the movement from Q_1 to Q_4.[6] In this instance, unit costs may be driven up substantially by the decision to adopt an

---

[6] The cigarette, soap, beer, and toiletries industries are good cases in point. Like the Red Queen in *Alice through the Looking Glass*, each firm has to run as fast as it can in its promotional activities just to keep up with where it is. This correctly recognizes that some promotional activity is defensive in nature and is undertaken to protect a firm's position as well as to enhance it.

which one will actually occur in a particular situation varies with the shape of the *LRAC* curve and the size of the effect of sales promotion upon demand and output.

A somewhat more interesting question relates to the effect of sales promotion activity upon a firm's price and profits. Consider Fig. 11-7. In panel (a) is illustrated a situation where sales promotion outlays have the effect of *lowering* a firm's price and *raising* a firm's profits. In the absense of promotion, the profit-maximizing price and output are P_1 and Q_1, respectively, and total profit equals $(P_1 - SRAC_{Q_1})Q_1$. Initiating promotional activity shifts the demand-*AR* curve rightward from (D_1, AR_1) to (D_2, AR_2) and the *LRAC* curve upward from $LRAC_1$ to $LRAC_2$. The firm will find it advantageous to expand output to Q_2 and to lower price to P_2; total profit will be $(P_2 - SRAC_{Q_2})Q_2$ dollars—an amount that dwarfs the profits earned when no promotional activity is undertaken. In panel (b) is shown a situation where promotional activity causes price to rise and profits to

FIGURE 11-7
Possible effects of sales promotion activity upon prices and profits

MATHEMATICAL CAPSULE 11

DETERMINING THE PROFIT-MAXIMIZING OUTPUT RATE AND LEVEL OF ADVERTISING EXPENDITURE

Advertising and promotional outlays necessarily affect the firm's profitability. Thus, we may say that

$$\pi = f(\text{output, advertising outlays}).$$

Suppose empirical analysis of a firm's operations indicates that the following relationship exists:

$$\pi = 600 - 4Q - Q^2 + 2QA + 116A - 5A^2,$$

where π = total profit per period of time, Q = the firm's output rate, and A = the firm's advertising outlay (in dollars) per period of time.

How can we determine the profit-maximizing output rate and the profit-maximizing amount of advertising expenditure? The answer to this question involves use of partial derivatives (Mathematical Capsule 2) and the principles of profit maximization. In mathematical terms we need to find the specific combination of values of Q and A that will maximize the value of π.

The first-order conditions for maximizing a multivariable function of this type are that

$$\frac{\partial \pi}{\partial Q} = 0 \quad \text{and} \quad \frac{\partial \pi}{\partial A} = 0.$$

Thus, the first step is to find the partial derivatives of π with respect to Q and A and set them equal to zero; this gives

$$\frac{\partial \pi}{\partial Q} = -4 - 2Q + 2A = 0,$$

$$\frac{\partial \pi}{\partial A} = 2Q + 116 - 10A = 0.$$

Solving these two equations simultaneously gives $Q = 12$ and $A = 14$.

To prove that these values represent maximum π rather than minimum π, we much check to see that the second-order conditions are met at $Q = 12$ and $A = 14$. The second-order conditions are that

$$\frac{\partial^2 \pi}{\partial Q^2} < 0, \quad \frac{\partial^2 \pi}{\partial A^2} < 0 \quad \text{and} \quad \left(\frac{\partial^2 \pi}{\partial Q^2}\right)\left(\frac{\partial^2 \pi}{\partial A^2}\right) > \left(\frac{\partial^2 \pi}{\partial Q \partial A}\right)^2.$$

Since

$$\frac{\partial^2 \pi}{\partial Q^2} = -2,$$

$$\frac{\partial^2 \pi}{\partial A^2} = -10,$$

$$\frac{\partial^2 \pi}{\partial Q \partial A} = 2,$$

> it is quickly verified that the profit-maximizing output rate is 12 units per period of time and the profit-maximizing advertising outlay is $14 per period of time.
>
> **EXERCISE**
>
> 1. Suppose that the functional relationship among profit, output, and advertising is given by the expression
>
> $$\pi = 1000 - 3Q^2 - 6Q + 6QA + 90A - 10A^2.$$
>
> Determine the profit-maximizing rates of output and advertising expenditure.

fall. Prior to initiating a promotional strategy, profit maximization occurs at P_1 and Q_1 with a resulting total profit of $(P_1 - SRAC_1)Q_1$ dollars. With promotion activity the profit-maximizing price and output are P_2 and Q_2 and total profit is only $(P_2 - SRAC_{Q_2})Q_2$ dollars. Other possibilities exist: Promotional activity can cause price to rise and profits to rise, price to fall and profits to fall, and so on. No general answer can be given as to the effect of promotional strategies upon a firm's costs, price, output, or profits. It all depends on the effect which promotional expenditures have upon the position and shape of the firm's demand-AR curve and its $LRAC$ curve.

A SUMMARY PROFILE OF COMPETITION
IN A MONOPOLISTICALLY COMPETITIVE MARKET

The distinguishing features of a monopolistically competitive market are: (1) a fragmented market structure whereby *many* suppliers are selling differentiated, yet similar, products; (2) no one seller has a significant or commanding market share; (3) each firm, because its product tends to be more or less different from what its rivals are offering, has some ability to influence its sales by changing its price; (4) downsloping, but highly elastic, demand-AR curves for the relevant output range of the firms; (5) the relative ease with which firms can enter and leave the industry; (6) the small effect the actions of any one firm have upon rival firms; and (7) firms which behave as if they seek to maximize profits.

Monopolistically competitive firms may earn short-run economic profits or incur short-run losses. The relative ease with which firms can enter the industry limits the opportunities for earning large economic profits over the long run. The exodus of firms from the industry tends to eliminate or at least reduce economic losses in the long run.

The firm in monopolistic competition has three basic competitive strategies for pursuing its principal goal of maximum profits: (1) using the appeal of a different (*usually lower*) price to create a clientele of buyers, (2) trying to set one's own product offering apart from those of rival sellers via differentiation and/or focus strategies, and (3) employing advertising and other sales promotion techniques to attract buyer attention and increase sales volume, revenues, and market share. Just what set of specific features and product attributes, selling at what price, and supplemented by what amount of promotional expenses will actually maximize profits is a complex issue. Each possible combination of price, product differentiation themes, and promotional outlay poses a different demand and cost situation for the firm, some one of which will yield the firm maximum profits. A trial-and-error procedure is virtually imperative in arriving at an optimum combination of price, product attributes, and promotional outlays.

Thus, the competitive strategies of firms can assume a variety of forms. Some firms may seek to compete mainly on price, while others aim at quality, and still others use heavier than usual advertising. Product differentiation themes may be aimed at making the item more durable or less durable; various performance features may be made standard or optional; the range of models, colors, and styles may be expanded or contracted; service after the sale may be increased or reduced; credit terms can be tightened or loosened; designs can be made plain or fancy; packaging may be made more or less elaborate and colorful. A stepped-up advertising campaign by one seller may be countered by another seller with improved guarantees to buyers. Lower prices may be met by improved customer services or adding new convenience features. Some products are so obviously different that sellers feel little pressure or derive little advantage from further promoting and proclaiming differences which most buyers are already well aware of. On the other hand, promotional activity plays a bigger role in those monopolistically competitive markets where product differentiation is slight or not readily apparent; here, rival firms are easily led to try to exploit and bolster the importance of differences.

It is important to observe that formulating a successful competitive strategy is inherently more complex in a monopolistically competitive market environment than it is in perfect competition. In a perfectly competitive market the products of different firms are all alike—the item is a "commodity" in the sense that buyers are purchasing *the industry's product*, not a given firm's product. Buyers do not care which seller they deal with, except if a particular seller's price is higher or lower than the going market price—in which case buyers will switch quickly to a lower-priced seller and away from a higher-priced seller. This "commodity" feature of a perfectly competitive marketplace creates a competitive environment wherein the most sensible strategy is that of striving to be *the low-cost producer* or at least *a low-cost producer*. Being in a low-cost position is the best single strategic defense against the price-cost style of competitive game that typifies a perfectly competitive market. Moreover, in a commodity market, there is no place for differentiation or focus types of competitive strategies since buyers have no basis for preferring to deal with any one seller and there is no buyer loyalty. Hence, the choice of how to compete is a very simple one insofar as a firm operating in a perfectly competitive environment is concerned. But this is not so in monopolistic competition. The differentiated product environment of a monopolistically competitive market gives a firm plenty of leeway in formulating an answer to the question of "how do we try to compete in this business?" There is space for many different competitive strategies to succeed, thus creating a situation where a firm must analyze carefully which of the many strategic options make the most sense to pursue. More about the choice of competitive strategy will be said in Chapters 15 and 16.

COMPETITION AMONG THE MANY: THEORY VERSUS PRACTICE

It turns out that the theoretical models of perfect competition and monopolistic competition are reasonably descriptive of firm and market behavior in certain industries. Where large numbers of relatively small firms sell a homogeneous product, market patterns *tend* to be in accord with the perfectly competitive model. Where large numbers of small firms sell differentiated products, firm behavior regarding prices, outputs, product variation, and promotion parallels the model of monopolistic competition.

Real-world examples of industries where near perfectly competitive conditions prevail include such agricultural markets as corn, wheat, cotton, wool, barley, oats, and livestock; the manufacture of cotton cloth; and some financial markets involving stocks, bonds, and loans to business. Conditions approaching monopolistic competition are found in such industries as machine tools, valves and pipe fittings, wood and upholstered furniture, wine, computer software, sawmills, screw machine products, paperboard boxes, shoes, paints and varnishes, millinery, costume jewelry, lighting fixtures, poultry processing, restaurants, burial caskets, men's and boys' suits and coats, and women's dresses, suits, coats, and skirts; monopolistic competition also typifies the wholesaling and retailing trades in more populated urban centers.

In addition, segments of other industries exhibit the characteristics of these two models. As we shall see in Chapter 12, in industries where numerous, comparatively small firms operate alongside a few large corporations, the competitive and market relationships between the two sets of firms often result in the small firms exhibiting behavior patterns closely akin to that of perfect or monopolistic competition—conditions in the steel, tire, dairy, retail grocery, soap, petroleum refining, plumbing fixtures, machinery, and electrical appliance industries serve as examples.

The behavior of prices, outputs, and profits in the above-mentioned industries (or segments thereof) compares favorably with the conclusions drawn from the two theoretical models of perfect and monopolistic competition. Rates of return on stockholder investment tend to run a bit below average. However, as might be anticipated, profits tend to be somewhat higher in the faster-growing industries and somewhat lower in the slow-growth industries. Supply is generally responsive to changes in consumer demand, rising most dramatically where market demand curves are shifting rapidly to the right. Outputs and prices respond rapidly to cost changes. Industries where technological change has tended to reduce unit costs show a relative decline in prices and a relatively large expansion of output. Consumer demand, output, and cost movements are correlated. Where consumer demand and output are vigorously expanding, technical progress is stimulated, and firms take advantage rather quickly of expansion opportunities. Unless scale economies dictate otherwise, the number of firms in the industry increases with demand. Cost reductions coupled with expanding production capabilities give rise to price cuts, which, in turn, reinforce the expansion process by triggering higher sales and output; this is a familiar cycle during the early and intermediate stages of the life cycle of a product or product group. It is clear, then, that the models of perfect and monopolistic competition have empirical validity; both are able to predict and explain market behavior in certain circumstances and both have something to say about the pros and cons of different ways a firm can try to compete successfully.

The Benefits of Competition among the Many

The conventional widsom in economics is that market conditions of perfect competition and monopolistic competition offer consumers the best of all possible worlds. If consumers are willing to accept homogeneous products, a perfectly competitive market structure will give it to them at the lowest possible price consistent with the costs of production. Under conditions of long-run equilibrium each firm operates at the minimum point of its short-run and long-run average cost curve and thus achieves maximum production efficiency. Price is driven to the level of minimum average cost, and investors receive a rate of return just sufficient to induce them to maintain their investment at levels adequate for producing the industry's equilibrium output most efficiently. Firms which fail to attain the lowest possible unit cost incur losses and eventually are driven from the industry. Consequently, resources *tend* to be employed at maximum production efficiency in a perfectly competitive industry.

If consumers exhibit a preference for differentiated products, as often they do because of the diversity of preferences and needs of buyers, then monopolistically competitive conditions are held to produce optimum consumer benefits. Competition is strong enough to keep prices down close to costs and profit margins slim. Although monopolistically competitive firms may not quite achieve maximum production efficiency (because at long-run equilibrium the demand-*AR* curve is tangent to the *LRAC* curve just short of the minimum point), unit costs still tend to be as low as can be achieved with differentiated products.

In both perfect and monopolistic competition, the output of goods and services automatically stays in close accord with consumer demand. Prices are no higher than necessary to maintain production. The market power of any one firm is negligible. For these reasons the market structures of perfect and monopolistic competition are commonly thought to yield an overall economic outcome that is most advantageous to consumers. The key benefit of "competition among the many" is having numerous relatively small firms competing under conditions where market forces are so dominant that buyers are well protected from exploitation by sellers and abuses of economic power on the supply side of the market. Firms are, for the most part, price-takers, not price-makers.

Some Disadvantages of Competition among the Many

However, competition among the many can produce some subtle disadvantages. To see why we have to go beyond industrywide prices, outputs, and profits and look critically at the specific traits that competition among the many can *sometimes* impose upon individual firms. Almost every real-world example of markets that are fragmented with many sellers involves industries where firms are small both relatively *and* absolutely. There is, in other words a very close correspondence between (1) the existence of near-perfect competition and of monopolistic competition and (2) the presence of small, entrepreneurial enterprises. This is more than mere circumstance. The representative firm operating under conditions of perfect or monopolistic competition *must* be small relatively because both models are predicated on the presence of large numbers of firms, no one of which has a sizable share of the market. In practice, the size of the representative firm is also absolutely small. Firm size is severely limited by the relatively quick appearance of diseconomies of scale. Were significant economies of scale present, firms would tend to be large—not small—relative to the total market because overall market demand is seldom big enough to accommodate the competitive existence of *large* numbers of *large* firms. Moreover, once existing firms take full advantage of scale economies, increased industry output is likely to be achieved *by the entry of new firms rather than by the expansion of existing firms.* In other words, the economic limitations on firm size tend to guarantee an atomistic structure of many small firms. This is not to say that conditions of perfect or monopolistic competition prevail wherever small firms exist, but it does say that perfect and monopolistic competition are found almost exclusively in markets comprised of firms that are small in an absolute sense. Billion-dollar corporations, commonplace in many industries, are the exception not the rule in markets approximating perfect and monopolistic competition.

The small size and enterpreneurial character of firms that operate in an atomistic or fragmented market environment, in conjunction with the nature of competition among the many, are what gives rise to the disadvantages. To begin with, the representative firm in an atomistic or fragmented market is thrust into a position of *reacting* and *responding* to changing market conditions. "The market" calls the shots, with the winds of change just as prone to blow in the direction of lower profits as in the direction of higher profits. Market forces can be harsh and unrelenting. Much like a small boat caught in the midst of a hurricane, the firm's security and survival is extremely tenuous—witness the comparatively precarious condition of many small businesses when market conditions are tough. As a consequence, the actions and strategies of such firms come to be aimed mainly at short-run profit maximization. Profit margins are too slim and too uncertain to allow otherwise. Weak demand may force severe financial retrenchment, bankruptcy, or exit from the industry. Strong demand, on the other hand, may offer limited prospects for above-average profits and growth because of the ease of entry of new firms and because of a lack of financial strength to pursue a large expansion program or gain a position of industry leadership.

In such an environment, profit incentives and financial capacities for risk-taking, for research, and for innovation are definitely impaired—both by the firm's small size and by its susceptibility to stringent treatment by market forces. There is, therefore, an increased likelihood that the pace of technological advance will be slower, not faster, where firms are small as compared to where they are large. A little bit of bigness—sales levels of $100 million to $250 million in most industries—is good for R & D and innovation. Firms of this size and larger find a well-rounded research and development program and the new ideas it generates to be an asset in maintaining their viability and growth. Moreover, they can better afford the talent needed to staff such an effort. Naturally, exceptions exist; some small entrepreneurial firms are known for their technological prowess, being extraordinarily prolific in generating new ideas and in developing relatively uncomplicated processes and products.[7] But, outside the so-called high-technology industries, small owner-managed firms tend not to be especially innovation-minded or technologically advanced. This is partially because the dominance of the market, competition, and ease of entry keep profits so slim and uncertain that firms are deprived of the venture capital requisite for financing technological research and for instituting sustained expansion. And it is partially because such firms operate on too small a scale to justify spending funds for formal research and development activities; R & D may not pay off from a short-run profit-and-loss viewpoint—the criterion employed by firms in atomistically competitive market environments. Even more significantly, a small firm may not be able to absorb the risk of failure that goes with venturesome R & D efforts.

This argument is supported by the fact that most industries exemplifying the characteristics of competition among the many are low-wage, low-skill industries where the levels of technological sophistication are minimal and capital investment requirements are small. Indeed, the *comparatively* slow pace of technological advance in sawmill operations, apparel, and segments of the food products, textile, fabricated metal products, and leather industries suggests that technological progress is more rapid where the rigors of short-run competitive forces are not so relentless as to make firms unwilling and unable to bear the risks and costs of research and innovation.

Furthermore, it is questionable whether the instability and insecurity of firms in a fragmented, supply-side environment promote rising incomes and noninflationary full employment. Less-advanced technology, low profits, and limited capital availability translate into low and slowly rising incomes for employees. Moreover, adjusting to market decline or stagnation is often a long, painful process— the prolonged death throes of the New England textile industry and the small farmer serve as cases in point. Over the long haul, it is the rates and quality of economic growth and technical progress, not low profits and maximum production efficiency, that *most* affect society's overall economic welfare.

Thus, upon closer examination competition among the many *can have* some side effects and long-term drawbacks that make the case for perfect competition and monopolistic competition weaker in actual practice than the theory seems to suggest. Basically, this is because rapid technical process, increases in productive capability, and attractive employment conditions are not always forthcoming on a long-term basis in a market environment where firms are thrown into a life-or-death competitive struggle, profits are minimal, risks are high, firms have less chance of long-term survival (owing either to competitive failure or death of the

---

[7] Apple Computer was nothing more than a back-of-the-house garage operation when it pioneered the development and use of small-scale personal computers.

owner-entrepreneur), capital investment is low, and little or no R & D efforts are undertaken.

Still, the two models of competition among the many do convincingly indicate the social value of a competitive market environment. The case for more competition *typically* outweighs the case for less competition.

SUGGESTED READINGS

ARCHIBALD, G. C., "Chamberlin *versus* Chicago," *Review of Economic Studies,* Vol. 29 (1961), pp. 2–28.

BISHOP, R. L., "The Theory of Monopolistic Competition after Thirty Years: The Impact on General Theory," *American Economic Review,* Vol. 54, No. 3 (May 1964), pp. 33–43.

CHAMBERLIN, E. H., *The Theory of Monopolistic Competition* (Cambridge, Mass.: Harvard University Press, 1933).

DOYLE, P., "Economic Aspects of Advertising: A Survey," *Economic Journal,* Vol. 78, No. 311 (September 1968), pp. 570–602.

KALDOR, N., "The Economic Aspects of Advertising," *Review of Economic Studies,* Vol. 18 (1949–1950), pp. 17–21.

KIRZNER, I. M., *Competition and Entrepreneurship* (Chicago: University of Chicago Press, 1973), Chapters 3 and 4.

ROBINSON, J., *The Economics of Imperfect Competition* (London: The Macmillan Company, 1933).

SCHERER, F. M., "Research and Development Resource Allocation under Rivalry," *Quarterly Journal of Economics,* Vol. 81, No. 3 (August 1967), pp. 359–394.

——, *Industrial Market Structure and Economic Performance,* 2nd ed. (Boston: Houghton Mifflin Company, 1980), Chapter 14.

STIGLER, G. J., "Monopolistic Competition in Retrospect," *The Organization of Industry* (Homewood, Ill.: Richard D. Irwin, Inc., 1968), pp. 71–94.

——, "Price and Non-price Competition," *Journal of Political Economy,* Vol. 76, No. 1 (January-February 1968), pp. 149–154.

TELSER, L. G., "Advertising and Competition," *Journal of Political Economy,* Vol. 72, No. 6 (December 1964), pp. 537–562.

PROBLEMS AND QUESTIONS FOR DISCUSSION

1. The Morgan Chair Company manufactures rocking chairs and sells them under conditions of monopolistic competition. The owner of the company has estimated its demand function as $P = 1625 - 6Q$, where P is in dollars and Q is in dozens of chairs sold per month. The company believes its monthly expenses vary with output according to the equation $TC = 25,000 + 25Q - 6Q^2 + \frac{1}{3}Q^3$.
   (a) Determine the firm's short-run profit-maximizing price and output rate.
   (b) How much profit will the firm earn at this price and output rate?
   (c) Suppose the Morgan Chair Company's total fixed costs rise by 10%. Calculate the impact upon the firm's price, output, and profits. How do you account for these results?

2. Using the unit cost and revenue curves, graphically illustrate the short-run profit-maximizing price and output for a monopolistically competitive firm which has a production function that exhibits constant returns to variable input over its entire range of output capability. (*Hint:* First determine the shape of the *ATC* and *MC* curves which correspond to a production function characterized by constant returns to variable input; then find the price and output at which *MR = MC*.) Indicate on your graph the area which represents the firm's total profits.

3. Using *TR-TC* analysis, graphically illustrate the short-run profit-maximizing output for a monopolistically competive firm which is faced with a linear, downsloping demand curve and which has a production function displaying decreasing returns to variable input over its entire range of output capability. Then derive the corresponding total profit function for the firm.

4. Suppose that a firm operating under conditions of monopolistic competition is faced with a linear, downward-sloping demand curve and that its production function is of cubic form $(a + bX + cX^2 - dX^3)$. Using the unit cost and revenue curves (*AR, MR, ATC, AVC,* and *MC*), graphically illustrate the price and output at which short-run profit will be maximized. Indicate on your graph the area which represents the firm's total profits.

5. In Chapter 5 it was shown that a linear, downsloping demand curve is half elastic and half inelastic; that is, the coefficient of price elasticity is greater than one along the top half of the demand curve and less than one along the bottom half. Is it possible for a monopolistically competitive firm which is confronted with a linear, downsloping demand curve to maximize short-run profits at a price and output corresponding to the inelastic portion of the demand curve? Why or why not?

6. Graphically illustrate a situation where the use of sales promotion activity by a monopolistically competitive firm results in a higher price and higher profits. The purpose of sales promotion expenditures is to shift the firm's demand-*AR* function to the right and, at the same time, to make it more steeply sloped (less elastic over the relevant price range). Assuming that a firm achieves this purpose, graphically illustrate the effect this has upon the shape and position of the firm's total revenue function.

7. (a) Under what conditions might a firm in a monopolistically competitive market be attracted to a strategy of striving to be the low-cost producer? What strengths do you see in such a competitive approach? What disadvantages might exist?

   (b) What are the pros and cons of employing a differentiation strategy in a monopolistically competitive market? Cite some of the different ways a firm can try to differentiate its product offering from those of its rivals.

   (c) What are the pros and cons of opting for a focus or specialization type of competitive strategy under conditions of monopolistic competition?

   (d) Explain why there is room for different firms to pursue different types of competitive strategies in a monopolistically competitive market.

12

HOW MARKETS FUNCTION
The many models of oligopoly

In this chapter we shift the spotlight from "competition among the many" to "competition among the few." Far and away the most prominent and economically important examples of competition among the few are found in the corporate sector. The list of markets where a *few* very large corporate enterprises supply most of the industry output is a veritable *Who's Who* of American manufacturing. It includes the markets for such goods as aircraft, aluminum, automobiles, alcoholic beverages, appliances, cigarettes, computers, copying machines, copper, farm equipment, flat glass, certain food products, gasoline, locomotives and railroad cars, metal cans, network television, sewing machines, steam engines and turbines, steel, synthetic fibers, telephone equipment, tires, and typewriters. Several geographic areas in the mining, construction, banking, insurance, retailing, and service industries also have just a few firms competing on the supply side of the market. The distinctive feature of *oligopoly* is that a few highly visible and usually well-known firms supply the lion's share of total output in a given market.

Oligopoly conditions often characterize the markets where big corporations operate. However, competition among the few is not limited to the corporate sector. It also arises in markets too small for more than a few firms to exist. For example, the small town with its two or three banks, auto repair shops, dry cleaners, building contractors, doctors, lawyers, accountants, and so on illustrates this situation. In manufacturing, a number of highly specialized tools, component parts, and novelty products have a total market demand (even nationwide) so limited that a few small firms can easily supply the entire output. Hence, conditions of competition among the few can arise where small firms are involved as well as where large corporations are involved. The zone of demarcation between competition among the many and competition among the few, therefore, does not correspond exactly with the zone between big firms and little firms.

Nonetheless, because of the visibility and importance of "big business," the presentation of oligopoly will be oriented to capture the specific facets of competition among large corporations. Small firm-dominated markets exhibiting the characteristics of competition among the few will be given less attention, but it should be emphasized that many of the conclusions we draw about competition among a few large firms will apply to competition among a few small firms.[1]

We begin our examination of the principles of competition among the few with a survey of contemporary models of oligopoly behavior. The assumption that the firm's overriding goal is to maximize profits will be continued; however, we shall relax this assumption in Chapter 14, and examine there the effect of alternative goals upon a firm's behavior.

THE DISTINGUISHING CHARACTERISTICS OF OLIGOPOLY

Oligopoly is synonymous with competition among the few. Markets are said to be oligopolistic whenever a small number of firms supply the dominant share of an industry's total output. In oligopoly, firms are *large* relative to the size of the total market they serve, and in the case of giant corporations they are large not just relatively but absolutely as well. The principal effect of fewness of firms is to give each firm such a prominent market position that its decisions and actions have significant repercussions on rival firms. What one firm does affects the others. If one firm announces a price change, its competitors take quick notice. If one firm brings out a new product or changes the attributes of its product offering or steps up its advertising, rival firms must take note and consider whether and how to respond. As a result, competition becomes highly personalized, with each firm recognizing that its own best course of action depends on the strategies its rivals elect. The interdependence among oligopolists extends to all facets of competition: price, sales volume and market share, product differentiation, promotional strategies, innovation, customer service policies, acquisitions and mergers, or whatever. Since rival firms may have numerous alternative courses of action,

---

[1] Recasting the traditional theory of oligopoly to focus on corporate enterprise has much to recommend it. Generalizing oligopoly theory to the point where it applies to both small, single-product firms and large, multiproduct enterprises forces one to exclude the rich institutional detail which supplies powerful understanding of the behavior of large corporations under conditions of corporate capitalism. Such an exclusion is a serious disadvantage when one is trying to explain the functioning of markets dominated by the presence of large corporations. It is very difficult to construct satisfactory models of business behavior which describe equally well the behavior of small proprietorships and the behavior of large managerial firms. After all, the behavior of a hardware store functioning as an oligopolistic firm in a small community differs in several important respects from IBM's behavior in the oligopolistic computer market. Thus, while orienting the presentation of oligopoly theory to capture specific facets of competition among market giants may suffer slightly from a lack of generality, this weakness is more than offset by the extra insight into the economics of corporate capitalism. The approach here is also strong pedagogically because it allows for a strong focus on the application of oligopoly theory to readily visible firms and industries.

anticipating their actions and reactions introduces a new and exceedingly complex dimension to the firm's decision process. But trying to anticipate the competitive response of rival firms is an exercise no oligopolist can afford to neglect, for the probability is high that a change in a firm's competitive tactics will elicit prompt and pointed reactions from rival firms. The great uncertainty is *how* one's rivals will react. As we shall see shortly, the interdependence and competitive interaction among firms is *the key feature* of oligopoly.

An oligopolistic market structure has several other characteristics. To begin with, rivalry among the few may involve either standardized or differentiated products. If the firms in an industry produce a standardized product, the industry is called a *pure oligopoly*. The most common examples of virtually uniform products marketed under conditions of oligopoly include steel, aluminum, lead, copper, cement, rayon, fuel oil, plywood, tin cans, newsprint, explosives, and industrial alcohol. If a few firms dominate the market for a differentiated product, the industry is called a *differentiated oligopoly*. The most visible differentiated oligopolies involve the production of automobiles, toothpaste, cereal, cigarettes, TV sets, electric razors, computers, farm implements, refrigerators, air conditioners, soft drinks, soap, and beer.

Entry into an oligopolistic industry is typically formidable, though by no means impossible. The most pervasive barrier to entry is the presence of substantial economies of scale. In industries where technology is complex, large machine units are used, and sales promotion requirements are substantial, the optimum scale of operation is large. Minimum average costs occur at output rates so large that a firm has to be big to be competitive; firms of lesser size incur unit costs so much higher that the entry of small-scale firms is generally not profitable. Moreover, the fact that existing firms produce well-known, highly advertised products and sell them through established marketing outlets works against the successful entrance of new firms. It is a hazardous undertaking for a relatively new or unknown firm to introduce a new product to compete directly against the brands of firms whose names are known to everyone. Often, entering such an industry entails so sizable a commitment of venture capital that small organizations are effectively foreclosed. The most likely candidates for entry into established oligopolies are other giant enterprises which do have the financial and organizational resources that it takes. This is not, however, an especially common occurrence in *mature* industries because the added production of another large-scale firm tends to increase supply to the point of driving price below average cost for all firms, thereby making the profit prospects for new entrants, large or small, rather dim. But in *young* or *rapidly growing* oligopolies the entry of new firms is fairly commonplace.

Like firms in monopolistic competition, oligopolistic firms, and especially those producing differentiated products, rely upon differences in price, quality, reliability, service, design, new product development, advanced technology, promotional outlays, and overall image to promote their sales and increase their profits. They attempt to create a very strong awareness among consumers of brands and product reputation. Everything that was said in Chapter 11 about the role of product differentiation and promotional outlays applies on an even grander

scale among corporate oligopolists. The dimensions of competition under oligopoly are limited only by the imagination of the firms themselves.

THE MANY MODELS OF OLIGOPOLY BEHAVIOR

In an oligopolistic market structure, there is no nice, neat, clear-cut equilibrium
position toward which all firms tend to move—such as we found in perfect competition and monopolistic competition. Two reasons account for this. One, in
oligopoly a wide variety of materially different competitive circumstances can
and do exist, no one of which is demonstrably more typical than others. Two,
even in a given competitive situation, several different and entirely reasonable
courses of action may be open to firms in selecting a competitive strategy. Just
what firms will decide to do and how their rivals will react is often open-ended.
A number of outcomes is possible, and the end result may vary from case to case.
No single pattern of behavior stands out from the rest or is dominant.

As a consequence, oligopoly theory consists of dozens of models, each de-
picting certain facets of oligopolistic conduct and performance but none telling a
complete story of competition among the few. The range of oligopolistic behavior
is simply too diverse and too complex for one model to cover all the bases at
once. Accordingly, our survey of oligopoly will consist of a series of models, each
portraying a different set of behavior patterns, traits of firms, and competitive
conditions. Taken together, they offer a reasonably accurate survey of the varieties of oligopolistic competition among large corporations. The models in this
chapter focus on profit-maximizing aspects of oligopolistic behavior. In Chapter
14 we complete the picture by presenting models where the goals of an enterprise
deviate from simple profit maximization.

The Kinked Demand Curve Model

One of the key questions which an oligopolistic firm must consider is "How
will rival firms respond if we decide to alter our selling price?" One answer to
this question is contained in the *kinked demand curve model* of oligopoly behavior.[2]

Suppose that three large firms, A, B, and C, are selling their own versions
of an essentially identical product, with each firm having about one-third of the
total market. Suppose, too, that the firms are selling at a common price of P_1
dollars and that at this price Corporation A's sales volume is Q_1 units, as shown
in Fig. 12-1. What will happen now if A independently lowers its selling price to
P_2 dollars? One possibility is for B and C to ignore A's lower price, in which case
A can expect sharply increasing sales, say to Q_2 units, because by underselling

[2] The kinked demand curve model was first advanced by Paul Sweezy in 1939. For a more
extensive discussion of this model, see his article "Demand under Conditions of Oligopoly," *Journal
of Political Economy*, Vol. 47 (August 1939), pp. 568–738. For an evaluation of the model, see George
J. Stigler, "The Kinky Oligopoly Demand Curve and Rigid Prices," *Journal of Political Economy*,
Vol. 55 (October 1947), pp. 432–449.

FIGURE 12-1
The kinked demand curve

firms B and C it will attract many customers away from its higher-priced rivals. A second possibility is for the two rival firms to match A's price cut to prevent A from gaining sales, market share, and profits at their expense. Such a retaliatory move will tend to have the effect of limiting A's gain in sales to its customary share of the increased business which all three firms will tend to realize because of selling at a lower price. In terms of Fig. 12-1, matching price cuts by B and C will hold A's sales down to Q_3 units instead of Q_2 units. Thus, A's demand-*AR* curve for lower prices assumes a position along the path of the solid line extending down from point P_1Q_1 when rivals match the price cut but is positioned along the path of the dashed line when rivals ignore the price cut.

Now, what if A should decide to raise its selling price above P_1 dollars, say to P_3 dollars? Assuming B and C again elect to ignore A's price change, then A would find itself in the lonely position of being the high-priced seller. Firm A might well price itself out of the market and lose so many of its customers to B and C that its resulting sales would be only Q_4 units; the higher price would not cause A to lose all its customers because some buyers may have strong enough preferences for A's brand that they are willing to pay the higher price. Since B and C stand to gain sales and profits at A's expense, there is a strong chance that they will not follow A's price increase to P_3 dollars. But if they should decide to exactly match A's price increase, perhaps because rising costs or other factors motivate them to do so, A's sales will fall less drastically. Why? Firm A will be at no competitive disadvantage with respect to price, and its sales loss is restricted to its share of the decline in marketwide sales which all three firms will incur from selling at a higher price. Referring again to Fig. 12-1, matching price increases by B and C will result in a loss of sales for A from Q_1 to Q_5 units instead of from Q_1 to Q_4 units. Thus, A's expected sales volumes for prices above P_1 will tend to follow the path of the solid line extending up from P_1Q_1 when rivals ignore price increases and will tend to follow the dashed line when rivals follow price increases.

Unless the three firms have specific knowledge to the contrary, they can each expect that *price cuts will be matched* as rivals react to prevent the price-cutter from gaining customers at their expense but that *price increases will be ignored*, because rivals of the price-raising firm will gain the business lost by the price booster. This means that each firm will have a kinked demand curve for its product like the solid line (*DD*) in Fig. 12-1, with the kink occurring at the prevailing price. The competitive situation among the firms is therefore such that an *independent* price increase will cause a drastic decline in a firm's sales volume, while a price cut will result in only modest sales gains. In more technical language, the demand curve for each oligopolist tends to be highly elastic above the ruling price and much less elastic or even inelastic below the going price.

When the firm's demand-*AR* curve is kinked, its corresponding marginal revenue curve consists of two disjointed segments (see Fig. 12-2). The upper segment corresponds to the more elastic portion of the demand-*AR* curve, whereas the lower segment corresponds to the less elastic portion of the demand-*AR* curve. The vertical discontinuity in the *MR* curve is at the prevailing price and output rate.

To see how a kinked demand curve can affect a firm's price and output decision, suppose we look further at Fig. 12-2. Assume that a firm's marginal cost

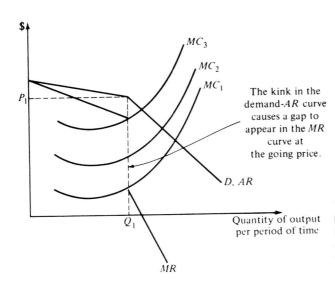

The kink in the demand-*AR* curve causes a gap to appear in the *MR* curve at the going price.

FIGURE 12-2
Profit-maximizing price and output for an oligopolistic firm faced with a kinked demand curve

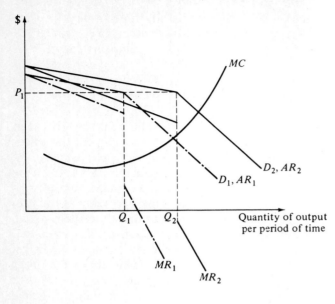

FIGURE 12-3
Effect of demand shifts upon an oligopolist's price and output rate

curve is MC_1. From previous chapters we know that profits are maximized where $MR = MC$. Thus, in Fig. 12-2 the short-run profit-maximizing output rate is Q_1 units, since at outputs less than Q_1 units $MR > MC$ and at outputs more than Q_1 units $MC > MR$. In the event that rising input prices (such as wage increases or increases in raw material prices) push the firm's marginal cost function up to MC_2, a selling price of P_1 dollars and an output of Q_1 units is still the most profitable price-output combination. In fact, the firm's marginal cost function must rise above MC_3 before it would be advantageous to change either price or output. As long as the MC function intersects the discontinuous portion of the MR function, the firm's profit-maximizing point is fixed at the kink in the demand-AR curve.

The same rigidity of prices but not of outputs may occur even though the demand for an oligopolist's product intensifies. In Fig. 12-3, for instance, the firm's demand-AR curve shifts rightward from D_1-AR_1 to D_2-AR_2, generating a new MR function (MR_2). However, the MC function intersects both the old and the new MR functions in the discontinuous segment. Hence, there is no incentive to change price from P_1 dollars, although the profit-maximizing output rate does rise from Q_1 to Q_2 units. So long as the shift in demand is not so large as to result in MC intersecting the new MR curve outside the discontinuous segment, no change in the firm's selling price is called for.

Several important predictions about the price and output strategies of oligopolists can be made when competing firms believe they are confronted with a kinked demand curve:

1.   Oligopolistic firms will refrain from *independently* raising price above the going rate for fear that charging a price higher than rivals will cause a substantial decline in sales, profits, and market share.

2.   Competing oligopolists will refrain from *independently* cutting price below the going level since rivals can be expected to match the price cut promptly, thus wiping out most of the potential the price-cutter would otherwise have for increasing sales, profits, and market share. (An exception can occur, however, when rivals' costs are unequal; then the low-cost producer may well seek to cut price and exploit the cost advantage it enjoys.)

3.   Competition forces rival oligopolists to charge the same or nearly the same prices for their products since the ease with which consumers can switch from one brand to another results in patronage flocking to the low-priced sellers. Firms simply cannot expect to survive by selling essentially the same product at significantly higher prices than rivals. The chief exception to this fundamental principle of competition is where firms have been so successful in differentiating their products and creating strong brand loyalties that their customers are willing to pay higher prices to obtain a "quality" product.

4.   The price and output rate of an oligopolistic firm *will not necessarily* change even though its costs change.

5.   An oligopolist's price will tend to be sticky, but its output rate will tend to be responsive to moderate shifts in demand.

All five predictions are consistent with observed corporate behavior in both pure and differentiated oligopolies. Past studies have shown that prices in corporate oligopolies appear to be generally more stable as compared to prices in perfectly and monopolistically competitive industries. Experience further indicates the prices charged by rival corporations tend to be *identical* where the products are standardized or else weakly differentiated—as in steel, aluminum, cement, newsprint, explosives, cast iron pipe, plywood, bread, and cigarettes. Where their products are strongly differentiated, oligopolists tend to charge prices which are *comparable* (tires, automobiles, household appliances, computers, TV sets). Moreover, executives have been found to evidence a strong conviction that price cuts *will* be matched.[3] Historically, during periods of recession and falling product demand, corporate oligopolies have been characterized by relatively small price declines and relatively large output declines.[4] Thus, the kinked demand curve model does help account for some significant facets of pricing and competitive behavior in the corporate sector.

[3] Actual examples may be found in Harold M. Fleming, *Gasoline Prices and Competition* (New York: Appleton-Century-Crofts, 1966), Chapter 5; R. B. Tennant, "The Cigarette Industry," in *The Structure of American Industry*, 3rd ed., Walter Adams, ed. (New York: The Macmillan Company, 1961), pp. 370–372; the records of the Salk vaccine case *(U.S. v. Eli Lilly et al.)* and the tetracycline case *(F.T.C. v. American Cyanamid et al.)*; and A. D. H. Kaplan, J. B. Dirlam, and R. F. Lanzilotti, *Pricing in Big Business* (Washington, D.C.: The Brookings Institution, 1958), p. 174.

[4] Gardiner C. Means, *Industrial Prices and Their Flexibility* (Washington, D.C.: U.S. Government Printing Office, 1935), p. 8: also, Gardiner C. Means, "The Administered Price Thesis Confirmed," *American Economic Review*, Vol. 62, No. 3 (June 1972), pp. 292–306. In contrast, in industries where firms were more numerous and the characteristics of competition among the many prevailed, price declines were relatively large, and production fell by relatively small amounts.

Nevertheless, the model is not without serious faults. In the first place, alternative explanations for price rigidity can be found. For instance, firms may hesitate to change prices frequently or independently so as not to disrupt customer relations by introducing an element of uncertainty as to future prices. Some firms profess that from the standpoint of buyer psychology it is better to raise prices in large doses and to do so infrequently than to raise prices frequently but by small amounts. Firms selling at "nationally advertised prices" face practical limitations upon the frequency with which prices can be altered. Obviously, recurrent price cuts run the danger that a price war will be triggered since rival firms may elect to teach the price-cutter a lesson by slashing their prices even lower, and all firms end up as losers.[5] In sum, oligopoly prices may be "sticky" because firms are cautious about making price changes *until cost or demand conditions have plainly changed in well-defined ways.*

A second important limitation of the kinked demand curve model is its inability to explain how oligopolists initially arrive at the prevailing prices. The model is much better at explaining why price persists at the kink than how it reached that level or why and how it might change. In other words, the kink is an *ex post* rationalization of price stability rather than an explanation of price determination.

Finally, the assumptions that price cuts will be matched and price increases ignored do not always hold. When a firm lowers its price, competitors need not interpret this to mean that the price-cutter is trying to steal the market. Rivals may take a price reduction to mean that the item has some fault and is not selling well, the item is about to be superceded by a later model, the company is in financial trouble and is trying to improve its sales, or that the company is hoping the whole industry will reduce its prices in the interests of stimulating total demand. Competitors may react differently depending on whether they view the price change as temporary or permanent. Each rival firm's reaction will be based upon what it *thinks* is motivating the company's price cut, and there is ample room for different firms to react differently.

Insofar as price increases are concerned, when rival firms experience similar shifts in cost or demand conditions, the incentive to change price may be generally recognized and mutually advantageous to all concerned. For example, industry-wide price adjustments frequently follow wage and tax increases imposed uniformly upon the firms by collective bargaining and government, respectively. Knowing that its rivals are confronted with comparable cost increases, a firm can boost price with more confidence that rivals will follow suit.[6] Indeed, when the

---

[5] The likelihood of a price war and the extent of damage it may do to the firms concerned tend to be greater (1) the more standardized are their products, (2) the more inelastic is the market demand for their output, and (3) the lower are the marginal costs of production. Industries such as petroleum, tires, and steel have a "high-risk" rating on all three counts.

[6] Linking price increases to wage or tax hikes has the added benefit of making it appear that the blame rests with greedy unions or a revenue-hungry government; such maneuvers help the firm to escape public criticism and charges of profiteering. However, in periods of rapidly inflating costs and prices, more than a few firms appear (to buyers, at least) to have engaged in price pyramiding—raising prices by more than the cost increases incurred in an effort to widen profit margins. Such practices have prompted government price-watchers to jawbone firms into cost-justifying their higher prices.

incentives for a price hike appear generally throughout the industry, the main problem becomes who will be bold enough to raise price first and wise enough to figure out what size price increase will be competitively acceptable. The tendency to ignore price increases also falls by the wayside in an inflationary economy when, after prices have been rising along a wide front for some time, consumers become resigned (however, grudgingly) to higher prices, and firms, both independently and as a group, find it easier to raise prices. In the case where incentives to cut price appear generally throughout the industry, however, there is usually little reluctance to be first to announce a lower price.

Market Share Models of Competitive Strategy

Another approach to price-output determination in oligopoly is based upon the competitive patterns emerging from variations in the market shares and cost of rival firms. Suppose that we start with a fairly simple competitive situation and then gradually introduce more variables.

Equal Market Shares and Equal Costs. Consider an industry comprised of only two firms, A and B, selling identical products, having exactly the same production costs, and dividing the market on a 50–50 basis. These conditions mean that the two firms will have identical demand-*AR, MR, ATC,* and *MC* curves, as shown in Fig. 12-4. With each firm having one-half the industry demand, the demand-*AR* curves of the two firms are located on top of one another, halfway between the vertical axis and the industrywide demand curve at each price. Since profits are maximum at the price and output rate where *MR = MC*, both A and B will be motivated to charge the same price ($P_{A, B}$) and to produce at the same output rate ($Q_{A, B}$). Each firm will earn a short-run economic profit equal to the shaded

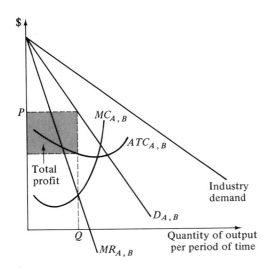

FIGURE 12-4
Competitive outcome for two firms with equal market shares and equal costs

area in Fig. 12-4. The significant point here is that no pricing conflict exists between the two firms because they maximize profits at the same price.

Each firm can be confident that its preferred price-output strategy will be "satisfactory" to its rival rather than provoking some sort of aggressive competitive activity. Why? Because if one firm initiates a price cut to try to gain increased sales, profits, and market share at the expense of the other, then it is merely inviting a costly price war. The other firm will have little option but to retaliate with price cuts of its own to keep from losing customers and absorbing the high costs of idle production capacity. Price cutting will mean both firms receive less for their product. And, if industry demand is price inelastic, then lower prices mean lower revenues will accompany the increased sales, and, clearly, the profits of both firms will drop. This accounts for why oligopolistic firms selling identical or weakly differentiated products are not usually excited by the prospect of price competition and, indeed, shy away from using price cuts as a competitive weapon.

Equal Market Shares and Different Costs.   Suppose, however, that we introduce a cost differential between the two firms, other factors remaining unchanged. Specifically, suppose firm B has a higher MC curve, as indicated in Fig. 12-5. Firm B's higher costs might reflect older, technologically inferior production facilities, higher raw material costs, higher labor costs, higher shipping costs due to an unfavorable geographic location, or managerial inefficiency. Examination of Fig. 12-5 indicates that firm A's profit-maximizing price and output are P_A and Q_A, whereas firm B will prefer P_B and Q_B.

A pricing conflict is immediately apparent. Each firm is worse off, profitwise, as its rival's favored price than at its own, and therefore each will prefer to see its own profit-maximizing price established on an industrywide basis. As long as the two firms continue to sell identical products, buyers are not likely to be as

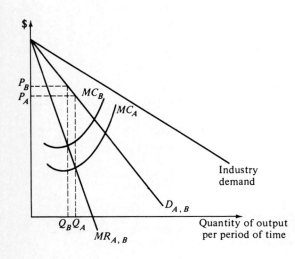

FIGURE 12-5
Competitive outcome for two firms with equal market shares and different costs

willing to buy from B, the higher-priced firm; patronage will flow quickly to the lower-priced seller. Competitive forces thus will soon drive the two firms to sell at the same price. But what price?

One obvious method by which the two firms may resolve their pricing difference is collusion. But collusion carries severe risk. Aside from the fact that price fixing is illegal under the antitrust laws, collusion can prove to be a fragile means of reaching a long-lasting solution.[7] Collusive arrangements of any variety are fragile because they give some firms an incentive to cheat on the other firms. A collusive price tends to be a compromise price and is certain to be higher than would prevail in the absence of collusion (it is most unlikely that the purpose of collusion is to lower the going price). The chances are good, therefore, that one or more firms will be sorely tempted to pick up a lot of profitable new business by discreetly negotiating secret price concessions with individual customers. Experience has shown that this temptation reaches monumental proportions when business slackens and the economy turns sour, although it is better contained when business is good enough to provide the colluding firms with at least a satisfactory sales volume and level of profitability. If and when one or more firms yield to the temptation to cheat, collusion quickly disintegrates. Mutual trust and faithful adherence to the bargain (as well as avoiding detection by the legal authorities) are essential for successful collusion—these are not easy to come by when cheating is lucrative and when more than four or five firms are involved.

A second alternative is for firm A, which prefers the lowest price, to try to force its preferred price upon firm B. Firm A is in a strong position to impose its price preference on B because of its cost advantage and because buyers flock to the low-priced seller. However, firm B is not entirely powerless. Should B's profits be unacceptable if it is forced to sell at A's lower price, then B may seek to intimidate A into a more "reasonable" price by slashing price below P_A and deliberately provoking a mutually unprofitable price war. This may indeed be a very viable option if firm B is a large diversified corporation, since any losses sustained by B from temporarily selling this product at a low price can be offset by profits from the sale of its other products. On the other hand, if firm A is also large or diversified or has ample financial resources, then it may be in as good or better position to weather a price war. So we cannot say for sure whether firm B will be able to "persuade" A to charge a price closer to P_B, whether the reverse will be true, or whether firm B will be forced to meet A's preferred price.

Only one thing is certain: *Whenever rival firms are selling essentially identical products, competitive forces will sooner or later drive them to sell at the same price.* Until this occurs, even a temporary "price equilibrium" cannot exist, simply because firms attempting to sell at prices above their rivals will face erosion of their sales, profits, and market shares and, conceivably, will be driven out of the market entirely over the long term. In general, then, a high-cost firm has the

---

[7] In fairness, it must be acknowledged that some people do not agree with the contention that collusion is either fragile or the exception rather than the rule. There is a body of doctrine which contends that whenever rival firms are few in number, an almost inherent attraction to collusion and monopolistic arrangements exists. The strong propensity to collude was noted almost 200 years ago by Adam Smith: "People of the same trade seldom meet together, even for merriment and diversion, but the conversation ends in a conspiracy against the public, or in some contrivance to raise prices."

following options for bringing about a price accommodation: (1) initiating some form of collusive action to raise price to an "acceptable" level, (2) threatening or actually initiating a price war so as to coerce lower-priced firms into adopting a compromise price somewhere in between the high and low end of the range, (3) revamping its production techniques to bring costs into line with (or even lower than) those of rival firms, (4) shifting into the production of other related items where expected profits are higher, and (5) doing the best it can at the price chosen by the low-cost firms.[8] Very likely options (3) and (5) will prove to be the most viable, short of shifting into some other business (option 4).

Analogous pricing conflicts arise where firms selling differentiated products have cost differences and thus different profit-maximizing prices. However, *the competitive imperative to sell at the same price is not so intense if the products are sufficiently differentiated that buyers can be persuaded to accept modest price differences.* Higher-cost firms preferring to sell at higher prices may be able to compete by successfully using the "ours is better than theirs" theme in promoting their products or by designing more "quality" into their products. To the extent such efforts win over enough buyers, firms are not so strongly compelled by competition to charge a uniform price and may be able to sell at their respective profit-maximizing prices. But if product differentiation results in sizable cost differences between firms and thereby drives a large wedge between their profit-maximizing prices, then a pricing conflict emerges, and competition will prod firms into reaching a more uniform price structure.

Different Market Shares and Equal Costs.   Next, consider the case where firms have identical costs but different market shares. All three panels of Fig. 12-6 illustrate demand situations where firm A has 60% of the total market at each price and firm B has the remaining 40% of the market. Here, the nature of the pricing conflict varies with the shape of the marginal cost function confronting the two firms. In Fig. 12-6(a) the products of the firms are produced under conditions of identically rising marginal costs. Firm A maximizes its profits by producing where $MC_{A,B} = MR_A$; accordingly, A's preferred price is P_A, and its preferred output rate is Q_A units. Firm B's profit-maximizing price and output are P_B and Q_B, respectively. A clash of pricing preferences is apparent, with the firm with the *larger* market share preferring the *higher* price. Other things being equal, this result holds not just for a 60–40 market split but also for any uneven market share split—60–40, 80–20, 55–45, or whatever. It turns out that the more divergent the market shares of the two firms, the greater is the gap between their respective profit-maximizing prices. In this situation, whether the large-share firm will accede to the price preference of the small-share firm, whether the reverse will be true, or whether some compromise price will evolve is open to question.

---

[8] Going out of business and dissolving the firm, while possible, is not a probable alternative—unless it is driven into bankruptcy by its inability to compete. The closing down of a large corporation is a rare event—much more so than in the case of small owner-managed companies. A large corporation normally responds to market adversity and unprofitable products by either withdrawing from the unprofitable market and redeploying its energies and resources into endeavors with higher expected profits or else undertaking a major overhaul of its production and marketing organization, which it believes will increase efficiency, reduce costs, and improve its long-term ability to compete successfully.

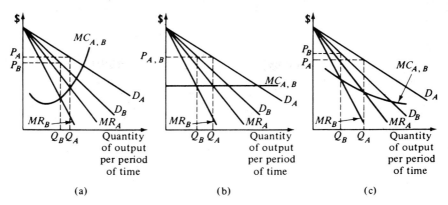

FIGURE 12-6
Competitive outcome for two firms with different market shares and equal costs

It all depends. The firm with the larger market share may try to intimidate the firm with the smaller share and coerce it into accepting a price close to the higher of the profit-maximizing prices. On the other hand, if the small-share firm is in a position to withstand pressure from the large-share firm, then it holds the upper hand, and price equilibrium is likely to be attained near the lower of the two profit-maximizing prices.

In Fig. 12-6(b) both firms produce under conditions of identical and constant marginal costs over the relevant output range. In this instance, firm A will maximize profits by producing Q_A units, and firm B will maximize profits by producing Q_B units. However, the profit-maximizing prices of the firms coincide at $P_{A,B}$. Such a result is not circumstantial but rather is an inherent geometrical trait of linear demand curves with a common vertical intercept. And it holds for a market share split of any combination. Therefore, when oligopolists have identical and constant marginal costs, no conflict over price arises, irrespective of the firms' market shares. Given that (1) cost studies of manufacturing enterprises have shown a fairly widespread tendency for MC to be constant up to 85 to 90% of capacity [refer back to Fig. 8-5(b)], (2) constant returns to scale may prevail as output expands over the long run [see Fig. 8-8(c)], and (3) competition forces rival firms to remain cost-competitive, the lack of a sizable differential among the respective profit-maximizing prices of rival firms as shown in Fig. 12-6(b) may not be uncommon.

Figure 12-6(c) shows declining marginal cost prevailing for both firms over the relevant output range. Here, firm A prefers a lower price (P_A) than firm B prefers (P_B). The firm with the larger market share prefers the lower price because of the lower marginal costs associated with higher outputs. The production economies stemming from larger outputs will likely make firm A less willing to compromise its lower price preference with firm B's preference for a higher price. However, both firms have an incentive to capture larger market shares in order to take advantage of declining costs. This is likely to result in persistent downward pressure on price, and the firm with the largest market share has the advantage of being in the best position to lower prices because of its lower marginal costs. While the antitrust laws will undoubtedly serve to restrain firm A from being so aggressive that antitrust action is invoked, the situation is ripe for one firm to grow larger at the expense of its rivals by initiating bold price cuts. Confronted with this threat, underdog firms may opt to defend or improve their position by making major product improvements (quality, service, convenience, etc.) in an attempt to divert buyers' attention away from price. Their major hope lies not in imitation but in achieving a differential advantage based upon a better product (Zenith's "the quality goes in before the name goes on"), or unconventional distribution outlets (Timex), or stronger appeal to special classes of buyers (Volkswagen), or a superior promotional campaign (Avis's "We're No. 2, We Try Harder"), or personal selling (Avon), or the like.

Different Market Shares and Different Costs.   Normally, product differentiation and varying degrees of product acceptance combine to give firms different market shares. At the same time, production technologies of differing vintage and efficiency and slight variations in wage rates, transportation costs, and raw material prices owing to geographic factors make it likely that corporate rivals will not have *identical* cost structures—though competition will force costs to be *comparable* from firm to firm. When both market shares and unit production costs are variable among rival firms, a wide range of outcomes exist. The small-share firms may have a lower profit-maximizing price, or it may be the large-share firms that have the lower profit-maximizing price. The variation in the preferred prices of rival firms may be wide or narrow. Conceivably, differences in market shares and costs will cancel out, and no material pricing conflict will emerge.

Yet, if price preferences do differ, some means will have to be found to decide what the going price (or band of prices) will be.[9] The ease with which buyers can switch to the lower-priced brands guarantees that this will be so. The existence of a pricing conflict occasionally surfaces in the form of short-term price wars, the uncovering of price-fixing arrangements, and competitive behavior with a cutthroat or predatory intent. More usually, pricing conflicts remain latent and are gradually resolved via intermediate- and long-term adjustments on the part of firms, including cost reduction schemes, plant relocations, technological innovation, increased attempts to achieve product differentiation, improved product design and performance, aggressive advertising and sales promotion tactics, and other forms of nonprice competition. Experience has shown that such adjustments are safer and more reliable forms of conflict resolution than mutually unprofitable price wars and collusive arrangements. In the meantime, firms that are at a competitive price disadvantage will suffer lower profits or even incur losses.

The major conclusion to be drawn from the market share models of competitive behavior is that, despite the difficulties involved, some attempt at reaching

---

[9] An experiment conducted by J. W. Friedman revealed a tendency for price equilibrium to be reached more than 75% of the time. Despite the opportunity to cheat once equilibrium agreements were reached, the agreed-to price was honored in nine out of ten cases. However, Friedman found that a price equilibrium was reached somewhat less often under conditions of different market shares and production costs as opposed to equal market shares and costs. For further details, see "An Experimental Study of Cooperative Duopoly," *Econometrica*, Vol. 35, No. 3–4 (July–October 1967), pp. 379–397.

a mutually acceptable price structure *must* and *will* be made by firms in oligopolistic competition. In either the short or the long run, *oligopolists have no realistic alternative to charging identical or comparable prices for their products, irrespective of market share and cost differences. Mutual interdependence and personalized rivalry quickly teach oligopolists that no firm can price blindly without regard for the prices charged by its rivals.* Thus, while corporate rivals may well decide to experiment with charging different prices, the responses of buyers to the prevailing price pattern will exert a natural and powerful force for a uniform price structure to emerge. Daily experience in the marketplace gives each firm a "feel" for what price it can charge and still compete, thereby making either formal or tacit agreements among firms quite superfluous as a mechanism for reaching an accommodation on the going price structure. Consequently, it is hard to tell from simple observation whether uniform pricing among rival corporations is indicative of competition or conspiracy.

Attempts at resolving differences in the preferred prices of oligopolistic rivals can entail any of several forms and results.[10] From an industrywide standpoint, the most attractive price compromise is *joint profit maximization* whereby firms cooperate (explicitly or implicitly) to arrive at a price (or range of prices) which is perceived to yield the largest possible *collective* profit. But while joint profit maximization may mean that all firms as a group are better off, some firms may feel they are giving up more than they are gaining; in fact, some firms may not fare well at all at the joint profit-maximizing price (because of cost or market share differences). In this case, attempts at joint profit maximization tend to break down because disadvantaged firms have a strong incentive to act independently on their own behalf.

Another basic approach is *independent profit maximization* where one firm (or a small group of firms) is sufficiently powerful and influential to impose its own profit-maximizing price upon rival firms. There are, of course, any number of forms of intermediate or *hybrid profit maximization* wherein via the market process a trial-and-error compromise is reached between pricing together for maximum joint profits and pricing independently for maximum individual profits. Although more disorganized and less purposeful than the previous two forms of price coordination, hybrid profit maximization may nonetheless entail *conscious parallelism* where competing firms, without any communication back and forth whatsoever, come to the realization that aggressive actions (such as price cutting) invite retaliation and, in the end, leave all firms worse off; thus, they adopt common prices and policies implicitly and in concert, with the conviction that their mutual interdependence makes it beneficial for like businesses to be run in like fashion.

Finally, price coordination efforts may lead to *formula pricing* whereby firms, by custom or agreement, adhere to the same rule-of-thumb procedure of

---

[10] For one fascinating version of how uniform prices can be attained without collusion or communication between the firms, see Thomas C. Schelling, *The Strategy of Conflict* (Cambridge, Mass.: Harvard University Press, 1960), Chapters 2 and 3. Schelling develops a theory of focal points in which it is contended that a tendency exists for choices among alternatives to converge on some prominent value intuitively perceived by those concerned. The focal point owes its prominence to precedent, analogy, an obvious split-the-difference situation, habit, institutional idiosyncracies, educated guess, or the like.

adding a "fair" profit margin to "normal" average total costs to reach a common price. All these price-coordinating procedures are observable in actual situations, but none seems to stand out as *the* predominant form of reconciling price differences among competing oligopolists.

However, perhaps the most significant issue in oligopoly pricing is not so much *how* pricing conflicts are resolved as whether the price equilibrium that is established is higher or lower than could reasonably be expected to prevail with some other form of competitive market structure. Or, to put it another way, is oligopoly as "competitive" as perfect or monopolistic competition? Although we shall postpone a final judgment until later, some preliminary generalizations are possible now. If collusive actions on the part of the rival oligopolists are feasible and maintainable, prices are sure to rise above "competitive" levels. However, in the absence of collusion and coercion, the price equilibrium is more likely to approach competitive levels and the lower end of the conflict range due to the upper hand which firms preferring a lower price have over those preferring a higher price.

Price Leadership Models of Competitive Strategy

Competitive pressures notwithstanding, one obvious way for corporate rivals to arrive at a common price is for one firm to seize the initiative and act as price leader for the industry. In such instances, it is customary for the price leader to announce a price change, with the remaining firms accepting the leader's judgment and promptly following suit. Two major forms of price leadership stand out: *dominant firm leadership* and *barometric firm leadership*.

Dominant Firm Price Leadership. Dominant firm price leadership arises when one firm accounts for a much larger market share than any of its rivals. Typically, the dominant firm is a large, vertically integrated corporation whose only rivals consist of numerous "competitive fringe" firms, none of which is able to exert a material influence on the market through its own price-output decisions. On rarer occasions, dominant firm industries are composed of one large firm, several medium-sized firms, and a host of small firms that operate on the competitive fringe of the market.

The assumption underlying the dominant-firm model is that the dominant firm establishes its own preferred price as the going market price and allows the competitive fringe firms to sell all they wish at that price; the dominant firm then produces an amount sufficient to meet the remaining demand at the chosen price. In essence, the competitive fringe firms behave just like perfectly competitive firms. They can sell all they want at the price set by the dominant firm and therefore face a horizontal demand curve at the established price. Each of the fringe firms pegs its output at the rate where $MC = MR$; MR is equal to the price set by the dominant firm since the latter lets the fringe firms sell all they please.

The determination of the dominant firm's optimum price is illustrated in Fig. 12-7. Suppose that the dominant firm believes the total market demand curve to be D_m. Suppose further that it estimates the amount of output which will be supplied by the competitive fringe firms at various alternative prices to be S_{cf} —

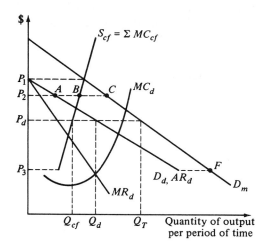

FIGURE 12-7
Outcome for a situation of dominant firm price leadership

found by summing together the portions of the marginal cost curves lying above average variable cost for each fringe producer. Once the dominant firm estimates how much of the total market demand will be served by the competitive fringe, it can calculate how much will be left over for itself. For example, at prices of P_1 and higher, the competitive fringe is willing to supply all the output the market will absorb, leaving no sales potential for the dominant firm. At price P_2 total market demand is P_2C units; of this, the fringe producers would produce P_2B units, leaving BC units for the dominant firm. To locate the dominant firm's demand curve at price P_2 we set point A such that BC units equals P_2A units of output. This procedure can be repeated for other assumed prices. In each case the dominant firm's demand is found by subtracting the fringe firms' output at a given price from the total industry demand at that price. The result is a series of points which, when connected, gives the curve D_d, AR_d. Observe that at prices below P_3 the dominant firm has the entire market to itself; no output will be supplied by the fringe firms when price is less than the minimum average variable cost of every fringe firm. Thus, the dominant firm's demand curve below price P_3 coincides with the segment of the industry demand curve labeled FD_m. The dominant firm's entire demand curve is D_d, AR_d plus the segment FD_m.

The dominant firm determines its profit-maximizing price and output in the customary fashion of equating marginal revenue and marginal cost. The marginal revenue curve corresponding to D_d, AR_d is MR_d, and the dominant firm's marginal cost curve is shown as MC_d. Its profit-maximizing output rate is therefore Q_d units, and its profit-maximizing price is P_d dollars. Total market demand at price P_d is Q_T units. Of this, the dominant firm supplies Q_d units, and the competitive fringe firms supply the remainder ($Q_T - Q_d$), which equals Q_{cf} units in Fig. 12-7.

One of the better current examples of dominant firm price leadership arises in retailing where a nationally known seller (such as K Mart, IBM, or Sears) competes with numerous small, locally owned retail firms carrying comparable products. The local firms must at least meet the prices of the dominant marketer or risk loss of a major portion of their customers. And they must be wary of trying to undercut the dominant firm's prices because if they get far out of line and begin to cut heavily into the leader's business, they can be certain of retaliatory action. The leader may well decide to discipline small maverick competitors by discreetly cutting its prices in those areas where its most aggressive rivals are strongest. A large firm serving many geographically distinct markets can afford to cut prices to the bone in one or a few areas and still make out with the profits it earns elsewhere.[11] The local firm has no such option. Here, the followership of small firms stems from implicit coercion and potential punishment from the dominant firm and not from genuine popularity of the leader's price.

However, it need not at all be the case that the dominant firm prefers a price higher than its smaller rivals and must throw its weight around to keep potential price-cutters in line. The price leader may well have secured its dominant position because of cost economies derived from large-scale production and because its cost advantage produces a profit-maximizing price *below* that of its smaller rivals. In other words, the dominant firm's market position may be due to its greater ability to attract customers by underselling everybody else. In this case, minor firms must match the leader's price or face the prospects of an even smaller market share.

In times past, dominant firm price leaders have included International Harvester in farm implements, U.S. Steel in steel, Firestone in tires, Exxon in petroleum, Alcoa in aluminum, General Motors in autos, Western Electric in telephone equipment, Birdseye in frozen foods, R. J. Reynolds in cigarettes, IBM in computers, Coca-Cola in soft drinks, American Can in tin cans, and International Paper in paper products. However, with the possible exception of IBM, the position of these dominant firms has gradually been eroded by growth and expansion of once-lesser rivals and stronger competitive forces now prevail.

The number of occasions where dominant firms have lost their dominance suggests that a dominant firm market structure may be short-lived and will eventually disintegrate into highly competitive oligopoly. The reasons are straightforward. When the dominant firm's price allows fringe firms to realize positive economic profits, then, over time, they are encouraged to take advantage of scale economies and expand their outputs.[12] Since the dominant firm is a "quantity-follower" and in effect makes room for fringe firm expansion by curbing its own output, the most aggressive smaller firms, via steady expansion, will begin to increase their market shares at the expense of the dominant firm. Sooner or later, the dominant firm will find itself confronted with several emerging rivals of growing influence and power, and its dominant position will be effectively undermined.

---

[11] This is not to say, however, that large firms will readily resort to local price warfare. The profit sacrifices of the dominant firm are likely to be quite large relative to the harm it inflicts upon small rivals. Price wars to discipline minor firms and to teach them the value of cooperation are worthwhile only if the aftermath produces an environment much more conducive to the earning of profits. Otherwise, it may take an inordinately long time to recoup the sacrifices of profit which a price war entails.

[12] The steel industry provides a classic example. In 1901 U.S. Steel controlled 65% of the industry's ingot capacity. As the dominant firm and price leader, it established a high price policy which stimulated the entry and expansion of smaller steel firms. By 1915 U.S. Steel's share of ingot capacity was down to 52%; its share has since eroded to 28% in 1960 and 21% in 1968.

The major point here is that *a dominant firm, if it wishes to retain its position of advantage in the market, must deviate from the pattern of letting smaller firms produce as much as they please. It is "suicide" for it to buy price leadership at the cost of quantity followership.* Instead, to preserve its position a dominant firm must abandon the short-run profit-maximizing behavior portrayed in the dominant firm model in favor of long-run profit maximization. Among other things, this means adjusting its short-run profit-maximizing price downward so as to deter small-firm expansion and the entry of new rivals. The dominant firm must be wary of creating short-run market conditions conducive to the growth of the competitive fringe. Of course, it may be that it has no choice in this regard. The antitrust laws and the shape of the long-run average cost curve may preclude the establishment of a price that will perpetuate the dominant firm's position.[13] But even should this happen (as obviously it has), all is not lost. The dominant firm can continue to outperform its lesser rivals by being the source of new product ideas, cost-saving discoveries, customer service improvements, and new distribution techniques. By maintaining a leadership posture on nonprice variables as well as price, it may succeed in discouraging upstart competitors. The principle that the best defense is a good offense applies well in this situation.

Another competitive approach the dominant firm can use is the multibrand strategy whereby it introduces a number of new product variations with different brand names. Although its own brands may be similar and compete with one another, the effect may still be to lock out room for other firms to bring out their brands. Procter & Gamble has used this technique to good advantage. It has several major brands of soaps (Ivory, Zest, Safeguard, Camay, and Lava) and household cleaners (Top Job, Mr. Clean, Comet, and Spic'n Span); this gives P&G a sizable overall market share and reduces the amount of shelf space available to competitors.

Occasionally, when a dominant firm has grown sluggish, inefficient, and complacent and then is challenged by smaller upstarts, it will try to protect its position by throwing its weight around with suppliers, distributors, or legislators and by initiating maneuvers to discipline firms which have "gotten out of line." For instance, it may threaten major suppliers with backward integration unless they give it more favorable prices than smaller competitors; it may pressure distributors to give less attention to competitor's products; its salesmen may gossip with buyers about how the fringe firms' products are "really inferior"; it may lobby with legislators for the passage of bills that will make it harder for small firms to compete. Alternatively, it may give special under-the-table price discounts to competitors' best customers or launch a massive promotional campaign which small firms cannot hope to match.

Thus, a dominant firm has several options for maintaining its dominance: (1) keeping the industry price low enough to deter entry and to make expansion of fringe firms unattractive, (2) an innovational offensive on nonprice competitive variables, and (3) a defensive strategy involving confrontation, disciplinary action, and persecution of maverick aggressors.

The smaller "underdog" firm's best hope in successfully competing with a

---

[13] A penetrating analysis of dominant firm pricing is found in Dean A. Worcester, "Why 'Dominant Firms' Decline," *Journal of Political Economy*, Vol. 65, No. 4 (August 1957), pp. 338–347.

dominant firm usually lies not in mounting a head-on attack but rather in striking suddenly and with a concentrated effort to catch the dominant firm by surprise. Innovation and product differentiation are an underdog's best strategies. The innovation may involve developing a superior product, cutting costs, finding new ways to distribute goods that offer substantial economies or reach particular buyer segments more effectively, or instituting unique customer services. When one or several of these are coupled with clever advertising, the result will usually suffice to give underdog firms a viable and perhaps increasing market share.

Barometric Price Leadership.   Barometric price leadership exists when there are *several* principal firms (surrounded or not, as the case may be, by a competitive fringe of small firms) and when one of the large firms is not powerful enough to impose its will upon the other consistently. Sometimes one, sometimes another of the principal firms will take the lead in initiating price changes. For instance, in rayon yarn, American Viscose (the largest seller) and DuPont (the second largest seller) have in recent years shared the role of leader. In copper, price leadership has been exercised by all of the Big Three—Anaconda, Kennecott, and Phelps Dodge. Anheuser-Busch and Miller Brewing share the lead in beer. U.S. Steel, Bethlehem, and various foreign steel firms bear the burden of price leadership in steel.

By and large, the barometric price leader appears to do little more than become the first firm to announce new prices consistent with current market conditions. Seldom does the barometric firm possess power to coerce the rest of the industry into accepting its lead, despite the fact that it may aspire to wield such control. In the usual case, the barometric firm acquires its status as leader because of its experience and respect throughout the industry, because other firms may be unable or unwilling to accept the responsibility of continuously appraising industry demand and supply conditions, or because other firms are hesitant to stick their necks out and formally recognize what is already being acknowledged in private. Thus, the barometric firm commands adherence of rivals to its price announcements only to the extent that it has accurately perceived the winds of change in industry demand and supply conditions. But even then, industrywide assent to the price change may not be forthcoming immediately; rival firms often temporize with a wait-and-see strategy for days or weeks or months.

The Significance of Price Leadership.   Successful price leadership has the important effect of eliminating any perceived kink in the demand curves of oligopolists. The firm whose leadership role is widely and consistently accepted can count upon rivals to follow price increases as well as price cuts. However, for barometric firms whose lead is sometimes undermined by failure to follow, the inhibitions of a perceived kink still lurk close by.

The evidence is not clear whether price leadership results in the establishment of a price structure higher than it would otherwise be. On some occasions, price leadership undoubtedly facilitates the raising of prices. Yet, when the price leader is the lowest-cost producer, it may hold price below levels preferred by rival firms. Then, too, price leaders may sometimes be "statesmanlike" and postpone price increases during inflationary periods so as to cooperate with (or not antagonize) inflation-fighting policy-makers and consumer advocates.

Game Theory Models of Competitive Strategy

It should by now be evident that the mutual interdependence which characterizes oligopoly prompts each competitor to consider most carefully the strategies and counterstrategies that rival firms may adopt. With only a few firms in the market, competition pits each firm head-on against rivals whose interests are in direct conflict with its own (much as occurs in chess or poker). In such a situation, *game theory* becomes a useful analytical device for determining a firm's own "best" course of action, the "best" course of action of rival firms, and thereby the optimal solution to the competitive conflict existing between the firms concerned.

Game theory utilizes a convenient device known as a *payoff matrix* to tabulate the alternative strategies being considered by rival firms and the estimated outcomes associated with each possible strategy combination. Use of a payoff matrix has two valuable benefits. First, it forces a firm to give systematic consideration to its own strategic alternatives. Second, it forces a firm to assess how each competitor perceives its own self-interest. From the standpoint of predicting how a rival will react, the latter exercise is most important; it means researching the rival's current financial status, sales trends, the basis of its product's appeal to buyers, its corporate strategy, and so on to try to anticipate what the rival firm's options are and how its management thinks. Does the rival have a set competitive-reaction policy? Can its behavior be predicted accurately on the basis of past actions? Or does the competitor appear to decide afresh on each occasion what sort of competitive response would be in its best interest?

Suppose that two firms, A and B, are faced with a pricing conflict such that firm A's profit-maximizing price is $100 and firm B's profit-maximizing price is $90. For the moment, assume that these are the only two alternative prices under consideration by the two firms. The payoff matrices below summarize the annual expected profit payoffs (in millions of dollars) for each firm:

Firm A's Payoff Matrix

		Firm B's Price Strategies	
		$90	$100
Firm A's Price Strategies	$ 90	$25 m.	$45 m.
	$100	$10 m.	$70 m.

Firm B's Payoff Matrix

		Firm B's Price Strategies	
		$90	$100
Firm A's Price Strategies	$ 90	$50 m.	$10 m.
	$100	$75 m.	$20 m.

Looking first at firm B's payoff matrix, we see that B's expected profits are higher at its preferred price of $90 irrespective of whether A chooses a $90 price or a $100 price. This means that firm B will almost certainly choose a price of $90. Looking next at A's payoff matrix we see that if firm B picks the $90 price, firm A is forced to do likewise because A's profits are $25 million at a $90 price and only $10 million at a $100 price. However, firm A will probably find this price combination unacceptable, since its profits are far below what could be earned if B chose the $100 price. In trying to decide how to "persuade" B to deviate from a $90 price, suppose that firm A considers two additional prices: a "compromise price" of $95 and a "war price" of $70 with payoffs as shown below:

Firm A's Payoff Matrix

		Firm B's Price Strategies			
		$70	$90	$95	$100
Firm A's	$ 70	−$ 7 m.	−$ 4 m.	$ 0	$ 2 m.
Price	$ 90	−$10 m.	$25 m.	$40 m.	$45 m.
Strategies	$ 95	−$25 m.	$20 m.	$50 m.	$65 m.
	$100	−$40 m.	$10 m.	$45 m.	$70 m.

Firm B's Payoff Matrix

		Firm B's Price Strategies			
		$70	$90	$95	$100
Firm A's	$ 70	−$5 m.	−$15 m.	−$25 m.	−$50 m.
Price	$ 90	−$1 m.	$50 m.	$30 m.	$10 m.
Strategies	$ 95	$0	$65 m.	$35 m.	$15 m.
	$100	$2 m.	$75 m.	$40 m.	$20 m.

Inspection of the expanded payoff matrices reveals that by selecting a $70 price firm A can "punish" firm B for choosing a $90 price, though not without inflicting losses upon itself as well. Yet if firm A becomes desperate or if it is better able financially to sustain temporary losses than is firm B, then provoking a price war is firm A's best response to B's choice of a $90 price. Faced with the prospect of a price war if it pursues its own self-interest at the expense of firm A, firm B may be persuaded to adopt the compromise price of $95.[14] Although both firms earn less-than-maximum profits at $95, the compromise price in this instance yields profits which both firms may view as more palatable than warfare.

Consider another situation where two firms, A and B, are forced to choose between prices of $10 and $15. The annual expected profits (in millions of dollars) for each firm appear in matrix form as follows:

Firm A's Payoff Matrix

		Firm B's Price Strategies	
		$10	$15
Firm A's	$10	$100 m.	$180 m.
Price			
Strategies	$15	$ 50 m.	$150 m.

Firm B's Payoff Matrix

		Firm B's Price Strategies	
		$10	$15
Firm A's	$10	$ 80 m.	$ 30 m.
Price			
Strategies	$15	$170 m.	$120 m.

Examination of firm A's payoff matrix indicates that firm A will prefer the $10 price strategy to the $15 price strategy. And if firm A selects the $10 price, firm

[14] J. L. Murphy reported a finding of higher prices and higher profits when rivals faced a threat of flagrant price cutting than when they did not. See his article, "Effects of the Threat of Losses on Duopoly Bargaining," *Quarterly Journal of Economics*, Vol. 80, No. 2 (May 1966), pp. 296–313.

B's best act is to choose the $10 price also. However, the apparent rationality of such a mental process is misleading; both firms will end up with lower profits by selling at a price of $10 than they could earn by selling at a price of $15. This apparent paradox is known in game theory as "the prisoner's dilemma."[15]

The solution to such a dilemma rests with information and experience. Provided that market conditions are reasonably stable, the dynamics of continuous rivalry among oligopolists afford ample opportunity for firms to study one another's behavior and to begin to anticipate one another's moves. It cannot be too long before one or both of the firms recognize the value of information sharing and communication.[16] When this happens, a cooperative pricing strategy may emerge, and competition becomes more a function of nonprice factors.

APPLICATIONS CAPSULE

OLIGOPOLISTIC COMPETITION AND MILITARY STRATEGY

It is not uncommon for oligopolistic firms to describe their competitive environment in military terms. The analogies are, in fact, very close. In both oligopoly and war there are two or more "sides." Each side seeks to increase its welfare, almost always at the expense of the other. Each side can employ various strategies and tactics to expose or injure the other. Each side has an incentive to resort to decoys, surprises, traps, and other maneuvers to gain an advantage.

Military terms are a standard part of competitive rhetoric. Executives speak of "invading" markets, of competitive "attacks," of developing new sales "weapons," of marketing research as "intelligence," of salesmen as "troops in the field," and of using "secret code names" for special projects. Price "wars" break out in a number of industries from time to time; firms have been known to engage in industrial "espionage" and "spying" with respect to one another's plant facilities, trade secrets, patents, and R & D efforts; advertising is referred to as a "propaganda campaign." Business magazines have talked about "border clashes" and "skirmishes" among computer manufacturers, the "escalating arms budgets" of soap and detergent companies, "guerilla warfare" by Purex against the soap firms, the "battle" over market share in countless industries, and of "takeovers" by acquisition-minded enterprises.

Often lying behind this talk is a conscious application of military principles to gain a competitive edge. Six well-known military maxims have particular relevance:

---

[15] The prisoner's dilemma gets its name from a situation where two suspects are taken into custody and interrogated separately. Owing to weaknesses in the evidence against them, each believes they may both go free or at worst receive a light sentence on reduced charges if neither prisoner talks. However, they are both informed by the district attorney that if one confesses and the other does not, the one who fails to confess will receive a particularly stiff penalty and the confessor will receive lenient treatment for turning state's evidence. Hence the dilemma: Should each place confidence in the other's strength of character to not confess, or should each prisoner, not having any assurance about what the other will do, protect only himself and confess?

[16] Several controlled experiments have been conducted which tend to confirm the ability of players to "solve" the prisoners dilemma type of game as they acquire experience and information. See Lester B. Lave, "An Empirical Approach to the Prisoners' Dilemma Game," *Quarterly Journal of Economics*, Vol. 76, No. 3 (August 1962), pp. 424–436; L. E. Fouraker and Sidney Siegel, *Bargaining Behavior* (New York: McGraw-Hill Book Company, 1963), pp. 50–51, 165–166, 199.

1. *Principle of the objective.* Every military operation must be directed toward a clearly defined, decisive, and attainable objective.

2. *Principle of mass.* Superior combat power must be concentrated at the critical time and place for a decisive purpose.

3. *Principle of flexibility of maneuver.* Flexibility must be a major consideration in the selection of plans, although the costs and dangers of flexibility must be weighed against its advantages.

4. *Principle of security.* Security is essential and is achieved by measures taken to prevent surprise, preserve freedom of action, and deny the enemy information.

5. *Principle of the offensive.* The commander must exercise initiative, set the pace, and exploit enemy weaknesses.

6. *Principle of surprise.* Surprise results from striking an enemy at a time, place, and in a manner for which he is not prepared.

Out of these principles emerge a number of strategic and competitive considerations. Should a firm concentrate its competitive resources on rivals' weaknesses or their strengths? Is it more strategically advantageous to defend a position of market strength or to attack a position of market weakness? Does a narrow, concentrated *focus strategy* offer a better chance of success than a broad "hit 'em on all fronts" approach? Does success breed success with respect to winning future competitive struggles? How rapidly should a "victory" be followed up on and the gains consolidated?

However, two major differences between military strategy and business competition should be noted. Whereas wars are fought for "total victory" in which the enemy is either to surrender or be destroyed, competition among firms must be conducted so that no one firm emerges a winner. Winning in oligopolistic competition means becoming a monopolist, and that is a violation of the antitrust laws. In fact, the antitrust apparatus is aimed at *preserving* competition, the philosophy being that competition is properly vigorous and spirited but no one firm is supposed to be so good at competing that it wins the struggle or gains a clear upper hand. Second, whereas "all is fair in love and war," in business competition there are important constraints on the weapon or tactics a firm can use. The antitrust statutes proscribe the rules of "fair competition" and specifically prohibit discriminatory pricing, restraints of trade, predatory tactics to drive another firm out of business, exclusive or tying arrangements, reciprocal dealing, misrepresentations, fraud, deception, and other such attempts to monopolize and/or weaken competitive forces.

Sources: Taken in part from Robert H. Caplan, "Appendix B: Relationships between Principles of Military Strategy and Principles of Business Planning," in *Planning and Control: A Framework for Analysis*, Robert N. Anthony, ed. (Boston: Division of Research, Graduate School of Business Administration, Harvard University, 1965), pp. 148–156, and Philip Kotler, *Marketing Management: Analysis, Planning and Control*, 2nd ed. (Englewood Cliffs, N.J.: Prentice-Hall, Inc., 1972), pp. 250–254.

Using Public Announcements to Accomplish Price Coordination

A firm's public announcements of its future pricing intentions can be a very effective way of communicating indirectly with rival firms and thereby achieving a coordinated pricing move. For example, firm A, believing that a price increase is warranted, may decide to issue a press release announcing a 10% price increase to take effect in 60 days. By timing its announcement well in advance of when it will take effect and by making its announcement public (so that it will likely be reported in the *Wall Street Journal,* leading trade publications, and similar media), a firm is able to test the sentiments of competitors. If other firms respond favorably to this new pricing development by shortly announcing an equal price increase, A can follow through with the price change as planned and be reasonably confident that its competitors will do the same. However, if the rival firms send signals of disagreement by making no announcement or by announcing a lesser increase, A can opt to withdraw its announced price rise or revise it downward to match those of its competitors. Whichever the case, using the media to communicate pricing desires and decisions can be a useful tactic for learning to what extent a price increase will be matched or ignored by firms in the industry.

An alternative way of signaling pleasure or displeasure with an initiating firm's price announcement is by offering one's opinion of the move in interviews with reporters, speeches to securities analysts, and the like. When B disagrees with A's price announcement, it can use speeches and interviews to offer reasons and views about market conditions aimed at persuading A to alter its decision ("if firm A's objective is to make higher profits, its scheduled pricing move is ill-conceived and ill-timed because . . ."). If B's arguments are unsuccessful and if B thinks it is better to go along with A rather than provoke conflict, B can in the due course of events announce it will follow A's lead on price. Using speeches and interviews to communicate reactions and opinions have the advantage of being a less binding commitment to a given course of action because they do not involve making a formal public announcement to actually change or not change one's own price. Doing something later that is inconsistent with opinions expressed earlier does not entail the same loss of credibility that goes with reneging on a prior price commitment.

Publicly announced price changes can also serve as threats. Suppose that firm A announces intentions to lower its prices on certain selected items in its product line. Firm B might elect to retaliate by announcing it is considering lowering its prices significantly below A's. This may suffice to deter A from going through with its intended price cuts because A now has ample indication that B is displeased with the price cuts and is willing to enter into a price war if need be.

On the other hand, a firm can employ public announcements in an effort to minimize the provocation that a price change can have. For instance, firm A may believe that the industry needs to adjust price levels downward. By announcing its intentions ahead of time and taking care to explain its move in terms of evolving market and cost conditions, it can avoid having other firms interpret the price-cutting move as an aggressive bid for increased market share. At the same time, these explanations serve as an attempt to get rival firms to see the logic and benefits of a lower price structure and to follow the move downward.

Quite often, firms comment publicly on their perceptions of current market conditions, what they believe the trend of demand and prices will be in the months and years ahead, how changes in raw material prices and wage rates will affect costs, and so on. Such commentaries can act as a coordinating tactic because

APPLICATIONS CAPSULE

USING THE MEDIA TO SEND "PRICE SIGNALS" TO COMPETITORS— LEGAL OR ILLEGAL?

In 1979 the Federal Trade Commission charged the four major companies selling lead additives for gasoline with using the media to fix prices. The FTC complaint alleged that by publicly announcing their prices and pricing policies the four companies—Ethyl Corporation, DuPont, PPG Industries, and Nalco Chemical—were guilty of "price signaling." The idea behind the FTC complaint was that oligopolistic firms desirous of coordinating any price adjustments do not have to meet secretly in obscure locations to negotiate a common course of action; rather, all one firm has to do is just tell the whole market—buyers and sellers alike—what it plans to do; other sellers will get the message and via a series of press releases back and forth—all duly reported in one place or another—eventually coordinate their actions with just as effective an outcome as if they had formally met face to face and hammered out a collusive scheme.

In addition, the FTC complaint against the four producers alleged other related anticompetitive activities—namely that they sold their additives only at a transportation-cost-included price; that some of the four promised their customers as low a price as anyone got; that all four used a 30-day-advance-notice-of-price-change clause in their contracts with customers; and that they often told the press and *potential* customers of coming price changes. According to the director of the FTC's Bureau of Competition, "the practices amount, under the circumstances in this industry, to a modern form of price-fixing. . . . Sophisticated price signaling usually coupled with other practices, achieves similar results while avoiding traditional agreements." In support of its case, the FTC claimed that there were 18 lockstep price increases in the industry in 4 years (DuPont claimed that this was untrue, saying that there were 18 price changes, including 6 price cuts, and that 9 changes were connected to changes in the price of lead).

The FTC's proposed remedies for the allegedly illegal and collusive price signaling were (1) to forbid firms from making advance announcements on price available to anyone but customers, (2) to forbid the four firms from selling at delivered prices, and (3) to forbid them from promising any customer as low a price as they give to any other customer. In 1978 an assistant attorney general for antitrust in the Justice Department indicated support for the conspiracy theory of price signaling, suggesting that it would be sufficient for a firm to just report its pricing plans to the government; *Forbes* quoted the official as saying "As to whether it's [a public price announcement] a fit subject for general public consideration, I'm not sure."

The FTC case against the sellers of lead additives was not the first of its kind; in 1972 the Justice Department brought a Sherman antitrust case against General Motors and Ford Motor Company for their "coordinated" action to eliminate price discounts on fleet sales of cars; the alleged mechanism for the price-fixing scheme, according to the Justice Department complaint, was that the two companies signaled each other about their positions and coming actions through speeches and press reports. However, both the criminal and civil cases against these two companies were later dismissed by the federal judge and jury because the government failed to prove any conspiracy. Under FTC rules, though, no proof of conspiracy is necessary; it need only be shown that the practice is sufficiently anticompetitive that it is in the public interest to ban sellers from making announcements of pending price changes public.

QUESTIONS FOR DISCUSSION

1. Should firms be allowed to inform their present customers about pending price changes? What about *potential* customers? If firms are restrained from using the media to announce future price adjustments to *potential* customers, then what avenues should they be able to use?

2. Do you see a potential conflict between the FTC's proposed ban on public price announcements and the freedom of speech guarantees provided by the First Amendment to the Constitution?

3. If the FTC wins its case and implements a ban on advance announcements of price increases, then do you think the effect will be procompetitive or anticompetitive? How important is knowledge about firms' prices and pricing policies to an efficient functioning of the market—especially from the standpoint of buyers and from the standpoint of sellers being alert to a need to match the price cuts of rival firms?

4. Suppose that the FTC is able to ban public announcements but permits sellers to inform their customers (by letter or personal contact with salespersons) and then certain customers turn around and "leak" notice of the pending changes either to the press or to rival sellers or to both. What then? Should such leaks also be banned?

Source: Adapted from information reported in "No Body Language, Please," *Forbes*, June 25, 1979, p. 37.

they reveal a firm's assumptions and beliefs about key market factors. As other competitors speak out and make their views known, it can be determined whether firms in the industry are operating under common assumptions and market perceptions. By trading views and opinions back and forth by means of the media and the customer-distributor grapevine, a consensus can be developed about what actions and changes are appropriate.

Are Prices in Oligopolistic Markets "Competitive"?

The foregoing discussion of oligopoly pricing suggests that the selling prices of rivals will gravitate toward a uniform level. No firm can price its product blindly without regard for what competitors are charging. Although competing firms may well have different profit-maximizing prices (owing to variations in demand or costs), they still have no realistic alternative to selling their products at equivalent prices in the case of identical products or at comparable prices in the case of differentiated products. Only when a firm is successful in differentiating its product to a point where its customers are willing to pay a higher price is it feasible for differences in selling price to persist. Otherwise, patronage flocks to the low-priced sellers—an outcome which prompts either the establishment of a more uniform price structure or efforts to achieve more successful product differentiation.

Competitive pressures not withstanding, collusion is obviously one avenue for deciding upon a "mutually acceptable" price structure. Price leadership is another. Conscious parallelism is still another. And price signaling through media channels is yet another. Of these, collusion is the riskiest and most fragile because it is outlawed by the antitrust statutes and because of the temptations to cheat.[17] In addition, the presence of "maverick" firms, periodic adoptions of new corporate strategies (such as a move to accelerate growth of sales or to assume a leadership position in product innovation), the entry or potential entry of strong competition, and frequently changing demand-supply conditions all tend to make successful price collusion tenuous and often unworkable.

In general, price leadership, conscious parallelism, and collusive arrangements are more likely to be found in *mature oligopolies* where established corporations sell similar or identical products under *stable* market conditions. In an *immature oligopoly* where firms are new and inexperienced and/or where oligopolists sell differentiated or rapidly changing products under conditions of variable demand, price competition is more active. This generalization has empirical validity. Despite a long record of price uniformity among standard brands of cigarettes, the introduction of new filter-tip and king-sized cigarettes by the major firms during the 1950's was accompanied by several years of frequent price adjusting before the firms again settled upon a uniform price structure.[18] The tire industry, where eight firms account for almost 90% of total output, is noted for its unstable price structure; not only is pricing complicated by a maze of grades, qualities, and innovations, but retail tire outlets also feature a procession of sales, special discounts, and guarantees on name-brand and private-label tires.[19] Pricing in the steel industry, though generally stable, typically breaks down when vigorous competition from foreign imports or depressed business conditions appear.[20] Other examples pertaining to electrical equipment, railroading, rayon, copper, glassmaking, and petroleum could be cited.[21]

---

[17] Although both formal and informal collusion (spontaneous meetings in smoke-filled backrooms, secret agreements, publicized pricing formulas, predetermined splitting of the market, prearranged output quotas, cooperation through an exclusive selling agency, and so on) is illegal in the United States, in Japan and in many European countries collusive arrangements are permitted and sometimes even encouraged.

The most spectacular example of outright price fixing among American firms occurred in the electrical equipment industry, when General Electric, Westinghouse, and a number of other firms were convicted in 1960 of fixing prices and dividing up the market for circuit breakers, switchgears, and related products. Other examples of *price fixing* have been uncovered in enameled cast iron and vitreous china bathroom and plumbing fixtures, wallboard, bread, cast iron water and gas pipe, cigarettes, cement, steel conduit, and polio vaccine. Companies that in recent years have pleaded "no contest" and declined to fight price-fixing charges include DuPont, Armco Steel, International Paper, Diamond International, PepsiCo, Pet, Sunshine Biscuits, Ciba-Geigy, H. K. Porter, American Cyanamid, Genesco, and Combustion Engineering.

From an international standpoint, the most prominent conspiracy to fix prices has occured not among business firms but among the governments of the oil-producing exporting countries (OPEC) in fixing the world market price of crude oil.

[18] Tennant, "The Cigarette Industry," pp. 376–377.

[19] Kaplan, Dirlam, and Lanzilotti, *Pricing in Big Business*, p. 203.

[20] *Ibid.*, pp. 19–24.

[21] See Harold C. Passer, *The Electrical Manufacturers: 1875–1900* (Cambridge, Mass.: Harvard University Press, 1953), pp. 62, 161–162, 263–264, 352–353; Jesse W. Markham, *Competition in the Rayon Industry* (Cambridge, Mass.: Harvard University Press, 1952), pp. 103, 130, 127–136, 150–153; J. L. McCarthy, "The American Copper Industry: 1947–1955," *Yale Economic Essays*, (Spring 1964), pp. 64–130; G. W. Stocking and M. W. Watkins, *Monopoly and Free Enterprise* (New York: Twentieth Century Fund, 1951), pp. 121–126; and E. P. Learned and Catherine C. Ellsworth, *Gasoline Pricing in Ohio* (Boston: Harvard Business School, 1959), pp. 108, 131–135, 147–149, 237–252.

At the same time, a number of factors act to impede "anticompetitive" price coordination among oligopolistic rivals: (1) the entry into the industry of new firms which ignore current customs and practices or which otherwise disturb established buyer-seller relationships, (2) volatile industry demand conditions, (3) the frequency with which producers' cost functions are modified by technological change and the extent to which these changes make for unequal costs among firms in the industry, (4) different market shares among the firms, (5) extreme product differentiation, (6) frequent product variations, and (7) the emergence of a new industry in which firms have not had time to size up rivals' behavior. Even so, given that one or more of these price-destabilizing factors appear often in almost every oligopolistic market, the fact that rivals still price uniformly is powerful testimony to the imperatives of pricing together—whether for reasons of competition or mutual "cooperation."

MULTIPLANT, MULTIMARKET, AND MULTIPRODUCT ASPECTS OF COMPETITIVE STRATEGY

The preceding models of oligopoly have focused upon the knotty problem of price conflict resolution and the strategies for reaching price equilibrium under conditions of competition among the few. We turn now to matters of internal operations within large corporations and their effects upon price and output decisions. Previously, we have indicated that large corporate enterprises operate many plants, sell in many different markets, and produce many products; in addition, they deal with market uncertainty and changing demand conditions in ways fundamentally different from small firms competing in fragmented or atomistic markets. The time has come to bring these facets into our analysis of corporate enterprise and competitive strategy.

Multiplant Operations and Production Strategy

The market demand for such items as tin cans, storage batteries, biscuits and crackers, cement, building materials, dairy products, tires, beer, disposable diapers, apparel, computers, floor coverings, and steel, among others, is far larger than the existing number of firms can accommodate by operating one plant.[22] As a result, firms operate several plants to manufacture the same product. American Can and Continental Can, for instance, manufacture containers in over 100 domestic locations, often at sites very close to major customers. Boise Cascade in a recent year operated 14 pulp and paper mills, 20 lumber mills, 24 plywood plants, 20 composite can plants, 6 envelope plants, 20 corrugated container plants, 2 particle board plants, 6 kitchen cabinet plants, 2 door plants, and 13 manufactured-housing plants. One decision peculiar to the multiplant firm concerns how to allocate the optimum total output of a product among its several plants in order to minimize costs and maximize profits.

---

[22] In contrast, in producing typewriters, soup, sewing machines, photographic equipment, steam turbines, transformers, and locomotives, plants are quite large relative to the size of the total market, and multiplant operations are much less in evidence.

TABLE 12-1 Allocation of Output among Plants

(1) Total Output of the Firm	(2) Marginal Cost, Plant 1	(3) Marginal Cost, Plant 2	(4) Marginal Cost for the Firm	(5) Price	(6) Total Revenue	(7) Marginal Revenue
0				$30	$ 0	
1	$ 3	$8	3	29	29	$29
2	5	8	5	28	56	27
3	7	8	7	27	81	25
4	9	8	8	26	104	23
5	10	8	8	25	125	21
6	11	8	8	24	144	19
7	12	9	8	23	161	17
8	Capacity	Capacity	8	22	176	15
9			8	21	189	13
10			9	20	200	11
11			9	19	209	9
12			10	18	216	7
13			11	17	221	5
14			12	16	224	3

The chances are that the various plants of a particular firm are not only located in different regions but also incorporate different technologies, obtain raw materials and labor inputs at varying prices, and therefore have different cost structures. An illustrative case is indicated in Table 12-1. The firm operates two plants with marginal costs as shown in columns (2) and (3). Inspection of the marginal cost functions of the two plants shows that if the firm wishes to produce three or less units of output it should use plant 1 exclusively, since it has the lowest marginal cost ($3, $5, and $7 compared to $8 for plant 2). However, the fourth through ninth units should definitely be produced in plant 2. Continuing in this fashion, the combined marginal cost curve for the firm can be derived [column (4)]. As usual, profit maximization requires that the firm select the output rate at which the marginal revenue from the last unit sold equals the marginal cost of the last unit produced. This occurs at an output of 11 units and a price of $19; here, the marginal cost of the eleventh unit is $9, and the marginal revenue from selling the eleventh unit is $9.

Given that the optimum total output of the firm is 11 units, how should production of the 11 units be divided between the two plants? The answer is as follows: produce 4 units at plant 1 and 7 units at plant 2. *Production must be allocated among the various plants such that the marginal costs of the last units produced at each plant are equal both to each other and to the value at which the firm's overall marginal cost equals the marginal revenue of the last unit sold.* Unless the marginal costs of the last units produced at each plant are equal, the firm can lower its total production costs for a given output by shifting units of production from the plant where marginal cost is higher to the plant where marginal cost is lower.

In general, then, whenever a firm operates a number of plants to produce a given item, proper application of the profit-maximizing rule involves three sequential steps. Step 1 is to determine the firm's overall marginal cost curve from the marginal cost curves of the various plants. Step 2 is to pinpoint the firm's most profitable output by finding the output rate where overall marginal cost equals marginal revenue. Step 3 is to allocate the profit-maximizing output among the various plants so that the marginal costs of the last units produced at each plant are equal. In mathematical terms, the firm should arrange its production activities so that

$$MR = MC = MC_{P_1} = MC_{P_2} = \cdots = MC_{P_n},$$

where MR is marginal revenue from all sales of the product, MC is the combined marginal cost, and $MC_{P_1}, MC_{P_2}, \ldots, MC_{P_n}$ are the marginal costs of the respective plants which the firm has for producing the item.

The effect of this rule in actual practice is that production activity is concentrated in the most efficient plants and that older, technologically inferior production facilities are used as sparingly as conditions will permit. The newest, most modern plants employing the latest technologies are nearly always operated at or near capacity levels, while older, less efficient plants are relied upon primarily to fill out the balance of the firm's total output and to help fill the firm's need for production capacity in periods of peak demand. In fact, it is partially because a firm's less efficient production facilities are used more intensively at higher output rates that marginal and average costs tend to rise at combined outputs beyond 90% of *total* capacity.

Multimarket Operations and Pricing Strategy

Up until now we have implicitly assumed that a firm sells a given product at a uniform price to all buyers. This is a tolerable first approximation, but many exceptions exist. Firms with big market coverage often sell their products in a variety of geographically separate markets (local, regional, national, and international), and they sell to diverse classes of customers (industrial users, commercial users, household users, large-quantity buyers, small-quantity buyers, regular customers, occasional customers, one-time customers, and so on). They sometimes find it more profitable to sell the same item to different customers at different prices depending on the market they are in and/or to sell to a single customer at different prices depending on the quantity purchased. They may also sell products with different costs at the same price (i.e., airlines serve full-course dinners on some flights but only snacks on others, yet ticket prices are the same; some manufacturers may charge all customers the same delivered price even though the freight costs are less for nearby customers than for distant customers).[23]

---

[23] Such practices are not restricted to business enterprises. Universities, for example, charge the same tuition for a large freshmen class taught by a graduate teaching assistant as they do for a small senior seminar taught by a premier professor.

These types of pricing practices are labeled by economists as *price discrimination*. Price discrimination may be said to occur whenever a particular product is sold at two or more prices; it can take several forms, depending on whether the basis for the different price is the class of customer, the place where it is sold, or the time at which it is sold.

For a firm to employ price discrimination tactics in a profitable fashion, three conditions must be satisfied. First, the firm must face a downsloping demand curve and thus have some discretion in the price or prices it charges buyers of the product. With a horizontal demand curve, the firm has no motive for selling at different prices; in fact, selling at less than the full market price involves a sacrifice of profits. Second, the firm must have easily identifiable groups of customers with different types of demand for the product in question. Put another way, the shape of the demand curve for one class of customers must differ from the shape of the demand curve for another class of customers. Third, the firm must be able to segregate its sales to each group of customers in such a way that customers paying the lower price cannot resell the item to customers paying a higher price; the different groups of customers must, in other words, be sealed off from one another so that resale of the product by one group to another is severely constrained or unprofitable.

Two distinct types of price discrimination serve to highlight the attractiveness of charging different prices for the same product. Consider first the case where the price the customer pays depends on the quantity purchased. Suppose that the individual customer has a demand curve DD', shown in Fig. 12-8. The firm charges a price of P_1 dollars per unit if the customer buys Q_1 or fewer units per period. The firm reduces its price to P_2 dollars per unit on those units purchased in excess of Q_1 but no greater than Q_2 units. For all units purchased in excess of Q_2, the firm charges a price of P_3 dollars. If a customer elects to purchase

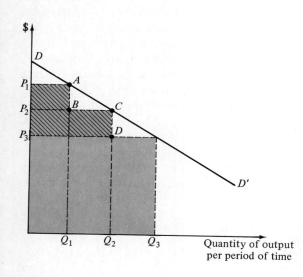

FIGURE 12-8
Revenue effect of pricing according to volume purchased

Quantity of output per period of time

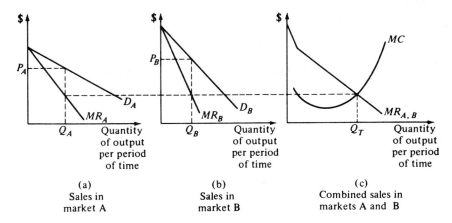

FIGURE 12-9
Two-market price discrimination

a total of Q_3 units in a given time period, the firm's total revenue (the customer's bill) is calculated as follows:

$$TR = P_1(Q_1) + P_2(Q_2 - Q_1) + P_3(Q_3 - Q_2).$$

This amount is equivalent to the shaded area in Fig. 12-8. The benefits to the firm of systematically reducing price as purchases increase should now be apparent. Under a single-price policy, sales of Q_3 units would call for charging a maximum of P_3 dollars per unit. Total revenue would amount to only $(P_3 \cdot Q_3)$ dollars, a figure P_1ABCDP_3 dollars less than obtained with a multiple-price policy.

Figure 12-9 illustrates a situation where a firm charges different prices to customers in two different markets, A and B. The respective demand and marginal revenue curves of the two classes of buyers are given in panels (a) and (b).[24] The firm must decide upon its most profitable combined sales volume, how much should be sold to buyers in each of the two markets, and the price to charge in each market. As usual, the most profitable output rate is where *MR* equals *MC*— however, the appropriate marginal revenue concept in this instance is not *MR* in *each* market *separately* but rather *MR* in both markets *combined*. The marginal revenue curves in markets A and B are summed *horizontally* to obtain combined *MR*, shown as $MR_{A,B}$ in Fig. 12-9(c). The intersection of $MR_{A,B}$ with *MC* in panel (c) defines the most profitable output rate (Q_T) for the firm. Next, a decision must be made as to how much of the total output of Q_T units to sell in market A and how much to sell in market B. The rule for profit maximization in such situations calls for allocating total sales between the markets in such a way that marginal

---

[24] Two-market price discrimination is quite common. Many firms sell their products at one price in international markets and at another price (sometimes higher, sometimes lower) in domestic markets. In the case of products sold nationwide, prices are often higher west than east of the Rocky Mountains. The rates for telephone service are quite different for business use as compared to residential use.

cost at the optimal output equals marginal revenue *in each market*. In terms of our example, the rule requires that

$$MC = MR_{A,B} = MR_A = MR_B.$$

To locate the equalizing value of marginal revenue in the two markets at the profit-maximizing output, a horizontal line is projected from the point in panel (c) where $MC = MR_{A,B}$ to panels (a) and (b) to find where $MC = MR_{A,B} = MR_A = MR_B$. This gives an optimal sales level of Q_A units in market A and Q_B units in market B ($Q_A + Q_B = Q_T$). The profit-maximizing prices, P_A and P_B, are found from the respective demand curves in each market. The firm will necessarily earn higher total profits by engaging in price discrimination than it could earn by following a single-price policy of charging the same price to all buyers. Furthermore, it can be proven mathematically (see Mathematical Capsule 12) that the firm's selling price is always higher in the market where demand is less elastic.

The case of two-market price discrimination is easily expanded to allow for any number of markets. Whenever the firm sells a product in a variety of markets for which demand is different, four steps are required for determining the profit-maximizing prices and outputs in each market. Step 1 is to ascertain the firm's combined marginal revenue curve by horizontally adding together the separate marginal revenue curves in each market. Step 2 is to pinpoint the firm's most profitable combined output rate for all markets by locating the output rate where marginal cost equals combined marginal revenue. Step 3 is to allocate the profit-maximizing output among the various markets in such a way that marginal cost at the optimal output rate is equal to the marginal revenues from the last units sold in each market. In mathematical terms, this means the firm must divide its output such that

$$MC = MR = MR_1 = MR_2 = \cdots = MR_n,$$

where MC is marginal cost, MR is the combined marginal revenue, and MR_1, $MR_2, \ldots, MR_n$ are the marginal revenues for the respective markets in which the product is sold. Step 4 is to determine the prices in each market from the respective market demand curves.

A tremendous variety of price discrimination practices can be found in the real world. Table 12-2 summarizes the principal types, along with examples of each. The information contained in this table provides a useful portrayal of pricing tactics often used by business firms.

Whether price discrimination is good or bad hinges upon subjective evaluations over which reasonable people may disagree. Value judgments inevitably creep into the picture. Most academic economists are suspicious of some forms of price discrimination because, if systematically practiced, they can facilitate adherence to a collusive price structure. In addition, since firms choose freely whether to use a single- or a multiple-price policy, the implication is clear that profits are higher with discrimination than without, thereby causing a redistribution of income from customers to the firm. On the positive side, charging dif-

TABLE 12-2 Types of Price Discrimination and Pricing Strategies

Individual Customer Discrimination

1. *Bargain-every-time.* Each sale is an individually negotiated deal. The classic case is the purchase of new and used cars; other examples include made-to-order sales and objects of art.
2. *Size-up-their-income.* Wealthier customers are charged more than less affluent customers; price is partially a function of income. Standard examples are the pricing of medical, legal, accounting, and management consulting services.
3. *Cut-price-if-you-must.* Departures from list price are made when buyers shop diligently for the best price; sellers grant secret concessions as a last resort. Examples include the transactions between steel firms and auto makers for hot and cold rolled sheet steel and virtually any industrial product sold to skilled purchasing agents who are always on the lookout for a lower price.
4. *Count-the-use.* Price is based upon the level of use, even though unit costs do not vary appreciably with volume. For example, the rental fees on Xerox copying machines are based upon the number of copies made.

Group Discrimination

1. *Promote-new-customers.* New customers are offered "special introductory prices" lower than those paid by established customers in the hopes of enlarging the firm's regular clientele. Record and book clubs and magazine publishers are avid practitioners of this pricing policy.
2. *Forget-the-freight.* All customers are charged the same delivered price, even though transportation costs vary from customer to customer according to the distance located from the production site. Nearby customers are discriminated against in favor of faraway customers. Examples include cement and steel pricing and, additionally, any commodity which is sold at "nationally advertised prices" irrespective of transportation cost differentials.
3. *Get-the-most-from-each-market.* Prices are persistently held higher in markets where competition is weak than where it is strong. Import quotas and tariff barriers allow some firms to charge higher prices in domestic markets than in international markets (sugar, oil, and domestic wool).
4. *Favor-the-big-buyer.* Large purchasers of a commodity are given price cuts perhaps geared to the cost savings derived from large-scale transactions. The large chain discount retailers buy many of their goods at prices below those of the small retailer; firms which purchase in "carload lots" obtain discounts not allowed to purchasers of just a few units.
5. *Skim-the-market.* A product is introduced at a high price within reach mainly of only high-income buyers. Periodically, price is then reduced step by step (and in conjunction with the availability of new production capacity) to allow steady, but gradual, penetration of broader markets. The pricing of TV sets and Polaroid cameras has followed this pattern.

Product Discrimination

1. *Make-them-pay-for-the-label.* Manufacturers sell a relatively homogeneous commodity under different brand names, charging higher prices for the better-known, more prestigious brand names. Automobile tires, paints, articles of clothing, and food products are examples.
2. *Appeal-to-quality.* Products are offered in packages ranging from the budget variety to the super deluxe. Differences in price are *more* than proportional to the differences in cost. Household appliances are an obvious example. Traveling first class as compared to tourist class is another example.
3. *Get-rid-of-the-dogs.* Price concessions in the form of "special" sales are made periodically, or continuously in the bargain department of the retail store, in order to reduce stocks of poorly selling items and to make room for new merchandise. The seemingly perpetual end-of-the-model sales, close-out specials, anniversary sales, and inventory reduction sales serve as good examples.
4. *Switch-them-to-off-peak-periods.* Lower prices are charged for services identical except for time of consumption in order to encourage fuller and more balanced use of capacity. Off-season rates at resorts and the lower rates for long-distance calls made at night and on Sundays are examples.

Sources: This table is a composite of the observations of several writers, including Fritz Machlup, "Characteristics and Types of Price Discrimination," contained in the National Bureau of Economic Research conference report, *Business Concentration and Price Policy* (Princeton, N.J.: Princeton University Press, 1955), pp. 397–435; Joel Dean, *Managerial Economics* (Englewood Cliffs, N.J.: Prentice-Hall, Inc., 1951), pp. 419–424, 503–548; and Ralph Cassady, Jr., "Techniques and Purposes of Price Discrimination," *Journal of Marketing*, Vol. 11, No. 2 (October 1946), pp. 135–150.

ferent prices in different markets affects the total output of the product little if at all.[25] And since customers with more elastic demands (and for whom price is lower) are likely to have incomes lower than the customers comprising the less elastic markets, price discrimination may work to the advantage of the economically weak and therefore produce "socially beneficial" effects. Moreover, situations may exist in which the costs of production cannot be covered unless revenues are enhanced by multiple pricing. Hence, where profits can be increased with multiple pricing, the added profits may be the margin between supplying a good or service and not doing so.[26] Finally, price discrimination can enhance competition by encouraging more price experimentation. Where producers are reluctant to engage in across-the-board price changes, they may be much more willing to test the consequences of a price change in one market or for one class of customers. On balance, the complex crosscurrents at work make it prudent to judge each particular instance of price discrimination on its merits.

Multiproduct Pricing

In the corporate sector almost every firm sells a variety of products. Even so-called single-product firms may have multiple models, sizes, and styles each of which, for pricing purposes, merits treatment as a separate product. In such cases, the single-product models examined to this point are not always adequate for assessing corporate pricing policies and corporate behavior.

Demand Interrelationships. Often, multiproduct enterprises find that the demands for their products are interrelated. They may be substitutes, as with General Motors' Buicks and Oldsmobiles, or they may be complements, as with Betty Crocker cake mixes and cake frostings. These demand interrelationships need to be taken into account in the firm's pricing decision since a change in the price of one has a bearing on the sales of the other. Determining the optimal prices of complementary and substitute products entails a careful assessment of the cross elasticity relationships and how various price combinations affect the combined revenues and profitability of the products in question.

Production Interrelationships. A firm's products can also be interrelated from a production standpoint. For instance, products may be jointly produced in a *fixed ratio* (as with leather hides and beef in a slaughterhouse operation) or in a *variable ratio* (as with gasoline and fuel oil in a crude oil refinery). Products may compete with one another in the sense of being alternatives—a butcher shop has to decide whether to cut beef quarters into roasts or grind it for hamburger; a paper producer must allocate paper pulp between making paperboard boxes and brown paper bags. Still another type of interrelationship arises when products are comple-

---

[25] For a treatment of the output effects of price discrimination, see E. O. Edwards, "The Analysis of Output under Discrimination," *Econometrica*, Vol. 18, No. 2 (April 1950), pp. 163–172, and Joan Robinson, *The Economics of Competition* (London: The Macmillan Company, 1933), pp. 188–195.

[26] George J. Stigler, *The Theory of Price*, 3rd ed. (New York: The Macmillan Company, 1966), pp. 213–214.

MATHEMATICAL CAPSULE 12

THE MATHEMATICS OF PRICE DISCRIMINATION

When a firm sells its product in markets that are economically isolated and when the respective market demand curves confronting the firm are different, the firm maximizes total profit by charging different prices in each market. The conditions for maximizing profits may be derived very simply. For illustrative convenience we shall restrict the analysis to a two-market situation.

Suppose that the firm's total revenue from sales of output in market A is represented as

$$TR_A = f(Q_A),$$

the firm's total revenue from sales of output in market B is represented as

$$TR_B = g(Q_B),$$

and the firm's total costs from combined sales in both markets is represented by

$$TC = h(Q_A + Q_B) = h(Q),$$

where Q is total output no matter in which market specific units are sold. In other words, TC depends on the output rate and not on where the output is sold.

As usual, total profit (π) is equal to total revenue minus total cost:

$$\pi = TR - TC.$$

Substituting into this expression gives

$$\pi = TR_A + TR_B - TC,$$

which can be rewritten as

$$\pi = f(Q_A) + g(Q_B) - h(Q).$$

The profit-maximizing conditions are

$$\frac{\partial \pi}{\partial Q_A} = \frac{\partial f}{\partial Q_A} - \frac{\partial h}{\partial Q} = \frac{df}{dQ_A} - \frac{dh}{dQ} = 0,$$

$$\frac{\partial \pi}{\partial Q_B} = \frac{\partial g}{\partial Q_B} - \frac{\partial h}{\partial Q} = \frac{dg}{dQ_B} - \frac{dh}{dQ} = 0.$$

But, by definition, $df/dQ_A = MR_A$, $dg/dQ_B = MR_B$, and $dh/dQ = MC$. Thus, *profit maximization requires that*

$$MR_A - MC = 0 \quad \text{and} \quad MR_B - MC = 0,$$

which in turn is equivalent to

$$MR_A = MR_B = MC.$$

Now let us prove that the higher of the two profit-maximizing prices is found in the market with the less elastic demand. Let $P = f(Q)$ represent any demand curve, where P is price and Q is the quantity demanded. The total revenue is

$$TR = PQ,$$

and marginal revenue, according to the rule of differential calculus for the derivative of a product of two variables, is

$$MR = \frac{dTR}{dQ} = P + Q\frac{dP}{dQ}.$$

Multiplying the last term of the expression by P/P gives

$$MR = P\left(1 + \frac{Q}{P} \cdot \frac{dP}{dQ}\right).$$

Recalling from our definition of point elasticity that $\epsilon_p = (dQ/dP) \cdot (P/Q)$ and substituting this into the expression, we get

$$MR = P\left(1 + \frac{1}{\epsilon_p}\right).$$

The latter expression can now be used to demonstrate our proof that price is higher in the market where demand is less elastic. From the expression above, it follows that

$$MR_A = P_A\left(1 + \frac{1}{\epsilon_A}\right)$$

$$MR_B = P_B\left(1 + \frac{1}{\epsilon_B}\right).$$

Since at the optimal output $MR_A = MR_B$, then

$$P_A\left(1 + \frac{1}{\epsilon_A}\right) = P_B\left(1 + \frac{1}{\epsilon_B}\right),$$

which can be rewritten as

$$\frac{P_A}{P_B} = \frac{1 + (1/\epsilon_B)}{1 + (1/\epsilon_A)}.$$

Suppose that $\epsilon_A = -4$ and $\epsilon_B = -2$ at the respective profit-maximizing prices of P_A and P_B; then demand is more elastic in market A than in market B. By substituting these values into the last expression, it is clear that $P_A/P_B < 1$ and that $P_B > P_A$. This result is obtained for any values of ϵ_A and ϵ_B such that $|\epsilon_A| > |\epsilon_B|$. Accordingly, two-market price discrimination always leads to a higher price in the market where demand is less elastic with regard to price.

mentary in production, as when one product incorporates wastes generated by the production of another (using wood chips left over from lumber production to make particle board).

The Pricing of Joint Products (Fixed Proportions).   The simplest case of multiproduct pricing concerns that of joint products produced in fixed proportions. Since joint products are produced as a package, their costs can likewise be considered as a package, and one set of cost curves suffices for both—in fact, it may not even be feasible to separate out their individual costs. Figure 12-10 illustrates

FIGURE 12-10
Price of joint products produced in fixed proportions (case 1)

the demand, marginal revenue, and marginal cost functions for two joint products, X and Y. Not surprisingly, the key to optimal pricing of joint products is still the *MR-MC* relationship. The *MC* curve in Fig. 12-10 represents the marginal cost of a 1-unit change in the joint output package of X and Y; MR_x and MR_y have the usual meaning. However, a *vertical summation* of the two *MR* curves is required in order to determine the combined marginal revenue change associated with output changes; the combined-*MR* curve appears as the dashed line MR_{x+y} for outputs up to Q_1 and coincides with MR_y for outputs greater than Q_1, since $MR_x < 0$. The intersection of *MC* and MR_{x+y} defines the short-run profit-maximizing joint output of X and Y; P_x and P_y are the respective profit-maximizing prices and are derived from the respective demand curves for X and Y.

But what if *MC* should happen to intersect MR_{x+y} at a joint output past Q_1 where MR_x is negative? This possibility is shown in Fig. 12-11. When *MC* intersects the combined *MR* at a joint output where the marginal revenue of one of the products (X in this case) is negative, profit maximization requires that the firm still produce where *MC* equals combined-*MR*—at Q_2 in Fig. 12-11. But, whereas the price for Y should be set to correspond with the $MC = MR_{x+y}$ intersection (at P_y), the price for X should be pegged at the demand where $MR_x = 0$, at P_x. Why? Because this is where TR_x is maximum; there is no point in setting a price below P_x in Fig. 12-11 so as to boost sales to Q_2 because TR_x is lower at Q_2 than at Q_1. In other words, to maximize the excess of joint revenues over joint costs, the firm should offer Q_2 units of Y for sale but should restrict sales of product X to Q_1 so as not to drive MR_x into the negative range. This will, of course, mean that the firm will have an excess of X on its hands, $Q_2 - Q_1$

FIGURE 12-11
Pricing of joint products produced in fixed proportions (case 2)

units to be specific. Naturally, some kind of revenue-producing outlet for the excess amount of X should be sought rather than having the surplus of X go to waste. The criterion here should be to dispose of the excess in ways which will not detract from the firm's primary market objective of selling Q_1 units of X at price P_x. However, in the long run, the firm might react to the excess supply of X by (1) advertising or otherwise promoting increased sales of X so as to shift D_x to the right or (2) seeking out technical means of altering the proportions of joint output in ways to increase Y and decrease X—for example, redesign papermaking processes to permit reductions in the output of cheaper grades of paper and increases in the output of finer grades.

The Pricing of Joint Products (Variable Proportions). Generally, multiproduct firms are not hemmed in by the constraints imposed by joint products produced under conditions of rigidly fixed proportions. Some flexibility in proportions is usually possible. When the firm can vary the proportions in which the joint output is produced, optimal pricing quickly becomes complex because of the number of alternative combinations which must be examined. Conceptually, what is required is the construction of a series of *isocost curves* showing the locus of all production combinations which can be produced for a given total cost outlay. Such a series of isocost curves is depicted in Fig. 12-12 as IC_1, IC_2, and IC_3, with total cost outlays of \$400, \$550, and \$800, respectively. The isocost curves are drawn concave to the origin because of the reasonable assumption that it is increasingly difficult to produce successively more units of one product and fewer units of the other, given the inherent limitations on varying the proportions. Next, a set of *isorevenue curves* (IR_1 = \$600, IR_2 = \$800, IR_3 = \$1000) must be derived to

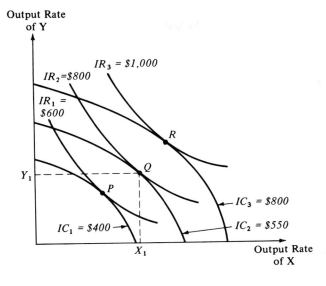

FIGURE 12-12
Price-output determination for joint products produced in variable proportions

show all combinations of the two products which, when sold, result in equivalent total revenues. The isorevenue lines are shown as being convex to the origin, reflecting the typical short-run market necessity of lowering price to sell a larger quantity.

Putting the isocost and isorevenue curves on the same graph defines a set of tangency points (each isocost curve will necessarily be tangent to some isorevenue curve). The tangency points (points P, Q, and R in Fig. 12-12) identify the relevant revenue-cost-output combinations since each point represents the lowest cost of reaching the associated total revenue combination. Which of the tangency points represents profit maximization is determined from a comparison of the revenue-cost-profit results at each point. In Fig. 12-12 profit maximization is at point Q, where total revenue from the sales of X and Y exceeds joint total cost by the greatest amount ($800 − $550 = $250); the profit-maximizing outputs of X and Y are X_1 units and Y_1 units. It can be shown that at point Q the marginal cost of producing each product equals the marginal revenue it generates.

Multiproduct Output with Resource Constraints

The odds are excellent that a multiproduct firm sells in markets of varying competitive intensity, has stronger positions of market advantage for some of its products than for others, and enjoys larger profit margins on some of its products than on others. However, since such a firm's production capacity is limited in the short run and since from time to time combined demand may exceed supply capability, the question arises as to how a multiproduct enterprise should best allocate scarce organizational resources so as to maximize the combined profits from all its products. Consider first the simplified case of a two-product firm operating at capacity and unable to increase the output of both items to their respective profit-maximizing rates.

For a two-product firm to maximize total profits from both products, it must divide its limited resource inputs between them in such a way that it receives an equivalent amount of extra profit from the last unit of input allocated to the production of each one. If the condition is violated, the firm can increase total profits by shifting units of input out of the production of the good where profit is less and into the production of the good where profit is greater. As a numerical illustration, consider a firm which has a total of 300 hours of skilled labor available for producing products A and B. The estimated profits from alternative uses of this labor are as indicated below:

Product A

Hours of Skilled Labor	Total Profit from A	Added Profit
0	0	
		$500
100	$ 500	
		600
200	1100	
		400
300	1500	

Product B

Hours of Skilled Labor	Total Profit from B	Added Profit
0	0	
		$600
100	$ 600	
		500
200	1100	
		400
300	1500	

Suppose that the firm is now using 100 hours of labor to produce A and 200 hours of labor to produce B, with resulting joint profits of $1600 ($500 from A and $1100 from B). Is the firm obtaining maximum total profit from both products? The answer is no. Combined profits can be increased by shifting 100 hours of skilled labor time out of producing B and into producing A. In doing so, the firm gives up $500 of profit from the production and sale of B but gains $600 profit from A—for a net gain of $100 and a joint profit total of $1700. By using 200 of the 300 hours of skilled labor to produce A and only 100 hours to produce B, the firm receives $600 profit from the last hundred units of skilled labor used to produce A and also $600 profit from the last hundred units of skilled labor used to produce B. It has equalized the added profit yields of the last batch of input allocated to each product.

The two-product situation is easily expanded to n number of items and restated as follows: *Limited resource inputs should be allocated among the production of goods G_1, G_2, G_3, . . . , G_n in such a way as to yield an equivalent amount of profit from the last unit of input allocated to the production of each good.* The significance of the profit-maximizing rule for multiproduct enterprises is that the limited availability of resource inputs often makes it more profitable to diversify into new products and to move into new markets *before* attempting to squeeze the last dollar's worth of profit from existing products and product markets. The most efficient and most profitable use of the firm's limited productive capabilities requires that the available resources be channeled into the production of items with high incremental profit prospects and out of items where incremental profits are low. Thus, short-run profit maximization for a multiproduct enterprise does not require that marginal revenue be equated to marginal cost for each and every product the firm produces *unless* the firm has adequate resources and sufficient production capacity in the short run to carry the production of *every* current and potential product to the rate where $MR = MC$. From a total organization viewpoint, price and output decisions require a careful balancing of adjustments among specific product markets to obtain the optimal divisional and companywide profits.[27]

The Competitive Significance of Inventories and Order Backlogs

The market environment in which oligopolists operate is typically characterized by ongoing changes in consumer tastes, incomes, technology, and resource prices. One effect of this is to make it hard for oligopolists to maintain precise equality in MR and MC, owing to the inhibitions against frequent price changes. At the same time, they are likely to find current sales and current production at least slightly out of balance because it is not always practical to continually fine-tune production rates to meet transitory demand conditions. Where technology is complex, with the various stages of the production process systematically connected and carefully harmonized, it takes time to readjust process flows, reschedule production, and realign workloads. More importantly, frequent production rate changes impair mass production efficiencies and cause unit costs to creep upward. As a result, a firm has reason to wait for well-defined demand changes before altering production rates. Instead, it is less disruptive, as well as cheaper, to respond to minor market fluctuations by adjusting inventory levels and/or unfilled order backlogs (promised delivery dates).[28]

This *modus operandi* is of special significance in oligopoly for its provides firms with a practical and readily invoked alternative to price and output changes

---

[27] A study of the pricing of steel products by U.S. Steel provides a good illustration. In the production of steel rails and steel cables, where demand was less elastic and also where competition was less intense, U.S. Steel charged proportionately higher prices and maintained wider profit margins. In the markets for stainless steel, galvanized sheets, and tin plate, where U.S. Steel was in strenuous direct and potential competition with aluminum and lumber as well as other steel producers, prices were more than proportionately lower and profit margins were much narrower. Thus, product market elasticities and profit margin differences were major decision variables in U.S. Steel's divisional price and output strategies. For greater detail, see Kaplan, Dirlam, and Lanzilotti, *Pricing in Big Business*, pp. 172–173.

[28] In perfect competition where the demand curve is horizontal, a firm can be confident of selling its entire output. To a lesser degree, monopolistically competitive firms can also anticipate selling their outputs, though perhaps after some price adjustment. In contrast, oligopolists with their downsloping demand-AR curves are less certain how much they can sell at a given price. The higher a firm's selling price relative to marginal cost, the more profitable it becomes for firms to carry sizable inventories to minimize the risk of losing sales in periods of peak demand. This is especially true for firms with high fixed costs and low variable costs; they clearly prefer building up inventories to shutting plants down. See Edwin S. Mills, *Price, Output, and Inventory Policy* (New York: John Wiley & Sons, Inc., 1962), pp. 82–83, 96, 116–117, and Merton J. Peck, *Competition in the Aluminum Industry* (Cambridge, Mass.: Harvard University Press, 1961), pp. 88, 92.

as a temporary means of balancing sales with production in any given period.[29] Although firms may base their output decision for the next period upon an attempt to bring projected *MR* into equality with expected *MC*, miscalculations will inevitably be made. If too much is produced relative to current sales at the prevailing price, inventory levels can be increased or unfilled order backlogs reduced. If production falls short of sales, inventories can be drawn down or delivery times extended. By keeping close tabs upon changes in new order flows, order backlogs, finished-goods inventory levels, and outgoing shipments, the firm can estimate the current position of its demand curve, the direction in which it is shifting, and expected future demand levels. The role of inventories and unfilled order backlogs is therefore twofold. They serve as *buffers* to compensate for fleeting production-sales imbalances, thereby avoiding zigzag production or price adjustments. And they serve as *feedback signals* to facilitate the coordination of future production with future demand. If and when the signals of changed demand and competitive conditions come through loud and clear, then substantive changes in production rates or prices are, of course, seriously entertained.

Inventory and order backlog adjustments thus introduce another element into accounting for price rigidity in oligopoly. Slight demand changes and market fluctuations can be accommodated via changes in inventories and backlogs—an alternative that is easier and more attractive than spending countless hours trying to make price-output changes that will keep *MR* equal to *MC*. In this sense, short-run profit maximization is abandoned in favor of long-run profit maximization (or some other goal), and price-output revisions are undertaken only in response to clear-cut changes in long-run demand and cost conditions.

Although evidence is limited, it does tend to confirm that oligopolistic corporations rely more heavily upon inventory and order backlog variations in adjusting to demand fluctuations than upon price variations. Professor Markham's study of the rayon industry revealed that only when sales declines persisted for several months was production trimmed back; price changes were resisted even longer.[30] The three major copper producers, Anaconda, Kennecott, and Phelps Dodge, have repeatedly maintained copper prices by building up their inventories in periods of slack demand.[31] In the durable consumer goods and capital goods industries where large corporations predominate, unfilled order backlogs may run in the hundreds of millions or even billions of dollars and inventory-sales ratios fluctuate over a relatively wide range. In contrast, in nondurable goods industries where small entrepreneurial firms are more numerous, order backlogs are virtually nonexistent; inventory levels are kept to a minimum to reduce the risk of perishability and style obsolescence. Additionally, price cuts in response to short-run demand conditions are discernibly more numerous and inventory-sales ratios are lower and less variable.[32]

---

[29] The material that follows draws heavily from the analysis of F. M. Scherer, *Industrial Market Structure and Economic Performance*, 2nd ed. (Boston: Houghton Mifflin Company, 1980), pp. 193–197.

[30] Markham, *Competition in the Rayon Industry*, Chapter 7.

[31] Kaplan, Dirlam and Lanzilotti, *Pricing in Big Business*, pp. 176–181.

[32] Scherer, *Industrial Market Structure*, pp. 195–196.

Other Dimensions of Competitive Strategy in Oligopolistic Markets

Although in some markets much of the competitive focus is on *price*, in many markets (and in oligopoly generally) the main force of competition relates to *nonprice* variables. Except when they have an important cost advantage, rival oligopolists are not prone to build their competitive strategy around successfully undercutting the prices of competitors so as to gain a market advantage. Why? For two reasons. One, a firm which uses price cuts to attract business away from rival firms accomplishes little more than to compel competitors in self-defense to match the lower price—a move which neutralizes the price cut, creates lower prices for all firms in the industry, and limits each firm's sales gain to its customary share of the increased business which flows from a lower industrywide price. Two, a price-cutting strategy is quickly and easily imitated by other firms; as a consequence, it is extremely hard for a firm to gain more than a fleeting competitive edge via price cutting. Mostly, what happens when firms try to use price as a primary competitive weapon is that they expose profit margins and total profits to a good possibility of sharp erosion. Consider a simple example which illustrates why this is so. Suppose a firm is selling an item for $1.00 and that *ATC* is 90 cents. If the firm tries to gain more business by cutting price, say to 95 cents, then its profit margin $(P - ATC)$ is only 5 cents compared to 10 cents before the price cut. For the firm to make as much profit at the 95-cent price as at the $1 price, it will have to sell *twice* as many units as before. In other words it will have to *double* sales just to recoup the loss of profit associated with earning only 5 cents per unit sold instead of 10 cents. True, unit costs are sometimes lowered by the increase in volume, but even if rising volume lowers unit costs to, say, 87 cents, the firm will still have to sell 20% *more* than before in order to earn as much as it was earning at the $1 price. Very likely demand will not be this price elastic $(\varepsilon_p = \%$ change in unit sales volume $\div \%$ change in price $= 20\% \div -5\% = -4)$—especially since rival firms will be sorely tempted to match the price cut in order to avoid losing market share to the price-cutter.

Consequently, unless a firm uses cost-saving technological innovations as the basis for its price-cutting strategy (so as not to impair profit margins with its price cuts) or unless it can realize major cost reductions from an increase in sales volume, using lower prices as a major competitive weapon tends to be an unprofitable strategy. The most attractive strategies for gaining sales, profits, and market share are thus grounded in market variables other than price. Successful nonprice strategies are harder to duplicate and tend to have a longer-lasting effect on strengthening a firm's market position. Hence, there exists a rational tendency among rival oligopolists to channel the main thrust of their head-to-head competitive efforts into forms of product differentiation: product innovation, customer service, quality, performance, convenience of use, terms of credit, styling and design, durability, advertising, and sales promotion. Indeed, billions of dollars are spent each year in efforts to maintain, strengthen, and promote product differentiation.

Aside from using a differentiation strategy, a firm can attempt to insulate itself from aggressive competition from rivals and from adverse cost changes by integrating vertically. Aside from converting a cost center into a profit center, backward vertical integration spares a firm the uncertainty of being dependent on suppliers for crucial inputs, as well as the uncertainty of what prices must be paid for the inputs. By bringing the production of raw materials and critical component goods under its ownership and control, a vertically integrated firm obtains *reliable* sources of supply at *reliable* prices. Such a move may be eminently desirable for defensive reasons if there is a good chance that corporate rivals will do the same or if favorable input prices are essential to preserving the firm's profit margins. Moreover, backward integration *internalizes* such problems as labor disputes, rising production costs, production breakdowns, and delays in scheduled deliveries. A firm is better able to control daily operating problems when they fall within the purview of its own management as opposed to when they are the problems of other managements. Integrating backward has the further advantage of allowing a firm to better coordinate and systematize the many facets of its overall production process, thus deriving efficiency and cost benefits. Holiday Inn, in rapidly expanding its number of inns, diversified into carpeting, candies, furniture items, foodstuffs, and a school of motel management—all of which complemented its main business by helping to supply its 1000-plus inns with basic support services. In general, the reductions of market uncertainty accompanying backward integration are valuable contributors to coordinating and routinizing production cycles, thereby allowing firms (1) to escape the disruptive influence of unreliable suppliers and supply prices, (2) to realize the potential of mass production efficiencies, and (3) to insulate themselves from the repercussions of tactical maneuvers of rival firms.

Also, for reasons of security and uncertainty reduction, firms with mass production capability may be motivated to integrate forward and develop their own distribution outlets. Access to product markets must be dependable. Where ownership of distribution channels is impractical, a firm may employ such strategic devices as franchise systems, leasing provisions, and exclusive-dealing arrangements to give it a stronger foothold in dealing with wholesale and retail outlets. For instance, while most gasoline service stations are independently operated, the facilities may be leased to the operator by the brand-name refiner under terms which permit the refiner to maintain a watchful eye over operating procedures and merchandising policies. In a similar vein, a large manufacturer often grants a wholesaler or a retailer an exclusive franchise to handle its product in a specified geographic area; in return, the franchisee agrees to conform to certain prices, terms of credit, customer service policies, and product guarantees and warranties. Exclusive dealerships are commonly found in tires, automobiles, fast-food firms, articles of clothing, sporting goods, appliances, and paints.

Finally, in order to strengthen its competitive market position a firm may expand its strategy to include a broader set of products related to its original line. For instance, Procter & Gamble took its successful Ivory Soap brand and followed it with Ivory Flakes and Ivory Snow. General Mills spent millions of dollars promoting Betty Crocker cake mixes and then used this brand identification to introduce Betty Crocker pie crusts, rolls, and dehydrated potatoes. The mounting of a competitively strong marketing effort frequently requires each producer to have a full line of products and thereby offer the customer a "total package." Specializing in the production of only one or two items can entail serious market disadvantages, as well as less than full utilization of organizational resources and expertise.

SUMMARY AND CONCLUSIONS

It should be apparent at this juncture that competition among the few has marked differences from competition among the many. Pricing and competition in oligopolistic markets proceed along lines dissimilar to atomistically structured markets. The fundamental economic reason for this is the high degree of mutual interdependence among competing oligopolists. In oligopoly each firm must try to anticipate the actions and reactions of rival firms in formulating and implementing its own competitive strategy. Nowhere is the effect of oligopolistic interdependence more apparent than in pricing. Where oligopolists produce standardized products, a uniform price is imperative, since firms which attempt to charge higher prices will be squeezed out of the market. Where rival oligopolists produce either weakly or strongly differentiated products, prices must be comparable, though not necessarily identical, since customers will tolerate price differentials they believe are justified.

Moreover, differences among rival firms regarding market shares and production costs give rise to divergent price preferences which somehow must be resolved. Whether firms with higher price preferences will win out over firms with lower price preferences or whether the reverse will occur varies with competitive and market circumstances. Collusion to maximize industry profits certainly is one possibility; however, collusive arrangements are fragile and run the risk of discovery and antitrust action. Price leadership is another possibility if follower firms are prone to cooperate with the leader's price judgment. Conscious parallelism, independent profit maximization, and formula pricing are still other possibilities. The ability of oligopolists to cooperate in the establishment of a monopolistic price structure is less likely to be successful the more firms there are in the industry, the larger is the output of competitive fringe firms, the more strongly differentiated and rapidly changing are the products of the firms, the more opportunities there are for secret price concessions, the more unstable are industrywide demand conditions, the more rapid is the rate of technical progress, and the greater is the degree of suspicion and mistrust among company executives. More importantly, the firms which perceive their profits to be greater at lower prices than at higher prices are frequently in a much stronger position to impose their preferences than are the firms which prefer higher prices. Long-run product substitution and the threat of entry by new firms also place a ceiling—and sometimes a low one—upon the ability of oligopolistic producers to peg price at a monopolistic level.

The extremely strong pricing interdependence among oligopolists is further demonstrated by the infrequency with which they change price individually; instead, prices are changed more or less simultaneously. The belief that competitors will ignore price increases and match price cuts and the practice of using inventory and order backlog changes to buffer minor demand fluctuations may combine to produce somewhat more stable prices in the corporate sector than where atomistically competitive conditions prevail.

Because of the imperative to charge comparable prices for their products, oligopolists have little incentive to rely heavily upon price as a strategic device for enhancing their market position in the short run. Rather, the competitive emphasis among oligopolists is aimed at product quality and performance, product innovation, design and styling, customer service, advertising, and other such means of achieving effective product differentiation.

SUGGESTED READINGS

BAIN, J. S., "Price Leaders, Barometers, and Kinks," *The Journal of Business,* Vol. 33, No. 3 (July 1960), pp. 193–203.

BISHOP, R. L., "Duopoly: Collusion or Warfare?" *American Economic Review,* Vol. 50, No. 5 (December 1960), pp. 933–961.

BOULDING, K. E., *Economic Analysis,* Vol. I, 4th ed. (New York: Harper & Row, Publishers, 1966), Chapter 22.

COX, E. P., "A Case for Price Discrimination," *Business Topics,* Vol. 23, No. 3 (Summer 1975), pp. 39–46.

DEWEY, D., *The Theory of Imperfect Competition: A Radical Reconstruction* (New York: Columbia University Press, 1969).

KAPLAN, A. D. H., J. B. DIRLAM, AND R. F. LANZILOTTI, *Pricing in Big Business* (Washington, D.C.: The Brookings Institution, 1958). Chapters 1 and 4.

LEIBENSTEIN, H., "Aspects of the X-Efficiency Theory of the Firm," *Bell Journal of Economics,* Vol. 6, No. 2 (Autumn 1975), pp. 580–606.

SCHERER, F. M., *Industrial Market Structure and Economic Performance,* 2nd ed. (Boston: Houghton Mifflin Company, 1980), Chapters 5–8.

SMITH, R. A., "The Incredible Electrical Conspiracy," *Fortune,* Vol. 63 (April and May 1961), pp. 132ff. (April) and pp. 161ff. (May).

STIGLER, G. J., "The Economics of Information," *Journal of Political Economy,* Vol. 69, No. 3 (June 1961), pp. 213–225.

———, "A Theory of Oligopoly," *Journal of Political Economy,* Vol. 72, No. 1 (February 1964), pp. 44–61.

WESTON, J. F., "Pricing Behavior of Large Firms," *Western Economic Journal,* Vol. 10, No. 1 (March 1972), pp. 1–18.

WORCESTER, D. A., "Why 'Dominant Firms' Decline," *Journal of Political Economy,* Vol. 65, No. 4 (August 1957), pp. 338–347.

PROBLEMS AND QUESTIONS FOR DISCUSSION

1. **(a)** Graphically illustrate the profit-maximizing price and output for an oligopolistic firm confronted with a kinked demand curve and whose production function reflects constant returns to variable input throughout the firm's range of output capability. Indicate on your graph the area which represents total profit.
   (b) Illustrate the effect upon the firm's optimum price and output of a decrease in the demand for its product.

2. Is it possible for an oligopolistic firm confronted with a kinked demand curve situation to increase its short-run profits by increasing its short-run expenditures on sales promotion? Justify your answer by means of a graph.

3. Titanic Corporation and Mammoth Enterprises are only two firms selling robots to perform selected domestic services. The Titanic Corporation believes that the annual demand for its particular style of robot is given by the equation $P_T = 2400 - 0.1Q_T$. Mammoth Enterprises estimates that the annual demand for its robots is given by $P_M = 2400 - 0.1Q_M$. Because their robots have different performance features, the cost of producing Titanic's robot differs from the cost of producing Mammoth's. The estimated total cost function for Titanic's robots is $TC_T = 400,000 + 600Q_T + 0.1Q_T^2$, where TC is in dollars per year and Q_T is Titanic's annual output of robots. The estimated total cost function for Mammoth's robots is $TC_M = 600,000 + 300Q_M + 0.2Q_M^2$, where TC is in dollars per year and Q_M is Mammoth's annual output of robots.
   (a) Determine the profit-maximizing price and output for both Titanic Corporation and Mammoth Enterprises.
   (b) Does a pricing conflict exist between the two firms?
   (c) If you were the president of Titanic Corporation, what price would you pick? Why?
   (d) If you were the president of Mammoth Enterprises, what price would you pick? Why?
   (e) Would a collusive arrangement between the firms be advantageous? Why or why not?

4. Reston Enterprises and Super-Technical Corporation are the only two firms producing pollution-free turbine engines for use in automobiles. Reston engines account for one-third of the total turbine engine sales, while Super-Technical engines account for two-thirds. Except for several minor features, both engines compare favorably in terms of quality, performance, and economy of operation.
   (a) Suppose that both firms produce their engines under conditions of identically rising marginal costs. Will there arise a conflict of price preferences between the two firms, assuming a goal of profit maximization? Illustrate graphically. Venture a judgment as to how the pricing conflict might be resolved in this particular situation. Is some form of collusion a distinct possibility here? Why or why not? Justify your reasoning.
   (b) Suppose that both firms produce their engines under conditions of identical and constant marginal costs. Will there then be a divergence of pricing preferences? Is it unreasonable to expect marginal costs to be constant?
   (c) Suppose that both firms produce their engines under conditions of identically declining marginal costs. Describe and graphically illustrate the nature of the pricing conflict, if any. If you were the president of Super-Technical Corporation, would you be willing to compromise your firm's preferred price with that of Reston Enterprises? Explain. Is some form of collusive arrangement likely to be reached under these circumstances? Why or why not?

5. The American Cracker Corporation has three plants for producing soda crackers. The marginal cost functions of the three plants and the firm's estimated demand-*AR* schedule are as follows:

Daily Output in Cartons	Marginal Cost of Plant 1	Marginal Cost of Plant 2	Marginal Cost of Plant 3	Price of Cartons of Soda Crackers
0	$0.14	$0.13	$0.10	$0.50
1	0.16	0.14	0.13	0.48
2	0.18	0.15	0.16	0.46
3	0.20	0.16	0.16	0.44
4	Capacity	Capacity	Capacity	0.42
5				0.40
6				0.38
7				0.36
8				0.34
9				0.32
10				0.30
11				0.28
12				0.26

Determine the most profitable price and output for the American Cracker Corporation. Then determine the optimal allocation of output among the firm's three plants.

6. Waxy Products, Inc., has discovered a new way to produce a "plastic wax" which, when once applied to hardwood floors, creates a permanent, waterproof, scuffproof, shiny surface absolutely guaranteed under any conditions to last for 12 months. Waxy Products, realizing the vast market potential for its plastic wax, has employed a market research team to estimate the demand function for plastic wax in both national and international markets. The market research team reports that its estimate of plastic wax demand in the domestic market is $P_D = 100 - 5Q_D$ and that its estimate of demand in the international market is $P_F = 60 - 5Q_F$, where P is in dollars and Q is daily sales in cases. Waxy Products estimates that the short-run production function for plastic wax is $Q = 10X$, where $X =$ units of variable input; units of variable input cost $220 each. The president of Waxy Products, not knowing very much about price policy, asks you to assist him in *maximizing* his firm's profits. Calculate for him the *specific* price and output levels that will maximize profits from the sale of plastic wax.

7. **(a)** Do you think competition among oligopolists is more strenuous, less strenuous, or about equally strenuous as compared to competition among perfectly competitive firms? Explain your reasoning.

   (b) Do you think competition among oligopolists is more strenuous or less strenuous as compared to competition among monopolistically competitive firms? Explain your reasoning.

8. Barrett Industries is considering reducing the price of its best-selling grease remover from $20 per gallon to $17. Barrett estimates its production costs of grease remover are $14 per gallon; the per-gallon cost is not thought to vary appreciably with volume, owing to constant returns. Currently, sales are running at an average of 20,000 gallons per month, and Barrett's volume, as well as the industry's as a whole, has remained stable for the past two years. Barrett has two major competitors in the grease remover market: Acme Chemical, which has an estimated market share of 40%, and Montana Products, which has approximately 25% of the market. Barrett's market share is thought to be 30%, and the remaining firms have about 5%. The going market price for grease remover is now $19 to $21 per gallon.

   (a) If Barrett cuts the price to $17, how many more gallons will it have to sell to earn just as much total profit after the price cut as before the price cut? What percentage gain in sales volume does this represent?

   (b) What would the value of the short-run price elasticity of demand have to be for the proposed price cut to be profitable for Barrett?

(c) Would you recommend that Barrett go ahead with the proposed price cut? Why or why not?

(d) Would your answer be different if the market for grease remover were expanding rapidly? If demand were viewed as being highly elastic and major cost reductions could be achieved if volume could be increased? Explain.

9. **(a)** What conditions would strongly attract an oligopolist to use price-cutting as a weapon to gain sales and market share at the expense of rival firms?

(b) What conditions argue for oligopolists to employ a differentiation type of competitive strategy?

(c) Would an oligopolist be inclined to pursue a focus or specialist type of competitive strategy? Under what circumstances?

13

HOW MARKETS FUNCTION
The case of monopoly

On rare occasions one firm is the sole supplier of a product in a given market area. Such a market situation is called *pure monopoly*. Strictly speaking, pure monopoly can exist only when there are no *close* substitutes for the product of the single seller. Not only can there be no rival firms producing the same product, but there can be no firms producing products varying in only minor ways. The pure monopolist's product must be clearly and substantially different. Thus, a monopolist faces no direct competition from rival firms and, as a consequence, has significant market power. In terms of market structure, monopoly is the extreme opposite of perfect competition.

Real-world examples of pure monopoly are few and far between. Firms in the business of providing electricity, natural gas, local telephone communications, cable TV service, and certain transportation services approach the position of pure monopoly. In years past, conditions approximating pure monopoly prevailed in the production of aluminum, nickel, magnesium, molybdenum, shoe machinery, and railroad passenger cars with sleeping accommodations. More recently, the companies which have held positions of market dominance approaching monopoly are General Motors (with a diesel locomotive market share averaging 77% between 1956 and 1971); IBM (with market shares of 72 to 82% in mainframe computers during the 1960s and early 1970s); AT&T's Western Electric division (with about 85% of the market for telephone equipment in the United States up until the early 1980s); Eastman Kodak (with about 90% of domestic amateur film production and roughly 65% of all film sales); Campbell Soup (with about 85% of canned soup sales); and Xerox (with about 75% of the copier market prior to the expiration of key patents in the 1970s).[1]

One reason for the occurrence of pure monopoly is the presence of pronounced economies of scale. The lowest unit costs and therefore the lowest consumer prices are achievable only when one firm supplies the entire market demand for the product. Substantially higher unit costs at small- or medium-scale outputs effectively bar the entry of new firms, and indeed, consumers are likely to be better off with just one producer from which to buy the product. Thus, although it may be technologically feasible to have two, three, or more firms, it is nevertheless economically inefficient to have more than one. Industries in which this occurs are called *natural monopolies*. In the normal case, natural monopolies are granted exclusive rights by government to serve a particular market or geographical area; in return the firm agrees to submit to government regulation as a measure for preventing abuses of its monopoly power. Public utility firms typify the natural monopoly type of enterprise.

Monopoly can also arise from situations where a firm has a patent on a product or on a low-cost technological process. Such monopolies are perfectly legal and give the inventor/innovator exclusive rights (for a period of 17 years in the United States). Patents can be very important in preventing the entry of competitors, although it is often possible to "invent around" a patent by developing a closely related product or process (as Kodak finally managed to do in coming up with an instant-developing camera film capable of competing head-on with Polaroid's instant film).

Three other sources of monopoly can be noted. One is where a firm obtains a franchise or license to be the exclusive producer/seller for a given geographical area. A second is the rare instance where a firm owns or controls the supply of a key raw material (the most oft-cited instance of this is the pre-World War II control that Aluminum Company of America had over bauxite—a key input in aluminum production). The third is where a firm becomes a monopolist by offering a superior product and outcompeting its rivals (as approximated by IBM in computers and Campbell in canned soups).

Despite the fact that pure monopoly is a limited market phenomenon, it is useful to examine the price and output decisions of a pure monopolist. Doing so illuminates the patterns of monopolistic business behavior, irrespective of whether a firm is a pure monopolist.

PRICE-OUTPUT BEHAVIOR FOR A MONOPOLISTIC FIRM

We shall assume for the time being that the pure monopolist's market price and output decisions are unconstrained by government regulation. We shall also continue to asssume that the principal objective of the firm is to maximize profits.

[1] F. M. Scherer, *Industrial Market Structure and Economic Performance*, 2nd ed. (Boston: Houghton Mifflin Company, 1980), p. 67.

The key difference between the market situation confronting a pure monopolist and that confronting other enterprises is that the firm's demand-*AR* curve
coincides with the industry demand curve. The firm is the industry. Being the
only seller of an item for which there is no close substitute allows a monopoly
firm great discretion in setting its prices. It is in a better position to be a *price-
maker* than any other firm. However, the demand for the product of a monopolist
is still subject to the law of demand—more units can be sold at lower prices than
at higher prices, so the monopolist's demand-*AR* curve is downsloping, as shown
in Fig. 13-1. Unless there is a shift in conditions on the demand side of the market,
a monopolist cannot raise price without losing sales, and it cannot gain sales
without reducing its price.

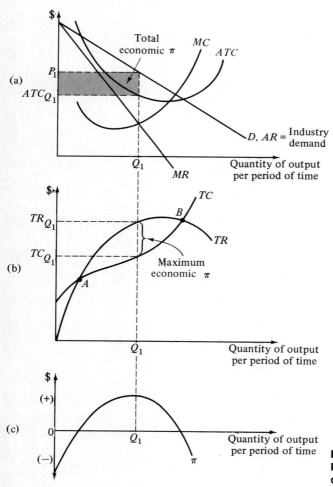

FIGURE 13-1
Profit-maximizing price and
output of a pure monopolist

Suppose that the cost structure of the monopolist is given by the *ATC* and *MC* curves in Fig. 13-1(a) and by the corresponding *TC* curve in Fig. 13-1(b). What, then, are the monopolist's optimal price and output levels?

Profit Maximization: The Total Cost–Total Revenue Approach

A monopolist, like any other firm, maximizes short-run profits at the output where total revenue exceeds total cost by the greatest amount. Given the *TR* and *TC* functions in Fig. 13-1(b), the monopolist will be able to earn an economic profit at any output rate between points *A* and *B*; but short-run profits will be maximum at an output of Q_1 units, where the vertical distance between *TR* and *TC* is the greatest. Geometrically, *TR* exceeds *TC* by the greatest amount at the output rate where a tangent to the *TC* curve has the same slope and is parallel to a tangent to the *TR* function. The total profit function in Fig. 13-1(c) is derived by subtracting *TC* from *TR* at each output rate. Logic dictates that the peak of the total profit function correspond to an output rate of Q_1 where *TR* exceeds *TC* by the largest amount.

Profit Maximization: The Unit Cost–Unit Revenue Approach

On a unit cost and unit revenue basis, short-run profits are maximized at the output rate where *MC* = *MR* and where marginal profit (*M*π) equals zero. The reasoning is precisely the same as in the case of firms operating in other types of markets. As long as an additional unit of output adds more to the firm's revenues than it does to the firm's costs, profit on that unit will be positive and total profits will be increased (or losses decreased) by producing and selling the unit. Alternatively, when *MR* exceeds *MC* and *M*π is positive, total profits can be increased (or losses decreased) by increasing output. In Fig. 13-1(a) short-run profits are maximum at an output of Q_1 units—where the marginal cost curve intersects the marginal revenue curve. Observe that this output rate coincides with the value of Q_1 in Fig. 13-1(b). At Q_1, the tangents to *TR* and *TC* have identical slopes. Since the slope of *TC* equals *MC* and the slope of *TR* equals *MR*, *MR* must equal *MC* at exactly the output where *TR* exceeds *TC* by the greatest amount.

The highest price that the monopolist can charge and still sell Q_1 units is P_1 dollars. The profit-maximizing price corresponds to the point on the demand–*AR* curve associated with the output at which *MC* = *MR* and short-run total profit equals $(P_1 - ATC_{Q_1})Q_1$, or the shaded area in Fig. 13-1(a). At outputs smaller than Q_1 units, *MR* exceeds *MC* and larger outputs up to Q_1 will add more to total revenue than to total costs; accordingly, total profit will rise. At an output rate beyond Q_1, *MC* exceeds *MR* and additional sales cause total costs to rise faster than total revenue, thereby decreasing total profit.

APPLICATIONS CAPSULE

THE MONOPOLY POWER OF BRAND NAMES AND TRADEMARKS: THE CASE OF THE PHARMACEUTICAL INDUSTRY

The pharmaceutical industry offers a dramatic example of how firms can exploit brand names and trademarks to their fullest. Even though patented drugs occupy center stage in the prescription drug industry (in 1974 no more than 15 to 20 of the 200 most frequently prescribed drugs were available from more than one supplier), trademarks and brand names are very valuable to manufacturers who market a drug that either cannot be patented or, if patented, has been so freely licensed as to allow considerable penetration of the competitive barrier of the patent itself.

Just how valuable brand names and trademarks can be is suggested by the findings of a governmental task force on prescription drugs. The task force reported that Squibb's Noctec brand of chloral hydrate (an unpatentable drug because it had been used medicinally as a sedative for a century) had better than a 50% market share even though the wholesale price of Noctec ran 3 to 4 times the prices of the same generic product offered by reliable small firms. The market for meprobamate (a freely licensed patented drug) was dominated by American Home Products' Equanil brand and Carter-Wallace's Miltown and Meprospan brands; the three brands accounted for nearly 80% of sales at prices to druggists that were more than double the prices charged by generic suppliers. Ciba's brand of reserpine (Serpasil) outsold generic reserpine by a wide margin, at wholesale prices up to 30 times greater than those charged by some of its competitors.

These are impressive price differentials considering that branded and generic versions of the same drug are nearly always chemically and biologically equivalent—in other words, the only real difference between branded and generic versions is that the former is sold under a registered trademark or brand name, whereas the generic version is sold by chemical name derived from the ingredients it contains. There is no other industry in which sellers gain such a wide market advantage from trademarks. Exxon, for example, despite being the largest corporation in the world and enjoying worldwide brand recognition of its products for years, is rarely able to command more than a 1- to 3-cent-per-gallon premium over the price of unbranded or off-brand gasoline. Procter & Gamble prices its best-selling Crest toothpaste at a level very comparable to other brands of toothpaste. Miller and Budweiser beers, the two market share leaders, sell at "popular prices."

One major explanation for the monopoly power of brands and trademarks in the prescription drug industry is that the physician makes the buying decision for the patient when the prescription is written. As the late Senator Estes Kefauver observed: "He who orders does not buy; he who buys does not order." Most physicians have little knowledge of the prices of different drugs (although almost all are aware that the branded version will cost the patient more than the generic version). This stems from what probably is a distortion of an excellent medical principle: prescribe whatever drug is deemed to be the best therapy for the patient. Given that the major drug companies flood doctors with advertising and promotional literature touting their brands of drugs (and seldom is price a featured item in such literature), it is somewhat understandable that doctors are prone to prescribe according to how familiar and knowledgeable they are about particular brand names.

The pharmacist is usually obligated to fill the prescription exactly as it is written—thus, if the doctor specifies Achrcmycin on the prescription, the druggist must supply American Cyanimid's brand of tetracycline and not the chemically identical products of Pfizer, Bristol, Squibb, or Upjohn. When getting a prescription filled, the average patient may not even know what he or she has purchased apart from the fact that it is a small bottle of yellow capsules; moreover, comparatively few people shop around for the lowest price—even though the most prevalent retail markup on prescriptions is 40% of the retail price (a 67% margin above the wholesale cost to the druggist).

All this combines to give the prescription drug firms an excellent position to reap good profits from trademarks and brand names. Interestingly enough, the basis of the value of trademarks and brand names derives more from the marketing aspects than from the manufacturing aspects. From a manufacturing standpoint, entry into the pharmaceutical industry is not overly difficult. The technical expertise and ability to maintain the high quality requisite for drug manufacturing are well within the reach of small firms. Nor are capital requirements a significant entry barrier (in 1968, 95% of the firms in the drug industry reported assets under $5 million). The key to business success lies not, therefore, in becoming an able producer but rather in achieving a high degree of marketing skill, most notably in the form of making physicians sufficiently aware of and knowledgeable about a firm's products that they will confidently prescribe its particular brand for their patients when the need arises.

Source: Based on information in Walter S. Measday, "The Pharmaceutical Industry," in *The Structure of American Industry*, 5th ed., Walter Adams, ed. (New York: Macmillan Publishing Co., Inc., 1977), pp. 250–284.

Calculating the Profit-Maximizing Output

The mathematics of determining the profit-maximizing price and output for a monopolist is analogous to the calculations for firms in competitive markets. Suppose that the monopolist's demand function is described by the equation $P = 5000 - 17Q$ and its total cost function by the equation $TC = 75,000 + 200Q - 17Q^2 + Q^3$. From the preceding discussion we know that profit is maximized at the output where $MR = MC$; both MR and MC can be obtained from the information given. If the demand function is $P = 5000 - 17Q$, then

$$TR = P \cdot Q = (5000 - 17Q)Q = 5000Q - 17Q^2$$

and

$$MR = \frac{dTR}{dQ} = 5000 - 34Q.$$

The *MC* function, being the first derivative of the *TC* function, is

$$MC = \frac{dTC}{dQ} = 200 - 34Q + 3Q^2$$

Equating *MR* with *MC* gives

$$5000 - 34Q = 200 - 34Q + 3Q^2,$$

which reduces to

$$3Q^2 = 4800.$$

Solving for *Q* yields the two roots $Q = -40$ and $Q = 40$. Since output can never be negative, the profit-maximizing rate of output is 40 units. (As indicated earlier, it can be proved that the larger of the two roots is always the profit-maximizing or loss-minimizing output rate.)

The profit-maximizing price is found by substituting the profit-maximizing output rate into the demand function and solving for *P*. In terms of our example, the profit-maximizing price is

$$P = 5000 - 17Q$$
$$P = 5000 - 17(40)$$
$$P = 5000 - 680$$
$$P = \$4320.$$

Total profit at this price and output can be calculated by subtracting *TC* at 40 units of output from *TR* at 40 units of output; this gives $52,000 per period of time.

LONG-RUN ADJUSTMENTS

In the long run a monopoly firm will tend to alter its scale of operations and the characteristics of its product in whatever ways it perceives will enhance profitability. Increases in demand for the monopolist's product will tend to prompt increases in production capacity—as long as there is a good prospect of larger profits. On the other hand, weak or declining market demand may warrant reductions in plant size and/or closing down inefficient production facilities. In general, the relation between the monopolist's market demand and its long-run average cost curve determines whether and to what extent it should alter plant scale and total production capacity. This same relationship also determines whether a monopolistic seller will find it most profitable to build and operate its production facilities just short of, at, or beyond the minimum point on its *LRAC* curve.

POPULAR MYTHS ABOUT MONOPOLY BEHAVIOR

Thoughtful scrutiny of Fig. 13-1 explodes a number of popular fallacies concerning the price and output behavior of monopolistic firms. A monopolist *does not* "charge the highest price it can get." There are many prices above P_1 in Fig. 13-1(a), but the seller has no incentive to pick them because of the lower profits which they entail.

Second, the demand curve for the monopolistic firm's product is not "inelastic." As discussed in Chapter 5, most demand curves are elastic at the upper end of the price range and inelastic at the lower end; linear demand curves are half elastic and half inelastic. The output that maximizes a monopolistic firm's profits will *always* fall within the elastic range of the demand curve—not the inelastic range. This proposition is quickly demonstrated. Since marginal cost is positive at all outputs, the output at which $MC = MR$ must necessarily correspond to outputs where MR is also positive and marginal revenue is positive only at output rates where the price elasticity of demand is greater than 1.[2]

A third common misconception about monopolistic firms is that they reap exorbitant profits. Weak demand and high costs are no less injurious to the profitability of a monopolist than they are to firms that face the rigors of direct competition. True, a monopolistic firm may be strategically positioned to earn sizable economic profits, but there is no guarantee that this will prove to be the case. It is quite possible for the monopolist's product to have such a weak demand that revenues are not high enough to cover operating costs (as illustrated in Fig. 11-4); alternatively, market demand may be just sufficient to allow only a normal profit (as illustrated in Fig. 11-5).

CONSTRAINTS UPON THE MARKET POWER
OF A MONOPOLISTIC FIRM

Although being the sole producer of a good or service for which there is no close substitute confers a great deal of economic power upon a firm, certain market restraints are nevertheless imposed upon an unregulated monopolist's behavior. Three such restraints deserve comment.

First, blatant, self-serving exercise of monopoly power is restrained by a fear of government intervention and regulation. A monopolistic firm producing what consumers view as a "necessity" will undoubtedly draw bitter outcries from consumers if it fully exploits its short-run profit opportunities. Widespread and persistent public criticism increases the risk of some form of government intervention—whether it be antitrust action, government support of new competitors, or direct regulation (as in the case of natural monopolies). Thus, a monopolist may hold back from charging the full amount of "what the traffic will bear" and curtail its pursuit of short-run profits in order to escape consumer resentment and

---

[2] The relationship between price elasticity, total revenue, and marginal revenue is described in the section "Elasticity and Total Revenue" in Chapter 5.

the likelihood of onerous government regulation—and thereby, perhaps, come closer to long-run profit maximization.

Second, a monopolist may deliberately limit its profits so as not to encourage direct competition. When a monopolistic firm exploits its market power fully and earns large economic profits in the short run, it risks attracting the attention of firms having the financial, technological, and organizational resources to crack the monopolist's entry barriers. The monopolist may also trigger efforts on the part of its customers or on the part of other firms to develop acceptable substitutes. In other words, high monopoly profits activate the forces of *potential competition* from both new firms and new products. This threat is very real. The business landscape is littered with ex-monopolists which have been the victims of emerging competition—Alcoa, American Can, Standard Oil, DuPont, United Shoe Machinery, Ford, International Nickel, Dow Chemical, and Gillette, not to mention the railroads, whose one-time monopoly profits have been reduced by competition from truck carriers and the airlines. Therefore, rather than set price at the level that maximizes short-run profits but invites competition (or regulation), the monopolistic firm may decide to lower price to a level that deters the threat of potential competition and wards off government regulation and antitrust action. Such a pricing practice is called *limit pricing.* The exact level of the limit price depends upon how effectively entry is blocked, the probability of government regulation, and the degree of technological difficulty in developing substitute products. The obvious purpose of limit pricing is to forego short-run profit maximization in favor of enhancing the firm's profits over the long term.

The third restraint upon the exercise of monopoly power is the systematic propensity for *countervailing power* to develop on the buying side of the market.[3] Large customers usually waste little time in attempting to negate the monopoly power of sellers with whom they must deal. Major food packers, for example, have repeatedly threatened to enter into tin-can manufacturing; to avoid the loss of these customers the two major tin can manufacturers have been forced to exercise price restraint. Electric utility firms have from time to time threatened to build nuclear-powered generating facilities to pressure railroad firms into reducing the freight rates on coal shipments to their coal-fired steam-generating facilities. In certain circumstances, therefore, "across-the market" competition may be successful in checking the power of a monopolistic firm and in reducing its price to levels more consistent with competition. Once price is lowered, the monopolistic firm has an incentive to increase output and make its product available to a broader segment of the market.

Taken together, these three restraints lessen the effective market power of monopolists to levels lower than they might otherwise obtain in the short run. True, at a given moment monopolists may possess substantial power to raise price above competitive levels; they may also earn sizable economic profits. But the situation can be short-lived. Monopolists that produce "necessities" and other

---

[3] The theory of countervailing power and its application to the corporate sector were highlighted by John Kenneth Galbraith in his book *American Capitalism: The Theory of Countervailing Power* (Boston: Houghton Mifflin Company, 1952), especially Chapter 9.

essential goods—public utility firms, for example—quickly find their rates regulated and their profits reduced to socially acceptable levels. Over time, technological change regularly undermines the market power of unregulated monopolists. And large buyers forced to do business with monopolistic sellers attempt to neutralize their market power through bargaining and threats of vertical integration.

BILATERAL MONOPOLY: THE SINGLE SELLER VERSUS THE SINGLE BUYER

In bilateral monopoly, a single seller is confronted with a single buyer. The seller has no other outlet for his product and the buyer has no other source. Such conditions are approximated when a particular defense contractor is the only firm in the United States with the technical capability of producing an advanced weapons system for the U.S. government. The question becomes one of analyzing the economics of what happens when monopoly power on the selling side of the market clashes against monopoly power on the buying side of the market.

Suppose that the buyer's demand is described by line D in Fig. 13-2; this demand is the same as the demand for the seller's product, given that a single buyer and a single seller constitute the market. Also suppose that the selling firm's marginal revenue curve is MR_S and its marginal cost curve is MC_S. Assuming

FIGURE 13-2
The economics of bilateral monopoly

that the monopolistic seller could exert its will and preference on the buyer, we could logically predict that the seller would produce Q_S units and charge a price of P_S, since these correspond to the profit-maximizing condition of $MR_S = MC_S$.

However, if the buying firm is able to exert its buying power to maximum advantage, the outcome will be different. Ideally, the single buyer would like to view the seller's marginal cost curve (MC_S) as a supply curve—the logic being that if the single buyer can control the market completely, the monopolistic seller can be forced into the position of a perfectly competitive industry; in this situation the marginal cost curve of the industry is also the industry supply curve (as was described and explained in Fig. 10-5). From the buyer's standpoint, the consequence of viewing MC_S as a supply curve is that it indicates the average cost (AC) to the buyer of purchasing various amounts of output. However, when a buyer is confronted with a rising supply curve, the curve marginal to MC, labeled as MC_B, represents the marginal cost of *buying* an additional unit.

Optimally, the single buyer would purchase additional units as long as the benefit of doing so (given by the buyer's demand curve) exceeds the marginal cost of purchasing the unit. The buyer would like, therefore, to set the purchase level at Q_B—the output at which MC_B intersects the demand curve; the buyer's preferred purchase price would be P_B, which is the lowest price the seller would be willing to accept for Q_B units.

The problem is that the single buyer can no more control the market completely by forcing the seller into the position of a perfectly competitive industry than the single seller can successfully impose its profit-maximizing price and output preference on a single buyer. What, then, is the outcome? Economic analysis provides no definite answer. It is not possible to predict by logical deduction just what terms the buyer and seller will finally agree to in a bilateral monopoly situation. We can say, though, that the range should be between P_B and P_S and between Q_B and Q_S, since neither party has an incentive to settle outside these limits. To a large extent the outcome is a function of (1) which party has the greatest bargaining strength and negotiating skill, (2) how well informed the buyer and seller are about each other, and (3) who aspires most—for whatever reason—to drive a hard bargain. Generally speaking, it is easier for the buyer and seller to agree on quantity than on price.

REGULATING MONOPOLY

In situations where pure monopoly and high degrees of monopoly power exist, government frequently elects to undertake some form of regulation so as to "protect the public interest" from undue economic abuse. Of the various alternatives to regulatory control, two approaches will be discussed here: (1) direct regulation of prices, services rendered, and profitability; and (2) indirect regulation through an "excess profits" tax.

Direct Regulation of Prices and Profits

The first serious attempts at regulating monopolies in the United States involved the attempts of city councils to specify the rates and services of electric,

APPLICATIONS CAPSULE

TO REGULATE OR TO DEREGULATE?

In January 1977, President Ford's Council of Economic Advisors offered the following diagnosis of government regulation in the U.S. economy and added impetus to growing sentiment for deregulating some "monopolistic" industries (Paul MacAvoy, a distinguished economist and expert in the economic aspects of regulation, was the Council member in charge of regulatory issues during most of the year covered by this report):

The Government regulates a substantial part of the economy in an effort to improve economic performance and promote individual welfare. Such regulation has created costs as well as benefits, and some anticipated benefits of regulation have never been realized. Regulation has also been difficult to reform or abandon, even when recognized as counterproductive, because elements of regulation frequently tend to satisfy certain special interests. Historically, some business enterprises have sought to avoid competition, and have sometimes been aided in doing so by regulation; other rules and procedures create vested interests and capital values which reform would endanger.

The motives behind efforts to regulate economic activity have generally been commendable, and the net effect of some Government regulatory activity has been positive. Unfortunately it often turns out that regulatory processes are not capable of achieving their intended goals or have generated greater costs than would result from the original problem. In some instances the problem prompting the adoption of regulation has passed but the regulations remain. In other cases the regulatory process has proved too inflexible to accommodate changes in the economy, and a previously beneficial regulatory activity may become ineffectual or harmful. In each of these instances reform of the regulations would lower the nonproductive use of Government resources and would free private resources for productive tasks. More important, some regulation is harmful as well as wasteful since it distorts the allocation of resources and thus lowers the potential output of the economy. The reform of such regulations would increase efficiency, thus making the economy better able to provide current consumers with goods and services and to ensure growth in output for the future.

A major purpose of regulation is to control prices charged and services rendered in industries considered to be natural monopolies, especially those in the transportation and public utility sectors, in order to prevent firms in these industries from exercising market power. The economic characteristics of these industries are such that it is more efficient for a single firm to supply the entire market. Price regulation is therefore usually accompanied by entry restrictions. Price and entry regulations have been extended, however, beyond the select cases where control of monopoly power justifies their implementation. They have been applied to many industries which seem capable of vigorous and healthy competition under less restrictive regulations: for example, trucking and airlines. In these cases it is appropriate to compare the results of price and entry regulation with the level of price and output that would be realized in a freely operating market.

If a regulated price exceeds the market-determined price, consumers will purchase less and output will be reduced. If a regulated price is below the competitive level, firms will provide less output than they would if they were not regulated. In both cases price and entry controls reduce the production of goods and services in the regulated markets. Resources are then reallocated to alternative uses which are less valuable to consumers. The result, coupled with the administrative costs of imposing and enforcing regulations, is to reduce efficiency and production.

Most regulatory legislation since the mid-1960s affects business activity in much more direct ways and in much greater detail than is true of simple price controls. The Federal Government has intervened in such matters as product quality, producer liability, conditions affecting the health and safety of employees, waste disposal, and equal employment opportunity. Much of this legislation is an attempt to deal with the problem of externalities—real costs or benefits that affect individuals other than those directly involved in a transaction. Economic efficiency requires that prices appropriately reflect the full cost to society of producing each good or service. External costs or benefits must be incorporated into each transaction, or internalized, for efficiency to be achieved. The internalization should be accomplished in the least costly manner. Unfortunately some of the regulations concerning health, safety, and the environment appear to be ineffective, and we bear their costs without enjoying much, if any, corresponding benefit. In other cases the benefits might have been achieved at a smaller sacrifice of other goods and services.

There are costs of extending regulation in a free-market economy that go beyond the direct impact on supply. First, the regulatory process itself uses public and private resources which could be used to produce other, more valuable, goods or services. Second, some regulatory procedures reduce the ability of industry to respond to changing supply and demand conditions and so create bottlenecks in regulated sectors of the economy. For example, the lag in implementing price adjustments to reflect the changing supply or demand conditions confronting public utilities can influence the timing of their investment decisions, causing shortages or excess capacity. Third, regulations which protect existing firms from potential competitors may reduce incentives for technological improvement and innovation. Fourth, the uncertainty introduced by the regulatory process itself will cause resources to be used in unproductive ways. Finally, if price controls lower the expected returns to new capital investment, capital formation will be retarded and the economy will grow more slowly.

Source: Reprinted from *The Economic Report of the President,* January 1977, pp. 146–148.

gas, and trolley companies. The political nature and makeup of city councils often resulted in franchise awards and terms of services becoming immersed in politics—which made the regulatory process a fertile area for corruption and economic mismanagement. Now, most direct regulation is undertaken by regulatory commissions with civil service staffs to investigate and audit the activities of the regulated firms. Every state has a public service commission, elected in some states and appointed in others, which supervises electric power, natural gas, telephone, and public transportation companies. There is, similarly, another set of regulatory commissions at the federal level to oversee interstate industries where monopoly power may exist—railroads, motor carriers, airlines, water carriers, oil pipelines, interstate telephone service, radio and TV broadcasting, communications satellites, interstate transmission of electricity and natural gas, and public utility holding companies are all subject to direct federal regulations.

The typical bread-and-butter issue in direct regulation is "rate-making"—establishing the prices that regulated firms can charge for their products or services. The traditional standard is that regulators should allow firms to charge rates that will cover all allowable operating expenses and yield the firm a "fair return on the fair value" of the capital investment made by the firm's owners.

In theory, rate regulation is supposed to result in lower prices and greater

FIGURE 13-3
Regulating a monopolist's price using the "fair return on fair value" concept

output than would be the case without regulation. The diagrammatics are shown in Fig. 13-3. An unregulated monopolist would prefer a price of P_1 dollars and an output of Q_1 units, thereby maximizing profits where $MR = MC$. However, with regulation, rates are often targeted toward a level such that price equals ATC, where ATC is defined to include a profit equal to a fair return on the company's capital investment; thus, in Fig. 13-3 regulators would aim at establishing a maximum price of P_2, in which case the company's customers would be inclined to purchase Q_2 units.

In applying the "fair return on fair value" concept, the regulatory focus is on (1) the *rate base*, which is defined to reflect the fair value of the capital invested by the company in conducting its business, and (2) the *allowed rate of return* on the rate base. Needless to say, controversy swirls around the definition of both what should be included in the rate base and what a "fair return" is. The search for an appropriate definition of the rate base has narrowed to essentially two measures: (1) the actual historical cost, adjusted for depreciation, of assets in use in the business; and (2) the reproduction value of assets employed (i.e., what it would cost the company to replace its capital assets at current price levels). Each has its pros and cons. Until the 1930s, the reproduction value approach predominated, but since then the original cost (or current depreciated book value) approach has the greatest following.[4] Even so, there still remains much debate over how to calculate the current book value of assets employed (there are no hard

---

[4] One of the current major issues in how the rate base should be defined concerns whether and how the value of construction work in progress should be treated. Some regulatory bodies allow construction work in progress to be included in the rate base, whereas others do not.

and fast rules governing what the "correct" depreciation method is); similarly, there is ample room to argue over what a company should be allowed to count as "legitimate" and "necessary" operating expenses (charitable contributions, advertising, and executives' salaries and expense accounts, for example, tend to provoke heated discussions). Quite often, public utility rate-making becomes mired down in nit-picking, emotionalism, and headline politics, even though the concept of regulation is a simple one of setting reasonable prices and profits.

What frequently gets lost in the debate is a clear concept of the functions a "fair profit" is intended to perform in a regulated environment. Three functions stand out. First and foremost, profit for a regulated company must be viewed as a payment to investors both for the use of their capital and for assuming the risk that attaches to this use. A regulated firm's profitability must be great enough over the long run that it can attract sufficient new capital to finance whatever new facilities are needed to serve its customers efficiently and reliably. A corollary consideration is that a regulated firm is entitled to a degree of profit that will maintain its financial integrity. By this is meant that the profit a firm is allowed to earn should be sufficient to avoid both an erosion of its stock price and a downgrading of its bond and preferred stock ratings. Second, profit performs the incentive function of rewarding excellent service to customers and punishing the opposite; in this sense a regulated firm's profit should not be viewed as a "guaranteed" rate of return but rather as an allowed rate of return under honest, economical, and efficient management. Third, profit serves to redistribute income from the firm's customers to its owners. Here is where standards of fairness enter the picture. How much profit is needed to ensure "fair" compensation of stockholders? How is this counterbalanced by the desirability of ensuring that the rates charged by the regulated firm do not place an "unfair" burden on the ratepayers—particularly when the good or service being supplied is a "necessity" such as electric power, natural gas, or telephone service? Financial theorists take the position that a "fair" rate of return to stockholders is governed by the prevailing rates of return in investments of comparable risk—an amount often judged to be in the range of 10 to 14% after taxes. Economists define a fair profit in opportunity cost terms too, but they may also consider consumers' ability to pay and what it will take to keep the firm in business in the long run.

Controlling Monopoly through Taxation

The other general approach to the social control of monopoly power is indirectly through taxation. Although there are several types of monopoly taxation, the one we shall present and discuss here is a profits tax.[5] The logic and rationale underlying a profits tax is very straightforward: allow the monopolist to set whatever price and output it choses, then tax away whatever resulting amount of profit is deemed "excessive." This could be done in principle by increasing the per-

---

[5] For a very readable discussion of other types of monopoly taxation, see David R. Kamerschen and Lloyd M. Valentine, *Intermediate Microeconomic Theory* (Cincinnati, Ohio: South-Western Publishing Company, 1977), pp. 371–374.

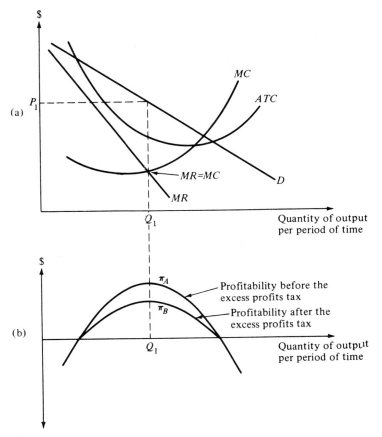

FIGURE 13-4
Regulating monopoly profits through an "excess profits" tax

centage of profits paid in taxes from, say, 50% to 75%. The objective would be to set a tax rate on a firm's reported before-tax profit (as measured in accounting terms) that would tax away all (or most) of the monopolist's economic profits and leave only a normal profit.

The effects of an "excess profits" tax on a monopolist's price and output are shown in Fig. 13-4. In panel 13-4(a), the profit-maximizing price and output values are P_1 and Q_1. The monopolist's total profit function is shown as π_A in panel (b) and is derived from calculating the profits at each price and output combination shown in panel (a). Suppose that the maximum profit at P_1 and Q_1 is viewed as "excessive" and that Congress passes legislation authorizing an excess profits tax on the monopolist's profits, with the form of the tax being one where the marginal *tax rate* on profits is increased sufficiently to bring the firm's after-tax profitability down close to a normal profit. Such a tax has the effect of lowering the firm's total after-tax profit from π_A to π_B.

Observe in this case that the monopolist's profit is still maximized at the same price and output after the excess profits tax is levied as before the tax. This is because a tax based on a certain fixed percentage of profits does not change the output at which $MR = MC$; therefore, it has no effect on the terms of exchange between buyers and sellers. Observe, further, that since the profit-maximizing price does not change, the seller absorbs the full brunt of the tax. None of the tax is passed on to buyers in the form of higher prices. This feature makes it particularly attractive as a policy alternative.[6]

APPLICATIONS CAPSULE

THE TRUCKING INDUSTRY'S EXPERIENCE WITH REGULATION AND WITH DEREGULATION

In a number of instances, government regulation has resulted in the establishment of prices that are *higher* than would prevail under free-market competition. Just how and why this proved to be the case in trucking was reported on by the President's Council of Economic Advisors in 1977:[a]

Trucking provides a good example of the economic costs of regulations that hold prices above the free-market level. In interstate trucking an antitrust exemption permits motor carriers to agree upon rates through rate bureaus, which are groups of truckers that function like private cartels. Rates tend to be set high enough to cover the costs of less efficient carriers. The result is higher prices to consumers. The Interstate Commerce Commission (ICC) regulates both the entry of new carriers and the expansion of route authority by existing carriers. These restrictions frequently require some trucks to drive extra miles on circuitous routes, prohibit access to intermediate points on routes, limit the commodities that can be handled by some carriers, and prohibit certain kinds of freight on the return trip. The result is excessive truck miles and unproductive consumption of motor fuel, labor time, and other resources.

Where more than one carrier gains a certificate to provide service, competition tends to occur on the basis of service quality—frequency of departure, faster delivery, and so on—rather than through prices. As a consequence trucks are often dispatched with smaller loads than they might otherwise haul. Equipment and labor costs are thus spread over fewer ton-miles and costs and prices are higher than necessary. The regulation of rates precludes price competition, and consequently the range of price-service options available to shippers is restricted. Those shippers who would have chosen less frequent service if it were offered at a lower price pay more for services they do not want. In markets where only one trucker has route authority, this process of rate setting may permit lower costs since the trucker, exercising his monopoly control, may reduce the frequency of scheduling, with the result that a higher proportion of trucks is dispatched fully loaded. However, because such a trucker has no competitors, he is unlikely to lower prices to fully reflect the lower-quality service.

---

[6] Such a result is not obtained when a per-unit-sold tax is levied on the monopolist's product. A per-unit tax is a variable cost to the monopolist because the amount of tax paid is a function of the number of units sold. Consequently, a per-unit tax raises both the monopolist's MC and ATC curves by the amount of the per-unit tax and results in a new intersection of MR and MC—at a higher price and a lower output. (Examples of per-unit taxes are cigarette, liquor, and gasoline taxes; however, the purpose of these taxes is not to control monopoly.) Because consumers bear part of the burden of a per-unit tax, it is generally not viewed as being appropriate for monopoly control.

A comparison of the transportation of small parcels with large or bulky shipments illustrates the advantages of multiple price-service options. Shippers of small parcels have several options. The scheduled airlines carry small packages as baggage at substantial prices but with a guarantee of delivery the same day. Some air freight firms collect packages at various cities, fly them first to a central sorting location, then on to their final destination each evening, and provide overnight service at slightly lower prices than those charged by the scheduled airlines. Intercity bus lines and special firms that deliver small packages use surface transportation to furnish delivery service at even cheaper rates. Finally, the U.S. Postal Service offers slower but widely available parcel delivery. The advantage of having multiple options is that shippers of small parcels may choose between various degrees of service at different prices. Although shippers of large or bulky freight have some flexibility, many are chiefly limited to motor carriers, where the range of price-service options is much more limited because of regulation.

The problems of excess capacity, higher prices, and too few price-service options would be reduced if entry into the trucking industry were not restricted. Unlike public utilities, trucking does not exhibit scale economies. Thus price competition is not likely to result in a single survivor—a monopolist. In trucking, fixed costs are low and except for Government restrictions entry is relatively easy. Competition, not monopoly, would be the natural condition in the trucking industry if it were not for Government regulation.

Recent research has demonstrated that common carrier truck regulations cause large losses in production and efficiency. Freight rates in countries that do not regulate motor carriers are significantly lower than rates in countries like West Germany and the United States where regulation is strict. Excessively high motor carrier rates cause some shippers to substitute alternative modes of transportation, or to provide their own transportation services. These responses to regulation reduce economic efficiency.

Subsequently, a consensus emerged that trucking and other surface transportation industries were ripe for deregulation. In 1983 the President's Council of Economic Advisors assessed the deregulatory efforts in trucking, railroads, and airlines as follows:[b]

The traditional rate and entry regulation of the trucking, freight-forwarder, intercity bus, barge, and maritime industries is now largely out of date. Many studies have demonstrated the absence of significant economies of scale in these industries, weakening the "natural monopoly" rationale for entry restrictions. The high degree of capital mobility in these industries implies that individual city-pair and port-pair markets are highly contestable. The existence of intermodal sources of competition and competitive international output markets for transported commodities further reduces any misallocations resulting from monopoly behavior. Additionally, the high rate of technological development in the transportation sector renders many regulations inapplicable. The experience since the recent deregulation of airlines and the partial deregulation of surface transportation indicates that a competitive industry structure would not reduce the financial viability of firms in these industries.

The effects of the partial deregulation of trucking—initiated by the Interstate Commerce Commission and affirmed by the Motor Carrier Act of 1980—have proven very encouraging. Published trucking rates are now subject to large and widely available discounts. Shippers appear to be overwhelmingly satisfied with the rates, service options, and competition for their business. Service to small communities has not deteriorated, as was originally predicted by the opponents of deregulation, and most shippers in small communities also appear to support deregulation. Both the number of new firms and failing firms have increased substantially, the latter due in part to the recession. Concerns have been expressed over the last year that the Interstate Commerce Commission may be slowing the deregulatory process. For example, the percentage of applications for grants of operating authority approved by the ICC declined slightly in both fiscal years since the passage of the Motor Carrier Act. On net, however, the ICC has facilitated increased competition in the trucking industry. The chaos predicted by the opponents of deregulation has not materialized, even during a sustained recession. The experience to date clearly supports the case for more general deregulation of surface transport.

The experience since the partial deregulation of railroads is similar. Although direct evidence on rail rates is not available, the number of contracts negotiated between rail carriers and shippers (a measure of the operating flexibility granted by the Staggers Rail Act) increased from 580 in fiscal 1980 to 2907 in fiscal 1982. Railroads have increased their share of total freight traffic and have substantially increased their shipments of some commodities, such as fruits and vegetables, that were previously carried almost exclusively by trucks. Railroad profits remained essentially steady despite the sustained recession.

While recent partial deregulation of the surface transportation industries has increased the competitiveness of these industries, the opportunity remains for significant gains from further deregulation. There seems to be little danger that further deregulation would enhance the monopoly power of carriers. The high degree of capital mobility in the trucking, bus, barge, and maritime industries should prevent monopoly pricing over a sustained period, even where there is only one carrier on a route.

[a] Taken from the 1977 Annual Report of the Council of Economic Advisors, as published in *The Economic Report of the President*, January 1977, pp. 148–150.

[b] Taken from the 1983 Annual Report of the Council of Economic Advisors, as published in *The Economic Report of the President*, January 1983, pp. 110–111.

MONOPOLISTIC AND ANTICOMPETITIVE PRACTICES

It has been astutely observed on numerous occasions that business executives think competition is a good thing—unless and until their firms become its victims. It should come as no surpise that firms, large and small, have been ingenious in devising ways to escape the discipline of competition. Scores of anticompetitive practices, some outlawed and some still legal, have been concocted to prop up profits and prices. Despite the illegality of nearly every form of collusive agreement, formal or informal, to fix prices, restrict output, restrain trade, or lessen competition, antitrust violations are uncovered each year and unknown numbers of schemes go undetected.

Collusive arrangements may pertain to base or list prices, shipping allowances, charges for extra features, guarantees, warranties, service policies, output quotas, market shares, or the specific geographic areas or product lines that are to be regarded as each firm's exclusive sphere of interest. In addition, firms may reach understandings regarding product standards, specifications, and the frequency with which products will be restyled and redesigned. Industry trade associations may be formed to promote information sharing among the member firms (these are popular in the lumber and wood products, electrical products, textile, aerospace, alcoholic beverage, utility, transportation, and insurance industries). Among steel, copper, oil, and chemical firms, joint ventures are a popular means of instituting interfirm cooperation and, at times, may have facilitated anticompetitive practices. Some firms have knowingly and willingly, although not necessarily collusively, acceded to price leadership in order to avoid price competition. Other firms have consciously engaged in parallel behavior to sidestep strong rivalries.

Some firms have abused the patent laws by aggressively buying up patents, licenses, and copyrights so as to preclude the emergence of competition from rival products.[7] Firms in such fields as plastics, cellophane, shoe machinery, photo supplies, electric lights, copying equipment, computers, tranquilizers, telephone equipment, television, and synthetic rubber have attempted to insulate themselves from competition by systematically building up an impregnable portfolio of patents. On other occasions, firms patent inventions which they have no real intention of using directly but which they do not want others to have.

A restrictive approach that is often used because of its effectiveness and compatibility with antitrust and patent laws is for firms holding a monopolistic patent position to insert competition-reducing provisions into the patent licenses which it may grant (willingly or unwillingly) to potential rival firms.[8] These provisions take several forms. First, firms to which licenses are granted may be constricted to sell only in a specified geographic area. Second, the price of the licensed product may be stipulated as one of the terms of the license. Third, direct or indirect output limitations may be incorporated into the licensing agreements. As a case in point, General Electric in the 1930s granted a license to Westinghouse to produce improved light bulbs that called for a royalty rate of 1 to 2% on the sales made by Westinghouse up to 25.4421% of the two firms' combined sales but a royalty rate of 30% for sales exceeding this quota.[9] Also, Westinghouse had to sell the bulbs at prices and terms set by General Electric.

To the extent that anticompetitive practices exist, they tend to be more prevalent in oligopolistic markets than in atomistic markets. Oligopolistic markets are inherently well suited to some sort of collusive agreement, since fewness of firms is a necessary prerequisite for reaching viable arrangements. Restrictive practices are virtually impossible to institute where markets are comprised of large numbers of firms, despite the fact that business executives in atomistically competitive markets may be equally desirous of escaping strong competitive forces. The more parties there are to a conspiracy the greater their diversity of situations and own best interests and the harder it is to reach a consensus—the hurdles of reaching an enforceable agreement are so difficult, in fact, that illegal collusion is almost totally absent in atomistic market structures. Such is one of the built-in social benefits of competition among the many. This is not to say, however, that small companies do not engage in monopolistic practices. At the local and regional level small firms may compete in small enough numbers that

[7] Scherer, *Industrial Market Structure and Economic Performance*, pp. 450–451.

[8] *Ibid.*, p. 173.

[9] George W. Stocking and Myron W. Watkins, *Cartels in Action* (New York: Twentieth Century Fund, 1947), p. 309.

oligopoly prevails, and thus they may well be in a position to exercise monopoly power.

Nevertheless, restrictive practices are more an exception than a norm—even in industries where there are only a few rival firms. The frailty of collusive agreements, firms' ambitions for growth and expansion, the general existence of spirited nonprice competition, the forces of technological change and innovation, a fear of potential entry, plus the antitrust laws all combine to make collusive arrangements more an illustration of deviant behavior than normal behavior. The antitrust laws, if vigorously enforced, can obviously be an effective deterrent to anticompetitive behavior because of the potential punishment, embarrassment, and loss of public image accompanying discovery of illegal practices. Indeed, the mere likelihood that antitrust officials will be diligent in prosecuting the parties to restrictive agreements, punishing abuses of monopoly power, opposing acquisitions and mergers that tend to consolidate market power and lessen competition, and blocking avenues for creating new kinds of monopolistic arrangements undeniably improves the functioning of markets in constructive ways.

THE COSTS TO SOCIETY OF MONOPOLY POWER

Several statistical studies have been made of the short-run economic impact of monopolistic practices, business inefficiency, and resource misallocation arising from competitive deficiencies and market imperfections.[10] These studies have found monopolistic price-output distortions giving rise to societal losses ranging from less than 1% to perhaps as much as 12% of the gross national product; however, most of these studies place the losses at less than 6% and probably less than 3% of GNP.

Scherer's study has produced the most explicit sources of output loss associated with the exercise of market power; his estimates are summarized in Table 13-1. Although Scherer admits that each of his individual category estimates is subject to a wide margin of error, he concludes that if the "true" output loss could be ascertained, it would probably fall within the range 3 to 12%. This is higher than the estimates of other experts, who have concluded that the static annual monopoly loss is "small" and perhaps even "trivial" and "inconsequential."

---

[10] Arnold Harberger, "Monopoly and Resource Allocation," *American Economic Review*, Vol. 44, No. 2 (May 1954), pp. 77–87; David Schwartzman, "The Burden of Monopoly," *Journal of Political Economy*, Vol. 68, No. 6 (December 1960), pp. 627–630; David R. Kamerschen, "An Estimation of the 'Welfare Losses' from Monopoly in the American Economy," *Western Economic Journal*, Vol. 4, No. 3 (Summer 1966), pp. 221–236; William G. Shepherd, *Market Power and Economic Welfare* (New York: Random House, Inc., 1970), pp. 195–198; Scherer, *Industrial Market Structure and Economic Performance* (Chicago: Rand McNally & Company, 1970), pp. 400–409; John J. Siegfried and T. K. Tiemann, "The Welfare Cost of Monopoly: An Interindustry Analysis," *Economic Inquiry*, Vol. 12, No. 2 (June 1974), pp. 190–202; Dean A. Worcester, Jr., "On Monopoly Welfare Losses: Comment," *American Economic Review*, Vol. 65, No. 5 (December 1975), pp. 1015–1023; R. A. Posner, "The Social Costs of Monopoly and Regulation," *Journal of Political Economy*, Vol. 83, No. 4 (August 1975), pp. 807–827.

TABLE 13-1   Best-Guess Estimates of the Output Losses Attributable to Collusion, the Exercise of Market Power, and Related Breakdowns in the Competitive Process, Expressed as a Percentage of 1966 GNP

Causes of Output Losses	Estimated Percentage Reduction in 1966 GNP
Output losses due to monopolistic resource allocation in the unregulated sectors of the U.S. economy	0.9
Output losses due to pricing distortions in the regulated sector of the U.S. economy	0.6
Inefficiencies in production and higher costs associated with enterprises insulated from competition and therefore not compelled to use the lowest-cost production technology	2.0
Inefficiencies due to deficient cost control by defense and space contractors	0.6
Wasteful advertising and sales promotion efforts	1.0
Producing at less than optimal scale for reasons other than product differentiation	0.3
Extra transportation costs stemming from inefficient plant locations	0.2
Idle and inefficient production capacity due to monopolistic practices and collusion	0.6
Total losses	6.2

Source: F. M. Scherer, *Industrial Market Structure and Economic Performance* (Chicago: Rand McNally & Company, 1970), p. 408.

The wide disparity in the estimates of the social costs of monopoly power correctly suggests that there are major statistical problems in determining the size of the monopolistic sector, the extent to which monopolistic prices exceed competitive levels, and the size of the relevant firm and industry demand elasticities—all of which are pertinent to the estimating procedure. Nonetheless, the weight of evidence is heavily on the side of studies indicating that the *static* effects of slack competitive pressures probably do not place an undue burden on the economy, especially considering that dynamic performance is the truly significant determinant of society's overall economic welfare. As it turns out, the static deadweight welfare loss from monopoly power and resource misallocation is overcome by technologically induced growth in the GNP in a surprisingly short time. The annual average economic welfare gain from innovation and technical change has been estimated to be in the range 1.2 to 1.5% as a minimum.[11] Accepting even the high figure of 12% welfare loss from monopoly power, the "worst-case" length of time required for innovation-related growth to surmount the adverse effects of monopoly power is about 9 years, with a more probable time being 1 to 4 years.

Why Innovation and Technological Change Are So Important.   The reason it is important to look at the rate of innovation and technological change in evaluating

[11] Jesse Markham, "Market Concentration and Innovation," in *Industrial Concentration: The New Learning* (New York: Columbia University Press, 1974).

the economic effects of monopoly is simply this: *An industry composed of many small firms whose rate of technological progress is "slow" will in the long run prove to be less efficient and will make less of a contribution to society's economic well-being than will a competitive industry composed of firms large enough to achieve a higher rate of technological achievement.* This result holds even though the technologically slow firms start from a position of lower costs and lower prices. Consider the following situation, which illustrates this point.

Assume that an industry is composed of 100 small companies, each producing 10 units of output and operating its facilities at peak efficiency and minimum ATC. Total industry output would therefore be 1000 units, which, let us say, could currently be sold at a price of $6 a unit. Suppose further that (1) the introduction of new technological innovations raises efficiency and permits the firms to increase production by 3% each year using the same amounts of resource inputs, and (2) competition causes any cost savings (exclusive of inflationary effects) to be passed on to consumers through price reductions of 1% annually. At the end of 5 years, then, industry output will have risen to 1159 units and the market price will have fallen to $5.71.

Now let us assume that this same industry is, instead, composed of three large corporations each producing 300 units of output but operating just short of minimum ATC at 333 units of output. Total industry output initially would total 900 units or 10% less than the output under a 100-firm market structure. The lesser initial output of the three large corporations, assuming identical market demand conditions, will allow them to obtain a higher price, say $6.30. But suppose that the large firms invest more heavily in R&D and, because of resulting efficiencies, are able to expand output by 5% per year using the same amount of resource inputs (but still producing short of ATC). Suppose also that competitive pressures are strong enough to force them to pass part of the cost-savings along to consumers in the form of price reductions of 2% per year.[12] At the end of 5 years the total output of the three large corporations will be 1149 units and price will have fallen to $5.70—results that are comparable to the small-firm market structure even though the three corporations started out with a lower total output and higher prices.

Moreover, every year thereafter the three-firm oligopolistic market will *outperform* the small-firm market on both *price* and *output* by an increasing amount. Prices in the oligopolistic market will fall by 2% compared to only 1% in the small-firm market; output in the oligopolistic market will expand by 5% compared to only 3% in the small-firm market. These results will occur without any economies-of-scale advantage and despite the fact that the three oligopolists may earn greater profits per unit of output and may not produce at minimum *ATC*.

---

[12] In many instances, of course, the fruits of technological progress are passed along to consumers in the form of increased quality rather than lower prices. (Color TV serves as a good example.) This alters the form but not the substance of the outcome insofar as the benefits to consumers are concerned. It could also be argued that none of the cost savings will be passed on to consumers, owing to the market power of large firms and the lack of price competition, which allows them to keep prices up and thereby earn greater economic profits. However, trends in the profit margins of large U.S. corporations do not indicate that such has historically been the case.

This example, although oversimplified, illustrates the importance of long-run performance in evaluating market performance. The rate of technical progress, not a snapshot of prices, profits, or efficiency at some moment of time, ultimately determines the quality and quantity of a product and the impact on the consumer's pocketbook. For this reason alone, it follows that *the socially optimum type of market structure is the one most conducive to achieving technological advance and innovation yet competitive enough to protect consumers against abuses of market power.* The terrific pressure that technological change brings to bear is illustrated every time a firm introduces a new product and rival firms scramble to bring out their versions. The same applies to technological breakthroughs which produce dramatic cost savings.

In a technologically dynamic environment new products are constantly replacing old products; new technologies are rendering older methods obsolete; some types of enterprises are prospering while others are dying out. The faster the procession of new innovations, the shorter becomes the life cycle of more products, technologies, and industries. Technological change and innovation produce a "perennial gale of creative destruction" and few firms and industries are sheltered from its winds over the long term.[13] Thus, like it or not, firms are drawn into competing on grounds of technological capability and product innovation.

Over the long run, whether a firm is technologically progressive is much more crucial to society than whether it is operating at the lowest possible unit cost at some moment of time. Long-run performance is ultimately what counts most because it is principally from technological change and innovation that society realizes gains in productivity (output per unit of input), gains in the quantity and quality of output, and gains in the level of per capita income. Hence, the truly effective enterprise must do enough research and development that it will be in a timely position to (1) improve its product or service, (2) install more efficient production processes, (3) adopt better methods of distribution, (4) move into new markets, and/or (5) take advantage of new sources of supply of raw materials and component parts. Simply trying to operate its *present* facilities most efficiently—at the minimum point of its short-run and long-run average total cost curve—is not enough.

Does Large Size Help Promote Technological Progress?   As a firm becomes larger, it becomes more able to undertake innovations and to compete on the basis of technology. Technological progress may be viewed as occurring in four steps: invention, development, implementation, and diffusion. *Invention* is the act of conceiving a new product or process and working out the details in its essential but rudimentary form. *Development* is the lengthy sequence of trial-and-error testing through which the invention is modified, perfected, and worked out in finest detail to make it technically ready for practical application. *Innovation* involves implementing the finalized version of the invention and putting it into practice for the first time. *Diffusion* relates to the rate and speed at which the innovation comes into widespread use as other enterprises follow the lead of the

---

[13] Joseph A. Schumpeter, *Capitalism, Socialism and Democracy*, 3rd ed. (New York: Harper & Brothers, 1950), p. 84.

innovator. The available evidence indicates that steps 1 and 2 (invention and development) are often relatively inexpensive and can be undertaken on a small scale.[14] They are thus within the reach of both small and large firms. There are important occasions, however, where the third step can be a costly, time-consuming process. The product may have to be test-marketed, unforeseen technical bugs eliminated, new productive facilities built or expanded, marketing channels organized, promotional campaigns designed and instituted, and competition from other products surmounted—a process that can take several years and require major organizational and financial commitments before a profit payoff is realized. Past experience shows that it is difficult for small firms to find the resources to support such efforts—especially if they are under the gun of intense competition.

The financial and organizational limitations of small firms explain why many inventions which originated in small companies have ended up as major products of large corporations. Well-known examples include air conditioning, the jet engine, cellophane, the cotton picker, the helicopter, power steering, and the cracking of petroleum.[15] This also explains why big companies may end up producing products discovered by academicians, independent inventors, and specialized R & D firms. Examples include the development of titanium metals, Eastman Kodak's Kodachrome color camera film, the development of Dacron fibers by DuPont, and Xerox's development of quick copiers. A number of other innovations have required such large-scale funding that only large firms could undertake them. The design and development costs of civilian jet airliners soared past the $100 million mark. Polaroid, over an 8-year period, invested $500 million to bring the SX-70 camera and film onto the market—a bold technical achievement that represents one of the biggest gambles ever on a consumer product. RCA sunk $65 million into R & D on color television before achieving a product with mass market potential. IBM staked its future and $5 billion over a 5-year period in designing, developing, and marketing its System/360 line of computers. Many millions were also spent by Alcoa in aircraft metals fabrication, by General Electric in refining X-ray equipment, by Westinghouse in designing nuclear-powered generating equipment, by steel firms in developing continuous casting of steel, and by General Motors in its development of diesel locomotives, automatic transmissions, liquid-cooled aircraft engines, and catalytic converters.[16]

[14] For an excellent discussion of this and related points, see F. M. Scherer, *Industrial Market Structure and Economic Performance*, 2nd ed., Chapter 15, especially pp. 413–422.

[15] John Jewkes, David Sawers, and Richard Stillerman, *The Sources of Invention* (New York: St. Martin's Press, 1958), pp. 71–85.

[16] A census of the various technological innovations in any one year would unquestionably reveal that the number of less-costly, minor innovations is far greater than the number of very expensive, more spectacular innovations. Thus, there are many technical challenges which can be successfully met by small entrepreneurial firms willing to bear the risks. Examples where small firms have been active in innovation include specialized applications of computer technology, semiconductors and electronic circuitry technology, numeric process control equipment, the use of bank credit cards, and retailing. Innovational opportunities for small firms also arise when the managers of large corporate enterprises are skeptical of the possibilities of proposed new products or new processes and when entrepreneur-minded scientists and researchers leave the employ of large firms to create their own enterprises. For these reasons, small enterprises cannot be relegated to an insignificant role in advancing the cause of technological progress. While a small firm is sometimes at a clear disadvantage in the process of technological and innovational competition, at other times and in other industries it is capable of competing on an almost equal footing.

It is indisputable that large-scale enterprises have made bigger financial and organizational commitment to technology than have small-scale firms. Statistics compiled by the National Science Foundation consistently show that the biggest firms undertake the lion's share of all formal industrial R & D activity. For many years firms having 5000 or more employees have accounted for 85 to 90% of industrial R & D spending; firms with fewer than 1000 employees account for only 5%.[17] Over 85% of the companies with 5000 or more employees have R & D budgets of at least $1,000,000, and over 200 of these companies spend more than $10 million for R & D activities. Moreover, in 1976 over 80% of the scientists and engineers engaged in R & D were employed in firms with 5000 or more employees. Fewer than 4% of these scientists and engineers were employed in R & D labs with budgets of less than $250,000. Very little formal scientific and engineering effort is in evidence in industries where the four largest firms have a combined market share below 15%.[18]

R & D outlays, of course, are only an input measure; they do not reflect innovational success or significance. Yet, it seems unlikely that innovation will occur as regularly where R & D is haphazard and casual as it will where it is organized and results-oriented. However, it is true that once a firm passes some threshold size there is room to question just how supportive bigness is of technical progress. Instances have occurred where companies dominating their markets have been slow to lead and quick to follow innovation. Sometimes progressiveness is as much the result of technological opportunity and profit potential as it is bigness, while on other occasions the largest firms' share of significant innovations has been found to be inversely correlated with high market shares.[19] Furthermore, where large firms are solidly entrenched, there is always the chance that technical progress will be retarded by monopolistic behavior and anticompetitive practices.

In general, it can be said that an industry's technological progress is potentially enhanced by the presence of large firms which have some degree of monopoly power. Big firms are capable of implementing technological and innovational changes of the highest order of magnitude; little companies can be at a severe disadvantage. The big firm's larger profits and cash flow, its ability to absorb the losses from research which proves unfruitful, its superior access to money capital for financing new investments, and its greater organizational capacity in terms of scientific, engineering, and managerial know-how necessarily place it ahead of small, financially-constrained rivals as the *potential pacesetter* for pushing back the barriers to technological progress.

[17] National Science Foundation, *Research and Development in Industry 1975* (Washington, D.C.: U.S. Government Printing Office, 1975).

[18] Jewkes, Sawers, and Stillerman, *The Sources of Invention*, p. 117; F. M. Scherer, "Market Structure and the Employment of Scientists and Engineers," *American Economic Review*, Vol. 57, No. 3 (June 1967), pp. 529–530.

[19] See, for instance, Scherer, *Industrial Market Structure and Economic Performance*, 2nd ed., pp. 413–422; Oliver E. Williamson, "Innovation and Market Structure," *Journal of Political Economy*, February 1965, pp. 67–73; W. S. Comanor, "Market Structure, Product Differentiation, and Industrial Research," *Quarterly Journal of Economics*, Vol. 81, No. 4 (November 1967), pp. 639–657; Almarin Phillips, "Patents, Potential Competition, and Technical Progress," *American Economic Review*, Vol. 56, No. 2 (May 1966), pp. 301–310; and Morton I. Kamien and Nancy L. Schwartz, "Market Structure and Innovation: A Survey," *Journal of Economic Literature*, Vol. 13, No. 1 (March 1975), pp. 22–26.

The conclusion to be drawn here about the monopoly consequences of large firm size is straightforward: if a large portion of technological progress is, in fact, attributable to the activities of large firms (some or many of which have monopoly power), the static monopoly welfare loss would have to be much larger than the presently indicated 3 to 12% of GNP before society could be made better off by breaking large firms up into many small companies in an effort to create allegedly more competitive market conditions.

THE SOCIAL CONTROL OF CORPORATE POWER

The antitrust laws, as written and applied, offer a reasonably sufficient body of rules for preventing anticompetitive practices and controlling monopoly power. But barring new interpretations, they leave almost untouched the troublesome issue of the kinds of corporate power that attach to merely being big. As yet, existing antitrust legislation has not been deemed applicable to the power that accrues to large *absolute* firm size. Historically, antitrust has aimed almost exclusively at combating the kinds of power that attach to restraints of trade and monopolizing the market for a particular product—problems of large *relative* firm size. But recently large size per se has become a point of public concern. The antibigness critics argue that:

1. Giant corporations have grown to a point where they are too large and too powerful. Vertical integration, diversification, and large-scale mergers are claimed to have been carried beyond the bounds justified by efficiency considerations.

2. The size and power of giant firms puts them in a position to manipulate markets rather than respond to them; this is evidenced by monopoly pricing, output restrictions, anticompetitive trade practices, tacit collusion, and conscious parallelism—each of which is the antithesis of free market economics.

3. Competitive forces are no longer strong enough or reliable enough to protect consumers from inflated prices, excessive profits, and self-serving corporate policies.

4. The oligopolistic structure of corporate-dominated markets diverts competitive rivalry away from price competition (the most desirable competitive form) into nonprice areas—a much less desirable competitive style that encourages over-emphasis on persuasive advertising, product proliferation, planned product obsolescence, and cosmetic production improvements.

5. Because of the political leverage which goes with bigness and which big firms deliberately cultivate, corporate enterprises are able to gain undue access to government in achieving private economic goals.

6. The motives and pressures for improved corporate performance (growth in sales, profits, etc.) have led to questionable mergers and acquisitions, manipulative accounting practices, and financial machinations that have doubtful social or economic value.

7. Reforms both from within and without are needed to curb corporate power, enliven competition, and make large firms more responsible and responsive to the general economic welfare of society.

Out of these concerns have emerged several proposals for the social control of corporate power; these may be grouped into four basic approaches: (1) the social responsibility model, (2) the regulatory model, (3) the public ownership model, and (4) the workable competition model.

The *social responsibility* approach to corporate power involves leaving power in the hands of corporate executives but persuading and teaching them to use this power in "socially responsible" ways. Much has been written and said about the need for corporations to assess the social impact of corporate activities and to formulate policies that are in accord with the goals and concerns of society at large. Some degree of corporate response to the call for social responsibility is visible, although it is debatable whether the response is enlightened and committed or whether it is the result of a fear of increased government regulation. More boards of directors are being constituted from a broader segment of society. A number of large firms have created new departments to analyze the social consequences of alternative corporate policies. Some corporations have deliberately located plants in urban ghettos; and many have instituted programs to increase corporation participation in community improvements. Irrespective of whether the actions are sincere or cosmetic, it is clear that corporations are increasingly inquiring into conflicts between corporate policy and the "general social welfare." Still, corporate social responsibility is inherently voluntary and can only be a partial answer to containing corporate power.

The *regulatory* approach to controlling both corporate power and anticompetitive practices essentially involves direct government approval of key corporate decisions. The use of formal wage and price controls in the early 1970s, along with legislation establishing federal controls over oil and natural gas prices and production rates, put the regulatory model back in the public spotlight. A few proposals advocated the two most extreme forms of regulation—rationing and government fixing of prices and wages—as being attractive and permanent weapons of corporate control. However, the majority of economists do not view regulation, rationing, or permanent wage-price controls as viable policies for remedying monopoly-related and other abuses of power. The reason lies basically in a strong conviction that bureaucratic fiat is a poor and often woefully ineffective substitute for a competitive price system. The freedom of buyers and sellers to exercise their own choices in a competitive marketplace *generally* has the durable property of yielding social results that are hard to improve on by public action.

This is not to say that the functioning of either oligopolistic or atomistic markets is without defect, for both can develop shortcomings requiring public action. But most economists are skeptical of the ability of government regulators to superimpose their judgments upon those of business managers and consumers and produce a result that is superior to the marketplace. To begin with, government regulation concentrates power in the hands of a few persons to an even greater extent than exists in oligopolistic markets. While the power of government regulators theoretically is deployed to serve "the public interest," there is ample room for disagreement and confusion as to what "the public interest" actually is.

More important, government policymakers can be every bit as prone to use power to serve their own purposes or those of special interests as they are to serve the larger "public purpose." This is shown by the frequency with which special interest groups have successfully lobbied for favored treatment and by the ambitions of government officials to enhance their own images and to expand the role and scope of their departments. Furthermore, the checks and balances on the actions of government regulators operate only in election years or when public opinion is strongly aroused. In contrast, the checks and balances imposed by vigorous competitive pressures operate daily and have the further advantage of keeping economic power diffused. Even though government regulators usually have good intentions, there still are few instances where it can be shown that making private decisions subordinate to government decree has yielded superior and less costly social results. In sum, the consensus view of economists is that the regulatory process is never likely to function so efficiently that government regulators understand and influence marketplace conditions better than buyers and sellers who are on the scene.

The *public ownership* model, although once popular among a modest number of economists, has fallen from favor. Nationalizing giant corporations and bringing their activities under the management and scrutiny of Congress and the president can create more problems than it solves. The British experience with nationalization of key industries has, to put it mildly, been ineffective in promoting the economic welfare of any but unionized employees of the nationalized firms; in Britian it is the politics of nationalization, not the economic advantages, that perpetuate public ownership. The chief trouble with public ownership is the lack of incentives to ensure efficient performance and prompt response to changes in consumer preferences and market conditions.

This leaves the fourth category—the model of *workable competition*—as being the approach with the greatest following. This model has as its goal making the structure of industry and the conduct of individual firms such that market performance over both the short run and the long run is as good as can be expected. The criteria for measuring market performance include whether output rates and the range of product qualities are in harmony with consumer demand, whether production activities are efficient and technologically progressive, whether competitive pressures are strong enough to keep profits down to a reasonable and fair minimum, whether the exercise of monopoly power is adequately contained, and whether private business activities are in accord with the broad public interest and national economic objectives.

These criteria are, for the most part, quite unobjectionable. Yet, problems exist. Value judgments can hardly fail to enter into drawing a line between too little and enough competition. In deciding whether a firm's production operations are efficient, one needs a yardstick indicating the highest achievable efficiency when, quite clearly, the boundaries of what is possible may never have been revealed in actual practice (this difficulty, however, can be skirted if comparisons with other national, international and publicly owned enterprises are available). Most important, there is difficulty in assessing the workability of competition when some but not all of the criteria are satisfied. This has led to the suggestion that competitive forces be judged workable and effective if and when no clearly indicated public policy measure could be implemented to produce superior competitive performance.[20] While this suggestion also runs afoul of the same value judgment and measurement difficulties, it does have the merit of focusing attention on the prescribing of constructive remedial actions.

SUMMARY AND CONCLUSIONS CONCERNING MONOPOLY BEHAVIOR

The major implications and predictions that flow from the market model of pure monopoly are:

1. A monopolistic firm will use its economic power to charge a higher price than would tend to prevail under competition.

2. Because a monopolist tends to charge a higher price, output will be less than in a competitive market; this is because customers will buy less of the product at the monopolist's higher price than they would be willing and able to buy at the lower prices that can be expected with competition.

3. An exception to the higher price/lower output predictions of the monopoly model is the case of *natural monopoly*, where economies of scale are so great that monopoly results in a lower price and a greater output than could be expected under competition. In such cases, there is clear conflict between promoting competition, on the one hand, and seeing that the marketplace provides consumers with the greatest possible output at the lowest feasible price, on the other hand.

Generally speaking, any form of unregulated monopoly and/or the exercise of monopoly power works against the best interests of consumers. Only in the case of natural monopoly is a monopolistic market preferable to a competitive market, and then only with some form of effective economic regulation.

The economic case against monopolistic markets and the unregulated exercise of monopoly power is exceedingly strong:

1. Monopoly tends to produce higher prices and restricted outputs as compared to competition.

2. Monopoly has the capability of producing "excessive" economic profits—an outcome that results in income and purchasing power being redistributed from the buying public to the monopolistic seller.

---

[20] For a more complete discussion of this concept, see Jesse W. Markham, "An Alternative Approach to the Concept of Workable Competition," *American Economic Review*, Vol. 40, No. 3 (June, 1950), pp. 349–361.

3.   Monopoly can prevent an optimal allocation of economic resources in the sense that monopolistic firms do not necessarily produce at the output rates where unit costs are lowest (the minimum point on the *LRAC* curve), as is the case in perfect competition.

4.   Such monopolistic practices as price-fixing, suppression of technological improvements, erecting artificial barriers to entry, tying contracts, exerting reciprocal purchasing leverage, refusing to sell, and attempting to drive rival firms out of business through predatory tactics are all without economic justification.

A monopolist obviously has a great deal of economic power, which it almost always will use to its own advantage. This can scarcely be condoned. However, the market power of a monopolist is seldom absolute. It can be weakened and even overcome completely by slack demand conditions, by actual or threatened government intervention and regulation, by potential competition from new firms and new products, by the exercise of countervailing power on the part of buyers, and by technological innovations which create new substitutes for the monopolist's product.

SUMMARY AND CONCLUSIONS CONCERNING THE FOUR MARKET MODELS

Despite the hazards of generalizations, the time has come to stand back and appraise the four models of market structure. As among perfect competition, monopolistic competition, oligopoly, and monopoly, which one produces the best outcome for consumers? Is competition among the many more socially optimum than competition among the few? Is an oligopolistically structured market less "contestable" than a monopolistically competitive market? What do the four models as a group tell us? What do we learn about real-world markets? What predictions are possible?

Make no mistake about it, these are very tough questions. They involve thorny issues about what benefits the overall economic welfare of society. Unfortunately, the answers are not categorically "black" or "white"; in most cases "it all depends." This is partly because real-world market conditions do not neatly correspond to the theoretical models of perfect competition, monopolistic competition, oligopoly, or pure monopoly. There is more to the sources and forces of competition than just how many firms comprise the selling side of the marketplace—as we shall see in Chapters 15 and 16.

In addition, the four formal models of market structure and behavior are *static* in their analytical approach; that is, they examine how firms and markets will behave under a particular set of circumstances. The models are presented as operating toward an equilibrium, the essence of which varies with the original set of market circumstances. The character of the equilibrium position is what commands the center of attention, with only incidental concern for the time and the path for reaching equilibrium. The fact is, however, that the static equilibrium results of particular competitive patterns are just snapshots of an ongoing process. Market conditions and competitive pressures are always in a state of flux. New equilibrium positions are constantly in the process of being created. Disequilibrium conditions are thus the norm, not the exception, as markets respond and react. In short, *competition is a dynamic process, not an equilibrium outcome.* Consequently, the strength of competition is not fully revealed from statically oriented models of market behavior. An economically advantageous equilibrium outcome in the short run may prove to be unfavorable in the long run, or vice versa. This means that rendering a judgment about the effects of competition on society's economic welfare requires extending the time frame of the evaluation period and examining business performance as it unfolds over a period of years.

For these reasons, caution is warranted in using the conclusions of the four static models of market behavior to project the ultimate impact on society's economic welfare over the long term. While static theoretical models do yield valuable insights into competitive processes (and for that alone they are worthwhile), they are far from being the last word in analyzing how industries function and in assessing the nature and strength of competition.

However, we shall not use these reasons as an excuse to dodge the issues. Having come this far, we shall proceed to try to tie things together—if only provisionally—and to arrive at some conclusions—even if they are tentative and subject to argument. The following generalizations are offered:

1.   Competition among the many (as epitomized by perfect and monopolistic competition) is likely to produce relatively lower prices and relatively narrower profit margins *in the short run* as compared to competition among the few. Herein lies the fundamental social benefit of atomistic competition. When this is coupled with the general inability of atomistic firms to exercise monopoly power or otherwise exploit consumers, the static short-run results of competition among large numbers of relatively small enterprises tend to be more advantageous to consumers than is oligopolistic competition—*provided that economies of scale are not such as to make oligopoly more cost efficient.*

2.   In the long run, however, a technologically progressive oligopolistic market can outperform an atomistically competitive industry having a slow rate of technological change and innovation. As one keen observer put it almost 40 years ago, inquiry into the origins of high living standards "leads not to the doors of those firms that work under conditions of comparatively free competition, but precisely to the doors of the large concerns . . . and a shocking suspicion dawns upon us that big business may have had more to do with creating that standard of life than with keeping it down."[21] Large enterprises are well positioned to act as pacesetters in implementing new product innovations and in pushing back the barriers to technological progress; they tend to achieve above-average gains in output per unit of input; and they have been in the forefront of enterprises that have raised wages faster than prices. It is precisely on such performance features

---

[21] Schumpeter, *Capitalism, Socialism and Democracy*, p. 82.

that the principal foundations of economic progress and rising standards of living rest. Hence, the dynamic patterns of corporate-dominated oligopolies can have socially beneficial results that may offset the superior short-run performance of atomistic competition.

Yet, some qualification is clearly needed. Although competitive forces can have a restraining effect upon arbitrary corporate policies and upon the self-serving exercise of power, the strengths of competitive forces can also operate unevenly in corporate-dominated markets. Some giant corporations are able to exercise a considerable degree of market power while others exercise little or none. Some large corporations have maneuvered themselves into a strong market position and are able to earn substantial profits while others possess no particular unique advantage and earn average or subpar profits. The winds of technological and innovational progress blow strongly in some corporate oligopolies but only occasionally in others. Cross currents such as these mean that long-run performance where there is competition among the few varies from "not so good" to "fair" to "very good" to, occasionally, "excellent."

3.   Ideally, the socially optimum "contestable" market would combine the short-term results of competition among large numbers of small firms with the long-term performance of competition among technologically progressive enterprises. The benefits to consumers are greatest when there are enough firms producing competing products so that short-run competitive forces are strong enough (a) to prevent abuses of market power, (b) to prevent collusion, (c) to keep price close to average cost and not allow firms to earn "excessive" profits, and (d) to force firms to operate at maximum efficiency and minimum costs. However, firms should be allowed to become large enough and diversified enough to capitalize on scale economies and experience curve effects and to fund major technological advances so that competition will result in superior long-run market performance. Improving the economic well-being of consumers ultimately depends upon a style of competition that promotes optimum dynamic performance.

4.   The most important shortcomings of competition among the few revolve around the potential accumulation of power by large corporations and the potential for various anticompetitive practices to emerge. To remedy these, it is appropriate for policymakers to establish "fair competitive practice" codes to strengthen the forces of the short-run competition among giant corporations with the specific objective of (a) curtailing wasteful promotional activities which raise costs and prices, (b) minimizing the ability of firms to use their size and power to serve corporate purposes not compatible with the public interest, (c) causing firms to operate at or near full production capacity before they raise prices, and (d) encouraging the entry of rival firms into those markets where corporate profits appear unduly "excessive" or "monopolistic." Generally speaking, the thrust of antitrust policy and codes of fair competition should be geared toward (a) enforcing as much competition as is consistent with achieving realizable economies of scale, (b) having enough product differentiation to satisfy consumers, and (c) achieving rates of technological progress, innovation, and economic growth that are consistent with the national interest. Whenever conflicts appear between pol-

icies that stiffen short-run competitive pressures and policies that stiffen long-run competitive forces, the long-run-oriented policy should normally take precedence, since sacrifices in short-run performance are sooner or later overwhelmed by improvements in long-run performance.

5. Without question, any sort of anticompetitive practice among sellers to fix prices, restrict production, divide markets, suppress innovation, or foreclose the entry of new firms should be prohibited and any violation vigorously prosecuted. Aggressive enforcement of antitrust laws can go far toward discouraging business firms from restraining competition or attempting to monopolize a product. However, it is doubtful whether the public interest is served by specifying any particular limits to the size of firms or to the market shares which they are allowed to achieve. The presence of economies of scale and experience curve effects may well result in larger firms being more cost efficient than smaller firms. Thus, larger firm sizes can be consistent with the public interest, unless, of course, they involve a manifest attempt to subvert competitive forces. The optimum number of firms in an industry is different, depending on technological considerations, the importance of research and innovation, the size of the relevant market, the diversity of buyer tastes and needs, scale economies, and experience curve effects.

SUGGESTED READINGS

BERRY, C. H., *Corporate Growth and Diversification* (Princeton, N.J.: Princeton University Press, 1974).

BORK, R. H., *The Antitrust Paradox: A Policy at War with Itself* (New York: Basic Books, Inc., 1978).

CLARK, J. M., *Competition as a Dynamic Process* (Washington, D.C.: The Brookings Institution, 1961), Chapters 4, 8, 10, and 19.

FELTON, J. R., "The Costs and Benefits of Motor Truck Regulation," *Quarterly Review of Economics and Business*, Vol. 18, No. 2 (Summer 1978), pp. 7–20.

GALBRAITH, J. K., *American Capitalism: The Theory of Countervailing Power* (Boston: Houghton Mifflin Company, 1951), Chapter 9.

HARBERGER, A. C., "Monopoly and Resource Allocation," *American Economic Review*, Vol. 44, No. 2 (May 1954), pp. 77–87.

LERNER, A. P., "The Concept of Monopoly and the Measurement of Monopoly Power," *Review of Economic Studies* (June 1943), pp. 157–175.

MARRIS, R., AND D. C. MUELLER, "The Corporation, Competition, and the Invisible Hand," *Journal of Economic Literature*, Vol. 18, No. 1 (March 1980), pp. 32–63.

REEKIE, W. D., "Price and Quality Competition in the United States Drug Industry," *Journal of Industrial Economics*, Vol. 26, No. 1 (March 1978), pp. 223–237.

SCHERER, F. M., *Industrial Market Structure and Economic Performance*, 2nd ed. (Boston: Houghton Mifflin Company, 1980), Chapters 2, 8, 15, 17, and 18.

SCHUMPETER, J. A., *Capitalism, Socialism and Democracy*, 3rd ed. (New York: Harper & Brothers, 1950), Chapters 7 and 8.

SILBERSTON, A., "Price Behavior of Firms," *Economic Journal*, Vol. 80, No. 319 (September 1970), pp. 511–575.

Sosnick, S., "A Critique of Concepts of Workable Competition," *Quarterly Journal of Economics*, Vol. 72, No. 3 (August 1958), pp. 380–423.

Telser, L. G., "Advertising and Competition," *Journal of Political Economy*, Vol. 72, No. 6 (December 1964), pp. 537–562.

Temin, P., "Technology, Regulation, and Market Structure in the Modern Pharmaceutical Industry," *Bell Journal of Economics*, Vol. 10, No. 2 (Autumn 1979), pp. 429–446.

Thompson, A. A., "Absolute Firm Size, Administered Prices, and Inflation," *Economic Inquiry*, Vol. 12, No. 2 (June 1974), pp. 240–254.

——, "Corporate Bigness—For Better or for Worse?" *Sloan Management Review*, Vol. 17, No. 1 (Fall 1975), pp. 37–62.

Worchester, D. A., Jr., "On Monopoly Welfare Losses: Comment," *American Economic Review*, Vol. 65, No. 5 (December 1975), pp. 1015–1023.

PROBLEMS AND QUESTIONS FOR DISCUSSION

1. Suppose that a pure monopolist's demand schedule and total cost function are as follows:

Selling Price	Quantity Demanded	Total Costs
$20	9,000	$160,000
19	10,000	165,000
18	11,000	171,000
17	12,000	178,000
16	13,000	186,000
15	14,000	195,000

What price should the monopolist charge in order to maximize profits?

2. The XQT Concessions Company paid $35,000 for exclusive rights to sell beer at the seven home games of the local pro football team. Attendance generally averages 60,000 persons per game. The variable costs of obtaining and selling a 12-ounce cup of draft beer are estimated to be 22 cents. The manager of the XQT company has estimated demand for beer at each home game to be the following:

Selling Price	Quantity Demanded (cups)
$0.75	36,000
1.00	32,000
1.25	26,000
1.50	18,000

What price should be selected in order to maximize XQT's profits?

3. Is it possible for a pure monopolist to benefit from sales promotion and advertising, given that there are no close substitutes for the monopolist's product? Explain and justify your answer graphically.

4. How can a firm have monopoly power without being a pure monopolist? How could one measure the strength of a firm's monopolistic position?

5. Why might a monopolist charge a price below what would maximize short-run profits? In practice how important are these considerations likely to be?

6. "The more profitable a firm, the greater its monopoly power." True or false? Explain.

7. What reasons can you give for why a monopolistic firm's price might be higher under regulation than if it were not regulated? How often and where do you think this might occur?

8. Does a profit-maximizing monopolist typically produce at an output rate which is optimal from a standpoint of cost and efficiency? Why or why not? Illustrate graphically.

9. Does a monopolistic firm have less incentive to be efficient than a firm confronted with vigorous price competition? Why or why not?

10. Does monopoly always result in higher prices and lower outputs than a competitively structured industry? Illustrate graphically. (*Hint*: Consider the result that might occur if the monopolist has access to economies of scale that are not available if there is competitive rivalry among many small firms.)

11. Explain why the *incentive* for undertaking technological advance may be weak in industries where firms are small and the market is atomistically structured.

12. Is the number of firms an important determinant of the degree of competition that will tend to exist in the market for a product? Is the size of the firms comprising an industry an important determinant of the degree of competition?

14

PRICING STRATEGIES AND MULTIPLE-GOAL MODELS OF BUSINESS BEHAVIOR

The managers of business enterprises, although very profit-conscious, are not always inclined to base their decisions solely upon profit criteria. As we saw in Chapter 9, other goals can influence what a firm does, especially when profits reach acceptable levels and a firm's long-term profitability does not appear to be in jeopardy. And even where profit is a prime consideration, it does not appear that corporate prices are keyed to the output where $MC = MR$; other factors enter into play. In this chapter we shall look briefly at pricing strategies where short-run profit maximization is not the overriding criterion. Then we shall explore some of the more prominent multiple-goal models of contemporary business behavior. In all these models, business decisions and strategies are predicated upon a hierachy of goals. Particular attention will be given to longer-run sales and growth goals and how these are conditioned by new product development, technological change, and competitive pressures.

HOW FIRMS DETERMINE PRICE: THEORY VERSUS PRACTICE

Although economists traditionally view price as *the* dominant competitive variable, in practice it is not clear that pricing receives the greatest amount of strategic attention. Pricing is a major strategic issue in essentially only four types of situations: (1) when a firm must set a price for the first time, as occurs when it introduces a new product, moves into a new market, or regularly enters competitive sealed bids on contract work; (2) when market or competitive circumstances prompt a firm to consider initiating a price change; (3) when one or more rival firms initiate a price change and some response is required; and (4) when the firm produces two or more products having interrelated demands and/or costs, thus posing problems of optimal price coordination. These situations are, of course, not rare, but neither are they so pervasive as to take up the bulk of management's time.

Firms have developed a wide variety of strategic approaches for addressing pricing. Interestingly enough, while profit is unquestionably a major concern in the pricing decision, the evidence is not strong that managerial estimates of the relationship between *MR* and *MC* actually form the basis for price selection.[1]

Pricing to Earn a Target Rate of Return

Studies of business pricing practices indicate a widespread use of target return pricing methods. A *target return price* is a price designed to yield the firm a predetermined profit from the sale of specific products or product groups. The desired profit is typically based upon dollar sales (total revenue) or upon some measure of invested capital and may be expressed either as a percentage rate or as a dollar amount. For example, the desired profit target may be stated as a profit on sales of 5%, a profit return equal to 10% of total assets, a profit return equal to 15% of net worth (stockholders' equity), a profit equal to X dollars per share of common stock, or as simply a specific dollar figure. The size of the profit target tends to hinge upon such considerations as (1) industry custom, (2) competitive pressures, (3) what managers believe to be a "fair" or "reasonable" return given the associated business risk, (4) a desire to equal or better the firm's recent profit performance, (5) a desire to stabilize industry prices, (6) whether the firm's product is new or a unique specialty item, and (7) the firm's related goals of sales, market share, and growth. Specific profit targets tend to differ among industries and firms, reflecting differing degrees of competition and differing priorities among alternative goals. Normally, however, *after-tax* profit targets tend to fall within a range of 3 to 7% of sales and 10 to 20% of invested capital.

The mechanics of target return pricing may be set forth briefly in terms of two examples—the first illustrating pricing to achieve a target return on investment and the second illustrating what is commonly referred to as cost-plus pricing.

[1] The literature on the subject is immense. Among the more definitive studies are R. L. Hall and Charles J. Hitch, "Price Theory and Business Behavior," *Oxford Economic Papers*, Vol. 2 (May 1939), pp. 12–45; A. D. H. Kaplan, J. B. Dirlam, and R. F. Lanzilotti, *Pricing in Big Business* (Washington, D. C.: The Brookings Institution, 1958), Chapter 2; Burnard H. Sord and Glenn A. Welsch, *Business Budgeting* (New York: Controllership Foundation, 1958), pp. 88–89 and 148; James H. Miller, "A Glimpse at Practice in Calculating and Using Return on Investment," *NAA Bulletin* June 1969, p. 73; W. W. Haynes, "Pricing Practices in Small Firms," *Southern Economic Journal*, Vol. 30, No. 4 (April 1964), pp. 315–324.

1. Assume that a firm has $100 million invested in the production of a particular product and desires to earn a long-run average annual return of 20% before taxes on its investment. This, of course, translates into an annual profit target of $20 million. The initial step is to determine average total cost at some "normal" output rate (often referred to as the standard volume). Usually, the normal output rate is arbitrarily pegged somewhere between two-thirds and four-fifths of the capacity rate, instead of being related to the firm's actual operating rate. Many firms base their normal output rate upon what they believe to be their long-run rate of plant utilization. Suppose *ATC* is estimated to be $50 at the normal output rate of 2 million units. Since the firm wishes a total profit of $20 million on sales of 2 million units, profit per unit must average $10. The target price is then calculated by adding the necessary profit margin of $10 to the projected average total cost of $50 at the normal output rate, giving a price of $60. The target price serves as the initial basis for the firm's price decision; it may be adjusted upward or downward according to prevailing business conditions, actual or potential competition, long-run strategic objectives, and other relevant factors of the moment. Once the target price is chosen, the firm sells whatever amount is then demanded at the target price.

2. *Cost-plus pricing* is a widely used procedure whereby price is calculated by adding a predetermined percentage markup to the estimated unit cost of the product. To determine unit cost, the firm first computes the costs of labor, raw materials, and other variable inputs to get an estimate of *AVC*; to this is added the projected *AFC* at the "normal" operating rate (or standard volume). To illustrate, suppose that the firm is producing a product under conditions of constant returns to variable input such that $MC = AVC = \$30$. Further suppose that 75% of capacity is viewed as the normal operating rate, and at this output rate *AFC* is estimated to be $15. Average total cost is therefore $45 at the normal output rate. To this figure is added a markup of 5, 10, 20, 50, or whatever percent is required to achieve the firm's target profit. The size of the markup frequently reflects what managers believe is an "equitable relation to cost." If the firm desires a 10% return on sales, it should add a margin of $5 to its unit cost estimate of $45 to give a selling price of $50, which in percentage terms is equivalent to a markup slightly in excess of 11% over cost. If the firm desires a 25% return on sales, it should add a margin of $15 to its $45 unit cost to give a price of $60—a percentage markup of $33\frac{1}{3}\%$ over cost. As with pricing to achieve a target return on investment, cost-plus prices are subject to modification by competitive conditions and other pertinent considerations.

There are numerous variations of these two approaches to pricing. Cost estimates may be based upon "normal" operating rates, forecasted costs, or costs for the most recent accounting period. The amount of the "plus" or the target profit may be based upon either short-run or long-run considerations; it may be fixed for all products of the firm or variable among products; it may be computed as a percentage of costs, invested capital, or sales. Normally, the specific "formula" is keyed to long-standing industry practices, competitive conditions, price-cost-volume relationships, capital investment requirements, and the like. It is not uncommon for diversified firms to have different profit targets and to use different pricing formulas for different types of products, depending on price elasticity considerations, competitive pressures, whether the item carries a name brand or a private label, the intricacy and originality of the product and its design, and the estimate of the product's economic worth and utility to the customer. For example, in the retail goods industry where *variable markup pricing* (a cost-plus hybrid) is common, the markups *over cost* have been reported as 67% for cosmetics, 30 to 35% for household appliances, 38% for cameras, 50% for books (though the markup is usually 25% for college textbooks), 85% for costume jewelry, 25% for tobacco products, 80 to 125% for furniture, from 15 to 87% for frozen foods, and 100% for light fixtures and cabinet hardware.[2]

Another common use of target return pricing is found in corporate strategies for new product development and product innovation.[3] In contemplating the introduction of a new product or the revamping of an existing product, a typical procedure is for the firm first to identify a target selling price using such criteria as the prices of similar products, competitor's prices, and the estimated performance value to the customer. Product design and planning then proceed toward producing at a cost that fits within the target market price and at the same time allows a margin of profit sufficient to yield the firm's target rate of return. Engineering and production personnel are assigned the task of designing a product which will conform as closely as possible to the targeted unit cost, price, and profit margin. Hence, the firm, in developing and pricing new products, starts from established or preconceived prices and works backward to see whether it can profitably offer the product at or below competitive prices. Failing this, the firm may pursue the question of whether higher costs can be justified by a product that on comparative performance can command a somewhat higher price than the ruling price average and still yield the desired target return. The attempt to design a product within the target cost-price-profit figures is sometimes successful and sometimes unsuccessful. In the unsuccessful instances whether the go-ahead is given depends on management's estimate of the nature of the product in its overall product line. If the product is one which strongly complements or creates a substantial demand for other of the firm's products, the firm may well decide to produce the item regardless of the estimated profits.

Attributes of Target Return Pricing.   In practice, both pricing to achieve a target return on investment and cost-plus offer relatively simple and expedient methods of price determination as well as a demonstrated ability to yield "adequate," "fair," or "reasonable" profits. The profitability of the two methods is evidenced by the avowed use of some sort of target return pricing by such "blue-chip" firms

---

[2] See, for instance, Lee E. Preston, *Profits, Competition and Rules of Thumb in Retail Food Pricing* (Berkeley: University of California Institute of Business and Economic Research, 1963), p. 31, and *Departmental Mechandising and Operating Results of 1966* (New York: National Retail Merchants Association, 1963), pp. 16, 28.

[3] An excellently documented example of International Harvester's use of this strategy is found in Kaplan, Dirlam, and Lanzilotti, *Pricing in Big Business*, pp. 69–79.

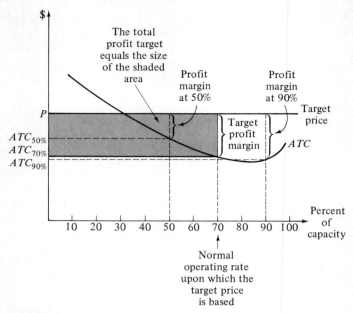

FIGURE 14-1
Effects of demand fluctuations upon achieving the target rate of return

as Alcoa, DuPont, Exxon, General Electric, General Foods, General Motors, International Harvester, Johns-Manville, Union Carbide, and U.S. Steel.[4]

Once the target price is chosen, the usual procedure is for the firm to stick by its price (barring major changes in market conditions) and sell whatever amounts of output that customers are willing to buy at the target price. The target return price is therefore a fairly stable price—an attribute that highly recommends itself to oligopoly situations where infrequent price changes are competitively helpful. This may partly explain the popularity of target return pricing among corporate oligopolists. However, target return pricing does have the effect of causing wide swings in profits when economic conditions turn up or down; on a year-to-year basis, actual profits may thus turn out to be either higher or lower than the target profit rate. Suppose, for example, that a firm has a short-run average total cost curve as illustrated in Fig. 14-1; the target price is P dollars, the "normal" operating rate is 70% of capacity, the target profit margin is $P - ATC_{70\%}$, and the target amount of total profit is equal to the shaded area. If in a particular year demand is especially strong and actual output corresponds to 90% of capacity, then total profits will be pushed up well above the targeted level. Two reasons can account for this. First, the firm's actual sales of output will exceed the rate required to achieve the profit target. Second, unit costs at 90% of capacity may be lower than at 70% of capacity because of the lower average

[4] R. F. Lanzilotti, "Pricing Objectives in Large Companies," *American Economic Review*, Vol. 48, No. 5 (December 1958), pp. 921–940.

fixed costs associated with higher production rates. The realized profit margin on each unit sold of $P - ATC_{90\%}$ may therefore be larger than the margin of $P - ATC_{70\%}$ needed to reach the target. The combined effect of wider profit margins and above-normal sales is a realized profit which may be considerably in excess of the target rate of return, as shown in Fig. 14-1. On the other hand, if demand for the firm's product is weak and actual sales of output amount to only 50% of capacity instead of the "normal" 70%, then the profit target will in all probability not be achieved. At production rates below the normal 70% figure, average fixed costs are sure to be higher, and average variable costs may be higher if the production process cannot be operated efficiently at less than normal rates. With average total cost at 50% of capacity exceeding that at 70%, the realized profit margin of $P - ATC_{50\%}$ will be narrower than the targeted margin of $P - ATC_{70\%}$. This, together with lower sales, produces total profits well below the target rate of return (see Fig. 14-1).

A firm using target pricing is well aware that profits in any given year may not correspond to the profit target because actual sales will almost certainly deviate to some extent from the output rate on which the target price is based. The target profit rate is something the firm hopes to achieve as a long-run average rather than in any particular year. This is apparent from the fact that the target price is predicated upon a normal rate of production instead of the forecasted sales volume for the upcoming period.

It follows from the discussion above that target return pricing is not a strategy for maximizing profits.[5] This is easily demonstrated. Since the target return price is keyed to the firm's normal operating rate (or standard volume), the target return price and the profit-maximizing price will coincide if and only if the normal operating rate just happens to correspond to the output rate where marginal cost equals marginal revenue. Certainly, there is no reason to expect this to occur—except by mere circumstance and coincidence.

Actually, the concept of target return pricing exemplifies a behavior pattern closely approximating satisficing. The target rate of return, according to the evidence available, tends to be based upon managerial concepts of what is an "equitable" or "reasonable" or "satisfactory" rate of return, given the degrees of risk and uncertainty involved. Few managers believe or, more accurately perhaps,

---

[5] Some economists have argued that if the firm's target rate of return is based upon some concept of the *largest* rate of return the firm perceives it can get, then the firm's behavior reflects a goal of profit maximization. This is misleading if not erroneous. To illustrate why, suppose a firm believes the maximum rate of return market conditions will allow is 20%. The critical question now becomes whether the perceived maximum rate of 20% can be obtained just as well via target return pricing as by marginal cost-marginal revenue pricing. The answer is only by rare circumstance. If 20% is truly the maximum profit rate, then the only way it can be attained is for the firm to elect the price and output corresponding to the intersection of *MC* and *MR*. Since the target return price is based upon the "normal" operating rate (or standard volume), the target return price and the profit-maximizing price will coincide only if the normal operating rate just happens to be the output rate where $MR = MC$. This is a little too much to expect. Thus, while a firm's managers may believe the target return price will yield the maximum rate of profit, the facts of the matter are to the contary. In a sense, the fallacy in their thinking is akin to the fallacy that maximum profit is achieved at the output where profit per unit ($P - ATC$) is greatest. As was demonstrated in Chapter 10, the output rate at which price exceeds ATC by the greatest amount *does not* correspond to the output rate where $MR = MC$.

admit that their profit targets are indicative of the "maximum" obtainable rate of return. Managers exhibit a propensity to use target return pricing techniques because information is often too sketchy or too expensive to obtain for a full analysis of the relevant factors to be conducted. In essence, target return pricing is an imperfect expedient designed to facilitate, in a rough but ready manner, the handling of a thorny decision problem under conditions of uncertainty. Parenthetically, it should be added that executives use similar "rules of thumb" in other decision situations. Advertising expenditures are frequently determined by setting aside some fixed percentage of total revenue; inventory levels may be pegged to some preset turnover norm. By translating complicated problems into simple routines, rule-of-thumb procedures economize on executive time and may even contribute to overall operating efficiency. In any event, they serve as classic examples of precisely what is meant by satisficing—the seeking of satisfactory workable solutions to complex decision problems.

Other Pricing Strategies

There are any number of other pricing strategies. Some of the most commonly used approaches are presented below.

Penetration Pricing.   In introducing new products and/or in moving into new geographical markets, firms sometimes deliberately set a relatively low price in order to develop the market for the item and to capture a large market share. Any of several conditions favor the use of penetration pricing: (1) when demand is very price elastic and many new customers can be attracted by a lower price (and then later induced to pay higher prices), (2) when major economies of scale and/or strong experience curve effects exist and large sales volumes are needed to achieve maximum efficiency-minimum unit cost, (3) when a low price will discourage the actual or potential entry of new firms as well as the development of substitute products, (4) when it is important for competitive and psychological reasons to get a lead on rival firms and capture as large a market share as quickly as possible, and (5) when a firm is trying to enter an industry and needs to have some basis for attracting buyers' attention and building up a clientele for its product.

Once the firm's market penetration objective is achieved, it can then turn attention to ways to increase profitability, including a planned gradual raising of price over a period of time. A penetration price thus deliberately sacrifices short-run profitability for long-run objectives (long-run profitability, growth in sales, market share, etc.).

Price Skimming.   On occasions, firms try to take advantage of the fact that some buyers are always willing and able to pay a premium price because the product, for any of several reasons, has a high immediate value to them. The objective of price skimming is initially to charge as much as these buyers will pay and then gradually to reduce price to gain access to lower-price market segments. In essence, price skimming is a form of price discrimination *over time*; starting with the price-inelastic buyer segments, the firm proceeds over time to draw in the more price-elastic market segments with progressively lower prices (often, the lower prices are keyed to the introduction of lower quality models so as not to interfere with continuing to realize substantially higher margins on top-of-the-line models).

APPLICATIONS CAPSULE

GENERAL MOTORS' PRICING STRATEGY

General Motors has for many years used target return pricing, attempting to achieve a long-run average rate of return of 20% on investment (after taxes). In figuring what price to announce for forthcoming models, GM typically considers production trends for its models, cost changes which it expects to experience, competitors' prices (including imports), the expected industrywide demand for autos, and general economic conditions.

With car prices having been boosted by unprecedented amounts during 1973–1975 and with auto sales slumping so badly in 1974 and 1975 (partly due to the sharp run-up in gasoline prices and partly due to the recession which began in late 1974), GM was particularly concerned about how to price its 1976 models. Being the trend setter in pricing in the auto industry, GM publicly expressed concern over having to announce sharp price increases for the third year in a row. Buyer resistance to the higher 1975 car prices (over $400 per car) was still much in evidence, and GM did not want to risk undermining the modest resurgence in car sales which appeared during mid-1975.

Although observers speculated that GM and the other auto manufacturers would announce increases of 6 to 7% on base sticker prices for their 1976 models, GM surprised the industry by trimming the discounts off sticker price to dealers and by removing various pieces of equipment as standard. The discount cut (estimated by GM to be equivalent to about one percentage point on a sales-weighted basis), together with the shift of some standard equipment to optional extras, still resulted in average base sticker price increases on 1976 cars of 4.4% (sales-weighted). But if GM had not made these moves, it was estimated that the price increases would have averaged about $275 per car instead of $206. In an attempt to pacify dealers over a reduction in their base sticker margins, GM raised the prices of optional equipment by 5% at wholesale and 6% at retail.

Small cars were the principal targets of GM's 1976 equipment deletions. Steel-belted radials were removed as standard from all of GM's six-cylinder compact models; power brakes were removed from Chevrolet Monza-type cars; and a number of deletions were applied to the Monza Towne Coupe. However, maintenance-free batteries were added as standard on Vegas, Astres, Monzas, Skylarks, Starfires, Corvettes, and all Cadillacs. GM's sticker price revisions ranged from a $211 cut on the Monza Towne Coupe to an increase of $808 on Corvettes.

In announcing the 1976 prices, GM Chairman Thomas Murphy indicated that during the past year GM had experienced or was committed to cost increases of about $375 per car. However, according to Murphy, "to increase prices to our customers by the full amount of these increases would, in our judgment, tend to dampen the returning demand in the market."

The table below shows GM's dealer discount structure on its various models:

GM's Dealer Discount Structure
(all figures represent dealer discounts from sticker prices)

Model Names	Historical	1975 Models[a]	1976 Models
Vega, Astre	17	15.5	15
Monza type	17	16.6	15
Compacts (Nova, Omega)	17	15.9	15
Camaro, Firebird	17	16.3	15
Intermediates (Cutlass, Century)	21	20.1	19
Monte Carlo	21	19.9	19
Chevrolet, Pontiac, Olds Delta, Buick LeSabre	25	24.1	22
Olds 98, Buick Electra	25	24.1	24
Toronado, Riviera, Corvette	25	23.8	24
Cadillac Seville	25	25	25
Other Cadillac	26	25.1	25

[a] The "historical" dealer discount was reduced by government-ordered pass-through of price increases for federally mandated equipment for safety and emission control. This occurred during the price-control period of 1971–1974.

QUESTIONS FOR DISCUSSION

1. What effect would you predict that GM's price strategy might have on dealer pricing?
2. What benefit, if any, did such a price revision offer to GM? To dealers? To GM car buyers?

Sources: A. D. H. Kaplan, J. B. Dirlam, and R. F. Lanzilotti, *Pricing in Big Business* (Washington, D.C.: The Brookings Institution, 1958), pp. 48–55, 131–135; and *Automotive News*, August 18, 1975, pp. 1, 7.

Price skimming makes good economic and business sense (from the standpoint of sellers) whenever (1) different classes of buyers have materially different price elasticities of demand and the firm has ample time to "ride" down the demand curve, charging each buyer segment as much as the traffic will bear; (2) the innovating firm has a lead time long enough that the initial high price will neither stimulate entry of rival firms nor the development of substitute products; (3) the diseconomies of producing at smaller volumes do not cancel out the advantage of premium prices; (4) high initial prices support the impression that the product is superior and of exceptional quality; and (5) there is substantial risk to setting an initial price that is too low (because demand is uncertain and may not materialize or because unit costs may exceed expectations). In addition, a high initial price leaves room for reducing price if things do not go as expected; usually, price cuts are easier to implement than price increases.[6]

[6] However, Kotler cites the case of a home permanent kit which did not sell well when priced at 39 cents and marketed through dimestores but which caught on when repriced at $1.98 and sold through drugstores. See Philip Kotler, *Marketing Management: Analysis, Planning, and Control*, 2nd ed. (Englewood Cliffs, N.J.: Prentice-Hall, Inc., 1972), p. 520, footnote.

Loss-Leader Pricing. Some firms, particularly food retailers and discount stores, price one or a few items at bargain levels (even below wholesale cost) in order to (1) increases future sales of the item or (2) attract customers to their stores and boost sales on other items. The objective, of course, is not to produce losses but rather to increase total profits. A successful loss-leader therefore is really a profit-leader. Loss-leader pricing can be defined as pricing an item at a level which generates a subpar or even negative unit contribution profit (i.e., $P - AVC$ will be less than the customary margin) but which is nonetheless expected to result in higher total profits through either increased future sales of the item or greater sales on the firm's entire line of items. Loss-leader pricing works well in situations where (1) it is desirable for buyers to become familiar with the product (or with the store), (2) it is apparent to buyers that the price represents a good value, (3) the price cut is sizable enough to cause buyers to respond, and (4) the lower price does not signify a reduction in quality.

Pricing for Early Recovery of Investment Costs. Some firms aim for a price that offers the quickest payback of sunk investment costs. This could mean pricing either "high" or "low," depending on such factors as buyer's sensitivity to price, whether the market is developed, the competitive threat from substitute products, barriers to entry, and so on. Firms may lean toward such a pricing strategy if they are cash-poor or if market change is too rapid to justify patiently cultivating demand.

Going-Rate Pricing. Competitive fringe firms, as well as larger firms which do not have a leadership position, may have a pricing strategy that consists of no more than simply charging the going price. This is referred to as going-rate pricing, imitative pricing, or price followership. In oligopolistic markets such a pricing strategy has obvious appeal for firms not in a position to exert price leadership or for firms whose products are not differentiated strongly enough to give them some price freedom. But the strategy is also used by firms unaffected by oligopolistic interdependence. Why? Because it is easy. The price imitator can sit back and let other firms worry about demand elasticities, changing market conditions, and what to do next; managers then have more time to devote to other decisions. This is a tenable position as long as acceptable profits can be earned being a price follower.

Sealed-Bid Pricing. In construction, defense contract work, and capital goods manufacture, firms compete for jobs on the basis of bid prices. Here, pricing strategy is necessarily keyed to expectations of how competitors will price. While overall market conditions and costs are relevant in deciding how hard to try to get a particular job, the firm's success is predicated upon being low bidder on a sufficient number of jobs to build a viable business. The firm thus confronts something of a dilemma: The higher its bid price is above variable costs, the higher are potential profits but the lower is the chance of getting the contract. On the other hand, if the firm consistently bids too close to variable costs, it may not earn enough contribution profit to cover total fixed costs.

Other Price Considerations. Some sellers believe that odd-number prices are more attractive to buyers than round-number prices. A $5.99 price may, for psychological or subconscious reasons, be more stimulating to sales than a $6.00 price. A 33-cent price may have more buyer appeal than a 32-cent or even a 30-cent price. Items may sell more rapidly at 3 for 88 cents than for 29 cents each. The problem here is to determine which numbers, if any, have more appeal and whether this appeal applies only to certain items or extends more broadly.

Still other pricing issues arise in special situations. For instance, food products firms which periodically offer buyers "cents-off" coupons and in-store "cents-off" specials face the problems of deciding upon seasonal timing, magnitude of the price discount, and competitive effect. Clothing stores regularly mark down the prices of fashion goods as the season progresses, giving rise to decisions about the appropriate size and timing of the mark-downs. Pricing also comes under serious scrutiny during periods of industrywide overcapacity, recession, and inflation.

Conclusions. The economist's marginal cost-marginal revenue models offer firms guidance in finding the short-run profit-maximizing price when estimates of demand and cost are available. Such models do not, however, allow for explicit consideration of long-run profit objectives, goals other than profit, nonprice competitive variables, and uncertainties as to demand and/or cost. In practice, quite a large number of enterprises orient their pricing toward cost (as in target return and cost-plus pricing) or toward demand (as in price skimming) or toward market share and sales growth (as in penetration pricing) or toward competition (as in going-rate pricing and sealed bids). Although marginal cost-marginal revenue considerations enter to some extent into these alternatives, they are not decisive in choosing the actual price.

MULTIPLE-GOAL MODELS OF BUSINESS BEHAVIOR

Revenue Maximization with a Profit Constraint

One of the best known of the multiple-goal models of business behavior is the model of sales revenue maximization with a profit constraint.[7] This model, first proposed by William Baumol, is founded upon the premise that once profits reach acceptable levels, the firm's profit goal becomes subordinate to its goal of increasing its sales revenue (the rationale underlying this goal hierarchy was presented in Chapter 9). According to Baumol, the drive to increase sales revenues assumes such strong proportions that the firm's managers are willing to forego higher profits to obtain greater sales revenues.

Figure 14-2 illustrates the revenue maximization model. The firm's *TR*, *TC*, and π curves are shown in their conventional shapes. Total profit is maximum at

---

[7] Baumol's model, with all of its price-output and strategy ramifications, is presented in his book *Business Behavior, Value and Growth*, rev. ed. (New York: Harcourt Brace Jovanovich, Inc., 1967), Chapters 6–8.

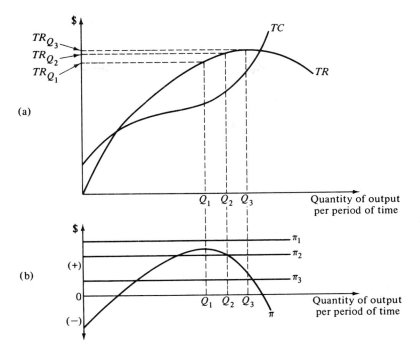

FIGURE 14-2
Revenue maximization model

an output rate of Q_1 units, and *TR* is maximum at an output rate of Q_3 units. Thus, it is evident that the firm cannot simultaneously maximize short-run profits *and* sales revenue. Profit is always maximum where $MR = MC$, whereas *TR* (or sales revenue) is maximum where $MR = 0$. The price and the output rate which maximize profits definitely do not correspond to the price and the output rate which maximize sales revenue. Suppose the firm has a profit target of π_1 dollars [Fig. 14-2(b)]. If profits of π_1 dollars are required before other objectives such as sales revenue maximization are pursued, then the firm is in no position to increase the sales of output beyond Q_1 units, since even at the profit-maximizing output the profit target is still out of reach. The firm must produce at Q_1 units just to come as close as possible to satisfying its profit constraint. However, if profits of π_2 dollars will fulfill its profit requirements, the firm is in a position to pursue a sales revenue goal as well as a profit goal. By a lowering of its price, the output rate can be expanded to Q_2 units and sales revenues pushed up to TR_{Q_2} dollars. Profits will still be the desired amount of π_2 dollars, though they will be below their potential maximum. Nonetheless, the firm is able to meet its profit objective, and it enjoys a higher level of sales revenues than it would at the profit-maximizing output of Q_1 units. This is what is meant by sales revenue maximization with a profit constraint. Finally, suppose the profit constraint is only π_3 dollars. Then price can be lowered yet further, the sales of output pushed to Q_3 units, and revenue pushed to the maximum value of TR_{Q_3} dollars. The firm has no motive to expand its output rate past Q_3, even though its profit goal of π_3 dollars is overfulfilled. The reason? Additional output can be absorbed in the market only at prices reduced so much that total revenue will fall. Hence, revenues are smaller at output rates greater than Q_3 than they are at Q_3, effectively undermining the firm's revenue incentive to push sales past Q_3 units.

Observe that at outputs below Q_1, a strategy of lowering price and increasing output enhances both profits and sales revenues. Up to an output of Q_1 units, the two goals are complementary in the sense that success in achieving higher sales is concomitant with success in achieving higher profits. On the other hand, between outputs of Q_1 and Q_3 units, lower prices and greater outputs cause profits to fall but sales revenues to rise. Therefore, between Q_1 and Q_3, greater sales revenues are achieved at the expense of profits—the two goals compete with one another. Beyond an output of Q_3 units, a lower price and consequently larger sales of output result in lower profits and in lower sales revenues.

A chief conclusion to be derived from the sales revenue maximization model is this: *If a firm has a goal of maximizing its sales revenue subject to a profit constraint and if the firm's profit constraint (or profit target) is below the maximum attainable profit, then the firm will charge lower prices for its products and will produce greater outputs than it would with a goal of profit maximization.*

Advertising Expenditures and the Goals of the Firm.   The decision as to how much to spend on advertising and sales promotion is also influenced by the firm's choice of goals. A revenue-maximizer tends to spend more money promoting its products than does a profit-maximizer. This proposition is illustrated in Fig. 14-3. The horizontal axis in panels (a) and (b) represents the dollar magnitude of advertising outlays; the vertical axis measures dollar costs, revenues, and profits. For simplicity, total cost is shown to increase linearly with advertising expenditures, starting from a value of TC_0 dollars where advertising is zero. The TC curve includes all production and selling costs, including advertising outlays. The total revenue curve is drawn on the reasonable assumption that increased advertising tends to increase sales of output and revenue, but by progressively lesser amounts. In other words, diminishing returns to promotion exist, and additional advertising expenditures result in ever more slowly increasing revenues. The total profit (π) curve in panel (b) is found by subtracting total costs from total revenues at each level of advertising outlay; it indicates the profitability of various-sized advertising outlays.

Figure 14-3 indicates that the profit-maximizing amount of advertising outlay is A_1 dollars. In contrast, a revenue-maximizing firm with a profit constraint of π_1 dollars has an optimal advertising outlay of A_2 dollars. The additional advertising pushes sales revenues from TR_{A1} dollars to TR_{A2} dollars without causing total profits to fall below the targeted level of π_1 dollars. As long as the revenue-maximizer's profit target is *less* than the maximum profit level, the revenue-maximizer will find it advantageous to spend more heavily on advertising than will a profit-maximizer. The revenue-maximizer's output rate will, accordingly, be greater than the profit-maximizer's output rate. However, the revenue-maximizing firm's selling price may be higher, lower, or equal to the profit-maximizing

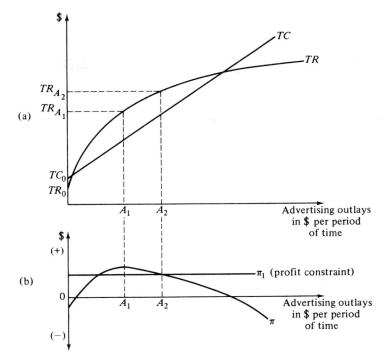

FIGURE 14-3
Advertising expenditures and the goals of the firm

firm's, depending on the effect advertising has upon unit costs and upon customer demand for the firm's products (see Fig. 11-7). On occasions, the extra advertising undertaken by the sales-maximizer may shift the firm's demand-*AR* curve so as to make it advantageous to charge a price slightly above that of rival firms. On other occasions, the additional advertising may simply result in selling more units at the prevailing price level. And on still other occasions, the extra advertising may entail a lower price as well as expanded sales.

The Effect of Fixed Cost Changes. One of the most surprising and interesting aspects of the economics of the firm is the effect of fixed cost changes upon price and output decisions. Consider Fig. 14-4, where the firm's initial cost-revenue-profit functions are given by TFC_1, TC_1, TR_1, and π_1. Note that if the firm's primary goal is profit maximization, then its optimum output rate is Q_1 units, but if its primary goal is sales revenue maximization with a profit constraint of π dollars, then its optimum output is Q_2 units. Now suppose the firm experiences a rise in the prices of its fixed inputs such that total fixed costs rise to a level indicated by TFC_2. This will cause the firm's total cost function to shift upward by the amount of the rise in fixed costs to TC_2. The rise in fixed costs will further cause the firm's profit function to shift downward from π_1 to π_2, with the amount of the downward shift being equal to the increase in fixed costs.

What effect does this sort of cost increase have upon the firm's optimum price and output rate if the firm's principal goal is profit maximization? The answer, surprisingly enough, is *none*. The rise in fixed costs *lowers* the peak of the total profit curve, but it moves the peak neither to the right nor to the left. Moreover, changes in fixed costs have no effect whatsoever upon *MC* or upon *MR*, thus leaving the point at which *MC* = *MR* completely undisturbed. Hence, total profit is maximized at precisely the same price and output as before the rise in total fixed costs. And we have the inescapable conclusion that changes in fixed costs do not influence the short-run price and output decisions of profit-maximizing firms so long as it is possible to earn positive contribution profits.

But what of the effect upon a revenue-maximizing firm? From Fig. 14-4 it is apparent that given the downward shift in the total profit curve an output of Q_2 units will result in profits below the minimum acceptable level. The revenue-maximizing firm will therefore be compelled to reduce output to Q_3 units to meet its profit constraint; concomitantly, it will raise price as the vehicle for effecting the reduction in unit sales. Thus, the goal of the firm is the pivotal factor in analyzing its response to a rise in fixed costs. Firms which seek to maximize profits will leave their price and output rates unchanged when fixed costs change, whereas firms which seek to maximize sales revenue subject to a profit constraint

FIGURE 14-4
Effect of fixed cost changes upon a firm's optimum price and output

will tend to reduce their outputs and raise their selling prices in response to an increase in fixed costs.

Insofar as actual business practice is concerned, there is little question which of the two responses to fixed cost increases is the more commonly observed. An increase in fixed costs is usually an occasion for serious consideration of a price increase.

The Effect of Tax Changes. Whether a firm is a profit-maximizer or a revenue-maximizer has significant public policy implications. An outstanding illustration concerns the use of federal taxation policies to control inflationary tendencies. Increases in corporate tax rates have on occasions been used to help contain inflationary forces and to promote price stability and full employment. The logic seems plain enough: With steeper corporate profits taxes, the business sector has fewer after-tax dollars to spend for new capital investment and less of a profit incentive to invest these dollars, so that investment spending is curtailed and the investment component of economywide spending is reduced. In turn, the pressure of total spending upon production capacity is relieved somewhat, and the motive of sellers to raise product prices is dampened.

However, the successful use of increases in corporate profits taxes as a weapon for fighting inflation depends implicitly on the principal goal of business enterprises. This can be seen from the cost-revenue-profit curves shown in Fig. 14-5. Given a total revenue curve of *TR*, a total cost curve of *TC*, a net-profit-after-taxes curve of π_1, and a profit target of *OA* dollars, the profit-maximizing and revenue-maximizing outputs are Q_1 units and Q_2 units, respectively. Now suppose an additional tax of 10% of all profits is imposed upon the firm. The effect of the tax is to shift the firm's after-tax profit curve downward at each level of *profitable output* by the amount of the additional tax, as shown by π_2. Observe that the peak of π_2 corresponds to the same output as does the peak of π_1. Hence, we may correctly conclude that the profit-maximizing output rate is the same after the additional tax is paid as it was before. The profit-maximizing firm therefore has no incentive to change either its output rate or its price. But the same cannot be said if the firm's goal is to maximize sales revenue subject to a profit constraint. Imposing additional corporate profits taxes upon a revenue-maximizing firm induces the firm to restrict its sales of output to Q_3 units and to raise its price as the means of reducing sales of output from Q_2 to Q_3 units. Raising price and restricting output allows the firm to cover the costs of higher taxes and still meet its after-tax profit constraint.

The preceding analysis highlights the effects of different goals upon the optimal price and output decisions of the firm. It indicates how seriously wrong predictions of business price and output behavior can be unless care is exercised first in determining the actual goals of business enterprises.

The Extent of Revenue-Maximizing Behavior. The evidence is inconclusive whether or not a significant number of business firms actually base their price and output decisions upon a goal of maximizing sales revenue subject to a profit constraint. The major obstacle is that the decision process of large corporations

FIGURE 14-5
Effect of tax changes upon the firm's optimum price and output

is exceedingly complex. Many factors influence and constrain corporate pricing decisions; it is quite difficult to know just what set of motivations and priorities are reflected in managerial decisions. In addition, the behavioral differences between profit maximization and revenue maximization are difficult to detect with the available empirical data because so many economic forces must be untangled. The few available studies of business behavior, the public pronouncements of business executives, and the consulting experiences which several academicians have had with major firms do, however, combine to give credence to the revenue maximization model.[8] The numerous examples of target return pricing are also quite consistent with a revenue-maximizing goal. Nevertheless, the final verdict is still out on the extent of revenue-maximizing behavior among business enterprises.

[8] See, for example, the instances cited by Baumol, *Business Behavior, Value and Growth*, Chapter 6; Marshall Hall, "Sales Revenue Maximization: An Empirical Examination," *Journal of Industrial Economics*, Vol. 15 (April 1967), pp. 143–154; J. W. McGuire, J. S. Y. Chiu, and A. D. Elbins, "Executive Income, Sales, and Profits," *American Economic Review*, Vol. 52, No. 4 (September 1962), pp. 753–761; B. D. Mabry and D. L. Siders, "An Empirical Test of the Sales Maximization Hypothesis," *Southern Economic Journal*, Vol. 33, No. 3 (January 1967), pp. 267–277; and Y. Amihud and J. Kamin, "Revenue vs. Profit Maximization: Differences in Behavior by the Type of Control and by Market Power," *Southern Economic Journal*, Vol. 45, No. 3 (January 1979), pp. 838–846.

The Related Goals of Revenue Growth, Profit, and Diversification: An Integrative Model

All the preceding models of corporate behavior have been largely *static* in their approach. They have concentrated upon pinpointing the firm's optimal price and output decisions at a particular moment, given some specified set of cost and revenue conditions. The result has been an illuminating snapshot description of firms and markets in motion. But a complete picture of business behavior and market performance requires that the time frame of our analysis be lengthened to include the long-run goals of business enterprise and the dynamic influences of such powerful forces as technological progress, shifts in consumer buying patterns, and long-run competitive pressures. Progress in raising the quality of economic life is best gauged by *trends* in prices, in product quality, in rates of growth in output, and in the pace of innovation, rather than by their respective values at some moment of time. Even more important, the growth of the economy as a whole presumably does not proceed in some mysterious fashion that is independent of the growth of its constituent parts.

As emphasized in Chapter 9, large corporate enterprises may exhibit interest in such goals as profits, revenue growth, market share, long-run survival, diversification, managerial autonomy, technological virtuosity, and rising dividend rates, as well as fulfillment of the personal objectives of top management. The surest strategy for achievement of these goals over the long term is maintaining the growth and expansion of the firm itself. Searching for some optimum short-run equilibrium condition and then seeking ways to maintain it is a strategy totally abhorrent and foreign to most corporate executives. Instead, their energies are almost always focused on how the corporation can escape the throes of a static state and the stagnation and decline which it soon entails. Every management is acutely aware that the activities upon which the firm presently relies will over time lose their sustaining power through changes in consumer tastes, the appearance of attractive substitutes, increased competition from foreign and domestic rivals, and growth in the market power of suppliers and customers. Change is certain, thereby making it imperative for firms to stay abreast of any new opportunities and expansion possibilities that change brings. Specifically, this means blueprinting the growth of the firm and deciding in what markets, with what products, at what speed, and with what competitive strategies growth should best be pursued. Expanding sales revenues and expanding profits—the two most focused upon measures of business growth—thus tend to be foremost in the typical corporation's goal hierarchy.

The concern with growth has very important implications for corporate behavior in the marketplace. In all probability, a growth-conscious management will avoid employing any sort of short-run strategy which interferes with the attainment of long-run goals. For example, firms commonly elect to deviate from their short-run profit-maximizing prices and output rates in order to better achieve long-run profit maximization. This was indicated in Chapters 12 and 13, where dominant firms and near monopolists were seen to have strong incentives for choosing actual selling prices below those at which $MC = MR$ and for increasing short-run output rates past the $MC = MR$ intersection. Via this short-run price-output strategy, these firms (1) discourage the entry and expansion of rival firms, (2) reduce the chances of government intervention, and (3) contain the motives for countervailing power. The intent of such a strategy is, of course, to forsake short-run for long-run profit maximization. In the same vein, firms may price new products below short-run profit-maximizing levels in order to open up more uses for the product, attract more new customers, and thereby enhance their long-term profits, sales, and market shares. Some firms may invest heavily in technologies which they know have little or no short-run payoff but which offer substantial long-run benefits in terms of costs and efficiency, given expected changes in input prices. Target return pricing, which makes use of long-run "normal" operating rates as the basis for price determination, is another situation where long-run considerations dominate those of the short run.

Growth and Diversification Strategy. Given that growth and diversification goals are so widespread in the business community, it is imperative that they be incorporated into our analysis of business behavior. Specifically, we shall concentrate upon the criteria for determining how rapidly the firm should expand its activities in pursuit of its goals. The analysis follows closely the lines proposed by Professor Baumol in his "growth-equilibrium" model.[9]

Consider first the effects of growth and diversification upon a firm's total costs. Two types of cost arising from the growth process are of particular interest: (1) *output cost*—ordinary fixed and variable costs stemming from the operation of production processes with greater output potential and (2) *diversification costs*—costs associated exclusively with expanding into new lines of business via acquisition or internal startup. Output costs can reasonably be expected to increase linearly as a firm's annual rate of growth in output rises—in other words, constant returns to scale may be said to characterize the expansion of production capacity. Once the optimum scale of plant for a productive activity is identified, a firm can build as many such plants as may be required to satisfy output needs. Technical progress also helps to ward off more-than-proportional increases in output costs as production rates are expanded.

Meanwhile, the faster a firm seeks to grow via diversification into new lines of business, the faster *costs* can be counted upon to rise. The reasons for this deserve brief mention. First, achieving diversification via rapid-fire acquisition of existing firms greatly enhances the probability of "not looking before leaping," thus contributing to a poorly thought out acquisition strategy, making one or more "bad" acquisitions, paying too much to "buy one's way" into a new line of business, and otherwise running up diversification costs by trying to get into too many new businesses too quickly—in other words, encountering all of the "too much, too soon" kinds of problems. Second, ever more rapid diversification requires ever more money to finance it. Beyond some point, firms generally find that the more money they must raise to diversify, the higher is the cost of obtaining it. The amount which can be funded by retained earnings is limited. Issuing large

---

[9] Baumol, *Business Behavior, Value and Growth*, Chapter 10.

amounts of new stock or selling bonds drives their prices down and so raises the cost of obtaining capital. Negotiating loans also tends to become more expensive, since lenders may well insist upon higher interest rates for larger and more leveraged loans. Third, internal startup of a brand new line of business entails the recruitment of more executives, middle- and lower-echelon managers, technical staff, and production workers. It takes time for them to be trained and to gain experience in their assignments. The more rapidly a firm tries to assimilate new personnel into the organization, the more opportunity there is for inefficiency, mistakes, false starts, and the lack of experience to result in added costs.

Consequently, as a firm seeks to accelerate the rate of expansion into new, unfamiliar lines of business, it typically finds it difficult to accommodate faster growth without encountering severe "growing pains" and a concomitant rise in inefficiency. Diversification costs, capital costs, and organizational staffing costs all increase disproportionately, causing the firm's total cost function to rise more and more sharply. Thus, while ordinary output costs tend to increase linearly in view of the prevalence of constant returns to scale, diversification costs can be counted upon to transform an otherwise linear total cost curve into one which increases at an increasing rate as a firm's annual growth in the size and scope of its operations become progressively larger. This is illustrated in Fig. 14-6.

Now, what about the effect of growth upon a firm's total revenues? Barring totally unfavorable market conditions, a firm's total revenues can be expected to rise as the rate of growth in output in existing lines of business rises above zero

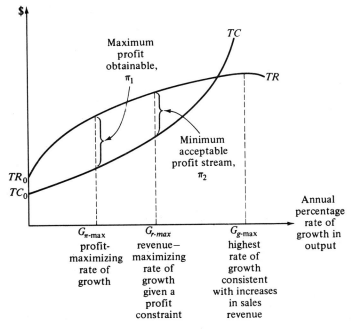

FIGURE 14-6
Growth equilibrium for the firm

and as diversification into new areas occurs. However, the ability to expand via internal growth and diversification over the near term is not boundless. Internally generated strategies to spur sales are likely to encounter diminishing success even in a favorable market environment and only so much new diversification can be handled. Hence, the firm's total revenue curve tends to increase at a decreasing rate, as shown in Fig. 14-6.

It is obvious from Fig. 14-6 that different rates of growth result in different degrees of profitability. The gap between TR and TC widens, then narrows, as the annual rate of growth increases. A firm will therefore find it unprofitable to expand either too slowly or too rapidly, and there is some rate of expansion that will maximize long-run profits. The profit-maximizing growth rate, shown as $G_{\pi-\max}$, results in a maximum profit stream of π_1 dollars. It follows from this analysis that a firm grows partly because growth makes the firm more profitable.[10]

However, as we have emphasized on numerous occasions, corporations may have objectives other than profit. One very plausible alternative to long-run profit maximization is maximization of the *rate of growth* of sales revenue subject to a profit constraint. Given that corporations stress the *percentage* by which sales and profits have grown rather than the *amount* of sales and profits, *growth rates* may more accurately describe corporate goals than absolute dollar values.

Referring again to Fig. 14-6, suppose a profit stream of π_2 dollars will suffice to meet the firm's capital needs as well as to satisfy stockholders' expectations. Then the firm can push its rate of growth past $G_{\pi-\max}$ to $G_{r-\max}$—$G_{r-\max}$ may be delineated as the maximum rate of expansion consistent with maximizing sales revenues *and* attaining the desired profit. Hence, a firm with an objective of maximizing its rate of growth of sales revenue will tend to expand faster than a profit-maximizing firm. It is apparent that past a growth rate of $G_{\pi-\max}$, profits and sales *compete*—higher revenues can be achieved only by sacrificing some profits. Yet, if growth is carried too far, the profit stream will be too small to generate the needed investment capital. This explains why the firm stops short of a growth rate corresponding to the peak of the *TR* curve (shown as $G_{g-\max}$ in Fig. 14-6).

Two very important conclusions are implied by this analysis. First, the corporation's behavior over the long term (as well as over the short term) varies according to its goals. The price and output decisions of profit-maximizers differ from those of revenue-maximizers; the decisions of growth-maximizers will result in yet a third outcome. The implication is strong that the pursuit of other goals will entail still different price-output decisions and growth strategy sets. In other words, price-output combinations, growth rates, and growth strategies all vary according to the priorities which a corporation may assign to its goal hierarchy.

Second, an enterprise has a very powerful motive to expand production and/or to diversify over time. Irrespective of whether the firm's ultimate goal is long-

---

[10] The motives for profitable growth are, of course, not the exclusive province of large corporations; small firms have growth ambitions too. Over the years a number of small firms have been so successful in executing a growth strategy that they now rank as large corporations—Control Data, Holiday Inn, Apple Computer, Textron, and Xerox are good examples.

run profit maximization or maximizing future sales revenues or something else, an increased size and scope of operation tends to be required. This is not to say that the output rate for each and every product must be increased, for obviously shifts in consumer demand may dictate otherwise, but it does say that the combined output of the firm's products and businesses will tend to rise over time. A positive rate of growth—and maybe a substantial rate—is a virtual prerequisite to achievement of multiple-goal hierarchies over the long-run.

Aspects of Corporate Growth.   The motives of rival firms for growth are highly contagious. One firm hell-bent on growth and a bigger market share can so jeopardize the market position of other firms in the industry that they must follow suit or face the unpleasant consequence of being squeezed into relative obscurity. Few firms opt for the latter; hence, the growth of one or a few firms catalyzes the growth of other firms and causes a strong growth psychology to pervade the entire industry. In addition, once growth competition appears, the posture of firms toward growth tends to become aggressive. Managers understand thoroughly the long-term strategic advantage a firm gains from staying in the ranks of the growth leaders. It is much more satisfactory to seize the initiative in pursuing growth because this permits the firm to pick the specific strategy and timing that seem most propitious.

SUMMARY AND CONCLUSIONS

We have seen that the firm's goals have a definite effect upon its price and output decisions. A profit goal in terms of target rates of return will not lead to the same price and output decisions as will one based upon marginal revenue and marginal cost concepts. A firm whose primary goal is revenue maximization subject to a profit constraint tends to produce at a greater output rate and to sell at a lower price than does a firm whose goal is profit maximization—other things being equal. Whereas a profit-maximizing firm has no incentive to alter its price and output in the face of increases in either fixed costs or taxes, a revenue-maximizing firm tends to respond by curtailing output and raising selling prices. A revenue maximizer also tends to spend greater amounts on advertising and sales promotion, which, if effective, will tend to push its output rate beyond that of a comparable profit-maximizing firm.

Unless confronted with an unfavorable economic environment, corporations will exhibit a strong propensity to grow. This holds whether their principal goal is long-run profit maximization or some combination of higher profit, greater sales revenues, and stronger market position. A powerful growth psychology tends to develop among corporate enterprises. Over the long term, growth tends to emerge as a major dimension of business behavior. The effect is to thrust the business sector into the role of being the driving force behind overall expansion of the economy. In a very real sense, business enterprises are a major engine of economic growth and economic progress.

SUGGESTED READINGS

BAUMOL, W. J., *Business Behavior, Value and Growth*, rev. ed. (New York: Harcourt Brace Jovanovich, Inc., 1967), Chapters 6–10.

KAMERSCHEN, D. R., "The Return of Target Pricing?" *Journal of Business*, Vol. 48, No. 2 (April 1975), pp. 242–252.

KAPLAN, A. D. H., J. B. DIRLAM, AND R. F. LANZILOTTI, *Pricing in Big Business* (Washington, D.C.: The Brookings Institution, 1958), Chapter 2.

MARRIS, R., "A Model of the 'Managerial' Enterprise," *Quarterly Journal of Economics*, Vol. 77, No. 2 (May 1963), pp. 185–209.

————, *The Economic Theory of 'Managerial' Capitalism* (New York: The Free Press, 1964).

MONROE, K. B., *Pricing: Making Profitable Decisions* (New York: McGraw-Hill Book Company, 1979).

PENROSE, E., *The Theory of the Growth of the Firm* (New York: John Wiley & Sons, Inc., 1959).

WESTON, J. F., "Pricing Behavior of Large Firms," *Western Economic Journal*, Vol. 10, No. 1 (March 1972), pp. 1–18.

WILLIAMSON, J., "Profit, Growth and Sales Maximization," *Economica*, Vol. 33, No. 129 (February 1966), pp. 1–16.

WILLIAMSON, O. E., "A Model of Rational Managerial Behavior," which appears as Chapter 9 of *A Behavioral Theory of the Firm*, R. M. Cyert and J. G. March, eds. (Englewood Cliffs, N.J.: Prentice-Hall, Inc., 1963), pp. 237–252.

————, *The Economics of Discretionary Behavior: Managerial Objectives in a Theory of the Firm* (Englewood Cliffs, N.J.: Prentice-Hall, Inc., 1964).

————, *Corporate Control and Business Behavior* (Englewood Cliffs, N.J.: Prentice-Hall, Inc., 1970).

PROBLEMS AND QUESTIONS FOR DISCUSSION

1. If a firm selects its selling price via some sort of "cost-plus" technique, is it possible for the firm to ever lose money? Why or why not?

2. Minnick Corporation has invested $50 million in facilities and equipment to produce miniature portable color TV sets with a 4-inch screen. Minnick's annual production capacity is 2 million sets. Over the last five years, Minnick's sales of these miniature TV sets have averaged 1.6 million per year. The company's fixed costs have remained relatively stable at $10 million per year. The firm estimates its annual total variable cost function to be $TVC = 120Q + 10Q^2$, where Q is *millions* of units of TV sets sold per year.

    (a) If Minnick desires to earn a target rate of return on its investment of 30% (before taxes), what target return price should Minnick select?

    (b) If Minnick's pricing policy is to add 15% to its normal production costs to determine selling price, what price should it charge, based upon the above information?

3. In the college textbook business, it is standard practice for the author's royalty to be some percentage of the total revenue which the publisher receives from sales of the book. The publisher, of course, incurs all costs of manufacturing, promoting, and distributing the book. Would the price and the sales volume (the number of books sold)

which maximize the publisher's profits on the book also maximize the author's royalty payments? Why or why not? Demonstrate your answer graphically.

4. Suppose that in the short run a firm produces under conditions of constant returns to variable input over the entire output range for which it has production capability. Suppose further that the firm selects its selling price in order to earn a target rate of return on its investment and follows the practice of selling at the target return price no matter what short-run demand conditions happen to be.
   (a) Graphically illustrate the firm's short-run AVC, MC, and ATC curves.
   (b) On the same graph, illustrate a target return price.
   (c) Under these circumstances what is the value of MR?
   (d) At what output rate would the firm maximize short-run profits?
   (e) At what output rate would the firm maximize sales revenues?

5. Suppose that a firm's short-run production function is characterized by constant returns to variable input. Suppose further that the firm faces a linear, downsloping demand curve for its product.
   (a) Graphically illustrate the firm's TR, TC, and π functions.
   (b) Indicate on your graph the profit-maximizing output.
   (c) Indicate on your graph a profit constraint which is smaller than the maximum amount of profit.
   (d) Indicate the revenue-maximizing output, given the profit constraint.

6. The Harco Instrument Corporation has estimated its monthly demand function to be $P = 416 - 7Q$ and its monthly total cost function to be $TC = 1700 + 16Q + Q^2$.
   (a) If Harco's goal is to maximize sales revenue subject to the constraint that profits equal no less than $3200 per month, what is Harco's optimum price and output rate? (*Hint:* Recalling that $\pi = TR - TC$, substitute the appropriate expressions into this equation and solve for Q.)
   (b) If Harco's goal is to maximize profits, then what is its optimum price and output rate? How does the profit-maximizing price and output compare with the revenue-maximizing price and output?
   (c) Suppose Harco's total fixed costs rise from $1700 to $1750. Determine the impact upon Harco's profit-maximizing price and ouput rate.
   (d) Determine the impact of the increase in total fixed costs from $1700 to $1750 upon Harco's revenue-maximizing price and output rate, given the profit constraint of $3200.

15

TECHNIQUES FOR ANALYZING INDUSTRIES AND COMPETITION

If one goes solely by what was said in the preceding five chapters about how firms compete, one might reasonably conclude that "everything" depends on the number of sellers comprising the supply side of the market. Indeed, a principal conclusion of the theory of how markets function is that the strength and effectiveness of competitive forces increases directly with the number of firms. But this conclusion is only part of the story. There is more to analyzing market structure and competitive interplay than just counting how many sellers make up the supply side of the market.

The task of this chapter is to complete the picture of industry and competitive analysis. The primary emphasis will be on expanding our understanding of the strategically relevant features of industry structure, examining some concepts and techniques that expose how an industry functions and where competitive forces come from, and indicating the kinds of factors that cause competitive forces to be strong or weak. Then, in Chapter 16, we will apply these ideas in surveying competition and competitive strategy in generic types of industry environments.

CONDUCTING AN INDUSTRY ANALYSIS

The first thing to realize about "industry analysis" is that the purpose is not just to accumulate anything one can find about the industry. An orderly, systematic approach is needed to expose how an industry functions and what economic factors govern the market. The spotlight needs to be trained on three key questions:

1. How is the industry structured?
2. Where is the industry headed, and what forces are driving it in this direction?
3. What are the underlying economics of the industry—most particularly, what are the key factors for competitive success?

With good, solid answers to these questions, it becomes possible to make predictions about what the industry structure will look like in the future, whether the industry's outlook is bright or dim, and what the principal competitive forces and competitive weapons are likely to be in the years ahead.

Analyzing Industry Structure

Industry analysis needs to start with an examination of industry structure. As a working definition, we shall use the word "industry" to mean a group of firms whose products are sufficiently close substitutes for each other that the member firms are drawn into competitive rivalry to serve much the same needs of some or all of the same types of buyers. The raw data for profiling industry structure are fairly standard: the number of sellers and their relative sizes, who the market leaders are and the extent to which they dominate the market, who the buyers are and the structure of the buying side of the market, what the channels of distribution are from manufacturer to final user, the prevalence of backward and forward integration within the industry, the ease of entry and exit, the size of the industry and its geographical boundaries (local, regional, national, or global), and any other basic characteristics (peculiar to the industry in question) that shape the industry arena in which firms compete. To the extent possible, one needs a grip on the generic type of industry environment—that is, whether the industry can be broadly characterized as fragmented or mature or in a young, emerging state or global in scope or dominated by rapidly moving technological developments. This information provides a general industry overview and lays the groundwork for greater in-depth probing of industry structure.

Strategic Group Mapping.   One of the newest and most revealing techniques for pushing beneath the surface of industry structure is *strategic group mapping.*[1] This technique is applicable whenever an industry is populated with several distinct *groups* of competitors, with each group occupying a different space in the overall market as well as having a different competitive approach. A *strategic group* consists of those rival firms with competitively similar market approaches.[2] Firms in the same strategic group can resemble one another in any of several ways, including having comparable product line breadth, utilizing the same kinds of distribution channels, being vertically integrated to much the same degree, offering buyers similar services and technical assistance, appealing to similar cus-

---

[1] Michael E. Porter, *Competitive Strategy: Techniques for Analyzing Industries and Competitors* (New York: The Free Press, 1980), Chapter 7.

[2] *Ibid.*, pp. 129–130.

tomer groups, emphasizing high quality, using extensive advertising, incorporating identical technological approaches, pursuing product differentiation, and so on.

An industry contains only one strategic group when all sellers approach the market in essentially identical ways and, at the other extreme, there are as many strategic groups as there are firms when each firm pursues its own unique and distinctive competitive market approach. The major home appliance industry, for example, contains three identifiable strategic groups. One cluster, composed of such firms as GE, Frigidaire, and Whirlpool, produces a full line of home appliances (refrigerators, freezers, clothes washers and dryers, dishwashers, stoves, cooking tops, ovens, garbage disposals, and microwaves), employs heavy national advertising, is vertically integrated, and has established a national network of distributors and dealers. Another cluster consists of limited product line or specialist firms (such as Amana in refrigerators and freezers, Maytag in washers and dryers, Kitchen Aid in dishwashers, and Jenn-Air in cooking tops) which focus on high-quality, high-price market segments and have selective distribution. A third cluster, consisting of such firms as Roper, Design and Manufacturing, and White, concentrates on supplying private-label retailers.

A *strategic group map* is constructed by judiciously selecting two key strategic variables as the basis for defining the industry's strategic groups and using these two variables as axes for a two-dimensional map, as shown in Fig. 15-1. The resulting map shows the market posture of each firm in the industry's overall "strategy space." In mapping strategic groups, several things need to be kept in mind.[3] First, it is important not to select two highly correlated variables as axes for the map; for instance, if those firms with broad product lines also use multiple distribution channels, the use of these two variables will fail to distinguish what is really different about the strategies and market postures of the groups. Second, the best variables to use as axes for the map are those that reveal how rivals really try to position themselves to compete against one another in the marketplace. The value of the map as an analytical device is its ability to reveal the competitive structure of the industry by looking at what is common and what is different about rival firms' competitive approaches. The map thus serves as a convenient bridge between looking at the industry as a whole and considering each firm separately. Third, the variables used as axes need not be either quantitative or continuous; rather, they can be discrete variables or defined in terms of distinct classes and combinations (just as was done in Fig. 15-1). Fourth, it is useful for the sizes of the circles on the map to be drawn proportional to the combined sales of the firms in each strategic group, thereby reflecting the relative sizes of each strategic group. A final consideration is that several maps can be drawn if need be, using different variables as axes, to represent the essential competitive relationships inherent in the industry's structure. There is not necessarily one "right" map that captures the structural and competitive makeup of an industry.

---

[3] *Ibid.*, pp. 152–154.

Note: The sizes of the circles are roughly proportional to the market shares of each group of competitors

FIGURE 15-1
Illustrative strategic group map of competitors in the retail jewelry business

Mapping the strategic groups in an industry adds to the understanding of industry structure in several ways:[4]

1. Because of their similar competitive approaches, firms in the same strategic group tend to be affected by and respond similarly to external events and to the

[4] *Ibid.,* pp. 132–138 and 154–155.

competitive moves of rival firms.[5] Recognizing the strengths and weaknesses in each strategic group's market position is helpful in predicting responses and reactions of the member firms to new competitive pressures and market developments.

2. The profit potential of firms in different strategic groups is often quite different because competitive forces are not the same from group to group. Strategic group maps help pinpoint those firms whose position is tenuous or marginal; firms in marginal groups are candidates for exit or for launching attempts to move into another strategic group.

3. Entry barriers vary according to the particular strategic group that an entrant seeks to join—entry into some strategic groups is easier than entry into others.

4. Firms in different strategic groups often enjoy differing degrees of bargaining power with suppliers and/or with customers and they may also face differing degrees of exposure to competition from substitute products outside the industry.

5. The existence of multiple strategic groups generally increases competitive rivalry in the industry because there is both intragroup and intergroup rivalry and because the greater diversity among competitive strategies tends to increase the likelihood that one or more firms will initiate "aggressive" competitive moves that, in turn, provoke retaliation.

6. Industry trends often have different implications for different strategic groups. It is worth thinking through each industry trend to explore (a) whether the trend is closing off the viability of one or more strategic groups and, if so, where will firms in the affected groups shift, (b) whether the trend will raise/lower the entry barriers into a group and the degree to which competitive pressures in the group will be increased/decreased, and (c) how the firms in each group will otherwise be affected by the trend and their probable response to the trend.

The Concept of Driving Forces

While it is necessary to develop an accurate profile of an industry's *current* structure, it is essential to recognize that any such picture is only a static snapshot. Industry structures evolve and sometimes they undergo dramatic shifts in direction. Any industry and any market is almost constantly in a state of flux—forces of change are either presently at work or lurking nearby. One popular hypothesis about how industries change is that they often go through observable evolutionary phases or life-cycle stages; the sequence of the stages usually proceeds from *early development* to *rapid growth and takeoff* to *competitive shakeout and consolidation* to *early maturity* to *saturation* to *decline and decay*.

Whether industries can be depended upon to evolve neatly according to the life-cycle hypothesis is debatable.[6] Many do, but some do not. There are cases where industries have skipped maturity, passing from growth to decline very

---

[5] *Ibid.*, p. 130.

[6] For a more extended discussion of this point, see Porter, *Competitive Strategy*, pp. 157–162.

quickly. Sometimes growth reappears after a period of decline, as has occurred in the radio broadcasting, bicycle, and motorcycle industries. Sometimes the paths of different industries collide, causing them to reform and merge as one industry (as is now occurring among banks, savings and loan associations, and brokerage firms—all of which used to be in distinctly separate industries, but which are now reforming into a single financial services industry). In addition, companies can influence the length of the growth phase through renewed product innovation.[7] Because of these facets, the character of industry evolution is capable of varying from industry to industry; there does not seem to be just one set pattern. Nothing in the life-cycle hypothesis permits reliable prediction as to when the "usual" cycle pattern will hold, when it will not, or how long the phases will last.

Hence, while it is worthwhile to be alert to signs as to where an industry might be in the cycle, it is more fruitful to search out what forces are driving the industry to change. *Industries evolve because some forces are in motion that create incentives or pressures for change.*[8] These can be called *the industry's driving forces*. Driving forces work to push the current industry structure into a new structure and they usually create new kinds of competitive pressures—both of which have implications for competitive strategy.

The Kinds of Driving Forces and How They Work. There are numerous types of driving forces which are capable of producing evolutionary changes in an industry:[9]

- *Changes in the long-term industry growth rate.* The rate at which an industry is growing is a powerful force for structural and competitive changes. Projected market growth is a key variable in the investment decisions of firms to expand capacity and at least maintain market share. How fast a market is expected to grow shapes the balance between industry supply and buyer demand and it affects the intensity of competition. An industry's long-term growth rate can change because of (1) changing buyer demographics (this is especially important in consumer goods industries), (2) trends in the need for and usage of the industry's products (rising property theft, for instance, has triggered increased demand for security alarms, safes, guards, and locks), (3) lower prices and/or new availability of substitute and/or complementary products, (4) a leveling off of demand owing to almost complete penetration of the *new customer market* (sales and growth then become a function of replacement demand), and (5) product innovation.

- *Changes in who buys the product and how they use it.* Increases or decreases in the kinds of customers who purchase the product have potential for changing customer service requirements (credit, technical services, maintenance and repair), creating a need to alter distribution channels, and precipitating broader/narrower product lines, increased/decreased capital requirements, and different

---

[7] For a discussion of how firms can accomplish this, see Theodore Levitt, "Exploit the Product Life Cycle," *Harvard Business Review*, Vol. 43, No. 6 (November–December 1965), pp. 81–94.

[8] Porter, *Competitive Strategy*, p. 162.

[9] *Ibid.*, pp. 164–183.

marketing practices. The hand calculator industry became a different market requiring different strategies when students and households began to use them as well as engineers and scientists. The computer industry was transformed by the surge of buyers for personal and home computers. The interest of some consumers in cordless telephones and mobile telephones for use in cars and trucks represents a major new buyer segment for telephone equipment manufacturers. Trying to ascertain the kinds of industry change to expect should, therefore, include an assessment of potential new buyer segments and their characteristics.

• *Product innovation.* Product innovation can broaden the market, promote industry growth, and enhance product differentiation among rival sellers. When an industry is characterized by rapid product introduction, product innovation is sure to be a key driving force—one that not only shapes what the industry's products are and will be but also affects manufacturing methods, economies of scale, marketing costs and practices, and distribution. Industries where product innovation has been a key driving force include copying equipment, cameras and photography equipment, computers, electronic video games, toys, soft drinks (sugar-free and caffeine-free), beer (low-calorie), and cigarettes (low-tar, low-nicotene).

• *Process innovation.* Frequent and important technological advances in manufacturing methods can also have a powerful impact on an industry. Rapid changes in manufacturing technology can dramatically alter unit costs, capital requirements, minimum efficient plant sizes, the desirability of vertical integration, and experience curve effects. All of these are capable of producing important changes in how large a firm needs to be and how many efficient-sized firms the market can support.

• *Marketing innovation.* The new ways that firms discover to market their products can sometimes revolutionize an industry. The shift in marketing wine from low-key magazine advertising to network television produced major gains in sales for wine and greatly increased the strategic position of large wineries with national distribution vis-à-vis small family wineries specializing in premium wines for local and regional markets. The use of a different advertising medium (advertising movies on TV), introduction of new advertising themes, discovery of new points of difference among products which can be exploited (less sugar or caffeine), the use of new distribution channels (the classic Timex decision to market low-priced watches through drugstores and discount outlets rather than through the traditional jewelry store) can widen demand, increase product differentiation, and/or lower unit costs, thus setting in motion new forces to alter the industry and the strategies of participant firms.

• *Entry and exit of major firms.* The entry of Philip Morris into beer and soft drinks and of Coca-Cola into wine proved to be important new driving forces because they resulted in the introduction of new marketing skills and financial resources that were applied to change competition and industry marketing practices. When an established firm from another industry enters a new market, it usually brings with it new ideas and perceptions about how its skills and resources can be innovatively applied. Hence, the entry of a large and different type of firm can result in a "new ballgame" with new rules and new key players. Similarly, exit of a major firm changes industry structure by reducing the number of market leaders and perhaps increasing the dominance of the leaders who remain.

- *Diffusion of proprietary knowledge.* As a technology becomes more established and knowledge about it spreads through the conduits of rival firms, suppliers, distributors, and customers, the advantage held by firms with proprietary technology erodes. This makes it easier for new competitors to spring up and, also, for suppliers or customers to integrate vertically into the industry. A well-known example is the technology of aerosol packaging; firms with proficiency in aerosol packaging gradually saw their business position erode as many large consumer marketing companies, armed with better understanding of aerosol packaging methods, integrated backward to form their own captive filling operations. As time passed and other aerosol users also turned to doing their own filling, the once strongly entrenched contract fillers found themselves left with the role of meeting emergency demand and in a very adverse bargaining position with large customers for aerosol cans. Even though the contract-filling firms invested in improving filling technology and in trying to invent new aerosol applications to restore their technological advantage, their strategy proved difficult to execute and their position weakened substantially over time. Except where strong patent protection effectively blockades the diffusion of an important technology, it is likely that rapid diffusion of proprietary knowledge will be an important driving force for industry change.

- *Changes in cost and efficiency.* In industries where new economies of scale are emerging or where experience curve effects cause unit costs to decline, large firm size becomes a distinct advantage and can cause all firms to adopt volume-building strategies—a "race for growth" emerges as the driving force. Similarly, sharply rising costs for a key ingredient input (either raw materials or necessary labor skills) can cause a scramble to either (1) line up reliable supplies of the input at affordable prices or else (2) search out lower-cost substitute inputs. The impact such cost increases can have is well illustrated by the recent experience of shifting from a condition of plentiful supplies of low-cost energy to a condition of depleting supplies and sharply higher energy costs. The strategic changes for both energy suppliers and energy users have been profound.

- *Moving from a differentiated to a commodity product emphasis (or vice versa).* In some industries there is a tendency for once-highly differentiated products of firms to become more like commodity products as buyers become more sophisticated and base purchasing decisions on better information. This has occurred in gasoline, where the once much-touted brands of the major oil companies are now largely perceived as identical to the products of the small independent retailers; the 3- to 5-cent per gallon differential between the major brands and the "discount" brands has virtually disappeared. Now the market focus is largely on price—the key characteristic of the market for a commodity product. On the other hand, when sellers are repeatedly successful in catering to the needs and tastes of different buyer segments by bringing out new performance features, making style changes, offering options and accessories, and creating image differences via advertising and packaging, "the name of the game" becomes one of effective product differentiation (examples include cigarettes, soft drinks, automobiles, and magazine publishing). Competitive strategies evolve differently depending on whether the forces in motion in the industry are acting to increase or decrease the emphasis upon product differentiation.

• *Regulatory influences and government policy changes.* Regulatory and governmental influences can significantly affect where an industry is headed and the character of the changes taking place. Medicare/Medicaid provisions affect hospital and nursing home operations. Government regulations weigh heavy on the natural gas industry and the trucking industry; a shift to deregulation would quickly become *the* driving force in these two industries, calling for far-reaching strategic adjustments on participant firms. Safety and pollution regulations have been key forces in the automobile industry and in the nuclear power industry.

• *Reductions in uncertainty and business risk.* A young, emerging industry is typically characterized by much uncertainty over potential market size, technological bugs, an unproven cost structure, what to do about product development, how to distribute the products and access potential buyers, and what competitive strategy to employ. The risks of failure can be high, despite the fact that rapid expansion of the market may for a time allow firms the luxury of employing widely divergent strategies and market approaches (each representing a different "bet" about the future road ahead). Over time, however, the uncertainties get resolved and the poor strategies are abandoned while the successful ones are imitated and improved—an evolutionary process that tends to stiffen competitive pressures. Meanwhile, as uncertainty about the industry's viability and prospects dissipates, new firms may be enticed to enter the industry. Often, the new entrants are larger, established firms with a preference for lower-risk ventures that have a proven track record. The entry of bigger firms is especially likely when it becomes clear that the new industry's potential is large and that the existing hurdles can be overcome. As uncertainty and business risk are reduced, those firms which have grown up with the industry must prepare to defend against the potential entry of bigger rivals and to modify competitive strategy (as earlier judgments about how best to try to compete become obsolete).

The foregoing list of the different types of driving forces which exist, together with the rather obvious unpredictability as to when some of these forces will be triggered in an industry and how strong they will be, make a convincing case for why an industry can suddenly switch gears and head off in a new direction and why it can deviate from the set path put forth in the life-cycle hypothesis. Not only are there any number of different types of driving forces but driving forces also vary from industry to industry and from time to time in a given industry. Hence, analyzing what the driving forces in a given industry are, how and why they are causing the industry to head in a given direction, and what the implications are for competition and competitive strategy all become an integral part of the picture of the industry environment.

Diagnosing an Industry's Economics

Every industry has an underlying set of economic characteristics. These economic characteristics consist of such things as capital requirments, the nature of internal cash flows, the cost structure, typical operating profit margins, pricing practices, economies of scale, price-cost relationships at various percentages of capacity utilization, break-even volumes, and the like. A command of the economics of the business is fundamental to industry and competitive analysis since revenue-cost-profit relationships effectively establish boundaries upon what a firm can and cannot do.

Take the convenience food store business, for example. A breakdown of the margins, expenses, and net profit for a representative convenience food store for a recent year showed:

Sales	$400,000	100.0%
Cost of goods sold	284,800	71.2
Gross profit margin	115,200	28.8
Expenses:		
Wages and benefits	50,000	12.5
Advertising and promotion	2,800	0.7
Rents and property upkeep	13,200	3.3
Utility costs	12,800	3.2
Other expenses	22,800	5.7
Total expenses	101,600	25.4
Profit before taxes	$ 13,600	3.4%

A typical investment in an urban convenience store location was about $200,000, the bulk of which represented the cost of acquiring a choice location with adequate parking on a heavily traveled thoroughfare. Convenience stores tended to have about 600 customers daily; on the average, patrons spent about $2 and took 3 to 5 minutes to make their purchase. Convenience store prices were 10 to 15% above the levels in most supermarkets, a reflection of the fact that patrons were willing to pay extra for the convenience such stores offered (location, easy access, 24-hour service, popular selections, and quick checkout). Stores generally stocked 3000 items in their 2400-square foot space and could be staffed with a single clerk. With these underlying economic characteristics, it was generally agreed in the industry that success hinged upon:

1. *Choosing good store locations.* Visible, easily accessible sites on well-traveled routes were essential to drawing an ample clientele.

2. *Selecting the "right" products to stock and merchandising them effectively.* Customers expected to find what they were looking for and, in many instances, also made an impulse purchase (factors that made it important to stock popular, high-turnover items and to do a good job of merchandising and positioning them in the store).

3. *Pricing.* Given that operating expenses were mostly fixed (not sensitive to changes in sales volume), it was important for prices to be set high enough to produce an average 28 to 30% gross margin on the mix of goods sold, yet pricing had to be sensitive to any competition from supermarkets.

4. *Operating efficiency.* With only a 28 to 30% gross margin, sloppy management practices and inefficiencies in store operations could quickly erode the typically slim 3.0 to 3.5% pretax profit margin.

The point is this: unless and until there is real understanding of the basic economic features of an industry, a firm may misjudge the key factors for success in an industry. *Key success factors* squarely target what a firm must concentrate on doing well if it is to be a competitive success and capture enough patronage to make its business healthy and profitable. Key success factors suggest the specific kinds of skills and competences a firm will need to cope with competitive forces and how an industry works; they point toward which aspects of which internal operating activities are the most crucial and why; and they indicate what size volume and market share is needed to achieve acceptable profitability. Key success factors then are a top-priority industry analysis consideration. At the very least, a firm's operations and competitive strategy must not be at odds with the industry's key success factors. At the most, key success factors can serve as *the cornerstones* for a firm's competitive strategy.

Although it would be nice to be able to generalize about key success factors, the truth is that they vary from industry to industry and even from time to time within the same industry (as industry conditions and driving forces change). Even where two industries may have some of the same kinds of key success factors, the subtleties surrounding each factor can differ greatly as well as their *relative* role and rank in the overall industry scheme. For instance, the key success factors outlined above for the convenience food store industry differ from the key success factors in many other retailing businesses (such as jewelry, tires, gasoline, or appliances). Also, the kinds of key success factors in retailing businesses are not like those in manufacturing businesses. In beer, the keys are utilization of brewing capacity, ample distribution, and good advertising; in copying equipment, the keys are product innovation and service; in apparel manufacturing, the keys are fashion design and manufacturing efficiency. In industries with high transportation costs, the keys are plant location and the ability to market plant output within economical shipping distances (regional market share proves far more crucial than national share). Because the subtleties of key success factors vary significantly across industries and across time, this aspect of industry analysis is especially crucial to understanding why firms in an industry do what they do.

THE FIVE-FORCES MODEL OF COMPETITION: A KEY ANALYTICAL TOOL

Industry analysis sets the stage for really exploring the whole competitive process: the sources of competitive pressures in an industry, how strong these pressures are, whether and why they can be expected to change, which strategic groups and which firms are in the strongest market position, what kind of competitive advantage is the best to have in the industry in question, how the industry's competitive forces are shaping the strategies of rival firms, and how the competitive strategies of rival firms are shaping the industry's competitive forces.

Even though each industry has its own special blend of competition and competitive pressures, there are enough similarities in how competition works from industry to industry to permit generalizations about the main forces which drive competition in the marketplace. The *five-forces model*, shown in Fig. 15-2, is an excellent tool for understanding the sources of competitive pressure and how they interact. Nearly always, the principal competitive force in an industry emerges from the interplay of strategic moves and countermoves among rival firms. But, in addition, there are four other important sources of competitive pressure: (1) whether and to what extent the participant firms are confronted with competitive threats from the substitute products of firms in other industries, (2) the potential entry of new competitors, (3) the economic power of suppliers, and (4) the economic power of customers. The relative strength and influence of these five forces and the pattern of interaction among them largely determine the nature

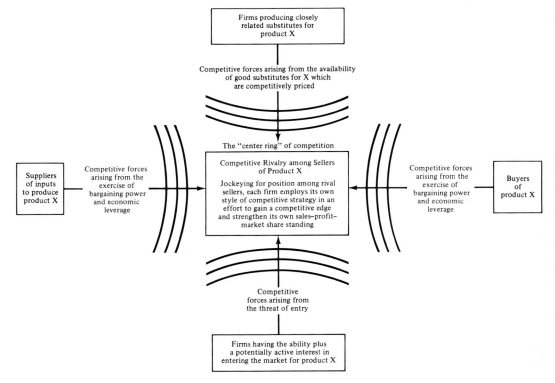

FIGURE 15-2
The five-forces model of competition

Source: Reprinted by permission of the *Harvard Business Review*. An exhibit from "How Competitive Forces Shape Strategy" by Michael E. Porter (March/April 1979). Copyright © 1979 by the President and Fellows of Harvard College; all rights reserved.

and intensity of competition in an industry. Indeed, the five forces model is a welcome ally in diagnosing what competitive pressures are at work in a market-place and how a competitive market really operates; it is the best single tool available for this purpose and it was developed by Michael E. Porter of the Harvard Business School.[10]

The Competitive Force of Rival Firms' Strategies

The center ring of the competitive arena is nearly always dominated by the strategic moves and countermoves of rival firms. Indeed, the jockeying of sellers for a stronger market position and for increased buyer patronage and loyalty is the best single indicator of the pulse of competition.[11] Every firm has reason to try to build a lasting competitive edge over its rivals and thus is well advised to formulate a well-thought-out strategy or plan for competing successfully. A firm's *competitive strategy* can thus be regarded as its *action plan for achieving market success* and, to the extent it can, *for winning a competitive edge over rival firms.*[12] Plainly, the most interesting competitive strategies are those that offer the prospects of allowing a firm to outdo its rivals, gain a stronger market foothold, and reap the rewards of increased buyer favor. Plainly, *every firm in an industry is motivated to formulate a competitive strategy that it believes will, at worst, ensure its survival in the marketplace and, at best, produce a sustainable competitive edge and overall market leadership.* Out of this motivation to employ a "winning" competitive strategy comes a competitive market process with the following dimensions:

1. Rival firms are more or less constantly jockeying for improved market position. The struggle for better position manifests in an *independent striving for patronage* whereby rivals formulate and reformulate their own competitive strat-

---

[10] For a more thoroughgoing treatment than is offered here, see Porter, *Competitive Strategy*, Chapter 1.

[11] Elements of the strategic aspects of competition go as far back in the economics literature as Adam Smith's *The Wealth of Nations* published in 1776. Cournot, Bertrand, and Edgeworth, all well-known classical economists, incorporated competitive strategy aspects in their writings, but their models were based on assumptions so foreign to contemporary strategic behavior as to render them void of much explanatory power. More modern treatments can be found in Edward H. Chamberlin, *The Theory of Monopolistic Competition* (Cambridge, Mass.: Harvard University Press, 1933), p. 6; Fritz Machlup, *The Economics of Sellers' Competition* (Baltimore: The Johns Hopkins Press, 1952); J. M. Schumpeter, *Capitalism, Socialism, and Democracy*, 3rd ed. (New York: Harper & Brothers, 1950); and J. M. Clark, *Competition as a Dynamic Process* (Washington, D.C.: The Brookings Institution, 1961), pp. 471–476. Numerous other writers have recognized the strategic rivalry aspects of competition in the form of game theory models of oligopoly.

[12] Lest any confusion arise, suffice it to say that every firm has a competitive strategy—however imperfect or unconscious it may be. A firm's strategy for competing may be explicit or it may have to be deduced from its actions and market conduct. The strategy may be carefully calculated and regularly assessed from every angle, or it may have emerged haphazardly and be mainly a product of luck and circumstance. Or it may have evolved gradually over time, standing as a result of trial and error and market feedback relative to what worked and what didn't. For a more complete survey of these elements of competitive strategy, see Arthur A. Thompson, Jr., and A. J. Strickland, *Strategic Management: Concepts and Cases*, 3rd ed. (Plano, Tex.: Business Publications, Inc., 1984), Chapters 2 and 5.

egies aimed at outmaneuvering one another and securing a more profitable market share.

2. The competitive strategies that rival firms may devise and the ways they may seek out new openings to compete are numerous, limited only by their imagination, by what will work in the marketplace (i.e., the constraints and reactions of buyers), and by what is legally permissible (based on antitrust legislation and definitions of "fair competitive practices").

3. Fresh competitive pressures are activated any time one or more competitors initiates a new "offensive" strategic move to increase sales and profits or launches a new "defensive" move to protect its established position.

4. The outcome of competitive rivalry entails both strategic successes and strategic failures; the strategic successes may, if they are sufficiently dramatic, influence or even "control" the direction of market forces and competitive pressures. Strategic failure, on the other hand, reflects a competitive approach that, in comparison with rival firms, was either poorly conceived, poorly executed, or both.

5. As the competitive process unfolds over the long term, active rivalry will result in firms both *creating* and *responding* to new driving forces, market trends, and customer preferences. In other words, the competitive strategies of rivals are to a degree both controlling and controlled by market events and by the sequence of moves and countermoves—*the behavior of rival firms affects the market and the market affects how rivals behave.*

These characteristics of strategic rivalry result in the following picture of how firms "play the game" of competition in the market arena.[13] Each rival tries to formulate a winning competitive strategy. A winning strategy is virtually always tied to gaining some sort of attractive competitive edge. The real challenge in formulating a winning competitive strategy is thus *how to gain an edge over rivals*, given that the success of any one firm's strategy hinges in large part on what strategies its rivals employ. What is the "best" strategy for firm A in its struggle for competitive advantage depends partly (or mostly) on rivals' choices of strategy and rivals, in turn, may elect to fine-tune their strategies in light of A's strategic moves.

The motivation of rival firms to secure a competitive advantage, in conjunction with the interdependence of their approaches to the market, produces market rivalry and competitive pressures of varying types and degrees. This rivalry manifests in an ongoing series of competitive strategies and maneuvering, some offensive and some defensive, on the part of each seller in the market.[14]

---

[13] What follows is drawn from the discussion in Arthur A. Thompson, "Competition as a Strategic Process," *Antitrust Bulletin*, Vol. 25, No. 4 (Winter 1980), pp. 777–803.

[14] Classical treatments of competitive strategy simplified the crucial matter of rival's responses to a new strategic move to two extreme cases: the firm acting as if rivals will not respond or as if they will respond so promptly as to neutralize any gain the initiating firm might make. Such oversimplification misses the really characteristic cases, which lie between the extremes and need more to explain them than can be represented by a curve on a diagram. See Clark, *Competition as a Dynamic Process*, p. 472.

Each firm's competitive moves and countermoves are an integral part of its overall corporate strategy for developing a viable business organization and for achieving a degree of market success at least sufficient to stay in business over the long run. Normally, a firm's competitive strategy incorporates both price and nonprice features, with the exact mix being a function of management perceptions as to what combination will have the most desirable market impact, given the prevailing strategies (and anticipated counterstrategies) of rival firms. How long a firm goes without fine-tuning its strategy or subjecting it to major overhaul is a function of the firm's market successes (or failures) and the durability of its competitive approach in withstanding strategic challenges from rival firms.

But the key point here is that the launching of new competitive strategies triggers a new and sometimes powerful round of competitive pressures in the marketplace. When a firm makes a successful strategic move, it can expect increased rewards, largely at the expense of rivals' market shares and rates of sales growth. The speed and extent of the initiator's competitive encroachment varies with whether the industry's product is standardized or differentiated, the initiator's competence and resources to capitalize on any advantage the strategy has produced, how difficult it is for sellers to shift buyer loyalties, and the ease with which the new strategy initiative can be copied or else blunted. The pressures on rivals to respond are, in addition, a function of whether the initiator is (1) a major firm with considerable market visibility, (2) a fringe firm whose efforts can be ignored for some time, or (3) a firm in financial distress and thus whose strategy is predicated on desperation. For instance, if a firm's strategic offensive is keyed to a low price and quick market penetration but also carries with it a substantial risk that full costs will not be recovered, rivals may judge that the strategy will be short-lived; they may choose to respond or not, depending on their estimates of whether it will be better to meet the low price on a temporary basis or to ride out whatever buyer resistance may be encountered. If the initiating firm finds its move neutralized by rivals' countermoves, it is challenged to seek out a better strategy not as easily defeated or else remain content with the stalemate it has encountered.

The ease with which a firm's competitive strategy options can be neutralized is a major criterion of strategy selection; there is good reason for a firm to gravitate toward competitive strategies which are neither easily imitated nor easily defeated. Such considerations indicate why it is wise for a firm to push the development of a *distinctive competence* whereby it can compete on some basis that is not susceptible to successful imitation. The importance of a distinctive competence to competitive success can scarcely be overemphasized. The whole concept of a competitive edge pivots on a firm being able to do something especially well in comparison with its rivals. This something can cover a wide range of competitively significant variables: excelling in the manufacture of a "quality" product, offering customers superior service after the sale, finding innovative ways to achieve low-cost production efficiency and then offering customers the attractiveness of a lower price, being better at developing innovative new products, designing more clever advertising and sales promotion techniques, having the best technological expertise, being skilled at working with customers on new applications and uses of the product, having the best network of dealers and distributors, and so on. Generally, for a distinctive competence to really count for much in the marketplace, it needs to relate to one or more of the industry's *key success factors* and/or to entail some feature that potential customers will value highly enough to influence their purchase choice. By deliberately developing a distinctive competence, a firm acquires unique competitive capability, which, in turn, can become the cornerstone of its competitive strategy and, if the distinctive competence is well chosen, the basis for gaining a competitive edge that not only enhances sales and profits but also insulates it somewhat from the competitive pressures created by rival firms' strategies.

It may be that only a few firms (large or small) will tend to initiate fresh strategic moves, and they may not do it often. But to the extent that these few are able to impact the market with their strategic initiatives, the give-and-take of strategic move and competitive response spreads and continues.[15] A fresh move may come from a firm with ambitious growth objectives, from a firm with excess capacity, or from a firm under pressure to gain added business. More generally, though, the classic offensive strategies are made by firms that see market opportunities and a chance to improve their profit performance. Such firms, whether they be actual leaders, would-be leaders, or mavericks, tend to be aware of the risks of undertaking a bold strategic move but they usually exhibit confidence (1) that they are shrewd enough to keep ahead of the game and (2) that they will be better off making a bold move than they would be by holding back and letting others take the lead. The defensive responses that follow aggressive moves not only reflect time lags and uncertainties but their character differs according to whether the new offensive consists of a new promotional campaign, introduction of a new product or product variation, a new channel of distribution, a move toward vertical integration, or merger with another competitor.

Typically, the strategies of the participant firms cause the spotlight of competition to swing first to one combination of product attributes and then to another—in no set pattern or time interval. At any given time, the central focus of competition might be on one or several of the following: price, new and improved products, a broader product offering, technical sophistication, the adoption of new cost-saving methods of manufacture, customer service, promotion, guarantees, styling, function, economy of use, convenience, and so on—and the focus shifts as new driving forces and competitive responses appear.

Most of the time, lulls in the competitive storm tend to be temporary, owing to the stream of new possibilities for product differentiation, cost-related technological changes, new buyer needs and preferences, changing demographics and life-styles, shifts in buying power, the availability of new substitutes, and general economic change. Apart from these market-related variables, periodic changes can be expected in the host of complex institutional factors that mold a firm's strategy choices from the outside and the intrafirm considerations which shape strategy from the inside. From the standpoint of analyzing competition in an industry, the main thing to remember is that from time to time there will be fresh

[15] Clark, *Competition as a Dynamic Process*, pp. 473–474.

strategic moves and these are likely to so stir competitive forces as to compel reactions and responses from other firms in the market. This is why the essence of competitive strategy involves a never-ending task of trying to maneuver and position the firm in its target market environment in ways intended to enhance its distinctive and competitive capabilities relative to rival firms.

It follows from this characterization that strategic rivalry can assume many forms and shades of intensity. The present strategies of firms in a given industry are just shapshots of an ongoing process whereby markets and competitive rivalry affect firms' strategies and firms' strategies affects markets and competitive rivalry. New competitive pressures are regularly created by the never-ending sequence of strategic moves and countermoves of participant firms. Changes in the form and intensity of competitive rivalry are thus the norm not the exception.

APPLICATIONS CAPSULE

THE MOVES AND COUNTERMOVES OF COMPETITIVE RIVALRY: COCA-COLA VERSUS PEPSI-COLA

Historically, Coca-Cola has dominated the American soft-drink industry. Sales and profits have grown rapidly ever since Coke was first introduced. Until the 1950s there was really no second-place firm worth mentioning. Pepsi-Cola, Coca-Cola's nearest competitor, was a relatively new drink that cost less to manufacture, but its taste was generally thought to be less unique and satisfying than Coke's. Pepsi's major selling point was that it offered more cola for the same price; Pepsi came in a 12-ounce bottle that sold for approximately the same price as Coke's famous $6\frac{1}{2}$-ounce bottle. Pepsi exploited this difference by advertising "twice as much for a nickle, too." Nonetheless, with its plain bottle and paper label (that often got dirty in transit), Pepsi was generally looked upon as second-class. To many it was "the poor man's drink."

When Alfred N. Steele came to the presidency of Pepsi-Cola, he recognized that the company's main hope for competitive vitality lay in transforming Pepsi into a first-class soft drink and in not being a cheap imitator of Coke. Steele assembled a two-phase grand offensive for improving Pepsi's position relative to Coke. In the first phase, which lasted from 1950 to 1955, a determined effort was made to improve Pepsi's taste. The formula was desweetened. Greater quality control was established over local bottlers, who previously added varying amounts of carbonation to the syrup, with the result that Pepsi's taste varied from locale to locale. Pepsi's bottle and other corporate symbols were redesigned and unified. Following up on the product improvements, Pepsi launched an advertising campaign aimed at upgrading Pepsi's image. The ads featured attractive, well-dressed women and debonair men drinking Pepsi, against a background of high-income surroundings. Along with this went the advertising theme "the light refreshment," suggesting indirectly that Coke was "heavy." At the same time, Pepsi made the decision to take dead aim on the "take-home" segment of the soft-drink market in the first phase of its grand offensive. Coca-Cola was particularly strong in the "on-premise" segment (soda fountain sales, vending machines, and refrigerated sales). Pepsi felt that the rifle-shot approach, aimed where Coca-Cola was weakest, gave it the best chance for success. Thus, Pepsi massed its efforts at penetrating the market for grocery retail sales of soft drinks—where it already had a small foothold. The final aspect of Pepsi's phase-one offensive involved singling out 25 cities for special promotional efforts. In these "push" markets Pepsi added company funds to those of the local bottlers for advertising and promotion. The concentrated effort to win market share in these 25 cities was successful in increasing Pepsi's market share.

By 1955, Pepsi's phase-one programs had made enough headway to warrant beginning phase two of the grand offensive. It consisted of attempts to increase Pepsi's share of the "on-premise" market where Coke was so solidly entrenched. However, Pepsi limited its efforts to the vending machine and cold-bottle sales segments because the soda fountain segment showed signs of maturity and perhaps even decline. Pepsi introduced some new bottle sizes to go along with its standard 12-ounce bottle in an attempt to offer more convenience to customers in the take-home and cold-bottle market segments. Additionally, Pepsi offered financing to those bottlers who were willing to buy and install Pepsi vending machines and to begin to push this part of their business.

As Pepsi's phase two began to strike chords of success, Coke decided it was time to initiate some kind of response. Until the latter stages of Pepsi's grand offensive, Coke's attitude had been mostly "ho-hum." For the most part, Coke refused to acknowledge that Pepsi was a threat. Many of Coke's local bottlers had become well-to-do and complacent, owing to Coke's previous success, and were not accustomed to tough competition. Initially, Coke's response consisted of launching new advertising campaigns, using such themes as "the really refreshed" and "no wonder Coke refreshes best." Coke also introduced new bottle sizes. Both steps perked up Coke's sales.

In the early 1960s, Pepsi's rate of growth slowed, and Pepsi responded with two new advertising campaigns—"be sociable" and "think young." The latter was quite successful in tying Pepsi to the youth market, a segment which accounted for the highest per capita consumption of soft drinks. But the youth theme, by implication, also tended to mark Coke as an old-fashioned drink. Coke responded with its new advertising theme of "things go better with Coke."

Then competition, which in the past had revolved largely around taste, bottling, and advertising, moved to new arenas. The first concerned the no-deposit bottle and the use of aluminum and steel cans. Both companies found that it was critical to design their containers carefully and time their introduction astutely. For instance, it was discovered that the metal can affected the taste; it was also discovered by one soft-drink company that the aluminum can it was about to introduce was eaten through by its product within a few days.

The second competitive development concerned product innovation. Using the principle of surprise, Royal Crown Cola introduced what proved to be a major new product—the diet soft drink. RC's Diet Cola was formulated without real sugar and was intended to appeal to the calorie-conscious segment of the market. Originally, this class of buyers was thought to constitute a small part of the soft-drink market, but it turned out that diet drinks had very broad appeal. Royal Crown's major success quickly forced both Coke and Pepsi to formulate their own dietetic soft drinks.

The third new competitive arena emerged when the soft-drink companies realized that a whole set of other good-tasting drinks could be formulated besides colas. Seven-Up's "un-cola" theme was so successful that Coke brought out its version of the un-cola—Sprite. Attempting to capitalize upon this development, Dr Pepper sharply increased its advertising budget and market penetration efforts.

Although Coke continued to retain its number one position in the industry, Pepsi emerged with a much stronger second-place market share and the smaller firms—Royal Crown, Seven-Up, and Dr Pepper—also made inroads, mostly at Coke's expense.

Still a fourth competitive arena emerged in the 1980s when Philip Morris, a leader in the cigarette industry and also the parent of Miller Brewing Company, acquired The Seven-Up Company and began an aggressive marketing campaign to expand the market shares of 7-Up and Diet 7-Up. PM's strategy was to exploit the growing awareness and concerns among consumers about health and nutrition by calling attention to the fact that 7-Up and Diet 7-Up were caffeine-free. Seven-Up's "never had it, never will" ads about the caffeine-free attribute of its drinks struck hard at both Coke and Pepsi since all brands of colas then contained substantial amounts of caffeine. So threatening were the Seven-Up ads that within a period of months both Coke and Pepsi introduced caffeine-free versions of their regular and diet cola drinks.

Sources: Alvin Toffler, "The Competition that Refreshes," *Fortune*, May 1961; "Things Go Better with Coke," *Sales Management*, March 5, 1965, pp. 28ff.; and Philip Kotler, *Marketing Management: Analysis, Planning, and Control*, 2nd ed. (Englewood Cliffs, N.J.: Prentice-Hall, Inc., 1972), pp. 254–257.

The Competitive Force of Substitute Products

All firms selling a particular product are, in a broad sense, in competition with firms producing related substitutes. Steel producers are in competition with aluminum producers—in the case of some customers and end uses. The producers of fiberglass insulation are in competition with the producers of rock wool and cellulose insulation. Sugar producers are in competition with the firms that produce artificial sweeteners and high-fructose corn syrup. The producers of plastic containers are in competition with the makers of glass bottles and jars, the manufacturers of paperboard cartons, and the producers of tin cans and aluminum cans.

The competitive force of closely related substitute products affects sellers in several ways. First, the price and availability of acceptable substitutes for good X places a ceiling on the prices which the producers of good X can charge; at the same time, the ceiling price places a limit on the profit potential for good X.[16] Second, unless the sellers of good X can upgrade quality, reduce prices via cost reduction, or otherwise differentiate their product from its substitutes, they risk

[16] Michael E. Porter, "How Competitive Forces Shape Strategy," *Harvard Business Review*, Vol. 57, No. 2 (March–April 1979), p. 142.

a low growth rate in sales and profits owing to the inroads that substitutes may make. The more sensitive the sales of X are to changes in the prices of substitutes, the stronger is the competitive influence of the substitutes.

Third, the competition from substitutes is affected by the ease with which buyers can change over to the substitute. Hence, a key consideration is usually the buyer's *switching costs*—the one-time costs facing the buyer of switching from use of X over to a substitute for X.[17] Typical switching costs include employee retraining costs, the cost to purchase ancillary equipment, the need for technical help in making the changeover, the time and cost in testing the quality and reliability of the substitute, and the psychic costs of severing old supplier relationships and establishing new ones. If buyers' switching costs are high, the sellers of substitutes must offer a major cost or performance benefit in order to attract users away from X. If switching costs are low, it is easier for sellers of substitutes to be a strong competitive force in the market for product X.

As a rule, then, the lower the price, the higher the quality and performance of substitutes, and the lower the user's switching costs, the more intense are the competitive pressures posed by substitute products. One very telling indicator of the strength of competition emanating from the producers of substitutes is their growth rate in sales; other indicators are their plans for expansion of capacity and the profits they are earning.

The Potential for New Firms to Enter the Market

New entrants to a market bring new production capacity, the desire to establish a secure place in the market and a satisfactory market share, and often substantial resources with which to compete.[18] The entry of strong firms can cause a major market shake-up, particularly in the case of established companies which diversify through acquisition into new products and markets (a classic example being the way Philip Morris shook up the whole beer industry's approach to marketing when it acquired Miller Brewing Co. and the resulting shake-up in caffeine-free soft drinks when Philip Morris acquired Seven-Up and began aggressively promoting its ''never had it, never will'' caffeine-free feature for Seven-Up brand drinks).

Just how serious the competitive threat of entry is into a particular market depends on two classes of factors: *barriers to entry* and the *expected reaction of existing firms to new entry*. A barrier to entry exists whenever it is difficult for a newcomer to break into the market and/or if the economics of the business puts a potential entrant at a price/cost disadvantage relative to its competitors. There are several major sources of entry barriers:[19]

- *Economies of scale.* The presence of important scale economies deters entry because it forces the potential entrant to commit to entering on a large-scale basis

---

[17] Porter, *Competitive Strategy*, p. 10.
[18] Porter, ''How Competitive Forces Shape Strategy,'' p. 138.
[19] Porter, *Competitive Strategy*, pp. 7–17.

(a costly and perhaps risky move) or else to accept a cost disadvantage (and, consequently, lower profitability). Large-scale entry could result in chronic over-capacity in the industry and/or it could so threaten the market shares of existing firms that they are pushed into aggressive competitive retaliation (in the form of price cuts, increased advertising and sales promotion, and similar such steps) so as to maintain their position; either way, the entrant's outlook is for lower profits. Scale economies may be encountered not just in production, but in research, advertising, selling, financing, in-house servicing of products, and distribution as well.

• *The existence of experience curve effects.* When achieving lower unit costs depends upon experience in producing the product and other learning curve benefits, a new entrant is put at a disadvantage in competing with older established firms with more accumulated know-how.

• *Brand preferences and customer loyalty.* When the products of rival sellers are differentiated, buyers usually have some degree of preference and loyalties to existing brands. This means that a potential entrant must be prepared to spend enough money on advertising and sales promotion to overcome customer loyalties and build its own clientele. Substantial time, as well as money, can be involved. Not only may a new entrant have to budget more funds for marketing than existing firms (which gives existing firms a cost advantage), but also the capital invested in establishing a new brand (unlike the capital invested in facilities and equipment) has no resale or recoverable value, which makes such expenditures a riskier "in-vestment." In addition, product differentiation can entail costs to buyers of switching brands, in which case the new entrant must persuade buyers that the changeover or switching costs are worth incurring; this may require lower prices or better quality-service-performance—again leading to lower profit expectations.

• *Capital requirements.* The larger the total dollar investment needed to enter the market successfully, the more limited is the pool of potential entrants. The most obvious capital requirements are associated with manufacturing plant and equipment, working capital to finance inventories, offering credit to customers, establishing a clientele, and bearing startup losses.

• *Cost disadvantages independent of size.* Existing firms may have cost advantages not available to potential entrants, regardless of the entrant's size. These advantages relate to access to the best and cheapest raw materials, possession of patents and unique technological know-how, the effects of the learning curve and the experience curve, having purchased fixed assets at preinflation prices, favorable locations, and availability of financial capital at lower costs.

• *Access to distribution channels.* Where a product is distributed through established market channels, a potential entrant may face the barrier of gaining adequate distribution access. Some distributors may be reluctant to take on a product that lacks buyer recognition. The more limited the number of wholesale and retail outlets and the more that existing producers have these tied up, the tougher entry will be. To overcome this barrier, potential entrants may have to lure distribution access by offering better margins to dealers and distributors or by giving advertising allowances and other promotional incentives, with the result that the potential entrant's profits may be squeezed unless and until its product gains market acceptance.

- *Government actions and policies.* Government agencies can limit or even bar entry by instituting controls over licenses and permits. Regulated industries such as trucking, radio and television stations, liquor retailing, and railroads all feature government-controlled entry. Entry can also be restricted, and certainly made more expensive, by government safety regulations and environmental pollution standards.

Even if a potential entrant is willing to tackle the problems of entry barriers, it may be dissuaded by its expectations about how existing firms will react to new entry.[20] Will incumbent firms "move over" grudgingly and let the new entrant take a satisfactory share of the market, or will they launch a vigorous, "survival of the fittest" competitive battle for market position—including price cuts, increased advertising, product improvements, and whatever else is calculated to give a new entrant (as well as other rivals) a hard time? A firm is likely to have second thoughts about entry:

- When incumbent firms have previously been aggressive in defending their market positions against entry.
- When incumbent firms possess substantial financial resources with which to defend against new entry.
- When incumbent firms are in a position to use leverage with distributors and customers to keep their business.
- When incumbent firms are able and willing to cut prices to preserve their market shares.
- When product demand is expanding slowly, thus limiting the market's ability to absorb and accommodate the new entrant without adversely affecting the profit performance of all the participant firms.
- When it is more costly for existing firms to leave the market than to fight to the death (because the costs of exit are very high, owing to heavy investment in specialized technology and equipment, union agreements which contain high severance costs, or important shared relationships with other products).

Naturally, a potential entrant can only guess about how incumbent firms will react to entry. Reactions to past entry are one obvious indication. So is how existing firms behave competitively toward each other. Sometimes the "personality" of rival firms can provide clues to their probable reaction to entry; relevant personality indicators include (1) the propensity a firm may exhibit to be aggressive or conservative, a leader or a follower; (2) the backgrounds and experiences of their executives; (3) the priority that rival firms have historically given to research

---

[20] Porter, "How Competitive Forces Shape Strategy," p. 140.

and development, advertising, technology, and similar key competitive variables; and (4) the assumptions and perceptions which the managements of rival firms seem to have about themselves and their business, as revealed by speeches and interviews, the kinds of people they recruit, and how they tend to reward their executives.

One additional point needs to be made about the threat of entry as a competitive force: the threat of entry changes as economic and market conditions change. For example, the expiration of a key patent can greatly increase the threat of entry. Technological discovery can create such a scale economy as virtually to bar new entry. The decisions of incumbent firms to increase advertising or strengthen distributor-dealer relations or step up R & D or improve product quality can result in the erection of higher roadblocks to entry. Dramatic price increases which also produce sharply higher profits can enhance the attractiveness and probability of new entry.

The Economic Power of Suppliers

The competitive impact which suppliers can have upon an industry is chiefly a function of how significant the input they supply is to the buyer.[21] When the input of a particular group of suppliers makes up a sizable proportion of total costs, is crucial to the buyer's production process, or else significantly affects quality of the industry's product, suppliers tend to have greater bargaining power and influence over firms in the buying industry. The extent to which this potential leverage is realized depends upon a number of factors; in general, a group of supplier firms has more bargaining leverage:

• When the input is, in one way or another, important to the buyer.

• When the supplier group is dominated by a few large firms that are not confronted with intensely competitive conditions.

• When suppliers' respective products are differentiated to such an extent that it is difficult or costly for buyers to switch from one supplier to another.

• When the buying firms are *not* important customers of the suppliers. In such instances, suppliers are not constrained by the fact that their own well-being is tied to the industry they are supplying; hence, they have no big incentive to protect the consumer industry via reasonable prices, improved quality, or new products which might well enhance the buying industry's sales and profits.

• When the suppliers of an input do *not* have to compete with the substitute inputs of suppliers in other industries. (For instance, the power of the suppliers of glass bottles to the soft-drink bottlers is checked by the ability of the soft drink firms to use aluminum cans and plastic bottles.)

• When one or more suppliers pose a credible threat of forward integration into the business of the buyer industry (attracted, perhaps, by the prospect of higher profits than it can earn in its own market).

---

[21] Porter, *Competitive Strategy*, pp. 27–28.

• When the buying firms display no inclination toward backward integration into the suppliers' business.

The power of suppliers can be an important economic factor in the marketplace because of the impact they can have on customer profits. Powerful suppliers can squeeze the profits of a customer industry via price increases which the latter is unable to pass on fully to its own customers. They can also jeopardize a buyer's profits via reductions in the quality of the inputs—reductions which enhance their own profits at the expense of the buyer's profits.

The Economic Power of Customers

Just as powerful suppliers can exert a competitive influence over an industry, so can powerful customers.[22] The relative leverage and bargaining power of customers tends to be relatively greater:

• When customers are large and few in number and when they purchase in large quantities. Often large customers are successful in using their volume-buying leverage to obtain important price concessions and other favorable terms and conditions of sale.

• When customers' purchases are a sizable percentage of the selling industry's total sales.

• When the supplying industry is comprised of large numbers of relatively small sellers.

• When the item being purchased is sufficiently standardized among sellers that not only can customers find alternative sellers but also they can switch suppliers at virtually zero cost.

• When customers pose a credible threat of backward integration, being attracted by the prospects of earning greater profits or by the benefits of reliable prices and reliable delivery.

• When sellers post little threat of forward integration into the product market of their customers.

• When the item being bought is *not* an important input.

• When it is economically feasible for customers to follow the practice of purchasing the input from several suppliers rather than one.

• When the product/service being bought does not save the customer money.

A firm can enhance its profitability and market standing by seeking out suppliers and customers who are in a comparatively weak position to exercise adverse power. Especially is this feasible in the case of selecting the customer groups to target one's marketing efforts. Rarely are all buyer groups in a position to enjoy equal bargaining power, and some may be more price or quality or service sensitive than others. An example is the automobile tire industry, where the major

---

[22] *Ibid.*, pp. 24–27.

tire manufacturers on the one hand confront very significant customer power in selling original equipment tires to the automobile manufacturers and on the other hand find themselves in a position to exercise the upper hand when selling replacement tires to individual car owners through their own networks of retail stores. Also, Crown Cork and Seal has been very successful in concentrating its efforts on producing cans for two types of buyers—those who use aerosol cans and those who require cans for products with unique characteristics.

A Collective Picture of Competitive Forces

The discussion to this point has identified five major determinants of the strength of competitive forces in the marketplace: (1) the strategic rivalry among firms producing their own brands of a particular item, (2) the ease with which buyers can switch to closely related substitute items, (3) threats of entry of new competitors, (4) the economic power exercisable by suppliers, and (5) the economic power that customers can apply. The unique analytical contribution of Figure 15-2 is the simplicity with which it portrays how these five forces combine to create a spectrum of considerations called "competition."

The collective impact of these forces determines the intensity of competition in a given market and, ultimately, the profits which the participating firms will be able to earn. As a rule, the more intense is competition, the lower is the collective profitability of participant firms. From a profit standpoint, the sternest and most vigorous sort of competition is where the long-term prospects are for no more than a normal profit—the same result as obtained under perfect competition. On the other hand, when a market offers the prospect of superior profit performance, the inference is that competitive forces are not as strong, for whatever reason.

One way for a firm to assess what sort of competitive strategy it ought to employ in a given market is to try to position itself (1) to defend and insulate itself as much as possible from the forces of competition and (2) to influence the direction of competition in its favor by choosing a trendsetting, pacesetting strategy. Doing this requires insightful understanding of what the competitive pressures are and where they are coming from. It also requires careful evaluation of a firm's competitive strengths and weaknesses, market opportunities and threats, and areas where creative strategy can produce a superior payoff. Very likely, different firms will arrive at different evaluations as to what the "best" competitive strategy is—even though they may be in substantial agreement on what the relevant competitive forces are. This accounts partly for why firms in a given market generally do not follow the same competitive strategy and, thus, do not have the same market position.

COMPETITOR ANALYSIS

Competitor analysis is a necessary feature of diagnosing competition and market behavior because of the diverse, complex supply-side structure of most industries. Not only can an industry have several different strategic groups of rivals but it is also typical for the firms in an industry to occupy sharply different market positions—some have big market shares, others have small shares; some are technological leaders, others are followers; some are wellknown, others are new-comers; some have a reputation for quality, others are better known for service; some have a loyal clientele, others are trying to build one. The demand side of most markets usually consists of enough groups and types of buyers, each having a somewhat different set of needs, preferences, and buying habits, that rival firms have ample "strategy space" to pursue different competitive strategies. More-over, competitors are inclined to pursue different competitive approaches (1) be-cause their managers hold dissimilar views about industry trends, driving forces, and future prospects, (2) because their internal situations and market positions are different enough that what is a suitable strategy for one firm tends to be unsuitable or unattractive for another, and (3) because there is room for rival firms' managers to arrive at different judgments about what is the "best" way to try to compete for buyer patronage.

To gain an appreciation for the diversity which can exist among competitors, consider that there are at least three approaches a firm can have with respect to *market share strategy*:

- Grow and build (with a commitment to invest in new capacity as needed).
- Hold and maintain.
- Shrink and retreat.

There are at least six different postures a firm can take insofar as its *market position* objective is concerned:

- Seek to be a dominant leader (have the biggest market share, the best-known name and industry reputation, and be the acknowledged front-runner).
- Be one of the industry leaders (in, say, the top five).
- Be a follower, content with a middle-of-the-pack position.
- Be resigned to a position as an also-ran, or fringe firm.
- Reject the status of an underdog or trailing firm and try to move up a notch or two in market standing (an overhaul and reposition approach).
- Be an aggressive newcomer (for firms that have just entered the industry and need to establish an image and reputation).

When it comes to the issue of "how to compete," there are three generic types of *competitive strategies*:[23]

- Striving to be the low-cost producer (a *cost leadership strategy*).
- Seeking to differentiate one's product offering in one way or another from the offerings of rivals (a *differentiation strategy*).

---

[23] This classification of generic competitive strategies has been advanced by Michael E. Porter of the Harvard Business School. See his *Competitive Strategy*, Chapter 2, for a fuller treatment.

- Concentrating on catering to a particular group of buyers, segment of the product line, or geographic market rather than on serving the whole market (a *focus strategy*).

In general, *any firm's competitive behavior mirrors the offensive or defensive actions it judges are prudent in order to cope successfully with the five competitive forces*, the ultimate objectives being to earn a superior profit and to create an attractive, defendable position for the firm in the marketplace. Given that the actions and strategies of rival firms are usually center stage in a competitive market, the issue of how to analyze and predict the behavior of competitors is a key part of understanding how a competitive market functions. One cannot hope to explain the behavior of firms or to gauge the intensity of competitive rivalry without first diagnosing the whys and hows of competitors' strategies and market approaches. Without perceptive understanding of rivals' strategies, an analyst is "flying blind" in trying to decipher why firms are doing what they are doing and why some firms have been more successful in the marketplace than others.

Diagnosis and prediction of a competitor's behavior has five pieces: (1) the firm's performance goals, (2) the firm's assumptions and beliefs about the industry and about its competitors, (3) the firm's current competitive strategy, (4) the backgrounds and experiences of the firm's managers, and (5) the firm's competitive capabilities.[24]

A Firm's Priorities and Performance Objectives

Doing the detective work to uncover a competitor's priorities and goals has several payoffs. It can reveal whether the firm is satisfied with its current performance and thus its current strategy. It can aid in assessing the likelihood of a shift in competitive strategy, the reasons for and seriousness behind such a shift, and the speed and vigor with which the firm might respond to either changes in market conditions or new strategic moves by its rivals. The following questions suggest what to be alert for:

1.   What inferences can be made about the firm's goals besides increased profits and return on investment? In particular, does the firm aspire to industry leadership in pricing or technological proficiency or market share or product quality or some other aspect?

2.   Are the firm's management compensation packages tied loosely or closely to achievement of its goals? (The assumption here is that close ties will get management's attention and promote stronger efforts to achieve the firm's goals.)

3.   Is the competitor a subsidiary of a larger corporate parent? If so, what are the parent's performance goals, and how is its subsidiary unit expected to contribute to them in terms of profitability, growth, and cash flow? Does the parent view this industry as one of its main strategic interests, or is it a sideline or

---

[24] The following discussion of these five aspects of competitor analysis is based on Porter, *Competitive Strategy*, Chapter 3.

peripheral business? To what extent does the parent give its subsidiary financial support and management attention? Does the parent have an emotional attachment to the business?

4. Has the firm been involved in any antitrust actions that could condition its strategic responses or that could constrain its profit and market share goals? In the same vein, are the firm's actions constrained by other regulatory, environmental, or social considerations?

5. Is the firm under any new pressures from corporate headquarters, customers, or other rivals to improve its performance? Is the firm striving to regain lost ground? Can the firm meet its profit and other goals without doing anything different or without launching a major strategic offensive? Can the firm afford to be happy or content with its current performance?

The Firm's Beliefs About the Industry and About Rivals

Every firm's management operates on assumptions and beliefs about the industry and about how the business ought to be run. How a firm sees itself and its situation is often a good barometer of its strategic thinking. The relevant areas to probe here include: What does management appear to believe (based on speeches, advertising claims, representations by its sales force to customers, and so on) about the firm's standing in the marketplace relative to quality, cost, technological proficiency, and image with customers? Is its reputation tightly identified with some competitive aspect (superior service, quality of manufacture, product innovation, breadth of product line, or focus on particular products of market segments) and, if so, will it fight to keep its reputation intact? Do the firm's managers believe strongly in certain principles or values or ways of doing business that can be counted upon to condition what it does or does not do? Do the firm's managers adhere to industry customs or rule-of-thumb approaches (such as target return pricing) or "conventional wisdoms" (such as "you have to give customers great service," "buyers look for quality and performance, not low price," "the key is low-cost manufacture and full utilization of capacity," and "you have to offer a full product line")? What does the firm's management appear to believe about industry trends, future competitive conditions, and the strengths and weaknesses of its rivals in the industry? What has the firm tried that succeeded, what has it tried that failed, and are these experiences likely to shape future strategic moves? What does it believe its competitive strengths and weaknesses are? Does it use certain consultants, advertising agencies, banks, or other advisors that are known for particular techniques and approaches? What motivated the firm to get into this business? What reason does it have to stay in the business? How accurate are its perceptions about itself, about its competitive position, and about industry trends and conditions?

The Firm's Current Competitive Strategy

Assessments of a firm's competitive strategy should include the following: What generic strategy is the firm pursuing (cost leadership, differentiation, or focus)? Is the firm considered to be a leader in some respect (innovation, pricing, quality, service, management know-how), or is it a follower? Where does the firm concentrate its efforts in terms of products, customers, and geographic focus? Where is the firm strongest and where is it weakest as concerns products, customer groups, and geographic market penetration? Where are key strategy decisions made—in the business unit itself or at corporate headquarters? Is the business a free-standing unit or is it operated to blend in with the requirements of sister units in a larger corporate organization? Is the firm gaining or losing ground in the marketplace and why? Is it locked into its present strategies because of facilities commitments or some other factor?

The Backgrounds and Experiences of Senior Managers

Sometimes important clues about the behavior and strategies of a firm can be gleaned from the personal experiences and backgrounds of its senior-level managers. Hence although the information may be hard to come by, it is worth exerting an effort to get. The most important areas of inquiry include:

1. What are the work backgrounds of the key managers (accounting, finance, sales, production, R & D), and how likely is it that they lean toward strategies that emphasize their own areas of expertise and experience? What other businesses have these managers worked in and what strategic approaches were characteristic of those businesses?

2. What types of strategies have/have not worked for them personally in their previous jobs?

3. Has the firm's current chief executive held the position for a long time (which may suggest continuation of the same basic strategy) or have new senior-level managers come recently from outside the company? Is the firm known for selecting managers with a certain type of track record or managerial philosophy?

4. Is there reason to believe that managers' actions will be conditioned by some previous major event in their background or experience (a sharp recession, having managed a rapid growth business, a traumatic plant closing, a severe strike, or a near bankruptcy)?

5. Have any of the rival's managers offered clues about their current thinking in their speeches to securities analysts, program appearances at trade associations, interviews with the media, or conversations with customers? Do they seem to place a high value on technological leadership or stable pricing or manufacturing efficiency or some other strategic feature that may suggest what actions they are apt to take?

A Firm's Ability to Compete Effectively

Perhaps the thing that matters most about a competitor is its capacity for competing effectively in the marketplace. Its strengths and weaknesses regarding product line, marketing and selling, dealer distribution network, R & D, engineering, manufacturing, cost and efficiency, financial condition, and managerial competence are all important in determining its ability to respond to competitive moves or to deal with industry trends. In assessing a firm's competitive strength, attention has to be paid to what the firm is best and worst at doing, what flexibility it has to adapt to a change in competitive conditions, and why it is doing better/ worse than other rivals. Also pertinent is an appraisal of the degree to which it is likely to be a major factor in the marketplace over the long haul and why its market standing is likely to increase or decrease.

Predicting a Competitor's Next Moves

Gaining useful answers to the kinds of questions and issues posed above is not a simple, short-run task. Compiling a profile of a rival's competitive strength is a task in which the relevant information is gathered in bits and pieces and it takes both time and hard work to get a real feeling for both a firm's situation and how its management thinks. But if the task is done systematically, the result can be a good ability to predict:

- How a firm will respond to changes in market trends or economic conditions.
- How satisfied a firm is with its present market position and profitability, and thus whether it is likely to initiate a fresh strategic move.
- The most likely moves a firm will make, given its set of goals, its assumptions and beliefs about the market, its current strategy, its management approach, and its competitive strengths and weaknesses.
- How vulnerable a firm is to new strategic moves by rivals.
- How much a firm can be pushed before it will be provoked into retaliation.
- The meaning and intent of a rival's new strategic move and how seriously it should be taken.

Such predictive ability is immensely valuable in drawing conclusions about the strength of future competition and about what forces are driving the competitive rivalry among the industry participants.

FACTORS AFFECTING THE INTENSITY OF COMPETITION

Having identified the major competitive forces, we are in position to pinpoint what specific features relative to these forces cause competition to be more or less intense.[25] In general, any market characteristic that affects strategic rivalry, barriers to entry or exit, the economic power of buyers or sellers, and the price and availability of closely related substitutes affects the vigor of competition. But while there can be a wide range of specific characteristics directly influencing

[25] This section draws upon Porter, *Competitive Strategy*, pp. 17–21.

how strong competition will be, certain ones seem to crop up again and again. These are worth enumerating.

Competition tends to increase as the number of rival firms increases and as these firms become more equal in size and capability. The number of firms is important because, up to some point, more firms increase the probability for fresh, creative strategic initiatives and because greater numbers reduce the effects of any one firm's actions upon the others, thereby reducing somewhat the probability of direct retaliation. Also, economists have a strong bias toward more firms because this gives buyers more choice among sellers and thus reduces the likelihood of any one firm being able to rig the market to its own advantage. When rival firms are more equal in size and capability, the chances are better that the firms can compete on a fairly even footing, a feature that makes it harder for one or two firms to "win" the competitive battle and emerge as dominant firms in a position to exercise leadership and some degree of market control.

Market rivalry is usually stronger when demand for the product is growing slowly. In a rapidly expanding market, rivalry is weakened by the fact that there is enough business for everybody. Indeed, it may take all of a firm's financial and managerial resources just to keep abreast of market growth, much less devoting efforts to steal away the customers of its rivals. But when growth slows, expansion-minded firms tend to ignite a battle for market share that often results in a shakeout of the weak and less efficient firms. Market share competition can be counted upon to produce fresh strategic moves and countermoves directly aimed at taking customers away from rival firms.[26]

Competition is more intense when rival firms are tempted to use price cuts or other marketing tactics to boost unit volume. Whenever fixed costs are high and marginal costs are low, firms are under strong economic pressure to produce at or very near full capacity. Hence, if market demand weakens and capacity utilization begins to fall off, rival firms frequently resort to secret price concessions, special discounts, rebates, and other sales-increasing tactics. A similar situation arises when a product is perishable or seasonal or is costly or difficult to store or hold in inventory. It can also occur if an industry is characterized by long lead times in constructing new plant capacity or by scale economies which dictate that additions to capacity be made in large increments or by persistent ups and downs in market demand that periodically give rise to excess capacity throughout the industry.

Competition is stronger when the products/services of rival firms are not so strongly differentiated that buyers become locked in by the high costs of switching from one brand to another. Product differentiation per se is not a deterrent to competition; indeed, it has the capacity for enlivening rivalry by forcing firms to seek creative new ways of improving their price-quality-service-performance of-

---

[26] In average growth markets, aggressive firms may move to build new plant capacity *ahead* of the time it will be needed so as to discourage others from expansion and thereby capture a greater market share. Should rivals catch on to this tactic and decide to retaliate with capacity additions of their own, the outcome can be a vigorous competitive struggle in which overall industry profitability is reduced. Such situations usually occur in oligopolistic markets where increased market share is a key to increased profits.

fering. The strategic moves of one firm to differentiate its product may well require important countermoves from rival firms. However, when the nature of product differentiation begins to result in layers of insulation from rivalry—as occurs when switching becomes costly or difficult—then a firm may gain protection from raids on its customers by its rivals. Should this occur, competitive intensity is obviously lessened.

Market rivalry increases in proportion to the size of the payoff from a successful strategic move. The greater the potential reward, the more likely some firm will give in to the temptation of a particular strategic move. How big the strategic payoff is varies partly with the speed of retaliation. When competitors can be expected to respond slowly (or maybe even not at all), the initiator of a fresh competitive strategy can reap the benefits in the intervening period and perhaps gain a lead time advantage which is not easily surmounted; the greater the chance this will occur, the greater will the potential benefits justify the risk of eventual retaliation. Firms that have shrewdly assessed the "personality" of each rival firm and which also have probed the economics of their rivals' businesses are in the best position to predict correctly how and when rivals may respond to a given strategic move; such knowledge is advantageous in assessing the potential payoffs of strategic alternatives.[27]

Market rivalry tends to be more vigorous when it costs more to get out of a business than to stay in and compete. The higher are exit barriers (and thus the more costly it is to abandon a market), the stronger the incentive for firms to remain and compete as best they can, even though they may be earning low profits or even incurring a loss. A weaker set of competitive forces exists when the short-run costs of exit are low in comparison to the long-term costs of staying in, trying to carve out a defensible market position, and failing in the end to be successful.

Competition becomes more volatile and unpredictable the more diverse that rival firms are in terms of their strategies, their personalities, their corporate priorities, their resources, and their countries of origin. When rival firms differ on how to compete (whether this be due to different perceptions about the market or different corporate objectives and personalities), their strategies are likely to produce a head-on clash in the marketplace. Moreover, a diverse range of views and approaches enhances the probability that one or more firms will behave as "mavericks" and employ strategies which produce more market flux and uncertainty than would otherwise occur. In such an environment, it is difficult for firms to predict rivals' behavior accurately; the effects of signaling are uncertain; and the comfortable atmosphere of a "fraternity of insiders" does not prevail. Indeed, the mere presence of "outsiders" or mavericks (particularly foreign firms or new entrants) who either do not understand or else deliberately ignore conventional

---

[27] It is worth noting here that it is important for a firm to understand the reasons underlying any shifts in the competitive strategies of rival firms. Unless a firm correctly perceives what the intentions of its competitors are, it is less able to develop appropriate moves and countermoves of its own. When rival firms change their competitive strategy, management is thus obliged to ask: What are they up to, why are they doing this, and what do they expect to accomplish? Is this an aggressive move or it is something we should all be doing? The answers are almost certain to be relevant in figuring out the firm's own strategic response.

methods of competing has considerable potential for creating "a whole new ballgame."

At the same time, when firms gear their competitive strategies and counterstrategies to their own specific internal priorities, strengths, weaknesses, and financial capabilities, the more likely that the "right" strategy for one firm is the "wrong" strategy for another. Strategic diversity among rivals usually heightens competition because it stimulates fine-tuning and countermoves if buyers begin to respond to one firm's strategy more favorably than to another's. An exception arises when rival firms pursue narrow strategies aimed at catering to separate customer groups and market segments; then, each firm moves deliberately to carve out its own market niche and to build up its own loyal customer following in ways that do not directly threaten or overlap with the market segments being focused on by others in the industry. To the extent that rival firms pursue market segmentation or focus strategies and to the extent that each firm limits its competitive energies to only one or a few of these segments, competition in any one market segment tends to be weaker than is suggested by the total number of firms in the industry.

SUMMARY AND CONCLUSIONS

To explain and predict how a given market functions, it is necessary to go beyond the theoretical models of perfect competition, monopolistic competition, oligopoly, and monopoly and examine the specifics of industry structure and the specifics of competitive forces. The techniques of industry analysis include strategic group mapping, identification and assessment of the industry's driving forces, and a probing of the industry's cost-price-profit economics to ascertain what a firm must know and do to be competitively successful—the key success factors.

The "five forces model" of competition is an extremely useful tool for diagnosing the nature and strength of the competitive forces that are at work in the market. At the center of the market struggle is the competitive rivalry emerging from the interplay and sequence of their strategic moves and countermoves. From a firm's standpoint, the name of the game is to outmaneuver rival firms and capture a market position that not only is profitable but is also somewhat insulated from counterattack. However, the jockeying for position that goes on among competitors is just one indicator of the nature and strength of competition, albeit the most important one. Other major competitive forces include (1) threats of entry of new competitors, (2) pressures created by the availability of closely related substitutes which are attractively priced, (3) the economic power which can be wielded by suppliers, and (4) the economic power which can be wielded by customers.

Diagnosing and predicting the whys and hows of a particular firm's competitive strategy and market behavior entails a scrutiny of the firm's performance goals, its assumptions about the industry and about its key competitors, its current competitive strategy, the backgrounds and experiences of the firm's managers, and the firm's competitive capabilities. Such knowledge arms an analyst with added understanding and support for why firms are doing what they are doing and why some firms have been more successful in the marketplace than others.

The intensity of competition in a given market varies according to (1) how many firms compete against one another and whether they compete on a fairly equal footing relative to size, costs, and resources; (2) the rate of growth in market demand; (3) how strongly firms are tempted to use price cuts or other marketing tactics to try to boost unit volume; (4) whether the products of rival sellers are so differentiated that buyers become locked in by the costs of switching from one brand to another; (5) how much a firm stands to gain (relative to the risk involved) if it attempts a new strategic move; (6) whether it costs more to get out of a market than to remain and compete; and (7) how diverse rival firms are in terms of their strategies, personalities, priorities, resource capabilities, and countries of origin.

SUGGESTED READINGS

CASE, J. H., *Economics and the Competitive Process* (New York: New York University Press, 1979).

CLARK, J. M., *Competition as a Dynamic Process* (Washington, D.C.: The Brookings Institution, 1961).

MACHLUP, F., *The Economics of Sellers' Competition* (Baltimore: The Johns Hopkins Press, 1952).

PORTER, M. E., "How Competitive Forces Shape Strategy," *Harvard Business Review*, Vol. 57, No. 2 (March–April 1979), pp. 137–145.

——, *Competitive Strategy: Techniques for Analyzing Industries and Competitors* (New York: The Free Press, 1980), Chapters 1, 3, and 7.

——, *Competitive Advantage* (New York: The Free Press, 1985).

THOMPSON, A. A., "Competition as a Strategic Process," *Antitrust Bulletin*, Vol. 25, No. 4 (Winter 1980), pp. 777–803.

QUESTIONS FOR DISCUSSION

1. In which type of market structure would you expect competition to be more vigorous— monopolistic competition or oligopoly? Why?

2. Is the most important determinant of the strength of competition the number of rival firms in the market? Why or why not?

3. Why is it appropriate to view competition as a strategic process?

4. What is the competitive reasoning underlying the statement that "whenever fixed costs are high and marginal costs are low, firms are under strong economic pressure to produce at or very near full capacity"?

5. Explain how it is that the suppliers to the firms in a given industry can act as a competitive force in that industry.

6. The bottlers of soft drinks are customers of the manufacturers of glass bottles, the manufacturers of aluminum cans, and the manufacturers of plastic bottles. Explain

how, as customers, the soft-drink bottlers act as a competitive force in the "container industry."

7. Bayer and St. Joseph are the two leading sellers of aspirin; a number of other "no-name" firms supply aspirin for private-label sale by large retailers (drug and food chains). To what extent do you think competition among the aspirin manufacturers is affected by the competitive strategies employed by the firms making Excedrin, Anacin, Tylenol, Alka-Seltzer, and other brands of remedies for headache pain and discomfort? Draw a five-forces model for the "aspirin" market and assess the strength of each of the five forces.

16

GENERIC INDUSTRY ENVIRONMENTS AND COMPETITIVE STRATEGY

In Chapter 15 we explored some techniques and models for analyzing industries and competition. In this chapter we extend that discussion and focus on how and why competitive strategies tend to be tailored to fit the competitive peculiarities of particular types of industry environments and industry structure. Different industries can have fundamentally different structures (numbers of firms, barriers to entry and exit, kinds of strategic groups); they can be at much different stages of maturity (young versus mature versus declining); and they can be characterized by widely varying driving forces and by differing sets of competitive pressures. The overall industry environment, not surprisingly, shapes the context of how a firm competes and which competitive strategy options are really attractive. Depending on the nature of the industry environment, some competitive strategies make more sense than others.

We begin with a look at the generic types of competitive strategies, followed by how these various commonly encountered industry environments shape competitive strategy, and then conclude with an examination of some techniques for analyzing which competitive strategy fits which type of industry situation.

GENERIC TYPES OF COMPETITIVE STRATEGY

Competitive strategy has been defined as a firm's action plan for competing successfully in a given market—in plainer words, a firm's competitive strategy addresses how it plans to try to knock the socks off its competition. This plan, which *evolves* more or less continually in response to changing market and competitive conditions, consists of whatever offensive or defensive actions are deemed appropriate to cope with the five competitive forces (as portrayed in Fig. 15-2). The criteria for judging a well-formulated competitive strategy hinge chiefly on two things: (1) whether it creates a defendable and attractive long-term market position for the firm, and (2) whether it enables the firm to earn "superior" profits (at least more than a normal profit and something above the average of other firms in the industry).

It is no surprise that firms have discovered many different competitive approaches which produce acceptable results. With few exceptions, a firm's strategy is tailor-made to fit its particular circumstances and thus has at least some unique features and wrinkles. In this sense there are as many competitive strategies as there are competitors. However, from a broader and more general perspective, it is possible to single out three *generic approaches* to competing: (1) striving to be the overall low-cost producer in the industry, (2) seeking to differentiate one's product offering in one way or another from rivals' products, and (3) a focused approach based on catering to a narrow portion of the market rather than going out after the whole market.[1]

Striving to Be the Low-Cost Producer

The impetus for a strategy of striving to be the industry's low-cost producer can stem from the presence of sizable economies of scale, sizable learning curve effects, sizable experience curve effects, and sizable numbers of price-conscious buyers. Trying to be the industry leader in achieving an overall low-cost position typically entails being out front of rivals in constructing the most efficient-sized plants, in implementing cost-reducing technological advances, in getting the sales and market share needed to capitalize on learning and experience curve effects, in maintaining a tight rein on overhead and other administrative types of fixed costs, and in containing costs in such areas as R & D, advertising, service, and distribution. Low cost *relative to competitors* is the theme of the firm's entire strategy—although low cost is not so zealously pursued that a firm's product offering loses its competitiveness as concerns attributes upon which buyers place a high value (such as quality, service, and so on).

There are many attractive advantages to being the low-cost producer:

- As concerns *rival competitors*, the low-cost producer is in the best position to compete on the basis of price, to defend itself in a market where price competition is dominant, to use the attractiveness of a lower price as a weapon for attacking the differentiation and focus strategies of rivals, and to earn above-average profits.

- As concerns *customers*, the low-cost producer can protect its profit margin

---

[1] Michael E. Porter, *Competitive Strategy: Techniques for Analyzing Industries and Competitors* (New York: The Free Press, 1980), Chapter 2. The remainder of this section is drawn from Porter's discussion of these generic strategies, especially pp. 35–39 and 44–46.

to some degree since powerful buyers will be able to bargain price down only to the level of the next most efficient firm.

- As concerns *suppliers*, the low-cost producer is somewhat more insulated than competitors from powerful suppliers because it has more room to cope with increases in input costs.

- As concerns *potential entrants*, the low-cost producer is in a favorable competitive position because having the lowest costs not only acts as a barrier for a new entrant to hurdle but also provides the leeway to use price cutting to defend against market inroads made by a new competitor.

- As concerns *substitutes*, a low-cost producer is, compared to its rivals, in favorable position to defend against attractive substitutes.

Consequently, a low-cost position provides a measure of protection against all five types of competitive forces. To the extent that the pressures of price competition do arise, less efficient rivals will suffer first. Being the low-cost producer allows a firm to use its cost advantage to earn higher profit margins or to charge a lower price or both. Firms in a low-cost position relative to rivals are in excellent position to appeal to those buyers who are inclined to base their purchase decision on low price; plainly, *a low-cost producer is in position to exert a heavy hand in determining the industry's price floor.*

The strategy of trying to be the low-cost producer is a particularly powerful strategy when (1) demand is price elastic; (2) all firms in the industry produce essentially standardized, commodity-type products (newsprint, sheet steel, fertilizer, plastic pipe, lumber, and bulk chemicals) such that the marketplace is dominated by price competition and ''the name of the game'' is for sellers to be cost efficient; (3) there are not many ways to achieve product differentiation that have much value to buyers; (4) most buyers utilize the product in the same ways and thus have common user requirements; and (5) buyers incur few if any switching costs in changing suppliers and thus are strongly inclined to shop suppliers for the best price.

However, trying to be the low-cost leader is not without risk and disadvantage. Technological changes can result in cost or process breakthroughs that nullify past investments and learning. Rival firms may find it comparatively easy and/or inexpensive to imitate the leader's low-cost methods. A tunnel-vision approach to cost reduction can result in a firm overlooking important product or marketing changes, subtle shifts in buyer preferences and needs, and declining buyer sensitivity to price—thus getting left behind if competition swings more to nonprice variables and emphasis on differentiation. Finally, heavy investments in cost minimization can lock a firm in both to its present technology and present strategy, leaving it vulnerable to new state-of-the-art technologies and to new market directions. In short, being the low-cost leader imposes a significant burden in terms of staying on top of cost-saving technological improvements, scrapping existing equipment (even if it is not worn out) any time that something more efficient comes along, and risking technological and strategic inflexibility if buyers begin to be attracted by rivals' introduction of new product attributes.

Examples of firms which are well known for their cost leadership strategies are Lincoln Electric in arc welding equipment and supplies, Briggs and Stratton in small-horsepower gasoline engines, BIC in ballpoint pens, Black & Decker in tools, Texas Instruments in hand calculators and semiconductors, and Beaird-Poulan in chain saws.

Pursuing a Strategy of Differentiation

The approaches to differentiating one's product from rival firms take many forms: a different taste (Dr Pepper and Listerine), special features (Jenn-Air in cooking tops with a vented built-in grill for barbecuing), superior service (IBM in computers and Federal Express in overnight package delivery), spare-parts availability (Caterpillar guarantees that it will deliver spare parts for its construction equipment to any customer anywhere in the world within 24 hours or else the part is furnished free), overall value to the customer (Sears and McDonald's), engineering design and performance (Mercedes in automobiles), unusual quality and distinctiveness (Rolex in watches and Chivas Regal in scotch), product reliability (Johnson and Johnson in baby products), quality manufacture (Karastan in carpets and Curtis Mathes in TV sets), technological leadership (Hyster in lift trucks and 3M Company in bonding and coating products), convenient payment (American Express), a full range of services (Merrill Lynch), a complete line of products (General Motors in automobiles and Campbell in soups), and top-of-the-line image and reputation (Brooks Brothers and Ralph Lauren in menswear, Chanel in perfumes and fragrances, and Cross in writing instruments). Differentiation provides some insulation against the strategies of rivals because customers establish a preference or loyalty for a version of the product they think best suits them and may, in turn, be willing to pay a little (perhaps a lot!) more for it. In addition, successful differentiation (1) erects entry barriers in the form of customer loyalty and uniqueness for any newcomers to have to hurdle, (2) mitigates the bargaining power of buyers since alternative brands are less attractive, and (3) puts a firm in better position to ward off threats from substitutes to the extent that it has built a loyal clientele of customers. To the extent that differentiation allows a seller to charge a higher price and earn bigger profit margins, a seller is in a stronger economic position to deal with powerful suppliers. Thus, as with cost leadership, differentiation creates grounds on which to deal with the five competitive forces. However, the lines of defense for a differentiation strategy differ from those of a cost leadership strategy.

Employing a differentiation strategy has its risks, too:

- The extra cost of adding enough product attributes to achieve differentiation can result in a selling price that is far enough above the price of low-cost competitors to cause buyers to switch to lower-priced brands. Buyers are usually willing to pay only so much extra for differentiation; when this extra differential is exceeded, low-cost firms gain an edge over high-cost firms—despite the extra features that the products of the high-cost firms may have, a cost leadership strategy can defeat a differentiation strategy.

• Buyers may, over a period of time, decide that they do not need or want extra features, concluding that a basic or standard model serves their purpose just as well. Then the market emphasis shifts away from differentiation toward that of a commodity product situation where the "name of the game" is low-cost, efficient production.

• Rival firms may imitate the product attributes of the leaders to such an extent that buyers perceive that very little, if any, meaningful differentiation actually exists. The differentiation attempts of rivals thus cancel each other out and buyers place little value in the differences which are perceived to exist.

The types of differentiation strategies which are most appealing are those which are least subject to quick or inexpensive imitation. Here is where having a distinctive competence comes into play. To the extent that a firm has skills and competences which competitors cannot match easily, it can use its ability as a basis for successful differentiation. Those areas where efforts to differentiate are likely to produce an attractive, longer-lasting competitive edge are:

• Differentiation based on *technical superiority*.
• Differentiation based on *quality*.
• Differentiation based on *giving customers more support services*.
• Differentiation based on *the appeal of a lower price*.

As a rule, differentiation strategies are suited for situations where (1) there are many ways to differentiate the product or service and these differences are perceived by some buyers to have value, (2) buyer needs and uses of the item are diverse, and (3) not many rival firms are following a differentiation strategy. Often, the most attractive avenue for product differentiation is the one least traveled by rival firms—as the saying goes, "never follow the crowd." Also, experience indicates that it is hard to excel in more than one approach to differentiation simultaneously. Attempting to differentiate in many ways at once can deteriorate into trying to be too many things to too many people, thus blurring the image the firm presents to its target markets. In formulating a differentiation strategy it is usually wise to stress one key value and to develop a distinctive competence in delivering it. It can also be a good tactic to select a basis for differentiation which makes it easy for first-time buyers to try the product (because their switching costs are low) and which makes it hard for regular users to abandon (because the costs of switching to other brands or substitutes are high).

Focus and Specialization Strategies

A focus or specialization strategy aims at building a competitive edge and carving out a market position by catering to the special needs of a particular group of customers or by concentrating on a limited geographic market or by concentrating on certain uses for the product. The distinguishing feature of a focus strategy is that the firm specializes in serving only a portion of the total market. The underlying premise is that a firm can serve its narrow target market more effectively or more efficiently than rivals which spread their resources and competitive energies over a broad geographic area and/or over a broad spectrum of customer groups and customer uses of the product. The resulting competitive advantage is earned either by differentiation from better meeting the needs of the target market segment or by achieving lower costs in serving the segment or both. Hence, while a focus strategy does not achieve low cost or differentiation from the perspective of the market as a whole, it does produce one or both of these results in the target market segment. With its position of low cost, high differentiation, or both, a firm obtains defenses against the five competitive forces.

APPLICATIONS CAPSULE

CHEERLEADER SUPPLY COMPANY: A SUCCESSFUL USER OF A FOCUS STRATEGY

Cheerleader Supply Company, a Dallas-based company with 1982 sales of about $20 million, trains and outfits the lion's share of the 600,000-odd cheerleaders in the United States. Lawrence Herkimer, the company's founder, chairman, and principal owner, claims to be the only person to have a cheerleading move named after him—the "Herkie jump." Herkimer, now a portly 56 years old, regularly demonstrates the Herkie jump at his numerous cheerleader clinics, always to the delight of enthusiastic audiences.

Herkimer first got into cheerleading at Southern Methodist University. Herkimer was a gymnast in high school but tried out for the cheerleading squad at SMU because SMU didn't have a gymnastics team. With his jumping ability he was soon a crowd favorite, and by the time he graduated in 1948, national sportswriters had dubbed him "Mr. Cheerleader." After graduate school in physical education, Herkimer took a job teaching gymnastics at SMU; before long, schools began calling him to train their cheerleading squads on weekends. The weekend sessions soon evolved into cheerleading clinics and his reputation spread. One weekend at Ohio State netted him $21,000 when Ohio State, anxious to have Herkimer, agreed to pay him a fee of $5 per attendee (his usual fee was $1); 4200 teenagers showed up for the clinic. That prompted Herkimer to go into the cheerleading business full-time.

At first, Cheerleader Supply was a vehicle to promote the clinics and help Herkimer sell his books—*Championship Cheers and Chants* and *Pep Rally Skits and Stunts*. When schools started asking him to help line up uniforms, Herkimer saw an opportunity:

> Cheerleaders have very special requirements in clothes, not only in design but in delivery. You pick the squad in April, and the uniforms have to be there in August. And every school wants something special—braid trim on the sweater, two-color lining on the shirt. For four months of the year you're turning out special orders in small batches, and for eight months you're doing nothing.

Herkimer spent $100,000 in the early 1960s to buy a knitting mill and workshop in a rural town south of Dallas. Owning the plant offered the advantages of quality control and elimination of the high premium charged by subcontract apparel manufacturers for small custom orders. Low-wage labor was also plentiful because local farm women, who were needed at home in the spring and fall, were willing to work double-overtime shifts in the summer. Other products were added to the line as Herkimer ferreted out old buildings (at bargain prices) in which to set up production: a nearby milk-carton factory was converted into a plant to make plastic megaphones and drinking cups; an old warehouse was used to make plastic buttons and badges.

The company's strategy has evolved to where little is overlooked in training and outfitting cheerleaders:

1. Herkimer and 300 college-age assistants run clinics across the United States all summer long.
2. Cheerleader Supply knits sweaters, makes skirts and slacks, hand-hooks chenille emblems, distributes dyed-to-match saddle shoes, and carries matching knee socks—to provide complete cheerleading outfits.
3. The company holds a design patent on pompons which are made at a company-owned plant outside Houston.
4. Cheerleader Supply sells a line of spirit-building items (miniature megaphones stamped with school mascots, custom-made buttons and ribbons with any desired inscriptions), which in turn can be sold by school clubs or its cheerleaders to raise money (to help finance trips to the next cheerleading clinic).

Currently, Cheerleader Supply has succeeded in making sales to about two-thirds of the estimated 70,000 high school cheerleading squads and to over half of the 2500 college squads.

Source: "Go! Fight! Win!" *Forbes,* September 27, 1982, pp. 136–40.

A competitive strategy based on focus or specialization has merit (1) when there are distinctly different groups of buyers who either have different needs or else utilize the product in different ways; (2) when rival firms have not attempted to specialize, preferring instead to try to appeal to all types of buyers; or (3) when the firm's resources do not permit it to go after a wide segment of the total market.

Examples of firms employing a focus strategy include Tandem Computers (a specialist in "nonstop" computers for customers who need a "fail-safe" system that can support thousands of on-line terminals and preserve data integrity and reliability); Rolls-Royce (in super-luxury automobiles); Thermidor (a maker of premium-quality refrigerators, freezers, and cooking appliances); Fort Howard Paper (specializing in paper products for industrial and commercial enterprises only); and the numerous commuter airlines (which specialize in low-traffic, short-haul flights linking major airports with smaller population centers 50 to 250 miles away).

The risks of a focus strategy include (1) the possibility that broad-range competitors will find effective ways to match the focused firm in serving the narrow target market; (2) shifts in buyer preferences and needs such that the differences in product attributes desired by the target segment and the market as a whole become much narrower, allowing broad-range rivals a strong competitive footing in the target markets of the focused firms; and (3) the chance that competitors will find subsegments within the target segment and outfocus the focuser.

COMPETITIVE BEHAVIOR IN GENERIC TYPES OF INDUSTRY ENVIRONMENTS AND COMPETITIVE SITUATIONS

How firms tailor the generic approaches to competitive strategy is conditioned partly by the industry environment in which they compete and partly by each firm's situation in that environment. To highlight some of the considerations that shape how a firm can try to compete, we will survey the following types of generic industry environments and competitive situations:

1. Competitive strategies for "underdog" firms.
2. Competitive strategies for leaders and dominant firms.
3. Competitive strategies for weak or marginal firms.
4. Rescue strategies for firms in distress or crisis situations.
5. Competing in a young, emerging industry.
6. Competing during the transition to industry maturity.
7. Competitive strategies for firms in stagnant or declining industries.
8. Competitive strategies in fragmented industries.
9. Competitive strategy in global markets.

Competitive Strategies for Underdog Firms

Virtually every industry contains underdog or trailing firms. After all, every competitor cannot be the leader. Some firms, often a majority, occupy significantly weaker market positions than do the few which have found their way to the top of the industry. If a firm is content to be a follower, perhaps because profits are still adequate, it has no urgent strategic issue to confront beyond that of "how long can we continue to do what we are already doing and should we consider fine-tuning our present strategy?" However, an ambitious underdog firm may well be looking for opportunities to improve its market position by a little or by a lot. A firm with a subpar market share may need to increase sales volume and get to at least a "middle of the pack" position in order to realize scale economies, to capture more experience curve effects, to generate funding for an ample R & D budget, to gain stronger distribution, and, in general, to establish a more profitable market position. Normally, if an underdog firm is to make a credible attempt to improve its market standing, it will need a strategy aimed at building a competitive advantage; rarely can an underdog improve its competitive position just by imitating what leading firms in the industry are doing. Moreover, if an underdog has a 5% market share and needs a 20% share to earn attractive returns, it needs a more creative approach to competing than "try harder."

In cases where large size gives rise to significantly lower unit costs, a low-market-share business has only two strategic options: fight to increase share or withdraw from the business (gradually or quickly). The most-used competitive strategies to building market share are based on (1) striving to become the low-cost producer and, in turn, using the attractiveness of a lower price to win increased customer favor, and (2) differentiation strategies based on quality or technological superiority or better customer service. Striving to be the low-cost producer is usually open to an underdog only when one of the market leaders is not already successfully pursuing a cost leadership strategy.

In cases where scale economies or experience curve effects are small and a large market share produces no cost advantage of competitive consequence, the practical competitive strategy options for underdog and low-market-share companies boil down to six approaches:[2]

1. *Vacant niche strategy*—where a firm searches for customers and cultivates product-use applications that major firms have bypassed or neglected. The principle underlying this competitive approach is to focus on what the leaders are not interested in. An "ideal" vacant niche is of sufficient size and scope to be profitable, has some growth potential, and is well suited to a firm's own capabilities and skills, as well as being outside the realm of interest to the leading firms. Two examples of successful use of a vacant niche type of focus strategy are the regional commuter airlines, which serve small and medium-sized population centers having too few passengers to attract the interest of the major airlines, and the small tire manufacturers, which have managed to find enough holes in the market to survive alongside Goodyear, Firestone, B. F. Goodrich, Uniroyal, and Michelin.

2. *Specialist strategy*—where competitive efforts are aimed at only a few, carefully chosen product-customer-use segments. Rather than trying to compete for all types of customers with a full product line appealing to all different needs and functions, stress is placed only on those areas where the company has or can develop special expertise and where such expertise will be highly valued by customers. The success of a specialist strategy can turn on clever ways to approach segmentation (some interesting options are to segment by stage of production, performance characteristics of the product, the cost and speed of distribution, geographic location, the type of support services offered, product applications and uses, and manufacturing capability). Smaller companies which have successfully used a specialist type of focus strategy include Control Data (which developed a better computer for scientific research), Crown Cork and Seal (which concentrated on metal cans for hard-to-hold products and on aerosol cans), and American Tobacco (which specializes in chewing tobacco and snuff).

3. *"Ours-is-better-than-theirs" strategy*—where a firm uses a combination focus-differentiation strategy keyed to product quality. Sales and marketing efforts are focused on quality-conscious and performance-oriented buyers. Fine craftsmanship, prestige quality, product improvements, and working closely with customers to develop a better product can undergird this type of approach. Some

---

[2] For more details, see Philip Kotler, *Marketing Management: Analysis, Planning and Control*, 5th ed. (Englewood Cliffs, N.J.: Prentice-Hall, Inc., 1984), Chapter 12, and R. G. Hamermesh, M. J. Anderson, Jr., and J. E. Harris, "Strategies for Low Market Share Businesses," *Harvard Business Review*, Vol. 56, No. 3 (May–June 1978), pp. 95–102.

examples: Beefeater's approach to selling gin, Tiffany's stance in diamonds and jewelry, Chicago Cutlery in premium-quality kitchen knives, Baccarat in fine crystal, Mazola in cooking oil and margarine, Bally in shoes, Pennzoil in motor oil, and Neiman-Marcus's approach to department store retailing.

4.   *Content follower strategy*—where the firm avoids overt attempts to steal customers away from leading firms and grab a bigger market share. Instead, the firm uses focus and differentiation approaches that will not provoke competitive retaliation. Burroughs (in computers) and Union Camp (in paper products) have been successful market followers by consciously concentrating on selected product uses and applications for specific customer groups, effectively focused R & D, profit emphasis rather than market share emphasis, and strong top management.

5.   *Guppy strategy*—where an aggressive small firm seeks to grow at the expense of still smaller rivals either by taking sales away from them or by acquiring them outright to form an enterprise that is of a more competitive size. Several of the ten largest brewers of beer owe their sales and market share growth to having beaten out or acquired small regional and local breweries.

6.   *Distinctive image strategy*—where an underdog tries to develop a differential competitive advantage through a distinctive and visible appeal. This may take the form of lower prices achieved through cost reductions, prestige quality at a good price, better customer services, unique product attributes, innovative distribution channels, leadership in new product introduction, or unusually creative advertising. Examples include Dr. Pepper's strategy of calling attention to its distinctive taste, Seven-Up's campaign to promote caffeine-free soft drinks, Apple Computer's approach to making it easier and interesting for people to use a personal computer, and Hyatt's use of architecture and luxurious accommodations to appeal to upscale travelers and conventions.

Without a doubt, in volume-oriented, mass production industries, firms with low market shares have to overcome such obstacles as less access to economies of scale in manufacturing or distribution or sales promotion, smaller R & D budgets, less opportunity to distribute through internal channels, and more difficulty in meeting capital requirements, keeping good managerial and technical personnel, and gaining customer recognition.[3] But it is erroneous to view small firms as necessarily being unable to hold their own against the biggest firms or being less profitable. Many small firms earn healthy profits and enjoy good reputations with customers. Often, the handicaps of small size can be surmounted and a profitable competitive position established by (1) competing only in carefully chosen market segments where particular strengths can be developed and avoid attacking dominant firms head-on with price cuts and increased promotional expenditure; (2) focusing R & D budgets on developing a distinctive competence in new product development or technical capabilities, but only for the target market segments; (3) being content to remain small and refusing to be lured into a "something for

---

[3] Hamermesh, Anderson, and Harris, "Strategies for Low Market Share Businesses," p. 102.

everyone" grow-and-build approach; (4) pushing specialization rather than diversification (but if diversification is needed, entering closely related markets); and (5) managing the business in an innovative/"dare to be different"/"beat-the-odds" type of mode as opposed to an all-out grow-and-build strategy that attacks the market leaders across a wide front. Only when the economics of the business is such that large regional or national market share is crucial to profitability is a low-market-share firm pushed into a grow-and-build type of strategy extending over many market segments. Of course, a trailing firm may be able to make major market share gains if it makes a sudden technological breakthrough, or if the leaders stumble or become complacent, or if it has the patience to nibble away at the leaders and build up gains in its customer base over a long period.

Competitive Strategies for Leaders and Dominant Firms

The competitive position of a dominant firm is usually enviable. As a leader, it has a proven strategy and a well-known reputation. The main issue of competitive strategy for a dominant firm tends to revolve around how best to sustain what has been achieved and how to maintain or improve upon its present standing. At least three different competitive postures are open:[4]

1. *Keep-the-offensive strategy*—entails application of the principle that the best defense is a good offense. Hence, the firm continues to press the existing strategy (usually a cost leadership or differentiation type strategy) by exercising the initiative and setting standards that rivals have to meet. The strategic goal is to be *the* source of new product ideas, cost-cutting discoveries, innovative customer services, and/or better means of distribution. In addition, ways can be identified to lower buyer's switching costs, thereby making it easier and less costly for potential customers to switch their purchases from rival firms. The leader can also look for "first-mover advantages" and try to exploit them. In the process, the present strategy can be reformulated as necessary to signal follower firms of the leader's evaluation of changed industry circumstances.

2. *Hold and maintain strategy*—where the leader's competitive moves are geared to making it hard for rivals to make competitive inroads and hard for new firms to enter. Specific actions can include attempting to raise entry barriers; introducing more of the company's own brands to compete with those already successful company brands; figuring out ways to increase the costs of customers switching to rival products; keeping prices reasonable and quality attractive; preserving or even raising the level of customer service; investing enough to remain cost competitive, stay technologically progressive, and maintain the firm's existing share of new market growth, thus staving off any market share slippage and decline; and shifting any extra cash flows to profitable opportunities elsewhere. The primary appeals of "hold and maintain" are to lessen the chances of

---

[4] Kotler, *Marketing Management*, Chapter 12.

antitrust charges (if the dominant firm's market share is approaching monopoly proportions) and to "milk" the firm's present position for profits and cash flow (if the industry's long-term prospects are not very attractive or if further gains in market share do not appear profitable enough to go after).

3. *Confrontation strategy*—where the leader sends clear signals to rivals that any moves to cut into the leader's business will be "bloody" and will provoke heavy-handed retaliation. The strategic themes include meeting all competitive price cuts promptly (with even larger cuts if necessary), being quick to launch large-scale retaliatory promotional campaigns if smaller firms seek to increase their market shares, offering better deals to the major customers of next-in-line or "maverick" firms, and sending signals to aggressive-minded small firms regarding who should lead and who should follow (including, if necessary, pressuring distributors not to carry rivals' products, having salespersons bad-mouth the products of aggressive small firms, or trying to hire away the better executives of firms that "get out of line"). The objectives of the dominant firm's competitive strategy is to establish an unwritten but well-understood tradition among small firms of the importance of "playing follow the leader," thereby increasing its own strategic flexibility and preserving its leadership role.

APPLICATIONS CAPSULE

COMPETITIVE STRATEGY AT IBM

IBM's System/360 computer models included a wide range of central processing unit (CPU) sizes, together with numerous options for tying in input-output equipment (printers, readers) and memory storage. IBM priced its memory and input-output equipment separately from its central processing computer units so as to allow customers maximum flexibility in choosing the best equipment combinations. The design characteristics of the System/360 models, however, allowed rival computer manufacturers to produce almost identical copies of the IBM input-output units and memories; they could then sell these at lower prices directly to users having IBM central processing units. Generally, IBM's central processing units were protected from the competition of rival computer firms because IBM customers were very reluctant to discard their investment in specialized programming and because of the difficulty in manufacturing a CPU having programming logic compatible with IBM processors. There was no such compatibility problem with input-output equipment or with memory units. Potter Instrument Company in 1967 initiated competition with IBM by introducing a replacement for IBM tape drives; a short time later, other peripheral equipment manufacturers came out with replacements for IBM disc drives and then for main memory units.

Because sales of input-output equipment and memory units accounted for over half of IBM's computer revenue, IBM was concerned in early 1970 about the threat posed by the competitive products of the peripheral equipment manufacturers and the great success they were having in getting IBM users to switch to lower-priced non-IBM equipment. At the time, IBM was preparing to introduce its new System/370 line, and while the company felt it could safely ignore the threat to the System/360 memories, it wanted to avoid losing the new System/370 memories to rival firms. IBM assembled a task force to assess how well rival firms would fare in selling IBM-compatible memory units against IBM at various IBM prices; the study was done for a hypothetical new company and also for an established company having the capacity to produce IBM-compatible memory units. Insofar as the hypothetical new company was concerned, the analysis showed that IBM's primary protection from competition was the time required for a new company to become established in the marketplace. The IBM task force estimated that if IBM established a lease price of $16,000 to $18,000 per month per megabyte of memory (with initial shipments to begin in 1972), then a new company could not break even competing with IBM until around 1974, and, further, if the IBM lease price was $12,000 and above, the task force projected good profitability for a new company beyond 1976 but at prices of $10,000 and below no break-even point was envisioned until the far future.

For an established company, the task force projected that a firm could enter memory competition and reach the break-even point by 1973 at an IBM lease price of $18,000 per month per megabyte, and by 1975 with a price of $10,000 to $12,000, with high profitability in later years for all lease rentals of $12,000 and above. The task force concluded that if IBM went ahead with its planned $12,000-per-megabyte monthly fee that a new company could be only marginally profitable but that an established peripheral equipment company would be very likely to enter the field because they could make a 20% return on investment for a $10 million investment and would enjoy a healthy 23% profit margin.

However, additional studies indicated that of the $61 million-per-month rental value which IBM expected to have from its memory units by 1976, that 26% would be protected through minimum memory sizes tied directly to the CPU, 36% through customers who would resist mixing IBM equipment with that of other manufacturers, and 15% because of locations in outlying geographical areas where the smaller firms were not expected to compete. This left only 23% of IBM's memory business as a possible competitive target, regardless of the exact price set by IBM. Thus, based upon the expected customer resistance to using non-IBM equipment and upon the estimated lag time between IBM's introduction to System/370 memory units and the availability of competitive memory units, IBM decided to go ahead with its planned price of $12,000 per month per megabyte for memory units on its 155 and 165 System/370 models. The 370/155 and 165 memory units utilized magnetic cores—the standard computer memory technology. But when IBM came out with its next System/370 model, the 145, a new all-semiconductor memory was used; this semiconductor memory was much faster than magnetic cores, and because it was a new technology, it was not considered subject to immediate competitive attack. As a result, IBM priced its new semiconductor memory units 60% higher than its magnetic core memory units. Within less than a year, though, IBM became concerned about the ability of rival firms to introduce not only magnetic core replacements for the early System/370 models but also replacement equipment for the new semiconductor unit.

Meanwhile, IBM studies indicated lower prices for central processing units prompted users to install the largest possible system and thus generate the maximum demand for memory and input-output equipment (subject to replacement by competitors), while higher prices on central processing units increased CPU profits but reduced the demand and profit earned on peripheral equipment sales and leases. IBM's solution to this profit trade-off was to package a large amount of memory with a central processing unit and charge a lower CPU price. This had the advantage of raising overall profits, while protecting at least the packaged portion of memory from competition.

Even so, within a few months, IBM saw that its previous forecast had underestimated the ability of rival firms to keep pace, and still another task force was set up to study alternatives for reducing the competitive threat. Basically, the plans the task force considered were various combinations of minimum memories, lower memory unit prices, and increased CPU prices. The task force also looked at reducing the number of memory options obtainable with a central processing unit and then refusing to sell CPUs without at least the minimum memory. Nonetheless, the final decision was to raise the central processing unit prices by a maximum of 8%, cut the purchase price of memory units on 155 and 165 models, and make no change on the rental price of memory units.

This action shortly proved to be ineffective, and IBM reviewed the strategy of introducing upgraded 155 and 165 models as new machines having higher CPU prices and lower memory prices. This was to be accomplished by tying the announcement of "virtual memory" for CPU to the new 145 model semiconductor memory announcement, thus justifying the higher CPU prices through increased performance and the lower memory price through the reduced manufacturing cost of semiconductor memory. Accordingly, IBM in August 1972 announced new versions of its 155 and 165 models, to be known as the 158 and 168 models (a revision known inside IBM as the SMASH program). The basic CPU price was raised 36% on the 165 model and 54% on the model 155. The memory price was cut 57% and a larger minimum memory size was tied to the basic central processing unit on both models, neither of which could be acquired without the memory units. The effect of the changes was to make the total price of the 158 and 168 models higher in small configurations and lower in larger configurations than the original 155 and 165 models. The semiconductor memory was not made available to users of the original 155 and 165 models, thereby prohibiting users from buying the cheaper central process unit and putting on the cheaper memory as well. The SMASH program effectively foreclosed rival firms from the memory market for several months.

In trying to unravel IBM's actions it is important to understand that there are high barriers to entry in the full-line computer systems market but low barriers to entry in the peripheral equipment market. The barriers that do exist in the peripheral equipment market are related primarily to brand loyalty to IBM (including a fear of problems of mixing the equipment of different manufacturers) and the difficulty of producing IBM-compatible products which will match IBM interface specifications. The latter problem causes a lag between the time IBM introduces a product and the time it can be copied. This time lag reduces the rental life of the product of rival firms and gives IBM some time after a new product introduction without competition. Additional barriers to entry in the peripheral market include raising enough working capital to finance a rental business and some small manufacturing economies of scale. However, the disadvantages of small size are not so large as to preclude a satisfactory profit by undercutting IBM's existing price—unless and until IBM also cuts prices.

A second aspect of the computer equipment market is the disruption caused by equipment installation and removal, even if compatibility is not a problem. Normally, lower-priced equipment is introduced as a "new" product having essentially identical performance specifications as existing products. The customer can get the price cut only by physically removing the old model and installing the new one. The freight charges and disruption involved, as well as lack of information or lethargy on the part of some computer users, means IBM can come out with a competitive low-priced product while still receiving the higher rent from many users for some time after the price cut.

A third feature which IBM used to good advantage related to the time lag between IBM's introduction of a new product and a rival's introduction of its equivalent. As part of its introductory scheme, IBM induced users to agree to a fixed-term lease period, with heavy penalties for early termination. This effectively locked out competitors until users completed their lease agreements. Then, too, by making periodic design changes in its products (such as switching control functions between drive and control units), IBM was able to further reduce the marketing effectiveness of its competitors without reducing its own prices.

QUESTIONS FOR DISCUSSION

1. Based upon the description above, what would you say IBM's principal goal was? Why?
2. What type of competitive strategy does IBM seem to be using here?

Sources: Based upon documents released in the antitrust litigation between Telex and IBM and upon Gerald Brock, *The U.S. Computer Industry: A Study of Market Power* (Cambridge, Mass.: Ballinger Publishing Company, 1975).

Competitive Strategies for Weak or Marginal Firms

A firm in a weak or marginally competitive condition has essentially four options. It can employ a *grow-and-build* strategy based on either low-cost production or "new" differentiation themes, pouring enough money and talent into the effort to make the enterprise a stronger performer. It can adopt a *hold-and-maintain* mode, continuing the present strategy and assigning enough resources to keep sales, market share, profitability, and competitive position at present levels. It can opt for an *abandonment* strategy (divestiture or liquidation) and prepare to get out of the business quickly or gradually. Or it can resort to a "harvest strategy" whereby reinvestment in the business is held to a bare-bones minimum and the main objective is to "harvest" short-term profits and/or maximize short-term cash flow. The gist of the first three options is self-explanatory. The fourth deserves more explanation.

A *harvest strategy* steers a middle course between maintenance and abandonment. It entails a level of resource support in between what is required for maintenance and a decision to divest or liquidate. It is a phasing-down or endgame approach. Kotler has suggested seven indicators of when a business should consider a harvest strategy:[5]

1. When the business is in a saturated or declining market and the industry's long-term prospects are unattractive.
2. When the business has gained only a small market share, and building it up would be too costly or not profitable enough; or when it has a respectable market share that is becoming increasingly costly to maintain or defend.
3. When profit prospects are subpar, because of the firm's competitive weakness or because poor long-term market conditions are forecasted.
4. When reduced levels of competitive effort will not immediately trigger sharp declines in sales and market position.
5. When the enterprise can redeploy the freed-up resources in higher-opportunity areas.
6. When the business is not a major component of the organization's overall business portfolio.
7. When the business does not contribute other desired features (sales stability, prestige, a well-rounded product line) to the total business portfolio.

The more of these seven conditions which are present, the more ideal the business is for harvesting.

The features of a harvesting strategy are fairly clear cut. The operating budget is reduced to a bare-bones level; stringent cost cutting is undertaken. Capital investment in new equipment is given little, if any, financial priority—depending upon the current condition of fixed assets and upon whether the harvest is to be fast or slow. Price may be raised, promotional expenses cut, quality reduced, customer services curtailed, equipment maintenance decreased, and the like. The harvest objective is to *maximize short-term cash flow* and use the funds for other product lines or for diversification. It is understood that sales will fall to some core level of demand, but it may be that costs can be cut such that profits erode slowly rather than rapidly. Ideally, though, sales and market share will not fall far below their preharvest level in the near term. If the business cannot make money and/or generate positive cash flow when it reaches the lower core level of demand, it can then be divested or liquidated. A harvest strategy thus relegates a business to its sunset or twilight stage.

Although a harvest strategy calls for reduced budgets and cost cutting, there is value in implementing the associated moves in ways which do not alert competitors and customers to the harvesting intention. To do so merely precipitates a decline in sales and reduces the potential harvest. Generally, the first cutbacks should be in expenditures for R & D and for plant and equipment. Later, marketing expenditures can be reduced and prices raised slightly. Still later, product quality and customer services can be trimmed. Management may also elect to splash some advertising occasionally, since such sporadic bursts may recapture customer and dealer attention, thereby slowing sales decay. Such an approach may result in a smaller gain in cash flow, but one which lasts over a longer period. A fast

[5] Philip Kotler, "Harvesting Strategies for Weak Products," *Business Horizons*, Vol. 21, No. 5 (August 1978), pp. 17–18.

harvest, where deep cutbacks are made across the board, produces a large cash flow increase, but it doesn't last long.[6]

Harvesting strategies have much to recommend, especially in diversified companies having businesses which are in the declining stages of the life cycle or which are "dogs." Different lines of business deserve different levels of resource support depending on their profit potential, their life-cycle stage, and their importance to a diversified firm's overall business portfolio.

Rescue Strategies for Firms in Crisis or Distress Situations

Rescue strategies come into play when a business worth saving has fallen into disrepair and decline. The goal is to arrest and reverse the sources of competitive and financial weakness as quickly as possible. The first task of rescue is diagnosis. What lies at the root of poor performance? Is it bad competitive strategy? Or is it poor implementation and execution of an otherwise workable strategy? Or are the causes of decline beyond management control? Can the business be saved? Discerning what is wrong and sizing up the seriousness of the firm's competitive problems are prerequisites to formulating a rescue plan for a turnaround. There are five generic approaches to restoring a business to healthier conditions:[7]

- A fundamental rebuilding and repositioning of the enterprise through major revisions in competitive strategy.
- Revenue-increasing strategies.
- Cost-reduction strategies.
- Asset reduction/retrenchment strategies.
- A combination of these.

When the cause of weak performance is diagnosed as "bad" strategy, the task of rejuvenating the firm's business can assume several forms: (1) shifting to a new competitive approach and thus trying to reposition the business in the marketplace, (2) overhauling internal operations to produce better support of the same basic overall competitive strategy, (3) merger with another firm, and (4) retrenching into a reduced core of products and customers more closely matched to the firm's strengths. Which of these makes the most sense depends on conditions prevailing in the industry and on the firm's particular strengths and weaknesses vis-à-vis rival firms. This entails doing an intensive "situation analysis" of the industry, major competitors, the firm's own competitive position, and its

---

[6] *Ibid.*, p. 20.

[7] For an excellent survey discussion of all the ins and outs of rescuing distressed firms, see Charles W. Hofer, "Turnaround Strategies," *Journal of Business Strategy*, Vol. 1, No. 1 (Summer 1980), pp. 19–31.

skills and resources. Usually, successful rescue of an ailing business has to be based on a firm's strengths and what it is best at doing.

Revenue-increasing rescue efforts aim at how to increase sales volume (increased promotion, more emphasis on marketing, added customer services) and whether and how much of a price increase can be instituted. Attempts to increase sales revenues are necessary (1) when there is little or no room in the operating budget to cut back on expenses and still reach break even, and (2) when the key to restoring profitability is increased utilization of existing capacity.

An emphasis on cost reduction works best when an ailing firm's cost structure is flexible enough to permit radical surgery, when operating inefficiencies are identifiable and readily correctable, and when the firm is relatively close to its break-even point. Accompanying a general belt-tightening can be an increased emphasis on budgeting and cost control, elimination of jobs and hirings, modernization of existing plant and equipment to gain greater productivity, and postponement of capital expenditures.

Asset reduction/retrenchment efforts become essential to rescue when cash flow is a critical consideration and when the most practical way to generate cash is (1) through sale of some of the firm's assets (plant and equipment, land, patents, inventories, or profitable subsidiaries) and (2) through retrenchment (pruning of marginal products from the product line, closing or sale of older plants, a reduced work force, withdrawal from outlying markets, cutbacks in customer service, and the like). Sometimes, though, selling off some of a firm's assets is not so much for the purpose of unloading and stemming cash drains as it is for the purpose of raising funds to plow back into a strengthening of the remaining activities.

Combination rescue strategies are usually essential in grim situations where fast action on a broad front is required. Similarly, combination actions frequently come into play when the rescue effort entails bringing in new managers and giving them a relatively free hand to make whatever changes they see fit in restoring the business to a good condition. Attempts to retrench, rebuild, and reposition a business in the marketplace nearly always have to draw upon a multipronged approach rather than depend upon just one category of turnaround actions.

Many rescue efforts prove unsuccessful. A recent study of 64 companies found no successful turnarounds among the most troubled companies in eight basic industries.[8] Many waited too late to begin a turnaround and others found themselves short of both cash and entrepreneurial talent to compete in a mature industry characterized by a fierce battle for market share; better-positioned rivals simply proved too strong to defeat in head-to-head combat for the market share needed to survive. This study found that as market maturity approaches and competitive hostility intensifies a firm's range of strategic options narrows. For a crisis-ridden firm to be successful in a turnaround effort, its management has to be alert to the signs of an impending competitive shakeout and launch an early effort to reposition the firm and rebuild its competitive status.

---

[8] William K. Hall, "Survival Strategies in a Hostile Environment," *Harvard Business Review*, Vol. 58, No. 5 (September–October 1980), pp. 75–85.

Competing in Young, Emerging Industries

Two crucial strategic issues confront firms trying to participate in a young, emerging industry with high-growth potential: (1) how to acquire the resources needed to support a *grow-and-build strategy* aimed at gaining a position among the industry leaders, and (2) how to develop the sorts of distinctive competence and competitive stamina that will be needed when growth slows and weaker, inefficient firms fall prey to competitive shakeout and industry consolidation.[9] Ironclad prescriptions cannot be given for just how these two issues should be resolved since emerging industries are not all alike. The form of the grow-and-build strategy has to be geared to match the firm's situation and the character of the emerging industry itself—it can emphasize differentiation or low cost. The market environments of emerging industries have several distinctive features:[10]

- There are no "rules of the game;" the issue of how the market will function is open-ended.

- Much of the technological know-how tends to be proprietary, having been developed in-house by pioneering firms.

- There is uncertainty over which production technology will prove to be the most efficient and which product attributes will be preferred by buyers—the result is erratic product quality, an industry-wide absence of product and technological standardization, and a situation where each firm is, at least until a broader consensus develops, committed to pioneering its own approach to technology, product design, marketing, and distribution.

- Firms lack solid information about competitors, characteristics of customers, and industry conditions such that they are groping to find the "right" strategy, an efficient production technology, and an attractive combination of product attributes (not the least of which is usually dependable quality and performance).

- A steep learning curve exists, allowing major cost reductions as volume builds and better ideas emerge for plant layout, production procedures, job design, and productivity improvement.

- Opportunities exist for newly formed companies to enter the industry—entry barriers are low except in situations where investment costs in new technology create a high financial barrier.

- A market situation prevails where customers must be created (since all buyers will be first-time users), thus making the marketing task one of inducing initial purchase and eliminating customer confusion over the multiplicity of product attributes, technologies, and claims of rival firms. Many potential buyers may perceive that second- or third-generation technologies will make current products

[9] Charles W. Hofer and Dan Schendel, *Strategy Formulation: Analytical Concepts* (St. Paul, Minnesota: West Publishing Co., 1978), pp. 164–165.

[10] Porter, *Competitive Strategy*, pp. 216–223.

obsolete; hence, they may delay purchase until the product "matures" and a consensus emerges regarding design and technology.

• Difficulties in securing ample supplies of raw materials and components may be encountered (until suppliers gear up to meet the industry's needs).

• Because of the conditions listed above, firms in the industry are faced with unit costs much higher than they know will prevail later as volume builds and the market grows; this situation sometimes requires firms to price below cost initially or else severely limit sales. Firms thus need enough financial strength to "get over the hump" of startup and to begin to realize the cost-volume benefits of riding the cost curve downward.

Dealing with these conditions is a challenging competitive strategy problem. The experiences of firms in emerging industries suggest the following competitive approaches:[11]

1.   Manage the business in an entrepreneurial mode with the aim of positioning the firm for future growth. In an emerging industry there are no established "rules of the game" and a wide variety of strategic approaches are often tried by industry participants. Because firms enjoy wide strategic freedom, a pioneering firm which makes a good strategic choice can shape the rules of the game in areas such as product design and attributes, marketing, and pricing, thus enhancing its long-run standing.

2.   Be alert for "first-mover advantages" related to product quality, performance features, styling, early commitments to technologies and raw material suppliers, and learning and experience curve effects.

3.   Search out new customer groups, new geographical areas to enter, and new user applications. Recognize that getting first-time buyers to try the industry's new product can be pursued with promotional tactics aimed at lowering buyers' switching costs.

4.   Watch for openings to shift advertising and promotion from building product awareness to increasing frequency of use and to creating brand loyalty.

5.   Move quickly when technological uncertainty clears and a "dominant" technology emerges; try to get in position to pioneer the "dominant design" approach (but be cautious when technology is moving so rapidly that early investments are likely to be rendered obsolete).

6.   Consider being first to lower prices to attract the next layer of price-sensitive buyers into the market.

7.   Try to prepare for the time when large, established firms looking for growth opportunities are drawn to enter the industry, attracted by the more certain prospects the industry is offering. For an early participant in an emerging industry to prepare for the entry of powerful competitors, it needs to forecast (a) who the probable entrants will be (based on present and future entry barriers) and (b) the

[11] Kotler, *Marketing Management*, p. 366, and Porter, *Competitive Strategy*, Chapter 10.

types of strategies they are likely to employ. Often, the entry of new "key players" means that existing firms have to seek out new ways to defend their positions.

The issue of how a pioneering firm can maintain/improve its competitive market position during the takeoff stage should not blind management to the longer-range strategic need to prepare for the different types of competitive forces that will arise when the transition to a more mature market triggers vigorous competition and a battle for market share.[12] The concern for near-term growth has to be balanced against the longer-range need to build a competitive edge and a defendable market position. This can be accomplished most easily in diversified enterprises that have had experience in managing young businesses through the early stages of an industry's evolution. A single-business enterprise in an industry on the verge of takeoff does have some options for adding to its competitive strength: it can gain guidance by wise selection of members of its board of directors; it can hire skilled management personnel from firms that have recently passed through the developmental and takeoff stages; or it can try to gain added expertise and a stronger resource base through acquisition or merger with other firms in the industry.

Competing During the Transition to Industry Maturity

Rapid industry growth cannot go on forever. The transition to a slow-growth, mature industry environment does not occur after any fixed period of time and it can be forestalled by innovations or other driving forces that renew rapid growth. Nonetheless, when maturity occurs, the transition usually produces fundamental changes in the industry's competitive environment:[13]

1. *Slowing growth in buyer demand generates more head-to-head competition for market share.* Since firms are unable to maintain their historical rates of growth by merely holding the same market share, rivalry turns toward trying to take customers away from other firms. Outbreaks of price cutting, increased advertising, and other aggressive tactics are common.

2. *Buyers become more sophisticated, often driving a harder bargain on repeat purchases.* Since the product is no longer new but an established item with which buyers are familiar, the attention of buyers is on which of several brands to buy the next time around.

3. *Competition often produces a greater emphasis on cost and service.* Once buyers decide on the product attributes they prefer, the choice among competing brands hinges upon which seller offers the best combination of price and service.

4. *Firms have a "topping out" problem in adding production capacity.* Slower rates of industry growth mean slower rates of capacity additions—or else industry overcapacity results. Each firm has to monitor rivals' capacity additions

---

[12] Hofer and Schendel, *Strategy Formulation*, pp. 164–165.
[13] Porter, *Competitive Strategy*, pp. 238–240.

carefully and to time its own capacity additions so that excess capacity is minimized. Rapid industry growth no longer quickly covers up the mistake of adding too much capacity too soon.

5. *Product innovation and new uses and applications are harder to come by.* Whereas during the takeoff and rapid-growth stages R & D activities may produce a stream of new product attributes and applications, the ability to continue to generate marketable innovations tends to become more limited. Firms run out of big, new ideas.

6. *International competition increases.* As a consequence of technological maturity, product standardization, and increased competitive emphasis on low-cost production, a more globally competitive industry tends to emerge; growth-minded domestic firms seek out new foreign markets and become interested in locating plant facilities in countries where production costs are lower.

7. *Industry profitability falls, sometimes temporarily and sometimes permanently.* Slower growth, increased competition, more sophisticated buyers, and the associated need for shifts in competitive strategy frequently cause industry profits to decline from their levels during the rapid growth phase. Some firms may be more affected than others—and the losers are almost certain to be the weak, less efficient firms.

8. *The resulting competitive shakeout induces a number of mergers and acquisitions among former competitors, drives some firms out of the industry, and, in general, produces industry consolidation.* In a rapid-growth environment, even inefficient firms and firms with weak competitive strategies can survive. Strategic sloppiness is generally exposed by industry maturity, however, and rivals are forced to scramble to get in a defendable, long-term market position. Most mergers and acquisitions emerge out of the need of firms to benefit from enhanced competitive strength and market position.

These characteristics usually force firms to reexamine their competitive strategies, making numerous fine-tuning adjustments and sometimes undertaking a major overhaul. A refashioned competitive approach can be a matter of survival. There are several competitive strategy considerations which arise again and again in maturing industries.[14]

Sophisticated Cost Analysis. Although numerous models, sizes, and product options may have been competitively useful in a rapidly growing market, product line proliferation can be a liability in a mature environment characterized by price competition and battles for market share. Sophisticated product costing becomes the basis for pruning unprofitable items from the line and concentrating on items where margins are highest and/or where the firm has distinctive skills or a comparative advantage. Average costing for groups of products and arbitrary allocations of overhead become inadequate for evaluating the product line and for deciding what new items to add.

[14] The following discussion draws from Porter, *Competitive Strategy*, pp. 241–246.

A second aspect of sophisticated cost analysis is to recognize that more than one cost curve can prevail in an industry. The cost curve for a specialist firm concentrating on custom orders and short production runs can differ substantially from the cost curve for a firm pursuing a high-volume, low-cost strategy, as shown in Fig. 16-1. Small firms may well enjoy cost advantages for the small-volume, custom-order buyer segments, whereas the large-volume producer has an advantage in serving the mass market.

Pricing Correctly. Although rule-of-thumb formulas and simple target return pricing methods may suffice in an era of rapid market growth, the stiff competitive environment of a mature market requires increased capability to measure costs on individual items and to price them accordingly. Unwittingly subsidizing the losses on one item with above-average profits on another hides items whose demand does not support their true costs and invites price cutting or new product introductions by rivals against items that may be priced high. In general, a much enhanced "profit consciousness" is needed to be successful in intensely competitive markets.

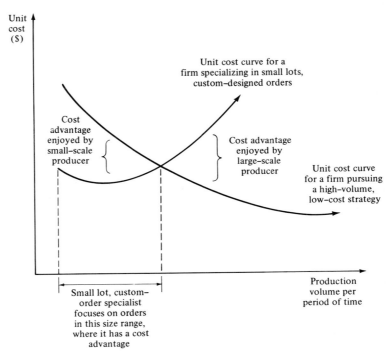

FIGURE 16-1

When a focus strategy can allow a small firm to be cost competitive with a large, mass production rival

Source: Adapted with permission of The Free Press, a division of Macmillan, Inc. from *Competitive Strategy: Techniques for Analyzing Industries and Competitors* by Michael E. Porter. Copyright © 1980 by The Free Press.

Process Innovation. With the shift to a competitive emphasis on low cost that accompanies market maturity also comes greater relative importance of process-oriented technological innovation. Innovations that permit lower-cost product design, lower-cost manufacturing methods, and lower-cost distribution have high competitive value in markets where the emphasis is on cost and service. Japanese firms have been quite successful emphasizing technological process strategies aimed at becoming the low-cost producer.

Increasing Sales to Present Customers. In a mature market, growing by finding new customers (taking them away from rivals) may not be as attractive as a strategy of expanding sales to existing customers. Increasing the purchases of existing customers can take the form of supplying peripheral equipment, upgrading product quality and performance, adding models and items to fit their needs, assembling components prior to shipment, and so on. A successful practitioner of this approach is Southland Corporation, which has added self-service gasoline, electronic games, and fast-food items to its 7-Eleven stores' product line in order to increase customers' total expenditures at 7-Eleven.

Purchase Other Firms at Bargain Prices. Sometimes the facilities and assets of distressed rivals can be acquired cheaply. Such acquisitions can improve margins and help create a low-cost position if these facilities are not inefficient or likely to be rendered obsolete by technological change. Heilman Brewing Company has risen from relative obscurity to become the fourth largest beer company by acquiring small regional brewers and used equipment at bargain prices.

Expanding Internationally. As its domestic market matures, a firm may seek to enter foreign markets where attractive growth potential still exists and where competitive pressures are not so strong. Philip Morris has recently begun to push international expansion of its cigarette business, as has Massey-Ferguson in farm implements and Holiday Inn in overnight lodging and conventions. Foreign markets can be attractive because equipment that has become obsolete domestically may be suitable for less-developed foreign markets (a condition that lowers entry costs), because foreign buyers are less sophisticated and have less bargaining power, because foreign competitors are smaller and less formidable, because cheaper production costs offer the prospects of bigger profit margins, and because a strong domestic firm's skills and reputation may be readily transferable to foreign markets.

Competitive Strategies for Firms in Stagnant or Declining Industries

Many firms do business in industries where demand is weakening or else growing at rates well below the economy-wide average. Although such businesses are sometimes "dogs" and thus prime candidates for harvesting, divestiture, or even liquidation, there are occasions when it is possible to work within a stagnant market environment and achieve modest growth and healthy profits.[15] The difficulty of finding a buyer who will pay an acceptable price often makes selling out impractical, and stagnant demand by itself is not enough to warrant liquidation. For example, even though the demand for coffee has decayed for almost two decades, General Foods still derives 40% of its sales and 33% of its profits from coffee products. Even more important, a decision to abandon businesses just because they are in tough, slow-growth markets is not always a profitable move for a diversified firm since, without the contribution margin generated by such businesses, a firm may find itself unable to cover corporate overhead and its whole portfolio may yield a consolidated loss.

Firms competing in slow-growth/mature industries have to accept the difficult realities of a continuing stagnant demand and they must resign themselves to performance goals consistent with the market opportunities that are available.[16] Cash flow and return on investment criteria are more appropriate than growth-oriented performance measures. Furthermore, head-to-head competition is usually more intense in markets where demand is stagnant than in markets where expansion is vigorous. In industries where market demand is growing rapidly, there tends to be enough opportunity for growth that firms need not launch aggressive attacks on rivals to gain higher sales; the major concern is with how to take advantage of market growth, not with how to take away customers from rival firms. However, in stagnant or declining industries, increases in sales volume have to come at the expense of one's competitors. The ensuing battle for market share frequently drives weaker firms out of the market, permitting market shares of the remaining companies to rise. For instance, in the cigar industry, where unit volume has been declining since the mid-sixties, the number of manufacturers declined from 283 in 1953 to 132 in 1972; in coffee, not only did the number of companies decline but the combined market shares of the top three firms rose from 47% in 1960 to 67% in 1976.[17]

In general, three themes characterize the strategies of firms which have succeeded in stagnant industries:[18]

1. *Pursue a focus strategy by identifying, creating, and exploiting the growth segments within the industry.* Mature or stagnant markets, just like other markets, are composed of numerous segments and subsegments (whether the segments are best identified by price, product use, geographic location, customer type, product attributes, or service requirements varies from case to case). Frequently, one or more of these segments is growing rapidly, despite a lack of growth in the industry as a whole. An astute competitor, by collecting and analyzing industry information in ways which pinpoint the segments with faster growth potential, can concentrate

---

[15] R. G. Hamermesh and S. B. Silk, "How to Compete in Stagnant Industries," *Harvard Business Review*, Vol. 57, No. 5 (September–October 1979), p. 161.

[16] *Ibid.*, p. 162.

[17] *Ibid.*

[18] *Ibid.*, pp. 163–165.

its efforts in the most attractive segments and thus escape being victimized by stagnating industry-wide trends. When successfully applied, this type of focus strategy yields healthy growth and increased profit, as well as a possible competitive advantage in serving the target segments.

2. *Emphasize quality improvement and product innovation.* The premise underlying this theme is that stagnant demand does not preclude significant innovation; indeed, innovation can rejuvenate demand by creating important new growth segments or otherwise postponing further stagnation in sales. From the standpoint of competitive strategy, successful product innovation opens up an avenue for competing besides that of meeting or beating the prices of rival sellers. Differentiation based on successful innovation has the additional advantage of being difficult and expensive for rival firms to imitate. An example is General Foods' introduction of freeze-dried coffee. Because many people viewed freeze-dried instant coffee as better tasting, demand grew rapidly (even though total consumption of coffee declined). Yet, with the notable exception of Nestlé, other producers resisted investing in the more expensive freeze-dry technology; as a consequence, the profit margins that General Foods earned on its freeze-dried business outpaced those of its other coffee products.

3. *Work diligently and persistently to improve production and distribution efficiency.* When increases in sales cannot be counted upon to generate increases in earnings, an alternative is to improve profit margins and return on investment by reducing operating costs. The paths for achieving a lower-cost position include (a) improving the manufacturing process via automation and increased specialization, (b) consolidating underutilized production facilities, (c) adding more distribution channels to ensure the unit volume needed for low-cost production, and (d) shifting sales away from low-volume, high-cost distribution outlets to high-volume, low-cost outlets.

Plainly enough, these three strategic themes are not mutually exclusive.[19] Attempts to introduce new innovative versions of a product can *create* a fast-growing market segment. Similarly, concentrating on operating efficiencies can stimulate the emergence of price-conscious growth segments. Note, also, that the three themes are all variations of the three generic competitive strategies—what is creative is how they have been applied so as to fit opportunities and conditions in an otherwise unattractive industry environment.

Competitive Strategy in Fragmented Industries

Many firms compete in fragmented, atomistically competitive industries where the selling side of the market is structured much like that portrayed in the models of perfect competition and monopolistic competition.[20] The competitive arena is populated with a large number of small and medium-sized companies,

---

[19] *Ibid.*, p. 165.

[20] This section is distilled from Porter, *Competitive Strategy*, Chapter 9.

many of which are privately held and none of which have a king-sized share of total industry sales. The key competitive feature of a fragmented industry is the absence of highly visible, well-known market leaders with the power to influence industry conditions and trends. Examples of fragmented industries include book publishing, photoengraving, kitchen cabinets, oil tanker shipping, garbage collection, the restaurant business, solar-powered equipment, women's dresses, poultry processing, metal foundries, meat packing, paperboard boxes, log homes, hotels and motels, and furniture.

Industries are structured with a host of fairly small competitors for many reasons, some historical and some economic:

- Low entry barriers.
- An absence of scale economies (and, often, diseconomies of scale in some important aspect such as a need to respond quickly to changes in style and fashion, customized production for individual users, the need for close local control, and the need for personal service).
- Diverse market needs for geographic area to geographic area, such that the demand for any particular product version is small, and adequate volume is not present to support producing, distributing, or marketing on a scale that yields advantages to a large firm.
- The need of buyers for customized products (as in the business forms industry, in advertising, and in interior design).
- High degrees of product differentiation based on image.
- High transportation costs (which limit the radius a plant can economically service—as in concrete blocks, mobile homes, milk, and gravel).
- Local regulatory requirements.
- Newness of the industry, such that no firms have yet developed the skills and resources to command a significant market share.

In fragmented industries, firms have a wide degree of strategic freedom. There is latitude for many different strategic approaches to exist side by side.

Some common approaches which firms can use to overcome fragmentation and gain a position of industry leadership include (1) trying to create scale economies by means of a technological breakthrough, (2) trying to standardize diverse market needs—creating a new product with broad appeal to buyers' tastes or making a design change that dramatically lowers the cost of a standardized item enough to attract buyers away from customized products, (3) making many acquisitions of local companies to attain a "critical mass" and thereby reach a threshold where new advantages of size can be created, and (4) using franchising to create a chain of outlets big enough to exploit potential economies of scale in purchasing, marketing, and the development of "formula" facilities that can be constructed, operated, and controlled in a very cost efficient manner (this strategic approach has spawned McDonald's, 7-Eleven, K mart, Pizza Hut, Baskin-Robbins, Holiday Inn, and numerous retail and fast-food chains).

Some fragmented industries consolidate naturally as they mature—the stiffer competition that comes with a slow-growth industry environment produces a shake-out of weak, inefficient firms and a greater concentration of fairly large, visible sellers. Other fragmented industries remain atomistically competitive for fundamental economic reasons. Still others become "stuck" in a fragmented state because existing firms either lack the resources and skills to employ a strategy that might promote industry consolidation or are complacently tied to traditional industry practices, willing to accept the status quo, and blind to opportunities for change. The historically fragmented U.S. wine industry has long been production-oriented, with little effort being made to achieve national distribution or win consumer brand recognition; this orientation was reversed when Coca-Cola and several other large consumer goods companies acquired wine producers and launched strategies based on potential economies of scale in production, national distribution, and national advertising.

In many situations, fragmentation and atomistic competition are the result of underlying economic factors that cannot be overcome by any one firm's strategy, however powerful and creative it might be. Then, the task of competitive strategy is to come up with an approach that deals with the prevailing competitive forces. Firms in fragmented industries usually are in a generally weak bargaining position with buyers and with suppliers. Entry is usually easy. Competition from substitutes may or may not be a major factor. In such an environment, about the best a firm can hope for is to rank among the most successful firms and to garner a modest market share. Competitive strategies based on low cost, on some kind of differentiation theme, or on focus approaches are all feasible in situations where the industry does not produce a commodity product. Where the fragmented industry's products or services are commodities or are otherwise difficult to differentiate, a firm is relegated to a strategy based on low cost or based on specialization and focus. Specific competitive strategy options include the following:

- *Constructing and operating "formula" facilities.* This is an attractive approach to achieving low cost when the firm must operate facilities at multiple locations. It involves designing a standard facility, constructing it in an optimum location at minimum cost, and then polishing to a science how to operate it in super-efficient manner. When well executed, this strategy gives a firm lower investment costs and lower operating costs than those of competitors. McDonald's and 7-Eleven have pursued this strategy to such perfection that they earn excellent profits in their respective industries.

- *A bare bones/no-frills posture.* When price competition is intense and profit margins are constantly under pressure, a lean operation based on low overhead, use of low-wage labor, tight budget control, and rigid adherence to a no-frills expenditure policy can place a firm in the best position to play the price-cutting game and still earn profits above the industry average.

- *Increasing value added through integration.* Selective backward or forward integration can increase the scope of a firm's position in the *total production-cost chain* and aim at lower costs or enhanced value to customers (such as cutting to size or by doing assembly of components before shipment to customers or by providing technical advice to customers). Sometimes forward integration into distribution or retailing can better control the conditions of sale, enhance reputation with final customers, neutralize buyers' power, or at least allow capture of a bigger profit and return on investment.

- *Specializing by product type.* When a fragmented industry is engaged in producing a broad product line with many models and styles, a focus strategy based on specialization in a particular area of the whole line can be very effective. Ethan Allen, a successful firm in the fragmented U.S. furniture industry, has specialized in early American furniture for all types of rooms. Using a network of independent retailers carrying only the Ethan Allen brand, the firm provides homeowners and interior designers with a one-stop showroom for decorating an entire home or office suite in this style. The company's product-based focus strategy, combined with its own exclusive retail distribution channel, yields a 20% price premium, adequate margins for television advertising of Ethan Allen brands and showroom locations, and a way to avoid hard bargaining with department stores, discount furniture outlets, and other powerful retailers to secure adequate retail coverage and distribution access. Ethan Allen has capitalized upon its strategy to win about a 3% market share and earn above-average profits.

- *Specializing by customer type.* A firm can try to cope with the intense competition of a fragmented industry by catering to customers with the least bargaining leverage (because they are small in size or because they purchase small annual volumes), by specializing in serving customers who are the least price sensitive, by going after those buyers who are interested in additional services or product attributes or other "extras," by serving customers who place custom orders, or by targeting buyers who have special needs or tastes.

- *Focusing on a limited geographic area.* Even though a firm in a fragmented industry is blocked from winning a big industry-wide market share, it may still be able to realize significant internal operating economies by blanketing a local/ regional geographic area. Concentrating facilities and marketing activities on a limited territory can produce greater sales force efficiency, allow use of a single distribution center, and permit stronger advertising saturation, while avoiding the diseconomies of trying to duplicate the strategy on a national scale. Local food store and convenience retailers have been successful in operating multiple locations within a limited geographic area.

Competitive Strategy in Global Industries

A global industry is one in which firms are required to compete on a worldwide scale or else face strategic disadvantages.[21] Global industries involve a worldwide market and require some type of worldwide competitive strategy. Global competition is most evident in oil, steel, automobiles, television receivers,

---

[21] This section is adapted from Porter, *Competitive Strategy*, Chapter 13.

motorcycles, sewing machines, heavy construction, aircraft, steam turbines, and oil tankers. Although the structural factors and market factors operating in global industries are essentially the same as those in national markets, there are some features that are unique to a globally competitive market environment:

- Differences in labor, capital, and other resource input costs among countries.
- Differences in markets from country to country.
- Different roles of foreign governments.
- Differences in competitors and competition from country to country.

There are three basic options for participating in a globally competitive industry: (1) licensing foreign firms to produce and distribute one's products, (2) maintaining a national (one-country) production base and exporting goods to foreign countries, and (3) establishing foreign-based plants and distribution networks to compete directly in the markets of foreign countries.

When there are important economic advantages (such as economies of scale, common uses of the product, similar buyer needs and requirements) to operating on a global scale, an industry is "driven" into global competition. However, there are forces that work *against* a globally competitive market: (1) high international transportation and storage costs, (2) differing product needs and customer requirements by country, (3) high barriers to gaining access to distribution channels in different countries, (4) the need to have a locally based sales force in each foreign market or submarket, (5) buyer preferences for a local repair service, (6) different approaches to buyer segmentation from country to country, (7) lack of a worldwide demand for the product, (8) differing technologies among country markets stemming from different rates of technological change, (9) government impediments, and (10) a need for intensive personal services on a locality-by-locality basis. In addition, globally competitive market environments are affected by the extent to which technology can flow freely from country to country, by the propensity of national governments to try to protect domestic industry from global competition, by the extent to which companies are inclined to participate in globally competitive markets, and by the size of any scale economies that accrue to firms which can capture a significant share of global market demand.

All these globally diverse factors give rise to four generic approaches to competing on a global scale:

1. *Broad line global competition*—where strategy is directed at competing worldwide with a full product line and many plant locations.

2. *A global focus strategy*—where competitive energies are aimed at serving the same identifiable market segment in each of many target countries.

3. *A nation-by-nation focus strategy*—where the firm sees important market and buyer differences from country to country and concludes that a single global-wide competitive approach is not as strong as a multiple country-by-country approach; the end result is a competitive approach which is flexible enough to be tailored to meet the particular needs of particular buyers in a particular country.

4. *A protected niche strategy*—where a firm seeks out situations having local government restrictions that preclude global or national approaches and, instead, require a localized geographic strategy that fits local government requirements; the aim is to achieve a local competitive advantage by being more responsive to local market variables and the customized requirements of particular localities within a country.

ANALYZING COMPETITIVE ADVANTAGE OPTIONS

Given that the acid test of successful business strategy is one of *positioning* the firm in the marketplace where it has some edge in coping with the five competitive forces, an important criterion for strategy selection is the magnitude and duration of any competitive advantage which various competitive approaches offer. The matrix shown in Fig. 16-2 presents an analytical framework developed by the Boston Consulting Group to help match competitive advantage strategies to prevailing market and competitive conditions.[22] Three premises underlie BCG's competitive advantage analysis: (1) some sort of competitive advantage is necessary for above-average profitability, (2) the number of ways an advantage can be gained and the potential size of the advantage vary according to certain industry characteristics, and (3) as industries evolve, so also do the sizes of any competitive advantages and the opportunities to build an advantage.

The vertical axis of the matrix is a scale of the number of ways firms have to create a differential competitive advantage. In the restaurant business, for example, firms have many ways to set themselves apart from rivals (location, menu selection, price, atmosphere, meal quality, service) whereas in commodity-type industries the standardized product features make for a price-oriented competitive environment and the overriding key success factor is being able to play the price-cost game. The horizontal axis in Fig. 16-2 represents the potential size of any advantage that can be gotten. This, too, varies by type of industry environment. For example, in a newly emerging industry, economies of scale often act to give big firms a major advantage over small firms but as that industry consolidates and the remaining firms by necessity invest in efficient, large-scale plants, the big advantage of large size disappears and a competitive edge has to be sought in other ways. In commodity-product industries and in other industries where buyers are not very sensitive to product differences and their switching costs are low, the size of any competitive advantage tends to be very small; the exception is when strategy is keyed to being the low-cost producer and lower price can be used as a competitive weapon.

As shown in Fig. 16-2, plotting the size of the advantage against the number of ways to achieve competitive advantage produces four distinct strategy spaces, each with its own set of dominating competitive features and resulting strategic

---

[22] This discussion is adapted from an approach used by the Boston Consulting Group as described in Walter Kiechel III, "Three (or Four, or More) Ways to Win," *Fortune*, October 19, 1981, pp. 181–188.

Size of the Competitive Advantage
That Can Be Achieved
(scaled from degrees of "small"
to degrees of "large")

	Small	Large
Many	**Key competitive feature:** Many ways to gain an edge, but the size of the edge counts for little in the marketplace. **Strategy prescriptions:** • Carve out a position and hold it. • Emphasize profits *now.* • Minimize investment. • Be cautious about expansion.	**Key competitive feature:** A specialized approach to the many market segments is essential, and so is creating and protecting the advantage in serving these segments. **Strategy prescriptions:** • Seek a niche. • Get in position to serve selected segments. Spend heavily to build and fortify the chosen advantage. • Stay ahead of rivals who aspire to gain the same advantage. • Watch out for change.
Few	**Key competitive feature:** Almost a pure cost–price game; on other factors, all firms are in about equal position. In the absence of price–cost differences, there is a virtual competitive stalemate. **Strategy prescriptions:** • Use aggressive cost–reduction strategies. • Emphasize ways to improve efficiency. • Seek to increase cash flow. • Look for diversification opportunities.	**Key competitive feature:** Only those who get and keep one of the large competitive advantages will survive; usually, low cost is the primary advantage that is available. Often, the name of the game is volume. **Strategy prescriptions:** • Pursue economies of scale. • Ride the experience curve downward by getting volume up. • Go after the customers of weak firms. • If weak, divest or look for new ways to compete.

Different Ways a Competitive Advantage Can Be Created (scaled from degrees of "many" to degrees of "few")

FIGURE 16-2
Analyzing competitive advantage opportunities

prescriptions. The content of the four cells in Fig. 16-2 is self-explanatory; how-ever, one additional point merits emphasis. A competitor who unleashes a pow-erful trendsetting strategy can change the structural character of an industry, establish new competitive rules, and alter the strategic prescriptions. McDonald's transformed the structure and competitive features of the low-volume, single-unit restaurant business during the 1960s and 1970s with a competitive strategy pred-icated on high-volume, "formula" facilities keyed to maximum efficiency, at-tractive prices, dependable quality, fast service, many locations, and national market coverage. A huge, new segment in the food-away-from-home industry was thus invented by a maverick strategy with such spectacular success that it quickly spawned new enterprises with imitative versions of the same basic strategy. The

**Customer Sensitivity to Differences in
the Product Offerings of
Rival Sellers**

	High (the differences make a big difference)	Low (the differences do not matter much)
High	**Key competitive features:** Competition is very active on all fronts; and there are frequent, bold moves by firms to introduce products with new features and/or to alter pricing. Buyers are very discriminating, have little brand loyalty, and shop around for the best overall deal. Key competitive variables can change rapidly. **Strategy prescriptions:** • Adopt a "flexible" strategy. • Promote both price and distinctive product features. • Push new product development. • Be creative and innovative. • Prepare for rapid change.	**Key competitive features:** A commodity–product business where low cost and low price are paramount. Gaining market share is often the key to higher profitability. **Strategy prescriptions:** • Pursue economies of scale. • Ride the experience curve downward by getting volume up. • Be aggressive in trying to capture market share. • Strive for cost leadership.
Low	**Key competitive features:** Having the product features that buyers are looking for and appreciate is essential. Must cater to the needs of distinct buyer segments. Success is usually keyed to the right kind of specialization. **Strategy prescriptions:** • Adopt a focus strategy. • Differentiate your products from those of rivals. • Build a distinctive competence. • Avoid blurring the firm's image with a broad coverage strategy (either many product versions or many target segments or, worst of all, both).	**Key competitive features:** Very difficult to build a meaningful competitive edge; competition is seldom intense. Rivalry is not active and the balance between market demand and market supply govern industry profitability. **Strategy prescriptions:** • Avoid price competition. • Promote differences but do not spend much on creating them. • Work on improving profit margin by cutting costs and increasing the size of the firm's clientele.

Customer Sensitivity to Price Differences among Rival Sellers (row axis, High / Low)

FIGURE 16-3
Matching competitive strategy to the variables of price and product differentiation

point here is that as an industry's driving forces and competitive rules evolve, it can move from one cell to another in Fig. 16-2, as opposed to being fixed in one position.

A somewhat different matrix approach is that used by Strategic Planning Associates and shown in Fig. 16-3.[23] Here the variables along the two axes are customer sensitivity to price and customer sensitivity to product differentiation. The issue is how to match competitive strategy to the various combinations of buyer sensitivity to pricing differences and to product differentiation efforts. The key competitive features and resulting strategic prescriptions displayed in the cells

[23] As described by Kiechel, "Three (or Four, or More) Ways to Win," p. 184.

of Fig. 16-3 offer further insights into what sorts of competitive approaches fit what sorts of market environments.

The main shortcomings of both matrixes are those associated with oversimplification and generalization. First, they are not particularly helpful in assessing conditions in the "middle" ranges between high and low or many and few. Second, the conclusions and prescriptions are only suggestive of broad themes and direction; specific details have to come from an assessment of the industry environment and a diagnosis of the five competitive forces that prevail. There are pitfalls in using "standard" game plans for situations which are similar in some respects (price sensitivity, importance of product differentiation, opportunities to gain competitive edges) but are different in other strategically important respects (industry structure and driving forces, strategic capabilities and positions of the leading firms, the intensity and interplay among the five competitive forces, the variety among strategic groups, buyer demographics, and so on). The situations of each industry and each firm are partly unique; these unique features have to be taken into account in formulating competitive strategy. Hence, the generalized strategy prescriptions shown in Figs. 16-2 and 16-3 should be viewed as overall themes and broad approaches that are subject to being tailored (in major or minor ways) to fit a firm's own industry environment and competitive position.

Other Competitive Strategy Considerations

Three other elements of the strategy selection problem can assume a pivotal import in shaping a firm's decision on how to compete:

- The risk/reward trade-off.
- Timing considerations and the strength of *first-mover advantages.*
- Contribution to performance and objectives.

Risk/Reward Considerations.   The relevance of the profitability versus risk trade-off is obvious. Risk-averters will be inclined toward "safe" strategies where external threats appear minimal, profits adequate but not spectacular, and in-house resources ample to meet the task ahead. Quite often, such firms insist upon following a financial approach that emphasizes internal financing rather than debt financing; similarly, they may opt to defer major financial commitments as long as possible or until the effects of uncertainty are deemed minimal. They may view pioneering-type innovations as "too chancy" relative to proven, well-established techniques, or they may simply prefer to be followers rather than leaders. In general, the risk-averter places a high premium on "conservative" strategies which minimize the downside risk.

On the other hand, eager risk-takers lean more toward opportunistic strategies where the payoffs are greater, the challenges more demanding, and the glamor more appealing, despite the pitfalls which may exist. Innovation is preferred to imitation. Launching a competitive offensive ranks ahead of defensive conservatism. A confident optimism about market prospects overrules pessimism. Attempts to improve the firm's market position are more attractive than maintaining the status quo.

Timing Considerations and First-Mover Advantages. Timing issues are partly a function of the risk-reward situation. For instance, where uncertainty is high, the risk-averter's tendency is to proceed with extreme caution or to stall, whereas the risk-taker is willing to move early and assume a trailblazing role. Where there are long lead times between initial action and result, there is enhanced risk of something "going wrong" in the meantime and fouling up an otherwise well-formulated strategy.

Yet the timing dilemma goes deeper than the risk/reward trade-off and a preference for an active or reactive style. It also relates to whether there are any *first-mover advantages* or *disadvantages*.[24] Being the first competitor to initiate a fresh strategy can have a high payoff when (1) pioneering adds greatly to a firm's image and reputation with buyers; (2) a steep experience curve exists, giving first-movers a decided cost advantage; (3) early commitments to supplies of raw materials, distribution channels, and so on can produce an absolute cost advantage over rivals; (4) customer loyalty is high, so that long-term benefits accrue to the firm that first convinces the customer to use its product; and (5) moving first can be a preemptive strike, making imitation extra hard or unlikely. The stronger any first-mover advantages are, the greater the danger of being late.

However, being late or following a "wait and see" approach is wise if first-mover disadvantages exist. Pioneering is risky when (1) the costs of opening up a new market are great but customer loyalty is weak, (2) technological change is so rapid that early investments can be rendered obsolete (thus allowing following firms to have the advantage of the newest products and processes), and (3) the industry is developing so rapidly that skills and know-how built up during the early competitive phase are easily bypassed and leapfrogged by late movers. "Good" timing, therefore, is an important ingredient in "good" competitive strategy formulation.

Contribution to Increased Profits and Other Goals. Frequently, a firm's competitive strategy is called into question by unsatisfactory performance. Thus, it makes sense that a firm's choice of how to compete in its target markets is heavily governed by the expected contribution of the various strategy options. The preferred competitive approach is likely to be the one with the greatest promise of improving the firm's profitability and long-term competitive position. But other goals can enter into play; maintaining historical rates of sales growth and a desire for technological leadership or market share leadership are among the nonprofit considerations that usually influence the choice of competitive strategy.

SUMMARY AND CONCLUSIONS

Understanding a firm's competitive behavior in the marketplace necessarily involves a case-by-case exercise of evaluating the specifics of the associated industry and competitive environment and relating these to the firm's own situation.

[24] Porter, *Competitive Strategy*, pp. 232–233.

Although each firm's approach to competing is a uniquely constructed game plan reflecting its particular circumstances, it is possible to generalize about the types of competitive approaches and the types of industry environments. There are three basic approaches to competing: (1) striving to be the low-cost producer and achieving overall cost leadership, (2) pursuit of some sort of product differentiation theme, and (3) specializing or focusing on selected market segments as opposed to an across-the-board approach. There are, however, numerous variations of these three basic approaches and there are a variety of ways to pursue each theme.

At least nine common types of industry and competitive environments can be singled out for analysis. Each one produces its own set of competitive strategy options for participant firms and each one tends to be associated with different combinations of the five competitive forces and different patterns of competitive behavior among industry rivals.

SUGGESTED READINGS

HALL, WILLIAM K., "Survival Strategies in a Hostile Environment," *Harvard Business Review*, Vol. 58, No. 5 (September–October 1980), pp. 75–85.

HAMERMESH, R. G., AND S. B. SILK, "How to Compete in Stagnant Industries," *Harvard Business Review*, Vol. 57, No. 5 (September–October 1979), pp. 161–168.

MACMILLAN, I. C., "How Business Strategies Can Use Guerilla Warfare Tactics," *Journal of Business Strategy*, Vol. 1. No. 2 (Fall 1980), pp. 63–65.

PORTER, M. E., *Competitive Strategy: Techniques for Analyzing Industries and Competitors* (New York: The Free Press, 1980), Chapters 9–13.

THOMPSON, A. A., "Strategies for Staying Cost Competitive," *Harvard Business Review*, Vol. 62, No. 1 (January–February 1984), pp. 110–117.

QUESTIONS FOR DISCUSSION

1. Under what kinds of competitive conditions would a firm be attracted to employ a competitive strategy aimed at striving to be the low-cost producer in the industry? What are the strengths of such a competitive strategy? What are the weaknesses of such a strategy?

2. What are the advantages of a differentiation strategy? In what kinds of industry and competitive environments is a differentiation strategy likely to work best?

3. What is a "focus" strategy? When does use of a focus strategy make sense?

4. Based upon your knowledge about the companies and the industry environments in which they compete, indicate which one of the three generic types of competitive strategy best describes the competitive approach employed for the following:
   (a) Seven-Up soft drinks
   (b) Chevrolet Corvette
   (c) Apple Computer
   (d) Liggett & Myers introduction of generic cigarettes
   (e) Pizza Hut
   (f) Michelob Light

  (g) Homestake Mining (a producer of gold)

  (h) Bostitch (a producer of staple guns, desktop staplers, and staples).

5. What reasons can you give for why the nature of competition and the types of prevailing competitive forces vary according to the type of industry environment?

6. What explanation can you give for why an industry goes through a period of "competitive shakeout" and otherwise "consolidates?"

7. Is it more correct to view competition in a mature industry as being "stronger" or "weaker" than in a young, emerging industry, or would it be more accurate to say that competition in these two types of industry environments is simply "different?"

17

HOW RESOURCE MARKETS FUNCTION
Prices, wages, and employment

In this chapter we shift attention from product markets to resource markets. The involvement of companies in the functioning of the markets for resource inputs is evident. Engaging in productive activity of any sort requires an enterprise to purchase resource inputs. Moreover, any change in output dictates a change in resource usage. What firms do in product markets thus quickly reverberates into resource markets, affecting both resource prices and resource employment.

The analysis of this chapter is aimed first at a firm's input decision, with the specific goal of identifying what determines the amount of a resource input a firm is willing to purchase at various input prices. The input decisions of enterprises are then used as the takeoff point for examining on a marketwide basis the employment rates of resources, the prices of resource inputs, and the incomes that accrue to resource owners.

To bring out the principles governing the operation of resource markets, it will be necessary to examine resource input decisions in three contexts: (1) when a firm sells its output in a perfectly competitive product market and buys its input in a perfectly competitive resource market, (2) when a firm sells its output in an imperfectly competitive market and buys its input in a perfectly competitive resource market, and (3) when a firm is confronted by imperfectly competitive conditions in both its product and resource markets. These are the three situations most frequently approximated in practice.

SOME PRELIMINARY CONSIDERATIONS

Before digging into the analysis of resource markets, three points warrant mention. First, the concepts and principles concerning demand, supply, revenue, production, and costs presented in earlier chapters have application in how resource markets function. The prices of resource inputs, for example, are in large measure determined by the interaction of demand and supply. However, as regards resource markets, the roles of the firm and the consumer are reversed. Resource inputs are demanded by firms, not consumers, and some important inputs, such as labor and managerial talents, are supplied by consumers, not firms.

Second, while a firm's inputs may be broadly classified as consisting of land, labor, capital, and managerial ability, the fact remains that each of these classifications contains an enormous variety of particular inputs. The range of labor inputs for a firm extends from the unskilled to the highly skilled; even within the same plant the types of labor services may include such diverse sorts as those provided by an aerospace engineer, a secretary, a machinist, a maintenance man, a computer programmer, a drill press operator, and a shipping clerk. Since each type of labor service is characterized by its own unique wage rate and demand and supply conditions, it is not really very meaningful to speak of *the* demand for labor or *the* price of labor. The analysis of resource markets will therefore be presented in terms of a "representative" and unspecified input. Because the principles underlying input decisions and the operation of resource markets are essentially the same, the models presented will have general applicability to almost every resource market—irrespective of whether the input is some type of land, labor, capital, or managerial talent.

Third, although firms may have a variety of goals, the principles of resource pricing and employment are indicated most easily by assuming that the only goal of the firm is to maximize profits. Accordingly, throughout this chapter, we shall assume a goal of profit maximization. This assumption in no way disturbs the thrust of the analysis and the resulting conclusions.[1]

RESOURCE PRICING AND EMPLOYMENT: THE CASE OF PERFECTLY COMPETITIVE PRODUCT AND RESOURCE MARKETS

The simplest case of resource pricing and employment arises in an environment where firms sell their products in a perfectly competitive market and buy their inputs under perfectly competitive conditions. For our purposes the most important aspect of a perfectly competitive *product* market is that the firm can sell additional units of output at the going price; consequently, the firm's demand-*AR*

---

[1] For an illustration of the effect which a goal of sales revenue maximization has upon the firm's input decision, see William J. Baumol, *Economic Theory and Operations Analysis*, 3rd ed. (Englewood Cliffs, N.J.: Prentice-Hall, Inc., 1972), pp. 328–330. Baumol demonstrates that a minor adjustment in the profit-maximizing input rules will give the revenue-maximizing input conditions.

curve is horizontal, and product price equals marginal revenue. In perfectly competitive *resource* markets the essential feature is that the firm can purchase as many units of an input as it may wish without affecting its price. In other words, the supply curve for an input which confronts the firm is horizontal at the prevailing input supply price.

A Perfectly Competitive Firm's Input Decision: The One-Variable Input Case

To identify the key factors underlying a perfectly competitive firm's input decision, suppose we consider first the situation where it has only one variable input, all the other resource inputs being fixed. The profit-conscious firm in a perfectly competitive environment will evaluate the outcomes of employing different quantities of its single variable resource—suppose we call it resource X—by their comparative effect upon total revenue and total cost. If using more units of resource X per period of time will add more to the firm's revenues than to its costs, then the extra input unit will increase the firm's total profits (or decrease its losses). On the other hand, if employing more units of resource X per period of time causes costs to rise by more than revenues, then using these input units will result in lower total profits (or larger losses). Hence, *to maximize profits a firm should purchase additional units of a resource input until the added costs associated with employing one more unit are equal to the added revenues it contributes*. This is the basic principle underlying the optimum input decision of a profit-maximizing firm; in fact, it is the $MC = MR$ rule applied to the firm's decision about how much of a resource to employ, depending on what the price it must pay happens to be.

The Revenue Gain from a Unit of Variable Input. When a firm employs another unit of variable input per period of time, its output rate rises by an amount equal to the marginal product of the variable input (MP_X). But the prime motivation of the firm for employing more of an input is not the output gain so much as the subsequent revenue gain. If the firm sells under conditions of a horizontal demand-AR curve, then each additional unit of output—suppose we call it product A—can be sold at the prevailing market price (P_A), which in turn equals marginal revenue (MR_A). The perfectly competitive firm's revenue gain from using one more unit of variable input may thus be calculated by multiplying the marginal product of the additional unit of input (MP_X) by the amount of revenue which the firm receives from selling another unit of the product (MR_A). For instance, if adding one more machine operator to the firm's production line causes the output rate to increase by 10 units per day and if each of these units can be sold for $5 each, then the firm's revenue gain is $50.

The change in total revenue associated with using one more unit of variable input (X) is called the *marginal revenue product* of the input (MRP_X), and it may be calculated according to the expression

$$MRP_X = MP_X \cdot MR_A.$$

Alternatively, marginal revenue product may be conceived as the change in total revenue resulting from a change in the use of variable input X, which in discrete mathematical terms is equivalent to the expression

$$MRP_X = \frac{\Delta TR}{\Delta X}.$$

As usual, MRP_X may be more rigorously defined as the rate of change in total revenue as the rate of usage of variable input X changes, or

$$MRP_X = \frac{dTR}{dX}.$$

Note carefully that the concept of *MRP* differs from that of *MR*. Whereas *MRP* refers to revenue changes which result from changes in the usage of *variable input*, *MR* refers to revenue changes associated with changes in the rate of *output*.

A second and more restricted concept of the revenue change from using more or less of variable input X may be referred to as the *sales value of the marginal product* of the input ($SVMP_X$). *SVMP* is just what its name implies— the dollar value of the increased output associated with using another unit of variable input. Put another way, $SVMP_X$ is the amount of extra output (MP_X) multiplied by the average price per unit at which it can be sold (P_A), or

$$SVMP_X = MP_X \cdot P_A.$$

Inasmuch as the perfectly competitive firm's selling price equals its marginal revenue ($P_A = MR_A$), it follows that $SVMP_X = MRP_X$. However, the equality between *SVMP* and *MRP* holds true only for a perfectly competitive firm. If the firm must reduce product price to sell the extra output (as is the case in all market situations other than perfect competition where firms face down-sloping demand-AR curves), then product price is always greater than marginal revenue, and the values of $SVMP_X$ will exceed the values for MRP_X at a given input rate. Thus, in reality, the concept of *SVMP* is only a special case of *MRP*: the case where price equals *MR*—a situation unique to a perfectly competitive product market.

Although in a perfectly competitive market structure *SVMP* equals *MRP*, we shall nevertheless use the concept of *MRP* to refer to the change in total revenue resulting from a change in input usage. The concept of *SVMP* will be reserved to apply only to the gross market value (in dollars) of the marginal product of a unit of input.

The Profit-Maximizing Rate of Input Usage. To illustrate how a firm can ascertain the profit-maximizing rate of usage of variable input X, consider the hypothetical production, cost, and revenue data in Table 17-1. The first three columns of the table show how the output of product A (Q_A) and the marginal product of variable input X (MP_X) change as successively larger doses of variable input X are com-

TABLE 17-1 Profit-Maximizing Rate of Resource Input Usage for a Firm Operating in Perfectly Competitive Product and Resource Markets[a]

(1) Units of Variable Input (X)	(2) Units of Output (Q_A)	(3) Marginal Product (MP_X)	(4) Price of Product A ($P_A = MR_A$)	(5) Total Revenue from the Sales of Product A ($TR_A = P_A \cdot Q_A$)	(6) Marginal Revenue Product ($MRP_X = MP_X \cdot MR_A = \Delta TR_A / \Delta X$)	(7) Supply Price of the Variable Input ($P_X = ARC_X = MRC_X$)	(8) Total Variable Cost ($TVC = P_X \cdot X$)	(9) Total Contribution Profit ($TCP = TR - TVC$)
0	0		$20	$ 0		$180	$ 0	$ 0
1	14	14	20	280	$280	180	180	100
2	40	26	20	800	520	180	360	440
3	60	20	20	1200	400	180	540	660
4	78	18	20	1560	360	180	720	840
5	94	16	20	1880	320	180	900	980
6	108	14	20	2160	280	180	1080	1080
7	120	12	20	2400	240	180	1260	1140
8	130	10	20	2600	200	180	1440	1160
9	138	8	20	2760	160	180	1620	1140
10	144	6	20	2880	120	180	1800	1080

[a] Observe that total contribution profit is maximized at an input of 8 units of resource X, which means that total profit is maximum (or losses minimum, depending on the amount of total fixed costs) at this input rate. By interpolation, it is seen that $MRP_X = MRC_X$ at 8 units of variable input.

bined with the available fixed inputs.[2] The price of product A (P_A) is constant at $20 [column (4)] because of the perfectly competitive product market, and the corresponding total revenue from the sale of product A (TR_A) is shown in column (5). The values for marginal revenue product (MRP_X) are shown in column (6) and are found by either (1) multiplying the gain in output from using another unit of X (MP_X) by the extra revenue the firm receives from the sale of a unit of output (MR_A) or (2) subtracting the successive values of TR_A in column (5) to find the change in total revenue per unit change in variable input. Column (7) indicates the price at which units of variable input can be purchased; the constant price of $180 correctly implies that the firm can buy as many units of variable input as it wants at the given price without inducing a change in the input price. Hence, the marginal cost of an additional unit of variable input is the same as its price. We shall find it convenient to refer to the amount which each additional unit of variable input adds to the firm's costs as the *marginal resource cost (MRC)*.[3] Since the supply price of X is fixed, $P_X = MRC_X$, and the supply function for X coincides precisely with the *MRC* function for X. Column (8) lists total variable costs (units of variable input X multiplied by its price per unit). The last column in the table shows the amounts of total contribution profit ($TR - TVC$) at each input rate; the value where total contribution profit is maximum also identifies where total profit is maximum inasmuch as the former differs from the latter only by the amount of total fixed costs.

As stated above, profit maximization requires that a firm purchase additional units of input until the added cost of one more unit just equals the added revenue it contributes. Given that the price of variable input remains unchanged irrespective of how many units the firm purchases, the cost of an additional unit of variable input is a constant equal to $180 [column (7)]. The revenue contribution of a unit of variable input is given by the *MRP* figures [column (6)]. A comparison of columns (6) and (7) in Table 17-1 indicates that it will pay the firm to employ 8 units of variable input. Increasing the usage of variable input from 7 to 8 units adds $200 to the firm's revenues but only $180 to costs. Should the firm employ the ninth unit of variable input, revenues will rise by $160 but costs will rise by $180; thus, the employment of 9 units of variable input is clearly a less profitable act. By interpolation, it is evident that at 8 units $MRP_X = MRC_X$, which satisfies the profit-maximizing condition and, in fact, is the rule by which the firm identifies

[2] Hypothetical amounts of fixed inputs, the prices of the fixed inputs, and the resulting amount of total fixed costs are not included in the table, since they do not really enter into the determination of the profit-maximizing rate of variable input.

[3] As with all other marginal concepts, marginal resource cost may be defined mathematically as the rate of change in the firm's costs as the rate of usage of variable input changes; in symbols this becomes

$$MRC_X = \frac{dTC}{dX} = \frac{dTVC}{dX},$$

where X refers to the units of variable input. Marginal resource cost differs from marginal cost in that the former refers to the changes in costs associated with a change in *input*, whereas the latter refers to a change in costs stemming from a change in *output*.

its profit-maximizing rate of input usage. Inspection of the total contribution profit figures in column (9) confirms that 8 units is the optimum amount of variable input. Total contribution profit is greatest when 8 units of variable input are used. Since total profit is maximum where total contribution profit is maximum, the profit-maximizing rate of variable input usage is 8 units per period of time.

The determination of the profit-maximizing rate of variable input can be illustrated graphically. We have just seen that a firm's input decision is based upon a comparison of how much an input is worth relative to what it costs. How much an input is worth in essence determines the firm's demand for the input, whereas what an input costs is a function of the available supplies of the input and the demand for it in the total market. A firm's profit-maximizing rate of input usage can therefore be approached by an analysis of the firm's demand and supply curves for the input.

The demand and supply approach to a firm's resource usage is shown in Fig. 17-1(a), using the same data as in Table 17-1. The firm's demand curve for a variable input is obtained by plotting the *MRP* figures in column (6) of the table. The *MRP* curve is synonymous with the demand curve for resource X if X is the only variable resource employed. The reason? A firm's demand for a resource input is necessarily predicated on what the resource is worth to the firm in terms of the revenue contribution it can make; this is precisely what is meant by *MRP*. The *MRP* curve rises briefly and then falls because the marginal product of the variable input first increases (due to increasing returns to variable input) and then decreases (due to the inevitable occurrence of diminishing marginal returns to variable input). The relevant portion of the *MRP* curve is the down-sloping seg-

FIGURE 17-1
The profit-maximizing rate of input usage for a firm operating in perfectly competitive product and resource markets.

ment where MP_X is declining but positive.[4] The firm's supply curve for the input is determined by the entries in column (7) of Table 17-1. It is a horizontal line at the level of $180—the prevailing market price of the input. Since the input supply price is a constant, the input's price is exactly equal to both the *average resource cost (ARC)* and the marginal resource cost *(MRC)* of adding more variable input. Or, to put it another way, when perfectly competitive conditions prevail for input X, it follows that $P_X = ARC_X = MRC_X$ and that the supply curve for X coincides with the *ARC* curve for X and the *MRC* curve for X. These relationships are so indicated in Fig. 17-1(a).

The firm's demand and supply curves [Fig. 17-1(a)] intersect at a point corresponding to 8 units of variable input. This intersection identifies the profit-maximizing amount of variable input. At inputs of fewer than 8 units per period of time an additional unit of variable input adds more to total revenue than it adds to total cost, thereby giving the firm a clear incentive to increase its variable input usage. This is the same as saying *MRP* exceeds *MRC* at inputs below 8 units. However, to go beyond 8 units per period of time will result in total costs rising faster than total revenues, and the additional variable input will fail to "pay its own way." Hence, the firm will reduce its total profits (or increase losses) by purchasing more than 8 units of variable input. Therefore, it can be concluded from the demand and supply analysis that *a perfectly competitive firm will maximize profits by employing additional units of variable input until the point is reached where the input's marginal revenue equals its marginal resource cost.* The rationale underlying the *MRP = MRC* rule is analogous to the *MR = MC* rule. The only real difference is that the former refers to the profit-maximizing rate of input usage and the latter to the profit-maximizing rate of output. The two rules give the same operating results in terms of price, output, and profit, but they approach the determination of the profit-maximizing conditions via a different route.

Plotting the total revenue and total variable cost data in columns (8) and (9) of the table verifies the *MRP = MRC* rule from another vantage point [see Fig. 17-1(b)]. Note that in Fig. 17-1(b) the horizontal axis has been drawn to represent units of variable input rather than units of output, thereby relating *TR* and *TVC* to the usage of variable input rather than to output. The maximum vertical distance between *TR* and *TVC* occurs when their slopes are equal. The slope of the *TR* curve when variable input (X) is plotted on the horizontal axis is dTR/dX, which, by definition, is MRP_X. Similarly, the slope of the *TVC* curve in these circumstances is $dTVC/dX$, which corresponds precisely to the meaning of MRC_X. Hence, the profit-maximizing rate of variable input usage is reached when the revenue gain from using more variable input (MRP_X) equals the added cost of purchasing the variable input (MRC_X). Can you explain the economics of the shapes of the *TR* and *TVC* curves in Fig. 17-1(b)? Why is the *TVC* curve linear?

---

[4] For reasons explored in Chapter 7 (pp. 206–208), the firm will find it profitable to use enough variable input to get beyond the point of diminishing marginal returns unless product demand is very weak or the cost of variable input so high as to make production unprofitable. Hence, the truly relevant portion of the *MRP* curve is the down-sloping segment.

MATHEMATICAL CAPSULE 13

DETERMINING A FIRM'S PROFIT-MAXIMIZING INPUT USAGE UNDER CONDITIONS OF PERFECTLY COMPETITIVE PRODUCT AND RESOURCE MARKETS

The proposition that a firm confronted with perfectly competitive product and resource markets will maximize profits by purchasing units of a variable input until the point is reached where *MRP* equals *MRC* is easily demonstrated in mathematical terms.

Let the firm's production function for producing product A be

$$Q_A = f(X),$$

where Q_A = units of output of product A and X = units of any variable resource input. Then the marginal product function for input X may be written as

$$MP_X = \frac{dQ_A}{dX} = f'(X).$$

The firm's profit function may be expressed as

$$\pi = TR - TC.$$

But by definition

$$TR = P_A Q_A$$

and

$$TC = TFC + TVC.$$

Since $TVC = P_X X$, we can rewrite the expression for *TC* as

$$TC = TFC + P_X X.$$

Substituting into the profit function gives

$$\pi = P_A Q_A - (TFC + P_X X).$$

However, since $Q_A = f(X)$, the expression for TR_A becomes $P_A \cdot f(X)$, which when substituted into the profit function gives

$$\pi = P_A \cdot f(X) - TFC - P_X X.$$

In mathematical terms, profit maximization requires that

$$\frac{d\pi}{dX} = 0,$$

which, translated into words, means variable input must be added to the point where profits cease to increase.

Taking the derivative of the profit function with respect to X gives

$$\frac{d\pi}{dX} = P_A \cdot f'(X) - P_X.$$

Setting this expression equal to zero to satisfy the profit-maximizing condition gives

$$P_A \cdot f'(X) - P_X = 0.$$

For this condition to be met, it is apparent that the first term of the above expression must equal the second term or that

$$P_A \cdot f'(X) = P_X.$$

But $f'(X)$ is, by definition, the same as MP_X, which gives

$$P_A \cdot MP_X = P_X.$$

The term $P_A \cdot MP_X$ is precisely equal to MRP_X, because in perfect competition $P_A = MR_A$; and $P_X = MRC_X$, because the input supply price in a perfectly competitive resource market is a constant value. So the condition for obtaining the profit-maximizing input rate becomes

$$MRP_X = MRC_X,$$

which is what we set out to establish.

Why does *TR* increase at a decreasing rate? (*Hint*: Your answers should concern the fact that the graph shows *TR* and *TVC* to be a function of the usage of variable input rather than the quantity of output.)

A Perfectly Competitive Firm's Input Decision: The Two-Variable Input Case

When a firm's production process utilizes two or more variable inputs, its input decisions become considerably more complex. The reason rests with the interdependence which exists among the variable inputs. A change in the price of one variable input not only affects the amount it will pay the firm to use of that input but it also alters the optimum amounts of the other variable inputs. Moreover, these alterations in the usage of the other variable inputs will trigger changes in the marginal product of the variable input whose price changed, thereby resulting in still further input adjustments.

To illustrate the nature of the firm's input decision when several resource inputs can be varied, consider the simplest case where the firm has only two variable inputs—X and Y. To keep things manageable, we shall restrict discussion to determining just the firm's optimum input rate for X. Suppose the price of input X is initially fixed at P_{X_1} and the amount of input X which will maximize the firm's profits is X_1, as shown in Fig. 17-2. When the amount of resource Y is held constant, the marginal revenue product curve for X is MRP_1. Now suppose a shift in the supply conditions for input X causes the price of X to fall from P_{X_1} to P_{X_2}. The change in the supply price of X has three effects which are pertinent to determining the new profit-maximizing input rate of X: the *substitution effect*, the *output effect*, and the *marginal cost effect*.

P_{X_1} —————————— S_1, ARC_1, MRC_1

P_{X_2} —————————— S_2, ARC_2, MRC_2

D_X

MRP_1 MRP_2

X_1 X_2 Units of
variable
input X
per period
of time

FIGURE 17-2
A perfectly competitive firm's input decision for two or more variable inputs

As explained in Chapter 7, when the price of one input falls, the firm will be induced to use more of it and less of other variable inputs.[5] Let the initial prices of inputs X and Y be P_{X_1} and P_{Y_1}, the initial output be on isoquant Q_1, and the equilibrium input rates be X_1 and Y_1 at point A, as shown in Fig. 17-3. If the price of X falls from P_{X_1} to P_{X_2}, the isocost line rotates to the right, allowing the firm to produce Q_2 units of output with the same total cost outlay, using X_2 units of variable input X and Y_2 units of variable input Y (point B).

The movement from A to B can be broken down into the substitution effect and the output effect. The substitution effect shows the change in the optimum input combination that would result if the firm decided to continue to produce Q_1 units of output; it is indicated graphically by the movement from point A to point C on isoquant Q_1 in Fig. 17-3. Point C is found by drawing a third isocost line tangent to isoquant Q_1 but parallel to the isocost line with extreme points TC_1/P_{Y_1} and TC_1/P_{X_2}. The isocost line tangent to Q_1 at point C has a slope equal to the new price ratio of inputs X and Y (P_{X_2}/P_{Y_1}) and serves to identify the optimum input combination for producing Q_1 units of output, given input prices of P_{X_2} and P_{Y_1}. The difference in the input combinations at A and C indicates the extent to which the firm is induced to use *more* of input X and *less* of input Y when the price of X falls from P_{X_1} to P_{X_2}, the price of Y remains fixed, and the firm decides to produce the *same* amount of output after the reduction in the price of X as before the price change. The relevance of the substitution effect to the firm's input decision is that substitution of input X for input Y will cause the marginal product curve for input X to shift downward, thereby making the values of MP_X smaller at each input rate of X than before. The lower marginal produc-

[5] For a review of the pertinent material, see the section in Chapter 7 on "The Impact of Changes in Resource Prices," pp. 224–227.

FIGURE 17-3
Substitution and output effects resulting from a change in an input's supply price

tivity of X arises from the fact that having fewer units of input Y to work with makes input X less productive.[6]

The output effect is represented by the movement from point C to point B in Fig. 17-3. It reflects the change in optimum input combination which is associated solely with a change in the firm's output rate, the ratio of input price being held constant. The output effect can be counted upon to result in an increase in the usage of both inputs X and Y.[7] Taken by itself, the output effect will shift the marginal product curve for input X upward because the presence of more of input Y will make X more productive. In other words, having more of input Y to work with will cause the values of MP_X to be higher at each input of X than they otherwise would be. (Note that the impact of the output effect upon MP_X is in the opposite direction as the impact of the substitution effect.)

The marginal cost effect stems from the lower price of input X. When the supply price of resource X falls from P_{X_1} to P_{X_2}, the marginal cost of producing

---

[6] The logical basis for this statement may be more apparent if one recalls that in situations where one input is variable and the remaining inputs are fixed, a reduction in the amount of fixed inputs causes the production function to shift downward, reflecting lower marginal productivity for the variable input. Consequently, it follows that reductions in the use of input Y will make input X less efficient because the units of X have fewer units of complementary input with which to produce the product.

[7] Only in rare and relatively unimportant cases will the output effect fail to affect both variable inputs in the same manner. Increases in the output rate normally require increased usage of all variable inputs. Similarly, decreases in output usually are accompanied by reductions in the use of each variable input.

each unit of output is reduced, because it costs less than before to obtain the variable input needed to produce more output. Thus, the marginal cost curve shifts downward, with the result that a firm's marginal cost curve will intersect its marginal revenue curve at a *larger* output than before (the reader should verify this statement by drawing a graph). Accordingly, the profit-maximizing rate of input is increased. The marginal cost effect thus leads to an expansion of output; in turn, more of both inputs X and Y will be required, and the marginal product curve for input X will shift upward.

To recapitulate, when the price of variable input X falls (the prices of all other variable inputs remaining constant), the substitution effect (by itself) tends to shift the marginal product curve for input X *downward*. In contrast, the output and marginal cost effects precipitate an *upward* shift of the MP_X curve. The net result will be a shift of MP_X upward (and quite possibly a change in its slope at each point as well).[8]

The consequently larger values of MP_X at each level of input, when multiplied by the firm's marginal revenue from additional sales, will cause the firm's *MRP* curve for input X to shift upward and to the right. Now, turning back to Fig. 17-2, suppose that the input adjustment and the subsequent changes in MP_X combine to shift the firm's marginal revenue product curve from MRP_1 to MRP_2. The new *MRP* curve, coupled with the new supply price of P_{X_2}, will generate a new profit-maximizing equilibrium input rate at X_2 units. By changing the price of X again, tracing through the substitution, output, and marginal cost effects upon MP_X, and then finding the new *MRP* curve for input X, other profit-maximizing input rates for X can be generated. The resulting equilibrium supply prices and input rates, when connected, form the firm's input demand curve for X, shown as line D_X in Fig. 17-2. The points along D_X show the quantities of input X which will maximize the firm's profits when the prices of other variable inputs are held constant and the usages of all other variable inputs are appropriately adjusted for changes in the supply price of X.

The Factors Influencing a Firm's Input Demand

We are now in a position to indicate explicitly the factors which ultimately determine a firm's demand for a resource input.[9] These factors may be grouped into two classes: (1) those which influence the *location* of the firm's input demand curve and which cause it to *shift* and (2) those which determine the sensitivity or elasticity of the firm's input demand to input price changes.

---

[8] Unfortunately, a proof of this statement involves an onerous mathematical exercise. The reader is thus asked to accept the statement on faith. Those who desire to pursue the point should consult Charles E. Ferguson, "Production, Price, and the Theory of Jointly Derived Input Demand Functions," *Economica*, Vol. 33, No. 132 (November 1966), pp. 454–461, and Charles E. Ferguson, "'Inferior Factors' and the Theories of Production and Input Demand," *Economica*, Vol. 35, No. 138 (May 1968), pp. 140–150. An additional treatment may be found in Charles E. Ferguson, *The Neoclassical Theory of Production and Distribution* (New York: Cambridge University Press, 1969), Chapters 6 and 9.

[9] This discussion is equally applicable to firms operating in either perfectly or imperfectly competitive product markets.

Changes in the Firm's Input Demand. As the previous discussion suggests, the determinants of a firm's input demand relate to the input's productivity and to the revenue contribution it makes to the firm's activities. However, we can be much more specific than this.

First, it is obvious that a firm's input demand is derived from the demand of consumers for the firm's products. The more intense is consumer demand for its products, the greater will be the firm's need for resource inputs to produce them. If improvements in a product or reductions in its price stimulate consumer demand, then the firm's input demand will also increase. A resource input that is very proficient in helping to produce a good in strong demand by consumers will itself have a strong demand. On the other hand, a firm's demand for an input will be slight if product demand is small, irrespective of the input's own productivity. There will be no demand for an input which is extraordinarily efficient at producing something no one wants to buy; thus high efficiency of an input, by itself, is insufficient to create a demand for that input.

Second, a firm's input demand is dependent on known technology and the directions of technological change. The technological character of a firm's production process is a fundamental factor in determining the marginal product function for each and every input. And, clearly enough, technological change alters the marginal productivity of a firm's resource inputs. Thus, technological progress that makes an input more productive also increases the demand for that input. Technological progress which makes an input less productive relative to other inputs ultimately reduces the demand for the input and may even eliminate demand for it entirely.

Third, the price of an input relative to other inputs influences input demand. As isoquant-isocost analysis demonstrates, the relative prices among substitutable inputs determine a firm's choice of production technologies from the array of known production recipes. If an input becomes cheaper relative to other inputs, the demand for it will gradually increase as producers alter their production techniques so as to substitute the lower-priced resource inputs for the relatively higher-priced ones.

Fourth, the demand for an input will be greater the higher is the marginal revenue which the firm receives from additional sales of output. Whatever the marginal product of an input is, the higher the value of *MR*, the larger will be the input's marginal revenue product. Since an input's *MR* values are of paramount importance in determining the profit-maximizing input rate, it necessarily must be true that anything which increases *MRP* will also increase the firm's input demand—other things being equal.

And last, the greater the quantity of cooperating inputs employed, the greater the demand for a given input. This proposition follows from the fact that giving an input more of other inputs with which to work and produce allows the input in question to be more productive and thereby have a higher marginal product at each input rate than otherwise. For example, providing automobile workers with more high-speed metal-stamping machines and robotic equipment will result in their being capable of achieving a greater output per labor-hour worked—which clearly means a higher marginal product of labor and, in turn, a higher marginal revenue product for labor.

The Firm's Elasticity of Demand for a Resource Input. Four important factors influence the degree to which a firm's input demand will respond to changes in the price of an input. As is customary in economics, we shall refer to this responsiveness or sensitivity as a firm's elasticity of demand for a resource input.[10]

First, the rate at which the marginal product of an input changes as the firm increases or decreases its usage has a bearing upon the degree to which a firm will alter its input rate as a consequence of a change in the input's supply price. This follows from the fact that the marginal revenue product of an input is equal to $MP \cdot MR$. Whatever the value of MR, the faster the value of MP declines, the more rapid will be the decline in MRP and the less elastic will be the firm's demand for the input. If, for example, the technological character of a firm's production function is such that the marginal product of variable input X declines slowly as larger doses of X are combined with the fixed inputs, then the effect will be to cause the MRP values for X to decline more slowly than otherwise. This will enhance the elasticity of the firm's demand for the input. On the other hand, if the marginal product of X falls off sharply as more of X is used, then the effect is to cause the MRP curve for X to decline more swiftly, thereby reducing the elasticity of the firm's input demand.

Second, the derived nature of resource demand necessarily makes the elasticity of a firm's input demand dependent on the elasticity of demand for the firm's product. A decline in the price of a product having an elastic demand will give rise to a sharper increase in output and therefore a stronger increase in the amounts of the variable inputs used to produce it than will a comparable decline in the price of a product having an inelastic demand.

Third, the degree to which resources can be substituted for one another determines an input's demand elasticity. The larger the number of substitutes for an input and the greater the ease with which substitution can be initiated and accomplished, the greater will be the elasticity of demand for that input. If a book publisher finds that some six or seven grades of paper are equally satisfactory in manufacturing college textbooks, then a rise in the price of any one grade of paper can be counted upon to cause a very sharp drop in its demand as other grades of paper are readily substituted. At the other extreme, where an input has few if any good substitutes, the demand for it tends to be highly inelastic. For instance, the lack of good substitutes for ink in printing books and magazines, for electricians in performing electric wiring functions for new construction projects, or for crude oil in the refining of motor fuels explains why their demands are relatively unresponsive in the short run to increases in their supply prices.

Finally, the elasticity of demand for a resource input is determined in part

---

[10] It will be recalled from Chapter 5 that the concept of elasticity is nothing more than a ratio of percentage changes. The elasticity of demand for a resource input X (ϵ_X) may be thought of as

$$\epsilon_X = \frac{\% \text{ change in the input rate of X}}{\% \text{ change in the supply price of input X}}.$$

by the fraction of total production costs accounted for by the input. The construction industry offers a good illustration of this propostion. In construction, labor costs are approximately 50% of total costs. If the wage rates of all the many types of construction labor rise by 10%, then total construction costs will rise by 5%. Rising construction costs will push the prices of new construction upward and reduce new construction activity. In turn, the demand of construction firms for construction labor will be weakened. However, suppose only the wage rates of bricklayers rise by 10%, the wage rates of other types of construction labor remaining fixed. Further suppose that the total wages paid to bricklayers amount to only 2% of total costs. Then a 10% rise in bricklayers' wages will cause total costs to rise by only 0.2%—an amount not likely to affect the demand for new construction to any important degree nor therefore the demand for bricklayers and other construction labor. Hence, as a general rule, the smaller the fraction of total costs accounted for by an input, the more inelastic will be a firm's demand for the input.[11]

Industry Demand for a Resource Input

The total industry demand for a resource input is found by combining the amounts of input that all firms in the industry will employ at a given price. This is slightly different from horizontally summing the individual firm demand curves for the input, because in perfect competition, when all firms change their output rates simultaneously, the market price of the product will also change. The resulting change in marginal revenue will trigger a shift in each firm's *MRP* curve for the input. Despite these complexities the industry demand curve for the input can be determined; the procedure is illustrated in Fig. 17-4.

The profit-maximizing input rates for a representative firm in a perfectly competitive industry are shown in panel (a). Given some market price for the firm's product, the firm's demand for input X is represented by the curve labeled D_1, derived according to the method described in Fig. 17-2. If the supply price of the input is P_1 dollars, the firm's equilibrium input is X_1 units. Adding together the optimum input usages of all the firms in the industry gives a total demand of X_{T_1} units at input price P_1, shown as point A in Fig. 17-4(b).

Now suppose the price of input X falls to P_2, perhaps because of greater available supplies of the input. This shifts the firm's marginal cost curve downward at each output rate and causes *MC* to intersect *MR* at a greater output rate. Assuming nothing else changes, the representative firm will expand its output rate by moving along D_1 in panel (a) and increasing its usage of X to X_3 units per period. However, we cannot assume that nothing else changes; what the representative firm does, the other firms will find it advantageous to do as well. The lower price of X affects the *MC* curves of all the firms. Hence, when the price

---

[11] It is, incidentally, the small portion of total costs coupled with a lack of good substitutes which explains why craft unions having more or less monopoly control over the supply of a specific type of labor have historically been able to negotiate attractive wage and fringe benefit packages for their members.

FIGURE 17-4
Deriving the industry demand for a resource input in a perfectly competitive environment

of input X falls, *all* firms will be induced to expand their output rates and thereby use more of input X. The industrywide expansion of output will shift the industry supply curve for the product to the right, causing the market price of the product to fall. In turn, the lower product price means a lower marginal revenue and thus a lower marginal revenue product for X at each input rate. The effect is to shift the firm's input demand curve for X down and to the left, say from D_1 to D_2. The new profit-maximizing input rate for the representative firm at input price P_2 therefore is X_2 units and not X_3 units. Aggregating for all firms in the industry gives a total industry demand of X_{T_2} units at input price P_2, shown as point B in Fig. 17-4(b). Points in addition to A and B can be determined by considering still other input prices. Connecting these points by a line gives the industry demand curve for input X.

Industry Supply of a Resource Input

The supply of a resource input to an industry refers to the various input quantities which owners of the input are willing and able to make available to firms in the industry at various prices. Since in a free economy resource owners have a choice of supplying their resources to one line of production or another, it is reasonable to presume that they will direct them to those uses and industries offering the best overall propsect of reward—and not necessarily just the greatest monetary reward, because the reward package often includes nonmonetary as well as monetary elements.

Insofar as capital and land inputs of various types are concerned, the expected monetary reward is generally the predominant consideration. However, the case of labor inputs is more complicated. Wage rates and salaries are certainly important, but so are such features as the time and expense in learning a job or entering a profession, the opportunity for obtaining personal satisfactions from the job, the prospects for promotion and advancement, the regularity of employment, the environmental conditions under which the work is performed, the specific community and geographical area in which the job is located, and the social status of the occupation. Each job type offers a package of monetary and nonmonetary considerations that each potential worker may evaluate differently in the light of his or her own preferences. Given a choice of occupation and jobs, each member of the labor force can reasonably be expected to choose the one perceived as offering the best total package relative to one's interests, skills, and capabilities. Nonetheless, since experience indicates that the nonmonetary elements affecting resource allocation change rather slowly and can therefore be treated as a constant for purposes of short-run analysis, it simplifies the analysis to express the supply of labor as a function of monetary rewards (or just "price"—where price encompasses both wages/salary and fringes).

Logic dictates that a positive relation between input prices and input supplies will exist for most all types of land, natural resources, labor, and capital goods inputs. As the amount of monetary reward accruing to an input rises, resource owners will ordinarily be induced to supply the input in larger quantities per period of time. For instance, higher prices for minerals and natural resources intensify efforts to discover and tap more sources of supply. As wage rates in one occupation rise relative to wage rates in other occupations, the number of people seeking employment in that occupation will tend to rise. The greater the wage differential between firms, the more will workers gravitate from low-paying to high-paying firms; similarly, the greater the wage differentials between industries and between geographical regions, the more mobile will workers become.[12] Accordingly, *input supply curves are upward sloping, owing to the tendency of inputs to be drawn to employments where the rewards are highest.*

How responsive input supplies will be to changes in input prices depends on several factors:

1. *The size of the economic unit under consideration—the total economy, a locality, an industry, or a single firm.* The supply of an input to the economy as a whole may be fixed in the short run, while at the same time the supply to a particular locality, industry, or firm may be highly elastic or even perfectly elastic. Although at any given time there is just so much land, labor, or capital input in the entire economy (or in a more restricted geographical area), one firm or industry may be able to obtain as much of the available supply of an input as it may need

---

[12] Sometimes substantial wage differentials exist and are maintained for long periods, but beyond some point a wage differential can become too great for a firm, or an industry, or a locality, or a region to maintain without affecting labor supply conditions. The wages workers expect from one firm bear some relationship to the wages similar workers elsewhere receive, and if workers' expectations are grossly unrealized, the supply of labor is bound to be affected. The supply of job applicants for firms paying subpar wages may not totally dry up, but the quality may deteriorate. Moreover, their labor turnover rates are likely to be above average as workers' dissatisfaction with their wages pushes them to look for alternative employment.

without changing its offer prices because, by itself, it may require only a negligible fraction of the available input supply.

2. *The period of time considered.* The response of input supplies to input price changes is greater over the long run than over the short run, primarily because the degree of resource mobility increases with time. It takes time to discover and develop new mineral deposits, to shift capital investment out of less profitable endeavors into more profitable endeavors, to convert land from one use to another, to retrain workers or induce them to move into areas where job opportunities are expanding, and to inform people preparing to enter the labor force of the changing prospects of economic reward in the various professions. Hence, the elasticity of supply of an input becomes greater with the expansion of the time frame under consideration.

3. *Whether the input is unique to a particular industry or whether it is widely used.* The supply of an input used only by a single industry tends to be less elastic than inputs which are used by a number of different industries. The more versatile and mobile an input is, the more elastic will be its supply to a particular industry.

The size of the coefficient of the elasticity of supply, however, is not of paramount importance for our purposes. The basic analysis will be the same whatever the shape and degree of elasticity of the industry supply curve—even if it is vertical or backward rising.[13]

Resource Pricing and Employment on an Industry-wide Basis

Demand and supply conditions for an input determine the equilibrium price which firms in an industry pay for the input and the equilibrium amount of the input employed in the industry. Figure 17-5 shows an industry's demand for input X and the quantity of X supplied to the industry; the resulting equilibrium input price is P_1 dollars and the equilibrium employment rate is X_{T_1} units per period of time. If the prevailing price exceeds P_1 dollars, the available supply of the input will exceed the quantity which firms are willing to employ. Some units of the input will be either idle altogether or else used only part of the time. The excess supply of the input will generate a downward pressure on its price. On the other hand, if the actual price of X falls below P_1, the quantity demanded by firms in the industry will exceed the quantity supplied to the industry, and firms will begin to bid up the input's price as they compete for the available supplies.

---

[13] A backward-bending supply curve for an input may arise from the fact that above certain input price levels, resource owners prefer to withdraw some units of input from the market to meet leisure-time or other personal preferences, since those units still being supplied will provide an income which is regarded as adequate. Hence, above some input price level, the higher the price, the smaller the quantity of the input supplied by resource owners. The effect is to cause the supply curve for the input to bend backward and upward—or to be backward rising. Generally, the concept of a backward rising supply curve is most applicable to the case of labor input.

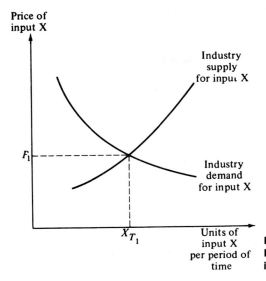

Price of
input X

FIGURE 17-5
Pricing and employment of a resource input

Thus, market forces push resource prices and employment rates toward levels that will clear the market. Multiplying the equilibrium input price by the equilibrium employment rate of X gives the amount of money income which the owners of input X will receive from the firms in the industry. Aggregating the income of input X over all industries which use input X gives the total money income received by the owners of X and the share of the economy's output they will earn from having supplied X. This explanation of how the income accruing to resource owners is determined is called the *marginal productivity theory of income distribution*. It derives this name from the fact that particular input prices and employment rates are a function of the input's marginal productivity.

However, keep in mind that when an input is used in many industries and when its supply to a particular industry is very sensitive to input price changes, it is inappropriate to examine input pricing and employment in the context of a single industry. The reason is that what firms in one industry pay for an input and the amounts they use of this input necessarily are related to the prices that firms in other industries pay and the amounts of that input they employ. In fact, input prices and employment rates among the various industries using that input are interconnected; price or employment adjustments in one industry transmit pressures and influences to other industries, though with "impulses" of varying degrees of intensity. The linkages between industries are usually sufficiently strong to cause an input's price to *tend* toward the same level in all industries. Different input prices for the same quality input can prevail without stimulating the movement of input supplies among firms and industries, but at some point the tolerance of resource owners for differentials becomes stretched so thin that firms and industries, in order to keep the inputs they need, will be forced to lessen the gap. Consequently, where an input is employed in several industries, the appropriate focal point for analyzing input prices is at the level of the total market for the input rather than at the level of the firm or industry.

The total market demand for an input on an economywide basis may be thought of as the sum of all the various industry demand curves, where the industries may be structured along any sort of lines and may contain any number of firms of various types and sizes. Similarly, the total market supply of an input is the result of combining the industry supply curves. Again, the intersection of market demand and market supply determines the input's economywide equilibrium price and rate of usage per period of time. The resulting price and employment rate form the basis for ascertaining the total amount of income which owners of the input in question will receive per period of time.

While it is generally agreed among economists that resource prices and employment rates are outcomes of supply and demand forces, in particular situations the operation of supply and demand forces may be suspended or modified. The presence of labor unions, the imposing of minimum wage requirements, a wage-price freeze, plus a host of other institutional considerations combine to cause input prices and employment rates to deviate from the free market results. We shall discuss some of the ramifications of these market interferences in the concluding section of this chapter.

The Applicability of the Perfectly Competitive Resource Input Model

Our conclusions about resource pricing and employment under conditions of perfect competition in both the product and resource markets apply mainly to those few markets where the products of the firms are homogeneous and where the number of firms comprising the product market is quite large. Only under these conditions is perfect competition in the product market even approximated. Thus, strictly speaking, the preceding model of resource pricing and resource employment provides a theoretical description of but a small segment of the economy. Nevertheless, many of the principles which characterize the model of perfectly competitive product and resource markets are much the same as in other types of market structures. In this sense, the perfectly competitive input model lays the groundwork for examining more widely applicable models of resource pricing and employment.

RESOURCE PRICING AND EMPLOYMENT: THE CASE OF IMPERFECTLY COMPETITIVE PRODUCT MARKETS AND PERFECTLY COMPETITIVE RESOURCE MARKETS

A somewhat more prevalent model of the functioning and behavior of resource input markets concerns the situation where the firm sells its product under conditions of imperfect competition (i.e., monopolistic competition, oligopoly, or monopoly) yet buys its inputs in a perfectly competitive resource market. This model characterizes many resource markets in the small business sector of the economy and some in the corporate sector.

The Imperfectly Competitive Firm's Input Decision: The One-Variable Input Case

When a firm sells its product in an imperfectly competitive market structure, its input decision is determined in a manner analogous to the perfectly competitive case, but with a slightly modified calculation procedure. In monopolistic competition, oligopoly, or pure monopoly the firm's product demand curve is downsloping, and, other competitive variables remaining unchanged, the firm must lower price in order to increase its sales volume. This has a very important consequence. Whereas the *MRP* curve of an input used by a perfectly competitive firm falls solely because the marginal product of the input declines, the *MRP* curve of an input used by an imperfectly competitive firm declines for two reasons: a declining marginal product and a lower marginal revenue from the sale of additional output. The perfectly competitive enterprise can sell additional output at a constant price and obtain a constant *MR*, so that its *MRP* curve falls at the same rate as does the *MP* curve of the variable input. But when an imperfectly competitive firm adds one more unit of variable input and output rises by the amount of its marginal product, it may have to lower selling price to sell the increased output. Barring the opportunity for price discrimination, any price decrease applies not just to the marginal product of the last unit of variable input but also to the units of output previously produced.[14] Hence, the marginal revenue received from additional sales is a decreasing function, and the firm's *MRP* curve for variable input falls faster than it otherwise would if the firm could sell all it pleased at an established market price—as occurs with the horizontal demand curve of a firm in perfect competition. However, in either case, *MRP* still equals the net addition to total revenue associated with a change in the variable input rate.

The Profit-Maximizing Rate of Input Usage.   To illustrate how a firm confronted with a downsloping demand-*AR* curve can ascertain the profit-maximizing rate of usage of a single variable input (X), consider the hypothetical production, cost, and revenue data in Table 17-2. Column (4) shows the extent to which the firm must lower price in order to sell the extra output of each successive unit of X, while columns (5) and (6) concern the corresponding *TR* and *MR* values. Column (7) contains the $SVMP_X$ figures, obtained by multiplying MP_X by the price at which the added output can be sold. Observe carefully that, unlike the perfectly competitive case, the figures for $SVMP_X$ in column (7) do *not* coincide with MRP_X values in column (8). The figures for the sales value of the marginal product represent the gross addition to total revenue attributable to an additional unit of

---

[14] We shall assume throughout the following discussion that the firm employs a single price policy and does not therefore engage in any of the several forms of price discrimination. We shall also assume that a firm lowers price to gain increased sales rather than depending upon increased efforts in nonprice areas to accommodate a rise in output.

TABLE 17-2 Profit-Maximizing Rate of Resource Input Usage for a Firm Operating in an Imperfectly Competitive Product Market and a Perfectly Competitive Resource Market

(1) Units of Variable Input (X)	(2) Units of Output (Q_A)	(3) Marginal Product (MP_X)	(4) Price of Product A (P_A)	(5) Total Revenue from Sales of Product A ($TR_A = P_A \cdot Q_A$)	(6) "Average" Marginal Revenue[a] (MR_A)	(7) Sales Value of Marginal Product ($SVMP_X = MP_X \cdot P_A$)	(8) Marginal Revenue Product ($MRP_X = MP_X \cdot MR_A = \Delta TR_A / \Delta X$)	(9) Supply Price of Variable Input ($P_X = ARC_X = MRC_X$)	(10) Total Variable Cost (TVC)	(11) Total Contribution Profit ($TCP = TR - TVC$)
0	0		$25	$ 0				$140	$ 0	$ 0
1	14	14	24	336	$24.00	$336	$336	140	140	196
2	40	26	23	920	22.46	598	584	140	280	640
3	60	20	22	1320	20.00	440	400	140	420	900
4	78	18	21	1638	17.67	378	318	140	560	1078
5	94	16	20	1880	15.12	320	242	140	700	1180
6	108	14	19	2052	12.29	266	172	140	840	1212
7	120	12	18	2160	9.00	216	108	140	980	1180
8	130	10	17	2210	5.00	170	50	140	1120	1090
9	138	8	16	2208	−0.25	128	−2	140	1260	948
10	144	6	15	2160	−8.00	90	−48	140	1400	760

[a] The term "average" marginal revenue is used here because, strictly speaking, the concept of MR refers to the extra revenue associated with a single-unit change in output; since the output changes in the table are multiunit, the only MR values which can be computed from the information in the table are the average MR values for the multiunit output increment in question.

X. However, the firm's total revenue does not rise by the amount of *SVMP*, because to sell the added output the firm must reduce its price on the preceding units of output, thereby causing the *net* addition to *TR* to be less than the gross addition. To illustrate: The eighth unit of X has a marginal product of 10 units of output; these can be sold for $17 apiece for a total of $170—the figure for *SVMP*. But this is not the *MRP* value for the eighth unit of X because, to sell these 10 units of output, the firm must accept a $1 price reduction on the 120 units of output produced by the preceding 7 units of X. Hence, the *MRP* of the eighth unit of X is [$170 − 120($1)] or $50, as shown in column (8). The other values in column (8) can be determined in like fashion. The figures in columns (9), (10), and (11) of the table are obtained in the usual way.

The principle upon which an imperfectly competitive firm's input decision is based is precisely the same as that of a perfectly competitive firm: *The firm should purchase additional units of a variable input up to the point where the added cost of more input equals the added revenue it contributes.* In short, the usage of variable input must be carried to the rate where *MRP* = *MRC*. A comparison of columns (8) and (9) in Table 17-2 indicates that the profit-maximizing input rate is 6 units of X. For the firm to go beyond this point and employ the seventh unit of X will result in revenues increasing by $108 but costs rising by $140—plainly an unprofitable act. For the firm to stop short of using 6 units of X will result in smaller total contribution profits [see column (11)] and hence smaller total profits (or greater losses).

The profit-maximizing input decision can be approached graphically in a somewhat more general fashion. Figure 17-6 shows an imperfectly competitive firm's *MRP* curve for a variable input. Suppose the input supply curve is S_1, with a resulting input price of P_1 dollars. The profit-maximizing input rate is X_1 units, where $MRP_X = MRC_X$. Should the input supply price fall to P_2 dollars, giving a new input supply curve at S_2, the firm's profit-maximizing input rate would

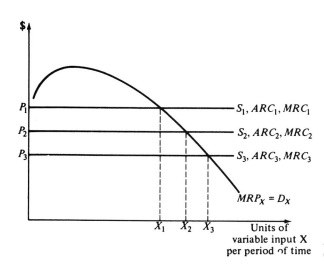

FIGURE 17-6
An imperfectly competitive firm's demand for a resource input

expand to X_2 units per period of time. And should the input supply curve shift downward to S_3, the new equilibrium input rate would become X_3 units. Consequently, the profit-maximizing input rate of X is found along the input's *MRP* curve, which makes the MRP_X curve the firm's demand curve for input X, provided that only one variable input is used in the firm's production process.

The Imperfectly Competitive Firm's Input Decision: The Two-Variable Input Case

The analysis for an imperfectly competitive firm using two or more variable inputs parallels that for the perfectly competitive firm. As portayed in Fig. 17-7, suppose that the supply price of input X is perfectly elastic and pegged at P_1 and that the input's marginal revenue product curve is MRP_1. The profit-maximizing rate of input is therefore X_1 units per period of time.

Now let the supply price of X fall to P_2. This change triggers four effects at the level of the firm; the substitution effect, the output effect, the marginal cost effect, and the marginal revenue effect. The substitution, output, and marginal cost effects operate in exactly the same way for firms in monopolistic competition, oligopoly, or pure monopoly as they do for firms in perfect competition.

However, the *marginal revenue effect* is unique to imperfectly competitive product markets and arises from the fact that the firm's marginal revenue will change as a consequence of the output changes induced by the shift in the price of input X. The decline in the price of X lowers the firm's marginal cost curve, causing a new intersection of *MC* and *MR* at a *larger* output, a *lower* price, and a *lower MR* value. (The reader should verify this statement by drawing a graph.) Since $MRP_X = MP_X \cdot MR$, a decline in *MR* necessarily acts to reduce MRP_X.

FIGURE 17-7

An imperfectly competitive firm's input decision when two or more inputs are variable

On balance, the output and marginal cost effects will override the substitution and marginal revenue effects, with the result that a decline in the supply price of X will shift the *MRP* curve for X upward and to the right, say from MRP_1 to MRP_2.[15] The profit-maximizing input rate for the imperfectly competitive firm thus becomes X_2 units at a supply price of P_2 dollars. Other profit-maximizing input rates for X can be generated by changing the price of X again and again, tracing through the substitution, output, marginal cost, and marginal revenue effects, and finding the new position of the firm's *MRP* curve. Connecting the points formed by the equilibrium input supply prices and input rates gives the firm's input demand curve for X, labeled as D_X in Fig. 17-7. The points along D_X show the various quantities of input X that maximize the firm's profits when the prices of other variable inputs remain constant and the usages of all other variable inputs are appropriately adjusted for changes in the supply price of input X.

The Input Demand of an Imperfectly Competitive Industry

To derive the industrywide demand for an input when the firms compete under conditions of imperfect competition requires that the demand curves of the individual firms somehow be combined into a single input demand curve for the industry. In an imperfectly competitive market of two or more firms, whatever shade of oligopoly or monopolistic competition may exist, the demand curves of the firms cannot simply be summed horizontally to give the industry demand curve.[16] This is invalid for the same reason it does not work for perfect competition. To begin with, a change in the input's supply price affects the optimum output rate of each firm in the industry. A change in the firm's output rate leads then to a price change. The price and output adjustments made by the firm will combine to shift the *MRP* curve of the input via the substitution, output, marginal cost, and marginal revenue effects. In turn, the shift in *MRP* alters the firm's optimum input demand at the new input supply price. In such situations, the industrywide input demand curve is derived by first finding the profit-maximizing input rate for each firm at each possible input price after allowing for shifts in the *MRP* curve and then by summing these optimum input amounts over all firms in the industry. The rationale and the graphical analysis are identical to that described in Fig. 17-4 and need not be reiterated here.

Once the industry demand for the input is determined, the industrywide equilibrium price and input rates are found at the intersection of the industry demand and supply curves for the input. The nature of an input's supply curve for a given industry, discussed in an earlier section of this chapter, is unaffected by the existence of imperfect competition in the product market. Again, however,

---

[15] For a formal proof of this claim the reader may consult the references in footnote 8.

[16] Obviously, if the industry is one of pure monopoly, no combining is necessary, because the firm's input demand and the industry input demand are one and the same.

the equilibrium price of an input on an industrywide basis is bound to be affected by the price of the input in other industries. When resource inputs are versatile enough to be used by several industries and when they are relatively mobile from industry to industry, the equilibrium price and employment rates of an input are best analyzed on a marketwide or economywide basis rather than on an industrywide basis. Barring the existence of resource immobility or other powerful institutional determinants of an input price, the tie between a resource input's price in one industry and its price in other industries is usually strong enough to cause the overall price of the input to *tend* toward the same level in all industries using that input. A valid explanation of how input prices are determined must therefore hinge upon overall market demand and supply conditions rather than upon demand and supply in any one industry.

RESOURCE PRICING AND EMPLOYMENT: THE CASE OF IMPERFECTLY COMPETITIVE PRODUCT AND RESOURCE MARKETS

In numerous geographical areas the supply of an input *in the short run* is relatively limited. Enterprises with large plants in the area may utilize such a sizable fraction of the local input supply that their decisions to employ more or less of the input have a discernible impact on the input's short-run local supply price. The effect is to make *the firm's* input supply curve upward sloping. The more of an input the firm wishes to obtain, the higher the price it must offer to bid supplies of the input away from alternative users.[17] The less of an input the firm needs, the smaller the price it can get by with paying, since it does not have to bid so high to attract the desired supply away from other firms.

Several types of input supply situations other than perfect competition may be delineated. A resource input market in which only *one* firm uses the input is referred to as *monopsony*.[18] If only a *few* firms are the predominant purchasers of the input, the resource market is designated as *oligopsony*. Where *many* firms are using an input but their numbers are still small enough to allow each firm a small influence over the input's supply price, the resource market may be characterized as *monopsonistic competition*. A particular firm can sell its output under conditions of oligopoly yet buy its inputs under conditions of monopsonistic com-

---

[17] As regards labor inputs, it should be recognized that a large firm may be able to expand the size of its labor force without raising the going wage rate by increasing recruiting efforts and/or by lowering its standards for hiring new employees. Either of these strategies, however, really means that the effective price of a given quantity and quality of labor is rising, even though the nominal wage scale remains the same.

[18] The term monopsony is on occasions also used to refer to product market situations where there is only a single buyer of a product. Hence, strictly speaking, monopsony refers to a single buyer—it matters not whether the buyer purchases an input or a final good or service. Similarly, pure monopoly refers to a single seller—whether the seller is selling a product or an input again really makes no difference. For example, the craft union which is able to unionize all persons having a particular skill is just as much as monopolist in "selling" the skill it controls as is the local telephone company in rendering telephone service. Analogous meanings and interpretations can be attached to the terms oligopoly, oligopsony, and so on.

it is possible for a firm to sell its product under conditions of [compe]tition and to obtain its inputs under conditions of monopsony; [if t]he numerous small producers were geographically dispersed [enough] to dominate the market for labor in a local area. Plainly, a [varie]d resource market combinations can result: monopoly-mon[opsony,] monopsony, oligopoly-monopsonistic competition, perfect [monops]ony, and so on. However, in any sort of imperfectly com[petitive marke]t, whether it be one of monopsony, oligopsony, or monop[sony], the analytical considerations governing the supply aspects [of the d]ecision are the same. Thus, it is sufficient merely to examine [the situati]on in the input market to learn about the firm's input decision [in a perf]ectly competitive resource market.

[Marginal] Resource Cost Curve and a Rising Input

[A featu]re of an imperfectly competitive input market is that *the firm* [faces a ri]sing input supply curve. With a rising supply curve the firm is [paying a hig]her price if it wishes to secure more of the input, and the firm [will be pa]ying a lower price for the input should it choose to use less of [it. Since th]e supply curve for an input represents the firm's average cost [of the in]put, the firm's *ARC* curve is also upward sloping and coincides [with the s]urve. This has a most important consequence insofar as the [marginal re]source cost is concerned.

[Under im]perfectly competitive input supply conditions, the *MRC* curve does [not correspo]nd to the input supply and average resource cost curve. Consider [the hypo]thetical data in Table 17-3. Columns (1) and (2) show how much the firm

TABLE 17-3 Marginal Resource Cost for a Firm Operating under Conditions of Imperfect Competition in Its Resource Input Market

(1) Units of Variable Input (X)	(2) Supply Price of Variable Input ($P_X = ARC_X$)	(3) Total Cost of Variable Input (TC_X)	(4) Marginal Resource Cost (MRC_X)
1	$5.00	$ 5.00	$ 6.00
2	5.50	11.00	7.00
3	6.00	18.00	8.00
4	6.50	26.00	9.00
5	7.00	35.00	10.00
6	7.50	45.00	11.00
7	8.00	56.00	12.00
8	8.50	68.00	13.00
9	9.00	81.00	14.00
10	9.50	95.00	

FIGURE 17-8
Relationships among the
curve, the average resource co
the marginal resource cur
perfectly competitive input mark

must increase its offer price in order to obtain additional units of
columns represent the firm's input supply and *ARC* schedules. Co
sents the total cost of input X associated with each of the various in
X. Column (4) shows the marginal resource cost of each additional un
can be calculated by successive subtraction of the TC_X figures; that is,
$\Delta TC_X/\Delta X$.

When the firm must pay a higher price to obtain larger amounts of in
the marginal resource cost of each extra unit will be higher than the input's s
price and average resource cost. As shown in Table 17-3, suppose the fir
creases its usage rate of X from 7 to 8 units per period. The price of the eig
unit is $8.50. But this value is not the marginal resource cost of the eighth un
To obtain the use of 8 units of X, the firm must pay $8.50 for *each* one.[19] Henc
the firm's cost of obtaining each of the previous 7 units of X rises from $8.00 to
$8.50 for an added cost of $3.50 (7 × $0.50). Adding this to the $8.50 cost of the
eighth unit gives a total increase of $12.00 in the firm's cost of upping the input
rate of X from 7 to 8 units. Thus, the marginal resource cost of the eighth unit is
$12.00. The *MRC* of the other units can be derived in the same fashion.

A graphical portrayal of the relationships among the firm's input supply
curve (S_X), the average resource cost curve (ARC_X), and the marginal resource
cost curve (MRC_X) is depicted in Fig. 17-8. The MRC_X curve lies above the input
supply and average resource cost curve at each and every input rate. The rationale

---

[19] This is not only required by the supply conditions, but it is also equitable. Since we assume
each unit of X is just alike, there is no cause for the firm to reward 1 unit of X any differently from
the others. If, for example, the firm has 8 identical units of input X, then the second unit (assuming
it can be picked out from the rest) is no more "valuable" than the fifth or the eighth unit. The *order*
in which the units of X are hired has no real bearing on their worth to the firm. Nor is it usually
feasible for the firm to pay different units of the same input a different price. Consequently, the price
which it takes to get the *total* amount of X that is desired is what determines the price *each unit* must
be paid.

is the same as for the relationship between ATC and MC; in fact, the ARC_X-MRC_X relation parallels that of ATC and MC. As is the usual case with marginal and average concepts, if the average cost (or supply price) of input X is rising, then the marginal cost of input X (MRC_X) must be greater than ARC_X and the MRC curve for X must lie above the input supply and average resource cost curve.

The mathematics of the relationship between S_X and MRC_X is easily indicated. Assume, for convenience of illustration, that the input supply curve for X is linear and upward-sloping. Then the general equation for the supply curve is

$$P_X = ARC_X = a + bX.$$

The total cost of the input at any input rate is

$$TC_X = P_X \cdot X = ARC_X \cdot X = (a + bX)X = aX + bX^2.$$

Marginal resource cost is, by definition, the rate of change in the total cost of the input as the input rate changes, which in terms of calculus is the first derivative of the input's total cost function. The equation for MRC_X thus becomes

$$MRC_X = \frac{dTC_X}{dX} = a + 2bX.$$

A comparison of the equation for the input supply-average resource cost curve and the equation for the MRC curve indicates that the MRC_X curve will rise twice as fast as S_X-ARC_X when S_X-ARC_X is linear and upward sloping. The marginal resource cost curve can be determined in like fashion for other types of input supply-average resource cost functions.

The Imperfectly Competitive Firm's Input Decision in an Imperfectly Competitive Resource Market: The One-Variable Input Case

Determining the firm's profit-maximizing input rate with respect to resource X follows the same principle when imperfect competition exists in the input market as it does when there is perfect competition. As we have just seen, the distinctive feature of an imperfectly competitive resource market is that each firm confronts an upward-rising input supply curve and an even more rapidly rising marginal resource cost curve. Nonetheless, a firm will still find it advantageous to increase the usage rate of X as long as additional units of X add more to revenues than to total costs. As before, the firm's net revenue gains from using additional units of an input are given by the input's MRP function, whereas the extra costs incurred are indicated by the input's MRC function as derived from the input's supply and ARC functions.

The relevant curves are shown in Fig. 17-9. The firm's profits will be maximum at an input rate of X_1 units, where $MRP_X = MRC_X$. To use more than X_1

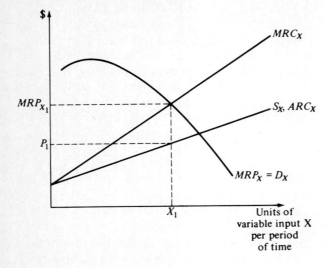

units of
variable input X
per period
of time

FIGURE 17-9
The profit-maximizing input rate for a firm operating in imperfectly competitive product and resource markets

units per period of time would add more to the firm's total costs than to its total revenues. To stop short of using X_1 units would mean a sacrifice of some profits, because the marginal revenue products of all units below X_1 exceed their respective marginal resource costs. Clearly, then, X_1 is the profit-maximizing input rate. But now the question becomes: What price must the firm pay to obtain X_1 units per period of time? Although the marginal revenue product at X_1 is MRP_{X_1}, this is not the price which the firm need pay to get X_1 units. The input supply curve (S_X) shows the price which the firm must pay for various quantities of the input. From S_X it is apparent that to obtain X_1 units of resource X, the firm will find it necessary to pay a price of P_1 dollars—this, then, is the firm's equilibrium input price.

The Imperfectly Competitive Firm's Input Decision in an Imperfectly Competitive Resource Market when Several Variable Inputs Are Used

Ordinarily, a firm's production technology will call for the use of several inputs—some fixed in the short run, others variable, but all subject to change in the long run. Consequently, it is important to consider how the firm's profit-maximizing input combination is determined when several inputs are variable.

In Chapter 7 it was shown that to minimize its total costs for a given output the firm must adjust its input mix so as to obtain an equivalent amount of output per dollar spent on the last unit of each input used. In more formal terms this requires the firm to combine its various inputs (X_a, X_b, X_c, . . . , X_n) such that

$$\frac{MP_{X_a}}{P_{X_a}} = \frac{MP_{X_b}}{P_{X_b}} = \frac{MP_{X_c}}{P_{X_c}} = \cdots = \frac{MP_{X_n}}{P_{X_n}} .$$

If the least-cost input combination rule is violated, the firm can either obtain more output for the same total cost or else get the same output for less total cost. Suppose, for instance, a dollar's worth of input X_a contributes more to output than a dollar's worth of input X_b. Then the firm would find it advantageous to shift its expenditures on inputs; more dollars should be allocated to the purchase of X_a and fewer to the purchase of X_b—the firm should substitute input X_a for input X_b. As the substitution is made, the marginal product of X_a declines and the marginal product of X_a rises; the subtitution process ceases when

$$\frac{MP_{X_a}}{P_{X_a}} = \frac{MP_{X_b}}{P_{X_b}}.$$

However, this propostion holds if and only if the inputs are purchased in perfectly competitive resource markets. If the firms' input supply curves are all upward sloping such that input prices vary with the quantity used, then a substitution of one input for another entails input price changes as well as marginal product changes. The firm must therefore consider an input's marginal resource cost (*MRC*) rather than its supply price when making its input decision. The rule for minimizing the cost of a given output under imperfectly competitive input conditions thus becomes

$$\frac{MP_{X_a}}{MRC_{X_a}} = \frac{MP_{X_b}}{MRC_{X_b}} = \frac{MP_{X_c}}{MRC_{X_c}} = \cdots = \frac{MP_{X_n}}{MRC_{X_n}}.$$

To see the rationale underlying this proposition consider the two-input case where inputs X_a and X_b are being used in such proportions that

$$\frac{MP_{X_a}}{MRC_{X_a}} > \frac{MP_{X_b}}{MRC_{X_b}}.$$

This inequality says that at the existing input combination the firm can realize a greater increase in output per additional dollar outlay on input X_a than on input X_b. Consequently, by substituting X_a for X_b the firm can realize more output for the same cost or else it can get the same output for less cost. As substitution is initiated, the marginal product of X_a declines and the MRC_{X_a} increases, whereas the marginal product of X_b increases and the MRC_{X_b} declines. Sooner or later the substitution of X_a for X_b will result in equality in the ratios of *MP* and *MRC*. At the point of equality, no further change in the firm's input mix will prove beneficial from the standpoint of costs or output.

The preceding discussion shows, albeit in a nonrigorous fashion, that if a firm *buying its inputs* under conditions of imperfect competition is to achieve the lowest possible total cost for a given output, then it should adjust its input combination to the point where the ratio of marginal product to marginal resource cost is the same for all inputs used. An interesting question now arises: What adjustments in the rule, if any, are necessary to identify *the profit-maximizing resource input combination*? Is the rule for attaining the least-cost resource combination for a given output also adequate for ascertaining the profit-maximizing input mix? The answer to the latter question is *no*, though the reason may not be apparent at first glance.

The rule for determining the least-cost resource combination for a *given output* reveals only the correct *proportions* in which to employ variable inputs. It says nothing about which output rate maximizes profits, and therefore it leaves unanswered the question as to the correct *absolute amounts* of each variable input. To illustrate the significance of this point, consider the following numerical example. Suppose that a firm is using 10 units of input X_a and 15 units of input X_b to produce 3500 units of a particular product per week. Suppose further that at this input combination the specific values of marginal product and marginal resource cost for X_a and X_b are $MP_{X_a} = 40$ units of output, $MRC_{X_a} = \$10$, $MP_{X_b} = 60$ units of output, and $MRC_{X_b} = \$15$. The least-cost rule that

$$\frac{MP_{X_a}}{MRC_{X_a}} = \frac{MP_{X_b}}{MRC_{X_b}}$$

is satisfied, as we can see by substituting the *MP* and *MRC* values into the above expression:

$$\frac{MP_{X_a}}{MRC_{X_a}} = \frac{40 \text{ units of output}}{\$10} = 4 \text{ units of output/\$,}$$

$$\frac{MRC_{X_b}}{MP_{X_b}} = \frac{60 \text{ units of output}}{\$15} = 4 \text{ units of output/\$.}$$

At the current input combination, the firm obtains 4 units of output per dollar spent on each input, which says that there is no advantage to be gained from shifting the input mix insofar as cost or output is concerned. However, how do we know whether or not it would be more *profitable* to use more (or less) of both inputs X_a and X_b? There is no way to tell from the information given. Thus, while it is clear that the firm is using its inputs to the best advantage to produce the current output of 3500 units, we do not know from the information given whether 3500 units is the profit-maximizing output rate and therefore whether 10 units of X_a and 15 units of X_b constitute the profit-maximizing input combination.

This shortcoming in the least-cost rule is easily disposed of by bringing the marginal revenue products of the two inputs into consideration. Suppose the marginal product of the tenth unit of input X_a (40 units of output) adds \$20 to the firm's total revenue and the marginal product of the fifteenth unit of X_b (60 units of output) adds \$30. Then, clearly, the *MRP* of both inputs exceeds their respective marginal resource costs of \$10 and \$15, and the firm will find it profitable to increase its usage of both X_a and X_b. As demonstrated previously, the firm should increase an input's usage to the point where $MRP = MRC$. This rationale applies to any and all resources. Thus, *in general it can be said that a firm attains the profit-maximizing input rate when each and every variable input is employed to the point where its marginal revenue product equals its marginal resource cost.*

In algebraic terms this becomes

$$\frac{MRP_{X_a}}{MRC_{X_a}} = \frac{MRP_{X_b}}{MRC_{X_b}} = \frac{MRP_{X_c}}{MRC_{X_c}} = \cdots = \frac{MRP_{X_n}}{MRC_{X_n}}.$$

Hence, converting the numerator of each term of the least-cost rule from a measure of marginal product to a measure of marginal revenue product gives the expression for the profit-maximizing input combination. The latter expression satisfies the need for determining both the absolute quantities and the proportions of the various inputs that will maximize total profits, since it incorporates measures of each input's productivity (marginal product), revenue contribution, and cost—all of which are essential for input optimization. However, since each input must be used at a rate such that its $MRP = MRC$, then it follows that the input ratios must not only be equal to each other but they must also be equal to 1. In other words, to use each variable input in the profit-maximizing *proportions* and in the profit-maximizing *absolute amounts*, the firm must adjust its input mix to the point where

$$\frac{MRP_{X_a}}{MRC_{X_a}} = \frac{MRP_{X_b}}{MRC_{X_b}} = \frac{MRP_{X_c}}{MRC_{X_c}} = \cdots = \frac{MRP_{X_n}}{MRC_{X_n}} = 1.$$

It should be recognized that (1) changes in an input's marginal productivity, (2) changes in the marginal revenue received from the sale of output, or (3) changes in an input's marginal resource cost will tend to change both the proportions and the absolute amounts of the inputs which a firm will find it most profitable to use.

The profit-maximizing rule derived above is applicable to firms operating under any and every type of product and resource market combination. This is necessarily so because, as we have seen, every firm—no matter whether the product and resource market circumstances it faces are perfectly or imperfectly competitive—finds it advantageous to adjust its input rate of a variable resource to the point at which the input's marginal revenue product equals its marginal resource cost.

AN EVALUATION OF THE MARGINAL PRODUCTIVITY APPROACH TO RESOURCE PRICING AND EMPLOYMENT

The discussion in this chapter has so far been chiefly theoretical with little emphasis on actual practice. The principal reason is that something of an abnormal gap exists between theoretical models of the functioning of resource input markets on the one hand and what goes on in the real world on the other hand. This gap has left the economic theories of input pricing, input employment, and income distribution in a very unsettled state, with a host of honest differences prevailing among various authorities.

The problem lies partly with the almost countless number of institutional interferences, market imperfections, and artificially imposed restraints that have gradually become an integral feature of input markets. A representative sample of some of the most important of these interferences and imperfections includes (1) the enactment of minimum wage laws; (2) the exercise of whatever monopoly power unions have to obtain wage increases in excess of productivity gains; (3) the imposing of wage-price controls; (4) restrictive union work rules and featherbedding practices; (5) the long-standing traditions regarding the size of wage differentials between certain types of occupations; (6) job discrimination and wage discrimination based upon race or sex; (7) the educational, apprenticeship, and license-to-practice requirements for entering an occupation; (8) the regulation of rates of return to monopolistic enterprise; (9) the effects of monetary policy upon interest rates; (10) zoning regulations which preclude the use of land for certain types of activities; and (11) the relative immobility of resource inputs among firms, industries, and geographical areas—at least in the short run.

The effects which such factors have upon input prices and employment are well worth illustrating. Two examples will be given, both taken from the labor input sector because of their widespread applicability to real-world events.

THE IMPACT OF MINIMUM WAGE LAWS
UPON LABOR MARKETS

Minimum wage legislation is generally aimed at accomplishing three things: (1) reducing the poverty associated with wage payments which do not afford workers a "decent" standard of living; (2) curtailing the practice whereby marginal firms pay substandard wages to a relatively immobile work force, thus keeping production costs low enough to enable them to compete with other enterprises (this practice is sometimes labeled as "unfair competition"); and (3) increasing the purchasing power of low-income families. For the most part, the firms affected by minimum wage laws are small companies operating on slim profit margins and stressing short-run profits, their work force is non-union, and they have a relatively low capital investment per worker.

The higher wages and higher labor costs which minimum wage laws impose upon the affected firms put them under severe pressure to correct their already precarious cost-price-profit position. When higher minimum wages are legislated, there is likely to arise a sort of "shock effect" which forces the affected firms to upgrade management practices, implement new production technologies, and increase labor performance and efficiency if they are to survive. Several specific responses present themselves, and each has, in fact, been observed to occur in practice. Management can improve plant layout and the quality of supervision; laborsaving equipment can be installed; jobs can be redesigned and streamlined so as to cut back on overall labor requirements; inefficient employees can be weeded out; new employee selection standards can be raised; working conditions can be improved so as to reduce labor turnover and to increase the general efficiency and morale of the firm's labor force; the amount of overtime work offered

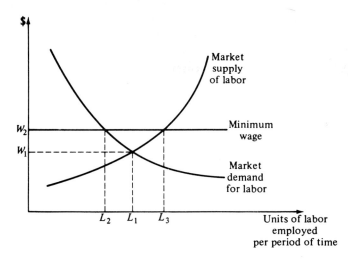

FIGURE 17-10
Employment effect of a minimum wage law

employees can be cut back; jobs which no longer pay their way can be eliminated entirely; and selling prices can be raised to cover the increased labor costs.

But whatever response set each affected firm elects, one important outcome is almost certain to emerge: the opportunities for employment in the affected occupations will be less than otherwise. The minimum wage law will peg the supply price for such labor above the level which would be determined by the forces of market demand and supply for such labor—otherwise the minimum wage has no *raison d'être*. The outcome of a higher-than-equilibrium input supply price is a reduced optimum employment rate, as depicted in Fig. 17-10.[20] If the minimum wage is set at W_2 dollars, given the market demand and supply curves for labor of a particular type, then firms will adjust their employment rate downward from L_1 to L_2 units per period of time, and $L_2 L_3$ units of labor will be involuntarily unemployed. The reduction in employment takes the form of dismissal of the least efficient employees, the closing down of marginal firms, cutbacks in the average number of hours worked per employee, or reductions in the number of new job opportunities in the affected occupations. Studies indicate that the groups hit hardest by the lower employment rates tend to be teenagers, blacks, and persons lacking in skills and training.

[20] Empirical studies of this phenomenon are numerous. See, for instance, *Studies of the Economic Effects of the $1 Minimum Wage: Effects in Selected Low Wage Industries and Localities*, Wage and Hour and Public Contracts Divisions, U.S. Department of Labor, January 1959; H. M. Douty, "Some Effects of the $1.00 Minimum Wage in the United States," *Economica*, Vol. 27, No. 106 (May 1960), pp. 137–147; N. Arnold Tolles, "American Mininum Wage Laws: Their Purposes and Results," *Proceedings of the Twelfth Annual Meeting of the Industrial Relations Research Association* (Madison, Wis.: Industrial Relations Research Association, 1960), pp. 116–133; Neil W. Chamberlain, *The Labor Sector* (New York: McGraw-Hill Book Company, 1965), pp. 529–533; Finis Welch and Marvin Kosters, "The Effects of Minimum Wages on the Distribution of Changes in Aggregate Employment," *American Economic Review*, Vol. 62, No. 3 (June 1972), pp. 323–332; and Finis Welch, "Minimum Wage Legislation in the United States," *Economic Inquiry*, Vol. 12, No. 3 (September 1974), pp. 285–318.

Hence, the economic effect of minimum wage laws upon resource pricing and employment is (1) to push wage rates for the lowest-paid occupations up above the equilibrium rates that would prevail in their absence and (2) to suppress employment rates in the affected occupations. On the other hand, many workers can benefit from a higher minimum wage, owing to the progress made in achieving the three aforementioned objectives of such legislation.[21] Inefficient firms are also forced to bring their operations up to par or else face the penalty of lower profits or even losses. For our purposes, the major point to be noted about minimum wage legislation is that it *artificially* causes the supply prices of low-skill, low-productivity types of labor to be higher than they would be if the forces of market demand and market supply were allowed to function freely. In this sense, governmental policy toward minimum wage rates, as well as labor's marginal productivity, are major factors in determining wages, employment, and income in the affected occupational categories.

It is also worth noting that minimum wage laws can affect wage rates in occupations which carry higher than the minimum wage. A higher minimum wage allows unions to press for further wage increases through collective bargaining. The unions' philosophy is that while they will use their bargaining power to become wage leaders, upward adjustments in the federal minimum rates provide them with a new platform from which they can launch demands for still higher union wages on the grounds of maintaining historical wage differentials.

APPLICATIONS CAPSULE

HOW THE MINIMUM WAGE DESTROYS JOBS
Fortune's Interview with J. Willard Marriott, Jr.

Over the last forty years, six different Administrations have tried to improve the lot of the workingman by raising the minimum wage. The most ambitious of these efforts was a bill signed by President Carter in 1977 that advances the minimum, through annual stepups, to a level of $3.35 by January, 1981—an increase totaling nearly 46 percent. Recently, however, the Administration has been paying some attention to the majority view among economists, which is that the minimum wage worsens inflation and destroys jobs.

With this issue back on the public agenda, FORTUNE'S Aimêe Morner paid a call recently on J. Willard Marriott Jr. As president and chief executive of a hotel and restaurant chain that pays the minimum wage to some 20,000 employees, he has learned a lot about the effects of this well-meaning social legislation on the real world of jobs and prices.

---

[21] When the demand for labor is *inelastic*, a rise in the minimum wage may lessen employment opportunities, but the total income of those who remain employed will definitely be greater than before. However, when the demand for labor is *elastic*, increases in the minimum wage will reduce both employment and the total income accruing to those who remain employed. Hence, only when labor demand is relatively inelastic do increases in the minimum wage have their most beneficial impact.

Q. With two successive jumps in the minimum wage, from $2.30 an hour in 1977 to $2.90 last January 1, what's happened at Marriott?

A. Several months before Congress passed the legislation, we felt it was imminent, so we got ready to combat the effect it would have on our costs. We first set up what I would call productivity specialists, who analyzed primarily how managers in each Marriott unit were utilizing and scheduling labor. Then we organized teams to find ways to reduce the number of man-hours, and the amount of work being done, in order to become more productive—to serve the same number of customers in fewer labor hours, and in some cases with fewer people.

Unlike many other restaurant chains, we did not open our restaurants later, or close them earlier. However, in some cases we closed parts of a restaurant, opening one dining room instead of two. For years we have been shifting to self-service salad bars in our Dinner Houses and other restaurants to cut down the number of waitress hours, and we accelerated that shift.

We achieved what I think are good, though not dramatic, results. Overall, we eliminated more than two million manhours, or about 5 percent of the total. It's very difficult for me to be too precise, because of the growth in our business, and the change in its mix. But we stopped hiring at many locations, and so cut our work force by 2 to 3 percent.

Q. So the increase in the minimum wage wiped out perhaps 1,500 jobs at Marriott?

A. Yes. And though we got a slight increase in productivity, it was not enough to make up for our higher costs. Wages rose by 15 percent in 1978 for employees at the minimum level, and our food costs went up, too. We estimate that we got back less than half of these added costs from gains in productivity, so we had to increase prices in some restaurants by as much as 10 percent.

Unfortunately, as we raise prices, we often lose customers; it's axiomatic. Throughout the restaurant industry, customer counts have not been as strong during the last twelve months as before, and in many of our restaurants customer counts have been down slightly. And as we serve fewer customers, we lay off more people; it becomes cyclical. The National Restaurant Association recently surveyed 2,000 of its members and found that after the minimum wage was increased on January 1, 1978, 95 percent of them raised prices, 78 percent reduced man-hours, 63 percent laid off people, and more than half bought equipment that would help them reduce their labor force. But it's hard to automate restaurants and hotels—they haven't invented a machine yet that makes beds.

Q. Who gets hit the hardest when the minimum goes up?

A. What's happening as it keeps rising is that more people such as wives are coming into the work force, replacing teenagers. Restaurant owners screen people better, and by and large hire more mature, more productive people at the higher rates.

Q. Of course, that is to your advantage.

A. True, but as we pay those higher rates, we in turn have to raise our prices, and nobody wants to do that. Given the option, I would prefer to hire people at a more reasonable wage and train them.

Q. Economists now agree that increases in the minimum wage reduce employment, mostly among minorities and teenagers, and yet they have little empirical evidence to prove their theory. Do you have any definitive proof that the phenomenon occurs?

A. I can give you a concrete example. We used to have about twenty restaurants in the District of Columbia, which has traditionally had one of the highest minimum-wage levels in the U.S.—until recently even higher than the federal minimum. The cost of wages is our highest cost of doing business. And during the last three or four years, as the minimum wage increased in Washington, our wage situation became so acute that we had to close fourteen restaurants and terminate 1,300 people, about a third of whom were minority youths.

When we close restaurants located in a center city, the minorities who lose their jobs often are unable to find other work nearby, or in the suburbs. The few jobs that are available in the suburbs go to the most productive workers, and in most cases these minority youths are just not as experienced as other workers. It's a terrible social problem.

What happens if 37 percent of the minority youths in this country reach age twenty and have never worked and are on the government dole? There is already a tremendous number of these people enrolled in government make-work programs. In fact, it's estimated that the government's bill for programs like CETA—the Comprehensive Employment and Training Act—will increase by $135 million this year because the minimum wage rose to $2.90. The government doesn't want to be in the business of hiring people and training people—it wants business to do that. But it's not economic for business to do that as long as the minimum wage keeps going up.

Q. The minimum wage for employees who work for tips stood at $1.33 last year, and rose to $1.60 on January 1. How will that increase of 20 percent affect operations at Marriott?

A. The tip credit, as it is called, is a serious concern of ours. This year it is being reduced for the first time, from 50 percent of the minimum wage, to 45 percent. That is, employees who get tips must be paid 55 percent of the regular minimum wage. Most tipped employees earn between three and five times their base wage as tips. So a 20 percent increase in their hourly base pay, or $2.16 a day, is peanuts compared with their earnings from tips, which can run more than $50 a day. But an increase of 27 cents an hour in the base wage is very costly to the employer. It's going to change the way the restaurant business is run, and eliminate many minimum-wage jobs.

There will be less specialization. In the past, a waitress only waited on tables. Today she makes fountain items, cuts pie, and clears tables. That reduces the need for fountain boys and busboys. As the minimum wage continues to rise, there will be more self-service, which will cut down the number of waitresses needed, too. We have to continue to improve efficiency, but I don't know how much more creative we can be without hurting the service.

Q. Does a higher minimum kick up wages all along the line of Marriott?

A. Yes. On January 1, 1978, the minimum wage rose by 15.2 percent, to $2.65. At Marriott, many workers at the next higher level got an automatic 10 percent increase, and at the next higher level, an 8 percent increase. A person in our Houston hotel earning $3, for example, got a raise to $3.25; a person making $2.60 got a raise to $2.85. The reason is very simple: if you've had a person working for you for a year or so, doing a good job, and making $2.75 an hour in 1978, and you hire a youngster off the street at $2.65 an hour, you've got an inequitable situation. That longer-term employee will come to you and say he's worth more than that kid is, and wants an increase in pay. We tell him we can't give him 15.2 percent, but we recognize the inequitable situation, and so we'll give him 10 percent. And, of course, our costs for Social Security and benefits rise because of the higher wages paid.

Q. Union leaders, notably George Meany, argue that as the minimum wage is increased the lowest-paid workers will have more money to spend, and so the entire economy benefits. Do you agree?

A. That's just a superficial argument. The labor unions want the minimum wage to increase because that gives them a better floor from which to bargain for higher wages for their members. Most of our workers are not unionized, but we know that the higher the minimum wage is, the greater the ripple effect—and the same thing occurs among unionized workers.

You must consider the fact that people who earn the minimum wage do not take home as much money after each increase, because they work fewer hours. Very few of our employees are putting in forty hours a week, though they may have done so two years ago; most of them work about thirty hours a week. We now schedule our workers so that we don't pay overtime, and neither do most companies in our industry.

Q. Then who benefits from an increase in the minimum wage?

A. I think everybody loses. Employees lose because their hours are shortened, so they take home fewer dollars. And at the same time, the minimum wage is inflationary, and inflation hits each worker in the pocketbook. People coming into the labor force lose because there is a strong tendency on the part of employers to hire more productive workers instead. And in a downturn in the economy, the less productive workers are the first to be put out of their jobs and onto welfare. In the end, the minimum wage practically wrecks the people it is supposed to help.

Q. So you would agree with Finis Welch, an economist at U.C.L.A., that the time for a mandated minimum wage has passed?

A. I think there needs to be a maintenance-level minimum wage to protect people from unscrupulous employers, of which there are probably some throughout the country. But a federal minimum wage at any level fails to take into account the characteristics of different regions. In many southern cities, we could probably hire quite a few people for $2.30 an hour, but we have to pay $2.90 an hour because somebody in Washington tells us to, and so we hire fewer workers.

I think a minimum-wage level should be set by each state, instead of by the federal government, and it should be based on a fair wage for each geographical area. Some forty-one states have a minimum wage, but in most cases it applies only if it is higher than the federal level. Only Alaska and Connecticut now have a higher minimum than the federal minimum. So, let each state determine its own minimum wage—or roll back the federal minimum to a level, say $2.30, that would not prevent people from coming into the work force.

Source: Reprinted from the January 29, 1979 issue of *Fortune* magazine by special permission; © Time, Inc.

UNION IMPACTS ON LABOR MARKETS

In modern industrial economies trade unions are an integral and accepted part of the functioning of labor markets, especially in the manufacturing sector. In the United States, nearly 85% of the workers in plants employing 100 workers or more are unionized; union membership totals approximately 18 million persons; and the pattern-setting wage settlements reached in certain key industries are quickly transmitted to other sectors of the economy. Thus, unions have a major impact upon national labor markets; their presence does make a difference. The added power workers gain by union organization creates a very strong presumption that the resulting wage and employment rates will be different from what they would have been had workers remained unorganized. Consequently, any analysis of wage rates and employment which ignores the impact of collective bargaining is suspect in its ability to explain and to predict the behavior of real-world labor markets.

Incorporating union behavior into the analysis of labor markets first requires some notion of the economic goals of unions. Casual observation suggests that unions pursue some satisfactory, and perhaps quite complex, balance of increased wages and incomes, increased leisure, and an adequate number of job opportunities for current and potential union members. However, depending on their own unique circumstances, different unions may place differing emphases and priorities on these goals; collective bargaining is by no means a uniform process whereby each union consistently pursues the same goals with the same intensity.

The Wage-Employment Preference Path

A union's preferred trade-off between wages and employment can be viewed graphically. Suppose collective negotiations between a firm and a union result in the establishment of an average wage of W_1 dollars and an equilibrium employment rate of L_1 units of labor per period of time, as shown in Fig. 17-11(a). Now consider the combination of wage and employment rates which the union would prefer and which it will attempt to attain in its negotiations with the firm. If the firm's product demand should shift in such a manner that its demand for labor input shifts from D_{L_1} to D_{L_2}, the union's preference is generally for substantial wage increases, say from W_1 to W_2 (which may, incidentally, be in the form of overtime wages), and modest increases in the number of persons employed, say from L_1 to L_2. This reflects the usual union attitude that its first responsibility is to the existing membership and that it is obliged to win them higher wages whenever the opportunity presents. Hence, the union's preference path is a steeply rising curve above the initial wage-employment combination.[22] However, the stronger the rise in the firm's demand for labor, the more the union is ordinarily willing to temper its wage demands in return for increases in employment (and

---

[22] An exception to this general case arises in instances where large numbers of union members are unemployed at the prevailing wage-employment combination. Here the union will probably pursue a policy of getting the unemployed members back to work before seeking major wage advances.

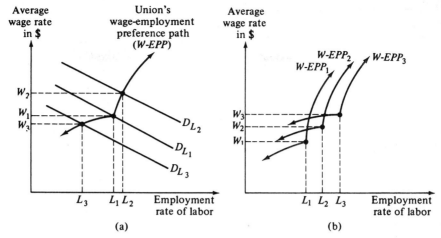

FIGURE 17-11
Wage-employment preference path of a typical union

gains in union membership). For this reason the portion of the union's preferred wage-employment path above the prevailing wage-employment combination is shown as rising at a decreasing rate.

If economic conditions should shift the firm's demand for labor input downward, say from D_{L_1} to D_{L_2}, the union usually exhibits a strong preference for larger cutbacks in employment (say from L_1 to L_3) relative to wages (which might be reduced from W_1 to W_3). The reasoning behind such a preference is that wage reductions weaken the ability of the union to win wage gains in future bargaining sessions, whereas employment cutbacks are self-correcting as soon as business conditions pick up again.[23] Hence, the lower section of the wage-employment preference path falls slowly and at a rate commensurate with employment reductions that are more than proportional to the wage reductions.[24] The union's wage-employment preferences therefore tend to produce a curvilinear pattern, kinked at the current wage-employment position. As new wage negotiations are consummated, the curve shifts to a new position, and a kink appears at the newly instituted wage-employment combination, as depicted in Fig. 17-11(b).

In viewing the union's wage-employment preferences, care must be taken not to view employment as referring solely to the number of workers employed. A firm's employment *rate* (L) is composed of n number of workers working h

[23] An excellent discussion of the tactical advantages which the union receives from following such a policy is found in Allan M. Cartter and F. Ray Marshall, *Labor Economics: Wages, Employment, and Trade Unionism*, rev. ed. (Homewood, Ill.: Richard D. Irwin, Inc., 1972), pp. 245–246.

[24] The preferred wage-employment path may fall off to the left more sharply if significant employment cutbacks have been recently imposed and many union members are already laid off. In such instances a union often is more amenable to cutting wages and maintaining employment, in which case the lower section of the curve reflects a preference for relatively larger wage cuts and relatively smaller employment cuts.

number of hours per period of time. Thus, a reduction in the union's preferred employment rate may reflect preferences for cutbacks in the number of workers *or* in the number of hours worked by each worker *or* both. Similarly, increases in the union's preferred employment rate may mean more workers *or* more hours worked by each worker *or* both. By observing the composition of the employment rate the union bargains for over a period of time, it is possible to infer what the union's preference is toward greater membership versus more leisure time for the rank and file. Therefore, the union's wage-employment preference curve is indicative not only of the union's wage (and income) goal and its employment (and membership) goal but also of its leisure-time goal.[25]

To the extent that unions are successful in imposing their wage-employment preferences upon firms we have at least a partial explanation of why wages rise at above-average rates in periods of strong business expansion, yet employment gains are modest, and why wage cutbacks are usually agreed to only when a union confronts severe layoffs and permanent employment reductions or when an employer is in great financial distress. Such wage-employment behavior is particularly prevalent in the corporate sector where most firms have unionized labor forces.

The Effects of Unions on a Firm's Use of Labor

From a supply standpoint the effect of union-negotiated wage rates is to make the firm's supply curve for union labor horizontal (or perfectly elastic) at the agreed-to wage scale, at least until the supply of labor runs out at these wage rates. This is illustrated in Fig. 17-12, where the firm's supply curve for labor in a nonunion (though still imperfectly competitive) labor market is S_L, the corresponding marginal resource cost curve for labor is MRC_L, and the firm's demand for labor is D_L, the last reflecting the firm's marginal revenue product of labor in an imperfectly competitive product market. The intersection of MRC_L and MRP_L determine the equilibrium wage and employment rates for the firm—W_1 and L_1, respectively.

But if a union organizes the firm's employees and uses its bargaining power to push the effective average wage rate to W_2, the firm's supply curve for labor becomes the kinked line W_2CAS_L, which is horizontal over the range W_2CA. Observe the effect this has upon the unionized firm's optimum employment rate. Since the unionized firm's labor supply curve is the line W_2CAS_L, the firm's marginal resource cost curve for labor becomes $W_2CABMRC_L$. A new intersec-

---

[25] Unions historically have shown a keen interest in shortening the standard workday and workweek. During periods of depressed business conditions, shorter working hours are a means of sharing the available work among greater numbers of people. During periods of prosperity, the shorter workweek is a means of raising wage rates by instituting time-and-a-half overtime rates after fewer hours worked. On occasions, unions may find it easier to persuade firms to pay workers the same total income but allow them to work fewer hours to earn it (which is equivalent to raising the average wage rate) than to persuade them to pay workers a higher wage rate for working the same number of hours as before. The former does not raise the firm's total labor costs provided the same amount of work can be accomplished in the fewer working hours, whereas the latter is sure to increase the firm's total wage bill.

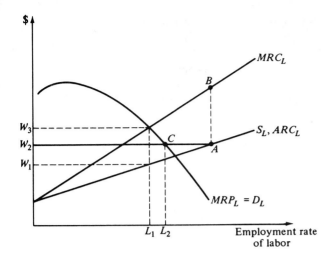

FIGURE 17-12
Effect of union-negotiated wage rates upon the firm's labor input decision

tion of MRC_L and MRP_L occurs at point C, giving an equilibrium employment rate of L_2 units. Thus, not only can the union benefit its members by increasing wages, but it can also increase employment rates because of the effect which contract wage rates have upon the shape of the firm's labor supply curve. Actually, the union can push the average wage rate all the way up to W_3 before the firm finds it advantageous to reduce its labor employment rate below the preunionization rate of L_1 units. Thus, we have the rather surprising conclusion that a union *may* initially have the effect of increasing both a firm's average wage rate and its employment rate, provided it does not insist upon pushing the wage rate up too far. This indeed constitutes a powerful argument in favor of unions—at least from the standpoint of union members.

Referring again to Fig. 17-12, suppose that the union bargains for and gets wage increases that push the average wage above W_3, thereby making it advantageous for the firm to cut its employment rate below L_1. Further suppose that the union views this cutback as undesirable. The union can then use its bargaining power to preclude the firm from so reducing labor employment. A major aspect of collective negotiations between unions and managements concerns working conditions and, in particular, such matters as the content of jobs, how certain operations are to be performed, the size of work crews, the quantity of work which can be expected, safety rules, the length of paid vacations, the number of paid holidays, seniority provisions, guaranteed annual wages, and supplemental unemployment benefits. In other words, there is a *work and effort bargain* in the contract, just as there is a wage bargain. A principal effect of the provisions relating to the work and effort bargain is to give unions a measure of influence over the firm's employment rate, either directly or indirectly—at least in the short run.

Experience clearly indicates that unions use these provisions to "make work" and to keep the number of persons employed in specific jobs, firms, and industries higher than managements might otherwise maintain. The notorious instances of featherbedding in the railroad industry and the output quotas in the construction industry are classic cases in point. Consequently, in a unionized firm the mere fact that labor's *MRC* exceeds its *MRP* is no guarantee that the firm will adjust its input of labor downward. The discretionary action of the firm's managers in regard to the labor input decision is heavily constrained by the provisions of its collective bargaining contract. Because of this, managers of unionized firms find strict adherence to the *MRC = MRP* rule a practical impossibility; work schedules, job assignments, and work loads can be altered only within limits. To some extent, therefore, the marginal productivity approach to input pricing and input employment is impeded, if not replaced, by the institutional mechanism of collective bargaining insofar as unionized firms are concerned. However, since most managements retain authority over the capital-labor input mix in building new production facilities, the power of unions to influence employment rates in the long run is somewhat less; and some companies try to escape high labor costs by relocating plants to foreign countries where wages are much lower.

The Effects of Unions on Economy-wide Wage Rates and Employment Rates

Few economists would deny that unions in certain firms and industries have won favorable wage and benefit packages for their members. But whether unions have pushed wages up faster than they would have risen anyway is a much trickier (and hotly contested) issue.[26] Significantly, the issue defies precise resolution, since it involves a comparison of what has actually happened with what might have happened under another set of circumstances. There simply is no way of knowing for sure what the relative wages of various industries would be if all industries were nonunion; any estimates to this effect are little better than educated conjectures.[27] Even so, it seems fair to say that unions are in a good position

[26] The literature on this issue is large and contains a number of studies with conflicting findings. The interested reader should consult, among others, Arthur Ross and William Goldner, "Forces Affecting the Interindustry Wage Structure," *Quarterly Journal of Economics*, Vol. 64, No. 2 (May 1950), pp. 254–281; Harry Douty, "Union and Nonunion Wages," in *Employment and Wages in the United States*, W. S. Woytinsky and Associates, eds. (New York: Twentieth Century Fund, 1953), pp. 493–501; Frank C. Pierson, "The Economic Influence of Big Unions," in *Labor Relations in an Expanding Economy*, Annals of the American Academy of Political and Social Science, January 1961, pp. 96–107; Martin Segal, "Unionism and Wage Movements," *Southern Economic Journal*, Vol. 28, No. 2 (October 1961), pp. 174–181; Albert Rees, *The Economics of Trade Unions* (Chicago: University of Chicago Press, 1962), Chapter 4; Gregg Lewis, *Unionism and Relative Wages in the United States* (Chicago: University of Chicago Press, 1963); and Vernon T. Clover, "Compensation in Union and Nonunion Plants 1960–1965," *Industrial and Labor Relations Review*, Vol. 21, No. 2 (January 1968), pp. 226–233.

[27] Comparisons of wage movements between union and nonunion firms and industries are not really very satisfactory because of the differences which exist in geographical location, sizes and types of firms, competitive pressures, technological processes, the proportion of labor costs to total costs, productivity changes, and so on. These factors, as well as the presence or absence of a union, affect wage movements and parceling out their separate effects presents almost insurmountable statistical difficulties.

to win "above-average" wage gains on a consistent basis when (1) the percentage of unionized firms in the industry is high and it is difficult for nonunion firms to enter; (2) bargaining is on an industrywide basis so that all firms in the industry are equally affected; (3) industry and firm profits are high enough that the firms can "afford" substantial wage increases without endangering their competitive position; (4) the industry is a strategic one such that work stoppages have serious economy-wide implications; and (5) the union controls entry to the trade via apprenticeship and other regulations.

In most occupational categories, wage rates in unionized firms exceed those in nonunion enterprises—even after allowing for differences in regional location, size of firm, size of community, and type of pay system (incentive wages or hourly wages).[28] Moreover, it is in the corporate sector where unions are strongest and where newly negotiated collective bargaining pacts often set the pattern of wage changes for blue-collar workers throughout the economy. In manufacturing, large-scale firms have proven easier to organize than small companies mainly because some of the above conditions appear more frequently in the corporate sector than in small-firm-dominated industries. The capacity of corporate oligopolists to pass along higher wage costs in the form of higher prices offers unions an attractive target.

The wage-raising effects of collective bargaining, to whatever extent they exist, therefore usually fall most heavily upon corporate oligopolists. As a consequence, the supply price of the blue-collar labor services to large corporations *tends* to be higher than for small entrepreneurial firms—a trait which partially accounts for the propensity of large-scale firms to substitute capital for production labor.

SUMMARY AND CONCLUSIONS

The marginal productivity approach to input pricing and input employment is a systematic attempt to analyze the principles governing a firm's input decision and to explain the functioning of the markets for resource inputs. Three basic models of input pricing and employment stand out: (1) the model of perfect competition in both product and resource markets, (2) the model of imperfect competition in the product market and perfect competition in the resource market, and (3) the model of imperfect competition in both product and resource markets. In all three models, one theme underlies the firm's input decision: To maximize profits a firm should adjust the usage of each input to the point where the added revenue it receives from using the last unit of the input equals the added costs associated with employing the input. A firm's usage of an input depends on what the input is worth to the firm relative to the costs of using it. This principle holds irrespective of the type of market circumstance in which the firm's product is sold or in which the input is purchased. It is from the $MRP = MRC$ rule that input prices and

---

[28] Douty, "Union and Nonunion Wages," pp. 496–497.

input employment rates are ultimately determined and the incomes accruing to resource owners are ultimately derived.

As a first approximation to the functioning of input markets, the demand and supply analyses of the three marginal productivity models is relatively sound. However, there exist numerous imperfections in and barriers to the free interplay of market forces. Collective bargaining, minimum wage laws, wage-price controls, and resource immobility, to mention only the more important, impede the attainment of free market equilibrium and cause outcomes which may deviate far and long from the equilibrium position suggested by marginal productivity analysis.

SUGGESTED READINGS

BAUMOL, W. J., *Economic Theory and Operations Analysis*, 3rd ed. (Englewood Cliffs, N.J.: Prentice-Hall, Inc., 1972), Chapters 16, and 17.

BISHOP, R. L., "A Firm's Short-Run and Long-Run Demands for a Factor," *Western Economic Journal*, Vol. 5 No. 1 (March 1967), pp. 122–140.

CARTTER, A. M., AND F. R. MARSHALL, *Labor Economics: Wages, Employment and Trade Unionism*, rev. ed. (Homewood, Ill.: Richard D. Irwin, Inc., 1972), Chapters 8–11 and 13.

FERGUSON, C. E., *The Neoclassical Theory of Production and Distribution* (New York: Cambridge University Press, 1969), Chapters 6, 7, 9, 11, and 12.

PIERSON, F. C., "An Evaluation of Wage Theory," *New Concepts in Wage Determination*, G. W. Taylor and C. Pierson, eds. (New York: McGraw-Hill Book Company, 1957), pp. 3–31.

REDER, M., "The Theory of Union Wage Policy," *Review of Economics and Statistics*, Vol. 34, No. 1 (February 1952), pp. 34–55.

REES, A., "The Effects of Unions on Resource Allocation," *Journal of Law and Economics*, Vol. 6 (October 1963), pp. 69–78.

———, *The Economics of Work and Pay* (New York: Harper & Row, Publishers, 1973).

RUSSELL, R. R., "A Graphical Proof of the Impossibility of a Positively Inclined Demand Curve for a Factor of Production," *American Economic Review*, Vol. 54, No. 5 (September 1964), pp. 726–732, and the critique of this proof by D. M. Winch, "The Demand Curve for a Factor of Production: Comment," *American Economic Review*, Vol. 55, No. 4 (September 1965), pp. 856–861.

WELCH, F., "Minimum Wage Legislation in the United States," *Economic Inquiry*, Vol. 12, No. 3 (September 1974), pp. 285–318.

PROBLEMS AND QUESTIONS FOR DISCUSSION

1. **(a)** Explain the difference between marginal revenue and marginal revenue product.
   (b) Explain the difference between marginal cost and marginal resource cost.

(c) What is the relationship between an input's *SVMP* and its *MRP* when the output is sold under conditions of perfect competition? Under conditions of imperfect competition?

2. Complete the following table:

Units of Variable Input X	Quantity of Output	MP$_X$	Product Price	TR	MRP$_X$	Supply Price of X	MRC$_X$
0	0	———	$5	———	———	$50	———
1	20	———	5	———	———	50	———
2	44	———	5	———	———	50	———
3	64	———	5	———	———	50	———
4	80	———	5	———	———	50	———
5	92	———	5	———	———	50	———
6	100	———	5	———	———	50	———
7	104	———	5	———	———	50	———

(a) Do the figures in the table suggest a perfectly or imperfectly competitive product market? Why? Do the figures indicate a perfectly or imperfectly competitive input market? Why?

(b) What is the profit-maximizing input of X?

3. Suppose that a firm employs only one variable input (X) and that the equation expressing the firm's marginal revenue product function for X is $MRP_X = 60 + 4X - X^2$. Suppose the firm's supply price for input X is fixed at $28 per unit. What is the firm's profit-maximizing input rate of X?

4. Complete the following table showing production, cost, and revenue data for a firm having only one variable input:

Units of Variable Input X	Quantity of Output	MP$_X$	Product Price	TR	"Average" MR	MRP$_X$	Supply Price of X	TVC	MRC$_X$
0	0	———	$25	———	———	———	$400	———	———
1	50	———	24	———	———	———	420	———	———
2	110	———	23	———	———	———	440	———	———
3	160	———	22	———	———	———	460	———	———
4	200	———	21	———	———	———	480	———	———
5	230	———	20	———	———	———	500	———	———
6	250	———	19	———	———	———	520	———	———
7	260	———	18	———	———	———	540	———	———

(a) What type of product and resource markets are indicated by the figures in the table?

(b) What is the profit-maximizing input rate of X?

5. The Alpha-Omega Corporation uses only one variable input in its production process—input X. Studies of the firm's revenue data indicate the following relationship between *TR* and the input rate of X: $TR = 144 + 70X - X^2$. Studies also indicate that the input supply curve for X which confronts Alpha-Omega may be expressed by the equation $P_X = 13 + 0.5X$. Determine the profit-maximizing input rate for X.

6. Given the following data for labor input, product prices, and wage rates:

Number of Workers of a Given Skill and Training	"Average" MP_L	Product Price	Daily Wage ($P_L = ARC_L$)
0	—	$2	—
10	18	2	$12
20	17	2	14
30	16	2	16
40	15	2	18
50	14	2	20
60	13	2	22
70	12	2	24
80	11	2	26

(a) Determine the profit-maximizing employment rate of labor and the equilibrium daily wage for a firm faced with the above schedules.

(b) Suppose a minimum daily wage of $24 is imposed upon the firm. Determine the profit-maximizing employment rate of labor.

(c) How do you reconcile the differences, if any, in your answers to parts (a) and (b)? Explain fully.

7. Consider the following two statements:

"An increase in the demand for an input raises its price."
"An increase in an input's price reduces demand for the input."

How can this pair of statements be reconciled? Does it make any difference in your answer whether perfect or imperfect competition characterizes the input market? The product market?

8. It has sometimes been advocated that firms should reward inputs according to their respective marginal products. That is, if the last unit of an input has a marginal product of 10 units and if these 10 units have a market value of $50, then the input is entitled to a monetary reward of $50. Any payment less than $50 entails "exploitation" of the input. What validity, if any, do you see in this position?

9. Suppose that input X is the only variable input which a firm uses to produce product A. The firm sells product A under conditions of imperfect competition and buys input X under conditions of imperfect competition. What effect would you expect each of the following to have upon the firm's usage of input X? Be sure to distinguish between a movement along the firm's demand curve for X and a shift in the location of the demand curve. If any uncertainty exists as to the impact upon the usage of X, then specify the causes of the uncertainty.

(a) An increase in the demand for product A.

(b) The appearance of a new and very good substitute for product A.

(c) A technological improvement in the capital equipment which input X works with in producing product A.

(d) An increase in the supply of input X.

10. Average wage rates in the United States are higher than in most foreign countries. Business executives in the U.S. often lament that this puts their firms at a severe cost disadvantage in competing with foreign firms. Unions reply that U.S. workers are generally healthier and better trained than workers in foreign nations and, further, that U.S. workers generally have more and better capital equipment with which to work. These factors, the unions claim, offset the wage rate differential.

(a) Explain the rationale of the union argument in terms of marginal productivity analysis.

(b) In recent years, Japan and several Western European nations have greatly closed the gap in worker productivity by raising the living standards of their population and by adopting the very latest production technologies. What implications does this have for the ability of U.S. firms to continue to pay higher wages and still compete in world markets?

(c) Would you expect that some U.S. firms paying higher wages and incurring greater labor costs than key foreign competitors might eventually be forced to negotiate *lower* wage and fringe benefit packages with unions in order to remain cost competitive? What posture would you expect union officials to take with regard to wage reduction proposals? What sort of wage-employment preference path would you expect unions to have in these situations?

18

GENERAL EQUILIBRIUM
Consumers, firms, markets, the economy

Preceding chapters have examined the individually made economic decisions of consumers, firms, and resource owners and the functioning of both product and resource markets. The behavior of consumers, firms, and specific types of markets has been viewed in isolation from the rest of the economy, mainly because one cannot undertake a detailed analysis of everything at once and not because it actually works this way in the real world. In fact, of course, the decisions and behavior of consumers interact with and affect the decisions and behavior of firms; the decisions and behavior of firms interact with and affect the functioning of product and resource markets; and the operations of product and resource markets interact with and affect economic activity as a whole. Indeed, whatever goes on in one part of the economy affects, either directly or indirectly, what goes on in another part, though sometimes the relationship is negligible or imperceptible. The point is that individual economic units and markets, taken together, make up an economy. Microeconomics is ultimately very concerned about how these units and markets fit together and how well the resulting *economic system* functions.

This chapter explores the branch of microeconomics that deals with the interactions and interrelationships among consumers, firms, and markets as part of a whole economy. Attention is first directed toward the conditions requisite for establishing static general equilibrium throughout the economy. Next, the analysis shifts to the problem of maintaining economywide equilibrium over time, with emphasis on stable, long-term growth.

STATIC EQUILIBRIUM ON AN ECONOMY-WIDE BASIS

In broad terms, *general equilibrium* for an entire economy exists when all economic units simultaneously achieve equilibrium positions, when the quantity demanded equals the quantity supplied in each and every product and resource market, and when the major economic sectors are in balance. Suppose we examine these conditions in a bit more detail.

The Conditions of General Equilibrium

Given the limitations of income and the prices that must be paid in exchange for goods and services, a consumer is in equilibrium when his expenditure-saving mix yields maximum satisfaction. This requires not only that a consumer make full utilization of income but that purchases be arranged such that the marginal utility per dollar spent on the last unit of each item is equal for all goods and services actually purchased. For general equilibrium to prevail, all consumers must be at their perceived utility-maximizing equilibrium positions. However, this is not to say that consumers are guaranteed complete satisfaction or happiness in this mechanism. All that is implied is that they are doing the very best they can do, given the prevailing set of circumstances.

A business firm is in equilibrium when its product prices, output rates, and input rates have been adjusted to the point where the firm attains its set of goals (profit, sales, market share, and so on) to the fullest extent that demand and cost conditions will permit. As a point of clarification, it is long-run, not short-run, equilibrium that is the pertinent equilibrium state for the firm, because short-run equilibrium positions are temporary and market forces are working to move the firm to the long-run equilibrium position. Firms cannot really be said to be in a state of rest with no incentive or opportunity to make adjustments unless the markets in which they operate are in long-run equilibrium.

A resource owner is in equilibrium when the resource inputs owned or controlled are employed to their maximum advantage, balancing the consideration of monetary reward with nonmonetary preferences. More specifically, workers are supplying labor at equilibrium rates when they have attained the most advantageous combination of work, leisure, and income, subject to the constraints imposed by their skills and abilities and the realizable opportunities for employment. The owners of property resources, being less affected by nonmonetary elements in deploying such resources, may be viewed as supplying property resources at equilibrium rates when the latter are allocated to the uses yielding the highest long-run monetary income and taking into consideration the attitudes of resource owners toward risk.

For the equilibrium conditions of consumers, business firms, and resource owners to be met simultaneously, a number of other less apparent conditions must be present. First, general equilibrium requires the price and output rate for each separate product to be pegged at levels consistent with demand and supply. Neither surplus nor shortage conditions for a good or service can exist, since the presence of either will elicit price and/or output rate adjustments by the firms concerned.

Second, the equilibrium which emerges in each product market must be based not only upon the particular demand and supply conditions for that product in isolation but also upon demand and supply conditions for complementary and substitute products. That is, the various prices and output rates for all items must be mutually consistent. The flows of goods and services through the economy must not result in the accumulation of surpluses in one sector and the appearance of shortages in another. This requirement is in recognition of the interdependencies among goods and services. (We shall elaborate upon the specifics of this requirement later in the chapter.)

Third, the same equilibrium characteristics of product markets must be present in resource input markets. Input prices and employment rates must be at positions which allow for a mutually consistent equilibrium *across* resource markets as well as for equilibrium in a particular resource market. The average price of each input must call forth an overall supply of that input which, when allocated among the alternative uses of the input, results both in equilibrium employment rates in each of the alternative firms and industries and in an equilibrium demand-supply combination for the input on an economywide bais. Given the prevailing patterns of input prices, firms must have no motive for changing their input mix.

Although the market mechanisms of changing prices, output rates, and input rates are most prominent in the process of reaching equilibrium, other factors are present. Underneath the surface are the guiding forces of consumer tastes and preferences, production and managerial technologies, limitations of resource supplies, business goals, and national priorities. In a static analysis, these forces are generally assumed to be constant. Provided that they remain fixed long enough, it is conceivable that the entire pattern of economic activity could adjust to them. Then each product and resource market would reach its own unique equilibrium, the equilibrium results in all markets would be consistent, and no forces would be acting to cause further adjustments. The economic system would settle into a fixed pattern whereby the same amount of the same good/service would be produced via the same technology-input mix by the same firms and would be bought by the same consumers with the same-sized incomes. The overall rate of economic activity would neither rise nor fall. This state of affairs is what is meant by *static general equilibrium.*[1]

---

[1] Economic theorists have spent a great deal of time and energy formulating mathematical models and deriving sets of equations in an effort to determine whether general equilibrium is possible. Most of the modern work has concerned general equilibrium in a *perfectly competitive environment*, primarily because of the mathematical simplicity and neatness of the perfectly competitive model. The results of these efforts do indicate that in a perfectly competitive economy it is possible to achieve general equilibrium without imposing unacceptable constraints upon the values of the relevant economic variables. However, no set of reasonably realistic, sufficient conditions for a stable equilibrium has yet been presented. For a simplified mathematical treatment of the theory of general equilibrium in a perfectly competitive economy, the reader is referred to K. J. Cohen and R. M. Cyert, *Theory of the Firm: Resource Allocation in a Market Economy*, 2nd ed. (Englewood Cliffs, N.J.: Prentice-Hall, Inc., 1975), Chapter 11. For more advanced discussions, see J. Quirk and R. Saposnik, *Introduction to General Equilibrium Theory and Welfare Economics* (New York: McGraw-Hill Book Company, 1968); R. E. Kuenne, *The Theory of General Economic Equilibrium* (Princeton, N.J.: Princeton

The Interrelationships of Industries and Markets

The complexities of static general equilibrium are worth further exploration, especially as concerns the interrelatedness of product and resource markets. Suppose initially that a state of static general equilibrium exists and there then occurs a significant increase in the demand of consumers for mobile homes. Let us trace through some of the chief effects of this "disturbance" upon the system of markets.

The first response to the demand increase will be a shift in the optimum price of mobile homes. Most likely, the retail prices of mobile homes will stiffen (the discounts from list prices will be smaller) as retailers discover the greater willingness of consumers to pay a higher net price. The brisk sales stemming from the rise in demand will prompt the sellers of mobile homes to increase the orders they place with manufacturers. The mobile home manufacturers can be counted upon to react to the influx of new orders by stepping up production rates and perhaps by raising wholesale prices, depending on how hard pressed they are to fill the additional orders from retailers and depending on their relative preferences for more profits, faster growth, a larger market share, and so on. The rise in the output of mobile homes will affect the demand of those firms manufacturing the resource inputs used in the production of mobile homes—sheet aluminum, window glass, axles, tires, sinks, shower stalls, carpeting, electric wiring supplies, and light fixtures, as well as the labor services of the various semiskilled and skilled construction workers needed for the mobile home assembling process. Since these resource inputs will have to be bid away from other uses, their prices will tend to be pulled upward. The mobile home manufacturers, by intensifying the competition for the needed resource inputs, will be forced to increase their offer prices for inputs. As this occurs, the firms losing the inputs may find it necessary to increase their offer prices in order to counteract the shift of needed inputs to the mobile home industry. The higher input prices imply rising costs and narrowing profit margins in the affected firms and industries.

University Press, 1963); Kenneth J. Arrow and Gerard Debreu, "Existence of an Equilibrium for a Competitive Economy," *Econometrica*, Vol. 22, No. 3 (July 1954), pp. 265–289; and Lionel McKenzie, "On the Existence of General Equilibrium for a Competitive Market," *Econometrica*, Vol. 27, No. 1 (January 1959), pp. 54–71.

But while it is valuable to be able to demonstrate that general equilibrium can exist in a perfectly competitive economy, the fact remains that real-world economies are far removed from being perfectly competitive and are becoming even further removed as the trend toward a corporate economy proceeds to run its course. Thus, the more relevant theoretical question revolves around the possibilities of an internally consistent general equilibrium in an *imperfectly competitive environment*. This problem so far has not been satisfactorily resolved by economic theorists, although in recent years it has received increasing attention. See Wassily Leontief, *The Structure of the American Economy* (New York: Oxford University Press, 1951), and the articles by Kenneth Arrow, John Lintner, and Robert Solow in *The Corporate Economy: Growth, Competition, and Innovative Potential*, Robin Marris and Adrian Wood, eds. (Cambridge, Mass.: Harvard University Press, 1971).

Since the mathematics of general equilibrium in an imperfectly competitive environment entails a degree of sophistication well beyond the scope of this book, we shall confine our discussion to presenting a conceptual framework for economy-wide equilibrium in a competitive (but not perfectly so) market economy, sidestepping the issue of whether the conditions required are in fact wholly compatible with each other.

Furthermore, should the induced shift of labor to the mobile home industry entail either a geographic relocation of workers and their families or the construction of new mobile home production facilities in areas where the needed supply of labor is available, the construction firms and the suppliers of building materials will experience an increase in the demand for their products (either from the demand for new housing or from the demand for new production facilities). This will further enlarge the affected product and resource markets, requiring additional price, output, and input adjustments.

However, the effects of the increase in the demand for mobile homes do not just reverberate back through the shifts in the input demands of the mobile home manufacturers. The higher demand for mobile homes will increase the demand for mobile home spaces in trailer parks, for compactly styled furniture, for equipment and accessories to transport mobile homes, and for the extension of more utility services to mobile homes. In addition, increases in mobile home ownership will elicit changes in the demand for other types of living accommodations—apartments, rental dwellings, and family-owned residences—thereby causing further adjustments in the residential construction and building materials industry. All the businesses catering to consumer loans, home mortgages, and real estate financing (banks, savings and loan associations, and finance companies) will feel the effects of the resulting rise in the demand for credit to finance the purchase of mobile homes in comparison with the demand for credit to finance other dwellings. Insurance companies will need to respond to the shift in the demand for various types of homeowner's policies regarding fire, theft, property liability, and damage from acts of nature, perhaps by changing policy coverages and premium rates to cover the special risks of mobile home ownership. The higher demand for mobile homes also implies a shift in life-styles and consumption habits which may have ramifications in such markets as those for household appliances, lawn and garden accessories, recreation goods, automobiles, camping equipment, tourism, and local convenience services. The resulting market demand changes not only will entail additional price and output rate adjustments by the affected firms but also will be transmitted back into the resource input markets relevant to all these products.

This is still not all: An increase in the number of mobile home owners has important consequences for the supplies of labor and land. Greater use of mobile homes should make workers more mobile, thus rendering the supplies of some labor services more elastic over time. More land will be needed for mobile home parks, mobile home communities, mobile home campsites, and sales display facilities; relatively less land will be needed for permanently located single- and multiple-family residences. In the public sector, the changing makeup of housing and living patterns will alter the nature of the demand for local government services and the structure of property taxation, the latter having implications for shifting the relative profitabilities of various types of housing investments and causing a realignment in real estate investment patterns. Finally, the whole array of price-output-input adjustments will affect wages, salaries, profits, rents, and interest rates in the affected firms and industries, causing some redistribution of personal income. These income changes will prompt yet another series of price-output-input reactions as the affected consumers revise their expenditure patterns and saving rates to confirm to the new income constraints.

If one had the tenacity and the inclination, the entire sequence of equilibrium adjustments and market linkages could be pursued to its ultimate conclusion and the entire set of market interrelationships pinned down. But the major point is already apparent. Product and resource markets are linked together directly and indirectly to form a *market network*. Given a state of static general equilibrium, any initial disturbance, whether it be a change in product demand, a change in resource supply conditions, an increase in population, a breakthrough in production technology, or a new product innovation, will trigger a complex chain reaction through the network of product and resource markets. The initial disturbance creates effects which spill over into adjacent markets and causes them to move toward new equilibrium positions. These secondary effects in turn generate new waves and ripples, which are carried by the various market linkages into a third set of product and resource markets. The third-order changes may extend back into the primary market where the initial disturbance occurred or back into the secondary markets and may also generate still higher-order effects transcending yet more distant markets. Barring further disturbances, the effects of the initial disturbance will eventually dissipate, new equilibrium positions will be reached, and a state of general equilibrium will be restored.

The Interrelationships of Economic Sectors

The foregoing paragraphs explain how markets are linked together. We now turn to the linkages between economic sectors. The term *economic sector* refers simply to a grouping of related markets and parts of a whole economy.

Figure 18-1 provides a convenient graphical summary and synthesis of the flow of dollars and products through the economy, showing how the major economic sectors are related. Starting at the box on the left, we see that the process of producing goods and services gives rise to an aggregate amount of income equal to the market value of what has been produced. This simple, but crucial, proposition follows from the fact that the monetary value of a product is determined by the market value of the economic resources required to produce it.[2] Four basic things can be done with the income which economic units (firms and households) receive from the production process: (1) a portion is paid to government in the form of taxes (T); (2) a portion is saved (S) and, temporarily at least, deposited in various financial institutions; (3) a portion may be used to pay for goods imported from foreign countries (M); and (4) far and away the major portion goes to purchase consumer goods and services (C).

Obviously enough, governmental units use the tax revenues they receive to pay for the goods and services required for carrying out governmental functions and for various income redistribution programs. Foreign countries use the dollars

---

[2] This is a fundamental proposition of macroeconomics, usually explained in detail in principles of economics texts. See, among others, Campbell R. McConnell, *Economics*, 9th ed. (New York: McGraw-Hill Book Company, 1984), Chapter 9, and G. L. Bach, *Economics*, 11th ed. (Englewood Cliffs, N.J.: Prentice-Hall, Inc., 1984), Chapters 7–9.

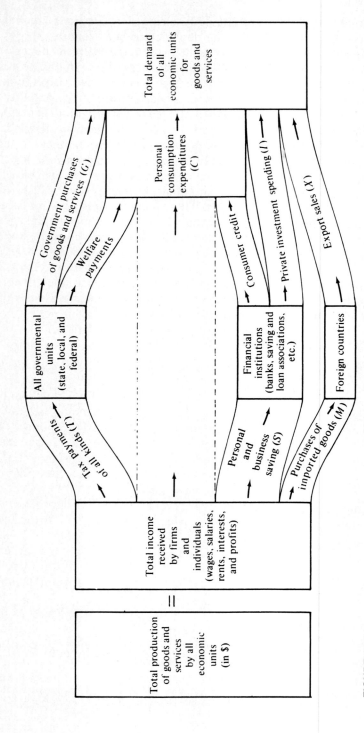

FIGURE 18-1
Simplified model of the operation of a market economy

they receive from the sale of goods to U.S. citizens to purchase goods which they desire to buy from us; hence, the leakage of income out of the economy via imports is offset to some greater or lesser extent by an inflow of money back into the economy from export sales. The flow of savings into financial institutions comes out in the form of funds for consumer credit and for private investment spending; the latter includes financing the replacement of worn-out production facilities, the expansion of production capacity, and new housing (considered as investment spending by national income accountants). The demand side of the economic picture therefore consists of four major components: (1) personal consumption expenditures (C), (2) government spending for goods and services (G), (3) private investment spending (I), and (4) sales of goods to foreign countries or exports (X). Figure 18-1 thus presents a model of the linkages between the major economic sectors, emphasizing the flows of dollars and products and the relationships between total supply and total demand.[3]

For analytical convenience suppose we refer to the tax, savings, and import flows as "leakages" and the government spending, investment, and export flows as "injections." The rectangular boxes across the diagram may be viewed as the main income-spending stream. It is evident that the balance between the leakages and the injections provides the key to overall economic stability and to the direction of change in the rate of economic activity. If during some period of time (a month, a quarter, a year, or whatever) the dollar sum of the leakages $(T + S + M)$ is just equal to the dollar sum of the injections $(G + I + X)$, then the total dollar value of the goods and services produced will be equal to the dollar value of total spending on goods and services. To put it differently, when the leakages equal the injections, then the income generated from the current rate of production is, after being allocated to the various spending components, converted into a volume of expenditures just sufficient to provide a matching total demand; the total demand for goods and services is exactly equal to the total supply of goods and services. Assuming, not unrealistically, that the composition of these goods and services is in accord with buyer preferences, all markets will be cleared of their output, and the economy may be said to be in equilibrium—no forces will operate to cause the overall rate of economic activity to either increase or decrease. Such is the nature of general equilibrium at the level of the whole economy.

On the other hand, whenever the leakages and the injections do not balance, a state of disequilibrium exists, and forces immediately and automatically spring into action to rectify the situation. Suppose, for instance, that a portion of the dollars flowing into government, or foreign countries, or financial institutions somehow gets trapped and is not spent. Then the size of the leakage flow will exceed the size of the injection flow. This has the effect of causing the prevailing production rates to exceed the rates at which goods are being purchased. Total supply will exceed total demand. As business firms see sales slipping and inventories of unsold goods piling up, they will respond by cutting prices and/or cur-

---

[3] This model can easily be expanded to portray in more detail the ties between various subsectors of the economy. However, for our purposes the simplified model of Fig. 15-1 will suffice.

tailing production rates. Typically, the prices of perishable, seasonal, and faddish items, as well as those which are expensive to store, will be reduced in an effort to stimulate buying and eliminate unwanted surpluses. But, in the cases of durable and easily stockpiled items, firms may find it more profitable to maintain prices and cut back on production rates until demand conditions become more favorable. The combination of falling prices and lower production rates will reduce incomes—wages and salary incomes will be lower because of the lessened need for labor inputs, and profits will be lower because of lower sales volumes and slimmer profit margins. The decline in incomes and profits will cause tax revenues to fall and will also cause business firms to review the profitability of new investment spending, probably revising investment spending plans downward unless the downturn in economic activity is viewed as clearly a short-term disturbance. In general, then, when the leakages exceed the injections, the rate of economic activity will fall. The economic decline will continue until production rates and spending rates are brought into line and supply-demand equilibrium is restored in the various product markets.

At the other extreme, it is quite conceivable that the sum of the injections $(G + I + X)$ will exceed the sum of the leakages $(S + T + M)$. There are several ways in which this can occur. Governments, of course, can spend more than they collect in tax revenues by borrowing the difference; this practice, known as deficit spending, is commonly engaged in at all levels of government. Scarcely any unit of government has not at one time or another issued bonds to finance some project and then paid off the bonds over time with new tax revenues. Financial institutions can also provide new funds for investment and consumer credit in amounts which exceed current saving rates; banks, in fact, create new money whenever they exchange IOUs for demand deposits.[4] Thus, both the government sector and the investment spending sector are fully capable of causing the injections flow to exceed the leakage flow at some moment of time. When and if such circumstances occur, current output rates will be inadequate to meet the total demand for goods and services; total demand will, in other words, exceed total supply. Producers who find the demand for their products outstripping current production rates have three alternative responses, which they can employ singly or in combination: (1) they can draw down inventories to help meet the excess demand; (2) they can increase production rates, provided they have unused production capacity and provided they can obtain the necessary labor and raw material inputs; and (3) they can raise prices to ration the available supplies among those buyers most anxious to obtain their products. Whatever response set producers elect—and most likely it will be some combination of all three—incomes will tend to rise, thereby stimulating further spending and expansion of economic activity. The general rise in incomes and in the overall pace of economic activity will cause tax revenues to rise, saving rates to increase, and investment in new production capacity to increase. Whether government spending will rise, fall, or remain un-

---

[4] The money-creating activity of commercial banks is explained in all basic economics books. See, for example, McConnell, *Economics*, Chapter 15; Bach, *Economics*, Chapter 16.

changed is, of course, more a political than an economic question. The major point is that when the injections exceed the leakages, economic activity in the various economic sectors tends to be stimulated. The rise in economic activity will lose its steam when production catches up with demand and producers are just able to meet the demands for their products.

This thumbnail sketch of the interrelationships of the major economic sectors is sufficient to indicate why static general equilibrium requires not just equilibrium in each market and each related market but also balance between and among the major economic sectors. Spending patterns must be consistent with income patterns; production flows must in the aggregate match the rates at which outputs are purchased; the siphoning off of dollars in leakages must somehow be offset by the pumping of an equivalent amount of dollars back into the income-expenditure stream.

General Equilibrium and the Overall Rate of Economic Activity

From the standpoint of society's overall economic welfare, the level of economic activity at which general equilibrium occurs makes a great deal of difference. For instance, national goals and priorities call for the achievement of full employment. Full employment requires two things: (1) that an adequate number of jobs be available for those persons who are willing and able to work and (2) that the available human and property resources be deployed among alternative uses in an efficient manner. The question becomes: If general equilibrium is attained, then must it or does it occur at a level of activity consistent with full employment?

The answer to this question is "not necessarily." Certainly there is neither an economic "law" nor a compelling economic force operating to peg the level of economic activity at the full employment position. As we have seen earlier, static general equilibrium requires that the total supply of goods and services be equal to the total demand for goods and services; or, putting it another way, the leakages must equal the injections. This condition guarantees that the flow of products through the major economic sectors will be mutually consistent; no forces will be operating to cause the overall rate of economic activity to rise or fall. Moreover, the composition of total output must be such that the demand and supply conditions for each separate commodity are consistent with equilibrium. This condition has several dimensions. Business firms must have no motives for altering prices or output rates, given the existing demand conditions. Consumers must be allocating their incomes in the optimum fashion, given the existing price and income constraints. Resource owners must be deploying their resources in the optimum pattern, given the existing demand for resource inputs and prevailing resource prices.

However, the static equilibrium position reached under these conditions may or may not represent a full employment equilibrium. Too low a level of total spending will call forth an equilibrium production rate requiring less than a full employment rate of input usage; unemployment rates for labor will rise above the tolerable and expected 4 to 6% target rate, and the related static equilibrium will be below the full employment level of economic activity. Too high a level of total spending will strain resource supplies and production rates to the point where higher product prices and input prices will be necessary to curb total demand and artificially bring it into line with total supply.

Nevertheless, the insatiability of consumer wants tends to generate a consistently "high" rate of economic activity; this tendency is further reinforced by the drive of business firms for growth and expansion and by the want-creating effects of new product innovation and sales promotion. But whether total spending will automatically be high enough to generate full employment is another matter. For this reason it is deemed desirable for the federal government to take an active role in using monetary and fiscal policy to promote full employment.

Statics versus Dynamics

The concept of static general equilibrium has practical importance because it is a useful tool of economic analysis. It would be a mistake, however, to conceive of static general equilibrium as either achievable or desirable. It is not probable that underlying economic conditions will ever remain fixed long enough for the forces of change to adjust to a point where they are in balance. Indeed, change is a product of the normal operation of a modern economy, and this change in turn affects the operation of the economy. The milieu of change transcends population size, consumer tastes and preferences, incomes, costs, product prices, output rates, business strategies, national economic priorities, the pattern of international competition, and so on. New technological processes and product innovations are constantly injecting new disturbances into the economic picture. Population growth, education, and training programs produce persistent rises in the quantity and quality of labor services available to producers. The net effect of these wide-ranging and perpetually emerging tendencies for economic change is to prevent a static equilibrium from ever being achieved. Instead, new economic developments and new patterns of economic activity are constantly appearing in response to changing demand and supply conditions; in turn, product and resource markets are forever pursuing newly created general equilibrium positions.

As indicated previously, the direction and the pace of economic change determine the gains in society's economic welfare. In a static stationary economy, the standard of living is fixed, and society as a whole is doomed to exist at the prevailing output, income, and employment rates. Progress is nonexistent. But in modern industrial economies things are quite different. Change is commonplace and all-pervasive; technological advance and business growth strategies tilt the forces of change toward economic expansion—rising outputs, rising incomes, rising living standards, and a higher quality of life. Insofar, then, as economywide equilibrium in a progressive environment is concerned, the focus is not upon static general equilibrium but upon *dynamic growth equilibrium*—stable, long-term growth.

DYNAMIC GROWTH EQUILIBRIUM

The study of dynamic equilibrium growth paths for an economy and the associated equilibrium growth patterns for firms constitutes one of the newest and least explored areas of economics. Moreover, because of the vast array of variables that must be taken into account, the theoretical models dealing with these topics are especially complex. For this reason, the body of theory which does exist is highly mathematical, involving a degree of sophistication well beyond the scope of this book.[5] We shall therefore restrict our consideration of dynamic growth models and of the links between growth equilibrium for the firm and for the economy to a presentation of basic concepts, indicating in nonrigorous terms some of the basic relationships and some of the tentative conclusions which have been reached. Again, the reader is forewarned that what follows is in the fomulative stages; by no means has it survived sufficient empirical testing to warrant great confidence.

Growth Equilibrium for the Economy

In an industrialized economy the quality of economic performance is judged by how well the economy adheres to a path of stable growth and noninflationary full employment. The less frequent the deviations from a path of orderly economic expansion and the smaller such deviations from the full employment level of economic activity, the better an economy's performance is judged to be. As long as the pace of economic activity is proceeding at a rate commensurate with a stable growth path, the economy may be said to be in *growth equilibrium*.

The character of growth equilibrium on an economywide basis has a number of fundamental features. Ideally, the total output of goods and services must expand fast enough to provide employment opportunities for all persons seeking jobs but not so fast as to strain resource supplies to the point of unleashing wage-price-cost spirals and the knotty inflationary problems which such conditions present. Given an economy's resource capabilities, the optimum growth rate of

---

[5] A representative sample of the literature of microeconomic and macroeconomic growth models includes W. J. Baumol, *Economic Dynamics*, 3rd ed. (New York: The Macmillan Company, 1970); Bent Hansen, *A Survey of General Equilibrium Systems* (New York: McGraw-Hill Book Company, 1970); Robert Dorfman, Paul A. Samuelson, and Robert Solow, *Linear Programming and Economic Analysis* (New York: McGraw-Hill Book Company, 1958), Chapter 11; Edith Penrose, *The Theory of the Growth of the Firm* (New York: John Wiley & Sons, Inc., 1959); Joan Robinson, *Essays in the Theory of Economic Growth* (New York: St. Martin's Press, 1964); and Edwin Burmeister and Rodney Dobell, *Mathematical Theories of Economic Growth* (New York: The Macmillan Company, 1970). More specific studies and also more advanced mathematical discussions of economic growth paths include J. A. Mirrlees, "Optimum Growth When Technology Is Changing," *Review of Economic Studies*, Vol. 34, No. 97 (January 1967), pp. 95–124; T. C. Koopmans, "Objectives, Constraints, and Outcomes in Optimal Growth Models," *Econometrica*, Vol. 35, No. 1 (January 1967), pp. 1–15; T. C. Koopmans, "On the Concept of Optimal Economic Growth," in *The Econometric Approach to Development Planning* (Chicago: Rand McNally & Company and North-Holland Publishing Co., 1966); Robert Solow and Paul A. Samuelson, "Balanced Growth under Constant Returns to Scale," *Econometrica*, Vol. 21, No. 3 (July 1953), pp. 412–424; and the Symposium on the Theory of Economic Growth, *Journal of Political Economy*, Vol. 77, No. 4, Part II (July–August 1969).

total output is one that is consistent with the limits of technological progress and with the simultaneous achievement of price stability and full employment. Joan Robinson has called such a smooth, steady expansion "a golden age" of growth.[6]

For the optimum growth rate to be realized, the leakages $(S + T + M)$ and injections $(G + I + X)$ must be kept in balance, growing in step with each other as expansion occurs. The total demand for goods and services must grow at the same pace as does the overall output rate of producers; otherwise, the size of the market for the new output will be deficient. Ordinarily, the process of growth is capable of generating the increases in income and spending needed to sustain the growth of output over time, because economic expansion generates new investment spending and creates new employment opportunities in amounts sufficient to provide the income requisite for purchasing the additional goods and services produced. A steady state of expansion then rolls smoothly along, with technological progress and productivity gains paving the way for increases in real incomes. New production technologies are implemented as firms build new production capacity. Profits are sufficiently high to continue to attract and provide the money capital requisite for expansion. Firms may be said to be in growth equilibrium because their realized expansion rates are, on the average, compatible with what is possible.

One may further characterize an economy in growth equilibrium by supposing that technological advances, combined with gains in the quantity and quality of resource inputs, allow for a 5% annual increase in the total output of goods and services when production rates are maintained at the full employment rate of input usage. Investment spending for the new production capacity needed to increase output rates and an increased demand for raw material inputs will serve to push the incomes of suppliers upward. Similarly, the new production activity will give rise to new job opportunities for blue-and white-collar workers and for managers, thus increasing wage and salary incomes. Suppose the 5% increase in production yields a 5% gain in total income. If the leakages are in balance with the injections, then the 5% rise in total income will in turn produce a 5% increase in total spending, thereby providing ample market potential for selling the additional production. Repeating this process year after year would put the economy on a steady growth path of 5% which, if attained, would constitute a stable "golden age" growth equilibrium for the economy.

Growth Equilibrium for the Firm

Although growth equilibrium entails even and steady expansion of total output for the economy as a whole, it would be erroneous to view the output rates of each and every product as expanding at the economywide equilibrium growth rate. The very process of economic growth will give birth to changes in consumer tastes and preferences and to variations in the intensity of competitive pressures.

---

[6] Mrs. Robinson has attached corresponding nicknames to other possible phases of growth: a limping golden age, a leaden age, a restrained golden age, a galloping platinum age, a creeping platinum age, a bastard golden age, and a bastard platinum age. See her *Essays in the Theory of Economic Growth*, pp. 51–59.

Some products will die out, and others will rise to prominence via the perennial gale of creative destruction. The discovery and implementation of new production techniques will alter optimum input mixes and economies of scale. These changes will provoke a variety of responses in the business sector, and all of them will play a role in determining the growth equilibrium for particular firms.

Growth equilibrium for a firm may be thought of as the path along which the firm must continually adjust its prices, output rates, and input rates so as to optimize the attainment of its complement of goals (profits, sales revenue, market share, growth, technological virtuosity, security, and so on), given the constraints imposed by the economic environment. Whatever the particular goal set of the firm, management's function in attaining growth equilibrium is to search out the particular activity mix which yields the best perceived outcome insofar as the firm's goal set is concerned. Decision-makers must juggle price-output-input-diversification combinations so as to obtain the best performance, given the existing uncertainties. This is not to say that once an optimum price-output-input-diversification combination has been identified, it should be maintained into the indefinite future. Realistically, new developments arising from further economic growth of the economy will cause the optimum combination to change; thus, decision makers will continually be forced to modify the firm's strategy set, revising prices and output rates, adding new products and dropping old ones, implementing new technologies, shifting the organization's resources into new activities, and revamping the organization's structure and orientation to meet new priorities.

Where the demand for a product is increasing faster than average, firms will be motivated to respond with above-average increases in production rates. Where the demand for a product is increasing at below-average rates, production rates can be expected to rise more slowly than the average. Where demand is shrinking or on the verge of disappearing entirely, firms will be forced to cut back production and perhaps to go out of business or shift into the production of items with more attractive profit and sales opportunities. The variability in the growth rates of the demand for various goods and services will change the composition of the economy's total output. In turn, firms will have to realign the usage of the various resource inputs in accord with demand changes and technological developments. The chief requirement which economy-wide growth equilibrium imposes upon producers is that the required output and input adjustments for specific products be orderly. When slack appears in one firm or industry or economic sector, it must be absorbed by expansion elsewhere in the economy; otherwise the achievement of full employment is jeopardized. Individual product prices and input prices can be raised or lowered, but if on the average product prices rise or fall by more than 1 or 2% and input prices get out of line with productivity changes, then inflationary or deflationary pressures interfere with attainment of price stability.

The growth equilibrium position of particular firms will vary according to two factors: (1) the quantity and quality of the opportunities for expansion offered by the overall economic environment and (2) the respective organizational capabilities of firms regarding the quality of management, the financial resources they can marshal, and their propensities for undertaking new activities. These relationships warrant further attention, because they comprise the link between growth equilibrium for the firm and growth equilibrium for the economy.[7]

Insofar as any one product is concerned, a firm's optimum growth rate is a function of the market potential of that product, the rate at which demand is rising (or falling), the profit opportunities, the strength of competitive pressures in that product market, and the like. But firms are not restricted to producing a single product; they may widen the range of their activities to include any number of related or unrelated products and they may extend their activities to include producing and selling in international markets rather than just national markets. This is why the growth equilibrium path of a particular firm is a function of the *entire* set of economywide expansion opportunities which are open to it and not just growth in the demand for the items it currently produces. It is clear that the size of the set of opportunities for expansion is very much dependent on the growth equilibrium path of the economy as a whole. An economywide growth of 5% per year will necessarily offer firms greater expansion potential than a growth rate of only 2%. One may think of the economy's equilibrium growth path as opening up a certain amount of new expansion potential for firms each period which, if taken advantage of, will result in achievement of the equilibrium growth rate.

Given the full range of opportunities for expansion offered by growth equilibrium on an economywide basis, firms may be viewed as competing for the available new market potential, with each firm's own growth equilibrium being a function of (1) its perceived role in the economic setting, (2) the strategic position it has for meeting the new demands for goods and services generated by growth, and (3) its aggressiveness in committing resources to the available expansion opportunities. Some firms are content to continue to operate within the bounds of their current activities; thus, their growth rates are pegged directly to the expansion of the product markets in which they operate. Other firms take a broader view of their capacities and branch out into new products and new markets as they approach the limits of expansion in their present products—the popularity of this strategy is reflected by a continuing propensity for diversification on the part of U.S. firms since the late 1960s. Firms confronted by shrinking markets and declining profit opportunities are faced with the choice of accepting a negative growth equilibrium path or else breaking out of their traditional molds and launching into new activities and new markets. In some cases, firms are in position to initiate and shape the course of economic expansion by means of new product innovations and new managerial technologies; other firms will be growth followers. Some firms are able to achieve high growth rates not so much because of careful planning and foresight but because they just happen, fortuitously, to be engaged in activities for which demand vigorously increases. Some firms may lack the financial resources to exploit fully the new opportunities which present themselves, while others will expand cautiously, engaging only in those activities

---

[7] However, to the extent that the operations of firms take on an international character, rather than being constrained by the boundaries of a single national economy, the link between growth equilibrium for the firm and growth equilibrium for the economy is supplemented by a link between growth equilibrium for the firm and growth equilibrium of the international economy in which the firm operates.

which are viewed as low-risk. Thus, there is a variety of growth equilibrium patterns for firms.

National Economic Policy and Growth Equilibrium

It goes without saying that the achievement of a stable growth equilibrium on an economywide basis is an enormously complex task. Not only must the process of economic change be kept orderly and tidy and the proper degree of flexibility in the production mechanism be maintained, but the economic environment must also be kept conducive to just the right rate of business expansion. None of these is likely to be accomplished without design and carefully executed strategy, despite a tendency for the economy to move toward growth equilibrium. The only institution capable of promoting and coordinating growth equilibrium on an economywide front is the federal government.

In general terms, the aim of national economic policy is to see to it that the target rates of national economic growth and the associated growth equilibrium become a reality. When stimulation of investment or consumption spending is needed to provide a boost to the economy, it is the responsibility of the monetary and fiscal authorities to design an appropriate strategy and to implement it at the proper time. Such a strategy may include tax cuts, increases in government spending, increases in the money supply, and lower interest rates in whatever combination is deemed most appropriate for the particular situation. On the other hand, when growth proceeds so fast that inflation is a by-product, then the economic pulse must be slowed by means of some combination of tax increases, restraints upon government spending, a tightening up of the money supply, higher interest rates, and perhaps wage-price controls. In other words, the federal government has the responsibility of orchestrating national economic policy such that the economic throttle is kept turned to the right speed; otherwise, the possibility of attaining a stable growth equilibrium is remote.

Actually, of course, keeping a trillion-dollar economy directly on the path of a stable growth equilibrium over the long term is really too much to expect of policy-makers, given the uncertainties of economic change, the lack of well-defined and coordinated policies for maintaining economic stability, and the political constraints which are inevitably present. Steering a course of noninflationary full employment and at the same time keeping the rate of increase in economic activity steady is much like trying to guide a raft through swirling rapids on an unknown river—the course ahead is uncharted, the going is tricky, and the margin for error to either side is razor thin. Thus, a more realistic interpretation of the role and function of public policy is for it to attempt to minimize the size and the frequency of deviations from the target growth path. But even this objective is likely to prove elusive—as is amply testified to by the recurrent ups and downs in the pace of economic activity and by the frequently unrealized predictions of governmental policy-makers. Nevertheless, attempting to keep the economy as close to the target equilibrium growth path as is possible is a very reasonable way of conceiving the goal of national economic policy.

However, while there is general accord on the nature of a socially desirable type of growth equilibrium, there exists a wide diversity of opinion as to the specific national policies which ought to be deployed to support its achievement. Furthermore, differences exist as to priorities. Plainly enough, there is room for reasonable people to disagree about how much of which kinds of growth. For this reason, even if it could be assumed that policy-makers are wise enough to know just what sort of policy mix is called for in specific situations, it would not be possible to prescribe an "optimal" growth equilibrium strategy. Thus, economic policy issues will necessarily remain in the realm of conflict, despite the powers of economic analysis to explain and to predict economic phenomena.

SUMMARY AND CONCLUSIONS

The part of economic theory that concerns the interdependencies and linkages among prices, output rates, and input rates in all of the various markets and economic sectors is called general equilibrium analysis. The purpose of such analysis is to determine what the equilibrium configuration of prices, output rates, and input rates will be for each firm and in each market, given the guiding forces of consumer tastes and preferences, production technologies, available resource supplies, business goals, and national priorities.

In a state of static general equilibrium there are no forces operating to cause the pace of economic activity to rise or fall. The leakages equal the injections, and the total supply of goods and services equals the total demand for goods and services. At a lower level, each product market is in equilibrium; so is each input market. Consumers, business firms, and resource owners have no motives for changing what they are doing, given the prevailing economic circumstances. In theory, general equilibrium can occur at, above, or below full employment, depending on the level of total spending.

In practice, however, static general equilibrium is never attained because the underlying forces are never constant long enough for all product and resource markets to reach their respective equilibrium positions. The real world is very much dynamic, with changes occurring constantly in such basic economic forces as consumer tastes and preferences, the range of possible products and production technologies, the quantity and quality of available resource inputs, the distribution of income, the styles of managerial technologies, and so on. Over the long term in a progressive society, the most appropriate concept of general equilibrium is growth equilibrium—a state of stable growth and noninflationary full employment, the optimal growth rate being a function of technological progress, the availability of new resource supplies, and societal preferences.

Insofar as firms are concerned, the character of economy-wide growth equilibrium is important because it determines the extent of expansion opportunities open to enterprises and ultimately their own individual growth equilibrium positions. The individual firm's own growth equilibrium path depends on the strategic position it has for meeting the new market demands generated by growth and the aggressiveness with which managers commit organizational resources to the available expansion opportunities. Growth equilibrium for the firm thus may be thought of as the path along which the firm continually adjusts its prices, output rates, and input rates so as to optimize the attainment of its complement of goals.

Even though there are strong tendencies for the economy to move in the direction of the growth equilibrium path, deviations and lags in adjustment are inevitable. Change is too frequent, resource mobility too imperfect, and the adjustment mechanism too slow in responding to change for the economy to remain fixed on a steady, even growth path. For this reason, it is appropriate for the federal government to play an active role in promoting economy-wide growth equilibrium and in facilitating the process of adjustment to economic change.

SUGGESTED READINGS

Baumol, W. J., *Economic Dynamics*, 3rd ed. (New York: The Macmillan Company, 1970), Chapters 17 and 18.

Coddington, A., "The Rationale of General Equilibrium Theory," *Economic Inquiry*, Vol. 13, No. 4 (December 1975), pp. 539–558.

Cohen, K. J., and R. M. Cyert, *Theory of the Firm: Resource Allocation in a Market Economy*, 2nd ed. (Englewood Cliffs, N.J.: Prentice-Hall, Inc. 1975), Chapter 11.

Hahn, F. H., and R. C. O. Matthews, "The Theory of Economic Growth: A Survey," *Economic Journal*, Vol. 74, No. 296 (December 1964), pp. 779–902; reprinted in *Survey of Economic Theory*, Vol. II (New York: St. Martin's Press, 1965).

Hansen, B., *A Survey of General Equilibrium Systems* (New York: McGraw-Hill Book Company, 1970).

Koopmans, T. C., "Is the Theory of Competitive Equilibrium with It?" *American Economic Review*, Vol. 64, No. 2 (May 1974), pp. 325–329.

Schumpeter, J. A., *The Theory of Economic Development* (New York: Oxford University Press, 1961), Chapters 2, 4, and 6.

QUESTIONS FOR DISCUSSION

1. Trace through the chain of economic effects triggered by:
    (a) An innovation which allows waste paper to be recycled and made reusable.
    (b) A permanent increase in the demand for sports entertainment.
    (c) A sharp decline in the number of women seeking employment.
    (d) A precipitous decline in natural gas reserves.
2. Distinguish between static general equilibrium and dynamic growth equilibrium for an economy.
3. (a) Do you think that some deviations from economy-wide growth equilibrium are inevitable? Why or why not?
    (b) Would it be fair to state that the economy-wide pace of economic activity *tends* toward the growth equilibrium path?
    (c) Is it likely that the nature of an economy's growth equilibrium path can be (and is) altered by basic changes in the economic environment? If so, what sorts of basic changes can cause the growth equilibrium path to shift?

4. Explain the relationships and the linkages between growth equilibrium for the economy and growth equilibrium for the firm.

5. Do you think managers of firms are able to keep their respective firms steered on a course of steady growth? Why or why not? Do they try to do so even though they may not succeed? Why or why not?

6. What, if any, guarantee does society have that growth of the economy and of firms will proceed in directions consistent with societal preferences and priorities?

7. It has been observed that business enterprises thrive on "problems," that these problems typically precipitate a search for technological solutions, that the resulting technological discoveries point the way to new investment opportunities, and that the resulting new investment spending is the cornerstone of economic growth. Critically evaluate this sequence of events as an "explanation" or "cause" of economic growth and expansion.

INDEX

DATE DUE

AUG 1 1 '89			